Lecture Notes in Artificial Intelligence 13336

Subseries of Lecture Notes in Computer Science

More information about this subseries at https://link.springer.com/bookseries/1244

Helmut Degen · Stavroula Ntoa (Eds.)

Artificial Intelligence in HCI

3rd International Conference, AI-HCI 2022
Held as Part of the 24th HCI International Conference, HCII 2022
Virtual Event, June 26 – July 1, 2022
Proceedings

Editors
Helmut Degen
Siemens (United States)
Princeton, NJ, USA

Stavroula Ntoa
Foundation for Research and Technology – Hellas (FORTH)
Heraklion, Crete, Greece

ISSN 0302-9743 ISSN 1611-3349 (electronic)
Lecture Notes in Artificial Intelligence
ISBN 978-3-031-05642-0 ISBN 978-3-031-05643-7 (eBook)
https://doi.org/10.1007/978-3-031-05643-7

LNCS Sublibrary: SL7 – Artificial Intelligence

This Springer imprint is published by the registered company Springer Nature Switzerland AG
The registered company address is: Gewerbestrasse 11, 6330 Cham, Switzerland

Foreword

Human-computer interaction (HCI) is acquiring an ever-increasing scientific and industrial importance, as well as having more impact on people's everyday life, as an ever-growing number of human activities are progressively moving from the physical to the digital world. This process, which has been ongoing for some time now, has been dramatically accelerated by the COVID-19 pandemic. The HCI International (HCII) conference series, held yearly, aims to respond to the compelling need to advance the exchange of knowledge and research and development efforts on the human aspects of design and use of computing systems.

The 24th International Conference on Human-Computer Interaction, HCI International 2022 (HCII 2022), was planned to be held at the Gothia Towers Hotel and Swedish Exhibition & Congress Centre, Göteborg, Sweden, during June 26 to July 1, 2022. Due to the COVID-19 pandemic and with everyone's health and safety in mind, HCII 2022 was organized and run as a virtual conference. It incorporated the 21 thematic areas and affiliated conferences listed on the following page.

A total of 5583 individuals from academia, research institutes, industry, and governmental agencies from 88 countries submitted contributions, and 1276 papers and 275 posters were included in the proceedings to appear just before the start of the conference. The contributions thoroughly cover the entire field of human-computer interaction, addressing major advances in knowledge and effective use of computers in a variety of application areas. These papers provide academics, researchers, engineers, scientists, practitioners, and students with state-of-the-art information on the most recent advances in HCI. The volumes constituting the set of proceedings to appear before the start of the conference are listed in the following pages.

The HCI International (HCII) conference also offers the option of 'Late Breaking Work' which applies both for papers and posters, and the corresponding volume(s) of the proceedings will appear after the conference. Full papers will be included in the 'HCII 2022 - Late Breaking Papers' volumes of the proceedings to be published in the Springer LNCS series, while 'Poster Extended Abstracts' will be included as short research papers in the 'HCII 2022 - Late Breaking Posters' volumes to be published in the Springer CCIS series.

I would like to thank the Program Board Chairs and the members of the Program Boards of all thematic areas and affiliated conferences for their contribution and support towards the highest scientific quality and overall success of the HCI International 2022 conference; they have helped in so many ways, including session organization, paper reviewing (single-blind review process, with a minimum of two reviews per submission) and, more generally, acting as goodwill ambassadors for the HCII conference.

This conference would not have been possible without the continuous and unwavering support and advice of Gavriel Salvendy, founder, General Chair Emeritus, and Scientific Advisor. For his outstanding efforts, I would like to express my appreciation to Abbas Moallem, Communications Chair and Editor of HCI International News.

June 2022 Constantine Stephanidis

HCI International 2022 Thematic Areas and Affiliated Conferences

Thematic Areas

- HCI: Human-Computer Interaction
- HIMI: Human Interface and the Management of Information

Affiliated Conferences

- EPCE: 19th International Conference on Engineering Psychology and Cognitive Ergonomics
- AC: 16th International Conference on Augmented Cognition
- UAHCI: 16th International Conference on Universal Access in Human-Computer Interaction
- CCD: 14th International Conference on Cross-Cultural Design
- SCSM: 14th International Conference on Social Computing and Social Media
- VAMR: 14th International Conference on Virtual, Augmented and Mixed Reality
- DHM: 13th International Conference on Digital Human Modeling and Applications in Health, Safety, Ergonomics and Risk Management
- DUXU: 11th International Conference on Design, User Experience and Usability
- C&C: 10th International Conference on Culture and Computing
- DAPI: 10th International Conference on Distributed, Ambient and Pervasive Interactions
- HCIBGO: 9th International Conference on HCI in Business, Government and Organizations
- LCT: 9th International Conference on Learning and Collaboration Technologies
- ITAP: 8th International Conference on Human Aspects of IT for the Aged Population
- AIS: 4th International Conference on Adaptive Instructional Systems
- HCI-CPT: 4th International Conference on HCI for Cybersecurity, Privacy and Trust
- HCI-Games: 4th International Conference on HCI in Games
- MobiTAS: 4th International Conference on HCI in Mobility, Transport and Automotive Systems
- AI-HCI: 3rd International Conference on Artificial Intelligence in HCI
- MOBILE: 3rd International Conference on Design, Operation and Evaluation of Mobile Communications

List of Conference Proceedings Volumes Appearing Before the Conference

1. LNCS 13302, Human-Computer Interaction: Theoretical Approaches and Design Methods (Part I), edited by Masaaki Kurosu
2. LNCS 13303, Human-Computer Interaction: Technological Innovation (Part II), edited by Masaaki Kurosu
3. LNCS 13304, Human-Computer Interaction: User Experience and Behavior (Part III), edited by Masaaki Kurosu
4. LNCS 13305, Human Interface and the Management of Information: Visual and Information Design (Part I), edited by Sakae Yamamoto and Hirohiko Mori
5. LNCS 13306, Human Interface and the Management of Information: Applications in Complex Technological Environments (Part II), edited by Sakae Yamamoto and Hirohiko Mori
6. LNAI 13307, Engineering Psychology and Cognitive Ergonomics, edited by Don Harris and Wen-Chin Li
7. LNCS 13308, Universal Access in Human-Computer Interaction: Novel Design Approaches and Technologies (Part I), edited by Margherita Antona and Constantine Stephanidis
8. LNCS 13309, Universal Access in Human-Computer Interaction: User and Context Diversity (Part II), edited by Margherita Antona and Constantine Stephanidis
9. LNAI 13310, Augmented Cognition, edited by Dylan D. Schmorrow and Cali M. Fidopiastis
10. LNCS 13311, Cross-Cultural Design: Interaction Design Across Cultures (Part I), edited by Pei-Luen Patrick Rau
11. LNCS 13312, Cross-Cultural Design: Applications in Learning, Arts, Cultural Heritage, Creative Industries, and Virtual Reality (Part II), edited by Pei-Luen Patrick Rau
12. LNCS 13313, Cross-Cultural Design: Applications in Business, Communication, Health, Well-being, and Inclusiveness (Part III), edited by Pei-Luen Patrick Rau
13. LNCS 13314, Cross-Cultural Design: Product and Service Design, Mobility and Automotive Design, Cities, Urban Areas, and Intelligent Environments Design (Part IV), edited by Pei-Luen Patrick Rau
14. LNCS 13315, Social Computing and Social Media: Design, User Experience and Impact (Part I), edited by Gabriele Meiselwitz
15. LNCS 13316, Social Computing and Social Media: Applications in Education and Commerce (Part II), edited by Gabriele Meiselwitz
16. LNCS 13317, Virtual, Augmented and Mixed Reality: Design and Development (Part I), edited by Jessie Y. C. Chen and Gino Fragomeni
17. LNCS 13318, Virtual, Augmented and Mixed Reality: Applications in Education, Aviation and Industry (Part II), edited by Jessie Y. C. Chen and Gino Fragomeni

18. LNCS 13319, Digital Human Modeling and Applications in Health, Safety, Ergonomics and Risk Management: Anthropometry, Human Behavior, and Communication (Part I), edited by Vincent G. Duffy
19. LNCS 13320, Digital Human Modeling and Applications in Health, Safety, Ergonomics and Risk Management: Health, Operations Management, and Design (Part II), edited by Vincent G. Duffy
20. LNCS 13321, Design, User Experience, and Usability: UX Research, Design, and Assessment (Part I), edited by Marcelo M. Soares, Elizabeth Rosenzweig and Aaron Marcus
21. LNCS 13322, Design, User Experience, and Usability: Design for Emotion, Well-being and Health, Learning, and Culture (Part II), edited by Marcelo M. Soares, Elizabeth Rosenzweig and Aaron Marcus
22. LNCS 13323, Design, User Experience, and Usability: Design Thinking and Practice in Contemporary and Emerging Technologies (Part III), edited by Marcelo M. Soares, Elizabeth Rosenzweig and Aaron Marcus
23. LNCS 13324, Culture and Computing, edited by Matthias Rauterberg
24. LNCS 13325, Distributed, Ambient and Pervasive Interactions: Smart Environments, Ecosystems, and Cities (Part I), edited by Norbert A. Streitz and Shin'ichi Konomi
25. LNCS 13326, Distributed, Ambient and Pervasive Interactions: Smart Living, Learning, Well-being and Health, Art and Creativity (Part II), edited by Norbert A. Streitz and Shin'ichi Konomi
26. LNCS 13327, HCI in Business, Government and Organizations, edited by Fiona Fui-Hoon Nah and Keng Siau
27. LNCS 13328, Learning and Collaboration Technologies: Designing the Learner and Teacher Experience (Part I), edited by Panayiotis Zaphiris and Andri Ioannou
28. LNCS 13329, Learning and Collaboration Technologies: Novel Technological Environments (Part II), edited by Panayiotis Zaphiris and Andri Ioannou
29. LNCS 13330, Human Aspects of IT for the Aged Population: Design, Interaction and Technology Acceptance (Part I), edited by Qin Gao and Jia Zhou
30. LNCS 13331, Human Aspects of IT for the Aged Population: Technology in Everyday Living (Part II), edited by Qin Gao and Jia Zhou
31. LNCS 13332, Adaptive Instructional Systems, edited by Robert A. Sottilare and Jessica Schwarz
32. LNCS 13333, HCI for Cybersecurity, Privacy and Trust, edited by Abbas Moallem
33. LNCS 13334, HCI in Games, edited by Xiaowen Fang
34. LNCS 13335, HCI in Mobility, Transport and Automotive Systems, edited by Heidi Krömker
35. LNAI 13336, Artificial Intelligence in HCI, edited by Helmut Degen and Stavroula Ntoa
36. LNCS 13337, Design, Operation and Evaluation of Mobile Communications, edited by Gavriel Salvendy and June Wei
37. CCIS 1580, HCI International 2022 Posters - Part I, edited by Constantine Stephanidis, Margherita Antona and Stavroula Ntoa
38. CCIS 1581, HCI International 2022 Posters - Part II, edited by Constantine Stephanidis, Margherita Antona and Stavroula Ntoa

39. CCIS 1582, HCI International 2022 Posters - Part III, edited by Constantine Stephanidis, Margherita Antona and Stavroula Ntoa
40. CCIS 1583, HCI International 2022 Posters - Part IV, edited by Constantine Stephanidis, Margherita Antona and Stavroula Ntoa

Preface

The 3rd International Conference on Artificial Intelligence in HCI (AI-HCI 2022), an affiliated conference of the HCI International conference, aimed to bring together academics, practitioners, and students to exchange results from academic and industrial research, as well as industrial experiences, on the use of artificial intelligence (AI) technologies to enhance human-computer interaction (HCI). In particular, the following areas of research were considered: (i) ethical and trustworthy AI to provide a fair and unbiased experience; (ii) evolution of human-centered AI including models processes, and modalities; (iii) processes, methods, and technical frameworks in the area of generative UX/UI design and automatic creation and adaptation of user interfaces; (iv) consumer and industrial application domains including healthcare, finance, market places, manufacturing and robots, (semi-) autonomous transportation, personal and industrial dashboards, personalized education and learning, and security.

The AI-HCI conference is targeted at individuals and organizations who have performed research or developed industrial applications in the area of AI in HCI. The conference is also targeted at individuals and organizations which want to learn from those results, so they can (re-)use them in research or industrial applications.

Both artificial intelligence and human-computer interaction are fields that have a long history and remarkable achievements; their collaboration and joint evolution, however, is expected to revolutionize advancements in each field and establish new common ground. A considerable part of research work and innovation in this area currently revolves around values, methods, and approaches that would make AI usable, useful, reliable, and trustworthy, with human-centered AI constituting a pivotal landmark. At the same time, substantial work is being conducted in areas examining the interlacing of the two fields, such as AI-enhanced UX methods and practices, AI applications in HCI, and UX research, design, and evaluation of AI-empowered systems. All the aforementioned perspectives and currently active fields of research are reflected in the articles presented in this year's proceedings.

One volume of the HCII 2022 proceedings is dedicated to this year's edition of the AI-HCI conference and it focuses on topics related to human-centered AI, explainable and trustworthy AI, UX design and evaluation of AI-enabled systems, AI applications in HCI, and human-AI collaboration, as well as AI for speech and text analysis.

Papers of this volume are included for publication after a minimum of two single-blind reviews from the members of the AI-HCI Program Board or, in some cases, from members of the Program Boards of other affiliated conferences. We would like to thank all of them for their invaluable contribution, support and efforts.

June 2022

Helmut Degen
Stavroula Ntoa

3rd International Conference on Artificial Intelligence in HCI (AI-HCI 2022)

The full list with the Program Board Chairs and the members of the Program Boards of all thematic areas and affiliated conferences is available online at

http://www.hci.international/board-members-2022.php

HCI International 2023

The 25th International Conference on Human-Computer Interaction, HCI International 2023, will be held jointly with the affiliated conferences at the AC Bella Sky Hotel and Bella Center, Copenhagen, Denmark, 23–28 July 2023. It will cover a broad spectrum of themes related to human-computer interaction, including theoretical issues, methods, tools, processes, and case studies in HCI design, as well as novel interaction techniques, interfaces, and applications. The proceedings will be published by Springer. More information will be available on the conference website: http://2023.hci.international/.

General Chair
Constantine Stephanidis
University of Crete and ICS-FORTH
Heraklion, Crete, Greece
Email: general_chair@hcii2023.org

http://2023.hci.international/

Contents

Human-Centered AI

Explainable and Trustworthy AI

AI Applications in HCI

Human-Centered AI

Exploring the Design Context of AI-Powered Services: A Qualitative Investigation of Designers' Experiences with Machine Learning

Emil Bergström and Pontus Wärnestål(✉)

Department of Informatics, School of Information Technology, Halmstad University, Halmstad, Sweden
{emil.bergstrom,pontus.warnestal}@hh.se

Abstract. Artificial Intelligence (AI) has provided user experience (UX) designers with a richer toolset. To use technologies such as Machine Learning (ML) that can expand their creative capacity to design intelligent services. ML has the capability to enhance the user experience, for example, by improving efficiency, personalization, and context-aware adaptation. However, research suggests ML as a challenging design material in UX practice, such as difficulties in comprehending data dependencies when prototyping, or the lack of tools and methods for evaluating adaptive user experiences. Previous research indicates that lack of knowledge transfer into the UX design practice may hamper innovative potential. This work aims to provide new insights on how designers think about – and experience – design for AI-powered services. It is important to make ML-powered services beneficial and sustainable for end-users, organizations, and society. Therefore, we explore UX designers' reflections and experiences of using ML in a design context. We have performed nine deep explorative interviews with professional designers that work with ML. The respondents have different backgrounds, seniority, and work in different sectors. The collected interview material was qualitatively analyzed and resulted in five conceptual themes for how UX designers experience the design context surrounding AI-powered services: 1) Absence of competence, 2) Lack of incentive for competence development, 3) Challenges in articulating design criteria, 4) Mature vs. Immature clients, and 5) Lack of support for ethical concerns. We provide implications for how these themes affect the design context and practice.

Keywords: Machine learning · Design material · UX design practice · Interaction design

1 Introduction

Recent advances in Artificial Intelligence (AI) have provided user experience (UX) designers with rich opportunities to use technologies such as Machine Learning (ML) to

H. Degen and S. Ntoa (Eds.): HCII 2022, LNAI 13336, pp. 3–21, 2022.
https://doi.org/10.1007/978-3-031-05643-7_1

expand their creative capacity to design intelligent services. For example, recommendation algorithms use interaction history and user modeling to provide personalization in music, movie, and shopping services. Other examples include ML-powered stock robots that automatically invest and manages money on end-users' behalf. Within the health and wellness sectors AI applications range from medical systems, such as image identification, or predicting menstrual cycles based on user-logged historical data, to nutrition and physical fitness apps that track and analyze activity and food intake. Researchers and digital designers recognize that the ML trend has become especially interesting since it opens for many new design opportunities for UX designers [e.g., 5, 18–24].

Yang, Zimmerman, Steinfeld and Tomasic [19] suggest that ML is rapidly becoming an integrated part of UX design. Even though ML has shown capabilities to empower the UX in today's services and products, researchers report that the UX design practice struggles with complex challenges handling ML as a design material [e.g., 6, 22, 19]. Yang, Scuito, Zimmerman, Forlizzi and Steinfeld [22] published an overview of identified challenges of UX designers working with ML as a design material. For example, UX designers struggle to work with data scientists proactively, and they typically have not acquired efficient methods or skills to sketch and prototype ML-powered services. Working with ML is technically knowledge-demanding for designers, and the current design process consequently change due to the lack of design tools and methods to test the viability of ML-empowered solutions. Holmquist [7] report on several challenges in a survey on UX designers' situations working with ML. For example, UX designers voice concerns regarding whether ML-powered services have ethical and purposeful outcomes or not. It is also suggested that UX designers' challanges with working with ML hamper their potential for innovation and to ideate beyond the less obvious design solutions. Moreover, there has been an ongoing discussion in research about approaching UX design practice while working with ML as a new design material [e.g., 1, 6, 20].

Goodman, Stolterman and Wakkary [14] discuss the UX design practice as professionals who design digital things for people's use, designing for the user experience. Research describes UX design practice as rather complex as it involves tackling ill-defined design problems and wicked dilemmas [6, 14]. Thus, the research describes UX design practice complexity depending on several factors, such as type of context, clients [14], design material [23] and social and societal impact [9]. Goodman et al. [14] discusses how a UX designer needs to be prepared for complex design dilemmas and not guided through one. UX design practice does not involve any prescribed design process that would lead a designer to a particular result. They give an overview of rigorous and disciplined aspects, describing that despite design complexity, a "good" designerly approach can lead to successful or even innovative results. Designers need to comprehend the right competence and tools to support them in approaching a complex situation.

Several recent papers aim to inform how ML affects society within different contextual circumstances. For example, challenges of designing for explainable AI [24] and critical advances in recommender systems [11]. Research illustrates several challenges that can interrupt UX designers during their design practice [1, 5, 7, 20–23]. Thus, there have been previous concerns that less research aims to influence UX designers' practice concerning how to improve their situation of handling design problems [14]. This study explores the UX designers' reflections on their experience of using ML during their practice. The research question pursued in this paper is: "*How do UX designers experience ML as a design material?*" This paper contributes to UX design practice by providing a set of themes derived from interviews with UX designers where they reflect on their experiences of working with ML in their design practice. The contribution advances our current understanding of how UX design practice may need to evolve as AI technologies such as ML continue to influence UX design practice. New insights on this matter for the research community and UX design professionals are important to work more effectively and to make AI-powered services beneficial and sustainable for individual end-users, organizations, and society.

The rest of this paper is structured as follows. First, we provide a literature overview of UX design practice and design materials and how research addresses ML as a design material. Following, our research approach is described, followed by the development of these study findings from interviews on how UX designers reflect on their experience working with ML. The findings indicate that designers are facing different design challenges that seem to disrupt their design practice. The paper is concluded with a discussion of the identified challenges and ML as a design material in UX design practice.

2 Literature Review

2.1 UX Design Practice and the Concept of a Design Material

The user experience (UX) design practice is to design products or services by understanding how users interact with them to design for the UX [14]. Löwgren and Stolterman [9] proposes that UX design practice explores possible futures, often using participatory methods. A UX designers' education regarding design practice includes understanding the design process [13]. There are several different design processes, examples are Goal-directed Design [4] and User-centered design [3]. In general, education teaches practitioners a design process where the user of the product or service is in focus [13]. In other words, the user's goals and needs are in focus.

During the past decades, research has discussed design practice as a rather complicated task. According to Cross [6], design problems are often recognized as ill-defined and ill-structured. Goodman, Stolterman and Wakkary [14] describes the complex situations designers encounter with digital design as "wicked problems". The UX designer encounters "infinite" different factors in the design decisions, such as the type of the clients, the product's societal impact, or identifying user needs. The UX design practice involves assessing alternative designs in parallel to present arguments for considering a solution. The UX designer's practice requires addressing projects that seem to be poorly structured, subjective, and fuzzy to be rigorous and disciplined. A rational and disciplined designer should know what tools and methods to use to reach design rationality, as it is necessary to articulate the criteria for the assessment. For example, to achieve the users' goal or to fulfill a business value. The decisions a designer takes during the design process could significantly impact the UX of a service. Goodman et al. [14] prescribes different kinds of support that designers use to manage complex situations. The list is not exhaustive but illustrates a general overview based on previous studies in UX design practice:

- Precise and simple tools or techniques (sketching, prototypes, interviews, surveys, observations, etc.)
- Frameworks that do not prescribe but that support reflection and decision-making (design patterns, ways of using prototypes, styles of interaction, etc.)
- Individual concepts that are intriguing and open for interpretation and reflection on how they can be used (affordance, persona, probe, etc.)
- High-level theoretical and/or philosophical ideas and approaches expand design thinking but do not prescribe design action (reflective practice, human-centered design, experience design, design rationale, etc.).

A design material includes hardware and software such as a smartphone or laptop and the components that the digital thing is made from, such as sensors, algorithms, or touch screens. According to Fernaeus and Sundström [23], it is unrealistic that one designer should understand all different materials and how they interact with each other. Also, the design practice always differs in one way or another, either in a new context, limited by resources, type of clients, the user, or different types of design material [8]. A UX designer's practice involves exploring relationships between different design solutions involving different design materials [14]. They argue that a designer needs to be prepared for action rather than guided-in-action. They should respect and understand the complexity and richness of a design situation with the support of tools and methods and a positive state in mind. Rather than follow a prescriptive procedure. Cross's [6] paper illustrates the complexity a designer encounters that it is challenging to determine, that the "correct" knowledge informing the solution is not always to be found. Goodman, Stolterman and Wakkary [14] argues there is no such thing as a "right" way of proceeding with the design practice, which indicates that there could be more than one combination of design materials that could solve a design dilemma.

Löwgren [8] compares a UX designer deciding on a digital design material to a product designer who would need to be aware of the physical characteristics of materials such as plastic, wood, metal and how these components fit together. To fit the components together so that it, for example, looks aesthetically pleasing and so that it meets the user's expectations of what is experienced as ergonomic. A particular design value comes from the quality of a service or product fulfilling or exceeding the users' expectations. Löwgren and Stolterman [9] discusses the dilemma of responsibility from the UX designer and how design changes people's experience of things by shaping and implementing digital services and products into someone's life. Goodman et al. [14] illustrate the UX design practice as the middleman or the translator between people and with actors with different educational and professional backgrounds. That there is not just the users' needs and goals to meet but also the other actors involved.

Researchers claim that research should not just focus their study on the user's experience, but also aim to influence professional design practitioners [13, 14]. Goodman et al. [14] acknowledge three main concerns from research about influencing professional design practitioners: 1) the lack of knowledge transfer from research to design practice, 2) design practitioners do not apply theories or methods because of time, cost, or workplace constraints, and 3) The latter is that researchers misinterpret how designers perceive or experience design problems, which has led to the result that methods, tools, and techniques researchers contribute with sometimes are irrelevant for designers. This opens the gap of understanding the designer's reflection on their experience using new design materials during their practice.

2.2 Machine Learning as a Design Material

In the past decades, clients and UX designers have started to notice the potential of ML's UX-empowering capabilities, such as facilitating more accurate decisions or improving efficiency in achieving one's goals (10, 19). Even though ML empower the UX in today's services and products, other researchers claim that the design practice underlies complex challenges handling ML as a design material [e.g., 5, 18, 21]. Designers face challenges understanding ML limitations as it goes outside a designer's education and competence – forcing them to rely more on data experts [5]. Yang, Scuito, Zimmerman, Forlizzi and Steinfeld [21] also indicates that ML as a design material has shown to question the designer's education and design practice, if ML is too technically knowledge-demanding design material for designers and if a designer's education and current competence are enough to work with ML as a material. They claim that UX education needs a more data-driven culture to learn the basics of data science terminology. This would enhance designers' experience and open new doors for creativity, such as understanding user behavior through data or identifying design goals through telemetry data visualizations. Yang, Steinfeld, Rosé and Zimmerman [22] also raise the importance of environmental constraints, laws, and regulations when proposing a real-world ML solution. For example, to know who is responsible for the data or regulations depending on the target group. Dove, Halskov, Forlizzi and Zimmerman [5] claim that the complex technical knowledge with ML drives design-led innovation to become rare because designers need to focus more on collaboration with data scientists, which has led to designers having a more challenging time seeing ML features that are less obvious, imagining something in addition to previous ML trends.

Another challenge is the lack of existing tools and methods when working with ML. Yang [19] mentions the challenges to ideate with sketching or prototyping with large datasets, computational power, time, and dependency on data scientists. That "fail fast and fail often" does not apply to current design practice with ML as a design material. The effort of working with ML is too demanding. Designers have tools for prototyping responsive web services, and that makes it easy to simulate the behavior of an app on the smartphone, but they have nothing that helps them quickly prototype and understand the UX impact of false negative and false positive responses from an ML service [22]. Yang, Scuito, Zimmerman, Forlizzi and Steinfeld [21] question if the current design process should change to the lack of design tools and methods to effectively test the viability of ML-empowered solutions. Dove et al. [5] mention that digital designers usually do not have an effective way of working with ML features, that they sometimes simply just apply it at the end of the project. They also mention the lack of ways to ideate and evaluate interactive prototypes, that they currently work with storytelling, narratives, or films to prototype the experience of products that yet do not exist. They claim that designers clearly demand new ways to work with ML as a design material. Amershi et al. [1] claim that ML can bring with it everything from costs to benefits or uncertainties in a designer's practice and describes the designer's routine job to handle such trade-offs. They emphasize the concerns of designers requiring support to work efficiently with

ML, which does not currently exist. Another challenge that there is a risk that the design process gets constrained by available data and its quality from the current design project [21].

Another challenge is designers' concern if they create something ethical and purposeful. Dove et al. [5] claim that we need to bring the human voice into the solutions to facilitate understanding the ethical impacts. Yang et al. [22] points out the challenges to design for unpredictability. Such as trespassing integrity data or designing to prevent users from losing control because of the ML features. For many non-technical digital users, an ML-based system is a black box [15]. This black-box phenomenon can cause the users to question the system's decisions. This reflexive skepticism can directly affect users' trust and decision-making efficiency, affecting the adoption of ML-based solutions, consequently affecting the design decisions for designers.

Yang [19] argues that designers do not recognize where and how knowledge of ML can add value to their practice. Knowing how to work with ML must be better integrated into design practice for designers to understand the value of understanding it more fully. As it currently stands, designers face various challenges to exploit their full potential.

3 Method

We set out for a qualitative investigation of research for design, an approach to studying and informing complex situations in doing design [15]. We wanted to build on previous investigations in research on UX design practice working with ML as a design material. We choose to conduct an exploratory interview study with professional UX designers that had experience working with ML as a design material. The intention of choosing an interview study was to get a deeper insight into the current UX design practice and a general overview of what is now an arising research area.

3.1 Empirical Data Collection

This study's empirical material consisted of exploratory interviews with nine professional UX designers carried out online on Zoom during spring 2021. The recruitment was done with different design agencies to get various representing voices. The criteria of recruitment were that the designer had experience designing products or services that enhanced UX with ML in at least one project. We wanted to generate a representative empirical overview of how UX designers currently experience ML as a design material, thus establish an open and not-guided empirical material. Table 1 summarizes the representation of the recruited UX designers, for example what kind of schooling they had designing with ML and type of projects they worked with ML before.

All interviews were recorded with informed consent. The interviews were designed to be approximately one hour long and were audio-recorded. The preparation of the interviews followed Myers and Newman [12] way of discussing qualitative interviews. We designed the interview questions to be open and explorative. For example, "How would you describe ML?", "How did you learn about ML in the design?", or "Could you describe the process of considering ML in the digital design?".

The openness meant that we could follow up with improvised questions if anything interesting were discussed.

Table 1. Interviews with UX designers

ID	ML education	Design project example	UX experience	ML experience
P1	None	Recommender in clothing app	8 yrs	2 projects
P2	Learning by working and self-interest	Monitoring of production process	6 yrs	1 project
P3	Learning by working and self-interest	Crossword puzzle maker	5 yrs	3 projects
P4	Learning by working, self-interest and one ML course	Decision support app	5 yrs	2 projects
P5	Learning by working	Robot monitoring process	1 yrs	1 project
P6	Learning by working	Intelligent conversation robot	10+ yrs	2 projects
P7	Learning by working and self-interest	Intelligent client surveys	3 yrs	4 projects
P8	Some education, self-interest and learning by working	Medical facilitation service	4 yrs	1 project
P9	Research, learning by working, self-interest	An adaptive speaking dialogue system	10+ yrs	5+ projects

3.2 Thematic Analysis

The gathered empirical material was analyzed using the thematic analysis method described by Braun and Clarke [2]. It was considered as a suitable method for organizing and identifying patterns in the large empirical data set. We sought to provide a rich thematic analysis of the entire data set so that the themes would represent how UX designers experience using ML as a design material. The themes were identified inductively, meaning that they were strongly linked to the gathered empirical data and not towards any theoretical framework. First, the recordings were transcribed and read to identify meaing-bearing units of text relevant to the research question. Second, units of text were analyzed by attaching codes. The coding was conducted to show patterns from semantic content, meaning that there was no attempt to theorize or analyze the broader meaning of the text units. See Table 2 for an example of the coding process.

Third, we systematically grouped the codes into categories that were dealing with the same issue. For example, codes about education related to ethics were grouped up in "education about ethics". The same code could reappear in more than one category. Grouping the codes together were relatively flexible in that it relied upon what we interpreted as interesting. This was an iterative process, going back and forth about how the codes related to each other. Fourth, the thematic analysis resulted in 45 categories

Table 2. Interview data extract of meaing-bearing phrases, transformed with code applied

Data extract	With code applied
"it's a pretty big knowledge threshold to be able to feel comfortable putting things up in Github and testing things out"	Knowledge threshold
"Today you are not rewarded for taking risks, but you are rewarded for not doing anything and then you do nothing"	No reward for taking risks
"It is often based on a trust that one must earn"	Trust is something you earn
"the clients need to understand what an AI can do and not do"	Teaching clients

that we grouped into five themes. The theming process was done by grouping categories that were related to each other. The last step was defining the essence of the themes. This was done by analyzing and refining the data in each theme and giving the themes their final name. A short sentence that was obvious, had a clear meaning and that reflected the meaning of the collected data.

4 Findings

Below we demonstrate the result of the thematic analysis which ended up in five different themes: absence of competence, lack of incentive for competence development, challenges articulating design criteria, mature versus immature clients and lack of support for ethical concerns.

4.1 Absence of Competence

Eight out of nine UX designers stated that they had no school education on how to work with ML in UX design practice. They shared that they learned about it from their design projects they were working on, or that they themselves tried to learn about it in their free time like reading articles and watching YouTube clips. "*It's really just experiences from different companies where you have worked with machine learning as a design material"* (P4). Additionally, another designer stated, "*I learned about it partly through lectures on YouTube from MIT linked to human-centered AI"* (P7).

The designers expressed that working with ML as a design material required new methods and tools to work with it effectively. For example, sketching ideas during UX design practice involving ML becomes more like a dialog between the system and the user. P3 stated it as: "*When I sketch with other design materials, I think this is how it comes out. But when I draw something for AI, I rather think that this is a scenario, this is what a dialogue could look like*".

Designers also expressed that UX design practice involving ML requires competence in data and data science, in the design team but also that designers require competence within it to work with it effectively. UX designers that had some competence with data and data science expressed how helpful it was learning about the basics of technical techniques and methods. "*By communication, I do not mean one way but both ways. You as a designer must also be able to explain why onboarding is important, the other is that you must also listen. You also have to listen to the developers, aha! can you do such a regression or clustering, then we can build this functionality" (P9).*

The respondents also raised ethical concerns as an important but complex subject when working with ML as a design material. The designers shared different kinds of ethical concerns and their complexity. They stated uncertainty about how to work around complex ethical questions and expressed if it even was within a UX designer's responsibility to handle these kinds of questions. "*Just because you are a decision-maker in something does not mean that you always understand the consequences of the decision that is made*" (P7). P2 stated a complexed design situation if a ML solution replaced human competence: "*It is difficult for users to understand how different it would be as they might not even need to be in the workplace, they might lose their jobs […] I understand the complexity. But not at an application level. But you must draw the line somewhere, what it is you are supposed to know*".

The majority of the UX designers stated that ethics was more of a discussion in their workplace between colleges and that they did not work from a particular method or framework. This was something that they indicated as something that would be good to have. "*We do not have such an established process around ethics, which you may feel that we should have […] It is more of a thing that you discuss with colleagues*" (P2).

The designers also raised laws and regulations as one competence outside their own regarding ML as a design material. And that it makes them hesitate, which leads them not to dare to take any chances. P6 expressed it as: "*Machine learning is like the GDPR, like a big paper dragon that you pull out and no one really knows what the GDPR is. Everyone thinks it's scary, stupid and bad. […] Today you are not rewarded for taking risks, but you are rewarded for not doing anything and then you do nothing*".

All but one UX designer had any formal education of how to work with ML as a design material in UX design practice. According to the anecdotes provided in the interviews, working with ML often requires understanding within areas the UX designers did not have competence in, such as data science, laws and regulation, and ethical concerns. The overall picture is that UX designers working with ML expressed uncertainty because of absence of competence with it, consequently missing out on possible solutions.

4.2 Lack of Incentive for Competence Development

The UX designers shared that they recognized a greater desire to use ML from clients. However, there was currently both no clear incentive and responsibility for the UX designers' competence development with a new design material such as ML. "*There is a certain trend level of machine learning […] It can definitely be an area that will be much stronger. There is an ambition. But you get stuck in the fact that it's actually quite difficult. You need to try to sell through it to clients and meanwhile build up competence around it*" (P2).

The majority of UX designers expressed not being fully aware of what their rolc in UX design practice was when working with ML, or what competence they are expected to possess if they even needed to increase their skillset at all or if they could rely on other competences. "*It's a little too abstract and it's a little too much to understand for me to want to broaden my own skillset with it right now […] But if something happens? Who is responsible? It still goes a bit beyond my role"* (P6).

Some UX designers expressed different incentives with competence development with ML as a designer. Understanding data dependency from the existing digital service facilitated articulating the criteria of the assessment. P3 stated *"The most important thing is that you need to check with those who work with the data. Can we build this? Do we have data for this, or do we need to collect it?"*.

Other UX designers stated that competence development with ML would save time communicating with the developers and that it would facilitate testing design solutions *"It require that you as a designer need to orientate yourself about data science and machine learning and to understand the vocabulary […] To make the design concepts so concrete that they are helpful to a programmer […] You can save one month of time without understanding what they actually mean if you understand coding"* (P9). Also, that ML was expressed to involve a lot of complexed legal questions that the majority of the UX designers did not have competence with which resulted in that ideas was missed out on. *"Sometimes we round things up already at the idea stage […] This means that, unfortunately, ideas have been put away that could be incredibly helpful, if there are legal concerns, it may be that we do nothing.* (P6).

Most designers also expressed how developing competence with ML would facilitate various confidential skills as a professional UX designer. To be trustworthy in your design articulation that there is a business value using ML in your design. *You can talk, but you also must deliver […] It is often based on trust that one must earn […] Having the vocabulary for adaptivity, prediction and data strategy and data bias […] You need to prove that you understand their business problems.* (P9).

The UX designers voiced that the lack of competence development made them miss out on ideas that could be valuable for the design. Also, that they do not dare or have the confidence to move on with a design solution they do not fully understand. The UX designers expressed that ML is a new and demanding design material compared to their current design expertise. Clients' need is not enough, but it needs to be in the strategy that the company they work for.

4.3 Challenges Articulating Design Criteria

A common challenge lies in designing for MLs unpredictable capabilities. The respondents shared that ML involved anticipating users' actions and simultaneously the ML action. They expressed that it was challenging to articulate the design criteria for a design solution involving MLs unpredictable capabilities. *"What happens if you unleash an algorithm that is supposed to make decisions that can affect someone's health or someone's finances*?" (P1). A majority of designers expressed that when UX design practice involves MLs unpredictability capabilities some design criteria become more prioritized. Such as traceability and transparency, the users of a digital service may want to be aware of how ML bases its result on. Also, it involves designing for the user's experience to feel comfortable with the ML solution. The UX design practice involving ML is expressed entailing articulating design criteria that is based on anticipating users' expectations and needs, which was expressed as challenging. *"I think that is what also makes UX designers to have a very important role, as a change agent, to include fears and to be able to address them early in the process. Will this be a threat to a user's integrity? It feels stressful because I'm being monitored. Then it will not be a good project. I think that you as a UX designer need to consider this more than in other digitalization projectors that I have worked in"* (P6).

P6 statement also mentions the complexity of articulating assessments when it is okay or not regarding trespassing a user's integrity. The UX designers expressed different design dilemmas that ML entailed. Involving anticipating a user experience of a service and preventing the user from becoming afraid of the MLs unpredictable capabilities. The UX designers also stated that it creates communication issues of what it can possibly do, they described ML as disruptive, that it is challenging to articulate the service value, what it should and should not do, or if a ML solution was needed at all. "*We design what it should do if something goes wrong, but what happens when everything goes well? [...]There is no one who wants to sit and watch something that says that everything is good all day long, what do you show then? [...] I would call it disruptive. It changes the conditions in many ways. An app project may no longer be an app project, you realize after a while. Why should I have an app? Do I need an interface?* (P2).

The UX designers expressed different unpredictable design dilemmas that they encountered during design practice involving ML. The unpredictability entailed challenges to articulate what design criteria to fulfill to accomplish an successful design project. Some concepts are expressed as more prioritized when working with ML, such as, transparency, and traceability and to design for comfortability when trespassing a user's integrity. Also, MLs unpredictability involved articulating design criteria if the design solution brings enough value for the user to be used at all.

4.4 Mature Versus Immature Clients

The UX designers were concerned that ML is becoming "a big trend" or a "buzzword". They stated that this has caused the clients to become more interested in design projects that involved ML. Also, the UX designers expressed that ML was more interesting to use because it opens a lot of new value possibilities. "*There is a certain trend level of machine learning [...] I think the great interest in AI is that it feels like magic, that is, with machine learning*" (P2). However, designers expressed pressure from the client to use ML in their design solution. P5 was asked: "*Why do you choose to use their lead in the design?*" and simply answered: "*Because clients demand it*". Further, the designers expressed that the relationship with the client is important and that it is the designer's responsibility to help them understand what ML can and cannot do. "*The client needs to understand what an AI can do and not do. You are the one who needs to help with the conditions with what is possible and what is not possible. How do they need to think about data and then also present what it looks like when an AI makes a decision?" (P7).*

However, the majority of the UX designers expressed that their practice changed depending on the client's digital maturity, that implies for example, if they have an already working digital product or if they work in a digital industry. "*It probably goes hand in hand with how digital the client is [...] If the client already has a product that is very adapted for abstract things, then this will just be another [...] Some work more old-fashioned and are perhaps a little more conservative, then this will be another scary thing. There is a very big difference" (P6).*

P6 stated that a more mature client could be if they already acted in an industry and was used to working with data, and if they already had a stable digital infrastructure within the company. "*As if you work with an insurance company where you are used to and work a lot with data, where you are used to calculated risk and so on. They think we already know this. Then it will be quite easy[...]It is easier for companies that already have the infrastructure where this can just be pushed in, so it is much easier to find both who owns the data, who should be the security, classification of the data and all such things that it can be" (P6).*

P8 expressed the contrast of UX design practice that involves working with more mature and less mature clients. When talking about the more mature client: "*There is a goalkeeper in goal. There are laws and rules that one must abide by. It is a huge difference to work with a company that is aware of how ML affects people and the ethical" (P8). And when talking about a less mature company: "A company that has no hesitations at all, but just wants to make more money"* (P8).

A majority of designers expressed that the UX design practice differentiated with the more immature clients, they needed much closer contact and more guided communication. Also, to inform the client about the requirements about ML, and what the ML can and cannot do. "*Holding the client in the hand, especially those clients who do not have the knowledge. For them it is a bit scary and new, and they are afraid that the budget will run away" (P4).*

4.5 Lack of Support for Ethical Concerns

The designers expressed that they tried to work from putting the user in focus, identifying the user value, and that they wanted to enhance the user experience rather than automate. "*We talk a lot about human centered AI rather than just designing for AI*" (P7). The UX designers also stated that it is their responsibility to communicate ethical concerns. "*We have no work documentation for ethics, which I know in any case, but it's our own responsibility. To communicate with clients and users"* (P3). Several the designers also expressed that the ethical concern often was neglected due to no ways to communicate about it during design practice, that it ended up more of a discussion regarding their own moral values and knowledge and that it less often was followed up. "*We do not have an established process around ethics, which you may feel that we should have [...] It is more of a thing that you discuss with colleagues*" (P2).

The respondents also expressed concerns about the UX design practice involving ML and mentioned things like "dark patterns". The UX designers suggested several different examples where other companies had used so-called dark pattern design where ML was involved. "*Not to design according to dark patterns and other such ugly tricks it is. [...] Google face recognition did not identify people with skin color other than white so to speak. And that must not happen" (P1).*

The ability of ML to empower a business value might be too forceful so that a designer can not say no to feature suggestions. That it often falls on how someone can earn a business value on the solution. P2 stated it as: "*Some features may be so heavenly good that it does not really become a user value but more a business value. That the user disappears"*. P8 expressed that MLs ability to enhance the business value could lead UX designers to make decisions they do not honestly agree to. That there is an external pressure such as salary and design repetition that could affect the design decisions they make. Several designers expressed that they need to be able to communicate human value before business value. *"It affects the design. We design things that we may deep down feel this does not feel good. But I have to get my salary and in other countries it may even be my insurance [...] You represent a designer in some way [...] It is unreasonable to demand this from completely green and young designers; how should you be able to resist a client?" (P8).*

The designers also expressed concerns that ML solutions could have consequences to society in the long term. They expressed that government should take their responsibility and form rules and regulations about ML, which the UX designers can back up their arguments towards. P8 had worked with ML in areas with already existing boundaries and experienced this as helpful in his design practice. *"What knowledge are we as a society prepared to lose? Society and politics have a huge responsibility to produce rules and laws for us [...] The good thing about working in the medical field is that there are a lot of ethical rules. This affects my design. How I visualize, what functions should I build in to make it feel safe for the doctor to use the algorithm to make a diagnosis".*

The majority of the UX designers expressed that working with ML during design practice often involved ethical concerns. However, the UX designers also expressed that it was challenging to work around ethics, that they did not have support to communicate it, but that instead got neglected, or discussed between colleagues. The UX designers stated that they do not have much to rely on when it comes to advising in ethical concerns. Their company's ethical standards or their own or their colleagues' moral values are often undefined or of little use in practice. This lack of support could even affect the UX designer's personal life, as the borders between everyday life and work practice can be blurred.

4.6 Concluding Remarks

The thematic analysis was carried out from the empirical material that consists of nine professional UX designers describing their experiences of working in UX design practice with ML as a design material. From the empirical material collection, we identified five themes. They are reflected upon below and summarized in Table 3.

The first theme illustrates a general overview of UX designers' lack of competence working with ML UX design practice. This experience interconnects with all the other themes of experiences, which also illustrate the relevance of this theme. The absence of competence presents several examples of designers' abstractions when working with ML which could have challenging consequences. For example, the lack of data and data science competence creates extra communication hours between the designer and others involved in the design project, and how they currently do no not reason with the ethical consequences, such as replacing a human's intellectual skill. The absence of competence theme illustrates both a lack of education and knowledge within the UX field when working with ML as a design material.

The lack of incentives for competence development was identified because the UX designers did not express encouragement of wanting to learn more about working with ML during design practice. All the designers expressed that ML had interesting opportunities that could open new doors for creativity and could be valuable for the design.

Table 3. Summary of the five identified themes

UX designers' experience of ML	Description
Absence of competence	UX designers expressed working with ML as a design material requires other competencies than they previously needed during UX design practice. The UX designers indicated a need for competence development regarding new methods and tools, data science, ethics and how to work with legal issues
Lack of incentive for competence development	UX design practice involving ML shows to have less apparent incentives for designers to develop their competence. The findings show that competence development within ML in design practice could improve a UX designer. For example, basic knowledge of data and data science can have many significant rewards such as an increased credibility as a designer and an increased trust from the client
Challenges articulating design criteria	This finding illustrates the challenges for UX designers articulating design criteria working with ML. Design practice involves dealing with different unpredictable design situations that cause new complex design questions such as how to design around trespassing integrity and how to inform the user without threatening the user
Mature vs. immature client	Depending on the digital maturity of the client the UX designers expressed that the designers need to adapt their design practice. The designers described some of the different characteristics of what is a more mature client and less mature. A more mature client who works in a business where they are used to working with data such as insurance companies where they make risk analysis based on data. A less mature client was expressed as someone that does not have a finished product yet or where there is not a stable data infrastructure

(continued)

Table 3. (*continued*)

UX designers' experience of ML	Description
Lack of support for ethical concerns	A UX design practice that involves working with ML was expressed involving complex design situations involving ethical concerns. However, the UX designers expressed not having any tools and support to articulate and discuss ethical concerns, instead they stated that they were neglected or not taken seriously. The dilemma for the designer thus becomes how to handle the responsibility for sometimes large societal questions

Moreover, the UX designers stated that they instead learned to work with ML through projects and their own interest. The lack of incentive for competence development theme also illustrates examples of what could be incentives to learn. One example was that designer's that had competence with data and data science entailed credibility as a designer which enhanced trust from the client. Another dilemma that the UX designers expressed concerning lack of incentive for competence development was whether it was within their responsibility to learn about ML. Now, they seem to rely on the design agency they work for to encourage the UX designers to learn about ML as a design material. However, the UX designers stated no encouragement from the agencies to show that kind of effort.

Challenges articulating design criteria theme illustrates the challenge for UX designers to articulate design criteria while working with ML. ML gives rise to design dilemmas that are "unpredictable". The UX designers expressed that while working with ML, it entailed disorders in their design practice. Designers gave examples where they were puzzled with different design dilemmas, such as whether the ML-empowered solution even required an interface at all, and that a design solution could replace a user's intellectual skill, which the designers got confronted by as they have always been taught to put the user in the center. One of the designers expressed that working with ML included other types of responsibility, including being a "change agent" which means designing a sense of security or credibility in the ML that underpins the service to build trust among the users. The experience illustrates that MLs capabilities involve articulating criteria that the designer might not have the tools or methods to explore. Consequently, they end up in a design situation where they do not know how to proceed or what the rational approach should be.

The UX designers expressed that more clients want to use ML because of its "magic" capabilities. The mature vs. immature client theme illustrates that the UX designer needs to adapt their way of working with them depending on their digital maturity. The designer stated some of the different characteristics of a more mature client versus a less mature. For example, a more mature client works in an existing business where they are used to working with data, such as insurance companies where they makc risk analysis based on data. A less mature client was characterized as someone that does not have a finished product yet or where there is not a stable data infrastructure. Depending on the digital maturity of the client, the UX designers also expressed other types of preparation and design questions could vary. The UX designers expressed that the design practice with less mature clients implied more discussion if ML even were relevant, considering the client's goals and needs. For example, a futuristic sketch of what the ML could do when the service or product had collected enough data. The more mature clients could, for example, appreciate that the designer put the ethical consequences before the business value, or the communication with a more mature client communication was much more accessible. The respondents expressed that working with ML implies teaching the clients ML requirements, ethical consequences, and business value of AI in general.

The subject of ethics was one of the more common subjects during the interviews with the UX designers. Even though the majority of the UX designers advocated to put the user first during the UX design practice, they indicated a lack of support for ethical concerns. They expressed that the ethical concerns often got neglected and that they did not possess the right tools or support for articulating their arguments with ethics. They expressed that it is currently more of a discussion between colleagues about what their moral values were. Lack of support for ethical concerns indicates that the absence of competence can affect a designer's rational design decisions to build their arguments concerning ethics. They currently do not have support to back up ethical argumentation in design practice to build confidence for their actions.

5 Discussion

The thematic analysis identified five themes of experiences. The themes of experiences summarize the attitudes and complexities designers have when working with ML in design practice and illustrate opportunities for why we need to understand ML as a design material more thoroughly. The themes of experiences distinguish features to support the UX design practice and build on research regarding designers working with ML as a design material. The themes of experiences were:

1) **Absence of competence**, which illustrates UX designers expressing missing competencies to work with ML more effectively,
2) **Lack of incentive for competence development**. The UX designers expressed not having enough apparent incentive to learn about ML,
3) **Challenges articulating criteria**. UX designers expressed that working with ML as a design material entails challenges to articulate design criteria for assessment,
4) **Mature versus immature clients**. Designers need to adapt their design practice depending on the digital maturity of the clients,
5) **Lack of support for ethical concerns**. Ethical concerns were reported as frequently neglected and not discussed seriously in practice, and that the current UX design work contexts lack support for argumentation and discussion.

In line with Goodman, Stolterman and Wakkary's [14] claim that even poorly structured and fuzzy design projects can be rigorous and disciplined with the right tools and methods. This study suggests that the UX design practice lacks handling design situations involving ML effectively since robust tools, competencies, and project structures are not tailored to the specific qualities that ML as a design material introduces. However, in contrast to previous research on ML as a design material in UX design practice [e.g., 5, 7, 19–22], this study contributes with insights from a UX designer's perspective of what the field need to understand and address in practice. This study contributes to an understanding of why we need to learn more about UX designer's experiences of incentives to learn more about ML as a design material. This could inform the UX design industry how and why learning more about ML as a design material would be valuable for them. This could also inform educators to approach this from the right direction, whether it should be different from other design materials and considered as a new design material.

This study indicates that the absence of competence with ML in UX design practice could establish disordering consequences. For example, UX designers need to be able to articulate design criteria for the experience that puts the user in focus. To be able to go forward with ideas that could be valuable for clients and the users. One potential implication would be to prepare the UX design practice with better preparatory means of support. This is in line with Goodman, Stolterman and Wakkarys [14] claim that research needs to influence UX designers' practice. As mature vs. immature clients indicate the characterization of the client was expressed to be meaningful in how to approach a design project. This study calls for research characterizing clients that tend to use ML in their digital solution more fully. This would lead to better preparation of support depending on design the design project. Also, the lack of support for ethical concerns indicates that designers working with ML encounter situations where they express uncertainty in articulating and communicating the criteria for assessment. This study indicates a calling for supporting tools and methods that can back up ethical argumentation in UX design practice, strengthening the designer's confidence and actions. UX designers need to be prepared for action and arrive with the right kind of toolbox for the right design project.

This study investigates an emerging area of UX design practice and research. The majority of the UX designers participating in this research study had less experience working with ML as a design material. That indicates that some of these experiences have a possibility to come with the newness of working with ML as a design material. This might have affected the result, which also advocates for a follow-up study in the future. Still, this research study accounts for the experience of working with the material in the current time. What is also worth noting is that the UX designers who participated in the study were all consultants. This can affect the outcome of the grants that the study advocates. For example, mature vs. Immature can mostly be seen as an experience that a consultant pays attention to. However, it identifies outcomes for design practice in general.

6 Conclusion

Previous research suggests that design practice lacks understanding of how to work with ML as a design material effectively and how it can add value to their practice. This study reports an interview study with nine UX designers' current situation working with ML as a design material. It expands previous research by articulating insights from UX designer's perspectives of what we need to understand about ML in UX practice. It contributes with further insight for researchers studying this domain practice. And hopefully, inform the studied practice itself.

The findings put forward in this study support that ML opens new possibilities for creative and innovative design that can enhance the users' experience. The study indicates that UX design practice face challenges that seem to disrupt their way of working. These challenges are: Absence of competence, Lack of incentive for competence development, Challenges articulating criteria, Mature versus immature clients, and Lack of support for ethical concerns. The findings indicate professional development opportunities that are interesting to consider for design practitioners and researchers.

References

1. Amershi, S., et al.: Guidelines for human-AI interaction. In: CHI 2019, Glasgow, pp. 1–13 (2019)
2. Braun, V., Clarke, V.: Using thematic analysis in psychology. Qual. Res. Psychol. **3**, 77–101 (2006)
3. Courage, C., Baxter, K.: Understanding Your Users: A Practical Guide to User Requirements Methods, Tools, and Techniques, Gulf Professional Publishing, Amsterdam (2005)
4. Cooper, A., Reimann, R., Cronin, D., Noessel, C.: About Face: The Essentials of Interaction Design. Wiley, Indianapolis (2014)
5. Dove, G., Halskov, K., Forlizzi, J., Zimmerman, J.: UX design innovation: challenges for working with machine learning as a design material. In: CHI 2017, Denver, pp. 278–288 (2017)
6. Cross, N.: Designerly ways of knowing. Des. Stud. **3**(4), 221–227 (1982)
7. Holmquist, L.E.: Intelligence on tap: artificial intelligence as a new design material. Interactions **24**, 28–33 (2017)
8. Löwgren, J.: Interaction Design - brief intro, The encyclopedia of human-computer interaction, The Interaction Design Foundation (2012). https://www.interaction-design.org/literature/book/the-encyclopedia-of-human-computer-interaction-2nd-ed/interaction-design-brief-intro
9. Löwgren, J., Stolterman, E.: Design av informationsteknik: Materialet utan egenskaper, Studentlitteratur AB, Lund (2004)
10. Komischke, T.: Human-centered artificial intelligence considerations and implementations: a case study from software product development. In: Degen, H., Ntoa, S. (eds.) HCII 2021. LNCS, vol. 12797, pp. 260–268. Springer, Cham (2021). https://doi.org/10.1007/978-3-030-77772-2_17
11. Konstan, J.A., Riedl, J.: Recommender systems: from algorithms to user experience. User Model User Adapt. Interact. **22**, pp. 101–123 (2012)
12. Myers, M.D., Newman, M.: The qualitative interview in IS research: examining the craft. Inf. Organ. **17**, pp. 2–26 (2007)
13. Getto, G., Beecher, F.: Toward a model of UX education: training UX designers within the academy. IEEE Trans. Prof. Commun. **59**, 153–164 (2016)
14. Goodman, E., Stolterman, E., Wakkary, R.: Understanding interaction design practices. In: Proceedings of the SIGCHI Conference on Human Factors in Computing Systems, pp. 1061–1070 (2011)
15. Stappers, P.J., Giaccardi, E.: Research through design. In: The Encyclopedia of Human-Computer Interaction, The Interaction Design Foundation (2017). https://www.interaction-design.org/literature/book/the-encyclopedia-of-human-computer-interaction-2nd-ed/research-through-design
16. Rittel, H.W., Webber, M.M.: Dilemmas in a general theory of planning. Policy Sci. **4**, 155–169 (1973)

17. Xu, W.: Toward human-centered AI: a perspective from human-computer interaction. Interactions **26**, 42–46 (2019)
18. Yang, Q., Zimmerman, J., Steinfeld, A., Tomasic, A.: Planning adaptive mobile experiences when wireframing. In: DIS 2016, Brisbane, pp. 565–576 (2016)
19. Yang, Q.: Machine learning as a ux design material: how can we imagine beyond automation, recommenders, and reminders? In: AAAI 2018, Pennsylvania, March 2018
20. Yang, Q., Banovic, N., Zimmerman, J.: Mapping machine learning advances from HCI research to reveal starting places for design innovation. In: CHI 2018, Montréal, pp. 1–11, April 2018
21. Yang, Q., Scuito, A., Zimmerman, J., Forlizzi, J., Steinfeld, A.: Investigating how experienced UX designers effectively work with machine learning. In: DIS 2018, Hong Kong, pp. 585–596, June 2018
22. Yang, Q., Steinfeld, A., Rosé, C., Zimmerman, J.: Re-examining whether, why, and how human-AI interaction is uniquely difficult to design. In: CHI 202, Honolulu, pp. 1–13, April 2020
23. Fernaeus, Y., Sundström, P.: The material move how materials matter in interaction design research. In: DIS 2012, Newcastle, pp. 486–495 (2012)
24. Zhu, J., Liapis, A., Risi, S., Bidarra, R., Youngblood, G.M.: Explainable AI for designers: A human-centered perspective on mixed-initiative co-creation. In: IEEE 2018 (CIG), Maastricht, pp. 1–8 (2018)

Measuring and Predicting Human Trust in Recommendations from an AI Teammate

Nikolos Gurney[1], David V. Pynadath[1,2](✉), and Ning Wang[1,2]

[1] Institute for Creative Technologies, University of Southern California, Los Angeles 90094, USA
{gurney,pynadath,nwang}@ict.usc.edu

[2] Computer Science Department, University of Southern California, Los Angeles 90007, USA
http://ict.usc.edu/

Abstract. Predicting compliance with AI recommendations and knowing when to intervene are critical facets of human-AI teaming. AIs are typically deployed in settings where their abilities to evaluate decision variables far exceed the abilities of their human counterparts. However, even though AIs excel at weighing multiple issues and computing near optimal solutions with speed and accuracy beyond that of any human, they still make mistakes. Thus, perfect compliance may be undesirable. This means, just as individuals must know when to follow the advice of other people, it is critical for them to know when to adopt the recommendations from their AI. Well-calibrated trust is thought to be a fundamental aspect of this type of knowledge. We compare the ability of a common trust inventory and the ability of a behavioral measure of trust to predict compliance and success in a reconnaissance mission. We interpret the experimental results to suggest that the behavioral measure is a better predictor of overall mission compliance and success. We discuss how this measure could possibly be used in compliance interventions and related open questions.

Keywords: Trust in AI · Explainable machine learning · AI compliance

Researchers, technologists, and funding agencies simultaneously promote and seek after AI capable of teaming with humans [2,6,17,18]. AI commonly functions as a decision-aid while humans make final decisions in these teams. Although state-of-the-art AI excels at weighing multiple issues to compute optimal solutions, the inherent uncertainty of the real world means that AI will inevitably make mistakes [2]. This means, just as individuals must know when to follow the advice of other people, it is critical for them to know when to adopt the recommendations from their AI. Well-calibrated trust is thought to be a fundamental aspect of this type of knowledge [4,20].

H. Degen and S. Ntoa (Eds.): HCII 2022, LNAI 13336, pp. 22–34, 2022.
https://doi.org/10.1007/978-3-031-05643-7_2

We explored this space in a simulated military reconnaissance mission (a testbed adapted from [21]) where human participants work with an AI teammate to clear potentially dangerous buildings. We adapt and compare a trust inventory and a behavioral measure in their ability to predict participants' compliance, correct choices, and opinions of the AI teammate. We find that the trust measure has a negative correlation with compliance and correct choices. The trust measure does, however, have a positive correlation with participants' ultimate opinions of the AI teammate. Meanwhile, early human behavior within the mission, our behavioral measure, consistently predicts later compliance, including after the AI's mistakes. Moreover, participants who complied early on were also more likely to make correct choices than their non-compliant counterparts.

1 Trust in AI Teammates

Arguably, most human-AI interactions occur because the human wants to reduce some vulnerability and/or uncertainty that they face in the pursuit of a goal. Decision aid AI is often tasked with assessing the potential risk(s) associated with each option that a team faces. The instance that we study, for example, has an AI that assesses the dangers present in a building before human teammates enter and recommends whether they should wear protective equipment [21]. Trust is tightly woven into the decision to heed a recommendation from the robot in this setting and is contingent on a multitude of factors, such as quality of communications [4], perceived robot competence [5], and even embodiment [22]. It is common practice to treat trust as a unitary construct when studying these interactions. This broad conceptualization of trust, however, fails to appreciate that in-the-moment decision making is subject to a plethora of variables that may undermine otherwise healthy trust. With this in mind, we argue that conceptualizing trust as having two distinct types, situational and attitudinal, has outstanding merit for AI researchers. This is not so much a redefining of the construct of trust in AI as it is a bifurcation of instances in which trust is observed and then reflecting that back onto an existing construct.

The American Psychological Association defines trust as the degree to which a person feels that they can rely on somebody to do what they say they will do [1]. This holds for whether the action or effect promised by the other agent is simply implied or explicitly promised. When we refer to situational trust in an AI teammate, we are talking about the degree to which a person feels that they can rely on the AI to reduce the vulnerability and/or uncertainty in a given situation or instance. Whereas situational trust can be specific and fleeting, it can also give way to an attitude that is more enduring and general. This more general notion of trust in AI, having a trusting attitude towards it, is inline with what Lee and See defined as trust in their seminal work on trust in automation [12].

Other work has partitioned trust into situational, dispositional, and learned [9]. This three-layer model of trust is markedly similar to what we are proposing; however, we assume that both situational and attitudinal trust are subject to learning, as neither trust relationship will remain static throughout an interaction. We therefore do not address learned trust as a separate construct in this investigation. We also note that a disposition to trust, in the psychology literature, is a level of abstraction higher than an attitude. Whereas a psychological disposition is a behavioral tendency (often a distinguishing one), an attitude is usually thought of as an enduring and general evaluation of an object or concept in the negative to positive dimension [1].

Partitioning trust into an attitude as well as a specific, situational feeling forces a reevaluation of what it means to have well-calibrated trust in AI. Well-calibrated situational trust in AI suggests having a reliable feeling for whether or not to rely on an AI in a specific instance. On the other hand, well-calibrated attitudinal trust in AI suggests a general sense for when AI should or should not be trusted. It is feasible that a person may be well-calibrated in one, both, or neither form of trust. The study of well-calibrated trust in AI, under this formalization, takes on new challenges, including: predicting levels of each type of trust, how situational and attitudinal trust independently and collectively impact a choice, and how outcomes may alter levels of each.

Deciding whether to follow a recommendation from an AI means integrating attitudinal and situational trust. A person may experience a general suspicion when they interact with an AI, for example, but when the only recommendation available comes from an AI or they suspect that human recommendations are flawed, they may exhibit what appears to be high situational trust by complying with the AI. The flip side of the same coin, having high attitudinal trust in AI but exhibiting low situational trust, may occur when a person is privy to knowledge that the AI is missing. The joint challenges of predicting different trust type levels and how they may interact during the decision making process, we believe, force a reckoning for the trust measures that are so commonly used by the HCI community.

2 Experimental Paradigm

We adapted an online human-robot interaction simulation testbed from [21]. This testbed was developed to study how trust changes when an AI is endowed with the ability to explain its recommendations. The basic study paradigm has participants join a reconnaissance mission with a robot teammate. During the mission, the team works to clear potentially hazardous locations in a foreign city. The robot plays the role of a scout and enters each new location first to assess whether the human operator needs to don protective equipment prior to clearing the location. The robot is equipped with multiple sensors, each of which may or may not be faulty. It learns about their accuracy using reinforcement learning throughout the mission and is able to explain how it is updating its recommendation algorithm based on the learning. Participants are incentivized to complete the mission expediently and without their character dying, which can happen when a threat is present. Finally, researchers can control the richness of the robot's explanations, although the level of explanation is fixed throughout a mission.

We maintained the basic study design and teamed participants with a simulated robot for a reconnaissance mission. Whereas previous experiments have had multiple missions of fewer buildings, this experiment had a single mission of 45 buildings. As in prior implementations, the robot entered each building before the participants to assess risks, then made a recommendation that they enter the building with or without protective gear. This gear neutralized any threat in the building, but with a time cost incurred in the process of (un)equipping the gear. Entering without gear incurred no time cost, but would lead to death (incurring a much larger time cost and then respawning to continue the mission) if a threat was present. Mission success occurred if all buildings were cleared within a time limit.

The robot based its recommendations on noisy sensor readings as input to a policy computed through model-free reinforcement learning [10,19] using the reward signal of the time cost and deaths incurred. We chose the robot's initial Q values, learning rate, and sequence of sensor readings so that it would make mistakes on 5/45 buildings, with the RL converging to the optimal policy only after the fifth mistake. Although the problem space is simple and it would be possible to learn faster, hamstringing the robot in this way enables us to study the evolution (or lack thereof) of compliance and trust.

As noted, this testbed was developed around studying explainable AI. In our case, the robot is capable of explaining how it arrived at a given decision as well as what it learned since its last recommendation. At each building, the robot constructed a decision-tree representation of its current policy [16]. It could use the path through that tree to explain its decision and any changes to the tree to explain its learning. By toggling these decision and learning explanations, we assigned participants to one of three conditions: no explanation, explanation of decisions, and explanation of decisions and learning. These are controlled for in data analyses, but discussed elsewhere [8].

3 Measures

There is no direct measure for the psychological experience of trust. This is true for our conceptualizations of attitudinal and situational trust. The most straightforward measures are subjective, such as simply asking human operators whether they trust their AI counterparts. Self reports, however, often do not align with other beliefs and behaviors [11]. For example, a recent survey found that, although the vast majority of people reported being concerned about risks that different AIs pose for society at large, they also indicated that they thought AIs were better decision makers than humans [3]. One interpretation of these results is that the participants had low attitudinal trust in AI, but because their attitudinal trust for humans was even lower, they reported relative trust in the AI. A general measure of trust may miss this nuance.

Compliance is often used as a behavioral measure of trust [20], and in most instances, it is a good proxy for situational trust. Exceptions are feasible—if a recommendation from an AI echoes what a person would otherwise do in a given instance, for example, compliance clearly is not a measure of trust. Thus, when compliance is serving as a proxy of situational trust, being able to isolate its role in the decision process is critical. In the present work, we rely on regression models and control for other experimental variables. Obviously, we are not able to control for all of the factors impinging on a participant's choices; however, we are able to demonstrate that the compliance measures are able to account for a significant amount of variance in the models. We interpret this as suggesting that they are not entirely confounded with other factors. The two compliance measures we rely on are: (1) whether the participant complied at the first location, and (2) the percentage of times that they complied over the first seven locations. We chose the first seven because location six was always the robot's first mistake, thus seven locations will include participants' compliance immediately after the first time they saw the robot make a mistake.

We rely on a psychometric measure, known as the disposition to trust inventory (DTI) [14], as a subjective assessment of attitudinal trust. Note that we steer away from using the term *disposition* to describe the trust that we are studying, because the term's usage in psychology suggests a distinguishing tendency that an individual possesses, rather than an enduring and general evaluation of a concept such as AI [1]. The DTI, despite its name, is more of an attitudinal than a dispositional measure. Participants completed this measure prior to their mission. DTI is a subset of items from a larger inventory and is the composite of four sub measures: benevolence, integrity, competence, and trusting stance (each has three items, ordered respectively). Although this measure has been used numerous times in HCI and HRI settings, it is worth noting that it has not been validated for our particular experimental setting, as we discuss elsewhere [7]. DTI was originally developed as a way of investigating the impact of trust on purchase intentions in digital settings, specifically during an initial interaction. Moreover, in that early work, no actual purchases were made—not even in a lab setting. Rather, participants simply indicated their intentions. The scale uses responses on a one to seven interval which we average to extract a DTI score for each participant. Applying DTI in this human-agent interaction interactions implicitly assumes that there is a meaningful mapping of the trust relationship a consumer forms with an online retailer to that which people form with an AI teammate. As will become apparent from our results, we believe there is merit in verifying whether this is in fact the case.

After completing the mission, participants answered questions to assess their opinions of the robot's capabilities (trust-ability [15]), its concern for their well-being (trust-benevolence, adapted from [13]), and their subjective assessment of their own understanding of its function (awareness of self-limitation [15]). These questions used Likert-style responses on a 1–7 scale that were averaged for each area to yield a score in the same range. The first two measures offer insight into participants' attitudinal trust levels after completing the mission with the robot. We can correlate these with the initial measures to gain insight into how mission outcomes may alter trust perspectives etc. The latter allows us to control for understanding, however since no meaningful effects were present, we do not report on it.

Finally, we also compute two general outcome measures. Overall compliance ratio is the percentage of times a participant followed the robot's recommendation. The robot made five mistakes throughout the mission, therefore perfect compliance was not optimal. The correct choice ratio is the percentage of times that a participant donned the equipment when warranted and otherwise not. These two measure allow us to test the predictive value of the situational and attitudinal measures of trust. We compute each measure for the entirety of the mission as well as for locations eight through forty-five. Doing the latter enables us to use location one and the average decision of location one through seven as proxies for situational trust as described above.

4 Results

We used multiple linear regressions to test the predictive capabilities of the trust and compliance measures. Each table of statistics indicates the dependent measure above the columns that contain the fitted values for each model. Note that intercepts, or the coefficient values for the null model, are the last reported variable. In all our models, this accounts for participants who did not receive any explanation for the robot's behavior. *Decision*, *Decision & Learning*, and *Loc. 1 Behavior* are indicator variables that take one if true (for participants in a treatment condition or who followed the robot's advice) and zero otherwise. *Dispositional Trust* and *Loc. 1–7 Behavior* are continuous measures. Note that treatment conditions are included here for completeness but that we discuss them in other work [8]. Also note that all interpretations of the coefficients are under the assumption of all else being equal.

The DTI measure was consistently correlated with compliance, but its correlation was negative (see Table 1). This suggests a counter-intuitive relationship where higher levels of attitudinal trust would lead to less compliance. We report two models: (1) includes the compliance ratio for the entire mission, and (2) includes the compliance ratio after location seven. The overall fit of both models is better than the intercept-only model, as indicated by their respective F-test statistics; however, they account for only 9% and 10% of observed variance, respectively. Both models suggest that a one unit increase in DTI score was correlated with a decrease in compliance of approximately 5%.

The DTI measure was also negatively correlated with the overall percentage of correct choices, but only when we include behavior at all locations in the mission (see Table 2). Model (1) suggests that a one unit increase on the DTI scale would result in about 3.5%, or one and a half, fewer correct choices on average.

Despite these negative correlations with actual compliance behavior, the DTI was positively correlated with the three self-reported opinion measures (see Table 3). A one unit increase on the DTI was correlated with reporting 34% higher evaluation of the robot's ability (1), rating its benevolence 44% higher

Table 1. Predicting compliance from dispositional trust

	Dependent variable: compliance ratio	
	Overall (1)	Post 1st mistake (2)
Dispositional trust	-0.051^{***}	-0.056^{***}
	(0.017)	(0.018)
Decision	0.012	0.015
	(0.038)	(0.040)
Decision & learning	0.087^{**}	0.093^{**}
	(0.038)	(0.039)
Constant (no explanation)	0.932^{***}	0.966^{***}
	(0.095)	(0.099)
Observations	148	148
R^2	0.092	0.099
Adjusted R^2	0.074	0.080
Residual std. error (df = 144)	0.187	0.195
F Statistic (df = 3; 144)	4.892^{***}	5.258^{***}
Note	$^{*}p < 0.1$; $^{**}p < 0.05$; $^{***}p < 0.01$	

Table 2. Predicting correct choices from dispositional trust

	Dependent variable: correct choices ratio	
	Overall (1)	Post 1st mistake (2)
Dispositional trust	-0.035^{**}	-0.029
	(0.016)	(0.017)
Decision	0.033	0.034
	(0.035)	(0.038)
Decision & learning	0.093^{***}	0.096^{**}
	(0.035)	(0.038)
Constant (no explanation)	0.799^{***}	0.714^{***}
	(0.089)	(0.095)
Observations	148	148
R^2	0.073	0.058
Adjusted R^2	0.053	0.039
Residual std. error (df = 144)	0.174	0.186
F Statistic (df = 3; 144)	3.764^{**}	2.979^{**}
Note	$^{*}p < 0.1$; $^{**}p < 0.05$; $^{***}p < 0.01$	

(2), and 56% higher awareness of their own limitations in understanding its ability (3). All three models accounted for significantly more variance than their respective intercept-only models.

Table 3. Predicting opinions of the robot based on trust scores

	Dependent variable: self reported trust		
	Ability (1)	Benevolence (2)	Self-Limitation (3)
Dispositional trust score	0.343***	0.440***	0.559***
	(0.078)	(0.093)	(0.106)
Decision	0.505***	0.295	0.788***
	(0.170)	(0.204)	(0.233)
Decision & learning	0.753***	0.297	0.777***
	(0.168)	(0.202)	(0.230)
Constant (no explanation)	3.317***	2.806***	1.695***
	(0.424)	(0.510)	(0.581)
Observations	145	145	145
R^2	0.245	0.165	0.262
Adjusted R^2	0.229	0.147	0.247
Residual std. error (df = 141)	0.828	0.997	1.135
F Statistic (df = 3; 141)	15.284***	9.301***	16.706***
Note	*p < 0.1; **p < 0.05; ***p < 0.01		

Unlike the attitudinal measure of trust, the situational measure (i.e., prior behavior) is positively correlated with compliance and correct choices (see Tables 4 and 5). As noted, we report two early behavior predictors: an indicator for whether a participant followed the robot's advice in the very first building, and the ratio of times that a participant followed the robot's recommendation in the first seven interactions, which include the interaction immediately after the robot's first mistake (i.e. the first seven locations). These are reported as models (1) and (2), respectively, in Tables 4 and 5. All models, again, outperformed their intercept-only counterparts. Following the robot's recommendation in the first location was correlated with a 9% higher compliance ratio and 11% higher correct choice ratio for locations eight to forty-five. Similarly, the compliance and correct choice ratios for locations one to seven were also correlated with significantly higher compliance and correct choices across later locations. All else being equal, the models suggest that a person who was perfectly compliant over the initial interval would, on average, end up being 32% more compliant than a person who was perfectly non-compliant. Roughly the same is true for a person who made the correct choice versus a person who made the incorrect choice in the first seven locations: in expectation, the former would outperform the latter by 32%.

Table 4. Predicting later compliance from early behavior

	Dependent variable: Bldg. 8:45 compliance ratio	
	Compliance ratio	
	(1)	(2)
Loc. 1 behavior	0.087***	
	(0.031)	
Loc. 1–7 behavior		0.315***
		(0.051)
Decision	−0.008	−0.008
	(0.037)	(0.034)
Decision & learning	0.088**	0.063*
	(0.037)	(0.034)
Constant (no explanation)	0.623***	0.483***
	(0.031)	(0.039)
Observations	163	163
R^2	0.093	0.231
Adjusted R^2	0.076	0.217
Residual std. error (df = 159)	0.193	0.178
F Statistic (df = 3; 159)	5.433***	15.934***
Note	*p < 0.1; **p < 0.05; ***p < 0.01	

5 Discussion

The experiment that we conducted was not designed to validate, diagnosis, or debunk DTI. Rather, our goal was to understand how equipping a robot with the ability to explain its decision making affects compliance, which we report in [8]. We administered DTI because of its prominence in the field: many researchers, including us, have employed it as a means of investigating the role of trust in HRI [20]. We anticipated that DTI scores would be positively correlated with mission outcomes, however this was not what we observed. The experimental outcomes inspired us to investigate trust dynamics using this data.

Compliance, as we previously noted, is a classic and common measure of trust in AI. The Disposition to Trust Inventory, which was developed to be a measure of enduring and general trust in technology and has been adopted by AI researchers, was negatively correlated with participant compliance. On the other hand, early compliance was consistently predictive of later compliance. One way to interpret this outcome is that early trusting behavior predicted later trusting behaviors, which to many will sound like the often quoted and hard to attribute aphorism, "prior behavior is the best predictor of future behavior."

It seems a safe assumption that using DTI as a predictor of compliance in HRI setting was never the intent, if even a thought of, the researchers who developed it. Similarly, it is meant to measure a more general and enduring type

Table 5. Predicting later correct choices from early behavior

	Dependent variable: Bldg. 8:45 correct choice ratio	
	Choice ratio	
	(1)	(2)
Loc. 1 behavior	0.112***	
	(0.028)	
Loc. 1–7 behavior		0.324***
		(0.046)
Decision	0.023	0.024
	(0.034)	(0.031)
Decision& learning	0.092***	0.066**
	(0.034)	(0.031)
Constant (no explanation)	0.504***	0.373***
	(0.028)	(0.035)
Observations	163	163
R^2	0.134	0.271
Adjusted R^2	0.117	0.257
Residual std. error (df = 159)	0.175	0.161
F statistic (df = 3; 159)	8.181***	19.696***
Note:	*p < 0.1; **p < 0.05; ***p < 0.01	

of trust, not trust in specific instances. It is quite feasible that a meta study of many different types of HRI would reveal that, in aggregate, DTI is a better predictor of compliance than prior behavior. If this is borne out, then its use is warranted. However, if our results are predictive of a broader trend, then it behooves researchers studying how humans team with AI to invest resources in developing a more applicable measure of attitudinal trust.

We compared a behavioral measure of situational trust to a psychometric measure of attitudinal trust. This is an artifact of the experiment not being designed to explicitly study the relative performance of trust measures. There is merit in conducting a more complete comparison in which behavioral and psychometric measures of both situational and attitudinal trust are evaluated. It may be that a behavioral measure of attitudinal trust in AI, for example observing compliance with a number of different systems, is a robust predictor of compliance in HRI settings.

Our experimental paradigm was developed around the idea of a human-robot team completing multiple tasks and learning about each other during those interactions. Many interactions are one-off, meaning the behavioral measure of trust that we used would not be possible. Even if behavioral measures outperform psychometric measures, it is still valuable to develop psychometric or other means of predicting trust in AI, as there will always be instances when a behavioral measure is not possible.

We did not explore compliance corrections in this experiment. It is feasible that a DTI would prove a better predictor of how people respond to compliance corrections than our behavioral measure. Again, there are important nuances in this question. At least two questions need to be answered: is situational or attitudinal trust more important when correcting compliance and do behavioral or psychometric measures better predict responses to correction?

DTI did predict positive opinions of the AI. The behavioral measures did not account for similar variance nor did they wash out the ability of DTI to predict opinions. DTI may thus be useful as a way of identifying people likely to engage with the AI in the future, i.e., outside of an experimental setting where they are being forced to engage with it, assuming that self-reported positive opinions of a past interaction ultimately map to future use.

Finally, there is an opportunity to better understand the trust-compliance dynamic using behavioral measures of trust. It may be the case that correcting compliance behavior is an entirely different challenge than simply predicting future compliance. For example, early compliance may also predict failures to quickly and accurately adjust behavior when the AI is determined to be faulty. Having an AI make early mistakes could help identify human teammates that are likely to comply or not update their compliance behavior when warranted.

6 Conclusion

Our results suggest that, when available, early behavior may be a better indicator of the need for intervention than psychometric measures of trust. This supports other findings that show behavioral measures outperform subjective self reports [23,24]. Although the early behavior measure that included reactions to the robot's first mistake accounted for more variance in the data, even just the behavior from the first interaction consistently predicted compliance and correct choices. This insight opens up many research questions related to understanding trust dynamics in human-AI teams. It may even be advisable to have an AI make an early mistake to identify human teammates that are less likely to comply.

References

1. APA dictionary of psychology. American Psychological Association. https://dictionary.apa.org/trust
2. Amershi, S., et al.: Guidelines for human-AI interaction. In: Proceedings of the 2019 CHI Conference on Human Factors in Computing Systems, pp. 1–13 (2019)
3. Araujo, T., Helberger, N., Kruikemeier, S., De Vreese, C.H.: In AI we trust? Perceptions about automated decision-making by artificial intelligence. AI Soc. **35**(3), 611–623 (2020)
4. Barnes, M.J., Wang, N., Pynadath, D.V., Chen, J.Y.: Human-agent bidirectional transparency. In: Trust in Human-Robot Interaction, pp. 209–232. Elsevier (2021)
5. Christoforakos, L., Gallucci, A., Surmava-Große, T., Ullrich, D., Diefenbach, S.: Can robots earn our trust the same way humans do? A systematic exploration of competence, warmth, and anthropomorphism as determinants of trust development in HRI. Front. Robot. AI **8**, 79 (2021)

6. Elliot, J.: Artificial social intelligence for successful teams (ASIST) (2021). https://www.darpa.mil/program/artificial-social-intelligence-for-successful-teams
7. Gurney, N., Pynadath, D.V., Wang, N.: Compliance in human-robot interactions (2022). Submitted to the Conference on User Modeling, Adaptation and Personalization
8. Gurney, N., Pynadath, D.V., Wang, N.: Explainable reinforcement learning in human-machine teams: the impact of decision-tree based explanations on transparency communication and team performance (2022). Submitted to the International Symposium on Robot and Human Interactive Communication
9. Hoff, K.A., Bashir, M.: Trust in automation: integrating empirical evidence on factors that influence trust. Hum. Factors **57**(3), 407–434 (2015)
10. Kaelbling, L.P., Littman, M.L., Moore, A.W.: Reinforcement learning: a survey. J. Artif. Intell. Res. **4**, 237–285 (1996)
11. Kunkel, J., Donkers, T., Michael, L., Barbu, C.M., Ziegler, J.: Let me explain: impact of personal and impersonal explanations on trust in recommender systems. In: Proceedings of the 2019 CHI Conference on Human Factors in Computing Systems, pp. 1–12 (2019)
12. Lee, J.D., See, K.A.: Trust in automation: designing for appropriate reliance. Hum. Factors **46**(1), 50–80 (2004)
13. Mayer, R.C., Davis, J.H., Schoorman, F.D.: An integrative model of organizational trust. Acad. Manag. Rev. **20**(3), 709–734 (1995)
14. McKnight, D.H., Choudhury, V., Kacmar, C.: Developing and validating trust measures for e-commerce: an integrative typology. Inf. Syst. Res. **13**(3), 334–359 (2002)
15. Pynadath, D.V., Wang, N., Rovira, E., Barnes, M.J.: Clustering behavior to recognize subjective beliefs in human-agent teams. In: Proceedings of the 17th International Conference on Autonomous Agents and MultiAgent Systems, pp. 1495–1503 (2018)
16. Quinlan, J.R.: Induction of decision trees. Mach. Learn. **1**(1), 81–106 (1986)
17. Seeber, I., et al.: Machines as teammates: a research agenda on AI in team collaboration. Inf. Manage. **57**(2), 103174 (2020)
18. Shneiderman, B.: Human-centered artificial intelligence: reliable, safe & trustworthy. Int. J. Hum.-Comput. Interact. **36**(6), 495–504 (2020)
19. Sutton, R.S., Barto, A.G.: Reinforcement Learning: An Introduction. MIT Press, Cambridge (2018)
20. Wang, N., Pynadath, D.V., Hill, S.G.: Trust calibration within a human-robot team: comparing automatically generated explanations. In: 2016 11th ACM/IEEE International Conference on Human-Robot Interaction (HRI), pp. 109–116. IEEE (2016)
21. Wang, N., Pynadath, D.V., Hill, S.G., Ground, A.P.: Building trust in a human-robot team with automatically generated explanations. In: Proceedings of the Interservice/Industry Training, Simulation and Education Conference (I/ITSEC), vol. 15315, pp. 1–12 (2015)
22. Wang, N., Pynadath, D.V., Rovira, E., Barnes, M.J., Hill, S.G.: Is it my looks? Or something I said? The impact of explanations, embodiment, and expectations on trust and performance in human-robot teams. In: Ham, J., Karapanos, E., Morita, P.P., Burns, C.M. (eds.) PERSUASIVE 2018. LNCS, vol. 10809, pp. 56–69. Springer, Cham (2018). https://doi.org/10.1007/978-3-319-78978-1_5
23. Yin, M., Wortman Vaughan, J., Wallach, H.: Understanding the effect of accuracy on trust in machine learning models. In: Proceedings of the 2019 CHI Conference on Human Factors in Computing Systems, pp. 1–12 (2019)

24. Zhang, Y., Liao, Q.V., Bellamy, R.K.: Effect of confidence and explanation on accuracy and trust calibration in AI-assisted decision making. In: Proceedings of the 2020 Conference on Fairness, Accountability, and Transparency, pp. 295–305 (2020)

Promoting Human Competences by Appropriate Modes of Interaction for Human-Centered-AI

Thomas Herrmann(✉)

Information and Technology Management, IAW, Ruhr-Universität Bochum, Bochum, Germany
Thomas.herrmann@rub.de

Abstract. There is an ongoing discussion about human-centered AI (HCAI) that emphasizes the value of including humans in the loop. We focus on types of HCAI in the context of machine learning that synergistically combine the complementary strengths of humans and AI and seek to develop competencies and capabilities of both parts. The development of human competencies is a largely neglected aspect compared to criteria such as fairness, trust, or accountability. Based on early discussions about the role of humans in the use of expert systems, the current HCAI discourse, and a literature review, we identify 10 modes of interaction that represent a way of interacting with AI that has the potential to support the development of human competencies relevant to the domain itself, but also to its context and to the use of technologies.

Keywords: Human-centered AI · Interaction modes · Socio-technical design

1 Introduction

There is an ongoing discussion about human-centered AI (HCAI) emphasizing the value of keeping the human in the loop (Johnson et al. 2017; Zanzotto 2019). We distinguish two types of HCAI, which are mainly related to machine learning (ML): On the one hand, there are approaches that seek to keep the human in the loop for the main purpose of advancing AI. For example Kamar (2016) proposes a concept where AI can recognize its limitations and can ask the human for help. On the other hand, there are approaches –e.g., Dellermann et al. (2019)– that emphasize the complementary strengths of both, human and AI, and propose a type of HCAI that aims to develop the capabilities of both parts.

We focus on the second type of approach and suggest that HCAI, which seeks to advance human competencies together with the improvement of Machine Learning performance, requires specific interaction modes that are in accordance with the goal of advancing human capabilities. The term "interaction mode" is usually used intuitively. Similar terms are interaction paradigms or interaction style (Shneiderman 1995), interaction principles (Valverde 2011), interaction guidelines or interaction techniques. We consider the different paradigms of HCI as referring to more general and basic differences such as using the computer as a tool vs. a partner vs. a medium. This type of distinction has a longstanding tradition. For instance, the cartoon in Fig. 1 was found in

H. Degen and S. Ntoa (Eds.): HCII 2022, LNAI 13336, pp. 35–50, 2022.
https://doi.org/10.1007/978-3-031-05643-7_3

1982 and illustrates the tension between the partnership- and the tool-perspective. The paradoxical constellation of Fig. 1 can be resolved if we assume –as a first step– that the human side is represented not only by an individual, but by a group of people such as an organizational unit. From a socio-technical point of view, (Herrmann et al. 2017, 2021) various roles can emerge within such a unit representing different rights and duties assigned to different tasks. These are, for example, roles such as administrator or end-user. While these different roles are usually distributed among different people, –in a second step– we can imagine that one single person is authorized to play different roles, such as using as well as maintaining a machine. Obviously, these different roles imply different degrees of being in control or keeping the human in the loop.

While paradigms such as partner vs. tool are more general in nature, they correspond to different ways of interaction such as natural language dialogues vs. direct manipulation. We refer to these different ways as interaction modes. Consequently, interaction modes in our understanding focus not only on different types of sensory modalities (such as audio, visual, and haptic), but also on different types of activities that are required or possible to perform different tasks.

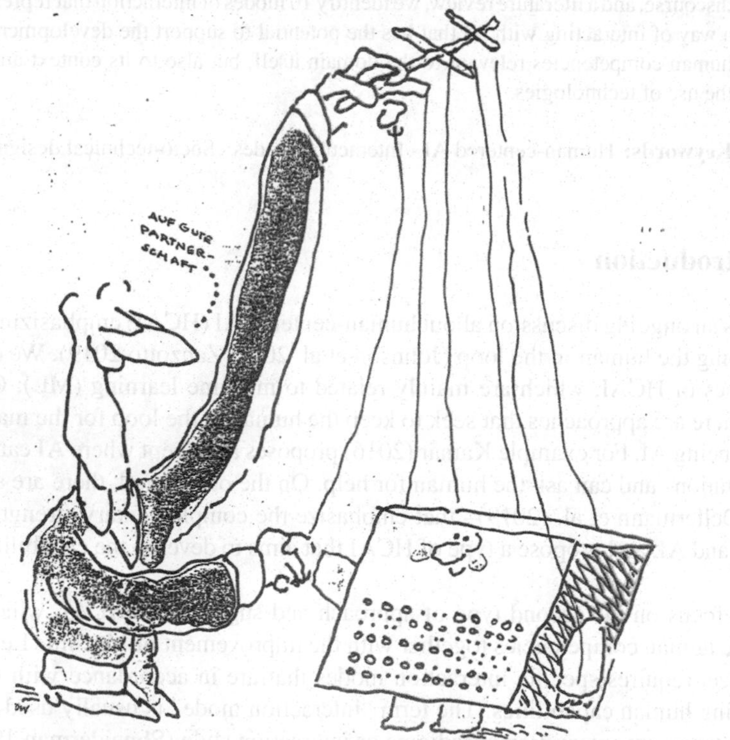

Fig. 1. The tension between partnership and tool-perspective (Herrmann 1983) (speech bubble says "on good partnership")

As a basis for further investigation, we assume that either different roles within an organizational unit or different roles taken by the same person must be supported by different modes of interaction.

In the field of AI, specific types of interaction modes are relevant in addition to simply entering case-descriptive data (e.g., entering a radiological image) and receiving an AI-based result (e.g., image analysis with malignant areas indicated). Examples for those specific modes are: implicit interaction (Schmidt 2000) where the stream form processed data is provided by the context; starting and monitoring automated processes with occasional intervention (Schmidt and Herrmann 2017); exploration and seeking for explanation (Ehsan et al. 2021); adaptation and re-training.

The research question guiding our further analysis asks about the modes of interaction that support people in using AI in roles that enable them to further develop their own competencies. We have identified ten types of such interaction modes and describe in general and examples. We assume, that the advancement of human competences is of specific relevance to support other criteria of HCAI such as fairness, trust, and accountability (Ehsan et al. 2021).

Competences and capabilities encompass various areas. They can be domain-specific, domain-independent (e.g., skills in handling technology or everyday knowledge), or meta-knowledge (Herrmann and Just 1995). Capabilities can have different foci, such as dealing with complexity, reflection and adaptation, creative problem solving or cooperation, and they refer to different levels, such as individuals vs. teams (Wilkens and Sprafke 2019). Competence development does not primarily mean the acquisition of knowledge, but rather learning to deal practically with problem solving in specific domains through the active application of existing knowledge and through collaborative, reflective feedback loops (Prilla et al. 2012).

2 Methodological Approach

The identification of interaction modes with AI that contribute to the development of human competencies is based on three backgrounds:

1. While doing research on the context of human-centered AI we found several hints on interaction modes that help to keep the human in the loop and to promote their competences (Herrmann and Pfeiffer 2022).
2. We referred to early discussions on AI that dealt with a human-centered design of knowledge- or rule-based expert systems (Fischer 1994, 2021; Herrmann and Just 1995; Shneiderman 2022), and took the insights of End-User development into account (Lieberman et al. 2006)
3. We conducted a literature research related to human-centered AI and to interacting with AI to find more sources that help identify and specify the possible interaction modes.

Table 1 presents the results of a research with google.scholar. The first column shows the search terms we applied, the second the number of hits and the third the number of relevant literature items selected.

Table 1. Literature research

Search terms	# of items found	Numbers of relevant items
"interaction paradigms" "human-centered AI"	11	3
"interaction styles" "human-centered AI"	1	0
"interaction principles" "human-centered AI"	3	0
"interaction mode" "human-centered AI"	4	0
"human-AI interaction" "human-centered AI"	170	14
"interaction techniques" "human-centered AI"	41	0
Sum	230	17

Table 2. Criteria for selecting literature

For exclusion:	For inclusion:
E1) Does not elaborate on different modes (or paradigms etc.)	I1) Elaborates on different modes
E2) Does not represent a full paper	I2) Elaborates a specific mode
E3) Although the paper mentions HCAI and/or interactive design, none of them represents the paper's focus	I3) Provides general background
E4) Paper is not in English	I4) Gives details to be considered when describing an interaction mode
E5) Paper is focused on a too narrow application field	I5) Points to more literature of interest

To identify the relevant items, we applied the selection criteria presented in Table 2. Typical example frameworks provided by Wright et al. (2020) or Margetis et al. (2021) help to examine in which areas human-centered interaction modes are relevant. We found that descriptions of interaction modes rarely address their impact on the development of human competences. Therefore, we take a general approach that assumes that challenging people to be in control and to understand how a technology works contributes to their cognitive abilities. Furthermore, we suggest that interaction modes that leave room for the application of typical human strengths, such as intuitive decision making, dealing with uncertainty and equivocality, or communicative negotiation (Jarrahi 2018), contribute to the further development of these strengths.

Table 3 provides an overview over the interaction mode that we have extracted from the three backgrounds mentioned above.

Table 3. Interaction modes

	Interaction modes	Literature sources
01	**Offering explanations and possibilities for exploration**	(Chromik and Butz 2021; Cirqueira et al. 2021; Ehsan et al. 2021; Ehsan et al. 2021; Herrmann and Just 1995; Kaluarachchi et al. 2021; Longo et al. 2020; Margetis et al. 2021; Schmidt and Herrmann 2017; Shin 2021; Shneiderman 2020, 2022; Wright et al. 2020)
02	**Testing**	(Margetis et al. 2021; Shneiderman 2020; Zhang et al. 2021)
03	**Initiating and performing re-training**	(Margetis et al. 2021; Serafini et al. 2021; Xu et al. 2021)
04	**Variation of underlying data sets and methods**	(Herrmann and Just 1995; Margetis et al. 2021; Wright et al. 2020; Y. Yang et al. 2019; Zhang et al. 2021)
05	**Flexible sequencing or filtering of data input**	(Beede et al. 2020; Endsley 2017; Herrmann and Just 1995; Shergadwala and El-Nasr 2021; Shneiderman 2020)
06	**Identification and comparison of similar cases**	(Cai et al. 2019; Cirqueira et al. 2021; Crowley et al. 2019; Herrmann and Just 1995)
07	**Refinement**	(Cai et al. 2019; Endsley 2017; Margetis et al. 2021; Shergadwala and El-Nasr 2021; Yang et al. 2020; Zhang et al. 2021)
08	**Intervention**	(Endsley 2017; Schmidt and Herrmann 2017; Xu et al. 2021)
09	**Vetoing**	(Rakova et al. 2021; Yang et al. 2020)
10	**Critiquing**	(Bond et al. 2019; Endsley 2017; Fischer 1994, 2021)

3 Interaction Modes

In the following, we present the identified interaction modes in more detail. Some of the literature found is of more general relevance and provides details that can be attributed to more than one mode. For example, Endsley (2017) provides a list of guidelines in the context of interaction between humans and autonomous systems that help specify the competency-oriented characteristics of interaction modes. Also, the work of Margetis et al. (2021) and Wright et al. (2020) provide overviews that serve as a resource to add details to most of the interaction modes. Within the field of HCAI, most literature we found is related to explainable AI (XAI). However, some of the concepts –for example as described by Chromik and Butz (2021)– include design principles that can be applied to more interaction modes than just offering explanations (see Sect. 3.1).

For each interaction mode we begin by describing its general characteristics and continue with providing details and examples, and we point out possible relationships for promoting human competence. We start with the mode that provides explanations and possibilities for exploration, as this plays a crucial role in building a human understanding of AI and is a foundation for enabling people to employ AI successfully. We continue with modes that help to prepare an AI-application (Sects. 3.2, 3.3 and 3.4) and continue with modes (Sects. 3.5, 3.6, 3.7, 3.8, 3.9 and 3.10) that relate to dealing with specific cases of problem solving or decision making.

3.1 Offering Explanations and Possibilities for Exploration

One of the main research areas within HCAI that seeks to help people use and interact with AI is the field of explainable AI. Explainability focusses on making the processes and results that are based on ML-models more transparent for users (Wright et al. 2020). XAI aims to reduce the complexity of ML systems and helps to explore the properties of the processed data so that the influence of certain elements of an ML-model can be understood (Margetis et al. 2021), e.g., by applying an interactive ranking mechanisms for the features that influence an AI-outcome (Cirqueira et al. 2021). XAI includes both, the transmission of comprehensive explanations of AI-processes and dialogues that offer an iterative conversation to build such an explanation step-by-step (Chromik and Butz 2021).

Explainability can be based on various output modalities:

- human-readable rules governing the AI-outcome (Cirqueira et al. 2021)
- natural language explanations (Ehsan et al. 2021)
- numbers that determine AI-processes (Ehsan et al. 2021)
- implicit explanations, e.g., by highlighting certain input or relevant parts, for example via heat-mapping (Longo et al. 2020)

These modalities can be flexibly combined e.g. by iterative strategies that allow going on after an initial explanations has been provided (Chromik and Butz 2021).

Providing explanations, which are mostly a post-hoc or retrospective reaction on users being surprised by an AI-result and therefore asking why a particular decision was made, may prove to be a suboptimal solution. Shneiderman (2020) points to alternatives such as step-by-step guidance that lead users gradually through the process of their decision making so that understanding of AI-behavior evolves implicitly. These approaches have already emerged in the context of rule-based knowledge- or expert-systems (Shneiderman 2022) (see also Sect. 3.7, Refinement). They include the possibility to go back and forward, allowing the user to stay in control while pursuing rapid convergence to desired AI-results (Chromik and Butz 2021).

We consider these possibilities as an exploration mode, where users seek to understand a system by experimenting with varying inputs. For example, the intervention mode (see Sect. 3.8) can be used to alter the parameters of an automated process or of rules or of input data to see the effects of these variations (Herrmann and Just 1995; Schmidt and Herrmann 2017). This can help not only to improve AI-results, but also to refine users' understanding or models of how an AI-algorithm works. For example: The

What-If Tool (Wexler et al. 2019) is designed for non-expert ML engineers to carry out interactive probing across different input variations (Kaluarachchi et al. 2021).

In summary, we propose an interaction mode that allows for a continuum between explanations that answer "what" and "why" questions (Ehsan et al. 2021) and exploration. We agree with Ehsan et al. (2021) that such an interaction mode should also provide social transparency to identify others who could help with explanations or exploration strategies. This would also address the promotion of cooperative capabilities including the team level (Wilkens and Sprafke 2019).

To promote human competences and understanding of AI, the models that humans already have, must be taken into account (Longo et al. 2020). This requirement is addressed by the concept of causability, which emphasizes that explanations can be provided by the system but that causal understanding is generated on the human side; causablity is a property of the user (Shin 2021). Therefore, an interaction mode for explanation and exploration has to include features for adjusting explanation strategies to the explainee's mental model (Chromik and Butz 2021), and, one step further, these features should contribute to the continuous development of this mental model. The development of critical reflection and thus new ways of understanding and dealing with AI does not happen by itself, but requires the stimulation of deliberative, analytical thinking (Ehsan et al. 2021), for example by Cognitive Forcing Functions (CFFs) (Croskerry 2003), such as prompts, delays etc.

3.2 Testing

While explanations may be sought and explored when using AI in specific decision-making situations, users may have a need to ascertain that the AI system is generally appropriate for the specific problems and decisions they face before they begin using the system. Therefore, a mode for testing an AI system is needed that allows users to perform their own quality assurance. Consequently, Shneiderman (2020) requires the possibility for in-depth testing of training datasets to check whether the data is appropriate.

An interaction mode of testing that includes these kinds of tools should also allow for detectability of faults so that the user can detect possible sources of AI errors within the context of her/his intended usage (Zhang et al. 2021).

Overall, testing serves the purpose of quality assessment by allowing validation of an ML-model's accuracy through the user interface, e.g., by methods of visualization (Margetis et al. 2021).

To put users in the role of testers, they need relevant capabilities on the one hand. On the other hand, this role also provides them with the opportunity to develop and refine strategies to recognize whether and under which conditions an AI tool may produce erroneous results.

3.3 Initiating and Performing Re-training

As soon as new or improved data sets are available for ML-training that appear to be helpful in overcoming current problems, it should be possible for users to start a re-training of the ML-System. Subsequently, they should be able to see how this alters the results of previously processed cases where the AI-system provided questionable or erroneous results. This interaction mode could be designed to allow for an involvement of end-users in the training cycle of an ML-model, including feature selection, review of available datasets etc. (Margetis et al. 2021). In essence, this mode is about ensuring that re-training is based on user feedback and that appropriate interactive features help users continuously collect training data that match the expected results that users hope to obtain from AI systems (Xu et al. 2021).

To support the development of competences, users must be able to recognize the differences achieved through the re-training. Even in the case of automatically initiated re-training (Serafini et al. 2021), users can see that it has taken place and must be able to influence when it should occur or that the re-training can be reversed if necessary. Experience made while participating in the re-training loops provides an essential basis for advancing domain-oriented knowledge in dealing with AI and for generating hypotheses about the relationship between problems, possible solutions, and the underlying data sets.

3.4 Variation of Underlying Data Sets and Methods

A more subtle method than re-training is to switch between different data sets used to train the ML-model or between the statistical methods used, e.g., to analyze medical images. Alternatively, the user can compare different results of AI-driven analyses based on different data sets or statistical methods (Margetis et al. 2021). This interaction mode contributes to correctability that allows users to actively overcome AI-errors, and to make the system learn from the corrections about user intentions and/or task characteristics (Zhang et al. 2021). This interaction mode allows users enriching the AI-systems with their knowledge about the world and their personal experience (Margetis et al. 2021). Compared to re-training, the variation of data sets and methods provide features for the fine-tuning of the available ML-models for specific users or tasks (Wright et al. 2020). This interaction mode thus represents a method for modifying or tailoring of AI systems. A practically relevant but widely neglected feature is the ability to add rules that help correct systematically occurring problems that are difficult to fix by retraining or switching between underlying datasets sets (Herrmann and Just 1995; Yang et al. 2019). These rules can help explicitly direct the searching or filtering of AI-generated solutions, or overrule certain choice made by the AI-system.

We hypothesize that these choices provide a way to learn and understand the implications of different features of datasets or statistical methods, and how switching between them can be used strategically and creatively to solve problems. In particular, the ability to add rules provides a way to apply one's own domain-specific knowledge and to advance this knowledge within the loops of modifying the AI-system's properties.

3.5 Flexible Sequencing or Filtering of Data Input

When working with rule-based expert systems, users typically had to enter the data that described a problem or case. To this end, expert systems usually controlled the way and sequence in which users entered data. In contrast, users should be able to change this order, omit data, and see the intermediate results to use as a guideline for their further data entry (Herrmann and Just 1995). This kind of flexibility complies with the more general requirement to avoid advanced queuing of tasks or information (Endsley 2017). Consequently, the user can decide whether s/he pursues a phase of producing divergent suggestions for a problem solution or whether to start a convergent search (Shergadwala and El-Nasr 2021).

This interaction mode can be aligned with the step-by-step method described by Shneiderman (2020). One might assume that the entering of data to describe a problem of decision making is largely replaced by automatically provided data streams such as radiology images, sensor data of plants, data extracted from customer-related files etc. However, there is always a need to filter data, to vary the amount of data, etc. that is required to trigger an AI-system to provide results or intermediate results that support the step-by-step approach. An impressive practical example is provided by Beede et al. (2020): An ML-system for medical image analysis rejected a scan because it was blurry at its edges. Although the nurse was already able to determine whether the image justifies further diagnosis, a new scan had to be made. This kind of inflexibility has to be overcome.

Flexibility in deciding the type, scope, and order of data entry is a basis for stimulating the users' own reflection on the cases they work on, and for training their capabilities to do so.

3.6 Identification and Comparison of Similar Cases

Instead of asking an AI system to directly suggest a solution for the case under consideration, the AI system can be asked to search for similar cases and the description of their treatment. This concept has already been discussed in the context of expert systems (Herrmann and Just 1995), and ML-approaches can also be used to find comparable cases (Cai et al. 2019). The idea here is to support a comparison of the characteristics of the current case with those of previously processed cases in order to find a way to handle the current case. The description of the cases being found by an AI-system could be designed in various way. For instance, narratives could be offered to describe complex situations in a way that humans can understand (Crowley et al. 2019). Thus, identifying and comparing similar cases can also contribute to explainability, especially if cases are identified that are slightly dissimilar and illustrate how subtle variations of the underlying situation can influence the AI-outcome (Cirqueira et al. 2021). To alert the user and to trigger deliberate reflection on an AI-result, case comparison could also provide examples where the system made unsuitable proposals.

Obviously, domain-specific capabilities are required and challenged to select the types of cases that are most similar or relevant to make a decision in the case under consideration, and to decide whether the solutions proposed for these similar cases should be iterated.

3.7 Refinement

Fine grained interaction with an AI-systems is made possible not only by deciding on the sequence in which to input case description data or on which data is submitted to the system (see Sect. 3.5), but also by purposefully varying the data to see the effects of the variation and have the system converge on the kind of decision that is most appropriate to a problem. This kind of refinement is a modification of AI-results that may differ from case to case whereas variations of the underlying data set (Sect. 3.4) or re-training (Sect. 3.3) imply a general modification of solution behavior. A convincing example for refinement has been designed and researched by Cai et al. (2019) in the field of medical image analysis where they employ a case comparison approach. Their system SMILY includes refinement by regions (of a medical image), by example and by medical concept, and it provides auxiliary functions such as narrowing hypotheses, augmenting variety and visualizing refinement procedures. This is again an example, where humans can follow a feedback-driven way to interactively construct an AI-based solution (Margetis et al. 2021). The search for solutions or similar cases can be refined step-by-step, and the user can see how a refinement step alters the space of possible solutions (Cai et al. 2019). Further advantages of the refinement mode are:

- It allows for flexibility since users can consider alternate interpretations of a constellation (Endsley 2017).
- It represents a strategy for avoiding that an error could hinder users in completing a task. In contrast, the system can support users even if a result is not entirely correct (Zhang et al. 2021).
- In the case of an incorrect output, the user has multiple options to react (Wright et al. 2020).
- Refinement can also be employed to reduce output complexity (Yang et al. 2020), especially if user wants to understand what details of the characteristics of the case lead to errors.
- It allows for switching between a divergent and convergent mode of seeking for diagnosis or decisions (Shergadwala and El-Nasr 2021).

Refinement has multiple effects on human capabilities: Users can learn how the conditions of a case influence the appropriate decision to be made – or they can understand how the system works and whether it proposes correct or at least consistent solutions. More importantly, they learn to deal with the uncertainties that are characteristic of their domain and, consequently, of the AI systems in their domain.

3.8 Intervention

The interaction mode of intervention (Schmidt and Herrmann 2017) allows users to interrupt or alter an automated, AI-based process on an exceptional basis. Intervention is only temporarily effective and the automated process is immediately resumed if it again complies with the user's need. Intervention can be considered as "…an effective human control mechanism … to enable human operators to monitor and quickly take over control of autonomous systems in emergencies (Xu et al. 2021, p. 40)".

Interventions have the following characteristics (Schmidt and Herrmann 2017): They occur only exceptionally and the occurrence is not planned in advance; they can be quickly initiated with an immediate impact on the system; they cyclically contribute to the improvement of AI-systems; they allow a time-limited phase of fine-grained interaction with the system. These characteristics are specified with respect to dealing with automated processes. However, we suggest that intervention can also be applied to situations where an AI-outcome is usually accepted but where phases of fine-grained refinement can be initiated exceptionally.

Intervention has to deal with an 'automation conundrum' (Endsley 2017): the longer a systems runs automatically, the more difficult it will be for humans to take control if necessary. Applying interventions helps to maintain the competences needed to exercise control. A prerequisite of intervention is the support of situation awareness by appropriate presentation of information (Endsley 2017) and that the users can recognize whether or not intervention is needed.

Intervention opens up the possibility for the user to move from monitoring to fine-grained interaction where they have the opportunity –frequently or at least occasionally– to apply their knowledge of how the system works, and to advance their capabilities to take control if needed.

3.9 Vetoing

The mode of vetoing allows users to ignore or reject an decision or finding proposed by AI (Rakova et al. 2021). Users are not coerced to include the AI-result in their own decision making and in the subsequent task handling. According to Bond et al. (2019), for an algorithmic decision it should be detectable if the certainty level is low. We assume that this feature triggers the users' attention and reflection and is a prerequisite for vetoing. Providing users with ways to deal with the uncertainty of AI systems' capabilities is a necessity (Yang et al. 2020).

Awareness of this uncertainty –also by the surrounding organization– has to be promoted to motivate the users' preparedness to apply vetoing. For this motivation, strategies that were mentioned in the context of stimulating users' interests in asking for explanations can be applied, such as Cognitive Forcing Functions (CFFs) (Croskerry 2003). The possibilities of vetoing have to be backed up by the surrounding organizations. To keep the organization in the loop (Herrmann and Pfeiffer 2022), the vetoing mode has to provide functionality for documentation so that each instance of a veto can become the subject of subsequent reflection and also trigger continuous improvement of an AI-application.

The possibility for vetoing also increases the responsibility of users and the need to use and advance their capabilities required to decide against an AI-system and to justify these decisions.

3.10 Critiquing

Critiquing systems (Fischer 1994) have been designed in the early phase of the discussion about the relationship between human and AI. This type of systems stands in the background, observing human work and only giving hints if crucial rules are violated, e.g. in the area of design or engineering. Thus, AI becomes a possibility to critically accompany human experts and helps them avoid mistakes and identify opportunities for improvement. Although this type of interactive mode is widely neglected, it can reasonably complement current HCAI-approaches (Fischer 2021). For instance, HCAI could provide users with the flexibility to decide for themselves whether to work in the refinement mode or in the critiquing mode. Furthermore, critiquing could provide cues to help users consider alternative interpretations of a constellation (Endsley 2017). Critiquing could be used to encourage the users to deliberately reflect on AI-outcome by presenting typical confounding AI-decisions or likely alternative decisions (Bond et al. 2019). Thus, critiquing prevents users from accepting AI-results too fast.

Critiquing is the opposite of intervention. Here, the user does not interrupt an automated process but the AI-system observes and interrupts the user – possibly a designer – to warn him about potential errors. This mode has a training effect per se by challenging the users to reflect on their activities.

4 Conclusion and Outlook

The detailed consideration of potential interaction modes for HCAI reveals that the combination of old approaches from the context of knowledge-based/rule-based expert systems with the current HCAI-concepts proves fruitful. For example, the critiquing mode or the exploratory step-by-step completion of solutions fits well into the context of refinement or XAI.

We need to distinguish between two instances of dealing with AI:

1. Preparing and improving the system before starting or proceeding with single cases. This is covered by the interaction modes of Sect. 3.2, 3.3 and 3.4.
2. Dealing with individual, specific cases to which the other modes apply (Sects. 3.1, 3.5, 3.6, 3.7, 3.8, 3.9 and 3.10).

However, dealing with the individual cases of decision making should provide a steady source of data that contributes to the continuous improvement of the AI solution.

Obviously, the interaction modes overlap or can complement each other. Critiquing, for example, could also be used to accompany the variation of data sets or the refinement mode, or when the user moves to fine grained interaction during an intervention –e.g. after interrupting the automated navigation of a car. The critiquing mode and intervention are two sides of the same coin: In the first case, the system observes the users and interrupts them from time to time, and vice versa, in the second case, the user monitors automated processes and decides if and when to take control or to change parameters. For HCAI it would be useful to develop rules and examples of how these two modes could alternate and can complement each other.

These kinds of modes assume that AI is characterized by uncertainty, and that users are tasked with compensating for that uncertainty, and that they must develop capabilities that help to do so. We suggest that the range of potential application of AI is much broader if we do not require that AI is 100% reliable, which in some way is not a realistic prospect. On the contrary, if we accept uncertainty, a broader vision for the use of AI opens up and assigns an appropriate role to the human workforce. However, humans must be empowered to play this role, and AI must be designed to contribute to this goal. The modes of interaction described above have the potential to support this purpose.

All of the modes require more activity from the users themselves and support learning by doing, learning by reflection and learning by errors either caused by humans or by AI. The instantiation of the described interaction modes and their positive impact on the advancement of human competencies and capabilities can only succeed if it is appropriately embedded in the organizational context. The perspective of keeping the human in the loop has to be indispensably aligned with keeping the organization in the loop (Herrmann and Pfeiffer 2022).

The criterion that HCAI should contribute to the development of human capabilities and competences is actually included in the hybrid intelligence systems perspective (Dellermann et al. 2019). However, it is not discussed as prominently as other criteria such as fairness, trust, or accountability (Ehsan et al. 2021; Zhou et al. 2021). Most of the modes discussed above are feasible to meet these criteria, if –and only if– the users involved have the capabilities to be in control of the development and application of AI-based solutions, and can continuously advance these competencies.

Possible foci for further research include:

- Providing more detailed example and guidelines of implementing the interaction modes,
- clarifying the interplay between the modes and how they can support each other,
- empirically reviewing of competences and capabilities needed and how they can be advanced,
- analyzing the interplay between competences and the fulfillment of other criteria such as fairness, trust or accountability,
- Examination of the alignment between the interaction modes and the organizational context.

Funding. This work was supported by the project Humaine (Human centered AI Network) that is funded by the Federal Ministry of Education and Research (BMBF), Germany within the "Zukunft der Wertschöpfung – Forschung zu Produktion, Dienstleistung und Arbeit" Program (funding-number: 02L19C200).

References

Beede, E., et al.: A human-centered evaluation of a deep learning system deployed in clinics for the detection of diabetic retinopathy. In: Proceedings of the 2020 CHI Conference on Human Factors in Computing Systems, pp. 1–12 (2020). https://doi.org/10.1145/3313831.3376718

Bond, R.R., Mulvenna, M., Wang, H.: Human centered artificial intelligence: weaving UX into algorithmic decision making. In: RoCHI, pp. 2–9 (2019)

Cai, C.J., et al.: Human-centered tools for coping with imperfect algorithms during medical decision-making. In: Proceedings of the 2019 CHI Conference on Human Factors in Computing Systems, pp. 1–14 (2019)

Chromik, M., Butz, A.: Human-XAI interaction: a review and design principles for explanation user interfaces. In: Ardito, C., et al. (eds.) INTERACT 2021. LNCS, vol. 12933, pp. 619–640. Springer, Cham (2021). https://doi.org/10.1007/978-3-030-85616-8_36

Cirqueira, D., Helfert, M., Bezbradica, M.: Towards design principles for user-centric explainable AI in fraud detection. In: Degen, H., Ntoa, S. (eds.) HCII 2021. LNCS (LNAI), vol. 12797, pp. 21–40. Springer, Cham (2021). https://doi.org/10.1007/978-3-030-77772-2_2

Croskerry, P.: Cognitive forcing strategies in clinical decisionmaking. Ann. Emerg. Med. **41**(1), 110–120 (2003). https://doi.org/10.1067/mem.2003.22

Crowley, J., et al.: Toward AI systems that augment and empower humans by understanding us, our society and the world around us. Report of 761758 EU Project HumaneAI, vol. 761758, pp. 1–32 (2019)

Dellermann, D., Calma, A., Lipusch, N., Weber, T., Weigel, S., Ebel, P.: The future of human-AI collaboration: a taxonomy of design knowledge for hybrid intelligence systems. In: Proceedings of the 52nd Hawaii International Conference on System Sciences (2019)

Ehsan, U., Liao, Q. V., Muller, M., Riedl, M.O., Weisz, J.D.: Expanding explainability: towards social transparency in AI systems. arXiv:2101.04719 [Cs], https://doi.org/10.1145/3411764.3445188 (2021)

Ehsan, U., et al.: The who in explainable AI: how AI background shapes perceptions of AI explanations. arXiv:2107.13509 [Cs] (2021)

Endsley, M.R.: From here to autonomy: lessons learned from human-automation research. Hum. Factors J. Hum. Factors Ergon. Soc. **59**(1), 5–27 (2017). https://doi.org/10.1177/0018720816681350

Fischer, G.: Domain-oriented design environments. Autom. Softw. Eng. **1**(2), 177–203 (1994)

Fischer, G.: End-user development: empowering stakeholders with artificial intelligence, meta-design, and cultures of participation. In: Fogli, D., Tetteroo, D., Barricelli, B.R., Borsci, S., Markopoulos, P., Papadopoulos, G.A. (eds.) IS-EUD 2021. LNCS, vol. 12724, pp. 3–16. Springer, Cham (2021). https://doi.org/10.1007/978-3-030-79840-6_1

Herrmann, T.: Rationalität und Irrationalität in der Mensch-Computer-Interaktion (Master Thesis). University of Bonn (1983). https://doi.org/10.13140/RG.2.2.35273.21607

Herrmann, T., Ackermann, M.S., Goggins, S.P., Stary, C., Prilla, M.: Designing health care that works – socio-technical conclusions. In: Designing Healthcare That Works. A Socio-technical Approach, S. 187–203. Academic Press (2017)

Herrmann, T., Jahnke, I., Nolte, A.: A problem-based approach to the advancement of heuristics for socio-technical evaluation. Behav. Inf. Technol., pp. 1–23 (2021). https://doi.org/10.1080/0144929X.2021.1972157

Herrmann, T., Just, K.: Experts' systems instead of expert systems. AI Soc. **9**(4), 321–355 (1995)

Herrmann, T., Pfeiffer, S.: Keeping the organization in the loop: a socio-technical extension of human-centered artificial intelligence (2022). https://doi.org/10.1007/s00146-022-01391-5

Jarrahi, M.H.: Artificial intelligence and the future of work: human-AI symbiosis in organizational decision making. Bus. Horiz. **61**(4), 577–586 (2018)

Johnson, A.W., Duda, K.R., Sheridan, T.B., Oman, C.M.: A closed-loop model of operator visual attention, situation awareness, and performance across automation mode transitions. Hum. Factors J. Hum. Factors Ergon. Soc. **59**(2), 229–241 (2017). https://doi.org/10.1177/0018720816665759

Kaluarachchi, T., Reis, A., Nanayakkara, S.: A review of recent deep learning approaches in human-centered machine learning. Sensors **21**(7), 2514 (2021). https://doi.org/10.3390/s21072514

Kamar, E.: Directions in hybrid intelligence: complementing AI systems with human intelligence. In: IJCAI, pp. 4070–4073 (2016)

Lieberman, H., Paterno, F., Klann, M., Wulf, V.: End-user development: an emerging paradigm. In: End User Development, pp. 1–8 (2006). https://doi.org/10.1007/1-4020-5386-X_1

Longo, L., Goebel, R., Lecue, F., Kieseberg, P., Holzinger, A.: Explainable artificial intelligence: concepts, applications, research challenges and visions. In: Holzinger, A., Kieseberg, P., Tjoa,

A.M., Weippl, E. (eds.) CD-MAKE 2020. LNCS, vol. 12279, pp. 1–16. Springer, Cham (2020). https://doi.org/10.1007/978-3-030-57321-8_1

Margetis, G., Ntoa, S., Antona, M., Stephanidis, C.: Human-centered design of artificial intelligence. In: Salvendy, G., Karwowski, W. (eds.), Handbook of Human Factors and Ergonomics, 1st edn., pp. 1085–1106. Wiley (2021). https://doi.org/10.1002/9781119636113.ch42

Prilla, M., Degeling, M., Herrmann, T.: Collaborative reflection at work: supporting informal learning at a healthcare workplace. In: Proceedings of the 17th ACM International Conference on Supporting Group Work, pp. 55–64 (2012). https://doi.org/10.1145/2389176.2389185

Rakova, B., Yang, J., Cramer, H., Chowdhury, R.: Where responsible AI meets reality: practitioner perspectives on enablers for shifting organizational practices. In: Proceedings of the ACM on Human-Computer Interaction, vol. 5, no. CSCW1, pp. 1–23 (2021)

Schmidt, A.: Implicit human computer interaction through context. Pers. Ubiquitous Comput. **4**(2/3), 191–199 (2000). https://doi.org/10.1007/BF01324126

Schmidt, A., Herrmann, T.: Intervention user interfaces: a new interaction paradigm for automated systems. Interactions **24**(5), 40–45 (2017)

Serafini, L., et al.: On some foundational aspects of human-centered artificial intelligence. arXiv: 2112.14480 [Cs] (2021)

Shergadwala, M.N., El-Nasr, M.S.: Human-centric design requirements and challenges for enabling human-AI Interaction in engineering design: an interview study. In: International Design Engineering Technical Conferences and Computers and Information in Engineering Conference, vol. 85420, p. V006T06A054. American Society of Mechanical Engineers (2021)

Shin, D.: The effects of explainability and causability on perception, trust, and acceptance: implications for explainable AI. Int. J. Hum. Comput. Stud. **146**, 102551 (2021). https://doi.org/10.1016/j.ijhcs.2020.102551

Shneiderman, B.: A taxonomy and rule base for the selection of interaction styles. In: Readings in Human–Computer Interaction, pp. 401–410 (1995). https://doi.org/10.1016/B978-0-08-051574-8.50042-X

Shneiderman, B.: Bridging the gap between ethics and practice: guidelines for reliable, safe, and trustworthy human-centered AI systems. ACM Trans. Interact. Intell. Syst. **10**(4), 1–31 (2020). https://doi.org/10.1145/3419764

Shneiderman, B.: Human-Centered AI. Oxford University Press, Oxford (2022)

Valverde, R.: Principles of Human Computer Interaction Design: HCI Design. LAP Lambert Academic Publishing, Sunnyvale (2011)

Wexler, J., Pushkarna, M., Bolukbasi, T., Wattenberg, M., Viegas, F., Wilson, J.: The what-if tool: interactive probing of machine learning models. IEEE Trans. Visual Comput. Graph. **26**, 56–65 (2019). https://doi.org/10.1109/TVCG.2019.2934619

Wilkens, U., Sprafke, N.: Micro-variables of dynamic capabilities and how they come into effect – exploring firm-specificity and cross-firm commonalities. Manag. Int. **23**(4), 30–49 (2019). https://doi.org/10.7202/1066068ar

Wright, A.P., et al.: A comparative analysis of industry human-AI interaction guidelines. arXiv: 2010.11761 [Cs] (2020)

Xu, W., Dainoff, M.J., Ge, L., Gao, Z.: Transitioning to human interaction with AI systems: new challenges and opportunities for HCI professionals to enable human-centered AI. arXiv:2105.05424 [Cs] (2021)

Yang, Q., Steinfeld, A., Rosé, C., Zimmerman, J.: Re-examining whether, why, and how human-AI interaction is uniquely difficult to design. In: Proceedings of the 2020 CHI Conference on Human Factors in Computing Systems, pp. 1–13 (2020). https://doi.org/10.1145/3313831.3376301

Yang, Y., Kandogan, E., Li, Y., Sen, P., Lasecki, W.S.: A study on interaction in human-in-the-loop machine learning for text analytics, Los Angeles, vol. 7 (2019)

Zanzotto, F.M.: Viewpoint: human-in-the-loop artificial intelligence. J. Artif. Intell. Res. **64**, 243–252 (2019). https://doi.org/10.1613/jair.1.11345

Zhang, Z.T., Liu, Y., Hussmann, H.: Forward reasoning decision support: toward a more complete view of the human-AI interaction design space. In: CHItaly 2021: 14th Biannual Conference of the Italian SIGCHI Chapter, pp. 1–5 (2021). https://doi.org/10.1145/3464385.3464696

Zhou, L., et al.: Intelligence augmentation: towards building human-machine symbiotic relationship. AIS Trans. Hum.-Comput. Interact. **13**(2), 243–264 (2021). https://doi.org/10.17705/1thci.00149

Artificial Intelligence Augmenting Human Teams. A Systematic Literature Review on the Opportunities and Concerns

Jayden Khakurel(✉) and Kirsimarja Blomqvist

LUT School of Business and Management, LUT University, Yliopistonkatu 34, 53850 Lappeenranta, Finland
{jayden.khakurel,kirsimarja.Blomqvist}@lut.fi

Abstract. Artificial intelligence (AI) that can augment human intelligence in teamwork has been addressed in many studies; however, the state-of-the art of scholarly knowledge of the topic itself is missing. Thus, this paper provides a systematic review of the current knowledge on AI in augmenting human teams. The systematic literature review shows that AI working as teammate could augment human teams in important ways in enhancing team coordination, enhancing knowledge sharing and learning, supporting decision making, as well as evaluation and team performance. Further, the review also reveals that there are concerns related with social and machine teammate interaction, design, privacy, and ethics, that need further research to unleash AI technologies' benefits in increasingly knowledge-intensive and diverse team collaboration.

Keywords: Artificial intelligence · Humans · Teams · AI-human collaboration · AI-augmenting human intelligence (HI) · AI-human teamwork (HT)

1 Introduction

In recent years, there has been a surge in interest and enthusiasm in artificial intelligence (AI) technologies, as the worldwide growth in AI technologies demonstrates [21]. Organisations have started incorporating "AI" as integral to their strategy in automating the collaborative organisational processes to perform more efficiently and effectively in gathering information, extracting data from internal and external sources to support knowledge processes and collaboration [1, 4, 16, 31]. The COVID-19 pandemic further provided a organizations a unique opportunity to prove that AI based applications could be beneficial to improve remote team collaboration by allowing analysis of real-time participants' facial expressions, head gestures and spotlights [9, 38].

AI technology undoubtedly creates new possibilities through Machine Learning (ML), Natural Language Processing (NLP) for teams in an organization in developing more innovative and creative ideas by transforming disparate data into relevant information, creating coherent and engaging personalized responses in real-time; however, its use has implications for actors involved [39]. Implications may include bias in AI:

H. Degen and S. Ntoa (Eds.): HCII 2022, LNAI 13336, pp. 51–68, 2022.
https://doi.org/10.1007/978-3-031-05643-7_4

algorithmic prejudice, negative legacy, and underestimation [27], threat to employees' autonomy, privacy rights, and risk discriminating against underserved communities [20]. These implications may vary depending upon the type of AI technology adopted [44].

Although researchers, practitioners, and policymakers are starting to pay attention whether AI will be used for developing knowledge worker for employer surveillance [16, 39], *a systematic overview of the opportunities and concerns related to AI in Augmenting Human Intelligence (HI) in the teamwork is still lacking.* For instance, Seeber et al. (2020) collaborated with 65 scientists and highlighted the future research agenda comprising three design areas – Machine artifact, Collaboration, and Institution – and 17 dualities, such as trust built/lost, health enabler/risk, job created/lost with significant effects with the potential for benefit or harm to organize early research in this new area of study. Author raised an important question as one of the future research agenda to be addressed *"what might the implications be for human team members, collaborative work practices, and outcomes, for organizations, and society when AI machines become teammates rather than tools?"*.

Thus, this study summarizes the current research on augmenting human intelligence in teamwork with AI, focusing especially on the trends, the range of AI technologies optimized tools, possibilities, concerns and state-of-the-art of the scholarly knowledge of the topic.

The review begins by an overview of the related work already conducted by scholars. Then, the research methodology section focusses on how this research was conducted and how relevant studies were gathered. The findings section presents the findings of this study and an interpretation of the results. Finally, we present the discussion that also outlines the path for future research, followed by conclusion and limitations.

2 Methods

This study adopts and applies a systematic literature review (SLR) approach to systematically assess existing literature following the guidelines presented by Kitchenham et al. [30]. Our research process consists of three phases: planning the review, conducting the review, reporting the review. Each phase was performed and reviewed by two members of the research team to confirm that the articles retrieved for the full-text assessment are accurate and appropriate for further analysis. The following section explains in detail the phases applied in this systematic literature review:

2.1 Planning the Literature Review

The following section provides an overview of the stages associated with planning this literature review study:

Identifying the Need for the Review. We evaluated the need for the review by performing the search on EBSCO Business Source Complete, PubMed, IEEE (Institute of Electrical and Electronics Engineers), ACM, Web of Science and Scopus online databases in including google scholar using the following initial search terms: keywords "artificial intelligence" "organization*"; "team collaboration" and "team*". The initial search result showed there is no single study comprehensively summarizing the current state of the research concerning Artificial Intelligence (AI) augmenting Human Intelligence in Teamwork.

Research Questions (RQ's): We formulated the research questions by using the PICO (population, intervention, control/comparison, and outcomes) criteria [47] which helps to organize search strategy [28]. For our purposes, PICO includes Population: Teams, organization Intervention: Artificial Intelligence (AI), AI-agents, Outcome: effectiveness and challenges. In this study, the focus was to find the opportunities and concerns related to AI for augmenting teams but not to compare them. Therefore, comparison was out of the scope and omitted. Thus, in view of the above, we frame the following four RQ's to obtain a more inclusive overview of the topic:

RQ1: What do the research activities conducted over time reveal the research and type of AI optimized tool for augmenting human intelligence in teamwork?

Rationale: *Identifies the research trends in recent times that have been the focus of the research including the range of AI technologies optimized tools that have been the focus of the research.*

RQ2: What opportunities does the literature mention on AI to augment human intelligence in teamwork?

Rationale: *Indicates the extent to which AI may add value to teams and organizations, which provides information about the development potential in AI augmenting human intelligence in teamwork.*

RQ3: What kind of concerns have been raised in augmenting team collaboration with AI and needs consideration by the research community?

Rationale: *Provides detailed information on the concerns that remain, and the improvements required; and serves as a basis for ascertaining future research directions.*

Conducting the Review. The guidelines [29] emphasize the importance of screening an initial set of articles by applying inclusion criteria (IC) and exclusion criteria (EC) to determine if a study should be included and how to classify the articles based on the keywords from the abstract. The following section presents the steps taken while conducting the review:

Identification of Research. In order to not miss, and identify as much relevant literature to research questions, it is crucial to initiate an optimum search strategy. Given that, the first step is to identify the search strings fed into digital libraries. Based on the guidelines [28], which comprises four phases,

In phase 1 the search terms were formulated based on the keywords used in the RQ's using PICO criteria. **In phase 2,** Synonyms and acronyms or alternative words were identified. (i.e., "artificial intelligence"; "AI" "machine learning"; "deep learning"; "intelligent agent"; "agent-human interaction"), ("organization"), ("team collaboration"; "team"). In phase 3, we merged all synonyms, acronyms, and alternative phrasings using

Boolean operator "or". Finally, in phase 4, all the major terms from the keywords were combined to construct the search string using "AND" operations: ("artificial intelligence" OR "AI" OR "machine learning" OR "deep learning" OR "intelligent agent*" OR "agent-human interaction") AND ("organization") AND ("team collaboration" OR "team*"). The search string went through multiple iterations (i.e., tested, modified, formulated, tested) and replicated to all databases until adequate results were obtained.

As the second step, the final search string and utilizing the search utilities of the digital databases, an initial search was conducted. The following search databases were included: EBSCO Business Source Complete, ACM Digital Library, IEEE Xplore, Scopus, Web of Science and PubMed. These databases were chosen because of their relevance in this research area (i.e., to the field of business, health, and technology). Additionally, from the identified papers, the citations were also manually browsed [57] as well as google scholar was used for citation chaining [3] to find any other relevant articles. The initial set of searches was performed utilizing the formulated search string and the search utility of the selected digital databases in January 2021 and final searches were made in April limiting the search to publications to 2009–2021.

Article Selection Process. The main objective of the article selection process is to check the eligibility of the identified articles based on the set of inclusion (IC) and exclusion (EC) criteria to extract publications relevant to the objective of this SLR. Thus, in this context, the following sets of inclusion criteria (IC) and exclusion criteria (EC) were applied:

- IC1: Publication is dated between 1/1/2009–04/15/2021; IC2: Includes answers for at least one of the research questions, which was determined by reading the title, and abstracts; IC3: Includes if the study conducted was related to the Artificial Intelligence, organization, and team; IC4: Only papers written in English.
- EC1: Paper that limited discussion about Artificial technology, team which was determined by reading the title, and abstracts; EC2: Technical documentation or reports that are available in the form of abstracts.

The automated search process led to 350 articles (see Fig. 2) on the following digital databases: EBSCO (2), PubMed (1), IEEE (4), ACM (23), and Web of Science (100) and Scopus (220). Each of which was performed and reviewed by two members of the research team to ascertain the articles retrieved. After refining the results based on the predefined criteria, removing duplicate articles, the final 30 studies were selected for data extraction and analysis. According to Impellizzeri and Bizzini (2012), "Data extraction must be accurate and unbiased and therefore, to reduce possible errors, it should be performed by at least two reviewers" (p. 499). Based on this recommendation, in the data sets were reviewed by other members of the research team to confirm that the intended meaning was accurate and appropriate for further analysis. The results were discussed among the authors, and no disagreements between the initial datasets (Fig. 1).

A template was developed to register all the relevant information from the final set of reviewed articles. The data extraction process included the following data for each primary source included in the study: Metadata: study ID (S1, S2, ...), author(s), year of publication, paper title, type of publication, name of the conference or journal in which

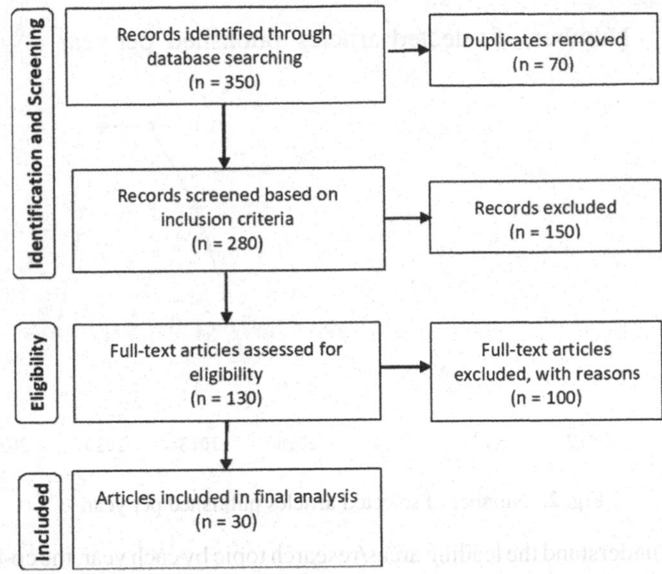

Fig. 1. Flow diagram of literature review process

the study was presented, keywords, topic, and database. In addition to general metadata, data relevant to the RQs were extracted as follows:

Type of AI technology (if applicable): RQ2; Opportunities (if applicable): RQ3; Concerns (if applicable): RQ4. All the extracted data were checked for accuracy and relevancy. Extracted data were recorded into data fields and be accessed online (https://doi/10.5281/zenodo.6284942).

3 Findings

We took an SLR approach to identify and present the preliminary results related to the opportunities and challenges in augmenting human intelligence with AI in team collaboration. The following section highlights the important results:

RQ1: What does the research activities over time reveal about the research and type of AI optimized tool for augmenting human intelligence in teamwork?

As shown on Fig. 2, even though the search was limited to between 2009 to 2021, the relevant articles only started to appear around 2015. One of the possibilities is due to the research on AI-related topics that has received more and more attention from researchers and industry. Examples include the launch of Tensor flow—an open-source platform for machine learning in 2015. From the analysis of the primary studies, the included studies originated from countries, predominantly the United States of America.

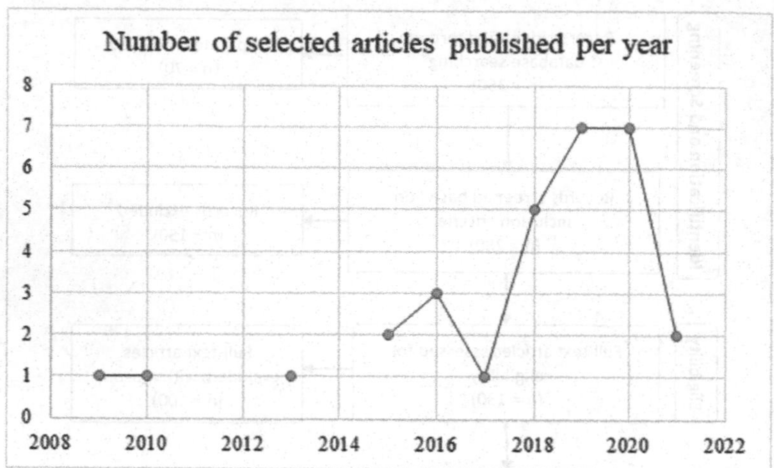

Fig. 2. Number of selected articles published per year

To further understand the leading areas/research topic by each year, the co-occurrence of the keywords within the selected primary studies were performed using KHCoder—a quantitative content analysis tool. In Fig. 3 the size of the bubble represents the frequency of occurrence of the keyword. Thus, the larger bubble size represents keywords that are most frequent in the primary studies.

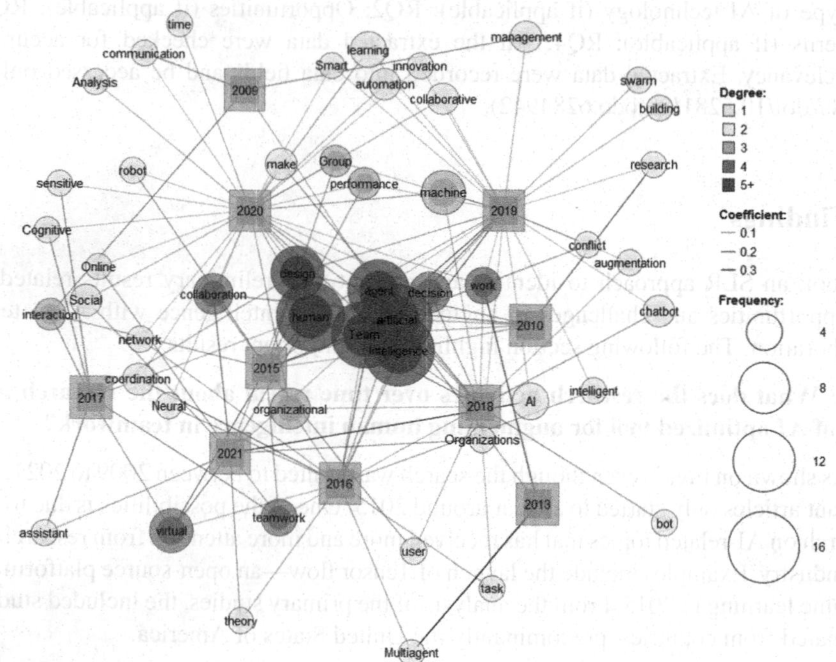

Fig. 3. Co-occurrence of the top research keywords based on 30 publications

From the analysis in Fig. 3, it is apparent that the Artificial Intelligence, human, team, AI as agent, and design were most encountered and important keywords in the reviewed literature. When looking at research carried through across time, we see that the relevant topics started to appear around 2015.

In addition, we analyzed the most frequently raised type of AI technologies from the literature that could augment human intelligence in team collaboration. Table 1 presents the AI optimized tool mapped with the AI technology that most primary studies discussed.

Table 1. Summary of AI optimized tool with type of AI technology identified in the literature

AI optimized tool	Type of AI technology
Decision support system [6, 7, 17, 19, 41]	Machine learning
Chatbot [5, 15, 36, 40, 42, 43, 54, 56, 58]	Natural language processing
AI-powered avatars [50]	Natural language processing
Sentiment analysis [23, 32]	Neural networks, deep learning

Most studies used Natural language processing and Machine learning, and contributed significantly to decision support system, chatbot and AI-powered avatars. Based on the current state of existing literature, AI optimized tool was used for sentiment analysis of the team members using deep learning and neural networks and were less discussed.

RQ2: What opportunities does the literature mention on AI to augment human intelligence in teamwork?

In our research context an AI is likely to work together with a human team and form a "human-AI team" to solve problems, gain insights, and recommend actions to a human responsible for final decisions, a context known as AI-supported decision making [15]. The following section presents the analysis of the 30 primary studies on the set of opportunities mentioned by the researchers studying augmenting team collaboration with AI.

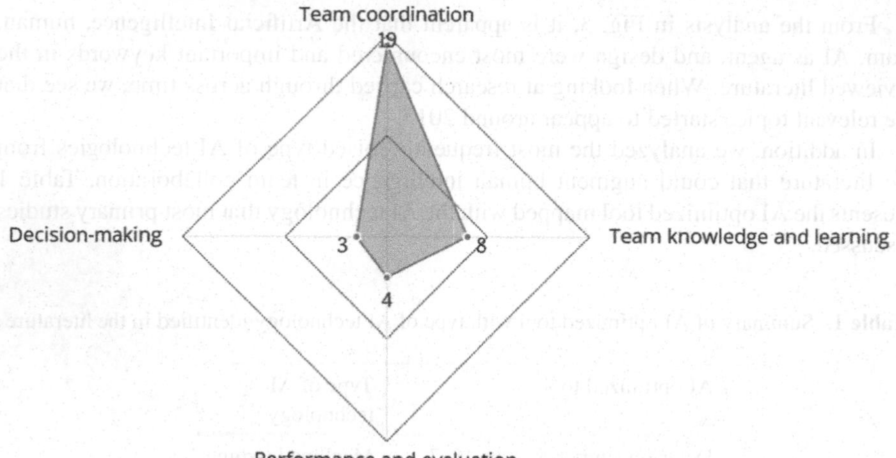

Fig. 4. Opportunities enabled by AI in augmenting team collaboration in the selected primary studies

Based on the analysis of the 30 studies four main common areas and opportunities enabled by AI in augmenting team collaboration can be seen (Fig. 4). More specifically, out of the four areas, most scholars discussed that AI could function as an agent supporting in team coordination, knowledge creation and learning in executing well-defined tasks. Less opportunities were seen in performance and evaluation as well as decision-making (number of the opportunities is larger than number of the papers, as some papers discussed several opportunities). The following section describes each opportunity in detail:

1. **Team Coordination.** In line with theoretical definition of team coordination [13, 49], 19 articles have studied [5, 7, 18, 24, 26, 32, 33, 36, 40, 42, 43, 48, 50, 51, 54–56, 59, 60] how AI could be used be used in managing the team member's action, knowledge, skills, and behaviors to achieve success. Review have identified six ways which AI can coordinate the Human teams in a timely manner—creating team situational awareness, creating conflict awareness, enhancing team communication, managing tasks and task interdependence, coordinating activities, facilitating team building.

Creating team situational awareness which is crucial factor and considered as "the degree to which every team member possesses the situation awareness required for his or her responsibilities" pp. 39 [12]. However, in a dynamic task environment, teams are challenged in identifying and mitigating the dynamic situation because of the multiple personalities, preconceptions, experiences, goals, roles, tasks, and skills. According to the literature reviewed AI tools may contribute to such circumstances by tracking the team activities, integrating the network of information (e.g., timeline, conversation, location, task progress) and utilize the machine learning model in identifying the patterns to support the overall team in a timely, adaptive constructive manner [18, 48, 59]. Such patterns may include the team's situation, focus areas and projection of future situations that may arise [56].

Creating Conflict Awareness. Communication gaps, interpersonal clashes, differences in work styles, task conflict and performance are usually the cause of team conflict which prevent team performance [33]. Paikari et al. [40] and Webber et al. [56] claim that AI tools can aid team functioning by detecting areas of potential direct and indirect conflict, notifying the emerging conflict within the team, and act as an emotion regulator for a team in resolving the conflicts [26].

Enhancing Team Communication. The literature review suggests that the AI tools such as chatbot could enhance team communication by increased understanding how the team interacts, how tasks are assigned to team members, and which levels of autonomous actions are possible within the team [50]. Zhang et al. [59] highlights that AI could support explicit communication via natural language processing during human-AI teamwork. Seeber et al [51] reports that AI could enhance the ability to interact and socialize with their peers. Similarly, Zoelen et al. [60] reports on the development of Machine learning (ML) enabled agents claiming that AI agents can enhance proactive communication in human-agent teaming using contextual factors that can reduce the cognitive load of team members anticipating their information need. We conclude that AI working as teammate could augment human teams in important ways in supporting decision making, creating team situational awareness, and team processes such as creating conflict awareness. However, research on AI regarding team knowledge processes is still scarce.

Managing Tasks and Task Interdependence. In the managing tasks and task interdependence context, scholars have pointed out that AI tools can support teams either as teammates or as leader/task assigners to facilitate internal processes in task management [7, 32, 36, 54]. The internal team processes include task allocation as per skills, capacities, and strengths [43], and coordinating updates regarding sequential and reciprocal task interdependence status. For example, Makarius et al. [32] asserted that "Advanced AI may have capabilities that enable it to work as a teammate with humans, even serve as a leader/task assigner" pp. 264. This new support or AI role as leader/assigner may enable teams to have more time and focus on the types of tasks they prefer and feel they can deliver more value [42].

Coordinating Various Team Activities. Several authors [7, 24, 32, 36, 54] have reported that AI agents can coordinate activities while augmenting human intelligence which includes notifying timely information to needy individual team members or the entire team (e.g., deadlines and tasks that they are responsible for), ensuring the task interdependence status are synchronized, measuring workload and redistributing the workload of individual team members to ensure that a team acts in a coherent manner.

Facilitating Team Building. Several studies highlighted that AI could facilitate the "pure" human-centered teambuilding activities before task performance on improving social relations, team affect, behavior, and performance [5, 43, 55]. For example, an AI agent can simulate the team building model in which an agent enters the human teams and vice versa, providing technical support, and running sociological/physiological experiments on interactions. [5].

2. **Team Knowledge and Learning.** Eight studies [6, 7, 11, 19, 23, 35, 48, 51] focused on how AI agents can mediate between human teams to develop their knowledge and skills by extracting, collecting, sharing, processing information and knowledge held by other individuals, set of knowledge entities. These opportunities are discussed below.

Knowledge Extraction. Howard et al. [19] indicate that AI extracts a set of knowledge entities from data, links the data sets across databases, and provides insights through visualization to empower teams in complex problem solving and support decision-making. In another study, Clauvice et al. [6] reported that AI agents could consolidate and provide access to integrate knowledge resulting from members' actions.

Extending Knowledge Base. AI can capture individual and collective knowledge available in large teams to build, extend and maintain a shared knowledge base [7, 51]. Metcalf et al. [35] point that these extended knowledge bases can enrich teams' knowledge base, improve their skills, derive more accurate answers to critical business questions, make better predictions, and make more effective decisions.

Co-learning. The study of Saenz et al. [48] points that AI has made it possible for the machine to learn from teams to improve its both "general" and "domain" knowledge through data, algorithms, equations, logic rules, and prior distribution [11]. At the same time, it offers opportunities for teams to acquire insights from AI (e.g., integrated knowledge resulting from members' actions) to enrich their knowledge base, skills, and ability [6, 23]. These studies suggest that both teams and AI learn from one another for facilitating AI-team collaboration on managing and diffusing complex situations.

3. **Performance and evaluation.** Of the 30 studies identified, four studies [10, 15, 17, 43] focused on how AI can (a) evaluate the standard workload, so that the team members don't feel overwhelmed, (b) factual data and carry out individuals within the team's performance reviews. Each of these identified opportunities are discussed below.

Evaluating and Reducing Workload. Team workload is a critical challenge [2] as uneven distribution can result in a suboptimal team performance and defective project results [17]. As a result, current research has examined how AI can augment team members in evaluating and reducing workload. A study conducted by Rajpurohit [43] showed that AI optimised tool can help in allocating team member roles based on their present work schedules and records along with their skill sets to make the projects more efficient. Other studies conducted by Maaike et al. [17], and Demir et al. [10] showed that AI tools such as virtual agent can manage and distribute work fairly and evenly across the team. For example, support workload harmonization in teams by measuring workload, informing team members about their own and other team members' workload, and supporting team members by automating task delegation to reduce the workload.

Monitoring Performance. The literature reviewed suggests that the AI algorithms can provide insight into the team performance on how quickly individuals within the team complete different tasks by analyzing the skills, attitudes, and actions of individual and team across the projects and different work scenarios [43]. Therefore, it appears that the ability of AI in monitoring team performance and providing insights would enable AI agents to serve as useful tools for the team and even in some leader roles for virtual teams [15].

4. **Decision Making.** Some of the studies [35, 43, 51] that have examined how AI can analyze large volumes of data, to summarize and suggest next steps to team members in decision making process are presented in this section.

Supporting Decision Making. Several authors have recognized [35, 43, 51] AI could uncover patterns from the data and support more objective and reliable team decision making in reducing human error. For example, Rajpurohit et al. [43] explained that "AI can enhance the working capacity of team members by reducing the focus from routine jobs that can be easily performed using AI techniques to strategic decision making …capacities" pp. 390. This means that the AI may, for example, provide a degree of autonomy to team members in terms of (i.) mining the new knowledge from the pool of resources either from the company's internal repositories or external sources, (ii.) supporting in summarizing the actions and organizing work that needs to be accomplished by the team.

Moreover, the study of Metcalf et al. [35] reveal that Artificial Swarm Intelligence (ASI), a branch of AI can mine knowledge from data and provide means for teams to combine their explicit and tacit knowledge in real time and to work synchronously to make predictions, to assess alternatives, and to reach decisions about known unknowns. Because of the potential of human swarming to enable groups to combine them knowledge and intuition in real-time, swarming likely offers the greatest benefit when human team members make complex decisions on topics that can be assessed from many unique perspectives, weighing their confidence and preferences [45].

Creating Recommendations. AI can provide data-driven recommendations to teams through the interfaces such as decision support system or chatbot. These outputs are crucial in making more effective decisions to maximize team performance [35, 51].

RQ4: What kind of concerns have been raised in augmenting team collaboration with AI and needs consideration by the research community?

Our literature review shows that there is enthusiasm about the opportunities with AI augmenting human teams on the one hand, but there are also concerns among employees and the scientific communities. Those concerns in relation to augmenting team with AI are presented below:

Design Teamwork in an organization is performed through conversation and communication practices, individuals within the team are expected to adapt the linguistic politeness which is an important and essential element of workplace interactions [8]. In the review, one of the concerns identified [54] was related to conversation design in terms of linguistic politeness. It was reported that AI chatbot sometimes failed to understand users when interacting in polite and human-like ways. The natural language understanding model had not been trained to handle those utterances beyond its capabilities in multi-threaded conversations. Wessel et al. [46] made observation where teams did not find current bots intelligent enough to handle and provide notification/awareness based on previous interaction tasks and challenges. Also, Metcalf et al. [35] raised a similar concern that current AI does not have access to tacit knowledge and mostly must rely on historical data from which patterns can be identified as significant limiting factors of AI predicated on machine learning.

The AI may connect physical and digital information to extract data, generate and deliver extensive new knowledge to the team through highly sophisticated systems with generated extensive detail and analysis. This could reduce the team members' interest in AI. For example, need of manual intervention, receiving reminders more often, suggesting wrong actions, lacking guidance for newcomers and lack of understanding of available resources [54, 56, 58]. Further, Seeber et al. [51] raise concern with algorithm design and point that the lack of methodological transparency inherent in Machine learning methods (ML) can impair the trust in the machine teammate.

Teammate interaction regarding human-human teammate interaction, studies reported that the AI could reduce social interaction. [36, 58] Thus, it may lower team members' identification with other team members, [36] who may find it challenging to build trust in team. For instance, Makarius et al. [32] note that "some employees may find issues in building trust with a system or teammate that does not actually feel emotions or have the same capability of empathy leaving managers with a difficult challenge on how to best integrate AI into the organization" pp. 264. Studies also indicate that loss of human-human team interaction may create the problem of reinforcing existing views, decreasing the out-of-the-box thinking, and losing collaborative creativity as it relies not just on inner time but also on social time [25, 51]. With regards to human-machine team interaction, Seeber et al. [51] also point that lack of sufficient reasoning and explaining by AI may lead to misunderstanding and exhibiting cognitive load on a human team.

Task management Toxtli et al. [54] experimental study found that handling multiple tasks simultaneously assigned by machine teammate adversely increased the cognitive demands on human teammates. By contrast, Crowston et al. [54] raised concerns about machine teammate effectiveness while performing an interdependent task that requires multiple humans to handle. Research also reported that human teaming with the machine must trot along at a pace dictated by the machine teammates speed to adapt to new tasks [25]. The study claims that this could be "overwhelming for human teammates as machine teammates are unable to deal with humans limited cognitive capacity" (pp. 8).

Privacy, Ethics Many of the privacy concerns reported in the literature were regarding data collection and feature extraction by AI tools from a data set and sharing that information for improving team performance. For example, Maaike et al. [17] point that AI may monitor the human team's workload and share the information with other team members or leaders, which can eventually lead to higher team performance; however, it may violate the individual team members' privacy. Similarly, Seeber et al. [51] point that data collection from various sources such as built-in cameras, human teammates, including confidential project information and processed by algorithms of machine teammates, raises privacy concern.

Current literature review raises concerns about algorithmic bias, accuracy, and algorithm transparency. For example, Jarrahi et al. [24] pointed, "As AI algorithms gradually penetrate more aspects of knowledge work, they can clash with knowledge workers and devalue workers' expertise due to their black-boxed performance". Gladden et al. [15] point that lack of extensive knowledge base of shared language and culture within the AI-mediated cross-culture human team members could create a spatial and temporal division between team members, resulting in unfair treatment.

Machine teammates behaviour Previous studies report that machine teammates learn more sophisticated behaviour including bad behaviours from human counterparts [51, 60]. As a result, machine teammates may replicate and exhibit negative or even aggressive behaviour, have prejudices, send nasty messages, or become biased [51]. Based on our review of the challenges it becomes clear that researchers and practitioners must continue their work to overcome the challenges so that teams are willing to explore the benefits of augmenting human teams with AI.

4 Discussion and Recommendation

As a general trend we find that the number of research articles on AI in teamwork has grown since 2015 and even more since 2018. Also, we find that technologies involved are machine learning, NLP, neural networks, and deep learning used mostly for chatbots, sentiment analysis and decision support systems. Team coordination is clearly the largest opportunity visible in 19 articles out of 30. In an increasingly remote work mode, an opportunity to enhance team situational awareness and managing team interdependence is highlighted. AI can have a key role also in mitigating conflicts and enhancing team communication and interaction.

Eight of the reviewed studies focused on team knowledge and learning helping teams to build a shared knowledge base and support team learning. Surprisingly, only four studies discussed team performance and evaluation as an opportunity. Especially related to coordinating team efforts, AI could support more equal sharing of teamwork load, support evaluation and enhance team-level performance. Regarding team decision-making AI's ability to uncover patterns and provide objective data for supporting human decision-making was seen as an opportunity. An interesting opportunity here is also a real-time possibility in combining explicit and tacit knowledge.

Researchers' concerns on AI in teams were first related to how AI chatbots can understand team members' use of natural language as well as provide meaningful notifications on previous tasks. Further, they may also replicate negative human behavior. Further, lack of access to human tacit knowledge means AI needs to rely on historical data to identify patterns. AI's lack of understanding of teamwork context such as available resources and experience may also have a negative impact on team members' interest in using it. AI may reduce team social interaction having negative implications on creative thinking and team identification. Also lack of reasoning and ability to adapt to human pace and cognitive capacity may overwhelm human team members. Finally, team members' privacy may be threatened, and ethical questions arise when AI uses human generated data and shares it with team members and lead. Algorithms may also devalue human experience by black-boxing performance.

For teams to benefit from AI there is clearly a need to carefully consider team processes to analyze where, how, and when AI can support team work optimally. Our findings show that researchers have started to actively explore different opportunities, yet acknowledge the potential drawbacks of AI itself, as well as the implications of introducing AI to teamwork.

5 Implications for Research and Practice

In future research, first the nature of human knowledge and related knowledge processes should be paid attention. Current research on team knowledge processes is still scarce, and research on the topic could yield major benefits for increasingly technology-enabled and knowledge-intensive team collaboration. Secondly, teams are increasingly diverse consisting of members from various professional and cultural backgrounds. At its best, AI could work together with team members to reduce obstacles related to cross-cultural teamwork and maximize trust between individual human team members from diverse professional and natural cultures creating a positive environment to improve team performance. The question arises, how can AI as a teammate facilitate team creativity processes in culturally diverse environment? To what extent can AI understand the different values, beliefs, attitudes, and behaviors shared by a diverse and cross-cultural team and act rationally and humanely to mitigate obstacles and improve team performance?

To augment human teams for any of the opportunities identified in this literature review, AI must be trained with a large dataset. Depending on the nature of the AI tool used in augmenting teams, the datasets may include employee generated data and outcomes from previous projects, and type of text used. However, workplace data may not be sufficient to boost a team's productivity and also complementary datasets from various digital devices including location, movement tracking at the workplace, time spent during breaks, meetings, time spent on applications installed on computers, mouse movements and keyboard typing patterns may be used. Thus, a collection of the "self-generated physiological and human performance" data aggregated with real-time workplace data brings opportunities but also challenges for teams using AI to enhance their performance: Which purposes will be collected data be used for? Who owns the data and with whom is the data shared what kinds of security measures will be taken to protect against internally unauthorized access by another member of the team? How can the AI model trained from the data be seen as trustworthy? Any uncertainty may seriously hinder the team members' acceptance of AI for augmenting human intelligence in teamwork. Thus, future research should focus on investigating how to collect employee self-generated physiological and human performance data, real-time "workplace" data for AI to augment human teams while maintaining team members' trust.

Too often, employees are not consulted during the implementation of AI as a teammate creating a potential trust issue. As suggested by Bentler et al. [37], organizations need to make sure that employees accept AI to become their teammate rather than tools to augment the process during teamwork. Further research should include empirical research to examine how employees feel about a future in which machines become teammates rather than tools.

6 Conclusion and Limitations

AI has the potential to empower human teams, yet we do not yet know exactly how and when. Current systematic literature review provides an overview of the development together with the opportunities and concerns in augmenting human intelligence. Fast technological development together with Covid-19 as a catalyst in increasing technology-mediated teamwork has received attention lately from researchers, practitioners, and policymakers. This study provides an overview of current research and highlights directions for future research. We conclude that to make maximum use of AI in augmenting human intelligence in teamwork, it is critical to judiciously maximize its opportunities and minimize concerns related to design, teammate interaction, task management, privacy, ethics, machine teammates behaviors, by developing and introducing AI-based applications in collaboration coordination between end-users, researchers, practitioners, and AI application developers.

The potential limitations of this literature review is [34, 53] that some relevant studies may have been omitted during the data collection process because of applied search strings, synonyms, anonyms, search exclusively in specific academic digital databases. However, in this review, this threat to validity has been reduced by utilizing the common rule within the systematic literature review method—the rigorous and transparent search process, interpreted data were quoted to validate the meaning of the results.

References

1. Amabile, T.: Creativity, artificial intelligence, and a world of surprises. Acad. Manag. Discov. **6**, 351–354 (2020)
2. Bedwell, W.L., et al.: Team workload. Organ. Psychol. Rev. **4**(2), 99–123 (2014). https://doi.org/10.1177/2041386613502665
3. Benedictine University: Google Scholar: Citation Chaining. https://researchguides.ben.edu/c.php?g=1136428&p=8295233. Accessed 5 Apr 2021
4. Bose, R.: Intelligent agents framework for developing knowledge-based decision support systems for collaborative organizational processes. Expert Syst. Appl. **11**(3), 247–261 (1996). https://doi.org/10.1016/S0957-4174(96)00042-5
5. Capone, C., et al.: Smart RogAgent: where agents and humans team up. In: Baldoni, M., Dastani, M., Liao, B., Sakurai, Y., Zalila Wenkstern, R. (eds.) PRIMA 2019. LNCS (LNAI), vol. 11873, pp. 541–549. Springer, Cham (2019). https://doi.org/10.1007/978-3-030-33792-6_39
6. Clauvice, K.: Modeling intermediation system based on intelligent agents for community of practices. In: 2009 13th International Conference on Computer Supported Cooperative Work in Design, pp. 270–275 IEEE (2009). https://doi.org/10.1109/CSCWD.2009.4968070
7. Consoli, A.: $_{AC}{}^{3}$M: the agent coordination and cooperation cognitive model. In: Tweedale, J.W., Neves-Silva, R., Jain, L.C., Phillips-Wren, G., Watada, J., Howlett, R.J. (eds.) Intelligent Decision Technology Support in Practice. SIST, vol. 42, pp. 141–168. Springer, Cham (2016). https://doi.org/10.1007/978-3-319-21209-8_9
8. Darics, E.: Politeness in computer-mediated discourse of a virtual team. J. Politeness Res. Lang. Behav. Cult. **6**, 1 (2010). https://doi.org/10.1515/jplr.2010.007
9. De, R., et al.: Impact of digital surge during Covid-19 pandemic: a viewpoint on research and practice. Int. J. Inf. Manage. **55**, 102171 (2020). https://doi.org/10.1016/j.ijinfomgt.2020.102171

10. Demir, M., et al.: Team synchrony in human-autonomy teaming. In: Advances in Intelligent Systems and Computing, pp. 303–312. Springer, Cham (2018). https://doi.org/10.1007/978-3-319-60384-1_29
11. Deng, C., et al.: Integrating machine learning with human knowledge. iScience **23**(11), 101656 (2020). https://doi.org/10.1016/j.isci.2020.101656
12. Endsley, M.R.: Measurement of situation awareness in dynamic systems. Hum. Factors J. Hum. Factors Ergon. Soc. **37**(1), 65–84 (1995). https://doi.org/10.1518/001872095779049499
13. Gabelica, C., et al.: Establishing team knowledge coordination from a learning perspective. Hum. Perform. **29**(1), 33–53 (2016). https://doi.org/10.1080/08959285.2015.1120304
14. Gatti, U.C., et al.: Using wearable physiological status monitors for analyzing the physical strain-productivity relationship for construction tasks. In: Congress on Computing in Civil Engineering, Proceedings (2012). https://doi.org/10.1061/9780784412343.0073
15. Gladden, M.: Leveraging the cross-cultural capacities of artificial agents as leaders of human virtual teams. In: 10th European Conference on Management Leadership and Governance, pp. 428–436 (2015)
16. Haefner, N., et al.: Artificial intelligence and innovation management: a review, framework, and research agenda. Technol. Forecast. Soc. Change. **162**, 120392 (2021). https://doi.org/10.1016/j.techfore.2020.120392
17. Harbers, M., Neerincx, M.A.: Value sensitive design of a virtual assistant for workload harmonization in teams. Cogn. Technol. Work **19**(2–3), 329–343 (2017). https://doi.org/10.1007/s10111-017-0408-4
18. Hong, M.-T., et al.: Coordinating agents. In: Companion of the 2018 ACM Conference on Computer Supported Cooperative Work and Social Computing, pp. 217–220 ACM, New York (2018). https://doi.org/10.1145/3272973.3274059
19. Howard, J.: Artificial intelligence: implications for the future of work. Am. J. Ind. Med. **62**(11), 917–926 (2019). https://doi.org/10.1002/ajim.23037
20. Hughes, C., et al.: Artificial intelligence, employee engagement, fairness, and job outcomes. In: Managing Technology and Middle- and Low-skilled Employees, pp. 61–68, August 2019. https://doi.org/10.1108/978-1-78973-077-720191005
21. IDC: IDC Forecasts Improved Growth for Global AI Market in 2021. https://www.idc.com/getdoc.jsp?containerId=prUS47482321
22. Impellizzeri, F.M., Bizzini, M.: Systematic review and meta-analysis: a primer. Int. J. Sports Phys. Ther. **7**(5), 493–503 (2012)
23. Jarrahi, M.H.: Artificial intelligence and the future of work: human-AI symbiosis in organizational decision making. Bus. Horiz. **61**(4), 577–586 (2018). https://doi.org/10.1016/j.bushor.2018.03.007
24. Jarrahi, M.H.: In the age of the smart artificial intelligence: AI's dual capacities for automating and informating work. Bus. Inf. Rev. **36**(4), 178–187 (2019). https://doi.org/10.1177/0266382119883999
25. Jarvenpaa, S.L., Välikangas, L.: Advanced technology and end-time in organizations: a doomsday for collaborative creativity? Acad. Manag. Perspect. **34**(4), 566–584 (2020). https://doi.org/10.5465/amp.2019.0040
26. Jung, M.F., et al.: Using robots to moderate team conflict: the case of repairing violations. In: ACM/IEEE International Conference on Human-Robot Interact, 2015-March, pp. 229–236, March 2015. https://doi.org/10.1145/2696454.2696460
27. Kamishima, T., et al.: Fairness-aware learning through regularization approach. In: 2011 IEEE 11th International Conference on Data Mining Workshops, pp. 643–650. IEEE (2011). https://doi.org/10.1109/ICDMW.2011.83

28. Khakurel, J., et al.: Tapping into the wearable device revolution in the work environment: a systematic review. Inf. Technol. People. **31**(3), 791–818 (2018). https://doi.org/10.1108/ITP-03-2017-0076
29. Kitchenham, B., et al.: Systematic literature reviews in software engineering – a systematic literature review. Inf. Softw. Technol. **51**(1), 7–15 (2009). https://doi.org/10.1016/j.infsof.2008.09.009
30. Kitchenham, B., et al.: Systematic literature reviews in software engineering – a tertiary study. Inf. Softw. Technol. **52**(8), 792–805 (2010). https://doi.org/10.1016/j.infsof.2010.03.006
31. von Krogh, G.: Artificial intelligence in organizations: new opportunities for phenomenon-based theorizing. Acad. Manag. Discov. **4**(4), 404–409 (2018). https://doi.org/10.5465/amd.2018.0084
32. Makarius, E.E., et al.: Rising with the machines: a sociotechnical framework for bringing artificial intelligence into the organization. J. Bus. Res. **120**, 262–273 (2020). https://doi.org/10.1016/j.jbusres.2020.07.045
33. Maltarich, M.A., et al.: Conflict in teams: modeling early and late conflict states and the interactive effects of conflict processes. Gr. Organ. Manag. **43**(1), 6–37 (2018). https://doi.org/10.1177/1059601116681127
34. Maxwell, J.: Understanding and validity in qualitative research. Harv. Educ. Rev. **62**(3), 279–301 (1992). https://doi.org/10.17763/haer.62.3.8323320856251826
35. Metcalf, L., et al.: Keeping humans in the loop: pooling knowledge through artificial swarm intelligence to improve business decision making. Calif. Manage. Rev. **61**(4), 84–109 (2019). https://doi.org/10.1177/0008125619862256
36. Mirbabaie, M., Stieglitz, S., Brünker, F., Hofeditz, L., Ross, B., Frick, N.R.J.: Understanding collaboration with virtual assistants – the role of social identity and the extended self. Bus. Inf. Syst. Eng. **63**(1), 21–37 (2020). https://doi.org/10.1007/s12599-020-00672-x
37. Mlekus, L., et al.: How to raise technology acceptance: user experience characteristics as technology-inherent determinants. Grup. Interaktion. Organ. Zeitschrift für Angew. Organ. **51**(3), 273–283 (2020). https://doi.org/10.1007/s11612-020-00529-7
38. Murali, P., et al.: AffectiveSpotlight: facilitating the communication of affective responses from audience members during online presentations. In: CHI 2021 (2021). https://doi.org/10.1145/3411764.3445235
39. Pachidi, S., et al.: Make way for the algorithms: symbolic actions and change in a regime of knowing, pp. 0–24, October 2020
40. Paikari, E., et al.: A chatbot for conflict detection and resolution. In: Proceedings - 2019 IEEE/ACM 1st International Workshop on Bots in Software Engineering BotSE 2019, pp. 29–33 (2019). https://doi.org/10.1109/BotSE.2019.00016
41. Parry, K., et al.: Rise of the machines: a critical consideration of automated leadership decision making in organizations. Gr. Organ. Manag. **41**(5), 571–594 (2016). https://doi.org/10.1177/1059601116643442
42. Sowa, K., Przegalinska, A.: Digital coworker: human-AI collaboration in work environment, on the example of virtual assistants for management professions. In: Przegalinska, A., Grippa, F., Gloor, P.A. (eds.) COINs 2019. SPC, pp. 179–201. Springer, Cham (2020). https://doi.org/10.1007/978-3-030-48993-9_13
43. Rajpurohit, N., et al.: Investigating impact of artificial intelligence in deployment of effective project teams. Int. J. Adv. Sci. Technol. **29**(8), 382–391 (2020)
44. Rhem, A.J.: AI ethics and its impact on knowledge management. AI Ethics **1**(1), 33–37 (2021). https://doi.org/10.1007/s43681-020-00015-2
45. Rosenberg, L.: Artificial swarm intelligence vs human experts. In: Proceedings of International Joint Conference on Neural Networks, 2016-October, pp. 2547–2551 (2016). https://doi.org/10.1109/IJCNN.2016.7727517

46. Rovinelli, A., et al.: Using machine learning and a data-driven approach to identify the small fatigue crack driving force in polycrystalline materials. npj Comput. Mater. **4**, 1–10 (2018). https://doi.org/10.1038/s41524-018-0094-7
47. Sackett, D.L.: Evidence-based medicine. In: Seminars in Perinatology (1997). https://doi.org/10.1016/S0146-0005(97)80013-4
48. Saenz, M.J., et al.: Designing AI systems with human-machine teams. MIT Sloan Manag. Rev. **61**(3), 1–5 (2020)
49. Salas, E., et al.: The wisdom of collectives in organizations: an update of the teamwork competencies. In: Team Effectiveness in Complex Organizations: Cross-Disciplinary Perspectives and Approaches, pp. 39–79. Routledge/Taylor & Francis Group (2009)
50. Schwartz, T., et al.: Hybrid teams: flexible collaboration between humans, robots and virtual agents. In: Klusch, M., Unland, R., Shehory, O., Pokahr, A., Ahrndt, S. (eds.) MATES 2016. LNCS (LNAI), vol. 9872, pp. 131–146. Springer, Cham (2016). https://doi.org/10.1007/978-3-319-45889-2_10
51. Seeber, I., et al.: Machines as teammates: a research agenda on AI in team collaboration. Inf. Manag. **57**, 2 (2020). https://doi.org/10.1016/j.im.2019.103174
52. Stahl, G.K., Maznevski, M.L.: Unraveling the effects of cultural diversity in teams: a retrospective of research on multicultural work groups and an agenda for future research. J. Int. Bus. Stud. **52**(1), 4–22 (2021). https://doi.org/10.1057/s41267-020-00389-9
53. Thomson, S.: Qualitative Research: Validity (2011)
54. Toxtli, C., et al.: Understanding chatbot-mediated task management, pp. 1–6. arXiv (2018)
55. Walliser, J.C., et al.: Team structure and team building improve human-machine teaming with autonomous agents. J. Cogn. Eng. Decis. Mak. **13**(4), 258–278 (2019). https://doi.org/10.1177/1555343419867563
56. Webber, S.S., et al.: Team challenges: is artificial intelligence the solution? Bus. Horiz. **62**(6), 741–750 (2019). https://doi.org/10.1016/j.bushor.2019.07.007
57. Webster, J., Watson, R.T.: Analyzing the past to prepare for the future: writing a literature review. MIS Q. **26**(2), pp. xiii–xxiii (2002). 10.1.1.104.6570
58. Wessel, M., et al.: The power of bots: understanding bots in OSS projects. In: Proceedings of ACM Human-Computer Interaction, CSCW, vol. 2, (2018). https://doi.org/10.1145/3274451
59. Zhang, R., et al.: "An ideal human": expectations of AI teammates in human-AI teaming. In: Proceedings of the ACM Human-Computer Interaction, CSCW3, vol. 4, pp. 1–25 (2021). https://doi.org/10.1145/3432945
60. van Zoelen, E.M., Cremers, A., Dignum, F.P.M., van Diggelen, J., Peeters, M.M.: Learning to communicate proactively in human-agent teaming. In: De La Prieta, F., et al. (eds.) PAAMS 2020. CCIS, vol. 1233, pp. 238–249. Springer, Cham (2020). https://doi.org/10.1007/978-3-030-51999-5_20

Adoption and Perception of Artificial Intelligence Technologies by Children and Teens in Education

Erin Li[1(✉)], Sean Li[1], and Xiaojun Yuan[2]

[1] Cherry Hill High School East, Cherry Hill, NJ 08003, USA
erinxinranli@gmail.com
[2] University at Albany, State University of New York, Albany, NY 12222, USA
xyuan@albany.edu

Abstract. Artificial intelligence (AI) technologies have been extensively used in education to improve the learning experience of students. We are particularly interested in AI in education for children and teens. This systematic review summarizes the state of the literature by exploring how AI technologies have been adopted and perceived by children and teens in education. Based on the PRISMA review framework [17], we performed three rounds of systematic selection in three databases: Education Source, ERIC (Educational Resources Information Center), and ACM Digital Library. The final sample includes 5 articles. The AI technologies involved in these studies include social robots, conversational agents, and AI-based educational games. It is noted that three of the studies focused on AI robots and related technologies. The analysis of these articles showed that it is important to study the use and perception of AI technologies by children and teens in education, and there is a research gap that must be addressed in this field.

Keywords: Artificial intelligence · Children · Education

1 Introduction

The development of artificial intelligence (AI) technologies has made it easier for us to accomplish many tasks. For example, we can easily talk to Amazon Echo, a personal intelligent agent, to instruct it to visit a website or play a song, while simultaneously viewing the progress visually. Generally speaking, AI "enables computers and other automated systems to perform tasks that have historically required human cognition and what we typically consider human decision-making abilities" ([13], p. 1). During the COVID-19 pandemic, AI is playing an increasingly more important role. For example, AI technologies have been used for social distancing detection and management [8] and to treat COVID-19 patients (e.g., using care robots or hospital robots) [11].

In 2018, Milena Marinova, the head of Artificial Intelligence (AI) at the digital education company Pearson said "Unlike other sectors, education is yet to fully realize the benefits of digital and advanced AI techniques, and there are great opportunities to improve learning outcomes and to enable better teaching… Pearson is committed

H. Degen and S. Ntoa (Eds.): HCII 2022, LNAI 13336, pp. 69–79, 2022.
https://doi.org/10.1007/978-3-031-05643-7_5

to transforming the learning experience and becoming the digital winner in education. As a strong believer in lifelong learning, I want to contribute and be a key part in that journey."

Artificial Intelligence in Education (AIED) is not a new concept. The use of AI technologies in the educational environment began about fifty years ago, and the application of AI has been growing exponentially in the recent years [5]. AI has been widely accepted and used by various educational institutions [1, 5]. Researchers have been focusing on designing AI systems or frameworks for children [10, 19, 23]. However, we are not clear how children or teens perceive the systems or technologies and use them in the educational setting. This systematic review mainly examined the adoption and perception of AI technologies by children and teens in the domain of education. Specifically, the review revolves around two research questions (RQs).

RQ1: What is the perception of AI technologies by children and teens in education?
RQ2: How did children and teens adopt AI technologies in education?

In the following, we present the previous work, followed by the methodology, results, and discussions. At the end, we conclude the paper with suggestions of future research.

2 Previous Work

In terms of [5], AIED includes "everything from AI-driven, step-by-step personalized instructional and dialogue systems, through AI-supported exploratory learning, the analysis of student writing, intelligent agents in game-based environments, and student-support chatbots, to AI-facilitated student/tutor matching that puts students firmly in control of their own learning ... students interacting one-to-one with computers, whole-school approaches, students using mobile phones outside the classroom, and much more besides" (p. 11). Timms [22] supported the idea of educational Cobots, a robot designed to help human teachers. Educational Cobot can be an educational technology or product responding to the need of combining the fields of robotics and AIED for the purpose of assisting teachers in the classrooms.

In 1971, Cynthia Solomon and Seymour Papert adopted the idea to teach children about AI [28], in particular they asked children to learn AI by LOGO programming and the Turtle robot [15]. Chen, Chen and Lin [1] evaluated how AI had an impact on education and claimed that incorporating AI technologies into early childhood education has improved the learning experience of students. Recently, researchers on children and AI have implemented ideas in various systems or programs, such as, Machine Learning for Kids [9], PopBots [28], AI Programming with eCraft2Learn [6], curriculums for middle school [20], and Cognimates [2]. Specifically, AI Programming with eCraft2Learn [6] showed that AI programming is not just for those with advanced degrees; instead, young children can be trained to creatively use AI programming to create apps that speak, listen, and learn. Sabuncuoglu [20] developed a 36-week open-source AI curriculum for middle school education to employ an interdisciplinary approach and showcase the entire picture of AI development.

It is important to understand what kind of factors may have an impact on children's perception of AI technologies in a learning environment. Researchers reported that age, familiarity, background, personal experience, social and cultural factors, and technological literacy have affected the perception of AI technologies by children [3, 4, 12, 21, 28]. [28] found that age affected the understanding of the AI concepts by children, especially if the activity involves multiple reasoning steps. They also reported that the familiarity of the related activities impacted the performance of children. When they were given more time and guidance on such activities, their performance increased. [12] carried out interviews with parent-child pairs in which they used Hello Barbie and CogniToys Dino, and found that children do not have a clear understanding of how smart toys work, indicating the importance of technological literacy. [21] claimed that with the development of children's understanding of robots and other AI technologies, their reasoning about such technologies become more sophisticated.

3 Methodology

Based on the PRISMA review framework [17], we performed three rounds of systematic selection in three databases: Education Source, ERIC (Educational Resources Information Center), and ACM Digital Library. These three databases were selected because they involved the first two to include articles on education, and the third one to include articles on technology. We performed three rounds of systematic selection in the selected databases. First, we searched predetermined keywords. Next, we screened the titles and abstracts using predetermined inclusion/exclusion criteria. Finally, we screened the full-text of selected articles to ensure that they met the same inclusion/exclusion criteria. In general, we chose English-written articles from journals and conferences, and excluded reviews, dissertations, commentaries, columns, etc. Studies about the perception of AI technologies by children and teens in education, the factors affecting children's perception of AI, and the adoption of AI technologies by children are included.

3.1 Keyword Search

First, we searched predetermined keywords. On February 19, 2022, we searched the Topic in the Education Source database in the title and abstract fields for articles using the following three sets of keywords ("artificial intelligence" OR "intelligent agent") AND (children OR child OR teenager OR kids OR teens) AND (education), and produced 23 results. We also searched the title and abstract fields in the ERIC and the ACM databases using the same keywords and produced 40 and 29 articles respectively. After excluding 5 duplicates and 1 non-English article, a total of 86 non-duplicate results remained for round two screening.

3.2 Screening the Titles and Abstracts

Next, we screened the titles and abstracts of these 86 articles independently. The three authors each independently screened approximately 1/3 of the titles and abstracts of the 86 articles. This screening resulted in the removal of 63 articles and 23 articles remained for round three screening (full-text screening). This round of screening was based on the rationale that the focus of our systematic literature review is about the use and perception of artificial intelligence technologies by children and teens in education. Other topics are outside of the scope of this review. Specifically, we removed an article if it met at least one of the following exclusion criteria:

- Use AI tools/techniques to build systems or demo ($n = 3$).
- Not empirical studies (e.g., literature review; book review; column/commentary/editorial; bulletin, books, speeches, symposium, collective works, reports, thesis, summary of events; proceedings; $n = 51$).
- Not AI-related ($n = 2$).
- Not children or teens related ($n = 3$).
- Not AI used by children or teens (models, algorithms, approaches) ($n = 4$).

After removing 63 articles, a total of 23 articles remained in the sample.

3.3 Screening the Full Text

We then screened the full text of all 23 remaining articles. During this round, we eliminated 18 more articles from our sample because they met at least one of the aforementioned exclusion criteria:

- Use AI tools/techniques to build systems ($n = 1$).
- Not empirical studies (e.g., literature review; reports, summary of events; interview; $n = 6$).
- Not AI-related ($n = 4$).
- Not children or teens related ($n = 1$).
- Not AI used by children or teens (models, algorithms, approaches) ($n = 6$).

A total of 5 articles remained in the final sample.

Following the PRISMA guidelines for reporting systematic reviews, we summarize the selection process in Fig. 4. During the first-round review of abstracts and titles, the articles were selected for inclusion based on the research focus. A total of 86 articles were included. During the second-round review, the articles were reviewed in their entirety and mapped by the research question, methodology, and type of technology included. Finally, 5 articles were selected for inclusion. Figure 1 shows the PRISMA review.

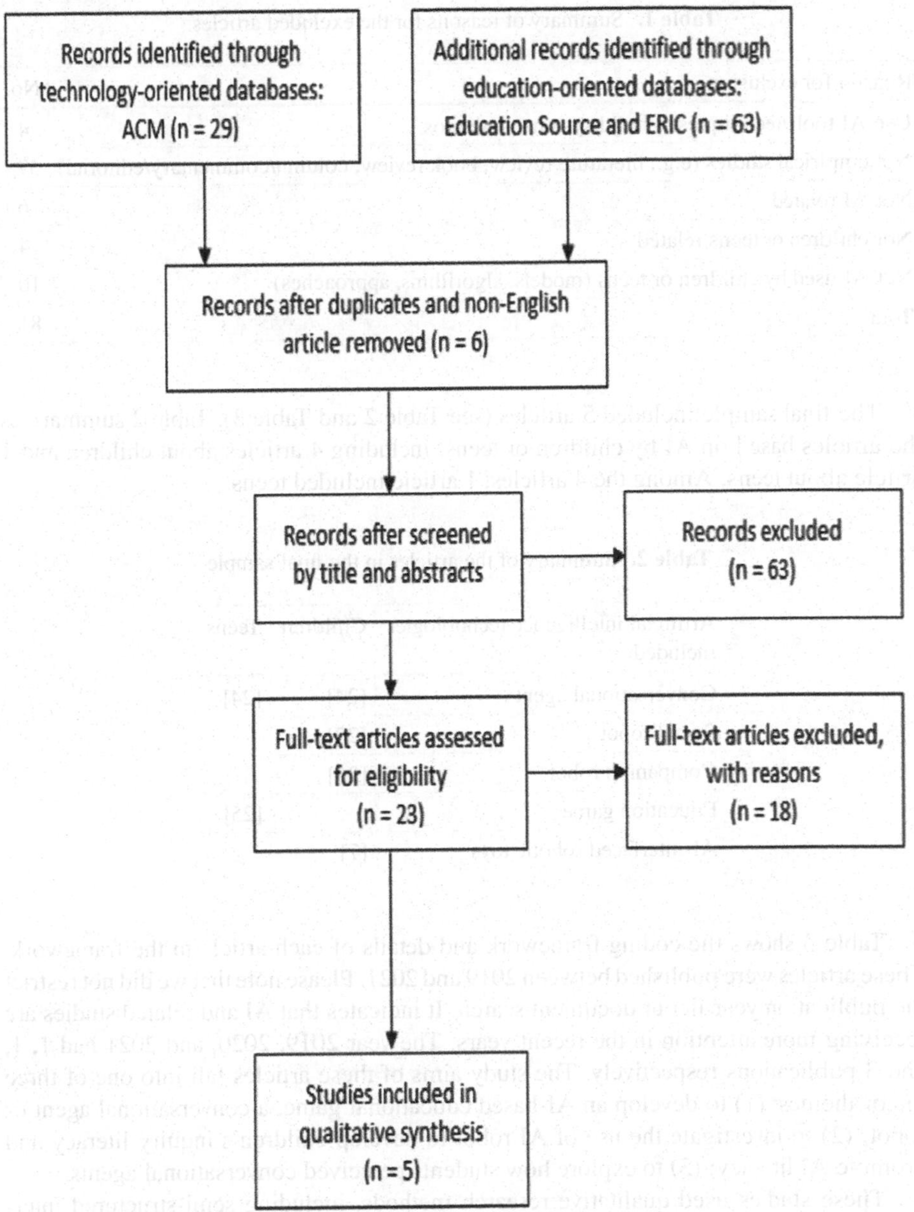

Fig. 1. PRISMA review

4 Results

Our initial searches found 86 articles. Through multiple rounds of screening, we removed 81 of them from our final sample. The reasons for excluding these 81 articles are summarized in Table 1.

Table 1. Summary of reasons for the excluded articles

Reason for exclusion	No.
Use AI tools/techniques to build systems or demos	4
Not empirical studies (e.g., literature review; book review; column/commentary/editorial)	57
Not AI related	6
Not children or teens related	4
Not AI used by children or teens (models, algorithms, approaches)	10
Total	81

The final sample included 5 articles (see Table 2 and Table 3). Table 2 summarizes the articles based on AI by children or teens, including 4 articles about children and 1 article about teens. Among the 4 articles, 1 article included teens.

Table 2. Summary of the articles in the final sample

Artificial intelligence technologies included	Children	Teens
Conversational agent	[24]	[24]
Social robot	[27]	
Companion robot	[26]	
Education game		[25]
AI-interfaced robotic toys	[7]	

Table 3 shows the coding framework and details of each article in the framework. These articles were published between 2019 and 2021. Please note that we did not restrict the publication year in our document search. It indicates that AI and related studies are receiving more attention in the recent years. The year 2019, 2020, and 2021 had 1, 1, and 3 publications respectively. The study aims of these articles fall into one of three major themes: (1) to develop an AI-based educational game, a conversational agent or robot; (2) to investigate the use of AI robot to develop children's inquiry literacy and promote AI literacy; (3) to explore how students perceived conversational agents.

These studies used qualitative research methods, including semi-structured interviews and focus group interviews, surveys, field notes, and video observations. The sample size of all the studies in our final sample was relatively small, ranging from 4 to 130. The AI technologies involved in these studies include social robots, conversational agents, and AI-based educational games. It is noted that three of the studies focused on AI robots and related technologies.

The studies were conducted in four different countries, including USA, UK, Taiwan and Greece. Researches related to the use and perception of AI technologies by children and teens are called for in USA. The five studies were conducted in different settings, including classroom (two studies), workshop (one study), online (one study), and development site (one study). Many studies reported positive outcomes in favor of the AI technologies or potential benefits for the children and teens.

Four out of five studies were designed for children (one of them included teens), and one was specifically designed for teens, indicating the importance of addressing the needs of children and teens in AI-related studies.

Table 3. Coding framework

Paper/Year	Study aims	Country	Method	AI technology	Participants	Setting	Key findings
[7] 2021	To investigate the use of AI-interfaced robotic toys within early childhood settings to develop children's inquiry literacy	UK	Semi-structured interviews, video observations, field notes	Interactive Artificial Intelligence (AI)-interfaced robotic toys	21 children, 2 teachers, 1 co-educator	Kindergarten classroom	Children's play with the AI robot stimulated inquiry literacies including creative inquiry, emotional inquiry and collaborative inquiry
[24] 2021	To explore how middle and high school students perceive Alexa change by programming their own conversational agents	USA	Questionnaire	Conversational agent	47 middle and high school students	Week-long AI education workshops	Students thought Alexa was more intelligent and felt closer to Alexa after the workshops; There were strong correlations between students' perceptions of Alexa's friendliness and trustworthiness, and safeness
[25] 2021	To develop a framework and game-based educational material for promoting AI literacy among primary and secondary education students	Greece	Online survey	Educational game	130 students (12–17 year old) and 17 teachers	Online	The "ArtBot" game was well received by students and teachers; It is critical to involve teachers and students from the early stages of design

(*continued*)

Table 3. (*continued*)

Paper/Year	Study aims	Country	Method	AI technology	Participants	Setting	Key findings
[26] 2020	To develop an AI robot math quiz game for primary school students	Taiwan	Focus group interviews	AI robot math quiz game	2 elementary school math teachers, a parent a 5th grade primary school student	Development site	Young children can use the robot for self-learning to improve the outcome of their learning
[27] 2019	To develop a novel early childhood AI platform, PopBots, where preschool children train and interact with social robots to learn AI concepts, and evaluate the childrens' perceptions of robots	USA	Questionnaire	Social robot	80 preschool children	Classroom	Younger children treated robots as smarter toys than themselves, but older children treated them more as people that were not as smart

5 Discussion

This paper conducted a systematic review of AI technologies used by children and teens and the possible factors that may affect their perception of AI technologies. Three databases (Education Source, ERIC, ACM digital library) were selected for literature search, and 86 non-duplicated articles came out. After the title/abstract and full paper screening, 5 articles were included in the final review sample. As can be seen, 4/5 of the articles in the final sample are about children. More research is called for teens and AI technologies.

Our review indicates a huge gap for research on the adoption, and perception of AI technologies by children and teens in education. This is evident in that a large number of the articles in our initial searches had no empirical data; instead, they reported technical specifics (e.g., algorithms, framework, conceptual design, hardware design, and software design) or system architecture for designing AI systems. In addition, most of the user studies that were relevant to AIED in the retrieved documents did not focus on children and teens; instead, they were targeted at college students and young adults. The lack of user studies and user evaluation of the AI technologies or systems for children and teens in education may be attributed to the fact that such an evaluation usually requires a restricted and time-consuming procedure to receive IRB approval.

The findings of these articles show positive results with the use of AI technologies or systems by children and teens. The five studies were conducted in 4 different countries, indicating the increased interest in this research area outside of the USA. One interesting finding from the review is that in the three studies related to social robots. It is recommended that users should be involved at the very beginning of the design stage. They also addressed the importance of interaction among teachers, parents, and students in designing AI-related educational materials or platforms or social robots for children and teens.

This systematic review has its limitations. The selection of our initial search terms was not exhaustive. We used only "artificial intelligence" or "intelligent" as our AI-related search terms and may have missed systems or technologies that did not use these terms but instead used AI. The children and teen-related search terms may not have been comprehensive either. There exists the potential for selection bias when articles were unintentionally selected to support the researchers' belief. We used three coders to reduce the potential for this bias. When it is related to the use and perception of AI technologies in education, ethical and privacy concerns from parents, teachers, and students have been discussed in many research articles. Because it is not the focus of this review, we did not discuss it in this paper. Despite these limitations, our systematic review is valuable, as it has identified existing work on AI with children and teens.

6 Conclusions

The findings of this systematic review indicate the existence of a huge research gap in how children and teens adopt AI technologies in education and how they perceive AI technologies. This research gap may have been exacerbated due to the ongoing COVID-19 global pandemic.

In the future, it would be beneficial to further explore one specific AI technology, e.g., a social robot or conversational agent, and examine how high school students adopt and perceive the technologies in their learning environment, and how to improve their satisfaction with the technologies. Studies of this kind may help to relieve the anxiety and stress of high school students and improve their learning experience. In addition, we feel that it is important to expand the AI-related researches to other socially vulnerable populations, including people of different races or ethnicities, low-income populations, or people with disabilities.

Acknowledgements. We thank all the reviewers for their constructive comments.

References

1. Chen, L., Chen, P., Lin, Z.: Artificial intelligence in education: a review. IEEE Access **8**, 75264–75278 (2020)
2. Druga, S.: Cognimate (2018)
3. Druga, S., Williams, R., Breazeal, C., Resnick, M.: Hey google is it ok if I eat you?: Initial explorations in childagent interaction. In: Proceedings of the 2017 Conference on Interaction Design and Children, pp. 595–600 (2017)

4. Druga, S., Williams, R., Park, H.W., Breazeal, C.: How smart are the smart toys?: children and parents' agent interaction and intelligence attribution. In: Proceedings of the 17th ACM Conference on Interaction Design and Children, pp. 231–240 (2018)
5. Holmes, W., Bialik, M., Fadel, C.: Artificial Intelligence in Education, pp. 1–35. Center for Curriculum Redesign, Boston (2019)
6. Kahn, K.M., Winters, N.: AI programming by children (2018). https://project.ecraft2learn.eu/wp-content/uploads/2018/08/Ai_programming_Constructionism_2018-v2.pdf
7. Kewalramani, S., Kidman, G., Palaiologou, I.: Using Artificial Intelligence (AI)-interfaced robotic toys in early childhood settings: a case for children's inquiry literacy. Eur. Early Child. Educ. Res. J. **29**(5), 652–668 (2021)
8. Landing AI: Landing A.I. Creates an AI Tool to Help Customers Monitor Social Distancing in the Workplace (2020). https://landing.ai/landing-ai-creates-an-ai-tool-to-help-customers-monitor-social-distancing-in-the-workplace/
9. Lane, D.: Machine learning for kids (2018)
10. Lin, P., Van Brummelen, J., Lukin, G., Williams, R., Breazeal, C.: Zhorai: designing a conversational agent for children to explore machine learning concepts. In: Proceedings of the AAAI Conference on Artificial Intelligence, vol. 34, no. 09, pp. 13381–13388 (2020)
11. Medical Device Network: What are the main types of robots used in healthcare? (2020). https://www.medicaldevice-network.com/comment/what-are-the-main-types-of-robots-used-in-healthcare/
12. McReynolds, E., Hubbard, S., Lau, T., Saraf, A., Cakmak, M., Roesner, F.: Toys that listen: a study of parents, children, and internet-connected toys. In: Proceedings of the 2017 CHI Conference on Human Factors in Computing Systems, pp. 5197–5207 (2017)
13. NITRD: The National Artificial Intelligence Research and Development Strategic Plan: 2019 Update (nitrd.gov) (2019)
14. Ouherrou, N., Elhammoumi, O., Benmarrakchi, F., El Kafi, J.: Comparative study on emotions analysis from facial expressions in children with and without learning disabilities in virtual learning environment. Educ. Inf. Technol. **24**(2), 1777–1792 (2019). https://doi.org/10.1007/s10639-018-09852-5
15. Papert, S., Solomon, C.: Twenty things to do with a computer, Cambridge, MA (1971)
16. Pearson: 'Pearson hires new head of artificial intelligence'. Press release, July 2018. https://plc.pearson.com/en-US/news/pearson-hires-new-head-artificial-intelligence
17. PRISMA Review. PRISMA (prisma-statement.org)
18. Porayska-Pomsta, K., et al.: Blending human and artificial intelligence to support autistic children's social communication skills. ACM Trans. Comput.-Hum. Interact. (TOCHI) **25**(6), 1–35 (2018)
19. Pueyo, V., et al.: Development of a system based on artificial intelligence to identify visual problems in children: study protocol of the TrackAI project. BMJ Open **10**(2), e033139 (2020)
20. Sabuncuoglu, A.: Designing one year curriculum to teach artificial intelligence for middle school. In: Proceedings of the 2020 ACM Conference on Innovation and Technology in Computer Science Education, pp. 96–102 (2020)
21. Severson, R.L., Carlson, S.M.: Behaving as or behaving as if? Childrens conceptions of personified robots and the emergence of a new ontological category. Neural Netw. **23**(8–9), 1099–1103 (2010)
22. Timms, M.J.: Letting artificial intelligence in education out of the box: educational cobots and smart classrooms. Int. J. Artif. Intell. Educ. **26**(2), 701–712 (2016)
23. Toivonen, T., Jormanainen, I., Kahila, J., Tedre, M., Valtonen, T., Vartiainen, H.: Co-designing machine learning apps in K-12 with primary school children. In: 2020 IEEE 20th International Conference on Advanced Learning Technologies (ICALT), pp. 308–310. IEEE (2020)

24. Van Brummelen, J., Tabunshchyk, V., Heng, T.: "Alexa, can I program you?": student perceptions of conversational artificial intelligence before and after programming Alexa. In: Interaction Design and Children, pp. 305–313 (2021)
25. Voulgari, I., Zammit, M., Stouraitis, E., Liapis, A., Yannakakis, G.: Learn to machine learn: designing a game based approach for teaching machine learning to primary and secondary education students. In: Interaction Design and Children, pp. 593–598 (2021)
26. Weng, T.S., Li, C.K., Hsu, M.H.: Development of robotic quiz games for self-regulated learning of primary school children. In: 2020 3rd Artificial Intelligence and Cloud Computing Conference, pp. 58–62 (2020)
27. Williams, R., Park, H.W., Breazeal, C.: A is for artificial intelligence: the impact of artificial intelligence activities on young children's perceptions of robots. In: Proceedings of the 2019 CHI Conference on Human Factors in Computing Systems, pp. 1–11 (2019)
28. Williams, R., Park, H.W., Oh, L., Breazeal, C.: PopBots: designing an artificial intelligence curriculum for early childhood education. In: Proceedings of the AAAI Conference on Artificial Intelligence, vol. 33, no. 1, pp. 9729–9736 (2019)

Analysis of the Impact of Applying UX Guidelines to Reduce Noise and Focus Attention

Jordán Pascual Espada[1](✉), Lucía Alonso-Virgós[2], and Rubén González Crespo[2]

[1] Department of Computer Science, University of Oviedo, Oviedo, Spain
pascualjordan@uniovi.com

[2] UNIR Universidad Internacional de La Rioja, La Rioja, Spain

Abstract. This research work is the continuation of previous, in which a set of usability guidelines where proposed. These guidelines were obtained from various authors and recommendations. The common part of those guides was that all of them were useful to reduce the noise and focus the attention of users in web interfaces. Some of these recommendations were evaluated in very confined environments, this research tries to evaluate the possible advantage of applying every one of these recommendations, quantifying in an experiment with real users what could be the potential time gain applying every of the recommendations. We have designed a set of web applications in which the user has to complete a simple task, some of the applications fill the usability guidelines and others not. With obtained data in the experiment, the web developers could choose in a more precise way which recommendations could be implemented in their interfaces to get a more efficient user interaction.

Keywords: Usability guidelines · Usability recommendations · Web usability · Data entry · User's behavior

1 Introduction

The websites not only have to be functional, they must also offer a good experience to the users. There are a lot of research works about why some things can improve the user experience in a website (Tezza et al. 2011). The "Usability" is the most common way to determine is a website is easy and comfortable to use by the users. The concept of usability could be very complex because it is something that this is conditioned by too many aspects, like navigation, performance, responsiveness, learnability, etc. The usability has also a great impact in the website functionalities, like what task users can do in every view and how they can do them, and also over the web design (Zimmerman et al. 2001). Measure the usability of a website could be a challenge (Mousa et al. 2021).

Create a web user interface with a good usability level is very often a great challenge for web developers. The only way to evaluate effectively the user experience of a website is analyzing the behavior of real users. These analyzes with real users are usually done in the design phase (Grady 2000; Yakunin and Bodrunova 2022) and also when the website is in final state (Retnani et al. 2017). There are many tools which are able to capture

H. Degen and S. Ntoa (Eds.): HCII 2022, LNAI 13336, pp. 80–99, 2022.
https://doi.org/10.1007/978-3-031-05643-7_6

and analyze the user behavior when the website is already in production (Solís-Martínez et al. 2020).

In addition to the information obtained from real users, the web developers could use other knowledges and techniques to create web users interfaces that enhance the user experience. The most common technique is following and validating usability guidelines, these guidelines could include concrete or generic advices or recommendations about the content, layouts, interactive elements, texts, etc. One the most popular is the Usability Heuristics for User Interface Design created by Jakob Nielsen (Nielsen 2020, 1990). The Research-Based Web Design & Usability Guidelines (Bevan 2005; Bevan and Spinhof 2007), usability.gov, There are other very extended guidelines like The Usability evaluation like Microsoft Usability Guidelines (Wang and Liu 2007). Among a lot of others, including guidelines for specific websites like B2C (Wang and Liu 2007).

Some authors consider that these guidelines could be very generic and based sometimes in just if theoretical approaches. There are other studies which collect and organize groups of user interface guidelines, for following conventions (Alonso-Virgós et al. 2020) create efficient and understandable controls (Alonso-Virgós et al. 2019a) and for reduce noise and focus the user attention in the important parts of the interface (Alonso-Virgós et al. 2019b). All these different groups of guidelines collect guides which come from many different sources, like compilations of general recommendations, books, experts, etc.

In addition to guidelines and real users also some automatic tools are useful to evaluate some aspects of usability (Solís-Martínez et al. 2020). Some of these tools are very popular like google analytics (Luo et al. 2015) Smartlook, Crazy Egg, etc. (Kumar and Hasteer 2017). Especially these tools are useful to understand the user behavior in the website. Almost all experts match in that these tools can used uniquely to evaluate the usability, but they can be a great support of help to other types of evaluations like the valuations done by experts or based in user interaction data. Some tools just show all the results of the users navigation, other works applies mechanisms of artificial intelligence and data mining (Duan and Liu 2012). In some cases, these automatic tools could be appropriate some very specific tasks like detect broken links (Ruiz-Rodriguez 2006) or manage the usability testing (Ahmad et al. 2010).

The most conflictive part of these guidelines is that, is seems that they say logical things but in very few scientific studies they were tested. We do not know what could be the improvement in the user interface if it contains every of these guidelines. Many research works about usability guidelines include evaluations which only are based on users opinions (Alonso-Virgós et al. 2020; Mahyavanshi et al. 2017), rarely a research work evaluates the effectiveness of each guide separately (Ma and Feng 2011). Most of research works evaluates if the website contains certain usability guidelines, or the complete website globally (Otaiza et al. 2010). Very few research works evaluate the impact of the use of a usability guide in a web, and even less evaluates each guide separately, they tend to consider the website as a pack. Have some results about the effectiveness of each guide could be extremely useful for web developers, so that they could know which guidelines represent a greater improvement in the user experience, even what guidelines should be avoided. Have an idea of the potential impact of every guideline could be used by web developers in the design and planning phases, also when web developers want to improve or analyze the user experience of a website in production.

This research work is focused in evaluate possible improvement of the guidelines that have the objective of "reduce noise and focus attention" (Alonso-Virgós et al. 2019b). For this objective a group of web applications will be created. These applications will include different versions of the users interfaces, some will comply with the guidelines and others will not. Every interface will be focused just in one guideline aiming to evaluate the effectiveness of each guide separately. The application will be used for a group of real users, they must have to accomplish a task in every interface. The application will automatically save the time and the mouse movement for every user. At the end of the research experiment, we can have an idea of which guidelines are better for reduce noise and focus attention, and also to know if the use of any of these guidelines could be counterproductive for users.

2 Proposal and Methodology

First step was analyzing the UX guidelines related to reduce noise and focus attention. We search in internet, using lists of most popular websites, in order to find some parts of the user Interface websites in which some of the guidelines could be apply. Each of the guidelines was processed in an independent way, locating a small part of the user interface or task in which the guideline could be applied.

As a result of previous step, we design 54 different web users interfaces. There were four different interfaces relative to each guidelines; in total, we analyze 13 different guidelines. Every user interface simulates a small real website and it has a small task associate, for example click in a word or a button. There are two versions of every web user interface. One version, which meet the guideline, and other version, which does not meet the guideline. In theory, the interface which include the guideline should be help for users to complete the task in a more efficient way. Test user must log in in the designed application and the test will start. The application works in a random way, the version of the interface which contains the usability guide can be shown first or second, in this way the test users don't really know. All user data is stored in a database, the time that the users take in every task and also the mouse movement. As a part of the application, we have implemented a JavaScript module for catching these user activity data.

Below this is a list of the guidelines evaluated and some of the web interfaces created for the research.

(1) **Blank space.** Views must have "blank space". Space not occupied by content, this blank space helps users read faster. The designed test show first a test with little white space between lines and a text with a more "adequate" blank space between lines. Users must follow a specific word and to do it the must read and analyze the text. The word that the user should find was exposed first in previous instructions in a popup window. This experiment tries to estimate what could be the loss of efficiency if a website does not include an adequate blank space between lines and paragraphs (Fig. 1).

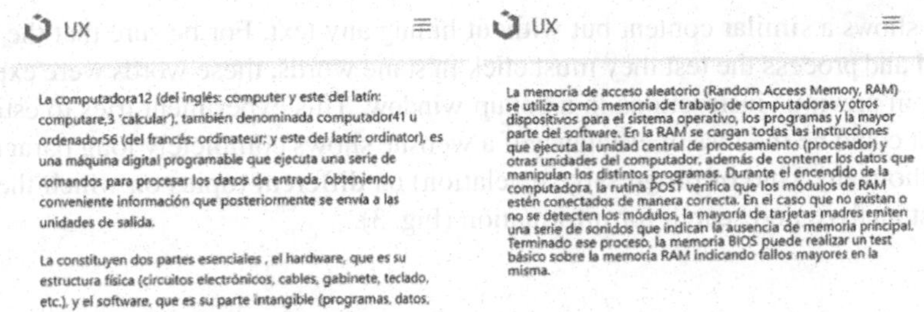

Fig. 1. One of the designed user interfaces for the evaluation of the guideline (1) Blank space.

(2) **Comprehensible and organized language.** In many situations, the texts can be organized using different structures, points, lists, grids, trees, etc. Even inside the organization structure, some extra techniques can be applied like priority, importance of a parameter, alphabetical order, etc. The structure could help the user to identify faster the relation among the textual information. The designed test show first a few elements to do a selection. One interface shows the elements strongly organized and the other version uses a minor level of organization. The word that the user should find was exposed first in previous instructions in a popup window. This experiment tries to estimate what could be the loss of efficiency if a website shows some information which could be organized in a logic way without any clear organization. It should be noted that maybe not all the information could be organized in all cases (Fig. 2).

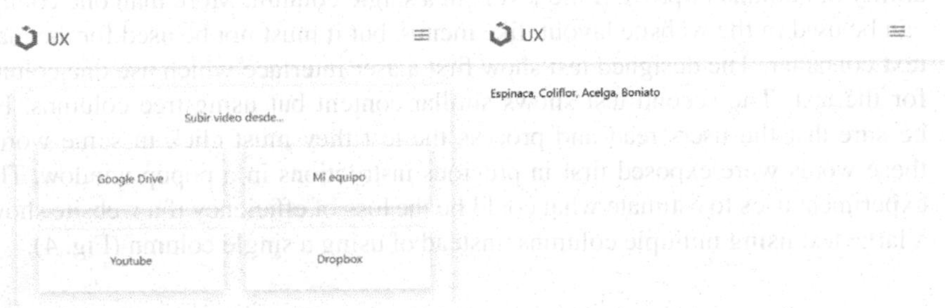

Fig. 2. One of the designed user interfaces for the evaluation of the guideline (2) Comprehensible and organized language.

(3) **Short texts and with highlighted elements.** Long paragraphs usually tire the users. The alternative is to reduce the paragraph lengths and it this is not completely possible trying to use techniques like the "progressive revelation". Using progressive revelation the user can read the main idea of the paragraph and extend it if he thinks he that the paragraph contains important information. The designed test show first a lot of information divided in paragraphs, just the abstract of the paragraph is shown and user must expand the paragraph if he want to continue reading. The second

test shows a similar content but without hiding any text. For be sure that the users read and process the test they must click in some words, these words were exposed first in previous instructions in a popup window. This experiment tries to estimate what could be the loss of efficiency if a website shows completely long paragraphs (without any kind of progressive revelation) on different topics on which the user must analyze and search for information (Fig. 3).

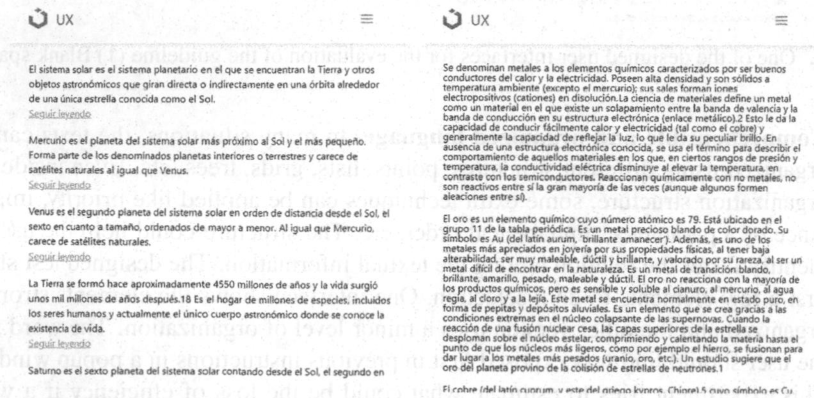

Fig. 3. One of the designed user interfaces for the evaluation of the guideline (3) Short texts and with highlighted elements.

(4) **Avoid multiple columns of text.** Some research work suggest that the reading ability of humans improve if the text is in a single column. More than one column can be used in the website layout, like menus, but it must not be used for the main text container. The designed test show first a user interface which use one column for the text. The second test shows similar content but using tree columns. For be sure that the users read and process the test they must click in some words, these words were exposed first in previous instructions in a popup window. This experiment tries to estimate what could be the loss of efficiency if a website shows a large text using multiple columns, instead of using a single column (Fig. 4).

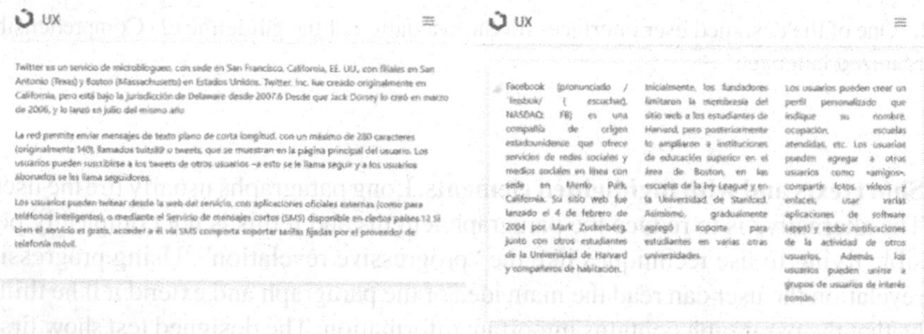

Fig. 4. One of the designed user interfaces for the evaluation of the guideline (4) Avoid multiple columns of text.

(5) **Limit the backgrounds and prominent edges.** When the interface contains many backgrounds or borders they catch the user attention, increasing the time users need to process the website. The number of backgrounds and strong borders must be very limited and used only for really relevant parts of the website. The designed test show first a user interface which contains a highlighted borders only in the most important sections, the second website is based on a similar content but uses highlighted borders in all elements. For be sure that the users read and process the information they must click in some words, these words were exposed first in previous instructions in a popup window. This experiment tries to estimate what could be the loss of efficiency if a user is searching for an important part of the website which is highlighted with a border, but there are too many parts highlighted in the view. We understand by "important" parts those links that are clicked more frequently in the interface, highlighting them makes it possible for the user to find them sooner (Fig. 5).

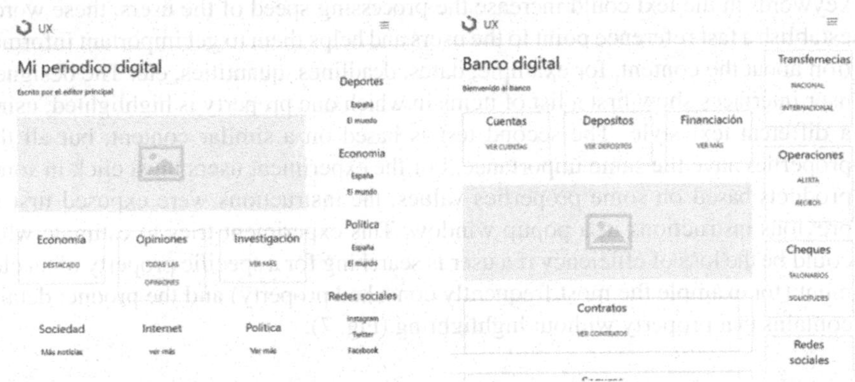

Fig. 5. One of the designed user interfaces for the evaluation of the guideline (5) Limit the backgrounds and prominent edges.

(6) **Key texts correctly highlighted.** These guideline is for users interfaces which include lists of products and elements and every of them have few or many properties. Usually the elements properties do not have the same level of importance for the web purpose, if the most important properties are highlighted the users could be analyze the content faster, or even make comparisons between the elements. The designed test show first a website interface which include some highlighted keywords in every paragraph, it uses bold. The second test is based on a similar content but without any bold word. For the experiment users must find some words in the text and click of them, these words were exposed first in previous instructions in a popup window. This experiment tries to estimate what could be the loss of efficiency if the most important parts of the text (keywords and important data) are not highlighted and the user want to get this information (Fig. 6).

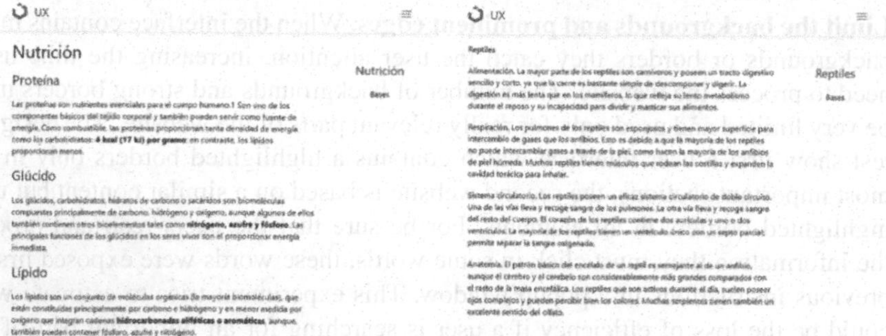

Fig. 6. One of the designed user interfaces for the evaluation of the guideline (6) Key texts correctly highlighted.

(7) **Highlight the key properties of a product or an element.** Highlighting some keywords in the text could increase the processing speed of the users, these words establish a fast reference point to the users and helps them to get important information about the content, for example, dates, deadlines, quantities, etc. The designed user interfaces show first a list of items in which one property is highlighted, using a different text style. The second test is based on a similar content, but all the properties have the same importance. For the experiment users must click in some products based on some properties values, the instructions were exposed first in previous instructions in a popup window. This experiment tries to estimate what could be the loss of efficiency if a user is searching for a specific property of an element (for example the most frequently consulted property) and the product details contains that property without highlighting (Fig. 7).

Fig. 7. One of the designed user interfaces for the evaluation of the guideline (7) Highlight the key properties of a product or an element.

(8) **Limit the number of featured items on each page.** For improving the analysis ability of users every view of the website must include some featured items. Interfaces usually include different types of featured content in order to guide the user on what elements he should explore and in what order. Include featured items is a good principle for improving the user experience but if the view contains to many featured items the effect may be just the opposite. To many featured elements can overload the user perception making that the user process the view in a slower way. The designed user interfaces show first interface which contains just few featured items. The second test is based on a similar content but contains many feature items. For the experiment users must click in some words, the instructions were exposed first in previous instructions in a popup window. This experiment tries to estimate what could be the loss of efficiency if a website shows all the actions featured rather than just the feature the action that is statistically most likely the user is going to choose (Fig. 8).

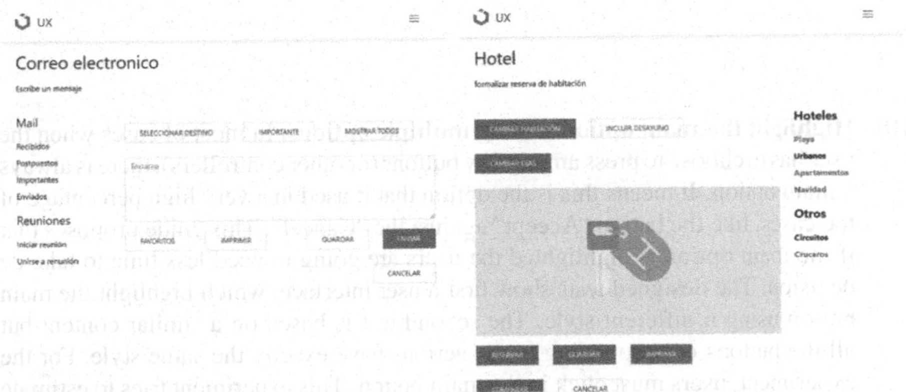

Fig. 8. One of the designed user interfaces for the evaluation of the guideline (8) Limit the number of featured items on each page.

(9) **Highlight the main task.** This guide is about the importance to highlight the main task in a view of a website web the view really contains a main task. It means this task must be completed to continue the interaction with the website. This guide shows the importance to highlight the main task in this kind of views. Applying this guide users can find the main task in a more efficient and faster way. The designed user interfaces show first interface which highlight the main task. The second test is based on a similar content but the main task is integrated in the content of the view. For the experiment users must click in a specific button to complete the task, to avoid include noise and variable elements in the test the users only have to press the button of the main task, the instructions were exposed first in previous instructions in a popup window. This experiment tries to estimate what could be the loss of

efficiency if it is sure the user must complete a task in a website and this task is not clearly highlighted over the other web content (Fig. 9).

Fig. 9. One of the designed user interfaces for the evaluation of the guideline (9) Highlight the main task.

(10) **Highlight the main option among multiple options.** In most of cases when the user has to choose to press among few buttons (or other controllers), there is always a main option. It means this is the option that it used in a very high percentage of the cases, like the button "Accept" against the "Cancel". This guide proposes that if the main option is highlighted the users are going to need less time to take de decision. The designed tests show first a user interface, which highlight the main button using a different style. The second test is based on a similar content but all the buttons corresponding to the actions have exactly the same style. For the experiment, users must click in the main button. This experiment tries to estimate what could be the loss of efficiency if the user must choose among few options and the statistically most used option is not highlighted (Fig. 10).

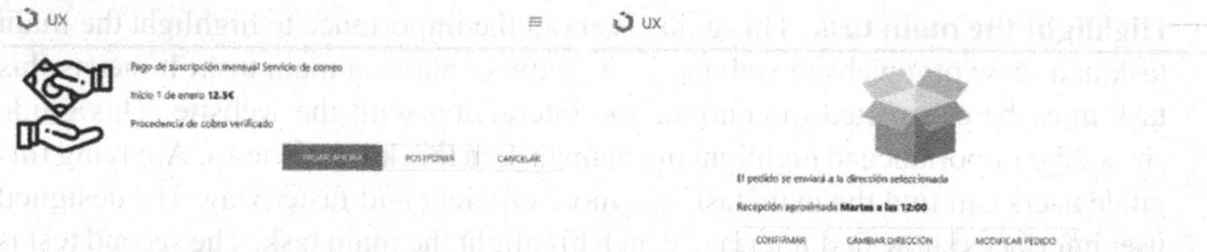

Fig. 10. One of the designed user interfaces for the evaluation of the guideline (10) Highlight the main option among multiple options.

(11) **Limit the number of options in a menu.** This guideline suggest that include a large number of options in a menu is counterproductive to user analytic ability. Instead of listing all the menu options at the same level, the options can be grouped, for example conceptually. In this way users will process the main groups and they explore the menu until the reach the appropriate option. This way of organizing a menu could reduce the time than users take to find a menu option. The designed user interfaces show first interface which highlight the main button using a different style. The second test is based on a similar content but all the buttons corresponding to the actions have exactly the same style. For the experiment, users must click in the main button. This experiment tries to estimate what could be the loss of efficiency if a website shows of elements including actions which are not used in a high percentage of the times. It could be probably that adding more actions (some of them a little used) the users will be more difficult find the most common actions (Fig. 11).

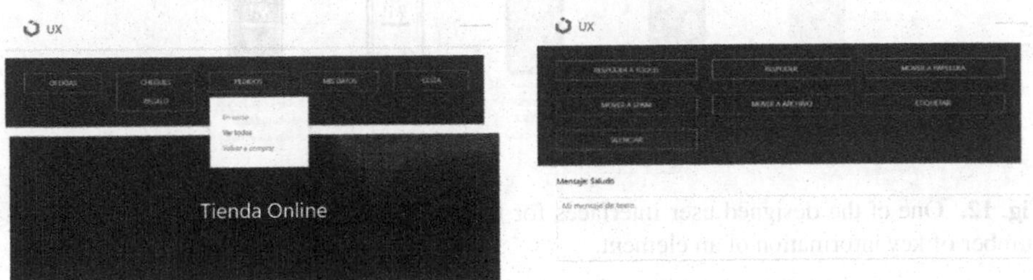

Fig. 11. One of the designed user interfaces for the evaluation of the guideline (11) Limit the number of options in a menu.

(12) **Limit the number of key information of an element.** Often web views that contains list of elements expose some of the key information of every element in the "miniature" or in the summary of the element that users can see in the list. A previous guide promotes the importance of include some of the key information in the list, but if the website includes too many key information, then it could start to be counterproductive for the users, dispersing their attention. They key information must be only these properties that are consulted very frequently by users, only those properties with a higher perfect. The designed user interfaces show first interface which highlight the two most important properties of every element. The second test is based on a similar content but highlight the most important six properties of every element. For the experiment, users must click in a specific element which have a specific information. This experiment tries to estimate what could be the loss of efficiency if a user is searching in a list of elements for a product with a specific information (statistically the most consulted information) and the product detail shows too much key properties (Fig. 12).

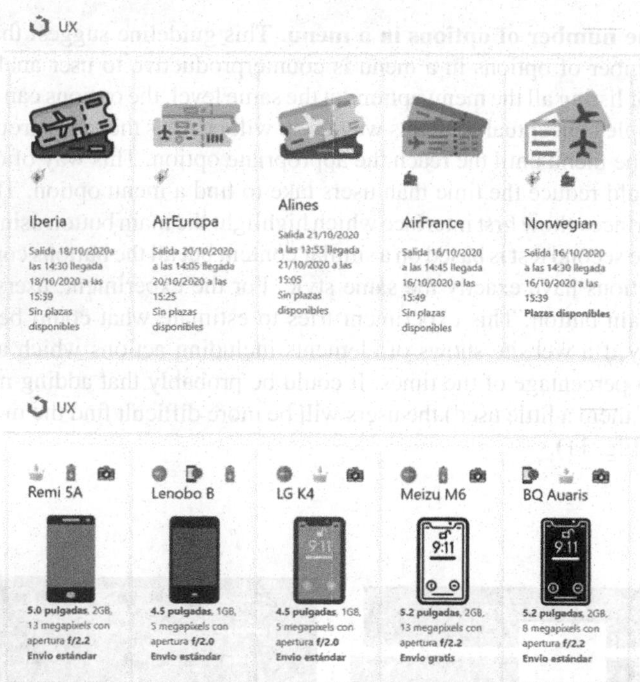

Fig. 12. One of the designed user interfaces for the evaluation of the guideline (12) Limit the number of key information of an element.

(13) **Limit the number of actions on elements.** Many websites contain list of elements, and the users can perform actions over these elements, por example: delete, deactivate, activate, see more details, change the value of some property, etc. This guideline suggests that only most common used actions show be showed in the list, including too many actions could be counterproductive for the users. The users could spend extra time analyzing actions which are not important. Non important actions can be grouped in other section or just include in the detailed view of the element. The designed user interfaces for the experiment show first interface which include a list of elements and only two actions for every element in the list. The second test is based on a similar content, but it shows four actions for every element, including some actions which are not so relevant. For the experiment, users must click in a specific action of an element. This experiment tries to estimate what could be the loss of efficiency if a user is searching in a list of elements for an action (statistically on the most used actions) and the product detail shows too many actions.

Each of "test user interfaces" has been developed in two versions, one, which meet the guideline, and other, which does not meet the requirement. We have tried that the interfaces are not so complex, in this way, a single interface should not be affected by more than one guideline.

Next, we show some on the test user interfaces designed for evaluate the guidelines. These test user interfaces have been developed using HTML, CSS, JavaScript and the UI Framework Uikit (Fig. 13).

Fig. 13. One of the designed user interfaces for the evaluation of the guideline (13) Limit the number of actions on elements.

We develop a full web application for test environment for users. This application is going to evaluate all of the guidelines. First the application choose one of the guidelines using a random order, then it randomly deice if it has to show first the test user interface which meet the guideline or which does not meet. For example if the application chose the (A) Test User interface for the first task, it is going to choose the (B) Test user interface for the second task. In a case, the application choose first the version of the user interface which does not meet the guideline them it will choose the version that does not meet the guideline.

3 Results and Evaluation

For the evaluation 18 users have been choose. They were people who commonly use internet and web applications. The profile of all people was very similar, first year students of an Engineering bachelor's degree. They opened the URL that was submitted and started to do the test. Next, we show the results in a individual way of the tests associated with each guideline. Charts show the average time and mouse movement (pixels * 50), the pixels of the mouse have been multiplied by 50 to get a scale like the time spend in the task (milliseconds). The times and the mouse movement has been obtained by the program using a JavaScript program. The user's activity starts to being register after the user press the "accept" button in the instructions prior to each test (Fig. 14).

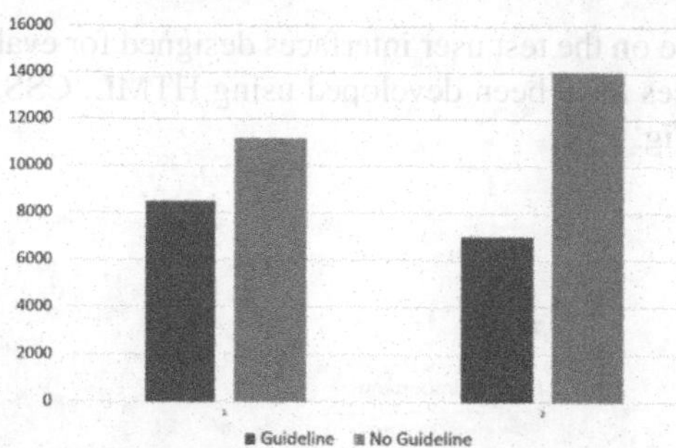

Fig. 14. Test results for guideline (1) Blank space.

The increment on the time for analyzing the paragraph when it does not include and adequate blank space between lines was the **31,6%** for this test, in the case of the mouse movement it was even greater (Fig. 15).

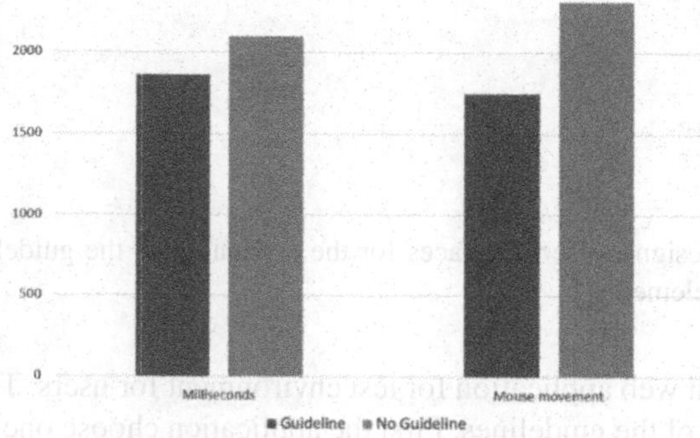

Fig. 15. Test results for guideline (2) Comprehensible and organized language.

When the information was organized in a clear way the users have been able to find the requested word a **12,63%** faster (Fig. 16).

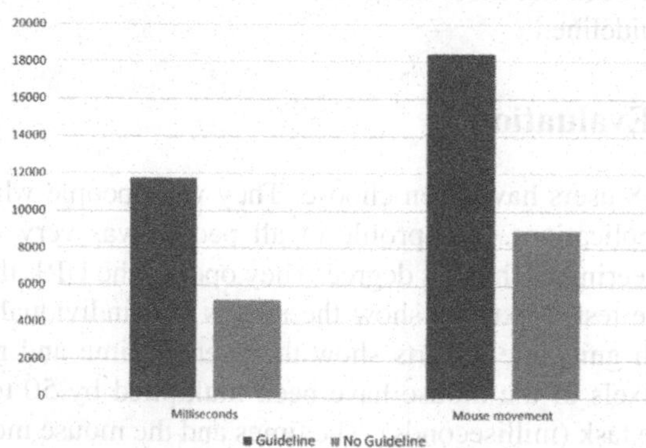

Fig. 16. Test results for guideline (3) Short texts and with highlighted elements.

In the tests the use of short test with progressive revelation did not seem to help the users to analyze the content in a more efficient way. Users must analyze the web content to find a specific paragraph and a specific word in it. The web which contains the full paragraphs without progressive revelation took a lot of less time **−55,63%**. In this case the compliance of the guideline did not seem to improve the user interface (Fig. 17).

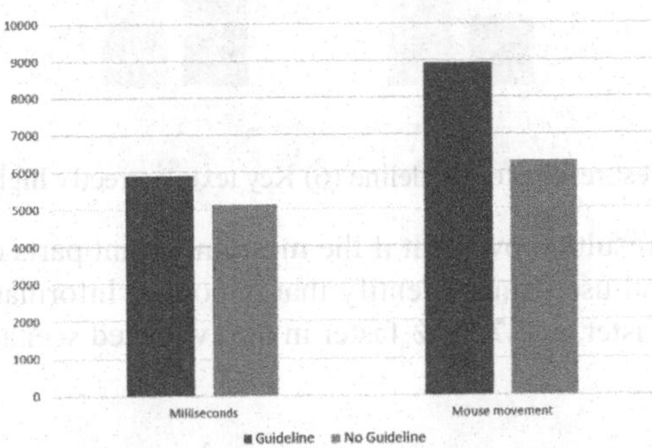

Fig. 17. Test results for guideline (4) Avoid multiple columns of text.

Results of the experiment show that users take more time to analyze the text when it was in a single column **−13,27%** In this case the compliance of the guideline did not seem to improve the user interface, although the time difference is quite small between the two alternatives (Fig. 18).

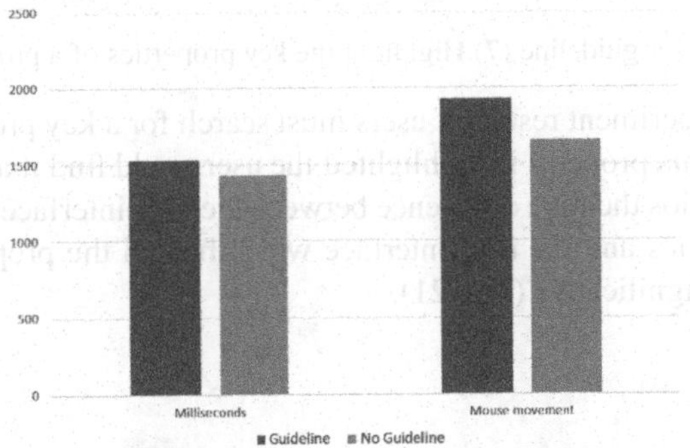

Fig. 18. Test results for guideline (5) Limit the backgrounds and prominent edges.

Based on the experiment results the excessive use of strong borders in the buttons of the website does not penalize interaction with users. Users found and press the required button using very similar times, only when the required button had a strong border and when all buttons had a strong edge (even the unimportant ones). The times differences were not significant in this experiment (Fig. 19).

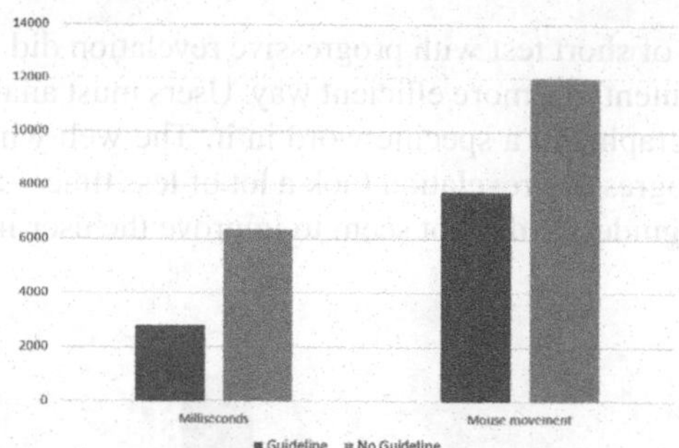

Fig. 19. Test results for guideline (6) Key texts correctly highlighted.

The experiments results shows that if the most important parts of the text are highlighted (bold fond) and users must identify that important information, they are going to do it significantly faster, a **127,59%** faster in the evaluated scenarios (Fig. 20).

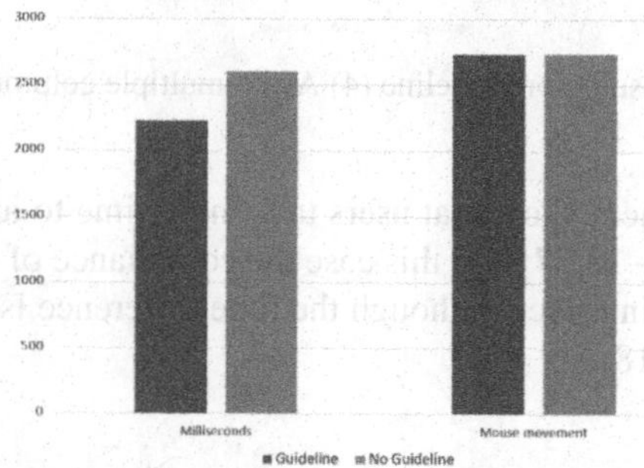

Fig. 20. Test results for guideline (7) Highlight the key properties of a product or an element.

Based on the experiment results if users must search for a key property of a product or an element and this property is highlighted the user could find it a **16,63%** faster. In the evaluated scenarios the time difference between the user interface which highlighted the required properties and the user interface which has all the properties at the same level was not very significative (Fig. 21).

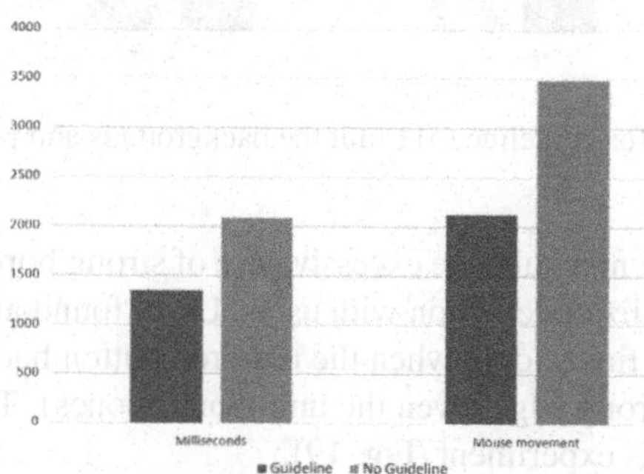

Fig. 21. Test results for guideline (8) Limit the number of featured items on each page.

Based on the experiment results if users must choose the action that is statistically most common in the view, and this action is highlighted over the other actions the interaction will be done a **54,89%** faster that if all the actions of the view were at the same level (Fig. 22).

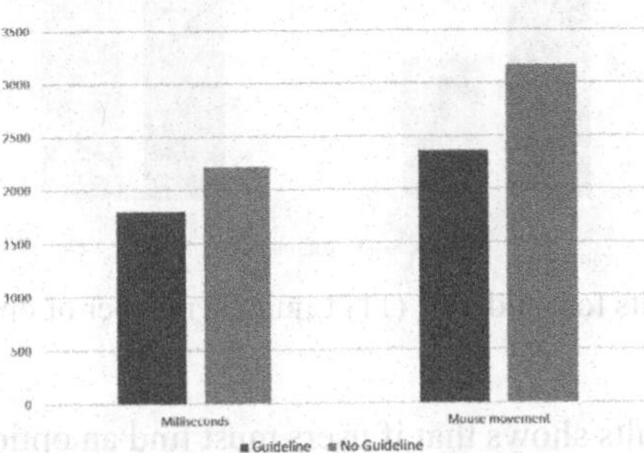

Fig. 22. Test results for guideline (9) Highlight the main task.

The experiments results shows that if users must complete a mandatory task in a view and this task is highlighted using a modal the users can identify and complete the task a **23,66%** faster than if the user interfaces of the task are integrated into the rest of the elements of the view (Fig. 23).

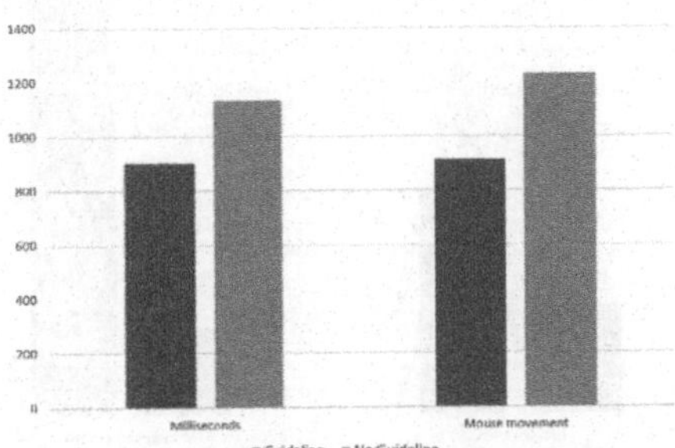

Fig. 23. Test results for guideline (10) Highlight the main option among multiple options.

Based on the experiment results if users must choose the action that is statistically most common among a group of actions, and this action is highlighted over the others the interaction will be done a **25,58%** faster that if all the options were at the same level (Fig. 24).

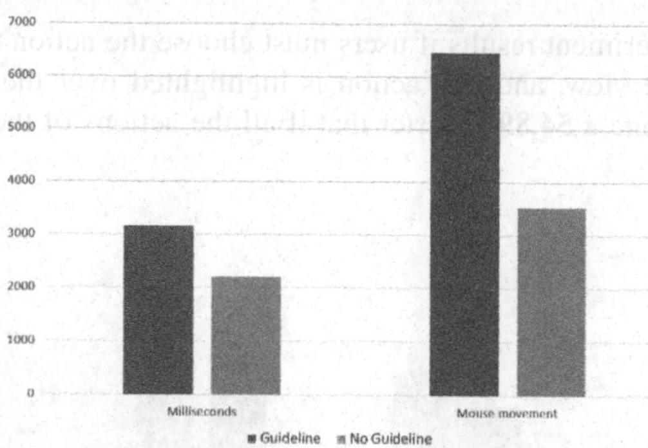

Fig. 24. Test results for guideline (11) Limit the number of options in a menu.

The experiments results shows that if users must find an option in a menu and these options are grouped in drop down menus the search process takes more time than if all menu actions are directly visible. The user interface which implements the guideline had worse interaction time **−30,37%** than the view which does not implement the guideline. The menus contain 8 and 11 options, many experts suggest that menu options should be grouped when they are more than 7 (Fig. 25).

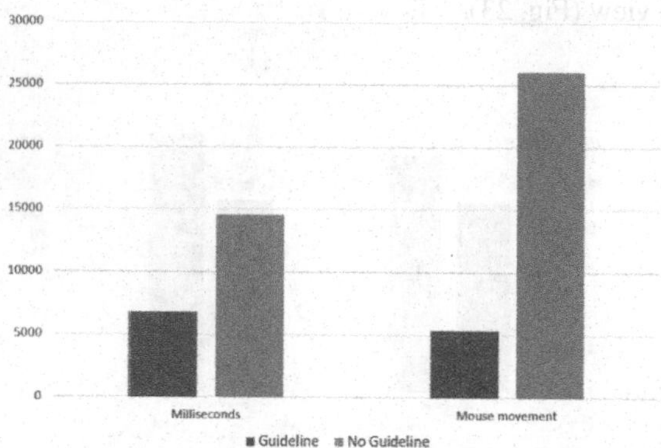

Fig. 25. Test results for guideline (12) Limit the number of key information of an element.

Based on the experiment results if users must search for an element with a key property (statistically the most consulted information) and the product detail shows just this key property the interaction will be **115,04%** faster that if the product detail shows too much key properties, including properties that are not so frequently consulted (Fig. 26).

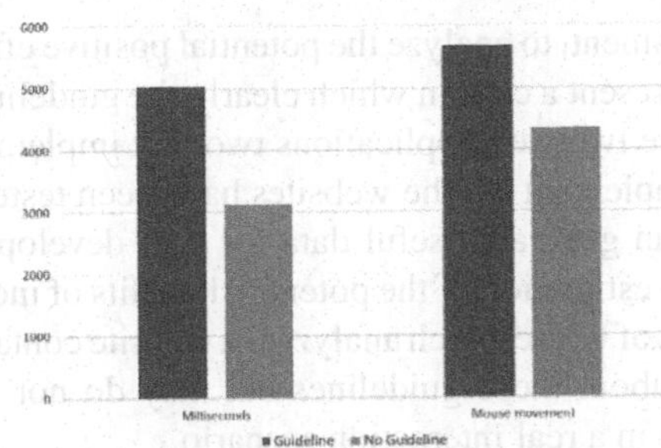

Fig. 26. Test results for guideline (13) Limit the number of actions on elements.

The experiments results shows that if users must find an attached action to an element of a list (statistically the most used actions) element shows too many actions this could increase interaction time. The user interface which implements the guideline had worse interaction time **−37,78%** than the view which does not implement the guideline. The implemented interfaces have 2 actions vs 4 actions (Table 1).

Table 1. Average time for every guideline.

Number	Guideline (ms)	No guideline (ms)	Difference
1	8502,41	11195,00	**31,66**
2	1863,70	2099,20	12,63
3	11745,70	5211,44	**−55,63**
4	5898,66	5115,44	−13,27
5	1531,25	1429,444	−6,64
6	2781,37	6330,25	**127,59**
7	2227,40	2598,00	16,63
8	1345,12	2083,50	**54,89**
9	1791,62	2215,62	23,66
10	901,55	1132,22	**25,58**
11	3160,75	2200,71	**−30,37**
12	6764,16	14546,25	**115,04**
13	5025,25	3125,75	**−37,79**

4 Conclusions

This research work analyzes the potential effect in the user experience of the usability guidelines which aim to reduce noise and focus user attention. Every of the guides have been analyzed in an independent way. A group of 54 web applications have been created to analyze in a test environment, to analyze the potential positive effect of each guideline. These web applications present a case in which clearly the guideline can be applied. For every guideline there were two web applications two that implement the guideline and two others that did not implement it. The websites have been tested with real users.

These experiments can generate useful data for web developers because previous research did not show any estimation of the potential benefits of include these guidelines in a web application. Most of UX research analyze if a website contains a ser of guidelines and the users' opinions about these guidelines but they do not analyze the potential benefits of each guideline in a real interaction scenario.

The obtained results for the evaluation scenario show that there are guidelines which arc cxtremely efficient in case that they could be applied in the user interface. The right use of (1) blank space, (5) limit the number of featured items on each page, (9) Highlight the main task, and (10) Highlight the main option among multiple options, showed that they made user interaction significantly faster 25%–60%. Other guidelines got an improvement in the time taken in the task of more than 100%. (6) Key texts correctly highlighted and (12) Limit the number of key information of an element. On the other side some guidelines showed that they were not useful to gain efficiency, they made users take longer in interact with the interface, (3) Short texts and with highlighted elements. (11) Limit the number of options in a menu. (13) Limit the number of actions on elements. In the case of study these guidelines increased the interaction time in 25%–60%.

References

Ahmad, W.F.W., Sulaiman, S., Johari, F.S.: Usability Management System (USEMATE): a web-based automated system for managing usability testing systematically. In: 2010 International Conference on User Science and Engineering (i-USEr), pp. 110–115 (2010). https://doi.org/10.1109/IUSER.2010.5716734

Alonso-Virgós, L., Espada, J.P., Crespo, R.G.: Analysing compliance and application of usability guidelines on efficient and understandable controls. Comput. Stand. Interfaces **66**, 103349 (2019a). https://doi.org/10.1016/j.csi.2019.04.008

Alonso-Virgós, L., Espada, J.P., Crespo, R.G.: Analyzing compliance and application of usability guidelines and recommendations by web developers. Comput. Stand. Interfaces **64**, 117–132 (2019b). https://doi.org/10.1016/j.csi.2019.01.004

Alonso-Virgós, L., Espada, J.P., Thomaschewski, J., Crespo, R.G.: Test usability guidelines and follow conventions. Useful recommendations from web developers. Comput. Stand. Interfaces **70**, 103423 (2020). https://doi.org/10.1016/j.csi.2020.103423

Bevan, N.: Guidelines and standards for web usability. In: Proceedings of HCI International (2005)

Bevan, N., Spinhof, L.: Are guidelines and standards for web usability comprehensive? In: Jacko, J.A. (ed.) HCI 2007. LNCS, vol. 4550, pp. 407–419. Springer, Heidelberg (2007). https://doi.org/10.1007/978-3-540-73105-4_45

Duan, J.-L., Liu, S.-X.: Application on web mining for web usability analysis. In: 2012 International Conference on Machine Learning and Cybernetics, vol. 5, pp. 1981–1985 (2012). https://doi.org/10.1109/ICMLC.2012.6359680

Grady, H.M.: Web site design: a case study in usability testing using paper prototypes. In: 18th Annual Conference on Computer Documentation. Ipcc Sigdoc 2000. Technology and Teamwork. Proceedings. IEEE Professional Communication Society International Professional Communication Conference an, pp. 39–45 (2000). https://doi.org/10.1109/IPCC.2000.887259

Kumar, R., Hasteer, N.: Evaluating usability of a web application: a comparative analysis of open-source tools. In: 2017 2nd International Conference on Communication and Electronics Systems (ICCES), pp. 350–354 (2017). https://doi.org/10.1109/CESYS.2017.8321296

Luo, H., Rocco, S., Schaad, C.: Using google analytics to understand online learning: a case study of a graduate-level online course. In: 2015 International Conference of Educational Innovation through Technology (EITT), pp. 264–268 (2015). https://doi.org/10.1109/EITT.2015.62

Ma, Y., Feng, J.: Evaluating usability of three authentication methods in web-based application. In: 2011 Ninth International Conference on Software Engineering Research, Management and Applications, pp. 81–88 (2011). https://doi.org/10.1109/SERA.2011.18

Mahyavanshi, N., Patil, M., Kulkarni, V.: A realistic study of user behavior for refining web usability. In: 2017 International Conference on I-SMAC (IoT in Social, Mobile, Analytics and Cloud) (I-SMAC), pp. 450–453 (2017). https://doi.org/10.1109/I-SMAC.2017.8058390

Mousa, A.H., Mohsen, M.K., Alnasrawi, A.M., Nasir, I.S.: IMUW-APP: an instrument for measuring the usability of web applications. Indones. J. Electr. Eng. Comput. Sci. **24**(2), 1183–1194 (2021). https://doi.org/10.11591/ijeecs.v24.i2.pp1183-1194

Nielsen, J.: Heuristic evaluation: How-to: Article by jakob nielsen. Nielson Norman GroupNorman, vol. 1995, pp. 1–11 (2020)

Nielsen, J.: Designing for international use (panel). In: BT - Conference on Human Factors in Computing Systems, CHI 1990, Proceedings, Seattle, WA, USA, 1–5 April 1990, pp. 291–294 (1990). https://doi.org/10.1145/97243.97298

Otaiza, R., Rusu, C., Roncagliolo, S.: Evaluating the usability of transactional web sites. In: 2010 Third International Conference on Advances in Computer-Human Interactions, pp. 32–37 (2010). https://doi.org/10.1109/ACHI.2010.27

Retnani, W.E.Y., Prasetyo, B., Prayogi, Y.P., Nizar, M.A., Abdul, R.M.: Usability testing to evaluate the library's academic web site. In: 2017 4th International Conference on Computer Applications and Information Processing Technology (CAIPT), pp. 1–4 (2017). https://doi.org/10.1109/CAIPT.2017.8320714

Ruiz-Rodriguez, R.: An auxiliary tool for usability and design guidelines validation of web sites. In: 2006 15th International Conference on Computing, pp. 304–308 (2006). https://doi.org/10.1109/CIC.2006.21

Solís-Martínez, J., Espada, J.P., González Crespo, R., Pelayo G-Bustelo, B.C., Cueva Lovelle, J.M.: UXJs: tracking and analyzing web usage information with a javascript oriented approach. IEEE Access **8**, 43725–43735 (2020). https://doi.org/10.1109/ACCESS.2020.2977879

Tezza, R., Bornia, A.C., de Andrade, D.F.: Measuring web usability using item response theory: principles, features and opportunities. Interact. Comput. **23**(2), 167–175 (2011). https://doi.org/10.1016/j.intcom.2011.02.004

Wang, X., Liu, J.: Usability evaluation of B2C web site. In: 2007 International Conference on Wireless Communications, Networking and Mobile Computing, pp. 3837–3840 (2007). https://doi.org/10.1109/WICOM.2007.949

Yakunin, A.V., Bodrunova, S.S.: Website aesthetics and functional user states as factors of web usability. In: Ahram, T., Taiar, R. (eds.) IHIET 2021. LNNS, vol. 319, pp. 394–401. Springer, Cham (2022). https://doi.org/10.1007/978-3-030-85540-6_51

Zimmerman, D., Slater, M., Kendall, P.: Risk communication and usability case study: implications for Web site design. In: IPCC 2001. Communication Dimensions. Proceedings IEEE International Professional Communication Conference (Cat. No. 01CH37271), pp. 445–452 (2001). https://doi.org/10.1109/IPCC.2001.971594

Gamifying the Human-in-the-Loop: Toward Increased Motivation for Training AI in Customer Service

Christina Wiethof(✉), Tim Roocks, and Eva A. C. Bittner

Universität Hamburg, 20146 Hamburg, Germany
{christina.wiethof,eva.bittner}@uni-hamburg.de,
tim.roocks@studium.uni-hamburg.de

Abstract. In this paper, we contribute to research on human-AI collaboration in the scope of Hybrid Intelligence Systems, which enable mutual augmentation and collaborative learning of both human and AI. Thereby, we address a research gap focusing on the continuance intention of customer service employees to teach AI during their work task. So far, the human-in-the-loop (HITL) approach is commonly applied to directly involve the human user in Machine Learning (ML) to actively advance AI. However, there is only little consideration of users' motivation regarding the extra effort of teaching AI during their work. To address this gap, we combine gamification and ML toward increased motivation to participate in HITL learning. Therefore, we follow the Design Science Research process and align to a framework for gamifying collaboration processes. Thus, we identify meta-requirements toward intended outcomes of gamified collaboration based on expert interviews, consequently derive design principles to gamify the process interactions and determine matching gamification elements. For demonstration, we implement the design principles with the according gamification elements in a prototype enabling customer service employees to provide feedback to an AI. Eventually, we evaluate the design principles with the prototype in user test simulations. The results reveal their successful implementation as well as the relevance of mixed gamification elements to trigger various motivation types. Additionally, we show applicability of the framework to gamify human-AI collaboration.

Keywords: Gamification · Human-in-the-loop · Customer service

1 Introduction

Artificial Intelligence (AI), specifically Machine Learning (ML) methods are increasingly implemented and used in customer service [1]. Thereby, companies aim to continuously elevate the efficiency of service delivery and customer satisfaction when processing customer requests. Therefore, AI-enabled technologies are deployed to autonomously reply to customers in the frontline or augment the employees in the back office [2–5]. To develop and establish AI-enabled

H. Degen and S. Ntoa (Eds.): HCII 2022, LNAI 13336, pp. 100–117, 2022.
https://doi.org/10.1007/978-3-031-05643-7_7

technologies in customer service, training through ML is necessary. Traditionally, automatic ML is applied to process and find patterns in big data, e.g., for speech recognition, recommender systems and autonomous vehicles [6,7]. However, in domains that are characterized by a limited amount of data and are thus complex for automatic ML on its own, recent research introduced interactive ML (iML) for immediate optimization and learning of an ML system through direct interactions with the human user [6,8–10]. With this, ML researchers seek to combine human and AI strengths toward so-called Hybrid Intelligence Systems (HIS) [11,12] to enable their collaboration as teammates working toward the same goal [13–15]. To ensure continuous improvement of a HIS, the "human-in-the-loop" (HITL) approach is determined to train AI based on iML approaches [8,16]. By putting the human user in the loop of AI and thus giving the user more control in the development and training of the ML system, additional complex training iterations with ML experts can be reduced [6,7,9,10]. Consequently, faster and more flexible learning cycles can be implemented [8]. However, iML comes with several risks to be considered. For the system to learn, it is dependent on expert users' feedback. Users might not enjoy this monotonous task, which interrupts their usual work task flow and does not show immediate progress [17]. In such iML settings, user engagement [17] as well as satisfaction and continuance intention to use and train the ML system [18] are of uttermost importance. Therefore, motives and motivation of individual expert users are crucial [18,19]. To increase engagement and motivation, there are several options to consider, e.g., social networks [18] or gamification [18,20,21]. However, so far, there is only little consideration of the expert users, who are in the loop of AI and interactively train an ML system as an additional work task. Thus, there is a lack of research on how to motivate and encourage expert users to actively participate in iML [7,22]. Accordingly, [22] call for future research on gamifying ML and disclose the potential of gamification to assist the optimization of ML and help human users to label data. Building on its wide variety of elements (e.g., leaderboards, badges, levels) [23], and its proven successful applicability to several domains (e.g., education, workplace, health care, software) [20], we investigate the use of gamification elements to incentivize expert users in the loop of AI based on a conceptual framework for gamifying collaboration processes [24]. Thereby, we combine gamification elements and the HITL approach in the scope of human-AI collaboration. To address the presented knowledge gap, we formulated the following research questions: **Q1:** *What effects do gamification elements have on expert users in customer service training an ML system?* **Q2:** *How can gamification elements be integrated into HITL learning in customer service toward higher user motivation?* **Q3:** *Which gamification elements are suitable for motivating expert users in customer service to train an ML system?* To answer the research questions, we conduct Design Science Research (DSR) [25,26] and follow the DSR process of [27]. Hence, the remainder of the paper proceeds as follows. First, we provide insights into related work covering research on human-AI-collaboration and HIS as well as gamification. Next, we describe our research approach. In the following sections, we present design knowledge and matching gamification elements for the design and development of gamified HITL learning. We demonstrate the implementation of the design knowledge and elements in a prototype in the next section and present the results of the evaluation afterwards. Finally, we conclude our study with a discussion of findings and future research implications.

2 Related Work

Research in human-AI teaming and collaboration is advancing rapidly as an advantageous alternative to human replacement through AI-enabled automation [13,15,28–30]. With this promising combination of both artificial and human intelligence in terms of human-AI collaboration, [12] introduced the concept of Hybrid Intelligence, and further contribute with design knowledge for HIS combining HITL with the computer-in-the-loop (CITL) [11]. They define HIS "*as systems that have the ability to accomplish complex goals by combining human and artificial intelligence to collectively achieve superior results than each of the[m] could have done in separation and continuously improve by learning from each other*" [11]. Thus, HIS enable and support mutual augmentation, i.e., the AI augments human intelligence through CITL, and the human augments AI through HITL [12]. Such augmentation scenarios are increasingly applied in organizations [31], especially in customer service [3,32]. However, existing research primarily focuses on how to best augment the employee disclosing a research gap on augmenting the AI toward mutual augmentation. As HIS demand continuous learning in terms of mutual learning [11,12,33], a high continuance intention to use needs to be ensured [18,19]. Still, a survey of HITL for ML found that studies do not address the factor of varying motivation, which is crucial for human involvement [34]. To address this issue, [22] see potential in the application of gamification to improve ML through HITL. [35] define gamification as "*the use of game design elements in non-game contexts*". So far, it has already been implemented in several domain applications, e.g., in commerce, education, health or ideation, toward psychological outcomes, e.g., enjoyment, engagement or motivation, as well as behavioral outcomes, e.g., level and quality of participation [36]. Besides, gamification also has been applied in collaboration scenarios, e.g., employee collaboration in social software solutions [23] or software engineering [21,37]. To enable systematic gamification of collaboration processes toward higher continuance intention to use, [24] developed an initial framework including theories of meaningful [38–41] and deep [18,39–41] engagement (see Fig. 1). The framework comprises three segments based on [38]: mechanics, dynamics, and user engagement. For each segment, there are elements to be considered for gamification, as well as according examples, e.g., mechanics - gamification affordances - status, competition, self-expression etc. The fourth part of the framework is intended to put the focus on digital collaboration processes, e.g., gamification elements in collaboration processes to support mechanics. Thus, the framework can be applied to gamify collaboration toward continuance intention to use. It can be systematically utilized by (1) defining intended outcomes for user engagement,

Gamification elements in collaboration processes		
Mechanics	Gamification affordances	Status, competition, self-expression, etc.
	Gamification objects	Items, characters, visual assets, etc.
	Gamification mechanics	Rules
Gamification principles for collaboration process interactions		
Dynamics	User-system-interactions	User-to-system, system-to-user, user-to-user
	Gameful interactions	Competition, cooperation
	Playful interactions	Exploration, creation, pretending
Intended outcomes of the gamified collaboration processes		
User engagement (aesthetic/flow experience)	Meaningful engagement (aesthetic experience)	Experiential outcomes: sensory and cognitive experiences (sensation, fantasy, narrative, challenge, fellowship, discovery, expression, submission, meaning, self-expansion), attachment to outcome, attachment to system
		Instrumental outcomes: functional, related to work context, prolonged use, increased use, increased learning
	Deep engagement (flow experience)	Hedonic motivation
Continuance intention to use gamified digital collaboration processes		

Fig. 1. Framework for gamifying collaboration processes [24]

(2) deriving gamification principles for dynamics, and (3) identifying appropriate gamification elements for mechanics. Although [24] only apply their framework to a collaboration process among humans, they call for research to prove applicability of their framework in other collaboration scenarios. Thus, we consider the framework for gamifying HITL in terms of human-AI collaboration within HIS. Additionally, [22] point out that the purpose of gamification is to optimize human-computer-interaction. Hence, it should be generally applicable to human involvement in ML through HITL in human-AI-collaboration. Furthermore, to support the potential of transferability from human-human to human-AI collaboration, we refer to Social Response Theory suggesting that humans equally apply certain rules, norms, and behaviors to humans as well as computers respectively [42]. Based on this, we eventually presume that gamification cannot only be applied to human-AI collaboration but can also be encouraged through AI. This is specifically the case, when we humanize AI to make it a teammate, as we consider fellowship as experiential outcome of gamification [24].

3 Research Approach

With this research, we aim to contribute prescriptive design knowledge in the form of applicable design principles (DPs) to the knowledge base connecting the research areas of Human-Computer-Interaction, Hybrid Intelligence, ML and Gamification in order to design a solution for the integration of gamification elements in HITL learning [25,26]. Therefore, we follow the DSR process by [27] (see Fig. 2). After the problem motivation in the introduction, we present related work including a conceptual framework for gamifying collaboration processes [24]. We apply the framework to systematically identify adequate gamification elements for HITL learning in customer service. First, we derive meta-requirements (MRs)

1. Problem Identification	2. Objectives of a Solution	3. Design and Development	4. Demonstration	5. Evaluation	6. Communication
Research gap of combining gamification with HITL to motivate expert users training AI.	Derivation of meta-requirements from expert interviews for the integration of gamification and HITL.	Design principles to implement gamification elements into the HITL process motivating expert users to interact with an ML system.	Instantiation of a customer service process prototype implementing HITL and gamification elements based on the design principles.	Evaluation through user test simulations and qualitative interviews with expert users in customer service assessing the implementation of the design principles.	Dissemination of design principles, and the gamified HITL process prototype in customer service.

Fig. 2. Structure along the DSR process [27]

from qualitative semi-structured interviews with domain experts [43] as objectives of a solution, i.e., expected effects of gamification (Q1). According to the findings, we formulate DPs [44] to ensure appropriate process integration and interactions (Q2). Based on these we determine matching gamification elements (Q3) and implement them within a HITL customer service process prototype for demonstration. We evaluate the DPs by using the developed prototype in user test simulations with domain experts and again conducting qualitative semi-structured interviews thereafter [43,45]. Communication will be completed with this paper.

4 Objectives of a Solution

By motivating expert users in customer service to train an ML system, we aim for a high continuance intention to use and train the ML system via HITL. To identify MRs, we considered the conceptual framework for gamifying collaboration processes [24] and conducted semi-structured qualitative expert interviews [43]. We interviewed nine domain experts (E1–E9) with experience in customer service. The interview guideline included questions toward user engagement [24] covering 1) the customer service process, thoughts and feelings about 2) collaborating with an AI, 3) the additional effort that comes with providing feedback, 4) ideas toward a more enjoyable way of giving feedback. To analyze the expert interviews, we conducted a thematic comparison [43] and inductively determined 16 MRs, 11 toward meaningful engagement, 5 toward deep engagement [24].

MRs Toward Meaningful Engagement. Regarding instrumental outcomes of user engagement, the trained system is expected to improve through provided feedback (E4, E6, E7) to "*ensure the process is in a good quality*" (E1) (**MR1**) and thus, will be able to not only make work more efficient and easier (E1 E5, E8, E9) (**MR2**), but also to educate users, especially to onboard and help new users (E1 E2, E4, E6–8) (**MR3**). Therefore, it is necessary, that all users are involved in the feedback process because "*if we get the feedback from all the experts [...] then we can really learn from everyone*" (E6) (**MR4**). Also, this contributes to an experiential outcome of fellowship and meaning. Apart from this, the duration of the feedback process could decrease motivation (E1, E9). Thus, if someone could "*calculate the effort [...] that would motivate [...] to also put effort in it*" (E4). Therefore, the required effort and time of the feedback process need to be assessable (**MR5**) and manageable (**MR6**). This comes along with the need to actually see results (E1, E3, E4, E6–9) making the progress of giving feedback visible (**MR7**) and thus further contributing to the instrumental outcomes of the user engagement. Besides that, it would be "*annoying*" (E1), if they would be enforced to give feedback in every interaction turn of the customer service process (E1, E2, E8), which is why users should be able to freely choose when to give feedback (**MR8**). In addition, in case they do provide feedback, this feedback should be confirmed, recognized, and appreciated toward the users (E1, E7) (**MR9**). However, qualitative feedback should be valued more than quantitative feedback (E2, E3) (**MR10**). At last, for meaningful engagement, it is important for the users to understand that the feedback process is not intended to replace any human user (E5) (**MR11**).

MRs Toward Deep Engagement. To trigger users' hedonic motivation, some experts suggested making the process of providing feedback a competition, e.g., to "*count your [...] feedback*" (E2), and to "*get points for using [the feedback feature]*" (E9), which will eventually be rewarded (E3, E9) (**MR12**). In addition, as "*working in a team is always more enjoyable*" (E1), the users should work in teams with other users giving feedback (E1, E3) (**MR13**). At last, one expert compared the process of providing feedback for the system with feedback giving among humans: "*as if I would talk to a human [...] because we also give feedback to them. And then they take it, and then they implement it directly. [...] And I think the same goes for the AI*" (E8). This supports Social Response Theory suggesting the application of social norms and behavior toward computers. To encourage this behavior, the AI should be equipped with a personality (E2) (**MR14**) as well as casually interact with the user including actively asking for feedback (E2) (**MR15**) and showing gratitude for users' feedback (E4) (**MR16**).

5 Artifact Design and Development

Based on the identified relevant MRs for user engagement with the gamified collaboration process, we derive and formulate seven action oriented DPs according to [44], which serve as gamification principles for collaboration process interactions [24] in the scope of HITL. Following the conceptual framework [24], we align our DPs with the three types of dynamics: gameful interactions, playful interactions, and user-system-interactions. Figure 3 depicts the derivation and classification of the DPs. We build on these DPs and refer to existing gamification research [21,24,36] to identify suitable gamification elements for motivating expert users in customer service to train an ML system. Following the conceptual framework for gamifying collaboration processes, we define specific gamification mechanics including affordances, objects, and rules [24] (see Fig. 4).

User-system-interactions	
DP1: Provide the system with the ability to improve itself and the process through the feedback in order for users, especially novices, to learn and work more efficiently, given that all users are involved in the feedback process.	MRs 1-4
DP2: Provide the system with an AI equipped with its own personality in order for users to get asked and thanked for giving feedback.	MRs 9, 14-16
DP3: Provide the system with an element ensuring the user's value and need for collaboration in order for the users to feel in charge of the feedback process and not fear any replacement.	MRs 8, 11
Gameful interactions	
DP4: Provide the system with a teamwork setting in order for users to work in a team.	MRs 4, 13
DP5: Provide the system with the ability to count, evaluate and compare users' feedback in order for users to be rewarded for giving feedback, given that their feedback is qualitatively valuable.	MRs 9, 10, 12
Playful interactions	
DP6: Provide the system with a visual representation of given and needed feedback in order for users to assess the progress.	MRs 5, 7
DP7: Provide the system with a mechanism for managing the progress in order for users to receive regular recognition for giving feedback.	MRs 5, 6, 9

Fig. 3. DPs with corresponding MRs

Affordances		
1	Epic Meaning – purpose, goals, overall progress of AI	DP1
2	Progress Bars – individual progress and team's progress	DP6
3	Points and Levels – points to reach lelvels, for user, team and AI	DP7
4	Competition – team competition, points per team, ranked, rewarded	DP5
Objects		
5	AI Personality – avatar, name, age, asking and thanking for feedback	DP2
Rules		
6	The better the feedback, the more points	DP5
7	Users are working in teams	DP4
8	Users are in charge – it's a collaboration, not an effort for replacement	DP3

Fig. 4. Gamification elements with corresponding DPs

6 Demonstration

We implement the identified gamification elements within an available use case scenario, which is provided by an organization selling projects and internships abroad to students. The use case is built upon customer service interaction between employee and customer. For each message sent by the customer, an

AI will provide the employee with an FAQ-based suggestion on how to reply to the customer. Due to AI's imperfection, we integrate HITL into the system at hand, i.e., including the user in the process of giving feedback to the AI. Figure 5 depicts the gamified HITL prototype for the customer service process of the organization.

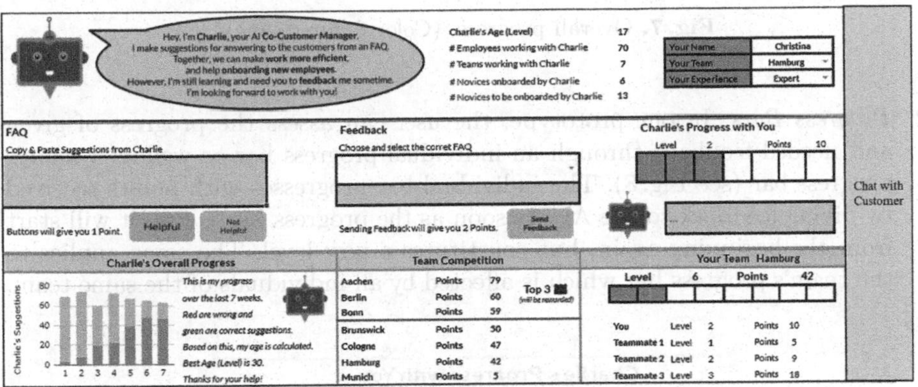

Fig. 5. Screenshot of the prototype user interface

1. *Epic Meaning.* In our prototype, the epic meaning is foremost conveyed by the AI, named Charlie, itself. Within a speech bubble, it explains the purpose of making work more efficient and especially helping to onboard new employees. Accordingly, next to it, numbers demonstrate how many novices are and still need to be onboarded as well as how many other employees are involved in working with Charlie (see Fig. 6). In addition, to confirm that the AI is improving, it has an age equivalent to its level determined by its overall progress, which is also visually represented in the prototype (see Fig. 7). It shows the AI's progress over the last seven weeks, which is measured by the number of helpful (green) and not helpful (wrong) suggestions given by the AI per week in the whole organization. The maximum age or level for the AI in this prototype is 30.

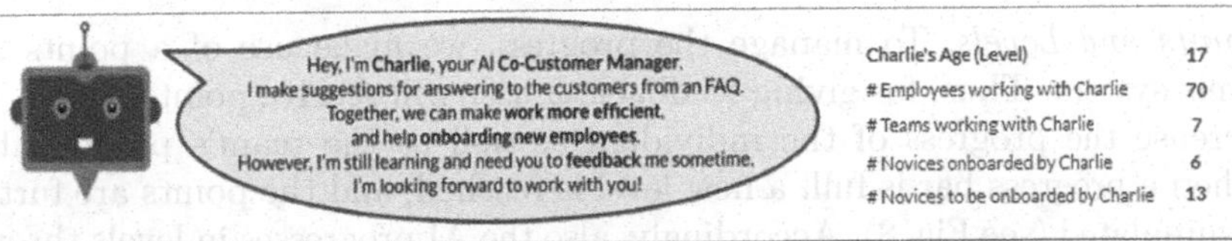

Fig. 6. Epic meaning

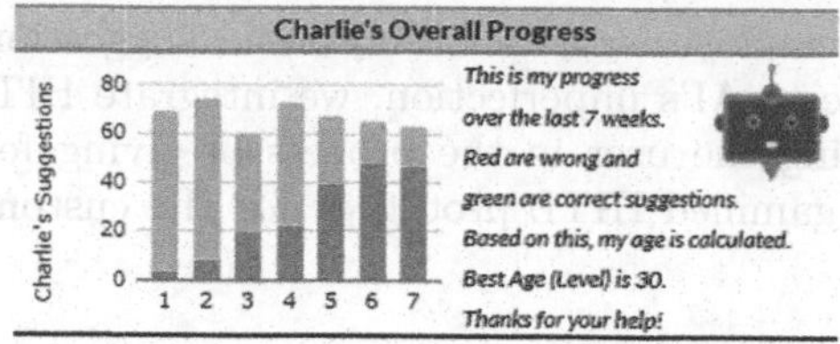

Fig. 7. Overall progress. (Color figure online)

2. *Progress Bars.* In our prototype, the user can assess the progress of given and needed feedback through an individual progress bar as well as a team's progress bar (see Fig. 8). The individual bar progresses with points received by giving feedback to the AI. As soon as the progress bar is full, it will start from the beginning again, but constitutes a new level. The same applies to the team's progress bar which is affected by all individuals of the same team.

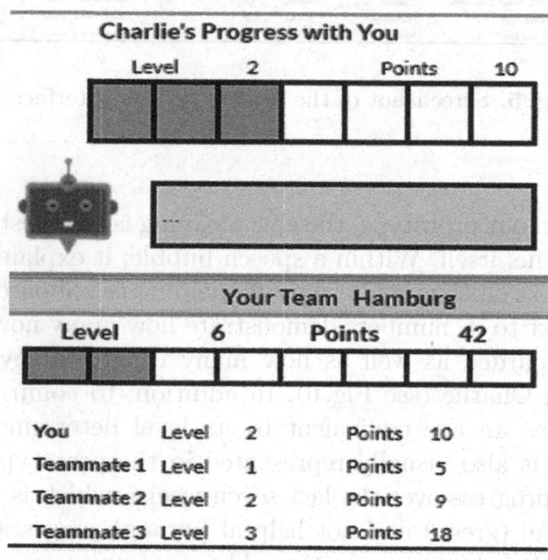

Fig. 8. Individual and team's progress bars

3. *Points and Levels.* To manage the progress, we make use of a points and levels system. Thus, for giving feedback, a user will receive points, which will increase the progress of the individual as well as the team's progress bar. When a progress bar is full, a new level is reached, and the points are further accumulated (see Fig. 8). Accordingly, also the AI progresses in levels through the feedback of all users.
4. *Competition.* The element of competition is implemented as a team competition. As the organization has several subsidiaries in different cities, the teams

are defined per city. As the prototype implements a points and levels system, each user contributes with the individual points to a specific team. These points are then used to rank the teams in the context of the team competition. The ranking is visually represented as depicted in Fig. 9. Furthermore, the top three teams will be rewarded, e.g., with internal organizational benefits.

Team Competition			
Aachen	Points	79	Top 3 (will be rewarded)
Berlin	Points	60	
Bonn	Points	59	
Braunschweig	Points	50	
Köln	Points	47	
Hamburg	Points	42	
München	Points	5	

Fig. 9. Team competition

5. *AI Personality.* The AI in our prototype is equipped with a personality including a name (Charlie), an avatar, and an age, which increases with its corresponding level. It also introduces itself as co-customer manager and asks for feedback to learn (see Fig. 6). Additionally, it also has the ability to thank users for feedback in a separate field below the individual progress bar (see Fig. 8). Hence, for provided feedback it will say "Thank you!". As an alternative, when the user does not provide feedback over a certain amount of time, the AI gives a reminder: "Please don't forget to feedback me". While the field is usually shaded in a greenish color, the latter statement will be highlighted with red color-coding.
6. *The better the feedback, the more points.* To ensure that feedback is not only good in quantitative numbers but also qualitatively valuable, we give users the opportunity to provide feedback in two different ways (see Fig. 10). For one thing, users can click a "helpful" or "not helpful" button based on their evaluation of the suggestion given by the AI. To make the feedback more valuable for the AI to learn, the users can also choose and select the correct FAQ according to the question asked by the customer. The field is populated with all relevant FAQ managed in a dropdown menu. When selecting an FAQ, a short answer to the question will appear in the field below. By clicking the "Send Feedback" button, the feedback will be submitted for the AI to learn by matching the customer question with the according FAQ. Both feedback versions can be used for helpful and for not helpful suggestions. To ensure that users will not only use the easier version of only clicking one "helpful/not helpful" button, we implement the rule that users will be rewarded for giving more qualitative feedback, i.e., they will receive two points instead of one.

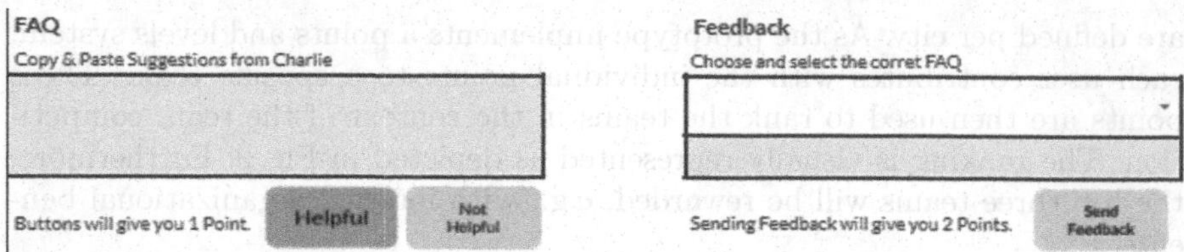

Fig. 10. Feedbacks

7. *Users are working in teams.* To encourage fellowship and enjoyment, users collect points together with other users within a team. As a team they further compete against the other teams. As of the organizational structures, users are allocated to a team based on their location. Thus, the prototype is equipped with three fields for the users to set their name, location and level of experience, i.e., expert or novice. The selected team will then show up in the team progress section of the prototype (see Fig. 8). It shows each member of the team, their points and levels, and thus, how they contributed to their team's progress.
8. *Users are in charge - it's a collaboration, not an effort for replacement.* The prototype ensures the need of the users' participation in the collaboration. With this, the user remains in charge and thus is also free to choose when to give feedback. While using the prototype, users should be aware of the collaborative aspect, its purpose of making work more efficient and onboarding new employees. They should not fear any human replacement.

7 Evaluation

We assess our derived DPs through an evaluation of our developed prototype implementing the according gamification elements [45]. Therefore, we conduct user test simulations with subsequent semi-structured expert interviews [43]. The simulation included a thorough presentation of the prototype as well as exemplary interactions with the prototype. Each user test run including simulation and interview lasted from around 40 to 60 min. We selected eleven domain expert users (U1–U11) (4 female, 7 male; average age of 23.64, SD = 2.19) with experience in customer service from the organization providing our use case for demonstration at hand. The interview guideline was designed to specifically address and evaluate our DPs and gamification effects. Overall, ten of the eleven participants recognized and were mostly positive about the prototype concluding a successful implementation of the DPs and gamification elements. However, one participant was rather negative about the prototype coming from a general skepticism toward human-AI collaboration ("*I don't want to participate in my eventual re-placement*" (U7)). We accordingly considered further respective remarks with carefulness.

DP1 - Epic Meaning. The main motivation of the majority of the participants is of intrinsic nature. Thus, they give feedback because it is necessary and relevant for the AI to learn (U2, U3, U5, U8, U11), especially from many people (U5, U11), which enables better support and education for novice employees (U2, U4, U5, U7, U9, U10). The element of the Epic Meaning supports this intrinsic motivation with numbers of employees and novices participating (U1, U3–5, U9) as it is "*good as an overview [for] the user to understand also their part in the development of the AI*" (U8). Apart from that, the introduction is "*pretty motivating as well because it's inviting you to give feedback and it's done in a nice way*" (U10).

DP2 - AI Personality. The personality attributes of the AI were mostly perceived as very likable, e.g., the smiling of the avatar, politeness, eagerness to learn, friendliness and respectfulness (U2–4, U9). Furthermore, the introduction text and greeting of the AI positively influenced this perception (U3, U4, U10). Also, the interaction itself with the AI was appreciated due to the manner of asking and thanking for feedback (U3–5, U9, U10). All in all, "*it doesn't give you the feeling that you are just talking to an algorithm*" (U1), but to kind of a partner (U4, U10). However, although the majority considered the AI as "cute" (U2, U4, U6, U8–10), the participants suggested adapting the age or level accordingly, as it is and should not be a child or teenager you are talking to (U6, U9). Additionally, the age should not be "*random*" (U7) or "*related to [...] the number of feedback*" (U4) but related to the ML.

DP3 - Users are in Charge. Though one participant predicted a decreasing relevance of the collaboration with increasing AI capabilities (U6), the intention for human-AI collaboration instead of human replacement was recognized and confirmed by most of the participants (U1–5, U8–11), e.g., "*on the one hand the AI is helping me, but on the other hand I can also shape and support the AI*" (U1) and "*the emphasis is so strongly on giving feedback, which I think is a very essential part of collaborating and getting better together*" (U2). Apart from that, the most skeptical participant emphasized the impossibility to "*collaborate with a non-human being*" (U7).

DP4 - Users are Working in Teams. The teamwork setting contributes to team feeling, spirit, and dynamics (U5, U6, U9, U10). Additionally, team members can hold each other accountable (U1, U6, U8). With the according competition (DP5) this makes the feedback process more enjoyable, satisfying, and motivating (U1–3, U8). What is more, it encourages the users to include Charlie in the team, e.g., "*It makes Charlie not only a co-worker but also a member of the team that everyone can support and should help*" (U4) and "*I see Charlie as a good addition to the team*" (U5). One aspect, which should be further discussed is the transparency of the individuals' points. It might discourage the employee being the last in the hierarchy of the team (U11).

DP5 - Competition and the Better the Feedback, the More Points. Most participants stated that the competition element contributes most to their continuance intention to use the feedback system (U2, U5, U6, U9–11). Eventually, they have fun participating in a competition (U1, U2, U4, U5, U8) and like that more effort will be rewarded (U3, U4). Thus, the rule for different feedback "*makes sense*" (U2, U3, U5, U6, U8, U10, U11). In general, they like to have two options for giving feedback in terms of efficiency, flexibility, and quality (U1, U4, U5, U8–10). However, there are two aspects to consider for improving the competition element. First, the scores should be calculated in relation to team size for a fair comparison of differently sized teams (U6). Second, manipulations of the feedback system need to be prevented (U11), e.g., checking, if correct feedback is provided (U5). At last, participants raised awareness on the fact that not all people are motivated by competitions (U7, U10, U11).

DP6 - Progress Bars. To visually see the progress and one's own contribution to it was perceived as both motivating and satisfying (U1, U3–6, U9, U10), e.g., "*I really like it because you can see your own contribution for yourself and also toward the team. And therefore I'm more motivated to use [the prototype] on a regular basis and to put more effort in it*" (U4). Additionally, it positively contributes to the team spirit, dynamics, and accountability (U3, U9–11). As the team aspect of the prototype was highly recognized, it is further suggested to improve the prototype by limiting the representation of the personal progress bar: "*For me, my personal progress bar is a bit over-represented, I think the team's progress bar seems cool as I contribute to something bigger than me kind of*" (U2).

DP7 - Points and Levels. The system of gaining points to reach levels positively contributed to the motivating game-aspects of the prototype, e.g., "*I really like it. I think it's a cool incentive system in itself to level up*" (U6). Besides, it makes sense as it is easy and transparent to understand and to track progress (U2, U3, U8–10), as "*it gives you check points that you can strive towards*" (U4). For improvement, it was suggested to increase the difficulty of reaching higher levels, i.e., with each higher level, more points are required to reach the next level (U4, U6). Also, to further contribute to the team aspect, it could be relevant to not be able to train the AI alone to a higher level (U4).

Design. Eventually, regarding the prototype itself, the participants especially appreciated the aesthetics and design as it is well-structured and therefore easy to handle and to understand (U2, U3, U5, U6, U8–11). Still, the prototype is perceived as a little crowded with all elements (U2–4). Thus, it is suggested to hide or separate the competition element on another site (U2, U4) as this element shifts the focus from the customer experience to educating the AI the most (U2).

8 Discussion and Conclusion

Overall, we formulated seven DPs based on 16 MRs to gamify HITL in customer service. We conducted our study along the DSR process [27] and systematically aligned it to the framework for gamifying collaboration processes [24]. Hence, we first identified intended outcomes as objectives of a solution through expert interviews (Q1). Then we derived DPs from the MRs as gamification principles for collaboration process interactions (Q2). Based on these, we could eventually identify matching gamification elements to gamify HITL in customer service (Q3). By implementing the DPs with the according gamification elements in a prototype, we could evaluate them and their effects through user test simulations and following interviews with domain experts (Q1). Based on the results of our evaluation, the DPs were successfully implemented to elevate users' motivation and with this their continuance intention to use. However, the evaluation also disclosed that one gamification element alone would not have reached the intended effects over a long time and not with all users, i.e., gamification effects strongly depend on the users and how to individually motivate them [36]. Thus, a good mixture of elements is required to trigger the motivation of the various individual users. For instance, while for some participants the rewarding nature of the competition (DP5) is the main motivator to give feedback to the AI and with this participate in the HITL, others do not feel affected at all by such extrinsic motivation. They mostly do not see the value in such a competition, as it does not have a bigger meaning for what they do. Hence, the Epic Meaning (DP1) is the most important and powerful element triggering intrinsic motivation and continuance intention to use. Thus, users give feedback because it has purpose affecting their work, e.g., making work more efficient and educating novices with an improved AI. Consequently, as progress bars (DP6) make users' contribution to the AI's improvement visible, they are considered equally meaningful and of intrinsically motivating nature. Seeing progress is of uttermost importance when training AI, otherwise the extra effort will be perceived useless leading to a lower continuance intention. The effects of the points and levels system to manage the progress (DP7) are twofold. For one thing, as it complements the progress visualization, it supports intrinsic motivation. For another thing, it is equally extrinsically motivating as the competition is based on the calculation of points for each team. Regarding the gamification rules, they positively supported the gamification affordances. First, it makes sense that users gain more points for more qualitative feedback (DP6). Second, as employees are still responsible for communicating with the customer and can choose, if and what feedback they want to provide to the AI, DP3 is successfully implemented to foster collaboration instead of human replacement. However, some people might hesitate to call it a "collaboration". They would rather call it a tool or support. This could come from a general disapproval, fear or inexperience toward AI and should be considered carefully. The third rule stating that users work in a team (DP4) positively impacts both the competition as well as the meaning behind the system as users are working together with their fellow colleagues to win as well as to improve the system together. At last, regarding the AI personality

(DP2), we successfully confirm the application of personality attributes to an AI as gamification object toward a more enjoyable experience. All in all, our results show potential for applying gamification in HITL learning. Thus, our study contributes to HIS research [12] combining the field of gamification with ML [22] in an augmentation scenario [31]. We therefore provide prescriptive design knowledge toward a theory of design and action in the form of seven DPs for gamifying HITL learning in customer service as well as an evaluated prototype implementing gamification elements following the DPs [25,26,45]. Additionally, we can confirm applicability of the framework for gamifying collaboration processes to human-AI collaboration processes [24]. We encourage both practitioners and researchers to draw on our findings to gamify HITL learning, as well as align with the framework to systematically gamify other collaboration process scenarios. Besides the promising results of this research, there are a few limitations to consider. First, the implementation for demonstration as well as evaluation is limited to only one organization. Additionally, we only performed user test simulations. Thus, we encourage future research to evaluate our DPs in various naturalistic settings. Second, we only conducted a qualitative situational evaluation. It would be valuable to quantitatively measure gamification effects on satisfaction, motivation, and continuance intention over a longer period of time using the system. Eventually, our DPs and prototype can serve as a fundament for combining gamification and ML as well as a complement to HIS research toward advancing HITL learning.

References

1. Statistik der Woche. https://www.heise.de/news/Statistik-der-Woche-Wo-KI-in-der-deutschen-Wirtschaft-boomt-6172430.html. Accessed 8 Feb 2021
2. Huang, M.-H., Rust, R.T.: Artificial intelligence in service. J. Serv. Res. **21**(2), 155–172 (2018)
3. de Keyser, A., Köcher, S., Alkire, L., Verbeeck, C., Kandampully, J.: Frontline service technology infusion: conceptual archetypes and future research directions. J. Serv. Manag. **30**(1), 156–183 (2019)
4. Robinson, S., et al.: Frontline encounters of the AI kind: an evolved service encounter framework. J. Bus. Res. **116**, 366–376 (2020)
5. Xu, Y., Shieh, C.-H., van Esch, P., Ling, I.-L.: AI customer service: task complexity, problem-solving ability, and usage intention. Australas. Mark. J. **28**(4), 189–199 (2020)
6. Holzinger, A.: Interactive Machine Learning (iML). Informatik Spektrum **39**(1), 64–68 (2016)
7. Holzinger, A., Plass, M., Holzinger, K., Crişan, G.C., Pintea, C.-M., Palade, V.: Towards interactive Machine Learning (iML): applying ant colony algorithms to solve the traveling salesman problem with the human-in-the-loop approach. In: Buccafurri, F., Holzinger, A., Kieseberg, P., Tjoa, A.M., Weippl, E. (eds.) CD-ARES 2016. LNCS, vol. 9817, pp. 81–95. Springer, Cham (2016). https://doi.org/10.1007/978-3-319-45507-5_6

8. Amershi, S., Cakmak, M., Knox, W.B., Kulesza, T.: Power to the people: the role of humans in interactive machine learning. AI Mag. **35**(4), 105–120 (2014)
9. Holzinger, A.: Interactive machine learning for health informatics: when do we need the human-in-the-loop? Brain Inform. **3**, 119–131 (2016)
10. Holzinger, A., Plass, M., Holzinger, K., Crisan, G.C., Pintea, C.-M., Palade, V.: A glass-box interactive machine learning approach for solving NP-hard problems with the human-in-the-loop. arXiv:1708.01104v1 (2017)
11. Dellermann, D., Calma, A., Lipusch, N., Weber, T., Weigel, S., Ebel, P.: The future of human-AI collaboration: a taxonomy of design knowledge for hybrid intelligence systems. In: Proceedings of the 52nd Hawaii International Conference on System Sciences (HICSS), Hawaii, USA (2019)
12. Dellermann, D., Ebel, P., Söllner, M., Leimeister, J.M.: Hybrid intelligence. Bus. Inf. Syst. Eng. **61**, 637–643 (2019)
13. Bittner, E., Oeste-Reiß, S., Leimeister, J.M.: Where is the bot in our team? Toward a taxonomy of design option combinations for conversational agents in collaborative work. In: Proceedings of the 52nd Hawaii International Conference on System Sciences (HICSS), Hawaii, USA (2019)
14. Frick, W.: When your boss wears metal pants. Harvard Bus. Rev. **93**, 84–89 (2015)
15. Seeber, I., et al.: Machines as teammates: a research agenda on AI in team collaboration. Inf. Manag. **57**, 103174 (2020)
16. Martínez, M.A.M., Nadj, M., Maedche, A.: Towards an integrative theoretical framework of interactive machine learning systems. In: Proceedings of the 27th European Conference on Information Systems, Stockholm-Uppsala, Sweden (2019)
17. Dudley, J.J., Kristensson, P.O.: A review of user interface design for interactive machine learning. ACM Trans. Interact. Intell. Syst. **8**(1), 1–37 (2018)
18. Lowry, P.B., Gaskin, J.E., Moody, G.D.: Proposing the Multi-Motive Information Systems Continuance Model (MISC) to better explain end-user system evaluations and continuance intentions. J. Assoc. Inf. Syst. **16**(7), 515–579 (2015)
19. Bhattacherjee, A., Premkumar, G.: Understanding changes in belief and attitude toward information technology usage. A theoretical model and longitudinal test. Manag. Inf. Syst. Q. **28**(2), 229–254 (2004)
20. Darejeh, A., Salim, S.S.: Gamification solutions to enhance software user engagement - a systematic review. Int. J. Hum.-Comput. Interact. **32**(8), 613–642 (2016)
21. Steffens, F., Marczak, S., Figueira Filho, F., Treude, C., Singer, L., Redmiles Ban Al-Ani, D.: Using gamification as a collaboration motivator for software development teams. A preliminary framework. In: Brazilian Symposium on Collaborative Systems, Salvador, Brazil (2015)
22. Khakpour, A., Colomo-Palacios, R.: Convergence of gamification and machine learning: a systematic literature review. Technol. Learn. **26**, 597–636 (2021)
23. Meske, C., Brockmann, T., Wilms, K., Stieglitz, S.: Gamify employee collaboration - a critical review of gamification elements in social software. In: Australasian Conference on Information Systems, Adelaide (2016)
24. Wiethof, C., Tavanapour, N., Bittner, E.: Designing and evaluating a collaborative writing process with gamification elements: toward a framework for gamifying collaboration processes. AIS Trans. Hum.-Comput. Interact. **13**(1), 38–61 (2021)
25. Gregor, S.: The nature of theory in information systems. MIS Q. **30**(3), 611–642 (2006)
26. Gregor, S., Hevner, A.: Positioning and presenting design science research for maximum impact. MIS Q. **37**(2), 337–355 (2013)

27. Peffers, K., et al.: The design science research process. A model for producing and presenting information systems research. In: Proceedings of the International Conference on Design Science Research in Information Systems and Technology, Claremont, CA (2006)
28. Cheng, X., Yin, G., Azadegan, A., Kolfschoten, G.: Trust evolvement in hybrid team collaboration: a longitudinal case study. Group Decis. Negot. **25**(2), 267–288 (2015). https://doi.org/10.1007/s10726-015-9442-x
29. Przybilla, L., Baar, L., Wiesche, M., Krcmar, H.: Machines as teammates in creative teams: digital facilitation of the dual pathway to creativity. In: Proceedings of SIGMIS-CPR, Nashville, TN, USA (2019)
30. Wiethof, C., Tavanapour, N., Bittner, E.: Implementing an intelligent collaborative agent as teammate in collaborative writing: toward a synergy of humans and AI. In: Proceedings of the 54th Hawaii International Conference on System Sciences (2021)
31. Benbya, H., Pachidi, S., Jarvenpaa, S.L.: Artificial intelligence in organizations: implications for information systems research. J. Assoc. Inf. Syst. **22**(2), 281–303 (2021)
32. Larivière, B., et al.: "Service Encounter 2.0": an investigation into the roles of technology, employees and customers. J. Bus. Res. **79**, 238–246 (2017)
33. Wiethof, C., Bittner, E.: Hybrid intelligence - combining the human in the loop with the computer in the loop: a systematic literature review. In: Forty-Second International Conference on Information Systems, Austin (2021)
34. Wu, X., Xiao, L., Sun, Y., Zhang, J., Ma, T., He, L.: A survey of human-in-the-loop for machine learning. arXiv:2108.00941v1 (2021)
35. Deterding, S., Dixon, D., Khaled, R., Nacke, L.: From game design elements to gamefulness: defining "gamification". In: MindTrek 2011, Tampere, Finland (2011)
36. Hamari, J., Koivisto, J., Sarsa, H.: Does gamification work? - A literature review of empirical studies on gamification. In: Proceedings of the 47th Hawaii International Conference on System Sciences, Hawaii, USA (2014)
37. Marczak, S., Filho, F.F., Singer, L, Treude, C., Steffens, F., Redmiles Ban Al-Ani, D.: Studying gamification as a collaboration motivator for virtual software teams. Social issues, cultural issues, and research methods. In: Proceedings of the 18th ACM Conference Companion on Computer Supported Cooperative Work and Social Computing, Vancouver, BC, Canada (2015)
38. Hunicke, R., LeBlanc, M., Zubek, R.: MDA: a formal approach to game design and game research. In: Proceedings of the Challenges in Games AI Workshop, Nineteenth National Conference of Artificial Intelligence, AAAI, San Jose, USA, pp. 1–5 (2004)
39. Liu, D., Santhanam, R., Webster, J.: Toward meaningful engagement: a framework for design and research of gamified information systems. Manag. Inf. Syst. Q. **41**(4), 1011–1034 (2017)
40. Suh, A., Cheung, C.M.K., Ahuja, M., Wagner, C.: Gamification in the workplace: the central role of the aesthetic experience. J. Manag. Inf. Syst. **34**(1), 268–305 (2017)
41. Tseng, S.-L., Sun, H.: Playful design elements and stages of player experience in gamification. In: Proceedings of the 38th International Conference on Information Systems, Seoul (2017)
42. Nass, C., Moon, Y.: Machines and mindlessness: social responses to computers. J. Soc. Issues **56**(1), 81–103 (2000)

43. Meuser, M., Nagel, U.: ExpertInneninterviews - vielfach erprobt, wenig bedacht. VS Verlag für Sozialwissenschaften, Wiesbaden (2002). https://doi.org/10.1007/978-3-322-93270-9_3
44. Chandra, L., Gregor, S., Seidel, S.: Prescriptive knowledge in IS research. Conceptualizing design principles in terms of materiality, action, and boundary conditions. In: Proceedings of the 48th Hawaii International Conference on System Sciences, Kauai, Hawaii, USA (2015)
45. Venable, J., Pries-Heje, J., Baskerville, R.: A comprehensive framework for evaluation in design science research. In: Peffers, K., Rothenberger, M., Kuechler, B. (eds.) DESRIST 2012. LNCS, vol. 7286, pp. 423–438. Springer, Heidelberg (2012). https://doi.org/10.1007/978-3-642-29863-9_31

Explainable and Trustworthy AI

Dominant View and Perception of Artificial Intelligence in Developing Economy

Elefelious Getachew Belay[1](✉), Getachew Hailemariam Mengesha[2], and Nuniyat Kifle[1]

[1] School of Information Technology and Engineering, Addis Ababa Institute of Technology, Addis Ababa University, Addis Ababa, Ethiopia
{elefelious.getachew,nuniyat.kifle}@aait.edu.et

[2] School of Information Science, Addis Ababa University, Addis Ababa, Ethiopia
getachew.hailemariam@aau.edu.et

Abstract. This study intends to explore the views and attitudes of scholars from different disciplines towards Artificial Intelligence (AI) and associated technologies. It attempts to assess and understand the phenomena related to AI views and perceptions held by scholars. A theoretical framework that contains seven independent and one dependent variable were used to guide the data collection, analysis, and reporting. A self-administered survey instrument was used to collect data from the sampled colleges, institutes, schools, and departments of Addis Ababa University. A total of 163 usable questionnaires were obtained. This paper presents the interim results of the study from six dimensions of AI indicators drawn from the research model. The overall result revealed a favorable attitude and perceptions about the AI systems. Nevertheless, regarding the potential colonization or decolonization rhetoric and in relation to the openness and explainability of the AI systems, divergent outcomes as compared to prior studies have been observed. Policymakers and AI champions in Ethiopia need to endeavor to clarify the clouded conceptions of AI through intellectual dialogue, research symposium workshops, and other AI awareness programs.

Keywords: AI dominant view · AI perception · AI4D · AI awareness

1 Introduction

Artificial Intelligence (AI) has started to impact various aspects of the human race and will continue to influence positively or otherwise. Over the years, various studies have been conducted with regard to the technical and economic implications of AI. However, the socio-technical consideration of AI in the African context remains unexplored at a sufficient level. Apparently, African countries' backbone telecom infrastructure constraints and lack of expertise in the domain have led to a staggering desire for AI technology adoption. Nevertheless, quite recently policymakers have recognized the potential benefits of AI to rectify the prevailing capacity limitations in vital sectors such as health, agriculture, and education. With a bid to harness AI in core economic sectors,

H. Degen and S. Ntoa (Eds.): HCII 2022, LNAI 13336, pp. 121–129, 2022.
https://doi.org/10.1007/978-3-031-05643-7_8

many African governments have begun to establish a government agency to oversee the proper adoption and use of the technology. Pursuant to this, Ethiopia established the Artificial Intelligence Center[1], a government agency, in 2020. The center is expected to mobilize scholars across a range of public, private, and research institutions and to create a platform in order to catalyze AI research and innovations. Further, the academic and research communities in Ethiopia are supposed to investigate how AI may be assimilated in the socioeconomic systems considering the peculiarities of AI and the Ethiopian context.

Such studies will have the advantage to initiate, guide, and inform policymaking and assist in the identification and consideration of AI intervention areas. On the other hand, researchers also claimed examining the various views, trust, and attitudes about AI impact and importance will affect how AI is going to be implemented [1]. Hence, scholars who can be considered as influential groups that involve in consulting the government in their special areas including policymaking have to be gauged. The development of digital technologies and the scholar community have to work in harmony to adequately prepare and address the inevitable changes of society and economics resulting from the progress of technology based on artificial intelligence. As a result, determining the main factors that influence the attitudes of scholars towards artificial intelligence, can help reduce various negative factors.

Although the intensity of negative attitudes on emerging Information Technology requires studies at different points in time and context, it has been an object of research for many scholars who have paid special attention to explore factors influencing the attitude towards technological changes [2]. Particularly, the views scholars hold on AI are critical and exert influence on how AI is accepted and implemented as technological discoveries in AI mainly emerge from the academic and research environment [3]. Ideally, universities are supposed to work in good coordination in order to prepare society for the inevitable AI-induced changes [4]. Societal and organizational attitudes towards technology are important as people tend to think AI is robotics and are perceived as human-like machines that wreak havoc on Earth [5].

Therefore, it is imperative in the first place to understand the perception and attitude of African scholars towards AI. A preliminary study we conducted indicates that some scholars consider AI as a fancy and luxury gadget to Africa, where conventional technologies have not yet diffused across the society at a grassroots level. Still, we do not know how far this view is widely shared across the scholar communities. The ultimate goal is to explore the views of scholars at Addis Ababa University that is supposed to reflect similar outlooks in similar setting in the African continent. The study is motivated to capture perceptions and attitudes of scholars using relevant indicators drawn from literature. We contend that the study is expected to elicit the gap between government strategies and the reality on the ground. In doing so, the study intends to feature misconceptions regarding AI and associated technologies and eventually recommend strategies to promote evidence based realistic understanding of AI along with its intended and unintended consequences. Various studies shows that AI exhibits algorithmic and data biases which leads to unfair discrimination against certain groups of people [6]. Righetti et al. mentioned that in 2015 Google photo service classified black

[1] Recently renamed Ethiopian Artificial Intelligence Institute.

people as gorillas echoing racist stereotypes. The problem could not be solved for more than two years until Google system developers simply remove the gorilla category from the classification. Moreover, several facial recognitions systems suffer from racial and gender stereotypes. For instance, Amazon's recognition system had about 30% classification errors for dark-skinned women while perfectly classifying light-skinned men [6].

Scholars from diverse fields of studies are supposed to be aware of potential algorithmic and data biases in AI systems and develop a mechanism whereby such flaws are detected and fixed. However, it would be extremely daunting when scholars themselves fall in prejudice and downplay the potential benefits of AI for rectifying socio-economic challenges.

Undoubtedly, African countries are likely to encounter another digital divide scenario if this sort of view is dominant among African scholars. Therefore, this study intends to explore the dominant views of educators and scholars at Addis Ababa University regarding the potential benefits and the associated risk of AI in Africa.

The remaining part of the paper is structured as follows. First, the method used for data gathering, analysis, and reporting are described. Then, the interim results of the study will be presented. This is followed by the discussion section. In the end, the paper concludes by reflecting on the major outcomes of the study.

2 Method

The study used the theoretical model presented in Fig. 1 below as a framework that guides the data collection, analysis, and reporting. The causal research model contains seven independent constructs along with seven hypothesized relationships and a total of 57 manifest variables that operationalized the eight constructs in the theoretical model. Table 1 lists construct included in the research model with their brief description.

Table 1. List of constructs and its description

#	Constructs	Description
1	General Understanding of AI	Which technologies are considered as AI and/or which of them apply/use AI technology
2	AI and information privacy	Views and perception whether AI systems respect privacy
3	AI and information security	Views, perception, and expectation whether AI systems respect security
4	AI systems transparency	Views, perception, and expectation of AI systems transparency
5	AI systems explicability	Views, perception, and expectation of AI systems explainability
6	Affection towards AI based systems	Affection towards AI based systems and associated technologies
7	Perception of AI systems	Perception and understanding of AI system
8	Overall view and perspectives of AI systems	Captures overall impressions towards AI

2.1 Participants

The sample consisted of 163 academic staff from Addis Ababa University in Ethiopia. The university has 14 campuses with a range of disciplines. The descriptive statistical result shows that respondents were distributed from engineering, health, natural science, social science, business, and law. Of the total participant, 112 were male, 48 female. With regards to academic status, 39 participants were Ph.D. and above, 81 participants were MSc/MA and 42 were BSc/BA. Further, the total participants 50 (30.7%) of them regarded themselves as an advanced IT guru, 58 (35.5%) are identified themselves as intermediate proficiency and the rest 55 (33.7%) identified themselves as IT literate.

2.2 Instruments

A survey questionnaire with a five-point Likert scale was developed to gather the data from the respondents at Addis Ababa University (AAU). This university is the oldest and largest university in Ethiopia and in East Africa. According to [7] 2021 AAU stood as one of the top ten best universities in Africa and ranked 517th from the world universities. Currently, AAU has 14 campuses, 70 undergraduate and 293 graduate programs. The university student population has reached over 50,000 and the total academic staff is about 3,000. A total of 200 survey instruments were distributed and 165 returned, which accounts for 82.5 response rates. After data cleaning was carried out 163 questionnaires were found to be usable.

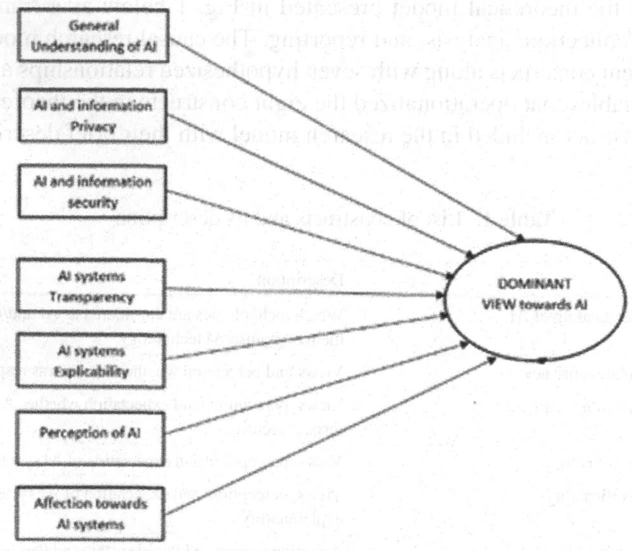

Fig. 1. Dominant view conceptual model

3 Results

This paper reports the work in progress of a bigger study. In the interest of time and space, limited descriptive statistical results are presented along six indicators drawn from the total of 15 indicators used to measure the dependent variable – "dominant view". The predictive statistical results will be presented in the upcoming publications. The six indicators selected to measure the dependent variables are as follows:

- AI Power African economic development
- AI creates more jobs than it eliminates
- Support the development of AI in Ethiopia and the African context
- AI induces algorithmic colonialism
- AI Systems are open about their operation
- Africa is not ready to adopt and use AI technologies

Table 2. Presents the descriptive statistical results in line with the selected indicators

#	Constructs	Strongly agree	Agree	Neutral	Disagree	Strongly disagree
1	AI Powers African economic development	49	70	35	6	3
2	AI creates more jobs than it eliminates	23	45	48	33	14
3	Support for the development of AI in Ethiopian and African context	62	78	16	7	–
4	AI induces algorithmic colonialism	21	43	63	27	9
5	AI systems are open about their operation	18	54	71	14	6
6	African is not ready to adopt and use AI technologies	14	25	43	65	16

The following section provides brief narrative descriptions and reflections on the results presented in Table 2.

3.1 AI Powers African Economic Development

The data in Table 2 reveals that from the total of 163 respondents 119, which accounts 73% agreed that AI technologies have the potential to power African economic development unleashing African natural and human resources. This is fully in line with the conviction and endeavor of the Ethiopian government to leverage AI to speed up economic development and transformation across key socio-economic sectors such as Agriculture health, environment, and manufacturing. Still, it is important to note that about 27% of respondents do not believe that AI would enhance African economic development. These scholars' views tend to be dominant when they get the opportunity to assume key government offices. Particularly, in Ethiopian cases quite recently the government has started recruiting scholars from higher educational institutions to serve at the top cabinet offices.

3.2 AI Systems Create More Jobs Than They Eliminate

In connection to job creations, people tend to be pessimists and consider AI as a monster that robs jobs from millions of people around the world. The survey result shows 68 (42%) of the total respondents believe that AI has the capability to create more jobs than it eliminates. In this regard, the overwhelming majority (58%) believe that AI eliminates existing jobs. As this is a response obtained from the scholar communities stationed in one of the African leading Universities, extensive awareness creation seminars, workshops, and research symposiums are required to increase the conceptions of scholars. This is timely and important because the images of physical manufacturing robots tend to come into the mind of people when one talks of artificial intelligence.

3.3 Support for AI System Development

Preliminary investigations we conducted reveal influential peoples at times regard AI as less important to Africa. This has provoked us to conduct large-scale studies in educational and research settings to understand the dominant view of influential scholars regarding the perceptions and beliefs they hold about AI. Accordingly, the survey result indicates that 140 (86%) of the total respondents support the design, development, and adoption of AI systems that fit the context of Africa.

3.4 AI Induce Algorithmic Colonialism

There has been a growing concern that AI technologies would be used by entities in the advanced world to trap and evade the privacy of African people. The survey result shows that 64 (39%) believe that AI can induce algorithmic colonialism. Conversely, only 36(22%) respondents openly disagreed with the tendency of AI inducing algorithmic colonialism. About 39% of respondents remained undecided on the matter. Perhaps, this indicator revealed a much more clouded conception AI as compared to the remaining five indicators selected for analysis.

3.5 Openness of AI Operation

Prior studies argue that AI systems, in general, appear to be a black box system, which makes it difficult to unpack and understand the inner operations. In this regard, 72 (44%) respondents believe that AI system operations are open and explainable. This result somehow diverges from what transpired in prior studies. In fact, this has been ascribed to be the cause for algorithmic and data biases implicated in AI systems.

3.6 African Readiness to Adopt AI

The survey item was worded negatively that Africa is not ready to adopt and use AI technologies. The survey result reveals that 39 (24%) believe that Africans are not ready to adopt and use AI systems. As opposed to this 81(50%) of respondents argue that Africans are ready to adopt and use AI technologies. However, as stated in the preceding section, the opinion of respondents who question the readiness of Africa to AI is likely to influence policymaking depending on the chance they get to hold policymaking positions in the nations they live in.

4 Discussion

In the previous section, we tried to present respondents' views and attitudes towards AI and associated technology. In this section, we will briefly present some discussion points in line with the results presented in the previous section.

The socio-technical oriented AI studies held mixed views and remained inconclusive with regards to the intended and unintended consequences of AI systems, particularly in less developed countries. For instance, research by [8] downplays the potential benefits of AI to Africa and casts AI technologies as an instrument for modern colonialism. Similarly, about 39% of the surveyed respondents echoed the position held by this particular research. Arguments on the impact of AI contribution in the African setting were dealt with in various literature from a different perspective. The viewpoints touch a range of areas that will trigger potential contentions among the research communities. One argument presented by the World Bank with respect to the digital divide that developing countries (listed some countries and that includes Ethiopia) has the portion of occupations that could experience significant automation is higher and a lot of jobs have already disappeared [9]. On the other side, researchers promote the power of AI in the area of agriculture to enhance the yield of the farmers where eighty-five percent of the population is involved in farming. Another research [10] states that sound AI for Africa will only be ensured when policymakers are cognizant of key dimensions such as gender equality, cultural and linguistic diversity, and labor market shift. The authors further note that when sound policies are in place African nations will be able to build socially beneficial and inclusive ecosystems that mirror the reality on the ground. Similarly, Hagerty and Rubinov state that while AI technologies have the potential to fix tremendous problems across diverse socio-economic sectors and improve life, the benefits come with the risk of entrenched and amplified social inequality [11]. Notwithstanding the position held by [8, 12] identified three discontent with AI basically rooted in the historical construction of race and ethnicity. First, a manifestation of racial and gender bias within AI technology. Second, is the tendency of commoditizing the human experience. Third, geopolitical issues in relation to the arms race and global leadership. These discontents are behind the notions of 'data colonialism' and 'digital colonialism' and the discourse surrounding it.

Eventually, the work of Adams [12] posits that the observed discontents would be reconciled considering ethical principles that would govern the development and applications of AI technologies. Implicitly, when ethical issues are regarded as design considerations, then AI systems are deemed to be decolonized making itself free from historical biases embedded in the technology. Although favorable responses are attained in relation to the extent of openness of AI systems in the current study, Nelson [13] also argues that AI systems suffer from Algorithmic and data bias which are not readily visible by the average user group.

Furthermore, to alleviate the observed potential bias and to align AI to the mores of society, other research [14] stressed the need to identify societal values and consider them as design parameters in order to come up with responsible AI systems. As a continuation of the previously mentioned work [14] propositions of developing value-oriented AI systems, the work by [15] recommended ethical principles required to capture and embed in AI systems. The views transpired by a number of scholars, some of them already cited in this study, signal that the views scholars at Addis Ababa University hold is likely to be shaped on two groundings. First, apparently, those who are close to the technology are already aware of the biases and pitfalls inherent in AI systems. This group of scholars has a strong theoretical and practical basis to oppose the hasty adoption of AI in the socioeconomic arena. Second, still, a number of scholars lack adequate awareness and knowledge about AI systems. As the conventional IT and the modern AI-based communication technologies are cross-cutting and impact all sectors and educational programs, educators and researchers at higher educational institutions need to have a solid understanding of the technology along with the intended and unintended consequences it may cause before taking a position without a sound understanding.

5 Conclusion

Arguably, mixed views were observed among influential persons around the world surrounding AI technologies. For years, the academic and research communities held diverse views on matters pertaining to AI. This study aimed to understand the dominant view of scholars at Addis Ababa University regarding the potential benefits of AI in the Ethiopian and African socio-economic arena. The overall outcome of the study along the six dimensions AI indicators revealed a favorable attitude and perceptions about the AI systems. Nevertheless, regarding the potential colonization, decolonization rhetoric, and in relation to the openness and explainability of the AI system, the study revealed divergent outcomes as compared to prior studies. Therefore, policymakers in Ethiopia who are currently advocating AI aggressively through the establishment of AI institutes need to work with universities and research centers to clarify the clouded conceptions of AI through intellectual dialogue, research symposiums, and workshops.

References

1. Shin, D.: The effects of explainability and causability on perception, trust, and acceptance: implications for explainable AI. Int. J. Hum. Comput. Stud. **1**(146), 102551 (2021)
2. Bean, R.: Why fear of disruption is driving investment in AI. MIT Sloan Manag. Rev. (2019)
3. Zhang, B., Dafoe, A.: US public opinion on the governance of artificial intelligence. In: Proceedings of the AAAI/ACM Conference on AI, Ethics, and Society 2020, pp. 187–193, 7 February 2020
4. Ilieva, R.: Contemporary tendencies in higher education–application of artificial intelligence. In: SHS Web of Conferences 2021, vol. 111, p. 01009. EDP Sciences (2021)
5. Frankenfield, J.: Investopedia. Artificial Intelligence (AI) (2021)
6. Righetti, L., Madhavan, R., Chatila, R.: Unintended consequences of biased robotic and artificial intelligence systems [ethical, legal, and societal issues]. IEEE Robot. Autom. Mag. **26**(3), 11–3 (2019)
7. Times Higher Education. https://www.timeshighereducation.com/student/best-universities/best-universities-africa. Accessed 21 Dec 2021
8. Birhane, A.: Algorithmic Colonization of Africa. Scripted **17**(2) (2020)
9. World Bank: World development report 2016: Digital dividends (2016). https://www.worldbank.org/en/publication/wdr2016. Accessed 12 Nov 2021
10. Gwagwa, A., Kraemer-Mbula, E., Rizk, N., Rutenberg, I., De Beer, J.: Artificial Intelligence (AI) deployments in Africa: benefits, challenges and policy dimensions. Afr. J. Inf. Commun. **26**, 1–28 (2020)
11. Hagerty, A., Rubinov, I.: Global AI ethics: a review of the social impacts and ethical implications of artificial intelligence. arXiv preprint arXiv:1907.07892 (2019)
12. Adams, R.: Can artificial intelligence be decolonized? Interdiscip. Sci. Rev. **46**, 1–2 (2021)
13. Nelson, G.: Bias in artificial intelligence. N. C. Med. J. **80**(4), 220–222 (2019)
14. Dignum, V.: Responsible artificial intelligence: designing AI for human values. ITU J. ICT Discov. Spec. Issue **1**, 25 (2017)
15. Floridi, L., Cowls, J., King, T.C., Taddeo, M.: How to design AI for social good: seven essential factors. Sci. Eng. Ethics **26**(3), 1771–1796 (2020). https://doi.org/10.1007/s11948-020-00213-5

MoReXAI - A Model to Reason About the eXplanation Design in AI Systems

Niltemberg de Oliveira Carvalho(✉), Andréia Libório Sampaio, and Davi Romero de Vasconcelos

Universidade Federal do Ceará, Campus de Quixadá, Ceará, Brazil
niltemberg@gmail.com
https://www.quixada.ufc.br/

Abstract. The interest in systems that use machine learning has been growing in recent years. Some algorithms implemented in these intelligent systems hide their fundamental assumptions, input information and parameters in black box models that are not directly observable. The adoption of these systems in sensitive and large-scale application domains involves several ethical issues. One way to promote these ethics requirements is to improve the explainability of these models. However, explainability may have different goals and content according to the intended audience (developers, domain experts, and end-users. Some explanations does not always represent the requirements of the end-users, because developers and users do not share the same social meaning system, making it difficult to build more effective explanations. This paper proposes a conceptual model, based on Semiotic Engineering, which explores the problem of explanation as a communicative process, in which designers and users work together on requirements on explanations. A Model to Reason about the eXplanation design in Artificial Intelligence Systems (MoReXAI) is based on a structured conversation, with promotes reflection on subjects such as Privacy, Fairness, Accountability, Equity and Explainability, aiming to help end-users understand how the systems work and supporting the explanation design system. The model can work as an epistemic tool, given the reflections raised in the conversations related to the topics of ethical principles, which helped in the process of raising important requirements for the design of the explanation.

Keywords: Semiotic Engineering · Ethics · Explanations · Artificial Intelligence

1 Introduction

In recent years, interest in Machine Learning (ML) systems has grown. One of the major challenges for the adoption of these systems in some contexts is that

This work is partially supported by the FUNCAP projects 04772314/2020.

H. Degen and S. Ntoa (Eds.): HCII 2022, LNAI 13336, pp. 130–148, 2022.
https://doi.org/10.1007/978-3-031-05643-7_9

many of the mathematical models implemented in these intelligent systems hide their fundamental assumptions, input information and parameters in black box models that are not directly observable, requiring specific techniques to improve the interpretation of the generated outputs [31].

EXplainable Artificial Intelligence (XAI) refers to a field of study of Artificial Intelligence (AI) that investigates techniques to improve the interpretability or explainability of machine learning models [28]. An interpretable system is one whose operations are understandable to humans, either through inspection of the system or some explanation produced during its operation. [6].

Current XAI tools do not fully capture the types of explanations many people want due to the complexity of the algorithms behind AI systems. Furthermore, there is a variety of audiences for which this explanation is intended. AI experts, domain experts and end-users need different levels of explanation and have different goals regarding the explainability of AI models [8]. For example, an AI expert seeks to improve explainability to obtain better performance from the algorithms, while domain experts seek explanation to improve confidence and gain greater knowledge about how the input data relates to the generated outputs [30]. In the context of end-users, explanations have several objectives: to improve transparency, reliability, trust, identify discriminatory bias and improve privacy awareness, given that the explanation helps users to assess the privacy of their data, revealing which of these data are being used in algorithmic decision making [27].

In addition to these objectives, the right to an explanation has already been regulated in several countries. These laws provide for the right to explanation, in the case of fully automated decisions that may have an impact on the life of the data subject.

Although the field of research on explainability of AI algorithms is not new, the opacity of machine learning algorithms brings new challenges in the quest to unravel the interior of these black boxes, or even to look for relationships between the input data and the outputs generated by these models. A lot of research has focused on technologies to visualize or expose the structures, features or decisions of these algorithms, or even the large data sets on which they are trained. These "explainable" systems usually present a simplified version of complex computational architecture, without providing evidence that justifies the use of the system or that it is effective [29]. According to [10], there is a gap between theories of construction of computing and theories of use of computing, and they propose the use of Semiotic Engineering Theory to explore the problem of explanations as a communicative process, in which designers and users are integrated into this process.

Semiotic Engineering (EngSem) is a theory based on communication. The Designer communicates to the user, through the system interface, who the user is, what problems he can solve, and how he should interact with the system [12]. For this communication to be effective, the designer needs to include in this communication the social meaning of the systems being designed, taking into account objectives, contexts of use, cultural and ethical aspects of the target audience. Often this social meaning is not thought of by AI developers, requiring a mediated process by another field of study, such as HCI. Reflect on the social meaning of AI systems, and include pragmatic thinking in the process of developing these systems and thinking about how they can affect end-users directly or indirectly [7].

The goal of this paper is to propose a model to support the design of explanations in AI systems. To this end, we promote reflection among stakeholders about the social meaning of AI systems, based on conversation topics on ethical principles and explanations, during the process of developing these AI models. The idea is that this reflection works as an epistemic tool for the design of explanations.

In Sect. 2 we present the theoretical foundations, the bibliography that support the construction of the model and related works. In Sect. 3 we present how the model was defined, specifying each of its elements. In Sect. 4 we present a case study, in which we apply the model in the context of developing a recommender system, and finally, in Sect. 5, some important points of discussion regarding the model and the conclusion in Sect. 6.

2 Foundations and Related Works

In this section we briefly introduce the key points of the foundation theory and background work that, has provided us with insights on either the problem we want to address, or the solution we propose.

2.1 Ethical Principles and Explainable Artificial Intelligence (XAI)

The growing advances in the area of AI and its increasing use in people's daily lives, has brought a lot of ethical discussions, in view of its increasing influence, in the most varied contexts. Thus, governments, intergovernmental organizations, private companies, professional associations, advocacy groups and multistakeholder initiatives that are related to these technologies have created, updated, or adopted a set of unethical principles for AI [17].

The goals for each of these sectors of society are varied. Civil society and multistakeholder documents [2,23,32,38] can serve to set a supporting agenda or set a direction for ongoing discussions, as well as establish a code of ethics and conduct for computing professionals. In government [13], these principles are often presented as part of an overall national AI strategy. In the private sector [20,21,25], the intention is to apply better governance for the organization's internal development and use of AI technology, as well as communicating its objectives to other relevant stakeholders, including customers and regulators.

Some authors carried out bibliographic reviews on ethical principles for AI, and defined sets of key themes, or main dimensions for these principles [9,17,18]. Explainability appears as one of the very important dimensions, from this it becomes easier to verify the adequacy of other ethical principles such as: privacy, accountability, fairness, reliability and safety.

Reflecting about these principles can happen within certain stages of the ML model development process. The development life cycle of ML models is divided into two major stages: one data-centric (data collection, data preparation and feature engineering) and another model-centric (training, testing and inferences) [37].

An example of data-centric development can be seen in [19]. They proposed data sheets for data sets, in which each data set is accompanied by a fact sheet that documents its motivation, composition, collection process, recommended uses, etc. Data sheets facilitate communication between data set creators and consumers and encourage the machine learning community to prioritize transparency and accountability, mitigate unwanted biases, facilitate greater reproducibility of results and help researchers and professionals to select the most appropriate data sets for the chosen tasks, considering that the characteristics of these data sets will influence the behavior of the model [19]. In this sense, data sheets help in the process of reflection, assessment of risk or potential harm and usage implications, as well as they can be valuable for policymakers, consumer advocates, individuals within the data set and those who may be affected by trained machine learning models [19].

In the model-centric stage, the model cards proposed by [26], are used to record reports and evaluate ML models, in addition to traditional evaluation metrics. In the structure of the model cards, it is possible, from a human-centered perspective [34], to record evaluations carried out in the construction of the model taking into account population, cultural, demographic and phenotypic groups. Model cards allow stakeholders to assess ethical, bias and fair issues, bringing varied perspectives to serve everyone involved in the project. Including group analysis as part of the reporting procedure prepares stakeholders to begin assessing fairness and including future machine learning system outcomes. Thus, in addition to supporting decision-making processes to determine the suitability of a given machine learning model in a given context, model reporting is an approach to transparent and trusted responsible practices in machine learning.

In the context of end-users, explanations may seek to achieve certain goals such as: (i) improving transparency to help users understand how the model works; (ii) improve reliability from assurance that the model will act as intended, generating reliable outputs in real-world scenarios, thus improving users' confidence in the system and its predictions; (iii) help end-users inspect whether systems are biased or have any discriminatory biases; and (iv) can also improve privacy awareness, given that explanation helps users evaluate the privacy of their data by revealing which of that data is being used in [27]. In addition to these goals, improving explainability can assist with auditability and accountability for damages caused by predictions generated in the context of users, and verification of compliance with regulatory standards. This list of goals is not exhaustive, nor are they exclusive to these types of users, and intersections can be found between the objectives of explainable AI and other types of users.

The above set of end-user explainability goals served as a basis for building the proposed model, presented in Sect. 3.

2.2 Semiotic Engineering

Semiotic Engineering (EngSem) is a theory that allows us to understand the phenomena involved in the design, use and evaluation of an interactive system [12]. The user's interaction with the system is seen as a conversation between the designer and the user, through the interface, at the moment the user makes use of it. The interface communicates to the user the designer's vision regarding who it is intended for, which problems it can solve and how to interact with it.

EngSem is grounded in Semiotics, and its ontology comprises the processes of signification and communication, the interlocutors involved in this process, and the HCI design space [12]. Signification is the process through which the expression and content of signs are established based on social and cultural conventions known to the people who will use them. Communication is the process through which people, using these signs, produce messages in order to express certain contents [12]. In this sense, culture influences human communication, considering the common sharing of signs and meanings that converge in the form of patterns of representation, used in the production and exchange of messages.

The HCI design space is structured in: context, sender, receiver, message, code and channel [22]. To design the meta-message, the designer must make decisions about each element of this model in order to identify: who are the interlocutors (receiver and sender) and what aspects of limitations, motivations, beliefs, and preferences should be taken into account for the benefit of meta-communication; what is the context of communication and what elements of interaction (psychological, sociocultural, technological, etc.) must be processed by the system; what is the communication code and how can or should be used to support efficient metacommunication; what is the available channel for designer-user metacommunication and what is the message that the designer must tell users, that is, what is the designer's communicative intention.

The designer has an active role in the interaction, considering that he/she is the interlocutor and must help users understand the meta-message contained in the interface. For this, he must reflect about the types of strategies he should use, the signs he can project on the interface, and the consequences that the limitations of the computational meanings bring to the interaction [3,11]. For this, he/she uses epistemic tools [1,5,33,35] that allow him/her to reflect on issues related to metacommunication artifacts and compare different proposed solutions.

Therefore, the process of interface design is a communicative act, in which the designer must make decisions about the solution that will be used to compose the interface (definition of signs and signification systems), it is necessary to have a better understanding of who the users are, their activities, experiences, values, and expectations, to allow a better transmission of the meta-message, from the interaction with the system. The designer has an active role in the interaction, considering that he/she is the interlocutor and must help users understand the meta-message contained in the interface. For this, it should reflect on the types of strategies it should use, the signs it can project onto the interface and the consequences that the limitations of computational meanings bring to the interaction [3,11].

2.3 Related Works

Design Based on EngSem. The work [4], is an example of the use of Semiotic Engineering to address ethical and social responsibility issues in the production of digital artifacts. They proposed an extension of the metacommunication template, an artifact used in Semiotic Engineering, to support human-centered design, in order that directly address moral responsibility and ethical issues. This extension works as an epistemic tool and can be used to create and elaborate knowledge related to these issues. The idea is to bring into the construction of the metacommunication message the vision not only of the designer, but of all those involved in the process of developing digital technology. The main actor is no longer "I" and becomes "We". The questions used to build the meta-message are now answered by all stakeholders, adding questions at each design step that bring an ethical reflection about the product they develop and how this technology can affect users.

Explanation Design with an End-Users Focus. There is recent work on explanation design with an end-users focus, for example in [15] they propose guidelines to improve the transparency of AI algorithms. The content of an explanation (what to explain) is elicited from the following steps: capturing the mental model of AI experts and what they consider ideal for users; capture of users' mental model; and target mental model synthesis, which the main components of the expert's mental model that are most relevant to users, and the level of detail preferred by them, are selected. However, there is no promotion of a reflection on the social aspects involved in AI systems. Furthermore, MoReXAI promotes a conversation so that decisions about what and how to explain are made together with end-users, AI experts and HCI experts.

In [29] the authors point out that there is a need for use-inspired human-focused guidelines for XAI. They propose a "Self-Explanation Scorecard", which can help developers understand how they can empower users by enabling self-explanation. In addition, they present a set of empirically-grounded, user-centered design principles that may guide developers to create successful explainable systems. In this work, we also use an approach involving end-users, however, we use communication focused design, where users and developers discuss explanations in a previously structured discussion model.

In [24] the authors present the development process of a multiperspective, user-centric tool for machine learning interpretability called Explain-ML. The tool was designed to implement a workflow in which the user can interactively perform the lifecycle steps of an ML model. For each project, it can create multiple runs, changing the model's definition and optimization settings of hyper-parameters, and generating a set of views that convey aspects of the model, the model's training data set and also instance-specific information. These views act as explanations for the model as it is designed to provide different perspectives that complement each other (global, database and local), which help the user to interpret the results of the model. A qualitative study was carried out to analyze in depth the users' perspective and perceptions of the tool. Based on an analysis of the results obtained in the evaluation of users' experience with Explain-ML, they observed potential relevance to meet the principles for designing Interactive Machine Learning interfaces [14], as well as consolidating them.

Users are the primary audiences for explanations in recommender systems. Explanations in this context usually reflect the goals that the designer wants to achieve with that explanation, such as: transparency, trust, scrutiny, persuasion, efficiency, effectiveness, and user satisfaction [36]. In [30], the authors propose to evaluate explanations of Facebook advertising recommendations using the semiotic inspection method, grounded in EngSem. They observe that although the explanations use good user-centered design practices, there are disruptions in interface communication due to the lack of meaning sharing of signs used in the explanation. Furthermore, users and designers have different goals with the explanations presented. Users are often concerned with ethical issues.

Explanation Design with an End-Users and EngSem Focus. Like our research, [16] is about XAI for end-users of AI systems. They argue that is need to discuss XAI early in the AI-system design process and with all stakeholders. They aimed at investigating how to operationalize the discussion about XAI scenarios and opportunities among designers and developers of AI and its end-users. They took the Semiotic Engineering as the theoretical background and the Signifying Message as our conceptual tool to structure the different dimensions that should be considered for XAI scenarios discussion.

3 The Model for Reasoning About AI Explanation Design

3.1 Model Questions

From the literature review related to the sets of unethical principles, those that are related to explainability were selected, based on the users' objectives, they are: **Privacy and Human Control(T1):, Responsibility and Accountability (T2):, Reliability and Security (T3):, Transparency and Explainability (T4):** e **Fairness, equity and non-discrimination (T5):**.

After this definition, we mapped them with the question sets addressed in the data sheets proposed in [19], and with the structure of the template cards proposed in [26], and the questions suggested by [7]. Then, we propose the following set of questions that act as a guide for MoReXAI. They are:

- **P1:** For what purpose was the data set created? Was there a specific task in mind? Was there a specific gap that needed to be filled? (T1)

- **P2:** What do the instances that make up the data set represent? Are there different types of instances? Are relationships between individual instances made explicit (e.g., user's movie ratings, social media links)? (T1, T3, T5)
- **P3:** Does the data set represent all instances, or is it a sample of a larger set? If it is a sample, what was the sampling strategy? (T3, T5)
- **P4:** Is there any information missing from individual instances? What strategy was used to balance the data set? How was this strategy validated? Are there errors, noise sources, or redundancies in the data set? (T3, T2, T5)
- **P5:** Do data sets remain constant or can they be modified or deleted over time? (T3)
- **P6:** Is the data set related to people? Does it contain data that could be considered confidential or sensitive? Does it contain data that, if viewed directly, could be offensive, insulting, threatening, or can cause anxiety? (T1, T2, T5)
- **P7:** Does the data set identify any sub populations (by age, gender)? If yes, how are these sub populations identified and how are they distributed in the data set? (T1, T3, T5)
- **P8:** Is it possible to identify individuals, directly or indirectly, from the data set? (T1, T2)
- **P9:** How was the data collection done? What mechanisms or procedures were used? How were these mechanisms or procedures validated? Who was involved in the data collection process? (T1, T2, T3, T4, T5)
- **P10:** Have the individuals in question been notified of the data collection? Did they consent to the collection and use of their data? How was consent sought? If consent has been obtained, have mechanisms been provided to revoke your consent in the future or for certain uses? (T1, T2)
- **P11:** Over what period of time was the data collected? Does this period of time correspond to the period of creation of the data associated with the instances? (T1, T3, T5)
- **P12:** Have ethical review processes been carried out (e.g. by an institutional review board)? (T1, T2, T3)
- **P13:** Has an analysis of the potential impact of the dataset and its use on data subjects been carried out (e.g. a data protection impact analysis)? (T1, T2, T5)
- **P14:** Is there anything about the composition of the dataset or the way it was collected and pre-processed/cleaned/labeled that could affect future uses? Is there anything a prospective user should know to avoid uses that could result in unfair treatment of individuals or groups or other undesirable harm? Is there anything a future user could do to mitigate this unwanted damage? (T2, T5)
- **P15:** Are there tasks for which the dataset should not be used? (T2)
- **P16:** What kind of ML model is being developed? Could you explain how it works? (T4)
- **P17:** Which algorithm is used to train the model? What is the degree of interpretability of the algorithm? Could you explain how it works? (T4)
- **P18:** What is the main internal use of the model? Who are the intended users that the model will serve? Any other usage scenarios outside this scope? (T1, T3)

- **P19:** Can the model affect demographic or phenotype groups in any way? What influence can these factors have on model performance? How is the influence of these factors on model performance evaluated? (T2, T3, T4, T5)
- **P20:** Can the instruments or the data set collection environment somehow influence the model's result? What influence can these factors have on model performance? How is the influence of these factors on model performance evaluated? (T1, T2, T3, T5)
- **P21:** What model performance metrics are being reported and why were they selected over other performance metrics? How are they calculated? (T3)
- **P22:** What data sets were used to evaluate the model? Why were these data sets used? How was the data pre-processed for evaluation? (T1, T2, T3, T5)
- **P23:** Are quantitative analyzes performed against disaggregated population subgroups of the data set? How did the model perform for each factor? How did the model perform in relation to the intersection of the factors evaluated? (T2, T3, T5)
- **P24:** What risks may be present in using the model? What risk mitigation strategies were used during model development? Are there any intended uses for the model that are ethically worrisome? (T2)
- **P25:** Is the model scalable? How to ensure that the initial model trained and evaluated, when applied in the real context of users, maintains the same results obtained previously? Can the model be transferred from the intended context to another? (T2, T3)
- **P26:** Is there documentation related to the data sets? And what about the model? (T2)
- **P27:** What is explainability? What is the purpose of an explanation? Who is this explanation for? How is it presented? When should it be presented? Where should it be presented? (T4)

3.2 MoReXAI Structure

The conceptual model proposed in this research aims to extract requirements for the design of explanations, based on structured conversations between stakeholders. It was based on Jakobson's communication model [22], thus having all the elements previously proposed by him:

- **Context:** involves the application domain, the topics of conversation (ethical principles and explanation) and how they can be impacted during the machine learning model development process. Thus, the conversation takes into account the collection and pre-processing of data, training, testing and evaluation of the ML model.
- **Interlocutors:** are all the stakeholders of the ML system under development. They can play the role of programmers, data scientists, academics, end-users, etc. It is important to capture the roles of the interlocutors in the conversation, in order that, in the analysis, it is possible to identify the perspective of each stakeholder on the topic discussed. Another important interlocutor in this process is the mediator, as it is, he/she who will initiate and lead the

conversation between the stakeholders, based on a set of pre-defined questions in the planning of application of the model. As it is a multidisciplinary conversation, it is up to the mediator to make interventions, in order to verify that the understanding of what is being talked about is understandable for everyone and to ask the sender to seek new ways to explain the subject being addressed.

- **Channel:** corresponds to the hardware and software where the conversation will run. As this is a conceptual model, it has not yet been defined which tools will best support the conversation within the model, taking into account that it can happen synchronously or asynchronously.
- **Message:** The message and model component that contains the communicated content. It is related to the typical conversations (ethical principles and explanation) that are proposed in the model. The set of messages exchanged from the answers to the questions raised by the mediator, bring a multidisciplinary perspective of the stakeholders, regarding how they think about ethical principles within the application domain, bringing to this conversation ways to explain the approaches used and that are understandable to those involved in the project. The message has the following structure:
  - **Sender:** identifier of the person sending the message. This could be, for example, the name of the person speaking and their role within the model development process.
  - **Receiver:** identifier of the person receiving the message. This message can be directed to everyone in the discussion, or to specific people.
  - **Date/Time:** date and time when the message was sent.
  - **Question:** This element is related to the development of the ML system, which is related to the application context and the typical conversation (ethical principles and explanation) as defined in Sect. 3.
  - **Answer:** text written in natural language that corresponds to the answer to a question in the model.
- **Code:** natural language is used.

3.3 MoReXai Use

Using the MoReXAI model involves 3 main steps:

1. **Planning:** This step is carried out by the person who will mediate the discussion and provides for the following actions:
   (a) meetings with the development team to obtain a vision of the project being developed, to know the domain, the context of use, which step of development it is in, which algorithms will be used, which database will be used to train the algorithm and who will be the users of the system.
   (b) selection of questions that will be used in the discussion.
   (c) Selection and recruitment of discussion participants.

(d) Interview with the participants: interviews are carried out with the recruited participants to learn about, in the case of the technical team, the time of development of ML applications, experience on the ML explanation project, what their role within the project. About users, what they use in this app and what they know about AI.

2. **Conversation - Exchange of Messages:** The mediator starts the conversation by introducing everyone in the group, presents the context of the application to be discussed and the dynamics of the conversation. Then the mediator leads the conversation, following the script of questions until all are exhausted. It is suggested that this step occurs in at least two moments in order that the conversation does not become tiring for the participants.
This step can happen in synchronous meetings (online or face-to-face) or in an asynchronous conversation through online discussion tools (e.g. WhatsApp, Telegram or email).
At the end, we seek to hold a focus group to capture general perceptions about what was discussed. The mediator should summarize what was discussed and close. These activities must be recorded (with everyone's permission) for further data analysis.
3. **Analysis of the results:** in this step, the collected data are organized, analyzed and a report is written with the directions obtained from the conversations for the design of explanations.

4 Case Study

We carried out an exploratory case study to observe the use of the model in a real context of developing an AI system.

The study was carried out during the development of a service recommendation system of the Government of the State of Ceará that will work within the Ceará App application. Ceará App is a mobile application with the objective of offering the main government services quickly and remotely in a single location. Through it, users can access services such as: 24-h online service for healthcare professionals, scheduling Covid-19 tests and vaccinations, issuing negative and regularity certificates, applying for a driver's license (CNH) and requesting 2nd via or renewal of CNH, advertisement, search and purchase of family farming products, among others.

4.1 Case Study Planning

The case study aimed to explore the use of the model in the real context of developing an AI system. In addition, to observe how the model can contribute to the design of explanations in the context of the application from the reflections on ethical principles within the development process. Evaluate the set of questions used in the model and their relationship with ethical principles. Also evaluate the process of applying the model, taking into account the roles of the interlocutors and the synchronous way in which the model was applied. The service recommendation system is in the initial step of development. Developers have a database of user accesses to government services, collected over a period of 3 months, with more than 130,000 data records. The database contains service access date, service name, user identifier, device brand-model, device type (smartphone, tablet), device platform (Android, iOS), operating system version, Ceará App on the day of access and SDK version. Developers are using Apple's Turicreate framework and mentioned that they are testing some algorithms like DBScan, K-nodes, K-prototype, K-means. The model questions were selected based on the application context and the development step it is in (Table 1). The conversation within the model was divided into two steps, one using questions focused on the datasets, and the other more focused on the training, testing and evaluation steps of the ML model. The two researchers involved in the development of the recommender system and three users of the App were recruited.

Table 1. Set of questions addressed in each meeting according to the step of the application development cycle

Development stage	Questions
Data-centric	(P1), (P2), (P3), (P4), (P5), (P6), (P7), (P8), (P9), (P10), (P11), (P12), (P26)
Centered on the ML model	(P16), (P17), (P18), (P19), (P20), (P21), (P24), (P26), (P27)

4.2 Model Application

From the interviews, it was verified that the researchers have experience in the area of development of ML systems, being a Ph.D. in computing, and an undergraduate student of the software engineering course, which we will refer to as (D1) and (D2) respectively. Developers are working together at all stages of the proposed system's development cycle and reported that they had not yet thought about explanations to users, or even about ethical principles. The three users (U1, U2 and U3) had experience in using the app, using services such as: scheduling exams, registering for Covid-19 vaccination, in addition to scheduling a second license. As for knowledge about AI, U1 and U2 said they had little knowledge, U3 knows a little more about AI concepts.

The model application conversations took place in two meetings through Google Meet. In addition to the mediator, the conversation had the participation of an HCI professional, who assisted in the information collection process, writing down data that he thought was relevant during the conversation. A focus group was held in order to evaluate the model. On that occasion, questions were asked related to the importance of reflecting on ethical principles in the context of machine learning models, and whether this reflection can influence the process of development and use of these systems and assist in the design of explanations.

4.3 Results: Talking About Explanations

Analyzing the case study with MoReXAI, we performed a discourse analysis on the conversations. We extract requirements on the 6 points that should compose a good explanation project (why? what? when? how? where? for whom?) The collected data and the full report are available at the following link: https://bityli.com/jRXhT.

Por Que Explicar? Questions from the MoReXAI model, in various topics, led stakeholders to realize that explanations are important because: (i) they guarantee rights (U1: *"You use an application and you no longer want your data to be used. If the law guarantees that, you will want it, then the system will have to find a way to solve it. I know there are technical limitations but I was thinking about the whole thing as a user"*); (ii) improve satisfaction in using the recommender system (D1: *"...if the user is satisfied with that (the explanation), then a duty for the system, providing this joy to him/her, would be an additional source of information..."*); (iii) they help to increase trust (U1: *"...I think it is the issue of credibility, trust, as I just said so you don't think it's just marketing..."*) and (iv) allow greater control over the data that is used (U1: *"...depending on the type of data they request, I don't even continue and end up changing platforms, I go to another environment that does not have so much of my data"*).

Os usuários estavam interessados em saber o que foi levado em consideração para gerar a recomendação, quais dados foram usados e se esses dados estão protegidos, por exemplo: U3 disse: *"como foi chegado a esse resultado, com base em que, quais dados estão sendo usados pra lidar com isso?"*; Apesar disso um dos usuários não sentiu necessidade em conhecer como é o funcionamento interno do modelo de ML, U1 disse: *"Se tiver uma orientação geral talvez eu leia, mas se tiver algo muito técnico, mais aprofundado, eu como usuária que não sou da TI, eu acredito que não iria aprofundar a leitura da explicação não."*.

What to Explain? As for the content that explanations should contain, there were several suggestions. One suggestion was to explain how the recommendation was made and based on what data, or even why the user is viewing a particular recommendation. In the case of informing the data used to generate the recommendation, emphasize those that had the most relevance in this prediction. In this sense, U1 said: *"I thought of indicators (...) The basic elements that make up that relevance and recommendation calculation. (...) if we take Spotify, the most listened, the most downloaded, the most played. I think it is possible to have simple indicators that are easy to understand, in order that people who do not even know that there is an indicator, but understand that it was from what generated a recommendation"*

An important point raised is in the case of applications that are not public, they must inform users if the recommendation is something related to marketing, if it is a sponsored recommendation, and say why, and based on what, they are recommending that product/service.

It was also suggested to insert in the explanation which date the recommended one was generated within the model. Because there may be recommendations based on old data. Furthermore, in the case of recommendations that consider these profiles similar, the importance of explaining the profile of the user group that is being used to associate with the profile of the person receiving the recommendation was discussed.

Still on what to explain, the model provided a conversation about inserting examples known to users in the explanations. In this sense U3 said: *"Yes, and similar to that recommendation system that we already have in some applications, based on what I always do, more videos will appear, for example on YouTube, similar to what I always see, why will they interest me, in this case will Ceará app be based on my history of use of the Ceará app, will there always be some function related to this use, similar, which is the next step, right?"*

How to Explain? There was talk about the explanation project: participants recognize that explanations should not be long and should be presented gradually, whenever possible using examples, and could also be presented in conversational forms, for example U3 said: *"I think, me as a user, having a little conversation, like a bot, a conversation with a little robot, some animation, as if it were a really informal conversation, could be more playful, even for lay users... and not that it was a boring reading that they most of the time they will not read"*.

Where Should These Explanations Be? Some places were suggested where the explanations should appear, being able to come along with the recommendations, staying in a specific place of the application where users can make this query whenever they feel the need. The place where the explanations should be presented came from questions related to the terms of authorization for the use of the data. For example, D1 said: *"I think it should be shown along with the recommendation, have a link on the side, understand more how this recommendation was generated, for example."* and D2 said: *"(...) to be available in some session of the application in case he/she curiously wants to go read it again"*.

When to Explain? It was also discussed when to explain, the participants had a consensus that the explanations should be presented close to the recommendations (in the case of a recommendation system). In this sense, D2 said: *"it has to appear right away to the user, at the moment he/she starts the application and also be available in some session of the application in case he/she curiously wants to read it again."* and U3 said: *"it could be a step by step when initializing the system, like a tutorial on how to move and within that tutorial, it is saying that this data will be used, what it will be used for and how it will be used, and it will be stored there for when he/she wants to look, or on some screen, right"*.

The idea of configurable controls for viewing explanations also came up. In this sense, U3 said: *"(...) I think it should be a configuration, like, when we are going to make a configuration, we allow it or not, for example on the cell phone, we allow or not the use of mobile data, in a certain situation, I think it should be in the profile, when the user goes to see the configuration. Because by law it has to be available to the user at any time, all information (...)"*

To Whom to Explain? During the conversation, it became very clear among all the participants that the explanations in the context of the recommender system should focus on the users who use this system.

5 Discussion

5.1 About the Epistemic Character of the MoReXAI

The case study carried out allowed us to reflect on elements of the model as well as its use. Leading developers to reflect on the artifact they are developing together with users is quite rich to build more effective explanations. The developers brought testimonials about the model's questions and how they can influence their development process, as observed in D2's statements: *"...I confess that most of the questions expanded my vision a little. I think a mistake I make a lot as a developer is to think only as a developer, and I forget that what I am doing is for a user, it is for a person, then these questions you asked helped me a lot to reflect on what I am working on and other concerns that you need to have"*, and in the speech of D1: *"I think these meetings were very relevant, it changes people's view of some things that were usually already in a cast, so I am going to change the way I did things based on these meetings, because I am going to try to facilitate, or at least try to leave a framework of how to do these things that we were talking about here, since I agree that they are good things"*.

In addition, the model brought a new look to users about the systems they use. For example, U1 said: *"I found it super interesting, I had not stopped to think about how much recommender systems are present in the applications I use. I found this bias of the ethical issue super interesting, generally speaking only about data confidentiality, but the ethical framework, until reaching this data, before having this data, should have an ethical concern for its use. Often we only worry about the end when the data is already there and we do not have this worrying about ethics before"*.

Still on the epistemic character of the model, we noticed that the explanations given by developers to users, in a technical format, brought terms that are not suitable to be used in explanation, such as: *"...predictive model, database, relationship of a matrix..."*. At this time, the mediator had the role of helping to translate the developers' explanation to the users and also to check with the users if it was understood. We understand that it was a rich moment to know which terms should or should not be used in the explanations of the system under development.

5.2 Improvements to the MoReXAI

New step identification for the model: In the case study we inserted the Focus Group to get feedback on the model. However, we realized that it was a space for gathering important information that helped to elaborate requirements for the explanation project. Therefore, we decided to insert the Focus Group at the end of the conversation in order that there is this moment to summarize what was discussed and to make a closing.

We noticed that some questions of the model need to be better explained to users. One way to do this is to use general examples, preferably from another system known to the group. For example, in the case study, some conversations took place using the Netflix movie recommendation system as an example. Therefore, we realize that it is important to guide the mediator to add examples related to the questions and the unethical principles they support.

We had anticipated that the model would be mediated by someone familiar with the elements of the model and who would organize the conversation. Among the roles we envisage are: defining the scope of the application to be discussed, defining and inviting discussion participants, scheduling and conducting the discussion, analyzing and compiling the data collected. However, in the case study we realized that an important role of the mediator is to assist in the communication between developers and users. During the experiment, we noticed that the developer used technical terms a few times. In these cases, the mediator must carry out a "translation" of what was said, or even intervene in order that the developers seek other ways to explain it to the users, and the mediator must follow what is being said by the technicians and check if the users are understanding. This process is interesting to capture the meaning system shared by the group. At first, we thought the mediator was an expert in Human-Computer Interaction, but we realized that he/she also needs to have basic knowledge of AI systems.

6 Conclusão

We propose a conceptual model to support the elicitation of explanations in ML projects. We use an approach that involves user participation and is based on communication-centered design.

We conclude that users' statements related to ethical principles topics (privacy, security, responsibility, reliability, transparency, explainability, justice, equity and non-discrimination) generated important requirements for the explanation design. The model promoted the conversation about these principles and then suggested ideas for explanations for the interface, given by the user himself/herself. It was possible to talk about What, Why, How, When and Whom to explain.

In addition, we noticed the epistemic character of the model, as all the participants in the conversation said they had changed their view on the points that were addressed. The case study brought us the opportunity to reflect on the synchronous or asynchronous use of the proposed model. The fact that the two meetings were synchronous was quite rich, as the contact between the stakeholders allowed for greater involvement and engagement in the conversation. In addition, the mediator had the opportunity to provoke the participants in order that everyone participated by giving their opinion. On the other hand, the main advantage of asynchronous conversation is giving people time to reflect on the questions.

Although the case study did not allow more time for participants to reflect on the questions of the conversation, as the conversations were synchronous, we realized that the fact that we had an interview days before starting the conversations already led the participants to think about what we were talking about. In addition, as the conversations took place in two sections, there was time between one section and the other, in this case it was two days, for those involved to reflect on the issues.

In further studies, we intend to explore the use of an asynchronous tool, or even a mixed methodology with synchronous and asynchronous moments, which allows those involved to have time to reflect on the model's questions. Regardless of whether the conversations are synchronous or asynchronous, the mediator will have the role of maintaining the group's engagement in the conversation, through targeted messages, ensuring that everyone participates.

We imagine the use of the proposed model in an AI system construction scenario where there is an interest in designing explanations. In this context, we envision an HCI expert interacting with the AI team to work together on this challenge of designing explanations. This team will invite users to join the conversations. These conversations can happen multiple times, with different users. In this context, the model works as an epistemic tool that generates knowledge, considering that with each application by this team, even in different and varied contexts, stakeholders will be adding knowledge about the design of explanations.

References

1. de A. Barbosa, C.M., Prates, R.O., de Souza, C.S.: Identifying potential social impact of collaborative systems at design time. In: Baranauskas, C., Palanque, P., Abascal, J., Barbosa, S.D.J. (eds.) INTERACT 2007. LNCS, vol. 4662, pp. 31–44. Springer, Heidelberg (2007). https://doi.org/10.1007/978-3-540-74796-3_6
2. The IEEE Global Initiative on Ethics of Autonomous and Intelligent Systems: Ethically Aligned Design - A Vision for Prioritizing Human Well-being with Autonomous and Intelligent Systems, 1st edn. IEEE (2019). https://standards.ieee.org/content/ieee-standards/en/industry-connections/ec/autonomous-systems.html
3. Barbosa, S., Silva, B.: Interação humano-computador. Elsevier, Brasil (2010)
4. Barbosa, S.D.J., Barbosa, G.D.J., de Souza, C.S., Leitão, C.F.: A semiotics-based epistemic tool to reason about ethical issues in digital technology design and development. In: Proceedings of the 2021 ACM Conference on Fairness, Accountability, and Transparency, FAccT 2021, pp. 363–374. Association for Computing Machinery, New York, NY, USA (2021). https://doi.org/10.1145/3442188.3445900

5. Barbosa, S.D.J., de Paula, M.G.: Designing and evaluating interaction as conversation: a modeling language based on semiotic engineering. In: Jorge, J.A., Jardim Nunes, N., Falcão e Cunha, J. (eds.) DSV-IS 2003. LNCS, vol. 2844, pp. 16–33. Springer, Heidelberg (2003). https://doi.org/10.1007/978-3-540-39929-2_2
6. Biran, O., Cotton, C.: Explanation and justification in machine learning: a survey. In: IJCAI-17 Workshop on Explainable AI (XAI), vol. 8 (2017)
7. Brandão, R., Carbonera, J., de Souza, C., Ferreira, J., Gonçalves, B., Leitão, C.: Mediation challenges and socio-technical gaps for explainable deep learning applications (2019)
8. Brennen, A.: What do people really want when they say they want "explainable AI?" we asked 60 stakeholders. In: Extended Abstracts of the 2020 CHI Conference on Human Factors in Computing Systems, CHI EA 2020, pp. 1–7. Association for Computing Machinery, New York, NY, USA (2020). https://doi.org/10.1145/3334480.3383047
9. Burle, C., Cortiz, D.: Mapping principles of artificial intelligence (November 2019)
10. Carbonera, J., Gonçalves, B., de Souza, C.: O problema da explicação em inteligência artificial: consideraçõees a partir da semiótica. TECCOGS: Revista Digital de Tecnologias Cognitivas (17) (2018)
11. De Souza, C.S., Leitão, C.F.: Semiotic engineering methods for scientific research in HCI. Synth. Lect. Hum. Centered Inf. **2**(1), 1–122 (2009)
12. De Souza, C.S., Nardi, B.A., Kaptelinin, V., Foot, K.A.: The Semiotic Engineering of Human-Computer Interaction. MIT Press (2005)
13. (DIB), D.I.B.: AI Principles: Recommendations on the Ethical Use of Artificial Intelligence by the Department of Defense. Department of Defense (DoD) (2019). https://media.defense.gov/2019/Oct/31/2002204458/-1/-1/0/DIB_AI_PRINCIPLES_PRIMARY_DOCUMENT.PDF
14. Dudley, J.J., Kristensson, P.O.: A review of user interface design for interactive machine learning. ACM Trans. Interact. Intell. Syst. (TiiS) **8**(2), 1–37 (2018)
15. Eiband, M., Schneider, H., Bilandzic, M., Fazekas-Con, J., Haug, M., Hussmann, H.: Bringing transparency design into practice. In: 23rd International Conference on Intelligent User Interfaces, IUI 2018, pp. 211–223. Association for Computing Machinery, New York, NY, USA (2018). https://doi.org/10.1145/3172944.3172961
16. Ferreira, J.J., Monteiro, M.: Designer-user communication for XAI: an epistemological approach to discuss XAI design. arXiv preprint arXiv:2105.07804 (2021)
17. Fjeld, J., Achten, N., Hilligoss, H., Nagy, A., Srikumar, M.: Principled artificial intelligence: Mapping consensus in ethical and rights-based approaches to principles for AI. Berkman Klein Center Research Publication (2020-1) (2020)
18. Floridi, L.: AI4People-an ethical framework for a good AI society: opportunities, risks, principles, and recommendations. Mind. Mach. **28**(4), 689–707 (2018)
19. Gebru, T., et al.: Datasheets for datasets. arXiv preprint arXiv:1803.09010 (2018)
20. Google: AI at Google: our principles (2018). https://www.blog.google/technology/ai/ai-principles/
21. IBM: Everyday ethics for artificial intelligence (2019). https://www.ibm.com/watson/assets/duo/pdf/everydayethics.pdf
22. Jakobson, R.: Linguistics and poetics. In: Style in Language, pp. 350–377. MIT Press, MA (1960)
23. Future of Life Institute, F.: Asilomar AI principles (2017). https://futureoflife.org/ai-principles/

24. Lopes, B.G., Soares, L.S., Prates, R.O., Gonçalves, M.A.: Analysis of the user experience with a multiperspective tool for explainable machine learning in light of interactive principles. In: Proceedings of the XX Brazilian Symposium on Human Factors in Computing Systems, pp. 1–11 (2021)
25. Microsoft: Microsoft AI principles (2019). https://www.microsoft.com/en-us/ai/our-approach-to-ai
26. Mitchell, M., et al.: Model cards for model reporting. In: Proceedings of the Conference on Fairness, Accountability, and Transparency, FAT* 2019, pp. 220–229. Association for Computing Machinery, New York, NY, USA (2019). https://doi.org/10.1145/3287560.3287596
27. Mohseni, S.: Toward design and evaluation framework for interpretable machine learning systems. In: Proceedings of the 2019 AAAI/ACM Conference on AI, Ethics, and Society, AIES 2019, pp. 553–554. Association for Computing Machinery, New York, NY, USA (2019). https://doi.org/10.1145/3306618.3314322
28. Molnar, C.: Interpretable Machine Learning. Lulu.com (2020)
29. Mueller, S.T., et al.: Principles of explanation in human-AI systems. arXiv preprint arXiv:2102.04972 (2021)
30. de O. Carvalho, N., Sampaio, A.L., Monteiro, I.T.: Evaluation of Facebook advertising recommendations explanations with the perspective of semiotic engineering. In: Proceedings of the 19th Brazilian Symposium on Human Factors in Computing Systems, IHC 2020. Association for Computing Machinery, New York, NY, USA (2020). https://doi.org/10.1145/3424953.3426632
31. O'Neil, C.: Weapons of Math Destruction: How Big Data Increases Inequality and Threatens Democracy, 1st edn. Crown, New York (2016)
32. ACM Code of Ethics and Professional Conduct: ACM Code of Ethics and Professional Conduct. Association for Computing Machinery (ACM) (2018). https://www.acm.org/binaries/content/assets/about/acm-code-of-ethics-booklet.pdf
33. Sampaio, A.L.: Um Modelo para Descrever e Negociar Modificaçoes em Sistemas Web. Ph.D. thesis, PUC-Rio (2010)
34. Shneiderman, B.: Human-centered artificial intelligence: reliable, safe & trustworthy. Int. J. Hum. Comput. Interact. **36**(6), 495–504 (2020)
35. Silveira, M.S., Barbosa, S.D.J., de Souza, C.S.: Model-based design of online help systems. In: Jacob, R.J.K., Limbourg, Q., Vanderdonckt, J. (eds.) Computer-Aided Design of User Interfaces IV, pp. 29–42. Springer, Dordrecht (2005). https://doi.org/10.1007/1-4020-3304-4_3
36. Tintarev, N., Masthoff, J.: Explaining recommendations: design and evaluation. In: Ricci, F., Rokach, L., Shapira, B. (eds.) Recommender Systems Handbook, pp. 353–382. Springer, Boston, MA (2015). https://doi.org/10.1007/978-1-4899-7637-6_10
37. Toreini, E., et al.: Technologies for trustworthy machine learning: a survey in a socio-technical context. arXiv preprint arXiv:2007.08911 (2020)
38. UNI Global Union: Top 10 principles for ethical artificial intelligence. Nyon, Switzerland (2017)

(De)Coding Social Practice in the Field of XAI: Towards a Co-constructive Framework of Explanations and Understanding Between Lay Users and Algorithmic Systems

Josefine Finke, Ilona Horwath, Tobias Matzner, and Christian Schulz(✉)

Paderborn University, Warburger Straße 100, 33098 Paderborn, Germany
{Josefine.finke,christian.schulz}@uni-paderborn.de

Abstract. Advances in the development of AI and its application in many areas of society have given rise to an ever-increasing need for society's members to understand at least to a certain degree how these technologies work. Where users are concerned, most approaches in *Explainable Artificial Intelligence* (XAI) assume a rather narrow view on the social process of explaining and show an undifferentiated assessment of explainees' understanding, which mostly are considered passive recipients of information. The actual knowledge, motives, needs and challenges of (lay)users in algorithmic environments remain mostly missing. We argue for the consideration of explanation as a *social practice* in which explainer and explainee *co-construct* understanding jointly. Therefore, we seek to enable lay users to document, evaluate, and reflect on distinct AI interactions and correspondingly on how *explainable* AI actually is in their daily lives. With this contribution we want to discuss our methodological approach that enhances the documentary method by the implementation of 'digital diaries' via the mobile instant messaging app WhatsApp – the most used instant messaging service worldwide. Furthermore, from a theoretical stance, we examine the socio-cultural patterns of orientation that guide users' interactions with AI and their imaginaries of the technologies – a sphere that is mostly obscured and hard to access for researchers. Finally, we complete our paper with empirical insights by referring to previous studies that point out the relevance of perspectives on explaining and understanding as a *co-constructive* social practice.

Keywords: XAI · Social practice · Co-construction

1 Introduction

Advances in the development of Artificial Intelligence (AI) and its application in many areas of society have given rise to an ever-increasing need for society's members to understand at least to a certain degree how these technologies work. In this respect, the goal of making algorithms accessible, transparent, and interpretable to different groups of users lies at the heart of *Explainable Artificial Intelligence* (XAI). However, current concepts of XAI very often just address epistemic problems within computer science. Where

H. Degen and S. Ntoa (Eds.): HCII 2022, LNAI 13336, pp. 149–160, 2022.
https://doi.org/10.1007/978-3-031-05643-7_10

users are concerned, most approaches in XAI assume a rather narrow view on the social process of explaining and show an undifferentiated assessment of explainees' understanding, which mostly are considered passive recipients of information [33]. The actual knowledge, motives, needs and challenges of (lay)users in algorithmic environments remain mostly missing [30, 31]. Given the growing need of explainability and interpretability, interest in research on XAI from a social science perspective has increased tremendously in recent years. Previous work refers to social contexts mainly by drawing on the literature and using common examples of "use case scenarios". Empirical validation of these models in real-world contexts and analyses of the sociomaterial contexts in which human-machine interactions take place are rather seldomly performed [2, 25]. In addition, existing explanation methods are usually tailored for expert users, whereas lay users' perspectives remain unexplored [29], although they are the addressees of most applications of AI.

The question arises: Which needs have to be met in order to obtain successful and responsible applications? (How) do such needs for explanation develop across social roles and how do they relate to categories of difference and social inequality, such as gender, age, and socio-economic background? How do users' imaginaries of technology and algorithms shape the practices of usage? Furthermore, how can we as researchers adequately collect, evaluate and use such data?

In terms of the prevalent exclusion of and paternalistic behavior towards lay users and narrow empirical work on the ways and means in which people experience and perceive algorithms in their everyday lives, we argue for the consideration of explanation as a *social practice* in which explainer and explainee *co-construct* understanding jointly [33]. Therefore, we seek to enable lay users to document, evaluate, and reflect on distinct AI interactions and correspondingly on how *explainable* AI actually is in their daily lives.

With this contribution we want to discuss our methodological approach that enhances the documentary method [3] by the implementation of 'digital diaries' via the mobile instant messaging app WhatsApp – the most used instant messaging service worldwide.[1] Digital methods [15, 31, 32] have experienced an enormous upswing during the past years and most recently, mobile instant messaging services have become increasingly promising for researchers since the outbreak of the Covid-19 pandemic [7, 13, 17, 18, 37]. Nevertheless, the potential of WhatsApp, Signal and others remain rather unexplored.

From a theoretical stance, we examine the socio-cultural patterns of orientation that guide users' interactions with AI and their imaginaries of the technologies – a sphere that is mostly obscured and hard to access for researchers. Since mobile messaging apps serve to a high degree as "the fabric in which people weave their everyday mobile-mediated social interactions" [1], they are particularly promising in terms of communication between researcher and recipient as well as the documentation of diverse AI interactions that are, to a high extend, performed on mobile platforms. We complete our paper with empirical insights by referring to previous studies by Schulz [35] that point out the relevance of perspectives on explaining and understanding as a *co-constructive* social practice.

[1] With reference to WhatsApp [39] it currently holds more than two billion users in 180 countries.

We seek to contribute not only to the ongoing endeavours to exploit the potential of mobile messaging apps for social research [17, 18] but also to advance the methodological foundation of the documentary method in the process of its digitization, i.e. the digitization of its reconstructive approach in complex real world settings, in a way that preserves its epistemic qualities [24].

2 Method

In regard of the continuing prevalence of mobile instant messaging in people's increasingly digital livelyhoods and in consideration of technology that can only be understood in the practice of its use [26, 38], we chose a methodological approach that acknowledges the value of mobile instant messaging apps in the field of qualitative social science. In order to gain insights into the socio-material lifeworlds and to systematically access, document and analyze the data produced by real-world users, we developed a reconstructive methodological framework that draws on the documentary method by Bohnsack [3] and combines qualitative and quantitative analyses (see Fig. 1). The documentary method is a highly reflective and sequential empirical-methodological approach, which originated in the methodological tradition of Karl Mannheim's sociology of culture and knowledge, elaborated in the 1920s and revisited in field of ethnomethodology by Harold Garfinkel in the 1960s. In its present form, the documentary method is closely attributed to the work of Ralf Bohnsack, who – in reference to Mannheim, phenomenological sociology and (at least partially) the Chicago School – made it applicable for empirical research in the social sciences, most prominently in regard to interview and group discussion processes.

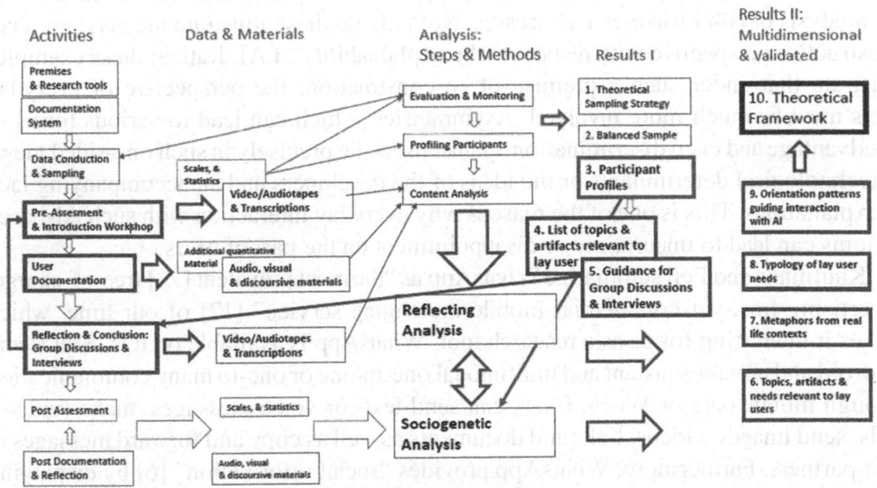

Fig. 1. Methodological framework

We have developed a mixed method approach that enables us to collect data *in situ*, over time, and obtain participants reflections. Thus, we will be able to tackle and analyze explicit as well as implicit knowledge guiding participants' interactions, as well as multi-layered social categories such as gender, age and class. Within this framework, up to a hundred participants are to record text, audio, and visual material regarding their everyday usage of algorithmic technologies and encounters with AI systems. Via the mobile instant messaging app WhatsApp participants create and share individual 'digital diaries' with us as researchers over a period of four weeks; supplemented by introductory talks beforehand. Based on the analysis of the diaries, we will then conduct interviews and focus groups in order to discuss common needs and challenges related to XAI.

When considering practices involving information technologies, a lot of the users' practices and in consequence their documentation will be influenced by the possibilities and impossibilities that these technologies afford. In this respect, interfaces play a central role, as users are confronted with very different interfaces in their everyday interactions with AI, which in turn are backed by different assumptions of developers. Nonetheless, and in the light of the reflections that we discuss in the introduction, technology should not be considered as mere conditions or even determinants of participants practices. Rather, as part of our co-constructive model, we amend Bohnsack's method to include Lucy Suchman's discussion of human-machine reconfigurations [39]. Based on ethnographic work with engineers, Suchman shows how machines and human practices mutually configure each other. We extend this approach to human-machine reconfigurations to users rather than engineers. Suchman shows that practices involving technologies do not only concern the actual technological affordances but also the *design imaginaries* of the persons involved. As we argue below in more detail, this has to be extended to the users' imaginaries of technology, because in many current applications of AI, programming and use are interactively connected.

Previous studies provided by Schulz [35] suggest important indications in terms of the analysis of *co-constructive* processes. Not only do these illustrate the need for a co-constructive perspective with respect to the explainability of AI. Rather, these examples illustrate that under such a premise of co-construction, the perspective of everyday users must be much more involved. Asymmetries, which can lead to various forms of disadvantage and even discrimination against users, lie precisely in such one-sided views of technological determinants or the ideas of the developers and an accompanying lack of explanations. This is one of the reasons why everyday interaction with such AI-based systems can lead to uncertainty or disappointment on the part of users.

Kaufmann and Peil summarize WhatsApp as "the most prevalent [...] free-of-charge, advertising-free, yet commercial mobile messaging service" [17] of our time, which makes it interesting for us as a research tool. WhatsApp is available on iOs, KaiOs and Android and provides instant and multimodal one-to-one or one-to many communication through mobile data or Wi-Fi. Users can send text- or voice messages, make (video-) calls, send images, videos, links and documents as well as copy and forward messages to chat partners. Furthermore, WhatsApp provides "social information" [6] by displaying when a user was last online, if they are currently writing or if they have received and read a message; unless restricted in the settings. Users and researchers respectively can also easily access a desktop version by scanning a QR code with their smartphone.

With respect to findings from a current preliminary test run[2] with volunteers, we perceive WhatsApp as a very easy-to-use and inherently well-structured documentation and communication tool that allows interacting with more than one participant at the same time.Nevertheless, researchers who draw on WhatsApp as a research tool also face significant challenges, as it requires a high degree of (self-)organization on the part of the researchers and limitations in regard of manageable group size. Moreover, WhatsApp in its current implementation is considered to violate the General Data Protection Regulation (GDPR) of the European Union (Data Protection Commission of Ireland 2021).[3] In particular, the information that WhatsApp provides to its customers is insufficient and WhatsApp regularly transfers the data about all contacts stored on a smartphone to both its European branch and its US-American parent company Meta Platforms. The contacts list usually contains personal information about many persons whose data is uploaded without these people noticing – let alone being able to consent. On the positive side, the high-quality encryption, which is standard for WhatsApp communication, offers a good level of protection for the contents of exchange. However, the inherent ties of mobile media to online storage, here in the form of online backups provided by the Android and iOS operating systems and WhatsApp itself, are another threat to the confidentiality of the contents of communication. Additional meta-data that accrues during communication is transferred to both Meta Platforms and the OS manufacturers Google or Apple respectively. There are thus three challenges to handle: Since data transfer (in particular metadata about the communication) to a third country with no GDPR compliant safeguards – the US – is involved, the use of WhatsApp is only permissible regarding the possibility of derogations for specific situations as specified in Art. 49 GDPR. This involves explicit consent to the data transfer of all involved subjects "after having been informed of the possible risks of such transfers for the data subject due to the absence of an adequacy decision and appropriate safeguards". This needs to be addressed in the consent forms. On the technical side, two challenges remain regarding the transfer of contacts and backups being uploaded which should be inhibited. We handle this by using a smartphone dedicated only for research with a clean install of both Android as operating system and WhatsApp. The contact list of the phone remains empty at all times. As a redundant safety measure, the permission of the WhatsApp app to access the contacts list is revoked directly after installation. All backup functions of the operation system and of WhatsApp are disabled. In addition, the operating system is disconnected from all Google accounts – thus disabling any possibility of cloud access that is not available in the configurations.

---

[2] More recent results regarding the suitability of our method as well as first insights into the diaries conducted will be provided during the HCI conference in June 2022.

[3] In consequence, the following might be legally required only for researches located in the EU as we are. However, research ethics suggest that the steps detailed here would be apt also for other researchers. See also [23].

3 Discussion/Empirical Insights

To stress the advantages of our methodological framework, we draw on results from Schulz [36] that further develop the concept of *algorithmic imaginaries* [5], providing two examples to illustrate the significance of users' perceptions in algorithmic environments such as Instagram and discuss how these can affect the conditions of '(un)successful' outcomes. Both examples refer to the introduction of an algorithmic ranking in the Instagram feed in March 2016 and are based on the *netnographic approach* [19, 20], which can be defined as "a form of qualitative research" and "a particular set of actions for doing research within and about social media" [20]. In this sense, netnography is congruent with an ethnographic approach, albeit limited exclusively to online spaces.

Importantly for the context of the examples discussed below, these imaginaries of users are not just any imaginaries of the algorithmic technologies behind them, but very concretely become part of the platform infrastructure itself, regardless of how accurate or correct these user imaginaries about the algorithms "real" functioning are [34]. It is particularly moments of disruption articulated by users during the use of Instagram that allow for a more detailed analysis of these algorithmic imaginaries. As will be shown, these user imaginaries cannot be attributed solely to Instagram's modification of the feed, but rather to the platform's (lack of) explanations of how it works.

The first example of user imaginations triggered by the altered feed can be found in a discussion Schulz observed in October 2017 on the account of a user named @U1[4] [35]. This user posted a selfie on 07 October 2017, which has since been deleted[5], presumably showing her in her bedroom. She is wearing casual clothes with a hoodie and in the background there is a mirror through which you can see that the shot is a selfie. The caption says:

> "*I'm a little perplexed why your comments & likes have dropped so much lately. Are you even seeing my posts anymore? [...] Are you guys having similar problems?*"

What initially looks like a personal address to followers about the lack of engagement on their part turns out to be a direct reaction to the lack of likes and comments in the wake of the feed change, as the following comment from a follower shows:

> "*I feel the same way. I'm also very sad. I feel like Instagram has changed something again. I still see your photos, but super delayed and not always, I guess.*"

The strange feeling the platform must have changed "something" is ubiquitous as further comments under the posted selfie reveal: "*I'd just be interested to know what the reason is,*" @U1 writes in response. And, according to another follower, in general "*it's unfair, because sometimes you put so much effort into a photo, which then gets so few*

[4] The user names are anonymized below for data protection reasons.

[5] The background is a wave of cease-and-desist letters circulating in 2018 with regard to influencers, which was instigated by the *Verband Sozialer Wettbewerb* (German Association of Social Competition) and initially culminated in a highly controversial preliminary injunction issued by the Berlin Regional Court against the popular influencer Vreni Frost in June 2018.

likes". A third follower finally gets to the point: "*That's the algorithm! Sometimes it just does what it wants*".

In a way, this last remark suggests a kind of temporary loss of control over "the" algorithm, which sometimes simply "goes nuts" and then just does what it wants. This not only humanizes the algorithmic systems in the users' imaginations. What is rather interesting here is that the framing of this statement suggests control over "the" algorithm (and that means the platform) as the normal state, and that it is only through this moment of disruption that agency is delegated to the algorithm. The gesture of humanization in the users' imaginations with an attributed autonomous will ("*sometimes it just does what it wants*") to the technology serves here as the simplest conceivable form of an explanation for the visibility problems lamented by @U1.

The second example deals with the topic of purchased likes and reaches (and that means followers). At the beginning of August 2018, a whole series of strange Instagram stories by an influencer named @U2 could be observed. At the urging of her followers, she posted several story clips, in which she takes a stand on the issue of purchased reach and justifies to her followers why many of them are from Brazil and speak Portuguese. In the course of this, she admits that she bought likes a few months ago and that the followers are most likely from tools that automatically give likes and follow other accounts. In particular, the discrepancy between the high number of followers and the constant interaction rates on her posts is a problem for some of her followers, to which she resolutely replies that she cannot explain it. All she can say is that it's up to everyone to believe her. "*All of you know how hard it is to grow on Instagram, and I think many of you just don't have enough patience*", she tries to deflect the problem away from herself.

Here it becomes clear that @U2, in contrast to @U1 from the first example, seems to be better informed about how the algorithm in the backend works and can explain certain parameters in the ranking, which is why she then also bought likes and followers to increase her position in the feed and the visibility that goes along with it. This is certainly also due to the personal goals of this influencer, who, unlike @U1 from the first example, also wants to earn money with it. However, what is particularly interesting here is that @U2's followers must also know about certain parameters in the way the algorithms work, otherwise they would not ask @U2 to account for purchased likes and followers. These purchased likes, which often involve social bots, can then be identified using easily accessible tools and apps such as *HypeAuditor*[6]. The followers of @U2 get their information from exactly such tools. Clearly, there are different qualities of knowledge that characterize @U1, @U2, and their peer groups. Which raises the question: how come these different qualities of knowledge regarding the algorithmic about?

First, it should be noted that due to the limitations of the *netnographic approach* [19, 20] with online-only field access used to conduct these examples, important information about the socioeconomic background of the two users is missing. Although indirect

[6] *HypeAuditor* is a software tool that has been available since 2018 and is mainly used by companies in the field of influencer marketing. It was originally intended for the precise analysis of accounts and, in particular, their reach. It is intended to enable companies to identify accounts with purchased reach (i.e., primarily purchased followers and/or likes) without much effort. It also serves companies in ongoing campaign analysis with influencers. See also: https://hypeauditor.com/.

assumptions can be made about the status on the platform via the profiles (e.g., through the number of followers and likes), a distinction must be made here between a user level and the real people behind the accounts. Therefore, unfortunately, no definitive statements can be made here about the people behind the accounts beyond speculation. Social media platforms such as Instagram and Facebook also only query such needs in the context of so-called A/B testing procedures in relation to the introduction of specific platform functions (e.g. for the like button). This patronizes users and puts them in a subordinate position, which can also be referred to as "platform paternalism" [28]. From this subordinate position of users and the lack of explanations by Instagram when it introduced its algorithmic ranking, the algorithmic imaginary feeds off in context of the first example.

At the time of @U1's first posting in October 2017, there was no detailed explanation for (lay) users of how the algorithm works, except for a short post on the official Instagram blog that accompanied the launch of the new algorithmic feed in March 2016. This blog post simply states: "*The order of photos and videos in your feed is based on how likely you are to be interested in the content, your relationship with the person who published the post, and how recent the post is*" (Instagram Blog, March 15, 2016). Although tech-savvy users could have imagined that there must be an algorithm at work here, users were not given any further information on the detailed functioning of this algorithm, and neither can the word "algorithm" be found in the blog post at all. Merely, tech journalists wrote about inaccurate recommendations they received within their feed [10] or anticipated a visibility contest [8] due to their experience with the Facebook News Feed algorithm [4]. For lay users, however, this explanation in the blog post by Instagram was coded and could not be deciphered. This causes irritation among users and also prompts @U1 to ask her community via selfie why her postings are invisible to large parts of her community.

Since June 2018 Instagram regularly briefs users how to act on the platform [9, 27]. Cues include six main categories (*interest*, *recency*, *relationship*, *frequency*, *following*, *usage*) and explain the most important ranking factors for different platform features (explore feed, stories, reels). Of these six key factors for assessing relevance, at least four are directly linked to the metrics of likes and followers. The *interest factor* is calculated on the basis of previous like behavior and the type of images liked, among other things. Depending on when the photo was posted and how many likes or comments it received in a certain period of time, the *recency factor* is calculated. The *relationship factor* is calculated via network analysis with the help of the social graph, in which accounts are ranked higher if one has liked or commented on their posts in the past or has received likes from other accounts. Finally, *the number of followers* determines how large the pool of corresponding accounts is in whose feeds one's own postings can appear [9]. Additionally, highly influential users with many followers often get special and more detailed information on ranking criteria [16].

When @U2 in August 2018, as shown in the second example, was urged by some of her followers to explain why so many of her followers are from Brazil and speak Portuguese, there were already more detailed explanations from Instagram about how its algorithm works. This knowledge spreads via multipliers such as particularly influential users or celebrities who are instructed by Instagram on how the algorithm works, so that this knowledge increasingly reaches non-tech-savvy users. In the case of @U2, who buys likes and followers based on such explanations of how the algorithm works, her followers also have at least rudimentary knowledge of the algorithms functioning.

From this perspective, Instagram decodes the functioning of certain parameters within the algorithm with these briefings. Yet, even this supposedly better knowledge about the algorithm as a result of Instagram's explanations can be described as imaginary, because the explanation is not only incomplete and serves only the economic interests of the platform. Moreover, it is precisely the asymmetry rooted in these economic interests that makes a true co-constructive explanation between users and platform impossible.

In this respect, these two examples show how explanations can shape user behavior in different manners according to their level of knowledge. However, they also show that successful explanations for the platform (explainers) do not necessarily have to be successful explanations for the users (explainees). From a research perspective it is important to consider not just the situatedness of knowledge with regard to the developers [39] or the different kinds of lay users [5], but in particular their permanent interplay. Not least for this reason, it is important to include the users' perspective more strongly in XAI, because the respective explanations by the developers or platforms do shape the users' imaginaries. However, these user imaginaries in turn also quite concretely influence how successful the respective AI applications are for users in everyday use, which is why there are so many A/B tests in the field of social media, for example. A co-constructive perspective is therefore suitable for taking into account these still prevailing asymmetries between explainers and explainees in XAI and, if necessary, also for critically questioning corresponding business models that prevent the co-construction of explanations as in the cases discussed in this paper.

4 Conclusion

The approach highlighted in this paper provides an essential step towards including the user perspective more strongly in research on XAI. It allows to observe (shared) orientation patterns, experiences, practices, expectations, and perceptions of (lay) users in real-world contexts and thus, in a second step, to analyze different explanatory needs of users regarding gender, age, and other markers of sociocultural diversity [12, 14, 21, 22].

We have shown that scientific data collected from the users themselves via WhatsApp is highly promising. Since users can communicate their problems and needs in dealing with algorithmic systems directly to researchers, much more accurate data can be obtained about users' explanatory needs, which is a research desideratum not only in computer science. However, direct contact between researchers and users that goes beyond (online) instant messages, e.g., via follow-up conversations, remains indispensable.

The documentary method proves to be a suitable approach to conduct our research since it provides sufficient scope and connectivity and permits to be extended towards digitally mediated interaction. We have discussed two examples that show that users' imaginaries of AI drive their usage, regardless of the quality or availability of explanations. If explanations are available they change the users' practices, yet not always towards their needs or desires. Our approach promises rich data to close this gap.

Our contribution is not least a plea for the necessity of empirical research within XAI that combines both qualitative and quantitative methods, as well as conventional and new digital methods. This enables the necessary stronger focus on (lay) users in co-constructively negotiated explanatory processes. In doing so, we aim to contribute to "achieving the goals of transparency and autonomy called for in research on XAI" [33].

Funding. The author(s) disclosed receipt of the following financial support for the research, authorship, and/or publication of this article: Research for this article was funded by the collaborative research centre "Constructing Explainability" (DFG TRR 318/1 2021 – 438445824) at Paderborn University and Bielefeld University.

References

1. Aguado, J.M., Martinez, I.J.: The message is the medium. Mobile instant messaging apps in the mobile communication ecosystem. In: Ling, R., Fortunati L., Goggin G, Lim, S.S., Li, Y. (eds.) Oxford Handbook of Mobile Communication and Society, pp. 439–454. Oxford University Press (2020)
2. Anjomshoae, S., Najjar, A., Calvares, D., Främling, K.: Explainable agents and robots. Results from a systematic literature review. Robotics track. In: International Foundation for Autonomous Agents and MultiAgent (eds.) Proceedings of the 18th International Conference on Autonomous Agents and MultiAgent Systems, AAMAS 19, Montreal, Canada, 13–17 May 2019, pp. 1078–1088. IFAAMAS (2019)
3. Bohnsack, R.: Rekonstruktive Sozialforschung. Einführung in qualitative Methoden, 9th edn. Budrich, Opladen (2014)
4. Bucher, T.: Want to be on the top? Algorithmic power and the threat of invisibility on Facebook. New Media Soc. **14**(7), 1164–1180 (2012)
5. Bucher, T.: The algorithmic imaginary: exploring the ordinary affects of Facebook algorithms. Inf. Commun. Soc. **20**(1), 30–44 (2017)
6. Church, K., de Oliveira, R.: What's up with WhatsApp? Comparing instant messaging behaviors with traditional SMS. In: Proceedings of the 15th International Conference on Human-Computer-Interaction with Mobile Devices and Services, Mobile HCI 2013, pp. 352–366 (2013)
7. Colom, A.: Using WhatsApp for focus group discussions: ecological validity, inclusion and deliberation. Qual. Res., 1–16 (2021)
8. Constine, J.: Instagram is switching its feed from chronological to best posts first. https://techcrunch.com/2016/03/15/filteredgram/. Accessed 24 Feb 2022
9. Constine, J.: How Instagram's algorithm works. https://techcrunch.com/2018/06/01/how-instagram-feed-works. Accessed 24 Feb 2022
10. Crook, J.: Instagram's algorithmic feed is the worst thing to happen to me all summer. https://techcrunch.com/2016/07/13/instagrams-algorithmic-feed-is-the-worst-thing-to-happen-to-me-all-summer/. Accessed 24 Feb 2022
11. Data Protection Commission of Ireland. Data Protection Commission announces decision in WhatsApp inquiry. https://www.dataprotection.ie/en/news-media/press-releases/data-protection-commission-announces-decision-whatsapp-inquiry. Accessed 24 Feb 2022
12. Ernst, W., Horwath, I. (eds.): Gender in Science and Technology: Interdisciplinary Approaches. transcript Verlag, Bielefeld (2014)
13. Gibson, K.: Bridging the digital divide: reflections on using WhatsApp instant messenger interviews in youth research. Qual. Res. Psychol., 1–21 (2020)
14. Holl, H.J., Horwath, I., Cojocaru, E.C., Hehenberger, P., Ernst, W.: Integration of gender in the design process of mechatronic products: an interdisciplinary approach. Mater. Today Proc. **5**(13), 26673–26679 (2019)

15. Hooley T., Marriott J., Wellens J.: Online interviews and focus groups. In: What Is Online Research? Using the Internet for Social Science Research, pp. 53–72. Bloomsbury Collections, London (2012)
16. Gevinson, T.: Who Would I Be Without Instagram? An Investigation. https://www.thecut.com/2019/09/who-would-tavi-gevinson-be-without-instagram.html. Accessed 24 Feb 2022
17. Kaufmann, K., Peil, C.: The mobile instant messaging interview (MIMI): using WhatsApp to enhance self-reporting and explore media usage in situ. Mob. Media Commun. **8**(2), 229–246 (2020)
18. Kaufmann, K., Peil, C., Bork-Hüffer, T.: Producing in situ data from a distance with mobile instant messaging interviews (MIMIs): examples from the COVID-19 pandemic. Int. J. Qual. Meth. **20**, 1–14 (2021)
19. Kozinets, R.V.: Netnography: Doing Ethnographic Research Online. Sage, London (2009)
20. Kozinets, R.V.: Netnography: The Essential Guide to Qualitative Social Media Research. Sage, London (2020)
21. Matzner, T.: Beyond data as representation: the performativity of big data in surveillance. Surveill. Soc. **14**(2), 197–210 (2016)
22. Matzner, T.: Opening black boxes is not enough: data-based surveillance in discipline and punish and today. Foucault Stud. **32**, 27–45 (2017)
23. Matzner, T., Ochs, C.: Sorting things out ethically: privacy as a research issue beyond the individual. In: Zimmer, M., Kinder-Kurlanda, K. (eds.): Internet Research Ethics for the Social Age. Peter Lang, New York (2017)
24. Marres, N.: Digital Sociology: The Reinvention of Social Research. Polity. Wiley, Cambridge (2017)
25. Miller, T.: Explanation in Artificial Intelligence: Insights from the Social Sciences. Preprint (2017)
26. Mol, A., Law, J.: Complexities: Social Studies of Knowledge Practices. Duke University Press, Durham (2002)
27. Mosseri, A.: Shedding More Light on How Instagram Works. https://about.instagram.com/blog/announcements/shedding-more-light-on-how-instagram-works. Accessed 24 Feb 2022
28. Petre, C., Duffy, B.E., Hund, E.: "Gaming the system": platform paternalism and the politics of algorithmic visibility. Soc. Media + Soc. **5**(4), 1–12 (2019)
29. Preece, A., Harborne, D., Braines, D., Tomsett, R., Chakraborty, S.: Stakeholders in explainable AI. arXiv (2018)
30. Ras, G., van Gerven, M., Haselager, P.: Explanation methods in deep learning: users, values, concerns and challenges. In: Escalante, H.J., et al. (eds.) Explainable and Interpretable Models in Computer Vision and Machine Learning. TSSCML, pp. 19–36. Springer, Cham (2018). https://doi.org/10.1007/978-3-319-98131-4_2
31. Rogers, R.: Digital Methods. MIT Press, Cambridge (2013)
32. Rogers, R.: Doing Digital Methods. Sage, London (2019)
33. Rohlfing, K.J., et al.: Explanation as a social practice: toward a conceptual framework for the social design of AI systems. IEEE Trans. Cogn. Dev. Syst. **13**(3), 717–728 (2021)
34. Schulz, C., Matzner, T.: Feed the interface. Social-media-feeds als schwellen. In: Navigationen – Zeitschrift für Medien- und Kulturwissenschaften, vol. 2, pp. 147–164 (2020)
35. Schulz, C.: In Likes We Trust oder die unmögliche Möglichkeit vom Like als Gabe zu sprechen. In: Koch, G., Rottgeri, A. (eds.) Populäre Artikulationen – Artikulationen des Populären. transcript, Bielefeld (2022, forthcoming)
36. Schulz, C.: (Re-)Konzeptualisierung eines algorithmisch Imaginären. Zeitschrift für Kulturwissenschaften. Radikale Imagination. Kulturen der Zukunft mit Castoriadis. transcript, Bielefeld (2022, forthcoming)

37. Singer, B., Walsh, C.M., Gondwe, L., Reynolds, K., Lawrence, E., Kasiya, A.: WhatsApp as a medium to collect qualitative data among adolescents: lessons learned and considerations for future use. Gates Open Res. **4**(130), 1–11 (2020)
38. Star, S.L.: The ethnography of infrastructure. Am. Behav. Sci. **43**(3), 377–391 (1999)
39. Suchman, L.: Human–Machine Reconfigurations: Plans and Situated Actions. Cambridge University Press, Cambridge (2006). https://doi.org/10.1017/CBO9780511808418
40. WhatsApp: About WhatsApp (2022). https://www.whatsapp.com/about/. Accessed 24 Feb 2022

Explainable AI for Suicide Risk Assessment Using Eye Activities and Head Gestures

Siyu Liu[1](✉), Catherine Lu[1], Sharifa Alghowinem[2], Lea Gotoh[3], Cynthia Breazeal[2], and Hae Won Park[2]

[1] Massachusetts Institute of Technology, Cambridge, MA 02139, USA
{eliu24,czlu}@mit.edu
[2] MIT Media Lab, Personal Robotics Group, Cambridge, MA 02139, USA
{sharifah,cynthiab,haewon}@media.mit.edu
[3] Japan Broadcasting Corporation, Tokyo, Japan
gotou.r-km@nhk.or.jp

Abstract. The prevalence of suicide has been on the rise since the 20th century, causing severe emotional damage to individuals, families, and communities alike. Despite the severity of this suicide epidemic, there is so far no reliable and systematic way to assess suicide intent of a given individual. Through efforts to automate and systematize diagnosis of mental illnesses over the past few years, verbal and acoustic behaviors have received increasing attention as biomarkers, but little has been done to study eyelids, gaze, and head pose in evaluating suicide risk. This study explores statistical analysis, feature selection, and machine learning classification as means of suicide risk evaluation and nonverbal behavioral interpretation. Applying these methods to the eye and head signals extracted from our unique dataset, this study finds that high-risk suicidal individuals experience psycho-motor retardation and symptoms of anxiety and depression, characterized by eye contact avoidance, slower blinks and a downward eye gaze. By comparing results from different methods of classification, we determined that these features are highly capable of automatically classifying different levels of suicide risk consistently and with high accuracy, above 98%. Our conclusion corroborates psychological studies, and shows great potential of a systematic approach in suicide risk evaluation that is adoptable by both healthcare providers and naïve observers.

Keywords: Affective computing · Suicide risk · Nonverbal behaviour · Explainable AI

1 Introduction

Among the many suicide attempts each year, 800,000 people die [37]. Often, they suffered from depression, anxiety, or have histories of self-injury for years [18]. Those that pass leave tremendous emotional strain to their families and communities. Japan is at the center of this suicide epidemic. Historical trauma, war,

H. Degen and S. Ntoa (Eds.): HCII 2022, LNAI 13336, pp. 161–178, 2022.
https://doi.org/10.1007/978-3-031-05643-7_11

unemployment, natural disasters, high stress, all contribute to the alarmingly high rate of 20,000 deaths per year [26]. Yet, suicide is preventable. Given the association between suicide inclination and mental disorder, early identification and intervention can mitigate many tragedies [28].

Current suicide assessment criteria—including Behavioral Health Screening (BHS), Manchester self harm rule (MSHR), and Södersjukhuset self-harm rule (SOS-4)—lack specificity and sensitivity, and are difficult to administrate, and those with suicide inclinations are often blamed for not seeking help [31,35]. This hinders early detection and intervention.

Recent efforts to automate suicide risk assessment using machine learning on metadata has shown promising results, yielding high classification accuracy (>90%) in suicide ideation prediction using electronic medical records and comorbidity biomarkers [6]. However, significant challenges exist in application of these results, as no model has successfully been transferred into new settings or populations [6,13]. While recent works have explored using objective verbal and acoustic markers for suicide risk assessment [9,15,20], to our best knowledge, the three studies led by Laksana [23], Eigbe [11] and Shah [33] are the only works that investigate observable facial behavior markers.

The purpose of this study is to construct a systematic and interpretable approach for suicide risk assessment. We investigate whether nonverbal behaviors from the eyelids, head pose, and eye gaze hold discriminative power for evaluating suicidal risks, considering a wider array of behavioral features than previous works using statistical analysis, feature selection, and classification with machine learning. Given the interpretability approach of this work, we hope to propose a systematic approach in suicide risk evaluation that is executable for both healthcare providers and naïve observers. The main contributions of this research are as follows:

- extract objective and interpretable behaviors that are discernible to naïve observers
- provide analyses using statistical methods, feature selection, and machine learning with a focus on explainability

2 Background

Nonverbal indicators of suicide ideation have received far less attention than verbal ones. Laksana et al. found simple facial features including smiling and head and eyebrow movement effective for suicide risk assessment [23], and that suicidal individuals produce more non-Duchenne smiles. Eigbe et al. verified this result and also found that suicidal subjects look down more often than their non-suicidal counterparts [11].

Suicidal intent have strong correlation with other mental disorders, including depression and anxiety. Symptoms of anxiety and depression—high stress, fatigue, and social withdrawal—have been observed among suicidal individuals as well [35]. Particularly, statistical analysis and machine learning classification of the movement of facial and ocular landmarks found that depressed patients have narrower eye openings, longer duration of blinks, and slower and less frequent head movements that signify fatigue or eye contact avoidance [2,3,36]. Fossi et al. attribute this phenomenon as a form of psycho-motor retardation [14]. Additionally, by analyzing data collected with eye trackers, infra-red corneal reflection techniques, or human observation, many studies have confirmed that patients with anxiety disorder avoid eye contact and direct gaze at the person's face in a photo, but scan non-facial features and the surrounding environment more extensively [19,22,27]. As depression and anxiety disorder are significant risk factors for suicidal thoughts and behaviors, we may leverage from nonverbal indicators of depression and anxiety to formulate our research.

To classify such indicators, machine learning has been utilized extensively. Automatic assessment of mental health disorders such as depression, schizophrenia, and bipolar disorder has primarily used machine learning classification to provide objective diagnosis [25]. These efforts have been successful. For instance, Cohn et al. [10], Abaei and Osman [1], and Shah et al. [33] classified for depression, bipolar disorder, and suicidal intent by analyzing visual, acoustic, and verbal features using machine learning techniques including support vector machines (SVMs), logistic regression, and convolutional neural-nets (CNNs). Given the correlation between these disorders and suicide, classification of verbal and nonverbal behaviors may yield good results for predicting suicidal risk.

Yet, few studies have attempted automatic machine learning classification of suicide risk. Laksana et al. [23] and Eigbe et al. [11] have achieved 40% and 69% accuracy in classifying suicidal, mentally ill, and control groups based on facial behaviors. In this paper, we explore combinations of different discriminative models (multi-layer perceptron and SVMs) and data processing methods to determine the best-performing classifier of suicide risk. We build upon the previous research by extracting an extensive array of nonverbal behaviors from head and eye movements. Then, we twice execute classification – once with all features and once with just 10% selected through feature selection and statistical analysis. Specifically, we chose 10% in order to only select the most prominent features. If the classification results obtained in both trials are similar, we deem the selected features to be representative of the task and capable of explaining the model.

3 Methodology

The overall process including pre-processing, low-level features extraction, post-processing and high-level feature summaries, and analysis is summarized in Fig. 1 and described in the following subsections.

3.1 Suicide Dataset Collection

The dataset was collected in collaboration with Japan Broadcasting Corporation (NHK), who conducted interviews with Japanese participants aged 15 to 25 who are suffering from suicidal thoughts as part of their suicide awareness

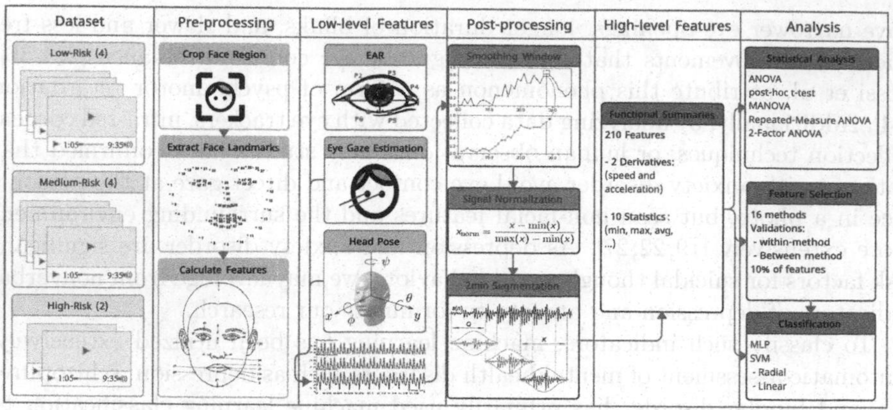

Fig. 1. The flowchart shows the general steps and their sub-steps start from dataset acquisition, pre-processing of signals (cropping image, facial landmark extraction, and basic feature calculation), low-level feature extraction (EAR, eye gaze, head pose estimation), post-processing of signals (window smoothing, signal normalization, thin-slicing), high-level feature extraction through functional summaries, and ending with analysis and interpretation of results through statistical analysis, features selection, and classification.

Table 1. Number of Subjects, Interview Duration and Total Segments in each Suicide Risk Level in the Sub-Dataset used in this Work

Risk level	# Subj	Interview duration (min)	# of 2 min segments
Low	4	60.80	54
Medium	4	88.00	63
High	2	31.16	27
Total	10	179.96	144

project. The project was advertised through social media, which invited people to share stories of their (or their loved ones') suffering on the project's website "Face to Suicide."[1]. People who were willing to be further interviewed were recruited for the project. All participants provided consent via email communication. The selected participants were pre-interviewed (without camera recording) by two project directors for screening and suicide risk assessment. During the pre-interview, the participants were assessed using the "Suicidal Risk" subsection of the M.I.N.I. (Mini-International Neuropsychiatric Interview) [24], which consists of 6 questions about their negative thoughts (e.g., suicidal ideation and intensity). Upon consultation with psychiatrists, another 5 questions were added to the pre-interview about their history of self-harm and clinical visits, environment (e.g., age, family, socioeconomic status), and positive thoughts (e.g., trusted persons, hobbies, coping mechanisms). The two directors then categorized

[1] http://www6.nhk.or.jp/heart-net/mukiau.

each participant as a low, medium, or high suicide risk individual. These assessments and potential conflicts were subsequently cross-validated and were resolved via discussion that accompanied psychiatrist consultation. A total of 14 participants were interviewed, once each; 4 of them requested to have their faces blurred for the recording. This work uses the 10 interviews with faces not blurred to study participants' nonverbal behaviors. Four participants were assessed as low risk, four at medium risk, and two at high risk (see Table 1). The interviews were conducted in several locations with different room layouts (e.g., window and door location, furniture), but the relative position of the interviewer-interviewee were consistent—both sat in chairs where they faced each other.

3.2 Feature Extraction

Pre-processing of Feature Extraction. High resolution videos were manually cropped to contain only the face region of the subject. For each frame of the processed video, we used single-shot face detection to locate a total of 68 facial landmarks, as proposed in [38]. Frames where the face is not fully captured were skipped. Additionally, using the facial landmarks, cropped images containing each eye were obtained from each valid frame, which served as inputs to calculate gaze direction (yaw and roll).

Low Level Feature Extraction. For each frame, Eye Aspect Ratio (EAR) and gaze direction were extracted for each eye, and head direction was extracted for the entire face image, as described below. Proposed by Soukupova and Cech, EAR characterize the openness of an eye as a scalar quantity in an image [7], where this ratio is normalized against distance of the eye to the camera and eye size differences between the subjects. A larger EAR value indicates a wider opening. A similar approach was taken by [2] for the analysis of eye movement for depression detection. Using the 6 eye-region landmark coordinates, EAR is computed based on the formula as follows, where p_i are the 2D landmark locations as depicted in Fig. 1 (EAR).

$$\frac{\|p_2 - p_6\| - \|p_3 - p_5\|}{2\,\|p_1 - p_4\|} \tag{1}$$

To describe each eye's angle of gaze, two scalar quantities, pitch and yaw, were extracted per frame. We used [40]'s multimodal CNN to estimate the eye gaze. The inputs of this CNN are the facial landmarks, normalized head angle vectors, and cropped eye images. This been trained on the MPIIGaze dataset that contains 213,659 images with diversity in appearance and illumination collected from everyday laptop usage of 15 participants [39].

Head pose was extracted in terms of three angle vectors—pitch, yaw, and roll for each frame—to represent the direction the subject is facing. Our study employed the technique outlined by [34] to estimate the 3D head pose using 6 facial landmarks—four eye corners and two mouth corners. By fitting generic 3D facial shape models onto our facial landmarks, we obtained angles of rotation of the head. Lastly, a distance to the face was calculated from the camera's focal point, based on the apparent size of the face.

Post-processing of the Signals. Low-level feature signals were post-processed to eliminate outliers and noise. For each low-level signal, a moving average was computed with a window size of 7 frames (window size 3–20 were attempted). The moving average window was chosen empirically to reduce noise without eliminating actual movements. For features that are applicable to both eyes (EAR, eye pitch, and eye yaw), results obtained from the left and right eye were averaged to reduce the variability and noise of the two signals. This final 7 low-level features (avg. EAR, avg. eye pitch, avg. eye yaw, head distance, head pitch, head yaw, and head roll) were used in further analysis. In order to eliminate inter-subject variability including the participant's personality, mannerism, and appearance, we linearly scaled each signal from 0 to 1.

High Level Feature Extraction. We segmented our data into small windows following the physiological thin-slicing theory [5], where a brief observation of a behavior (a thin slice) can be indicative to the physiological outcome at levels similar to the full observation. This process also serves as a mitigation for the small number of subjects in our dataset. As Shah et al.'s experiment has shown, 2-min slices are just as effective as 5-min slices in capturing features of the video [33]. Hence, we segmented each subject's signal into 2-min slices, with a one-minute overlap between two adjacent slices. The total number of segments per risk group is listed in Table 1. A total of 210 statistical features, i.e., "functionals", were extracted to summarize the segments. For each of the 7 post-process low-level features, 30 statistics were calculated, which are:

- The speed and acceleration at which the signal moves. This is computed by taking the first and second derivatives with regard to the frame index.
- Maximum, minimum, range, mean, variance, standard deviation, skewness, kurtosis, number of peaks and valleys for the original signal and its derivatives.

These functionals capture the frequency and velocity of the movement of each signal, as well as the duration of continuous movement and their direction. The compilations of statistical features from 2-min segments across videos from the same categories—a statistical summary—were used as samples for our classification, feature selection, and statistical analysis. One study employing a similar approach of statistical hypothesis testing and multimodal predictive modeling yielded promising results in predicting suicide intent using sliced videos from social media [33].

3.3 Feature Selection

A **feature selection framework (FS)** to systematically select the most representative features that are correlated to an independent variable, i.e. nonverbal behavior with suicide risks, was proposed in [4], which we replicated in this work. While extracting a large number of features as an exploration of behaviors is a common practice in the AI community, it is not commonly practiced in the psychology field for diagnoses without confirming an assumption or a hypothesis.

Such confirmation is done through statistical analysis that accounts for multi-test correction (e.g., Bonferroni correction), which might not be ideal for large feature spaces and small sample sizes. Therefore, the FS framework aimed to fill the gap by systematically aggregating the results from several statistical analyses with several methods of feature selection. The framework also serves as an interpretation tool through narrowing the feature space to the most meaningful features for a variable/class, not only by analyzing the features independently, but also analyzing the relationship between features (e.g., removing redundant features, finding a combination of features that correlate together, etc.). Given the two-step validation approach, i.e., within and between methods validation, the sensitivity of any method to the sample size is mitigated. That is, when a feature is not stable enough for the selection process, the framework excludes it.

In this work, we selected up to top 10% behavioral features using 16 feature selection methods (e.g., statistical-based, information theory-based) for the multi-class suicide risk assessment - high, medium, low. For the cross-validation method, we used 10-folds with two runs to measure both Jaccard Index (JI) and Between Threshold Stability (BTS), which were then used to validate and select the final feature set, as described in [4]. Notably, we treated the low, medium, and high categories as nominal instead of ordinal because we are more interested in categorical differences among the three clusters, without assuming that measurements from medium-risk participants always sit between those from low and high-risk counterparts. As such, we chose not to execute correlations analysis where both variables are ordinal or continuous.

3.4 Statistical Analysis

A one-way analysis of variance (ANOVA) test was performed for each functional to determine whether a systematic difference between the three suicide risk classes (low, medium, high) exists, followed by a post-hoc two-tailed t-test when statistical significance was found. For both tests, we chose a significance value threshold of 0.05 as alpha, and apply Bonferroni correction to obtain a corrected significance level of $0.05/210 = 2.3809 \cdot 10^{-4}$. We selected the functionals for which at least one of the three post-hoc p-values is within this corrected significance threshold. Additionally, we conducted a multivariate analysis of variance (MANOVA) and a two-factor ANOVA to understand subject dependence and selected for the most discriminating feature of suicide risk. Specifically, since the between-subject groups are unbalanced and there is an interaction between independent variables, type-III sums of squares estimation was utilized for the two-factor test. As more than one sample was taken from each video sample the due to the 2-min segmentation, we ran a repeated-measure ANOVA to determine features that are indicative of suicide risk, accounting for subject-dependence. Although assumptions for ANOVA and T-tests are not fully satisfied - normality and non-colinearity - as our sample size is enlarged with video segmentation, we proceed executing the tests with caution.

3.5 Classification

Our goal is to classify the statistical and selected features into three classes for suicide risk: low-risk, medium-risk, high-risk. To select the best model for this task, we tried variations on three discriminative models: a multilayer perceptron (MLP) with one hidden layer and SVMs with linear and radial kernels. To reduce potential bias caused by overrepresented classes, we tested two different sampling methods: oversampling and undersampling. For oversampling, we randomly duplicated samples from underpopulated classes, and for undersampling, we randomly removed samples from overrepresented classes. This is to ensure that all classes have the same number of samples for training.

For each combination of model and sampling method, we performed 10 random stratified trials using data from all 144 statistical summaries. In each trial, the data was randomly split into a stratified training set and testing set, with a split of around 75% training data and 25% test data. Both sets were normalized based on the training data and scaled to values between 0 and 1. The training set was then either left alone, balanced via oversampling, or balanced via undersampling before fitting the model.

Hyperparameter tuning was done via a grid search using 10-split cross-validation on the training data. For MLP, our only hyperparameter was the number of hidden units. We searched over an evenly spaced range of 10 values slightly greater than the number of features to ensure that a good spread of reasonable hypothesis classes were tested. For testing with 210 features, this range was from 22 to 232 hidden units, and for the selected 12 features, the range was 2 to 14. For SVM, we chose our C value by iteratively performing narrowing grid searches over intervals of values between 0 and 1, eventually narrowing down to values 0.01 apart, then selecting the best one. For SVM with radial kernels, we used several values for gamma, calculated using 1/(n_features * variance in training sample).

The final performance of each modeling process is represented by its performance on the test data, measured by the mean balanced accuracy score across all 10 trials. As false negatives are highly undesirable when classifying suicide risk, we took measures to ensure classification quality between classes. First, we selected hyperparameters based on balanced scores, which account for the number of samples in each class, and calculated a Matthews Correlation Coefficient (MCC) score for each trial. Accounting for the differences between class sample sizes, MCC is regarded as one of the best evaluators of classification quality in comparison with other measures like F1 score, since it is only high when good results are achieved from all classes [8]. We used a generalized multiclass version of MCC as described by Gorodkin [16].

We performed two additional randomized experiments. One experiment was done using randomly shuffled feature vectors and the original labels, and another with randomly shuffled labels and the original feature data. By comparing our classification results to these results obtained by chance, we ensure that our results are robust and meaningful. We report all of our results with the best-performing combinations of models and sampling methods.

Table 2. Interpretations of the Features that Passed Corrected p-values by Statistical Analysis: 69 behavioral features passed ANOVA and post-hoc t-tests.

Behavioral theme	Statistical features	Direction
Deminished Eye and Head movement	Var. of speed of EAR changes, var. of EAR, max. of speed of eye pitch movement, mean of speed of eye pitch movement, rang. of speed of eye pitch movement, std. of speed of eye pitch movement, var. of speed of eye pitch movement, max. of acc. of eye pitch movement, rang. of acc. of eye pitch movement, std. of acc. of eye pitch movement, var of acc. of eye pitch movement, std. of head pitch, var. of head pitch	L > M > H
	Std. of speed of EAR changes, std of acc. of EAR changes, max. of EAR, range of EAR, std. of EAR, mean of eye yaw	L > H > M
	Rang. of head roll, std. of head roll, rang. of head yaw, std. of head yaw, var. of head yaw	M > L > H
	Var. of head roll	M > H > L
	Kurt. of speed of head pitch movement, skew of speed of head pitch movement, skew of head roll movement, kurt. of head roll movement	H > L > M
	Min. of eye pitch movement, min. of acc. of eye pitch movement, kurt. of speed of head distance movement, skew of speed of head distance movement	H > M > L
Anxiety-related involuntary behaviors	Skew of speed of eye yaw movement	L > M > H
	Kurt. of head distance	M > L > H
	Skew of EAR changes	M > H > L
	Peaks of head roll, valys. of head roll	H > L > M
Engagement in conversation (head movement to signify emotion, eye contact, head distance)	Kurt. of eye yaw, max. of eye pitch, mean of eye pitch, rang. of eye pitch, std. of eye pitch, var. of eye pitch, kurt. of speed of eye yaw movement, kurt. of acc. of eye yaw movement	L > M > H
	Mean of head pitch	L > H > M
	Rang. of eye yaw, std. of eye yaw, var. of eye yaw, std. of speed of eye yaw movement, var. of speed of eye yaw movement	M > H > L
	Min. of head pitch	H > L > M
	Peaks of head pitch, valys. of head pitch	H > M > L
Miscellaneous	Min. of eye yaw, peaks of eye yaw, valys. of eye yaw	L > H > M
	Min. of head roll, head_roll-d1_kurt	H > L > M

var.: variance, **kurt.**: kurtosis, **valys.**: number of valleys, **acc.**: acceleration

4 Results and Discussion

4.1 Interpretation of Nonverbal Behavior

Statistical Analysis. ANOVA tests were performed for the 210 functionals collected over two-minute windows, among which, 123 were significant. To further verify the significance, we conducted post-hoc t-tests for each behavioral feature between the three groups. From this process, 69 functionals were found to be significant in at least one of the three intergroup comparisons (low/high, med/high, low/med). Moreover, we used the t-values to determine the direction of the correlations between the groups.

T-tests show that higher risk participants exhibit lower levels of ocular and head activity, as well as heightened anxiety and depression related symptoms, including "fight-or-flight" movements and social withdrawal. Table 2 enumerates all 69 features, from which the most prominent ones are discussed in this section. Higher risk individuals blink less often and have narrower eye-openings and less sudden movements of the eyelids. The minimum of the EAR is zero (when the eye is closed). As low-risk individuals have the highest maximum, range, and standard deviation in EAR, their ocular activity is more diverse. They have wider eye openings and more frequent blink. Additionally, given that the speed and acceleration of the EAR is near-zero when the eyes are open, low-risk participants' high standard deviations in their EAR's first and second derivatives also signify they blink more and faster. Assuming all interviewees have similar physical needs of blinking for lubricating the eye, the reduction in eyelid activity among high-risk individuals allude to their less robust nervous and muscular system around the eyes.

Low-risk subjects have higher levels of gaze movement, characterized by faster and more frequent up-down glancing. Among all three groups, low-risk individuals have the greatest mean, range, and standard deviation in their eye pitch movement speeds, highlighting they have the most significant gaze shift. The same statistics show that high-risk participant's up-down gaze shifts have much smaller magnitude. Similarly, low-risk individuals also have more jerky movements, as evidenced by high max., range, std., and var. in the acceleration of eye pitch. Analysis of head motions yields similar findings—high-risk subjects have the least range of motion when moving their heads in all directions. These trends are inferred from the low range and std. of head roll and yaw among the high-risk participants, and are in line with literature: the slower, diminished, and more sporadic movement of higher risk individuals exhibit signs of fatigue and lethargy that can be attributed to psycho-motor retardation—one of the most prominent identifiers of depression [2,3,14,36].

Statistical analysis also reveals that suicidal individuals have higher levels of anxiety. Notably, the low skew on the speed of high-risk subjects' eye yaw indicates that they have more frequent left-right movement in their eyes, as they spend more time move their eyes at higher speeds. This corroborates with findings in [19,22,27,35] that high risk subjects scan the room from left to right and rarely make eye contact with the interviewer. Moreover, despite having the smallest range in motion, high-risk group tilt, nod, and move their head more than their lower-risk counterparts, as signified by the low range, var. and std. of head roll and yaw.

This study observed augmented levels of social withdrawal among higher risk individuals. Statistics pertaining to the left-right movement of the gaze indicates that low-risk participants' gaze is often focused on the interviewer—they rarely look away, and even when they do so, their gaze would quickly come back to the interviewer. Additionally, low-risk subjects' gaze and head pose direction are the most elevated. These findings corroborate with the correlation between depression, anxiety, and eye contact avoidance found by previous studies [2,3,19,22,27,36].

Medium-risk participants' features frequently sit between low and high-risk groups in most behaviors. The level of their eyelid and gaze activity is higher

Table 3. Interpretations of the 21 behavioral features selected that passed the 2-factor ANOVA

Behavioral theme	Functional features	Direction
Engagement in conversation (head movement to signify emotion, eye contact, head distance)	Range of head pitch	L > M > H
	Skew of head distance	M > L > H
	Std. of head distance	M > H > L
	Skew of EAR	H > L > M
Room scanning (anxiety symptom)	Kurt. of acc. of eye pitch	L > H > M
	Min. of speed of head yaw	H > L > M
	Kurt. of head roll	
	Min. of speed of head yaw	
Diminished Eye and Head movement (depression symptom)	Skew of speed of eye pitch	L > H > M
	Range of head pitch	L > M > H
	Var. of speed of head pitch	
	Var. of acc. of head pitch	
	Var. of acc. of head roll	
	Var. of acc. of eye pitch	
	Min. of speed of EAR	M > H > L
	Skew of EAR	H > L > M
	Kurt. of head yaw	
	Min. of speed of head yaw	
Miscellaneous	Kurt. of speed of EAR	M > L > H
	Skew of head yaw	H > L > M
	Skew of head roll	

var.: variance, **valys.**: number of valleys, **acc.**: acceleration

than high-risk individuals, but lower than low-risk individuals; their vertical gaze direction is higher than high-risk, but lower than low-risk subjects. These trends affirm that medium-risk participants experience moderate drowsiness in movement and depression comparing to high and low-risk participants. Other trends pertaining to medium-risk participants, however, call for further investigation.They have the least front-back head movement, as they seldom lean forward or back to show engagement in the conversation. They blink the slowest, although the difference is not significant between high and medium-risk groups. They tilt their head the least often compare to low and high-risk group, which can be interpreted as either high level of focus or severe psycho-motor retardation. When scanning the room, medium-risk subjects' gaze diverges the furthest away from the interviewer, although their left-right gaze movement is sparse. This may be interpreted as fixation at a spot away from the interviewer, either due to curious distraction or eye contact avoidance. While these trends are insightful, additional information is required for further interpretation.

Multivariate Analysis of Variance (MANOVA) determines no significant difference in the extracted features for the three suicide levels. Roy's Greatest Root is the only statistic that yields a significant p-value[2]. This is expected, as the feature space is especially large. Using the repeated-measure ANOVA, we found suicide risk to have a significant effect in the number of sudden movements in participants' left-right eye gaze. T-tests subsequently found the low-risk group have the highest number of valys. of eye yaw acc., hence the most sudden movements, while high-risk group to have the least. This finding corroborates the depression-induced psycho-motor retardation hypothesis.

Two-factor ANOVAs were conducted for each feature in order to further understand subject and risk-level-based dependence. Specifically, we conducted type-III ANOVA, which assumes dependence between independent variables – risk level and identity of the participant – which are not independent. For all features, we compute the probability of the distribution being identical for both variables and their interaction, and selected 18 features that are both significant in level-identity interaction and insignificant for identity differences (alpha <0.05). As such, we deem the 18 features to be free of subject-dependence. Among the 18 features, one was selected by features selection, and one by t-tests.

Analysis of the 18 features using the group-wise t-statistic found remarkable trends. In general, participants at higher suicide risk exhibit more distinguishable depression symptoms, and those at lower risk, the least. Specifically, since head pitch's velocity, var. of acc., and range are high, we deem the low-risk group to have the most frequent sudden up-down head movements, the greatest range of head-nodding motion, and move their heads the quickest when they do so. The low-risk group also have the most sudden head tilts and fastest sudden up-down movements in their eye gaze, as signified by the variance in acceleration in head roll and max. acc. in eye pitch. Participants in the high-risk group display the least of these eye and head activities. Additionally, high-risk participants rarely turn or tilt their heads (high kurt. in head yaw and roll), and have low levels of eye openness (high skew in EAR). Such ocular and head movement reduction can be explained with depression-induced psycho-motor retardation and social disengagement. In contrast, the low-risk group often lean forward as they engage in conversation with the interviewer, as observed by the high std. of their head-distance. This signal, in combination with low-risk participants' higher activity level, signify their higher level of social engagement.

High and medium-risk groups also exhibit anxiety symptoms. Especially, medium-risk individuals have the quickest and most frequent head turns and tilts, given the low skew in head yaw and roll. As the interviewees' gaze is in the direction of the interview most of the time, the medium-risk group's least uniform velocity in their eyes' up-down movements signify that they frequently look away, up-down scanning the room.

Some findings of 2-factor ANOVA lack explanation. Medium-risk group have the highest kurt. of speed of EAR, meaning that the speed in their eyelid's movement is the most uniform. This implies they blink the least often. It was also found that medium-risk group have the lowest skew in head yaw and roll,

[2] Detailed MANOVA results are presented here: https://bit.ly/32h6CRa.

Table 4. Interpretations of the Features Selected by Feature Selection Framework: 12 behavioral features were narrowed down through the framework

Behavioral theme	Functional features	Direction
Engagement in conversation (head movement to signify emotion, eye contact, head distance)	Std. of head pitch	L > M > H
	Avg. of eye gaze pitch	
	Std. of head yaw	M > L > H
	Var. of head yaw	
	Min. of head distance	M > H > L
	Std. of eye gaze yaw	
	Var. of eye gaze yaw	
Room Scanning (anxiety related)	Var. of the speed of eye gaze yaw shift	M > H > L
Diminished Eye and Head movement	Std. of the speed of EAR change	L > H > L
	Valys of acc. of eye gaze yaw shifts	L > M > H
	Var. of acc. of head pitch change	
	Skewness of acc. of head roll change	M > H > L

var.: variance, **valys.**: number of valleys, **acc.**: acceleration

Table 5. The best classification results using statistical summaries obtained from 2-min windows

Features	All features			Selected features			Random features	Shuffled labels
Performance	Best model	2nd best	3rd best	Best model	2nd best	3rd best	Best model	Best model
Sampling method	None	None	Over-sample	None	None	Over-sample	Under-sample	Over-sample
Model	SVM (linear)	MLP	SVM (linear)	MLP	SVM (radial)	SVM (linear)	SVM (radial)	MLP
Avg accuracy	0.983	0.978	0.977	0.977	0.971	0.961	0.425	0.399
Std. accuracy	0.019	0.020	0.033	0.021	0.023	0.033	0.045	0.077
Avg MCC	0.966	0.970	0.957	0.966	0.974	0.943	0.138	0.106

and high-risk group have the highest. This implies that medium risk group tilt their heads to the right more often while the high risk group, more to the left. This may be due to fixation at a spot away from the interviewer, yet further investigation is required for a more meaningful interpretation.

Feature Selection. A feature selection method developed by [4] was applied on our suicide data set. Using the same 210 functionals' statistical summaries as inputs, a total of 12 features passed the FS framework. To investigate the direction of these features in each risk group, the state value of the t-test analysis was obtained as listed in Table 4. The results from FS align with those obtained from statistical analysis. We observed that, in comparison to the low and medium-risk participants, the high-risk group rarely nod and shake their heads. Their heads' range of up-down movements are the smallest; their sudden left-right movement of the gaze is the least frequent; their eyes' blinking velocity is the most uniform—indicating less and slower blinks. These observations lead us to conclude that, due to depression-induced psycho-motor retardation, higher-risk individuals exhibit reduced activity in their heads and eye regions [14].

Results from feature selection also shed light on the participants' emotional expression. The low mean in the eye-pitch and the high mean in the eye yaw indicate that medium and high-risk subjects spend significantly more time looking down and avoiding eye contact with the interviewer—strong signals of social withdrawal [14,36]. The low-risk group spent more time tilting their heads and leaning forwards as they engage with the interviewer. The eye's left-right moving speed is the most uniform among low-risk subjects, which parallels previous works—anxiety patients often have a hard time focusing on the interviewer and scan the room. Given the prevalence of depression and anxiety among suicidal patients, these results are in line with literature, that depression leads to psycho-motor retardation and anxiety gives rise to more frequent distraction from the conversation.

4.2 Classification Results

Table 5 shows the classification results using the best-performing classifiers, measured by balanced accuracy[3]. From our top 3 best-performing classifiers, we can see that all models performed similarly well. Still, the best model accuracy-wise for all features was an SVM with linear kernels, while the best for selected features was MLP. Even though the best balanced accuracies were 98.3% and 97.7% with full and selected features, respectively, the best MCC scores were obtained from our 2nd best models (0.970 and 0.974 for full and selected features respectively). Given that MCC accounts for the imbalanced samples from each class, we can argue that our 2nd best models performed better than the best (even though with small margin) since it has less confusion between the classes. For both all features and selected features, training using the original dataset worked far better than undersampling (4.5% absolute difference across all trials) and slightly better than oversampling (0.6% absolute difference).

Using all statistical features for training, our best model averaged 98% accuracy with a small standard deviation. The mean MCC was 0.967—almost perfect test performance across all three classes. We achieved similar numbers using the selected features with slightly greater standard deviation. Since we were able to immensely reduce the feature space with the FS framework without impacting classification accuracy, we conclude that the 12 selected behavioral features can indicate suicide risk level as well as represent the model for a behavioral interpretation.

[3] Full classification results are presented here: https://bit.ly/3tnqcY1.

For comparison, running the same tests using randomly switched labels resulted in far worse accuracy (ranging from 30–40%), as did the random feature vectors (also ranging from around 30–40%). Thus, we are confident that our results are indicative of the discriminative power of our features, not of any algorithm bias. In addition, achieving high accuracy with both MLP and SVM implies that our features are easily separable between classes, so they would hold good discriminative power regardless of the modeling method. Overall, our results indicate that both the entire statistical summary and the selected features are excellent at distinguishing between different levels of risk with high accuracy.

4.3 Limitations

We acknowledge the small sample size of the dataset, and our results necessitates further investigation upon features that cannot be explained. Particularly, high-risk participants have the greatest head tilt to their left, but the speed of their head tilt movement is the most uniform. Moreover, while our results support the psycho-motor retardation theory, we found the high-risk group to tilt and nod their head frequently but with the smallest range of motion. We hypothesized that such contradicting results stem from the association between suicide risk and bipolar disorder [21,30]. Since bipolar disorder patients experience both high and low energy episodes—which could sufficiently interpret our findings—we hope to also explore the biomarkers of bipolar disorder. Additionally, studies on eye gaze of people suffering from mental disorders shows nonspecific gaze [32], anxious gaze aversion [29], or simply gazing at the door during uncomfortable situations [12,17]. As the interviews were conducted in different locations, adding the room context to the feature set will provide insight into what the subject is gazing at.

5 Conclusion

Suicide poses significant risk, to those at risk, their families, and our society. Suicide is also often connected with depression, anxiety, and self-harm, but none of these factors alone is deterministic enough for an objective and effective suicide risk assessment. Additionally, due to privacy constraints, biomarkers of suicide have received very limited attention in academia and industry, as datasets that contain sensitive information are rarely available.

In this work, we aim to extend and fill the gap by systematically and objectively exploring nonverbal behaviors. We employ statistical analysis, feature selection, and machine learning classification to analyze signals from the eyes and head. Applying these three methods to our dataset, our conclusion corroborates previous psychological studies. Particularly, high-risk suicidal subjects exhibit lower activity levels in their eyes and head movements and are subject to a higher degree of psycho-motor retardation. Their eye gaze shows symptoms of anxiety and depression, including constant left-right scanning, difficulty of maintaining eye contact, and angling down their gaze and head pose.

Our classification results showed that these features are representative of suicidal intent. We achieved classification accuracy ranging from 96–98% for three risk levels across different modeling methods. We also highlight that since the results from statistical analysis and feature selection lead to the same conclusion, both are viable means of objective suicide risk assessment. Yet, conclusions from this work must be tested and verified against a larger and more diverse dataset. Future work will also extend to study body movements and speech prosody as potential biomarkers of suicide intents.

Acknowledgement. We thank and acknowledge the effort made by NHK, Nippon Hoso Kyokai (Japan Broadcasting Corporation) for conducting, recording and providing the interview dataset used in this work.

References

1. Abaei, N., Osman, H.A.: A hybrid model for bipolar disorder classification from visual information. In: 2020 IEEE International Conference on Acoustics, Speech and Signal Processing (ICASSP), ICASSP 2020, pp. 4107–4111 (2020). https://doi.org/10.1109/ICASSP40776.2020.9054648
2. Alghowinem, S., Goecke, R., Wagner, M., Parker, G., Breakspear, M.: Eye movement analysis for depression detection. In: 2013 IEEE International Conference on Image Processing, pp. 4220–4224 (2013). https://doi.org/10.1109/ICIP.2013.6738869
3. Alghowinem, S., Goecke, R., Wagner, M., Parkerx, G., Breakspear, M.: Head pose and movement analysis as an indicator of depression. In: 2013 Humaine Association Conference on Affective Computing and Intelligent Interaction, pp. 283–288. IEEE (2013)
4. Alghowinem, S.M., Gedeon, T., Goecke, R., Cohn, J., Parker, G.: Interpretation of depression detection models via feature selection methods. IEEE Trans. Affect. Comput. **1**(1), 1 (2020). https://doi.org/10.1109/TAFFC.2020.3035535
5. Ambady, N., Rosenthal, R.: Thin slices of expressive behavior as predictors of interpersonal consequences: a meta-analysis. Psychol. Bull. **111**(2), 256 (1992)
6. Bernert, R.A., Hilberg, A.M., Melia, R., Kim, J.P., Shah, N.H., Abnousi, F.: Artificial intelligence and suicide prevention: a systematic review of machine learning investigations. Int. J. Environ. Res. Public Health **17**(16), 5929 (2020). https://doi.org/10.3390/ijerph17165929
7. Cech, J., Soukupova, T.: Real-time eye blink detection using facial landmarks, pp. 1–8 (2016)
8. Chicco, D., Jurman, G.: The advantages of the Matthews correlation coefficient (MCC) over F1 score and accuracy in binary classification evaluation. BMC Genomics **21**(1) (2020). https://doi.org/10.1186/s12864-019-6413-7
9. Chowdhury, G.: TREC: Experiment and Evaluation in Information Retrieval (2007). Online information review
10. Cohn, J.F., et al.: Detecting depression from facial actions and vocal prosody. In: 2009 3rd International Conference on Affective Computing and Intelligent Interaction and Workshops. pp. 1–7 (2009). https://doi.org/10.1109/ACII.2009.5349358

11. Eigbe, N., Baltrusaitis, T., Morency, L., Pestian, J.: Toward visual behavior markers of suicidal ideation. In: 2018 13th IEEE International Conference on Automatic Face Gesture Recognition, FG 2018, pp. 530–534 (2018). https://doi.org/10.1109/FG.2018.00085
12. Eisenberg, N., Spinrad, T.L.: Emotion-related regulation: sharpening the definition. Child Dev. **75**(2), 334–339 (2004)
13. Fonseka, T.M., Bhat, V., Kennedy, S.H.: The utility of artificial intelligence in suicide risk prediction and the management of suicidal behaviors. Aust. NZ J. Psychiatry **53**(10), 954–964 (2019)
14. Fossi, L., Faravelli, C., Paoli, M.: The ethological approach to the assessment of depressive disorders. J. Nerv. Ment. Dis. **172**(6), 332–341 (1984). https://doi.org/10.1097/00005053-198406000-00004
15. Gómez, J.M.: Language technologies for suicide prevention in social media. In: Proceedings of the Workshop on Natural Language Processing in the 5th Information Systems Research Working Days (JISIC), pp. 21–29 (2014)
16. Gorodkin, J.: Comparing two k-category assignments by a k-category correlation coefficient. Comput. Biol. Chem. **28**(5–6), 367–374 (2004). https://doi.org/10.1016/j.compbiolchem.2004.09.006
17. Grandin, T.: How people with autism think. In: Schopler, E., Mesibov, G.B. (eds.) Learning and Cognition in Autism, pp. 137–156. Springer, Boston, MA (1995). https://doi.org/10.1007/978-1-4899-1286-2_8
18. Guan, K., Fox, K.R., Prinstein, M.J.: Nonsuicidal self-injury as a time-invariant predictor of adolescent suicide ideation and attempts in a diverse community sample. J. Consult. Clin. Psychol. **80**(5), 842 (2012)
19. Horley, K., Williams, L.M., Gonsalvez, C., Gordon, E.: Social phobics do not see eye to eye: a visual scanpath study of emotional expression processing. J. Anxiety Disord. **17**(1), 33–44 (2003). https://doi.org/10.1016/S0887-6185(02)00180-9. https://www.sciencedirect.com/science/article/pii/S0887618502001809
20. Huang, Y.P., Goh, T., Liew, C.L.: Hunting suicide notes in web 2.0-preliminary findings. In: 9th IEEE International Symposium on Multimedia Workshops, ISMW 2007, pp. 517–521. IEEE (2007)
21. Jamison, K.R., et al.: Suicide and bipolar disorder. J. Clin. Psychiatry **61**, 47–51 (2000)
22. Jun, Y.Y., Mareschal, I., Clifford, C.W., Dadds, M.R.: Cone of direct gaze as a marker of social anxiety in males. Psychiatry Res. **210**(1), 193–198 (2013). https://doi.org/10.1016/j.psychres.2013.05.020. https://www.sciencedirect.com/science/article/pii/S0165178113002795
23. Laksana, E., Baltrušaitis, T., Morency, L., Pestian, J.P.: Investigating facial behavior indicators of suicidal ideation. In: 2017 12th IEEE International Conference on Automatic Face Gesture Recognition, FG 2017, pp. 770–777 (2017). https://doi.org/10.1109/FG.2017.96
24. Lecrubier, Y., et al.: The mini international neuropsychiatric interview (MINI). A short diagnostic structured interview: reliability and validity according to the CIDI. Eur. Psychiatry **12**(5), 224–231 (1997)
25. Low, D.M., Bentley, K.H., Ghosh, S.S.: Automated assessment of psychiatric disorders using speech: a systematic review. Laryngoscope Invest. Otolaryngol. **5**(1), 96–116 (2020). https://doi.org/10.1002/lio2.354
26. Matsubayashi, T., Sekijima, K., Ueda, M.: Government spending, recession, and suicide: evidence from Japan. BMC Pub. Health **20**(1), 243 (2020). https://doi.org/10.1186/s12889-020-8264-1

27. Moukheiber, A., et al.: Gaze avoidance in social phobia: objective measure and correlates. Behav. Res. Ther. **48**(2), 147–151 (2010). https://doi.org/10.1016/j.brat.2009.09.012. https://www.sciencedirect.com/science/article/pii/S0005796709002265
28. NIH: Suicide prevention (2021). https://www.nimh.nih.gov/health/topics/suicide-prevention/index.shtml. Accessed 03 Apr 2021
29. Perez, J.E., Riggio, R.E.: Nonverbal social skills and psychopathology. In: Philippot, P., Feldman, R.S., Coats, E.J. (eds.) Nonverbal Behavior in Clinical Settings. Series in Affective Science, pp. 17–44. Oxford University Press (2003)
30. Plans, L.: Association between completed suicide and bipolar disorder: a systematic review of the literature. J. Affect. Disord. **242**, 111–122 (2019)
31. Runeson, B., Odeberg, J., Pettersson, A., Edbom, T., Jildevik Adamsson, I., Waern, M.: Instruments for the assessment of suicide risk: a systematic review evaluating the certainty of the evidence. PLoS ONE **12**(7), e0180292 (2017)
32. Schelde, J.T.M.: Major depression: behavioral markers of depression and recovery. J. Nerv. Ment. Dis. **186**(3), 133–140 (1998)
33. Shah, A.P., Vaibhav, V., Sharma, V., Al Ismail, M., Girard, J., Morency, L.P.: Multimodal behavioral markers exploring suicidal intent in social media videos. In: 2019 International Conference on Multimodal Interaction, pp. 409–413 (2019)
34. Sugano, Y., Matsushita, Y., Sato, Y.: Learning-by-synthesis for appearance-based 3D gaze estimation. In: Proceedings of the IEEE Computer Society Conference on Computer Vision and Pattern Recognition, June 2014, pp. 1821–1828 (2014). https://doi.org/10.1109/CVPR.2014.235
35. Waern, M., Kaiser, N., Renberg, E.S.: Psychiatrists' experiences of suicide assessment. BMC Psychiatry **16**(1), 440 (2016)
36. Waxer, P.H.: Nonverbal cues for anxiety: an examination of emotional leakage. J. Abnorm. Psychol. **86**(3), 306 (1977)
37. WHO: Suicide. https://www.who.int/news-room/fact-sheets/detail/suicide
38. Zhang, S., Zhu, X., Lei, Z., Shi, H., Wang, X., Li, S.Z.: S^3FD: single shot scale-invariant face detector. In: Proceedings of the IEEE International Conference on Computer Vision, pp. 192–201 (2017)
39. Zhang, X., Sugano, Y., Fritz, M., Bulling, A.: MPIIGaze: real-world dataset and deep appearance-based gaze estimation. IEEE Trans. Pattern Anal. Mach. Intell. **41**(1), 162–175 (2019). https://doi.org/10.1109/TPAMI.2017.2778103
40. Zhang, X., Sugano, Y., Fritz, M., Bulling, A.: Appearance-based gaze estimation in the wild. In: Proceedings of the IEEE Conference on Computer Vision and Pattern Recognition (CVPR), June 2015, pp. 4511–4520 (2015)

ExMo: *Ex*plainable AI *Mo*del Using Inverse Frequency Decision Rules

Pradip Mainali[1(✉)], Ismini Psychoula[1], and Fabien A. P. Petitcolas[2]

[1] OneSpan, Cambridge, United Kingdom
{pradip.mainali,ismini.psychoula}@onespan.com
[2] OneSpan, Brussels, Belgium
fabien.petitcolas@onespan.com

Abstract. In this paper, we present a novel method to compute decision rules to build a more accurate interpretable machine learning model, denoted as ExMo. The ExMo interpretable machine learning model consists of a list of IF...THEN... statements with a decision rule in the condition. This way, ExMo naturally provides an explanation for a prediction using the decision rule that was triggered. ExMo uses a new approach to extract decision rules from the training data using term frequency-inverse document frequency (TF-IDF) features. With TF-IDF, decision rules with feature values that are more relevant to each class are extracted. Hence, the decision rules obtained by ExMo can distinguish the positive and negative classes better than the decision rules used in the existing Bayesian Rule List (BRL) algorithm, obtained using the frequent pattern mining approach. The paper also shows that ExMo learns a qualitatively better model than BRL. Furthermore, ExMo demonstrates that the textual explanation can be provided in a human-friendly way so that the explanation can be easily understood by non-expert users. We validate ExMo on several datasets with different sizes to evaluate its efficacy. Experimental validation on a real-world fraud detection application shows that ExMo is ≈20% more accurate than BRL and that it achieves accuracy similar to those of deep learning models.

Keywords: Interpretable · Explainable · Decision rules

1 Introduction

Artificial intelligence (AI) and machine learning (ML) show promising results in many application domains. Accenture projects that AI will boost the global economy by 35% by 2035 [5,11] and that individuals will be 40% more productive by employing AI [5]. Currently, the adoption of AI is mainly for low-stake applications such as recommendation of products in e-commerce. However, in high-stake applications such as finance, medicine, justice, etc., the adoption of AI is not taking place at the same speed. One of the hurdles is the black-box nature of machine learning and deep learning methodologies. Complex deep learning models can achieve higher accuracy, but they are difficult to interpret and understand the rationale

H. Degen and S. Ntoa (Eds.): HCII 2022, LNAI 13336, pp. 179–198, 2022.
https://doi.org/10.1007/978-3-031-05643-7_12

behind their decision making. In high-stake applications, understanding the rationale behind decision making is important to build trust in the system. For example, doctors may want to scrutinize the decision of AI, if AI predicts surgery. Also, there is a legal obligation mentioned in the EU General Data Protection Regulation (GDPR) such as 'right to explain' [1], hence autonomous systems are required to provide explanations to meet the legal compliance.

The research directions to deal with this problem are Explainable AI and Interpretable AI. In the Explainable AI approach, the predictions are made using a complex black-box model, and a second simpler model is used to help explain what the black-box model is doing locally [12,25]. Well known model-agnostic approaches are SHAP [23] and LIME [30], which provide explanations for any machine learning model. Another method designed specifically for deep neural networks is called Integrated Gradients (IG) [35]. Interpretable AI models can be directly inspected and interpreted by human experts [25]. A study carried out in [32] strongly recommends using interpretable models for high-stake applications. It used to be a common myth that interpretable models were less accurate, however, recent advances with rule list algorithms have led to the ability to build more accurate interpretable models [32]. Our paper aims to improve the accuracy of interpretable models even further.

This paper proposes a new approach to compute decision rules and an interpretable model is built using them. The method is named ExMo. We compare ExMo with the existing BRL algorithm [22], which uses frequent pattern mining (FPGrowth) [19], and is commonly used for interpretability, and show that the decision rules provided by ExMo offer greater accuracy and quality. Basically, ExMo advances the research work in BRL further by adopting a new approach for computing the decision rules. The ExMo model is composed of a list of IF...THEN... statements with a decision rule in the 'IF' condition and the 'THEN' part providing the prediction score. Consequently, the model naturally provides an explanation because the features in the decision rule are the main reasons for that prediction. Moreover, the decision rule resembles very highly the human decision-making process where the human reasoning mostly starts with 'IF' and conditions, hence the model is highly interpretable [25]. To extract the decision rules from the training data, we use features extracted using the term frequency-inverse document frequency (TF-IDF) technique from natural language processing. First, two document classes (i.e., fraud and non-fraud) are created by converting the fraud and non-fraud samples into a text representation, and then the text represented samples are assembled to create two documents (one for each class). TF-IDF features are based on the number of times that features have occurred in each class, which is the term frequency (TF). After that, the inverse document frequency (IDF) is computed: it is a weight computed for the same features in TF and whether these features occur in both the documents or not. If the features occur in both documents, then the weights are small and vice-versa. Finally, TF-IDF features are computed by multiplying both the terms. In essence, IDF de-emphasizes the decision rules with the features that occur in both document classes. Consequently, our approach provides sharper decision rules than the decision rules extracted using frequent pattern mining such as FPGrowth [19] as used in the original BRL algorithm [22]. In the frequent pattern mining approach, decision rules are computed independently for each class and hence the decision rules are blurry and make the interpretable model less accurate.

The main advantages of the ExMo interpretable model are that the explanation is obtained at no additional computational cost, the ExMo model can be audited by the regulators, and the explanation in the textual form is also provided for non-expert users. Model-agnostic methods such as SHAP [23] and LIME [30] require perturbation of the training data and need to make predictions for all perturbed data samples to compute the explanation. Consequently, generating the explanation requires expensive computations. The second benefit of ExMo is that the model is readable by human experts, as for example, regulators who can simply read the model in text form to verify for bias and unfairness. AI explainers, such as SHAP, could also be used to provide explanation and auditability to regulators for black-box models. However recently it was shown that AI explainers can be tricked to hide bias [34], hence AI explainers may not be safe enough to be used in practice. Another advantage of ExMo is that it also provides an explanation in the textual form, that is, in a more human-friendly way suitable for non-expert users. For this, the decision rule is processed further to format the explanation in textual form. This will bring advantages such as ExMo will enable customer support teams to communicate a prediction to the end-user as to why the loan application was declined and help the doctors to scrutinize the decision in greater detail etc.

The main contribution of this paper is the proposal of a new scheme that uses TF-IDF to extract the decision rules from the training data. We validate the approach with experiments and show that the ExMo interpretable model built using these new decision rules achieves a higher classification accuracy. We also compared ExMo with a deep learning model for fraud detection application, ExMo achieves an accuracy that is close to the deep learning model, while proving an explanation without additional computation time. Furthermore, we also demonstrate that ExMo achieves a qualitatively better model than BRL, thanks to TF-IDF based decision rules. Finally, this paper also demonstrates that ExMo can provide a textual explanation for its prediction, so that non-expert users can also understand the explanation.

2 Related Work

In this section, the machine learning models and explanation approaches are reviewed. We also provide a literature study on how the explanation techniques are being adopted for the development and improvement of machine learning systems.

Explaining Fraud: There has been a sharp rise in the literature proposing the use of machine learning in real-life applications. Hence, the integration of explanation techniques is also growing [28]. Several machine learning models for credit card fraud detection are discussed in [24]. A deep learning approach using convolutional neural networks and Long Short-Term Memory Network (LSTM) sequence model was used for fraud detection in [26]. Authors of [16] developed two novel dashboards to visualize features and a Sankey diagram to visualize the decision rules used to explain the prediction made by machine learning models. The authors found that the adoption of this explanation can dramatically speed up the process of filtering potential fraud cases. The SHAP explanation technique was used in [17] to improve a fraud detection model. In their approach, specialists analyzed the output of a fraud detection model with the SHAP technique in each iteration to check whether the model had learned the desired pattern or not. xFraud [29] is proposed to detect fraud from the graph representation of data for online retail platforms. The explanation is generated using GNNExplainer and the results are fed to the business unit for further processing to understand predictions. A deep learning model is used for fault detection in [15] and SHAP explanation technique was used to understand the prediction of the model. Finally, in [37] the authors show how explanation techniques could be used to better identify adversarial attacks and help prevent fraud in the medical domain.

Explainable AI: The growing popularity of deep learning methodology and its black-box nature have led to the development of "Explainable AI". Model agnostic and model-specific explanation techniques are two different mechanisms for this. The model agnostic approach creates a second model to explain what the actual deep learning model is doing locally and can explain any machine learning or deep learning model. LIME [30] and SHAP [23] are popular techniques based on this category. LIME and SHAP provide an explanation based on feature importance, showing the different features that are contributing positively and negatively to the prediction. LIME approximates a local region with an interpretable model such as a linear model. SHAP uses a game-theoretic approach, namely Shapley values to assign credit to input features to generate feature importances. Anchors [31] improved upon LIME by replacing a linear model with a logical rule similar to the decision rule, providing a more selective explanation. Due to data perturbation, the explanation provided by LIME can have slightly different features on each run. To provide a consistent explanation for each run, DLIME [39] was proposed, which perturbs data based on clusters for more deterministic data perturbation rather than perturbing the whole dataset. GraphLIME [20] is another adaptation of LIME to provide an explanation for models applied to graph-represented data. RESP [14] provides an explanation based on causality and has also been validated on credit and fraud datasets. Methods to explain the output of deep neural networks (DNN) have also been developed. DeepLIFT [33] computes the importance scores for input features by comparing them with a reference entity. Layer-wise relevance propagation (LRP) [13] explains the classifier's decision by decomposition and by redistributing the prediction backwards through the layers until it assigns a relevance score to each input variable. Integrated Gradients [35] accumulate the gradients obtained after perturbing input from the reference value to the input value and provide an explanation as feature importance scores.

Interpretable AI: Interpretable models provide both a prediction and the reason for the prediction. Interpretable models are those that directly build a human-readable model from the data. Recently, interpretable models started to be built using decision rule lists [22,36,38]. The decision rules are extracted using a frequent pattern mining algorithm. Then the model is built using the decision rules. The decision rules are highly interpretable and naturally provide an explanation for the prediction. The method proposed in [27] replaces the last layer of the neural network and predicts over the decision rules, providing both prediction and explanation together. For high-stake applications, the paper [32] suggested following the path of building the interpretable model because it provides stable and truthful explanations.

3 Proposed Method

In this section, we explain ExMo in detail on how decision rules are computed from the training data and the interpretable model is built from these decision rules. We also briefly review the Bayesian rule list (BRL) algorithm in Sect. 3.1. Following that, our new approach for learning the decision rules using TF-IDF features is explained in Sect. 3.2.

3.1 Review of the Bayesian Rule List (BRL) Algorithm

The goal of the BRL algorithm [22] is to learn a model which consists of an ordered collection of decision rules ($d = \{a_i\}_{i=1}^{m}$) as shown in Table 1, where m is the number of rules in the decision list. The model is specified by a list of IF...THEN... statements with a decision rule (a_i) in the condition of the 'IF' part and a probability of classification in the 'THEN' part as shown in Table 1. The decision rule a_i is a condition on data sample x that evaluates to true or false. y is a prediction score which is a binomial distribution over labels $\boldsymbol{\theta}_i$, which is computed from prior $\boldsymbol{\alpha}$ and the likelihood specified with the beta distribution. The vector $\boldsymbol{\alpha} = [\alpha_1, \alpha_0]$ has a prior parameter for each class. The notation $\boldsymbol{N}_i$ is a two-dimensional vector of counts for positive and negative classes. The counts are computed from training data that satisfy the decision rule a_i and none of the previous decision rules from a_1 to a_{i-1} in the list.

Table 1. Interpretable model

if a_1	then $y \sim \text{Binomial}(\boldsymbol{\theta}_1)$,	$\boldsymbol{\theta}_1 \sim \text{Beta}(\boldsymbol{\alpha} + \boldsymbol{N}_1)$
else if a_2	then $y \sim \text{Binomial}(\boldsymbol{\theta}_2)$,	$\boldsymbol{\theta}_2 \sim \text{Beta}(\boldsymbol{\alpha} + \boldsymbol{N}_2)$
.		
else if a_m	then $y \sim \text{Binomial}(\boldsymbol{\theta}_m)$,	$\boldsymbol{\theta}_m \sim \text{Beta}(\boldsymbol{\alpha} + \boldsymbol{N}_m)$
else	$y \sim \text{Binomial}(\boldsymbol{\theta}_0)$,	$\boldsymbol{\theta}_0 \sim \text{Beta}(\boldsymbol{\alpha} + \boldsymbol{N}_0)$

In the BRL algorithm, the decision rules are mined from the training dataset using a frequent pattern mining algorithm such as FPGrowth, Apriori, etc. A frequent pattern mining algorithm computes frequent co-occurrence of feature values. Support is used to measure the occurrence of feature values as below:

$$\text{Support}(x, f) = \frac{1}{n}\sum_{i=1}^{n} I(x_i) \tag{1}$$

where f is the feature value, n is the number of samples in the training dataset and I the indicator function that returns 1 if the sample has feature value f, otherwise 0.

To extract the decision rules for binary classification, the training samples are grouped into positive and negative groups. Then, the frequent pattern mining algorithm is applied on each group to extract decision rules. Later, the decision rules with support values (as in Eq. 1) that are higher than some threshold values are extracted. Once the decision rules from each group are extracted, the decision rules are combined to create a pool of decision rules (A).

The BRL algorithm learns the interpretable model as stated above from the pool of decision rules that was obtained earlier. Bayesian statistics is used to compute the posterior over the decision list, which is computed from the likelihood and prior as below:

$$p(d|x, y, A, \alpha, \lambda, \eta) \propto p(y|x, d, \alpha)p(d|A, \lambda, \eta) \tag{2}$$

where d is an ordered decision list, x the data sample, y the label, A the pool of pre-mined decision rules, λ the prior expected length of the decision lists, η the prior expected number of conditions in a rule, and α the prior pseudo-count for the positive and negative classes which is fixed at $[1, 1]$ as in [22].

The likelihood for the model is given by:

$$p(y|x, d, \alpha) \propto \prod_{j=0}^{m} \frac{\Gamma(N_{j,0} + \alpha_0)\Gamma(N_{j,1} + \alpha_1)}{\Gamma(N_{j,0} + N_{j,1} + \alpha_0 + \alpha_1)} \tag{3}$$

$N_{j,0}$ and $N_{j,1}$ are counts of training observations with labels 0 and 1 respectively that satisfy the decision rule a_j and not a_1 to a_{j-1}. The likelihood of rule a_j is large if $N_{j,0}$ is large and $N_{j,1}$ is very small or vice versa.

The prior is given by:

$$p(d|A, \lambda, \eta) = p(m|A, \lambda) \prod_{j=0}^{m} p(c_j|c_{<j}, A, \eta)p(a_j|a_{<j}, c_j, A) \tag{4}$$

Here, c_j is the number of features in the rule or cardinality of each decision rule. The first and second terms in Eq. 4 are respectively the priors for the number of rules m in the model and the number of features c_j in a decision rule.

The BRL algorithm can be summarised in the following steps:

1. The decision rules (A) in Eq. 2 are pre-mined by using the FPGrowth algorithm.

2. The Decision list d is sampled randomly from the prior distribution.
3. Markov Chain Monte Carlo (MCMC) sampling with Metropolis-Hastings is used to compute posterior in Eq. 2, generating a chain of the posterior samples of decision list $d = \{a_i\}_{i=1}^{m}$. The posterior samples in the chain are added by generating the proposal sample d^* by modifying the current d and if the acceptance criteria are satisfied as specified in the Metropolis-Hastings algorithm. The decision list d is modified by adding, moving or removing the decision rule (a_i) from the list. The option to move, add or remove the decision rule (a_i) in the decision list is chosen randomly. The algorithm is executed for K (e.g., 30,000) iterations. The algorithm runs three different MCMC chains, each initialized randomly.
4. Select the decision list from the sampled lists (i.e., chain) with the highest probability according to the posterior distribution.

3.2 Decision Rules from TF-IDF

The quality of the decision rules plays an important role for the BRL algorithm to achieve higher accuracy. Therefore, we borrowed an idea from text mining to extract the best decision rules by using TF-IDF n-gram features. To enable the text processing of data, the training data is converted into two documents (i.e., positive and negative classes of documents) by combining all samples from the same class. For example, the text document for a positive class is created by concatenating all samples having positive labels. Before concatenating the samples, the numerical features are also discretized as mentioned in the BRL algorithm. The discretization of samples is done using the algorithm proposed in [18]. This allows treating the numerical feature as a categorical feature for text processing. The label is also used to find cut points for discretization. Once the data is represented in two text documents, n-gram TF-IDF features are computed. 'TF' is a term-frequency and measures how important a feature is to a document. 'IDF' is an inverse-document-frequency and identifies how important the features are to a specific document. The 'IDF' values are smaller for the feature values that are common to both documents. The 'IDF' values are larger for feature values that occur only in one document. The final weighting of feature values in a decision rule using the TF-IDF is computed by multiplying both the terms as follows:

$$\text{tf-idf}(f, l) = \text{tf}(f, l) \times \text{idf}(f) \tag{5}$$

where

$$\text{idf}(f) = 1 + \log \frac{1 + N}{1 + \text{df}(f)}, \tag{6}$$

l is the document class, N is the number of documents ($N = 2$ in our case), and where $\text{df}(f)$ is the number of documents that contain a term or feature value f. We can observe that 'TF' has a similar meaning to that of 'Support' in Eq. 1. In our approach, the term 'IDF' helps to emphasize the decision rules with feature values that occur in one document class only and de-emphasize the decision rules with feature values that occur in both the classes. Hence, the decision rules computed by our method are better in quality than those obtained by the frequent pattern mining algorithms as used in the original BRL algorithm.

Algorithm 1: Algorithm for computing decision rules

```
1: Initialize cardinality of decision rules, i.e. n-gram range setting for TF-IDF
2: Initialize maximum number of permutations P
3: Pool of decision rules A = [ ]
4: for t = 1...P do
5:     Permute position of feature columns in tabular data
6:     Convert samples to text and create positive and negative document classes
7:     Compute n-gram TF-IDF features
8:     Get top-k n-gram features from each document class
9:     Append the top-2k features to A
10: end for
11: Randomly shuffle the decision rules A
```

The algorithm to compute the decision rules using TF-IDF n-gram features is given in Algorithm 1. In the first step, the algorithm is initialized for cardinality and the number of permutations (P) to be performed. The cardinality mentioned in Eq. 4 corresponds to the maximum number of features in a decision rule. This also corresponds to a maximum value in n-gram range settings for the TF-IDF algorithm. For example with the n-gram range setting $(3, 5)$, a decision rule with a maximum number of 5 features are computed. The next parameter is P. We permute the position of the feature columns in the tabular data to compute the decision rules with different n-gram features. The number of times that the position of feature columns are permuted is defined by P. In each iteration from steps 3 to 9, the position of feature columns in tabular data is permuted and the data is converted to two document classes as discussed earlier. The k top n-gram features from each class are extracted. In total, $2 \times k$ decision rules are extracted from each iteration. The process is repeated for P number of permutations. In the end, the algorithm outputs $2k \times P$ decision rules. The pool of decision rules is randomly shuffled. This pool of decision rules is given as input to the BRL algorithm to learn the interpretable model.

4 Experimental Results

In this section, we provide the experimental results of classification accuracy, comparison of the models, comparison of explanations generated by different algorithms, and execution time to compute explanations. We also provide details of the datasets and the features present in the dataset. We compare the explanations generated by our algorithm with BRL, LIME [30], SHAP [23], Anchor [31] and IG [35].

4.1 Datasets

We evaluate the algorithms on small and large datasets to evaluate the efficacy of ExMo. The small dataset consists of a few samples and features. The large dataset consists of a huge number of samples and features so that the scalability of ExMo can be evaluated. The details of the datasets are given below. We also provide some information regarding the features in the dataset as well so that the explanations given by the algorithms can be illustrated better.

Small Dataset: We used Diabetes [9], Default Credit Card Payment [3] and Income over 50K (or adult) [7] datasets, having 769, 30,000 and 48,842 samples, respectively. In terms of the number of features, the datasets contain 8, 23 and 14, respectively. We used 80% of data for training and 20% of data for testing. We also use the diabetes dataset to compare the models and to compare textual explanations, hence we provide more information regarding the features. The features in the diabetes dataset are: the number of times pregnancy occurred (times_pregnant), plasma glucose level after 2 h (plasma_glucose), diastolic_blood_pressure, tricep_skin_fold_thickness, serum_insulin, body_mass_ index, diabetes_pedigree_function and age.

Large Dataset: We carried out the experiment on the large dataset so that the experiment demonstrates that ExMo can be applied in the large dataset as well. For this, we selected the IEEE-CIS Fraud Detection dataset [6], which is a real-world dataset consisting of 500K samples and 433 features for online payments collected by Vestas Corporation. The dataset provides labels: fraud and not-fraud. There are 433 features in the dataset. Most of the features are masked and their actual meanings are not provided due to privacy and security concerns. Therefore, we used 54 features for which the description of the features are known as the explanation could be more understandable. We now provide a brief explanation of the features that we kept. 'TransactionAMT' gives the transaction amount in USD. 'ProductCD' is the product category for each transaction. The device type such as mobile or desktop and information about the device such as operating system are given in 'DeviceType' and 'DeviceInfo' respectively. The features 'card1'–'card6' are card related features such as debit or credit card type, card category (e.g., Mastercard, Visa, or American Express), issue bank, country, etc. The purchaser's and receiver's email domains are given in 'R_emaildomain' and 'P_emaildomain' features respectively. 'M1'–'M9' are match features, whether the names on the card and address, etc. match or not. 'C1'–'C14' are count features such as how many addresses are found to be associated with the payment card. 'D1'–'D15' are time delta features, such as days between previous transactions, etc. The address features are given in 'addr1' and 'addr2' and are, respectively, billing region (zip code) and billing country. 'dist1' and 'dist2' are distance features and are distance between billing address and mailing address. The following features are categorical features: 'ProductCD', 'card1' 'card6', 'addr1', 'addr2', 'P_emaildomain', 'R_emaildomain',

'M1'–'M9' and the remaining features are numerical features. The data samples were divided into 60% for training (i.e., 377K samples), 20% (95K samples) for testing and 20% (95K samples) for validation.

4.2 Classification Accuracy

In this experiment, we compare the classification accuracy of ExMo, BRL and machine learning models on both small and large datasets. We used the AUC-ROC (area under ROC curve) score for comparison as used in [6,22,38].

Table 2. Classification scores on the small dataset

Dataset	BRL	XGBoost	Ours
Diabetes	0.66	0.79	0.81
Default credit card	0.70	0.77	0.76
Income over 50K	0.80	0.89	0.88

Small Dataset: Table 2 shows the classification accuracy comparison on the small dataset for BRL, XGBoost and ExMo. Both ExMo and BRL were set to learn 10, 20 and 50 decision rules, respectively, for diabetes, default credit card payment and income over 50K datasets. The training was also executed for $K = 30000$ iterations. Both ExMo and BRL were set to learn a maximum of 5 features in decision rules as well. The experimental result shows that ExMo achieves higher classification accuracy in all three datasets, thanks to TF-IDF based decision rules.

Large Dataset: To evaluate the classification accuracy, we also build a deep learning model to detect fraud. The details of the deep learning model, algorithm settings and classification scores are provided below.

Deep Learning Model for Fraud Detection: We used a three-layered neural network to build the model for fraud detection. Embeddings were used for the categorical features and the output of the embedding layer is provided as input to the first layer. The first and second layers have 16 and 8 neurons, respectively, and the final layer is a sigmoid. The model outputs the probability of being a fraud for the given input sample.

Algorithm Settings: We trained ExMo for three different n-gram settings of $(3, 5)$, $(5, 7)$, and $(7, 9)$ and these versions are referred, respectively, by 'Ours-5', 'Ours-7', and 'Ours-9'. We used $P = 200$ and $k = 10$ in our experiments. With these settings, we extracted 3049, 3110, 3090 decision rules for the three different settings. Our algorithm is also configured to learn a model with a list of 125 decision rules. For the BRL algorithm, we used the maximum cardinality of 7 and the minimum support values of 75 and 65, respectively, for the negative and positive classes. With these settings, we extracted 3,600 decision rules. We also set the BRL algorithm to learn a model with a list of 125 decision rules. We used these settings for BRL because we got the best classification accuracy.

Table 3. Classification scores on the IEEE-CIS Fraud dataset

Method	AUC-ROC
XGBoost	0.93
Neural	0.92
BRL	0.69
Ours-5	0.82
Ours-7	0.87
Ours-9	0.89

Classification Scores: Table 3 shows the classification accuracy comparison among different methods on test data. We also provide results for three versions of ExMo: ‘Ours-5’, ‘Ours-7’, and ‘Ours-9’. We also implemented the XGBoost model that had won the competition in Kaggle [6] and the result is given in the table for the comparison. The experimental results show that ExMo achieves a score that is very close to the deep neural network method and provides a significant improvement (20%) over the BRL algorithm. The score saturates around ‘Ours-7’, hence this model could be used in practice, which achieves a better trade-off of achieving higher accuracy and at the same time providing a compact explanation with fewer features.

4.3 Model Comparison

In this section, we give the comparison between the models learnt by our algorithm and the BRL algorithm for the diabetes dataset. For diabetes, the plasma or blood glucose level is the main factor that indicates whether someone has diabetes or not. A High blood glucose level is a sign of diabetes. A blood glucose level below 95 is considered normal, 95–152 is considered pre-diabetic, and above 153 is considered diabetic [4]. Therefore, the plasma glucose level is the primary feature whether some have diabetes or not. The higher value of body mass also increases the risk of being diabetic and a higher value not necessarily means diabetes. The risk of diabetes also increases with age. With these characteristics in mind, we will evaluate the model learnt by ExMo and BRL.

Table 4 shows the model learnt by ExMo and BRL for the diabetes dataset. The decision rules in the ExMo model uses plasma glucose levels extensively, which is almost in every decision rule in the model compared to the decision rules in the model obtained by BRL. The first decision rule in ExMo uses

Table 4. Model comparison

ExMo
IF plasma_glucose:127.5_to_166.5 AND body_mass_index:29.65_to_inf THEN probability of diabetes: 76.0%
ELSE IF plasma_glucose:127.5_to_166.5 THEN probability of diabetes: 41.5%
ELSE IF age:-inf_to_28.5 AND body_mass_index:-inf_to_29.65 THEN probability of diabetes: 2.7%
ELSE IF plasma_glucose:-inf_to_99.5 THEN probability of diabetes: 22.5%
ELSE IF plasma_glucose:99.5_to_127.5 AND age:-inf_to_28.5 AND times_pregnant:-inf_to_6.5 THEN probability of diabetes: 30.1%
ELSE IF plasma_glucose:99.5_to_127.5 THEN probability of diabetes: 60.9%
ELSE probability of diabetes: 54.1%
BRL
IF age:28.5_to_inf AND body_mass_index:29.65_to_inf THEN probability of diabetes: 74.9%
ELSE IF age:28.5_to_inf THEN probability of diabetes: 44.2%
ELSE IF serum_insulin:-inf_to_16.0 AND body_mass_index:29.65_to_inf THEN probability of diabetes: 59.6%
ELSE IF age:28.5_to_inf THEN probability of diabetes: 50.0%
ELSE IF body_mass_index:-inf_to_29.65 THEN probability of diabetes: 8.1%
ELSE IF plasma_glucose:99.5_to_127.5 THEN probability of diabetes: 16.7%
ELSE IF body_mass_index:-inf_to_29.65 THEN probability of diabetes: 50.0%
ELSE IF age:-inf_to_28.5 THEN probability of diabetes: 50.6%
ELSE probability of diabetes: 50.0%

plasma_glucose in the range 127 to 166 and body_mass_index above 29 features to give a prediction of 0.76. On the other hand, the first rule in BRL uses age above 28 and body_mass_index above 29 features to give a prediction of 0.75, completely ignoring the plasma glucose level to give such a high prediction score. Subsequently, the decision rules in the model obtained by ExMo consisted of plasma glucose and other features such as age, body mass index, and the number of times the pregnancy had occurred. The model obtained by BRL consists of plasma glucose only on the 6th decision rule. Most of the decisions are based on age and body mass index. Theoretically, it is more accurate to look at the plasma glucose level as it is a primary feature and ExMo has been rightfully using this feature for prediction. Therefore, qualitatively, ExMo is able to learn a better model than BRL, thanks to TF-IDF based decision rules.

4.4 Textual Explanation

In this section, we provide more details on how the textual explanation can also be generated, so that non-expert users can easily understand the explanation. Table 5 shows the template that is used to format the explanation from the decision rule that was triggered. The 'application name' is the name of the application (e.g. diabetes) and the 'probability' is the output of the ExMo model. Depending on the feature types in the triggered decision rule, the templates from 1 to 4 given in Table 5

Table 5. Template for the textual explanation depending on rule types 1–4

Template for Explanation	
Prob. of {application name} is {probability} because	
1. abs. value	{feature name} is {value}
2. -inf_to_value	{feature name}({feature value}) is below {value}
3. value_l_to_value_r	{feature name}({feature value}) is between {value_l} to {value_r}
4. value_to_inf	{feature name}({feature value}) is above {value}

are used to format the explanation. The first feature type is a feature with some absolute value, the second feature type considers a range of feature values from -infinity to some feature value, the third feature type considers a range of feature values from *value_l* to *value_r* and finally the fourth feature type considers a range of feature values from some feature value to infinity. The feature name and feature value are obtained from the input data sample.

Table 6. Data samples for a textual explanation

plasma_glucose	serum_insulin	body_mass_index	times_pregnant	Age	Label
152.0	171	34.2	9	33	1
108.0	0.0	30.8	2	21	0

Table 7 shows the explanations generated by ExMo and BRL for the positive and negative data samples given in Table 6. The template given in Table 5 is used to convert the triggered decision rule into the textual explanation. For the positive sample, the first decision rule in the model for both ExMo and BRL in Table 4 is triggered. The explanation generated by ExMo states that the probability of diabetes is 0.76 because the plasma glucose is in the higher range of 127 to 166 and body mass index is in the higher range and above the threshold value of 29. Similarly, for BRL, the first decision rule is triggered and the textual that is obtained using the template is shown in the table. For the negative sample, the 5th and 3rd rules are triggered, respectively for ExMo and BRL. The textual explanation generated by ExMo states that the probability of diabetes is 0.3 because the plasma glucose is between 99.5 to 127.5, the patient is young in the age of 21 which is below 28 and the number of pregnancies that occurred so far is 2.0 and below some threshold of 6.5. It is quite clear that the textual explanation is easily understandable and readable by non-experts.

4.5 Comparison with Model-Agnostic Explanation

In this section, we compare the explanations generated by our method, BRL and model agnostic explanation methods such as SHAP, LIME, Anchor and IG.

Table 7. Textual explanation of positive and negative samples in the diabetes dataset

Method	Textual explanation
Positive sample (label 1)	
BRL	Prob. of diabetes is 0.75 because age (33.0) is above 28.5 and body_mass_index (34.2) is above 29.65
Ours	Prob. of diabetes is 0.76 because plasma_glucose (152.0) is between 127.5 to 166.5 and body_mass_index (34.2) is above 29.65
Negative sample (label 0)	
BRL	Prob. of diabetes is 0.6 because serum_insulin (0.0) is below 16.0 and body_mass_index (30.8) is above 29.65
Ours	Prob. of diabetes is 0.3 because plasma_glucose (108.0) is between 99.5 to 127.5 and age (21.0) is below 28.5 and times_pregnant (2.0) is below 6.5

We used the large dataset of fraud detection for the experiment. For the model agnostic methods, we also need a deep learning model to explain the decision. Hence, we used a deep neural network for fraud detection as discussed earlier.

Algorithm Settings. We used the implementation provided by the authors for SHAP [10], LIME [8], Anchor [2] and BRL [22]. For Integrated Gradients, we used the implementation provided in [21]. For SHAP, we also needed to provide the background samples. We selected all fraud samples and the equal number of the non-fraud samples from the training data as the background samples. Since the dataset is unbalanced, providing the background samples in this way gives more stable explanations in our experiments.

Common Features in Explanations: In this experiment, we report how many matching features are found in the explanation given by different algorithms. Ideally, we would like to have same features in the explanation for all the algorithms. In this experiment, we used 10 thousand samples from the test set. All 4 thousand fraud samples and the remaining randomly sampled 6 thousand non-fraud samples are used. We used the 'Ours-7' version of our algorithm, which generates at most 7 features in explanation. The remaining algorithms (SHAP, LIME, IG, and Anchor) used in the comparison are also set to generate 7 features in the explanation. The number of matching features in the explanations are counted. Figure 1 shows a distribution of counts of features that are common in the explanations given by the different combinations of the algorithms. The result shows that ExMo finds significantly more matching features with other methods in explanation as compared to the BRL algorithm. For the BRL algorithm, around 85% of the samples did not have any matching features with the explanation generated by LIME, IG, and SHAP. For ExMo, only around 40% of the samples did not have any common features in the explanation.

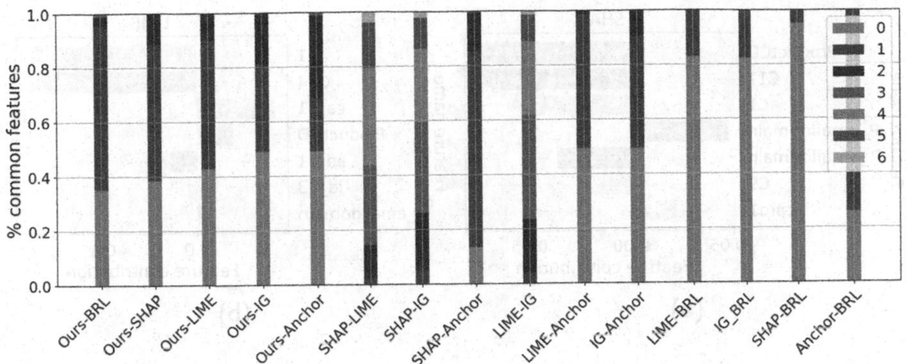

Fig. 1. The number of features that are common in explanation generated by the different algorithms.

Instance Explanations: In this section, we provide the results of the explanation generated by different algorithms. Figures 2 and 3 show explanations generated by SHAP, LIME, IG, Anchor, BRL, and our approach for non-fraudulent and fraudulent transactions, respectively. The model predictions for the non-fraudulent transaction used in Fig. 2 are 0.005, 0.512, and 0.345, respectively, for the deep learning model, BRL and ExMo. In this example, two and three common features in the explanation are found by ExMo and SHAP and IG, respectively. The features 'C11' and 'C1' are common in the explanation given by SHAP and ExMo. The three features 'C14', 'C11', and 'C1' are common in the explanation given by IG and our approach. For the fraudulent transaction given in Fig. 3, the predictions are 0.70, 0.89, and 0.95 for the deep learning model, BRL and ExMo. There are one and two common features in the explanation for SHAP and IG with ExMo, respectively.

Discussion: SHAP, LIME and IG provide explanations in terms of feature importance, providing positive and negative contributions. For example, the SHAP explanation shown in Fig. 2(a) gives the importance of each feature 'ProductCD', 'C11', 'C1', etc. that contribute positively to the prediction. The feature explanation only provides information in terms of importance. In our approach, BRL and Anchor provide explanations in the form of a decision rule, which is different from the feature importance. The explanation is given in terms of comparison, i.e., if the feature value is greater than or equal to some value. Therefore, the explanation of the decision rule is in the absolute sense (i.e., pointing out the feature value or feature value range), while the explanations in the form of feature importance are in the relative sense in terms of percentage of contribution. Therefore, the textual explanation as we discussed in Sect. 4.4 will not be possible for model agnostics explanation techniques as only feature importance's are known. One thing to note is that the features in the decision rule do not give importance to any features and also they are not presented in the sequence of their importance.

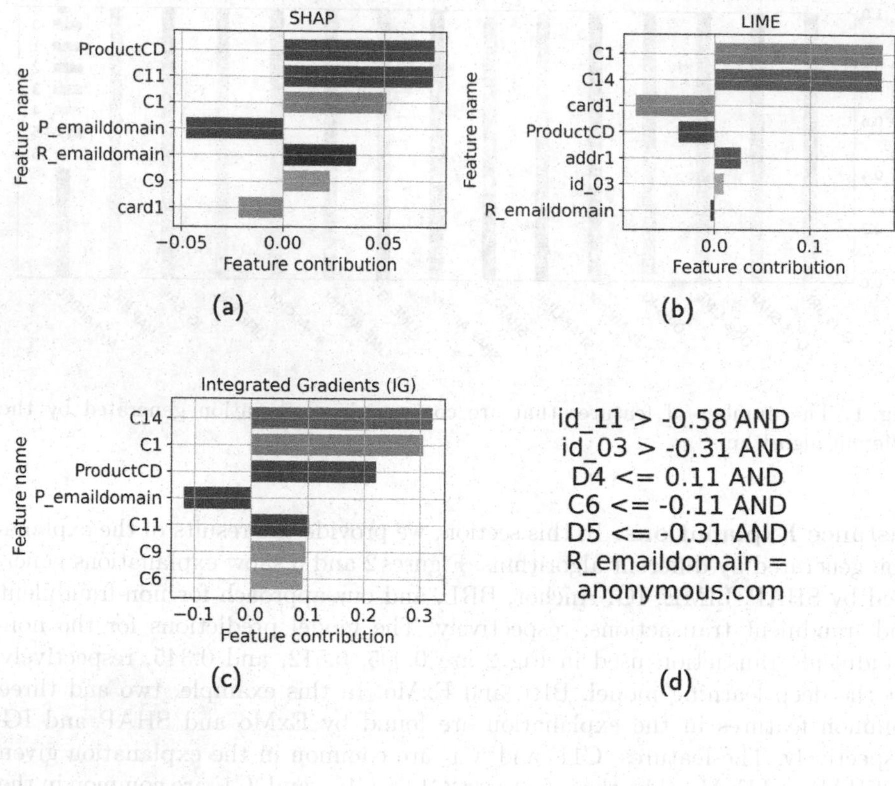

Fig. 2. Explanations computed for a non-fraud sample by: (a) SHAP, (b) LIME, (c) Anchor, (d) Integrated Gradients, (e) BRL and (f) Ours. The values of the features that appeared in the explanations are: ProductCD: S, C1: 1.0, C5: 0.0, C6: 0.0, C9: 0.0, C11: 1.0, C14: 1.0, P_emaildomain: NULL, R_emaildomain: anonymous.com, card1: 1675, card3: 150.0, aadr1: 330.0, addr2: 87.0, id_03: 0.0, id_11: 100.0, D4: NULL, D5: NULL.

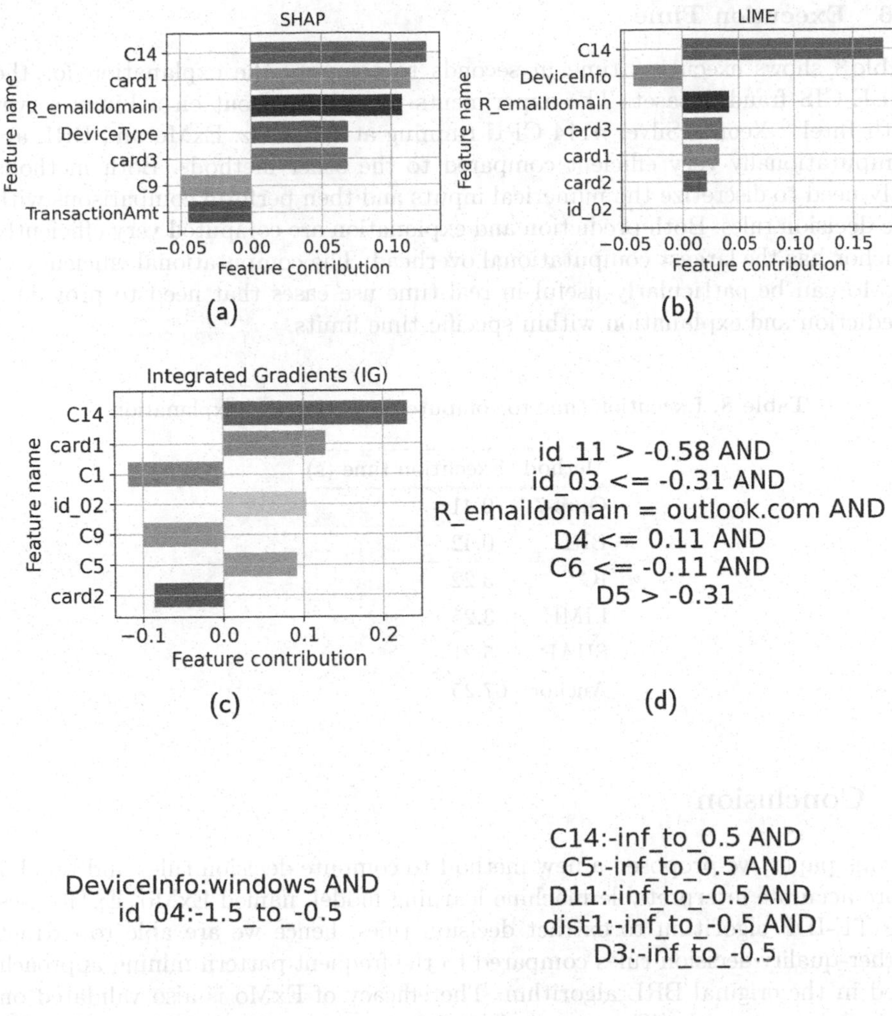

Fig. 3. Explanations computed for a fraud sample by: (a) SHAP, (b) LIME, (c) Anchor, (d) Integrated Gradients, (e) BRL and (f) Ours. The values of the features that appeared in the explanations are: ProductCD: C, C1: 3.0, C5: 0.0, C6: 1.0, C9:0.0, C14: 0.0, TransactionAmt: 36.581, R_emaildomain: outlook.com, card1: 9633, card2: 130.0, card3: 185.0, DeviceInfo: NULL, DeviceType: mobile, dist1: NULL, id_02: 522232.0, id_03: NULL, id_04: NULL, D3: NULL, D4: 0.0, D5: 0.0, D11: NULL.

4.6 Execution Time

Table 8 shows execution time in seconds to compute the explanation for the IEEE-CIS fraud dataset. The experiments were carried out on a Linux server with Intel® Xeon® Silver 4114 CPU running at 2.20 GHz. ExMo and BRL are computationally very efficient compared to the other methods. Both methods only need to discretize the numerical inputs and then perform comparisons with the decision rules. Both prediction and explanation are computed very efficiently. Anchor has the largest computational overhead. The computational efficiency of ExMo can be particularly useful in real-time use cases that need to provide a prediction and explanation within specific time limits.

Table 8. Execution time to compute prediction and explanation

Method	Execution time (s)
Ours-7	0.41
BRL	0.42
IG	3.22
LIME	3.25
SHAP	5.21
Anchor	67.25

5 Conclusion

In this paper, we proposed a new method to compute decision rules and build a more accurate interpretable machine learning model, named ExMo. ExMo uses the TF-IDF algorithm to extract decision rules, hence we are able to extract higher-quality decision rules compared to the frequent pattern mining approach used in the original BRL algorithm. The efficacy of ExMo is also validated on several datasets with different sample and feature sizes. The validation of ExMo on fraud detection, which is a very complex and challenging problem for machine learning systems, shows that ExMo can achieve accuracy very close to the black-box deep learning method. We also demonstrated with the experiments that with the use of these decision rules on fraud detection applications that ExMo can achieve ≈20% higher accuracy. We also demonstrated that the textual explanation can be provided by ExMo, which could be used to communicate decisions to non-expert users. We conclude that our approach will be useful for high-stake applications since it not only achieves better accuracy but also provides explanations in a more human-friendly way. An additional advantage is that the model can also be inspected by regulators for bias and fairness, in a way that is user friendly and easy to understand.

References

1. A right to explanation. https://www.europarl.europa.eu/RegData/etudes/STUD/2020/641530/EPRS_STU(2020)641530_EN.pdf. Accessed 7 May 2021
2. Anchor Implementation. https://github.com/marcotcr/anchor. Accessed 18 Apr 2021
3. Default credit card dataset. https://archive.ics.uci.edu/ml/datasets/default+of+credit+card+clients. Accessed 18 Oct 2021
4. Diabetes plasma glucose ranges. https://labtestsonline.org.uk/tests/glucose-tests, under: What does the test result mean? Accessed 18 Oct 2021
5. How AI Boosts Industry Profits and Innovation. https://www.accenture.com/fr-fr/_acnmedia/36dc7f76eab444cab6a7f44017cc3997.pdf. Accessed 18 Oct 2020
6. IEEE-CIS Fraud Dataset. https://www.kaggle.com/c/ieee-fraud-detection/overview. Accessed 30 Sept 2020
7. Income over 50K. https://archive.ics.uci.edu/ml/datasets/adult. Accessed 18 Oct 2021
8. LIME Implementation. https://github.com/marcotcr/lime. Accessed 18 Apr 2021
9. PIMA diabetes dataset. https://www.kaggle.com/kumargh/pimaindiansdiabetescsv. Accessed 18 Oct 2021
10. SHAP Implementation. https://github.com/slundberg/shap. Accessed 18 Apr 2021
11. Understanding Machines: Explainable AI. https://www.accenture.com/_acnmedia/PDF-85/Accenture-Understanding-Machines-Explainable-AI.pdf. Accessed 18 Oct 2020
12. Adadi, A., Berrada, M.: Peeking inside the black-box: a survey on explainable artificial intelligence (XAI). IEEE Access **6**, 52138–52160 (2018)
13. Bach, S., Binder, A., Montavon, G., Klauschen, F., Müller, K.R., Samek, W.: On pixel-wise explanations for non-linear classifier decisions by layer-wise relevance propagation. PLoS ONE **10**(7), 1–46 (2015)
14. Bertossi, L.E., Li, J., Schleich, M., Suciu, D., Vagena, Z.: Causality-based explanation of classification outcomes. CoRR abs/2003.06868 (2020). https://arxiv.org/abs/2003.06868
15. Brito, L.C., Susto, G.A., Brito, J.N., Duarte, M.A.V.: An explainable artificial intelligence approach for unsupervised fault detection and diagnosis in rotating machinery. CoRR (2021). https://arxiv.org/abs/2102.11848
16. Collaris, D., Vink, L.M., van Wijk, J.J.: Instance-level explanations for fraud detection: a case study. CoRR (2018). http://arxiv.org/abs/1806.07129
17. Coma-Puig, B., Carmona, J.: An iterative approach based on explainability to improve the learning of fraud detection models. CoRR abs/2009.13437 (2020). https://arxiv.org/abs/2009.13437
18. Fayyad, U.M., Irani, K.B.: Multi-interval discretization of continuous-valued attributes for classification learning. In: International Joint Conferences on Artificial Intelligence, pp. 1022–1029 (1993)
19. Han, J.: Mining frequent patterns without candidate generation: a frequent-pattern tree approach. Data Min. Knowl. Discov. **8**, 53–87 (2004)
20. Huang, Q., Yamada, M., Tian, Y., Singh, D., Yin, D., Chang, Y.: GraphLIME: local interpretable model explanations for graph neural networks. CoRR (2020). https://arxiv.org/abs/2001.06216
21. Klaise, J., Van Looveren, A., Vacanti, G., Coca, A.: Alibi: algorithms for monitoring and explaining machine learning models (2019). https://github.com/SeldonIO/alibi

22. Letham, B., Rudin, C., McCormick, T., Madigan, D.: Interpretable classifiers using rules and Bayesian analysis: building a better stroke prediction model. Ann. Appl. Stat. **9**, 1350–1371 (2015)
23. Lundberg, S.M., Lee, S.I.: A unified approach to interpreting model predictions. In: Proceedings of the 31st International Conference on Neural Information Processing Systems, NIPS 2017, pp. 4768–4777 (2017)
24. Makki, S., Assaghir, Z., Taher, Y., Haque, R., Hacid, M.S., Zeineddine, H.: An experimental study with imbalanced classification approaches for credit card fraud detection. IEEE Access **7**, 93010–93022 (2019)
25. Molnar, C.: Interpretable Machine Learning (2019). https://christophm.github.io/interpretable-ml-book/
26. Nguyen, T.T., Tahir, H., Abdelrazek, M., Babar, A.: Deep learning methods for credit card fraud detection. CoRR (2020). https://arxiv.org/abs/2012.03754
27. Okajima, Y., Sadamasa, K.: Deep neural networks constrained by decision rules. In: Proceedings of the AAAI Conference on Artificial Intelligence, July 2019, vol. 33, no. 01 (2019)
28. Psychoula, I., Gutmann, A., Mainali, P., Lee, S.H., Dunphy, P., Petitcolas, F.A.P.: Explainable machine learning for fraud detection. CoRR (2021). https://arxiv.org/abs/2105.06314
29. Rao, S.X., et al.: xFraud: explainable fraud transaction detection on heterogeneous graphs. CoRR (2020). https://arxiv.org/abs/2011.12193
30. Ribeiro, M.T., Singh, S., Guestrin, C.: "Why should I trust you?": explaining the predictions of any classifier. In: Proceedings of the 22nd ACM SIGKDD International Conference on Knowledge Discovery and Data Mining, San Francisco, CA, USA, 13–17 August 2016, pp. 1135–1144 (2016)
31. Ribeiro, M.T., Singh, S., Guestrin, C.: Anchors: high-precision model-agnostic explanations. In: AAAI Conference on Artificial Intelligence (AAAI) (2018)
32. Rudin, C.: Stop explaining black box machine learning models for high stakes decisions and use interpretable models instead. Nat. Mach. Intell. **1**, 206–215 (2019)
33. Shrikumar, A., Greenside, P., Kundaje, A.: Learning important features through propagating activation differences. In: Proceedings of the 34th International Conference on Machine Learning, vol. 70, pp. 3145–3153. JMLR.org (2017)
34. Slack, D., Hilgard, S., Jia, E., Singh, S., Lakkaraju, H.: Fooling LIME and SHA: adversarial attacks on post hoc explanation methods. In: Proceedings of the AAAI/ACM Conference on AI, Ethics, and Society, February 2020, pp. 180–186 (2020)
35. Sundararajan, M., Taly, A., Yan, Q.: Axiomatic attribution for deep networks. In: Proceedings of the 34th International Conference on Machine Learning. Proceedings of Machine Learning Research, 06–11 August 2017, vol. 70, pp. 3319–3328 (2017)
36. Wang, F., Rudin, C.: Falling rule lists. In: Proceedings of Artificial Intelligence and Statistics (AISTATS) (2015)
37. Watson, M., Moubayed, N.A.: Attack-agnostic adversarial detection on medical data using explainable machine learning (2021)
38. Yang, H., Rudin, C., Seltzer, M.: Scalable Bayesian rule lists. In: Proceedings of the 34th International Conference on Machine Learning, vol. 70, pp. 3921–3930. JMLR.org (2017)
39. Zafar, M.R., Khan, N.M.: DLIME: a deterministic local interpretable model-agnostic explanations approach for computer-aided diagnosis systems. CoRR (2019). http://arxiv.org/abs/1906.10263

UX Design and Evaluation of AI-Enabled Systems

A Model of Adaptive Gamification in Collaborative Location-Based Collecting Systems

María Dalponte Ayastuy[1,2(✉)], Diego Torres[1,2], and Alejandro Fernández[2]

[1] Depto CyT, Universidad Nacional de Quilmes, Bernal, Argentina
{mdalponte,diego.torres}@unq.edu.ar
[2] LIFIA, CICPBA-Facultad de Informática, Universidad Nacional de La Plata, La Plata, Argentina
{mdalponte,diego.torres,alejandro.fernandez}@lifia.info.unlp.edu.ar

Abstract. Gamification is a widely used resource to engage and retain users. It is about the use of game elements and mechanics in systems and domains that are not naturally games. Nevertheless, the usage of gamification does not always achieve the expected results due to the too much generalized approach that makes invisible the different motivations, characteristics and playing styles among the players. Currently, research on adaptive gamification deals with the gamification that each particular user needs at a particular moment, adapting gamification to users and contexts. Collaborative location-based collecting systems (CLCS) are a particular case of collaborative systems where a community of users collaboratively collect geo-referenced data. This article proposes an adapted gamification approach for CLCS, through the automatic game challenge generation. Particularly a model of user profile considering the space-time behavior and challenge completion, a model for the different types of challenges applicable in CLCS, a model for the CLCS objectives and coverage, and a strategy for the application of Machine Learning techniques for adaptation.

Keywords: Adaptive gamification · Collaborative location-based collecting systems · Game challenge

1 Introduction

Collaborative location-based collecting systems (CLCS) are a particular case of collaborative systems where a community of users collaboratively collect geo-referenced data [5]. CLCS bundle data records into datasets following a specific data schema that typically includes geographic coverage, submission date, creator, and data quality requirements [14]. CLCS frequently require the user to visit specific location to fulfill the sampling, and consequently, they are implemented with mobile applications.

H. Degen and S. Ntoa (Eds.): HCII 2022, LNAI 13336, pp. 201–216, 2022.
https://doi.org/10.1007/978-3-031-05643-7_13

Gamification (i.e., the usage of game elements in non-game contexts [6]) can be applied in CLCS as a strategy to attract participants, to sustain participation, and to motivate desired behaviours. However, gamification cannot be generalized to all users because of the different users' profiles, preferences, and playing contexts so it needs to be tailored to each one. [3,7,12,17]. Moreover, player engagement tends to decrease as the playing time passes [8], and so the desired behaviors must be reinforced [19].

The gamification of CLCS applies game elements related to space-time aspects to reach the project space-time objectives. This means to motivate the user community to collect data at certain times and places and to sustain that motivation over time. For example, the AppEar [4] citizen science project aims to survey the coasts of rivers, lakes and estuaries. For AppEar, it is important to ensure that the community visits certain geographic areas at certain times and do so with sufficient redundancy. Similarly, the iNaturalist project defines the "City campaign challenge" to promote in a specific city the collection of biodiversity data [11,16] within a certain period of time. This means that the sampling task has spatial and temporal conditions. Moreover, each different project should have specific criteria about the quality of sampling task. In some cases it may be important to achieve a certain sampling density and in other cases it is necessary to achieve a certain level of coverage.

One of the most used game elements in gamified collaborative systems is challenges [2]. A game challenge is a task or problem whose difficulty depends on the user's skills, abilities, motivation, and knowledge [9]. The player completes challenges for different reasons, but mainly because challenges allow to progress in the game and to get results (reach new levels, earn points, etc.). Although the skills, abilities, motivation of users vary, challenges (as game elements) are not frequently tailored.

There is a wide range of types of challenges detailed in the literature [21]. Particularly, those that require endurance or those that require commitment and rhythm can be mentioned, meaning that a space-time constraint must be set. Therefore, a strategy for adapting gamification in CLCS is to build game challenges tailored both to the player's space-time behavior as well to the needs of the CLCS.

The approach of Khoshkangini et al. [10] proposes a mechanism for generating personalized game challenges for each player at all times, based on their individual historical performance but also that of the community. They propose an automatic generation of game challenges using machine learning techniques that is personalized for the history and habits of each player and contextualized to their game state. Indeed, Khoshkangini et al. model and use it as input for adapting the policies or objectives intended to promote.

However, Khoshkangini et al. approach does not take into account the space-time behavior of the users, that is, when and where they interact with the CLCS. The work in [5] proposes a strategy to model the space-time behavior as a time series of behavioral atoms, where each behavioral atom synthesizes in a categorical value the intensity of gameplay based on the elicited frequency of interactions and the movement pattern within a time frame. The sequence of atoms potentially allows to identify space-time behavioral patterns shared between people and thus determine a criterion of similarity between them.

This article proposes an approach for adapting game challenges to the user and the game's objectives in a CLCS using Machine Learning strategies. This approach consists of four elements: 1) a representation of user profile considering the space-time behavior, and the challenge completion, 2) a model for the different types of challenges applicable in CLCS, 3) a model for the CLCS objectives and coverage, and 4) a strategy for the application of Machine Learning techniques for adaptation.

Also, this article presents an extension proposal of the approach in [10] specifically for CLCS, with two traits. On the one hand, using space-time goals, focusing in collecting tasks, and on the other hand modelling static as well dynamic project's objectives. A static objective is represented by goals' weights, and the dynamic objectives are computed goals priorities, considering a set of quality criteria over the sampling task. For instance, the quality criteria can be expressed in terms of collecting density (how many samples must an area have) or collecting coverage (how many different areas need to be sampled).

This article is organized as follows. In next section, a review of related work is presented. In Sect. 3 a concepts background is developed. The approach of CLCS game challenges recommendation is detailed in Sect. 4: and finally the Sect. 5 and 6 shares conclusions and future work.

2 Related Work

Research has been done on adapting gamification elements to the users, and it has been observed that users do not like repetition or uniformity, so dynamic content generation is considered to adapt the gaming experience based on the profiling of users' characteristics [15].

Among the research works that propose gamification adaptation mechanisms, it is possible to find approaches where the player profile (or the playing style) is statically modeled, or where an idea of a dynamic profile is implicitly derived and automatically adjusted over time. Among this first group the works in [10,13] can be included. On the other hand, there are studies that build a player profile based on a classification, usually determined by a questionnaire, to associate them with game preferences (game dynamics). For example, the work of [18] considers user's characteristic by means of Hexad scale [20] and relates it to the optimal game element from the known relationship between each player archetype and the game mechanics.

Contemporary video games frequently use procedural content generation to dynamically create new game elements and consequently grow the game diversity and the gaming experience, that can keep players engaged with the game. This can be used to dynamically adapt the game to player's preferences, skills and playing style [15].

3 Background

As was previously introduced, in a CLCS the community of users collaboratively collect geo-referenced data in a domain-specific data structure that includes, at least: geographic coordinates, submission date, creator, and sample data.

Some objectives of the CLCS can be: to summon a significant number of people/volunteers, to motivate certain behavior in people (for example, to make them travel in a certain manner, to make them participate in a sustained way), to reach a certain sampling quality level, get different samples of different people over the same area (to have different points of view), among others. Beyond the fact that these systems may have other objectives, those mentioned above are related to the space-time aspect, and particularly the present work focuses on the objective of reaching a target sampling quality level.

To specify the quality criteria that each CLCS needs to apply, a set of geographic areas and a set of temporal restrictions are defined to group the sampled data. This allows to express the collecting coverage or collecting density (presented in Sect. 1) in terms of the number of samples required for a given area, which meet a given time constraint. As an example, consider the Fig. 1, where areas are described as black boxes, the green dots describe weekend samples and yellow dots describe weekdays samples.

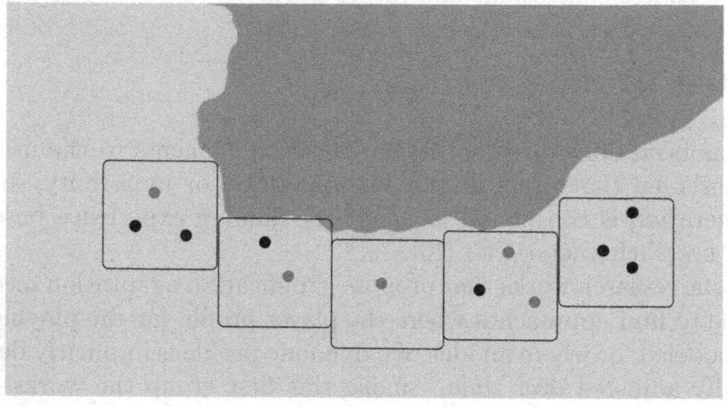

Fig. 1. Sampling example (Color figure online)

In this example, a coverage quality criteria could be to have five yellow samples and five green samples on each area. It can be understood observing the Fig. 1 that in the most left area four weekday samples and 3 weekend samples are still needed.

This section includes definitions that are necessary to understand the approach that is addressed in Sect. 4. Firstly, the definitions related to *Space-time Behaviour* are presented. Later the *Game Challenge* data structure is defined.

3.1 Space-Time Behaviour Definitions

Definition 1 (Sample). *The sample data of a CLCS is a tuple:*

$$SD = <u, T, LL, D>$$

where u *is de user,* T *is the sample timestamp,* LL *is the sample geographic coordinates (Latitude and longitude), and* D *is the domain-specific data (i.e., the content of the sample).*

The work in [5] presents an approach to the users' space-time profiling. As a first step to describe the space-time behavior of the user, the samples are grouped within timeframes, and based on the aggregation of these samples, a clustering technique is applied. This clusters represents the different interaction intensities within a time frame.

Definition 2 (Timeframe). *A time frame is identified by an integer value:*

$$t_i \in [1...n] \subset \mathbb{Z}$$

where $t_i < t_j$ *if* $i < j$

Definition 3 (Behavioural Atom). *A behavioral atom is a categorical value that describes the user's interaction with the CLCS within a time frame from a sample set [5].*

Notice that the input data is not modeled explicitly in the atom, because each possible atom value represents an abstraction of the space-time behavior in a given time period. Particularly, the clusters on a dataset of Fousquare application in New York city [1] gave rise to four atom types, read as Low, Medium, High and Max.

Definition 4 (UTB). *The User Traveling Behaviour series for a user* **u** *is a sequence*

$$UTB_u = \{a_1, ..., a_n\}$$

where each $\boldsymbol{a}_i$ *is a behavioral atom corresponding to the timeframe* ***i***.

3.2 Game Challenge Definitions

Goals characterize the sampling task through a spatial condition, a temporal condition, and a number of samples. Both in the spatial and temporal sense it is possible to define a discrete set of scenarios to characterize the sample. That is, define a set of geographical areas of interest to the CLCS and a set of time intervals that segment the temporal universe according to the sampling needs of the CLCS. To give an example, some system might need to break the time into weekdays vs. weekend days, and other might need smaller segments (morning, afternoon, or night), or more specific combinations. In addition, the goals define a number of samples that must be carried out fulfilling these space-time conditions. With this structure, a goal could be: "take 3 samples in zone number 1 between December 13 and 20". The objective of this number of samples field is to allow the *behavior improvement* of the users, growing this value through recommendations, based on the playing history.

Definition 5 (Goal). *The goal is a tuple:*

$$G = <SA, TR, \#S>$$

where `SA` *is the identification of an sampling area, and* `TR` *is a discrete value that describes a time restriction (interval) when the goal must be completed, and* `#S` *is the sample number that must be done in area* `SA` *and interval* `TR`*.*

A challenge goal can be, for instance:

g_1 : To complete one (`#S = 1`) sample in area 50 (`SA = 50`) on monday (`TR = monday`).

g_2 : To complete two (`#S = 2`) samples in area 6 (`SA = 6`) on a weekend day (`TR = weekend`).

Definition 6 (Game Challenge). *The Game Challenge is a tuple:*

$$GC = <u, g, d, r, w, i>$$

where `u` *is the user,* `g` *is the goal,* `d` *is the estimated difficulty category, and* `r`*,* `w` *and* `i` *are numbers that represents respectively the goal's computed reward, the weight and the percentage of improvement. The* `w` *value is the relevance that is statically configured for each goal.*

For instance, the game challenge $gc_1 = <alex, g_1, medium, 50, 8, 25>$ can be read as user Alex must complete goal g_1, which has an estimated *medium* difficulty for Alex, a reward of 50, a project relevance weight of 8 and an improvement of 25%. Another example is the game challenge $gc_2 = <chris, g_1, low, 20, 8, 50>$ that represents that the user Chris must complete goal g_1, which has an estimated *low* difficulty for Chris, a reward of 20, a project relevance weight of 8 and an improvement of 50%. With these two examples it can be seen that the same challenge goal has different difficulty, reward and improvement for two different users.

Definition 7 (Playing History). *The playing history of a user u is a list of tuples:*

$$PH_u = \{<gc, a>\}$$

where `gc` *is the game challenge and* `a` *is a real value in range* $[0...1] \subset R$ *that describes the challenge achievement*

Note that even though in Definition 7 the value A is presented as a real value in range [0...1], this allows to represent also the discrete Boolean values 0 and 1, that are useful for those goals that do not allow a partial completion (they are fully completed or not completed at all).

For instance, the playing history $ph_1 = \{<g_1, 1>, <g_2, 1>, <g_3, 0>, \}$ indicates that the user completed the first two challenges (g_1 and g_2) but not the third one (g_3).

Definition 8 (User profile). *The representation of user profile considering the traveling behaviour, the challenge preferences and completion is the following tuple:*

$$UP_u = <UTB_u, PH_u>$$

3.3 System Setup Definitions

The CLCS domain specification requires the setup of the samples areas set, the time restrictions set, the improvement scale, the static goal weights, the prize table and the area coverage requirements.

Definition 9 (Areas set). *The areas set is a set of integer values:*

$$a_i \in \mathbb{Z}$$

Definition 10 (Time restrictions). *The time restrictions are a set of categorical values:*

$$tr_i \in String$$

Definition 11 (Improvement scale). *The improvement scale is a set of percentage values:*

$$bi_i \in [0...100] \subset \mathbb{Z}$$

Definition 12 (Prize table). *A prize table is a list of tuples:*

$$prizes = \{<a, tr, d, i, p>\}$$

*where **a** is a sampling area, **tr** is a time restriction, **d** is the difficulty, **i** is the improvement and **p** is an integer number representing the prize for challenges with area **a**, time restriction **tr**, difficulty **d** and improvement **i**.*

Definition 13 (Static Weights). *The goals weights is a list of tuples:*

$$weights = \{<a, tr, w>\}$$

*where **a** is a sampling area, **tr** is a time restriction and **w** is the corresponding weight.*

Definition 14 (Required coverage). *The CLCS required coverage is a list of tuples:*

$$requiredCoverage = \{<a, tr, rs>\}$$

where ***a*** *is a sampling area,* ***tr*** *is a time restriction and* ***rs*** *is an integer number representing the required number of samples in area* ***a*** *within time restriction* ***tr***.

As an example, if a coverage quality criteria is to have, in each area, five samples for *weekday* time restriction and three samples for *weekend*, then the required coverage is:

$$\{<a_1, weekday, 5>, <a_1, weekend, 3>, ..., <a_3, weekend, 3>\}$$

4 CLCS Automatic Game Challenge Recommendation

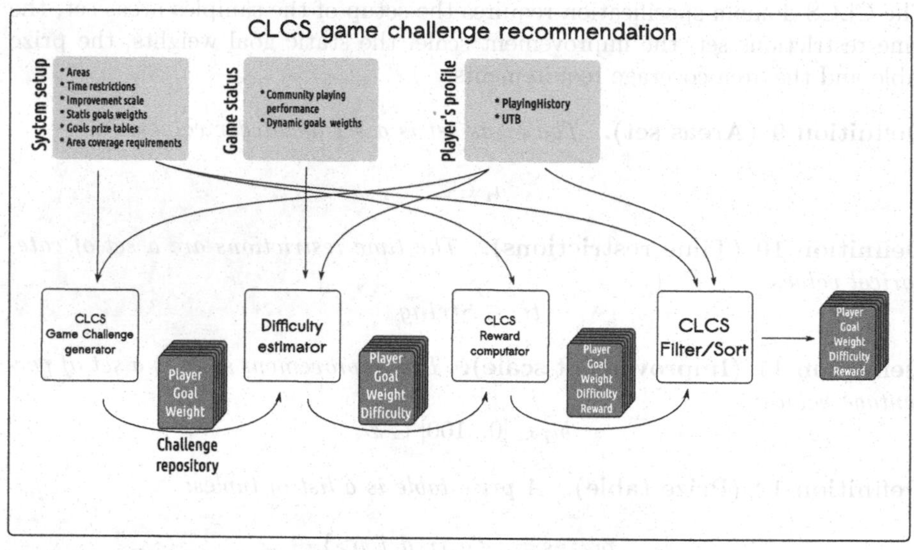

Fig. 2. Framework for CLCS game challenge recommendation

This game challenge recommendation is based on the generation of game challenges tailored to users within the restrictions and objectives presented by each CLCS. It can be seen as a pipeline process made up of 4 main processes which input is the user u_1, and the output is an ordered list of game challenges. The first step is the *challenge repository population*, when all the possible challenge goals that present to the user u_1 a behavioral improvement are built. Also, these challenges must be related to the CLCS specific requirements.

The second step is the *goal difficulty estimation* for each game challenge in the repository populated in the previous step, considering the user u_1 playing history and the community performance in relation to the game challenge goal. The third step is the *reward computation* for each game challenge, where given it's goal, difficulty value, and behavior improvement percentage, a reward amount is obtained. This is done considering the goal's prize table and the dynamically computed system priorities. Finally, the *filtering and sorting step* is done, where the all the potential game challenges are ordered by difficulty, reward and weight, to be recommended to the user u_1. This steps are depicted in Fig. 2.

As was mentioned in the introduction, the recommendation system presented in [10] can be suited to CLCS needs. Therefore this article proposes an extension that takes into account the characteristics and needs of the CLCS and incorporates the idea of space-time behavior modeled by the UTB. Specifically, it models an CLCS goal, extends the game status considering the sample quality related objectives of CLCS, and incorporates the dynamic calculation of goal weights and the users' UTB series at the moment of filtering and ordering the game challenges. To achieve this, the system setup provides a set of geographic areas and a set of time restrictions for the sampling goal.

As an example, a system setup is detailed in Table 1, with 3 geographical areas (a_i), 2 time restrictions (weekday and weekend) and 2 behavioral improvements (50% and 100%). In addition, goals are assigned with a weight that is configured in the system setup, and that allows a priority or relevance to be statically assigned to certain goals (certain areas in certain time restrictions). Also, the prizes tables for the goals $<a_1, weekday>$ and $<a_3, weekend>$ (area a_1, with *weekday* and area a_3 with *weekend* restriction) is shown.

Table 1. Example of system setup

Property	Values
Sample area (SA)	$\{a_1, a_2, a_3\}$
Time restriction (TR)	$\{weekday, weekend\}$
Improvement scale	$\{50\%, 100\%\}$

Goals weights

	a_1	a_2	a_3
Weekday	8	10	12
Weekend	6	8	9

Prizes tables

<a₁,weekday>				<a₃,weekend>		
dif\imp	50%	100%		dif\imp	50%	100%
Easy	100	125	(...)	Easy	111	130
Medium	133	156		Medium	144	161
Hard	166	186		Hard	177	192
Very hard	197	225		Very hard	211	230

4.1 Challenge Repository Population

Table 2. Step 1.a: game challenge repository population

sa	tr	i	w
a_1	Weekday	50%	8
a_1	Weekday	100%	8
a_1	Weekend	50%	6
a_1	Weekend	100%	6
⋮			
a_3	Weekend	50%	9
a_3	Weekend	100%	9

In the first step, the CLCS Game Challenge generator generates an initial repository of game challenges from all the combinations of areas and time restriction that are configured through the system setup. The game challenges must also suppose a level of improvement in the player's behavior that is forced by the $\#s$ parameter (see Definition 5), so each generated goal is replicated to be combined with each level of improvement configured by system setup. Considering the system setup example of Table 1, there are 12 combinations (see Table 2: 3 areas $\times$ 2 time restriction $\times$ 2 improvement scales). The *weight* field is filed out with the corresponding value in the system setup: $W(a_1, weekday) = 8$ (see Table 1).

The value for $\#s$ parameter is completed considering the playing history of the user. For instance, if in the last period the player could complete the goal $g_1 = <a_1, weekday, 2>$ (2 samples), then a 50% improvement means completing $\#s$ with the value 3, and a 100% improvement, the value 4. On the other hand, if the player has no previous activity on a given goal, this field is filled with 1. As an example consider that alex had solved g_1 and g_2:

$$g_1 = <a_1, weekday, 2>$$
$$g_2 = <a_2, weekend, 1>$$

With this historic input, $\#s$ parameter in the Game Challenge repository is filled as shown in Table 3). Notice that are only showed the goals based on g_1, in first and second row, with 50% and 100% respectively, and g_2 in third and fourth row, with 50% and 100%.

4.2 Challenge Difficulty Estimation

This module estimates the difficulty of each challenge c_1 in the repository for user u_1. The difficulty estimation has, as a central element, placing the performance of the user u_1 in the context of the performance of the community. For this, the

Table 3. Step 1.b: improvement application

sa	tr	i	w	#s
a_1	Weekday	50%	8	3
a_1	Weekday	100%	8	4
⋮				
a_2	Weekend	50%	8	2
a_2	Weekend	100%	8	2
⋮				

historical information is limited to those challenges associated with the same goal g_{c1}. Then the other users who have already solved the target challenge c_1 are identified and their distance from u_1 is quantified. Challenge's difficulty is defined as a categorical value between Easy, Medium, Hard and Very Hard, and is calculated from the distance between u_1 and the other players who had completed the target challenge c_1.

Particularly, with the aim of better adapting the challenge c_1 to capabilities or mobility style of the user u_1, he is placed in the context of a segment of the community, made up of people who have similar space-time behavior to that of u_1. The contribution of this article at this point is to narrow the community to this segment, by means of an unsupervised clustering on the UTB series of the entire community. This clustering allows the categorization of the users according to their space-time behavior as is modeled in the approach presented in [5]. Particularly, the difficulty estimation presented in [10] is adapted for the input that contains only the u_1's neighborhood. This adaptation takes into account a most specific context to tailor the challenge difficulty based on similar users with equivalent space-time behavior.

Table 4. Step 2: challenge difficulty estimation

sa	tr	i	w	#s	d	r
a_1	Weekday	50%	8	3	Medium	
a_1	Weekday	100%	8	4	Medium	
⋮						

For instance, consider that user Alex has in his playing history a completed challenge with goal: $g_1 = <a_1, weekday, 2>$. And considering a 100% improvement, the target goal is: $g_2 = <a_1, weekday, 4>$. On the other hand, comparing de current performance (#s = *2*) with the performance of his neighbors in relation to the goal $<a_1, weekday>$, his playing history is not so far from the zone where g_2 is. This means that the estimated difficulty for this challenge is *Medium.*

4.3 Challenge Reward Computation

Beyond representing a game element, the game challenge's reward is a vehicle to motivate the desired behavior, and particularly to meet the defined quality criteria in the CLCS setup. With this objective, in the goal reward computation step, the prizes tables that are statically defined in the system configurations are combined with the current goals' coverage. To compute the reward field, the static baseline reward is weighted with a computed goal priority, as is described in the following equation:

$$r_c = prize(g_c, i_c, d_c) \times w_c \tag{1}$$

where *prize* is a function that obtains from the prizes table the statically configured value for goal g_c, improvement i_c and difficulty d_c, where g_c, i_c and d_c are the goal, improvement and difficulty of challenge c respectively.

The value w_c is the dynamically computed goal weight, defined in the Eq. 2, which considers the required coverage and the current coverage of the goal g_c.

$$w_c = \frac{reqCoverage(a_c, tr_c)}{currentCoverage(a_c, tr_c)} \tag{2}$$

where $currentCoverage(a_c, tr_c)$ is an integer value that represents the sampling status in area a_c and time restriction tr_c, and $reqCoverage(a_c, tr_c)$ is the integer value corresponding to the configured coverage requirement for area a_c and time restriction tr_c. Notice that, while $reqCoverage(a_c, tr_c)$ is greater than $currentCoverage(a_c, tr_c)$ -which is fulfilled from the beginning of the game- w_c is a value that overscales $prize(g_c, i_c, d_c)$, and when $currentCoverage(a_c, tr_c)$ reaches $reqCoverage(a_c, tr_c)$, the value w_c starts to underscale $prize(g_c, i_c, d_c)$. This means that as long as the quality level is not reached, the reward is greater to motivate the challenge to be met.

Table 5. Required coverage configuration

A	TR	Required samples
a_1	Weekday	5
a_1	Weekend	5
⋮		

As an example, consider the required coverage configuration described in Table 5, the defined prizes in Table 1, and the scenario introduced by Fig. 1, where area a_1 had one sample on a weekday (yellow dot) and two weekend samples (green dots). The computed reward for a challenge c_1 = $<alex, g_1, medium, r, 8, 50>$, bounded to goal g_1 = $<a_1, weekday>$, needs to compute the dynamic goal weight (w_{c1}) as follows:

$$w_{c1} = \frac{reqCoverage(a_1, weekday)}{currentCoverage(a_1, weekday)} = \frac{5}{1} = 5$$

Secondly, this value is used in Eq. 1:

$$r_{c1} = p(g_1, 50, medium) \times w_{c1} = 133 \times 5 = 665$$

This formula is applied to the repository as is shown in Table 6.

Table 6. Step 3: reward calculation

sa	tr	i	w	#s	d	r
a_1	Weekday	50%	8	3	Medium	665
a_1	Weekday	100%	8	4	Medium	780
⋮						

The computation presented here considers the required and current level of coverage, through the criteria described in Eqs. 1 and 2, but it is important to note that it is not the only way to incorporate the objectives of the project in the computation of the challenge reward.

4.4 Challenge Sorting

This is the last stage of the CLCS game challenge recommendation process, where the different variables of the game challenges are taken into account to present the user with the elements of the repository in a certain order. There is not a single order criterion, and in particular it is important to consider the 2 dimensions that are proposed: the objectives of the CLCS and the space-time behavior in the definition of community.

In our proposal this is modeled through different data and processes. On the one hand, in relation to the CLCS objectives, there are the static goals weights, which are represented as a variable in the game challenge tuple, and the dynamic objectives that are calculated as was described in the Eq. 2. On the other hand, in relation to the space-time behavior of the users, there are the difficulty value (which considers the UTB series of the community) and the reward value, which takes into account the difficulty and, transitively, the UTB series.

Therefore, a possible strategy is to sort the set of challenges by least difficulty, then highest reward, then static weight. Considering the repository described in Table 7, the challenges order is: $\{c_2, c_3, c_1\}$.

However, the sorting strategy's efficiency must be measured, considering user acceptance through the challenge completion rate.

Table 7. Step 4: challenge sorting

Challenge	sa	tr	i	w	#s	d	r
c_1	a_1	Weekday	50%	8	3	Medium	665
⋮							
c_2	a_3	Weekend	50%	9	1	Easy	720
c_3	a_3	Weekend	100%	9	1	Medium	805

5 Discussion

This article adapted Khoshkangini et al.'s approach for CLCS, adding the user's and community space-time behavior. Nevertheless, different and specific goal models could be proposed for other domains, and some devices in the recommendation process can be replaced by others.

An important aspect that requires greater detail is the granularity of the areas. This topic was not analyzed in this article, however their size can generate differences over the user's engagement. Particularly, regarding the required sampling quality, it could be fitted by using an area set representing a finer grain tessellation (smaller poligons). Also, due to the way they have been modeled here, the areas are independent and different, but it could be useful to model the equivalence of areas and to generate the challenges based on these equivalences. This would allow having a greater number of challenges in the analysis and help to minimize the cold start.

Another aspect that can be exploited is the calculation of atoms. The proposal presented here considers only the set of tuples with coordinates and timestamps, but could include a wider variables set, to relate these samples to the game challenge (or other game element) that had been assigned to the user.

Considering the sorting step, a different sorting strategy can be applied, and the playing history could be taken into account to consider the completion of similar challenges. Finally, the modeling of the user's motivation and objective can be used here.

Lastly, this approach was focused on the generation of challenges, but the question remains of how much of this scheme can be reused to generate other game elements? Or even more, can several types of elements be generated in parallel?

6 Conclusions and Future Work

In this article an automatic game challenge generation approach for CLCS was presented. The needs and characteristics of the CLCS are presented, such as the space-time objectives and the space-time user behavior, to later be valued during the process of automatic generation of game challenges. The contributions are a model of user profile considering the space-time behavior and challenge completion, a model for the different types of challenges applicable in CLCS, a model for the CLCS objectives and coverage, and a strategy for the application of Machine Learning techniques for adaptation.

It is still pending for future work to consider the level of completion of the game challenges at some point in the process. Also, a potential challenge generation strategy could consider area equivalence for both difficulty estimation, reward estimation, or challenge sorting. Also, the quality criterion could consider in some way this notion of equivalence of areas.

Other work scheduled for the future is to detect the player's objectives or to establish a relationship between the type of challenge and the types of player (from a space-time behavior point of view).

References

1. Dalponte Ayastuy, M., Torres, D.: Behavioral atoms for NY foursquare users in 2012 (April 2021). https://doi.org/10.5281/zenodo.4728128
2. Dalponte Ayastuy, M., Torres, D., Fernández, A.: Adaptive gamification in Collaborative systems, a systematic mapping study. Comput. Sci. Rev. **39**, 100333 (2021). https://doi.org/10.1016/j.cosrev.2020.100333. https://www.sciencedirect.com/science/article/pii/S1574013720304330
3. Böckle, M., Novak, J., Bick, M.: Towards Adaptive Gamification: a Synthesis of Current Developments. Research Papers (July 2017)
4. Cochero, J.: Appear: a citizen science mobile app to map the habitat quality of continental waterbodies. Ecología Austral. **28**(02), 467–479 (2018)
5. Dalponte Ayastuy, M., Torres, D.: Relevance of non-activity representation in traveling user behavior profiling for adaptive gamification. In: Proceedings of the XXI International Conference on Human Computer Interaction. Interacción 2021. Association for Computing Machinery, New York (2021). https://doi.org/10.1145/3471391.3471431
6. Deterding, S., Dixon, D., Khaled, R., Nacke, L.: From game design elements to gamefulness: defining "gamification". In: Proceedings of the 15th International Academic MindTrek Conference: Envisioning Future Media Environments, MindTrek 2011, Tampere, Finland, pp. 9–15. ACM, New York (2011). https://doi.org/10.1145/2181037.2181040
7. Göbel, S., Wendel, V.: Personalization and adaptation. In: Dörner, R., Göbel, S., Effelsberg, W., Wiemeyer, J. (eds.) Serious Games, pp. 161–210. Springer, Cham (2016). https://doi.org/10.1007/978-3-319-40612-1_7
8. Hamari, J., Koivisto, J., Sarsa, H.: Does gamification work? A literature review of empirical studies on gamification. In: 2014 47th Hawaii International Conference on System Sciences, pp. 3025–3034. IEEE (2014)
9. Iversen, S.: In the double grip of the game: challenge and *fallout* 3. Game Stud. **12** (2012). http://www.gamestudies.org/1202/articles/in_the_double_grip_of_the_game
10. Khoshkangini, R., Valetto, G., Marconi, A., Pistore, M.: Automatic generation and recommendation of personalized challenges for gamification. User Model. User Adap. Inter. **31**(1), 1–34 (2020). https://doi.org/10.1007/s11257-019-09255-2

11. Kishimoto, K., Kobori, H.: Covid-19 pandemic drives changes in participation in citizen science project "city nature challenge" in Tokyo. Biol. Conserv. **255**, 109001 (2021). https://doi.org/10.1016/j.biocon.2021.109001. https://www.sciencedirect.com/science/article/pii/S0006320721000537
12. Tomé Klock, A.C., da Cunha, L.F., de Carvalho, M.F., Eduardo Rosa, B., Jaqueline Anton, A., Gasparini, I.: Gamification in e-learning systems: a conceptual model to engage students and its application in an adaptive e-learning system. In: Zaphiris, P., Ioannou, A. (eds.) LCT 2015. LNCS, vol. 9192, pp. 595–607. Springer, Cham (2015). https://doi.org/10.1007/978-3-319-20609-7_56
13. Lavoué, E., Monterrat, B., Desmarais, M., George, S.: Adaptive gamification for learning environments. IEEE Trans. Learn. Technol. **12**, 16–28 (2018). https://doi.org/10.1109/TLT.2018.2823710
14. Lemmens, R.: A conceptual model for participants and activities in citizen science projects. In: Vohland, K., et al. (eds.) The Science of Citizen Science, pp. 159–182. Springer, Cham (2021). https://doi.org/10.1007/978-3-030-58278-4_9
15. Lopes, R., Bidarra, R.: Adaptivity challenges in games and simulations: a survey. IEEE Trans. Comput. Intell. AI Games **3**(2), 85–99 (2011). https://doi.org/10.1109/TCIAIG.2011.2152841
16. Nugent, J.: Citizen science: iNaturalist. Sci. Scope **041**(07), 12–13 (2018)
17. Orji, R., Tondello, G.F., Nacke, L.E.: Personalizing persuasive strategies in gameful systems to gamification user types. In: Proceedings of the 2018 CHI Conference on Human Factors in Computing Systems, CHI 2018, pp. 1–14. Association for Computing Machinery, New York (2018). https://doi.org/10.1145/3173574.3174009
18. Sánchez-Anguix, V., Alberola, J.M., Julián, V.: Towards adaptive gamification in small online communities. In: Sanjurjo González, H., Pastor López, I., García Bringas, P., Quintián, H., Corchado, E. (eds.) SOCO 2021. AISC, vol. 1401, pp. 48–57. Springer, Cham (2022). https://doi.org/10.1007/978-3-030-87869-6_5
19. Thiebes, S., Lins, S., Basten, D.: Gamifying information systems - a synthesis of gamification mechanics and dynamics. In: ECIS 2014, June 2014 (2014)
20. Tondello, G., Wehbe, R., Diamond, L., Busch, M., Marczewski, A., Nacke, L.: The gamification user types hexad scale. In: CHI PLAY 2016, October 2016 (2016). https://doi.org/10.1145/2967934.2968082
21. Vahlo, J., Karhulahti, V.M.: Challenge types in gaming validation of video game challenge inventory (CHA). Int. J. Hum. Comput. Stud. **143**, 102473 (2020). https://doi.org/10.1016/j.ijhcs.2020.102473. https://www.sciencedirect.com/science/article/pii/S1071581920300756

Benchmarking Neural Networks-Based Approaches for Predicting Visual Perception of User Interfaces

Maxim Bakaev[1(✉)], Sebastian Heil[2], Leonid Chirkov[1], and Martin Gaedke[2]

[1] Novosibirsk State Technical University, Novosibirsk, Russia
bakaev@corp.nstu.ru
[2] Technische Universität Chemnitz, Chemnitz, Germany
{sebastian.heil,martin.gaedke}@informatik.tu-chemnitz.de

Abstract. Deep Learning techniques have become the mainstream and unquestioned standard in many fields, e.g. convolutional neural networks (CNN) for image analysis and recognition tasks. As testing and validation of graphical user interfaces (GUIs) is increasingly relying on computer vision, CNN models that predict such subjective and informal dimensions of user experience as aesthetic or complexity perception start to achieve decent accuracy. They however require huge amounts of human-labeled training data, which are costly or unavailable in the field of Human-Computer Interaction (HCI). More traditional approaches rely on manually engineered features that are extracted from UI images with domain-specific algorithms and are used in "traditional" Machine Learning models, such as feedforward artificial neural networks (ANN) that generally need fewer data. In our paper, we compare the prediction quality of CNN (a modified GoogLeNet architecture) and ANN models to predict visual perception per Aesthetics, Complexity, and Orderliness scales for about 2700 web UIs assessed by 137 users. Our results suggest that the ANN architecture produces smaller Mean Squared Error (MSE) for the training dataset size (N) available in our study, but that CNN should become superior with N > 2912. We also propose the regression model that can help HCI researchers to foretell MSE in their ML experiments.

Keywords: User Interfaces · Aesthetics · Visual Complexity · Deep Learning

1 Introduction

The currently ongoing "AI summer" is largely associated with advances in Deep Learning artificial neural networks (DNNs). For many non-specialists, the very term *neural network* (ANN) came to be synonymous with *Machine Learning* (ML) and even with *Artificial Intelligence* (AI) in general. Indeed, Deep Learning (DL) techniques have become the mainstream and unquestioned standard in many fields, a notable example being convolutional neural networks (CNN) in image analysis and recognition tasks.

H. Degen and S. Ntoa (Eds.): HCII 2022, LNAI 13336, pp. 217–231, 2022.
https://doi.org/10.1007/978-3-031-05643-7_14

One disadvantage of DL is that it is computationally expensive, but the current AI summer is facilitated by reasonably cheap and available hardware, so it becomes less of a problem. Another issue is that generally deep models are hungry for data, which is still a limitation for their application in certain fields. For instance, in HCI arguably the only source of abundant and nearly free data are interaction logs, but some aspects of user behavior cannot be reflected there in principle. Particularly, dimensions of subjective satisfaction are largely collected from users in surveys or dedicated experiments, so the corresponding datasets are limited in size, usually to 1000s of records.

In the last decade, HCI saw a rise in algorithms and tools for extracting various UI metrics, which could be provided as inputs for feature-based ML models. A notable example of software implementation is AIM [1], while the WUI Measurement Platform [2] was built upon several such online services. The popular outputs of UBMs are objective usability parameters, e.g., time on task or success rate, or dimensions of subjective satisfaction, for instance, aesthetic impression or visual complexity [3]. Unlike for the objective parameters, the R^2s in the models predicting subjective impressions in the ML regression task would typically not exceed the rather modest value of 0.7. So, a considerable number of research publications would focus on proposing new metrics affecting user perception of UIs and on polishing the algorithms for calculating the existing metrics [4].

In recent years though, this branch of HCI appears to be also turning towards featureless DL approaches. For instance, *Webthetics DNN* [5] has demonstrated superior performance in predicting webpage aesthetics. They relied on a dataset from 2013 that contained 40,000 user ratings averaged for about 400 web UI images (they were downsampled from the resolution of 1024 × 768 to 256 × 192, and the pixel intensities were rescaled). To compensate for the relatively modest size of the dataset, the authors employed a model pre-trained on 80,000 general images, which allowed them to report the linear correlation corresponding to $R^2 = 0.723$. At the same time, public datasets incorporating 10,000s of UI images start to emerge, e.g., *Rico* dataset [6], although their focus is still mostly on interaction logs, not on the rated subjective impressions. With this dataset, it was already demonstrated that the detection of elements in GUIs can achieve superior outcomes relying on DL approaches. However, though the accuracy in the detection of UI elements is important, it does not necessarily transform into the quality of UBMs predicting users' subjective impressions [7].

If the task is conventional detection or classification of objects in a UI screenshot, one probably wouldn't need to seek anything better than the mainstream CNN-based computer vision (although code-based approaches might be more effective). However, it so far remains unclear if a user interface, being designed for interaction, is just an image in terms of visual perception – and this may well define the suite of effective methods. For instance, the complexity of topographic maps can be duly estimated based on features, such as the number of graphical elements per unit map area [8]. Which particular subjective impression dimension is involved might also matter: e.g., a web page aesthetical perception could be universal, whereas assessment of its orderliness might be shaped by the previous user interactions on the web. Even for images, feature-based approaches work well for certain tasks: for instance, in [9] they achieved a classification success rate of about 95% with a dataset of just over 5000 images, which is comparable with a CNN model trained on 16,000 images [10]. In practical terms, this presents a challenge for the development of the field: **should it focus on selecting more meaningful metrics and polishing the respective algorithms or on creating larger and more robust datasets?**

So, in our current work we benchmark several neural network approaches: "conventional" ANN based on features that we extract from web UIs using our WUI Measurement Platform and CNN DL model operating on raw images of the same web UIs. The comparison is done on a dataset practically sized for the HCI field: about 3000 web UI images and about 35,000 user ratings for the subjective impressions of Complexity, Aesthetics, and Orderliness. The rest of our paper is structured as follows. In Sect. 2 we overview the usage of neural networks in various computer vision tasks and for different types of material. There we also briefly note the means for feature extraction from UIs. In Sect. 3 we describe our experimental study and detail the employed NN architectures. In Sect. 4 we compare the models having different architectures and study the effect of the additional factors. In the final section we summarize our contributions, discuss the limitations and outline the direction for further research.

2 Methods and Related Work

2.1 Neural Networks in Computer Vision

The "traditional" feed-forward artificial neural networks are generally limited in processing multidimensional data, such as videos, sound, etc. in its raw form. One might choose to rely on domain expertise and carefully engineer and extract the features to be subsequently fed into such ML model. Another possibility is employing DL, which allows automatic feature extraction, at the cost of needing more training data and being more computationally expensive. Architecture-wise, DNNs have many hidden layers with relatively a small number of neurons in each of them, which mathematically makes them superior approximators in real tasks, where the activation function cannot be implemented exactly [11]. Particularly, CNNs can have dozens of layers, each convolutional layer implementing a filter and producing feature maps.

Due to the high practical effectiveness of CNNs in dealing with imagery, which is also explained by their similarity to the organization of the animal visual cortex [12], this architecture is the current standard in computer vision. The most common tasks in this field include image classification and segmentation, but DL models can be used in regression tasks for more sophisticated and user-subjective parameters. For instance, it was demonstrated that human opinion scores on the images' quality can be predicted with a CNN [13]. Aesthetics and visual complexity are the other dimensions popular in the current research, whose values are mostly collected through surveys and are reasonably well predicted by DL models [14]. At the same time, even presumably invariant object detection tasks have been shown to benefit from additional feature-based tweaking for GUIs [15]. Thus, theoretical considerations do not give us a definite answer in favor of either approach, so practical benchmarking is deemed necessary.

Among the research publications that came to our attention, we could not find the ones comparing different NN architectures and ML approaches for image-based UI analysis. There is relevant work in text analysis [16] and document classification [17], which operate with dataset sizes (1000s of documents) comparable to the ones available in HCI practice. The general methodology is reasonably straightforward: "Classifiers are applied on raw and processed data separately and their accuracy is noted" [16]. Subsequently, we describe how we process the UIs and our experimental study.

2.2 UI Feature Extraction

Since software is essentially its code, code-based analysis appears natural for studying user interfaces. Indeed, they are reasonably successful in detecting problems with not just straightforward HTML/CSS and content correctness, but also with accessibility and even, with a certain degree of confidence, usability ("usability smells" [18]). However, code-based approaches are understandably less effective in extracting features meaningful for the dimensions of users' visual impressions: complexity, clutter, regularity of layouts, etc. In the attempt to teach computers to "see" and even "comprehend" graphical UIs, image-based approaches gained momentum in the last decade [19]. E.g., the same concept of "smells" can mean probable violation of visual design guidelines, which is detected based on selected features extracted from UI images [20]. A notable example of extending HTML DOM-based analysis with partial webpage rendering is the *ViCRAM* tool [21].

Some of the services capable of extracting meaningful features (*metrics*) from UI screenshots have been made accessible to researchers and designers by the authors. However, inputting many screenshots and saving the output in a consistent format might be problematic if one seeks to collect large volumes of data. So, we have developed a kind of meta-service, *WUI Measurement Integration Platform*[1], which can automate the collection of metrics provided by the various services [2]. As demonstrated in Fig. 1, it sends the specified website URIs or ready-made screenshots (the latter might be provided as a list in the platform's batch mode) to a remote service using its supported protocol and saves the metrics and other output in the platform's database in an ML-friendly form. The productivity of the platform is largely defined by the time needed for a remote service to process a screenshot.

The platform was used to extract the features for the material we used in the experimental study, with the two dedicated remote services, VA [22] and AIM [1].

[1] The web browser version is available at http://va.wuikb.info.

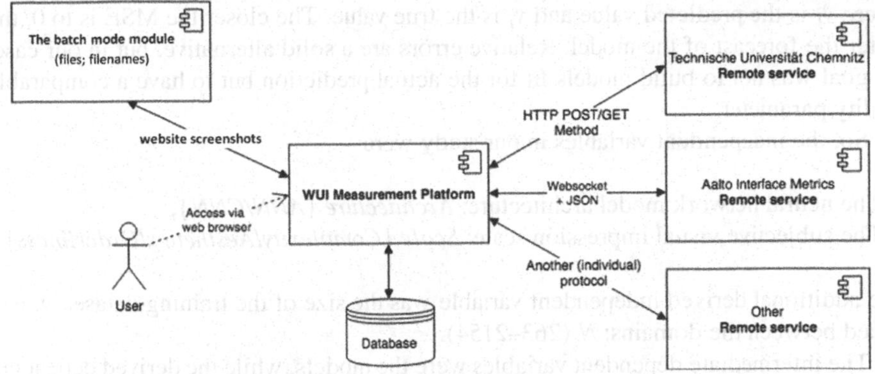

Fig. 1. The WUI Measurement Integration Platform with batch mode access.

3 The Experimental Study Description

3.1 Hypotheses and Design

The goal of our experiment was to compare the user behavior predictive ability of neural network models with two different architectures: "classical" feature-based ANNs and "deep" CNNs. Our previous studies suggest that the quality of the models can vary considerably depending on the dimension of visual perception being predicted, so we are controlling for this factor in the experiment, employing three different subjective impression scales: *Complexity*, *Aesthetics,* and *Orderliness* [23]. At the same time, the uniformity or diversity of the training data is an important issue as well – for instance, it has been shown that the models do not always work well across different topical domains [3]. Thus, we employed the websites purposefully selected from 6 different domains, although in this study we do not control specifically for this factor. To explore the effect of the dataset sizes, we have a different number of websites in each domain, and construct the training datasets for the models by merging the domains datasets in $2^6 - 1 = 63$ possible ways.

So, the experiment had a within-subject design, relying on the same training datasets for the two different architectures. In the ANN models, the input values were the normalized metrics obtained for the screenshots (the full list of the 32 metrics can be found in [3, Table 3]), whereas in the CNN models the input was the actual screenshot images. The outputs in both ANN and CNN models were the visual perception assessments per the 3 subjective impression scales. In accordance with the usual ML practices, 80% of the samples were used for training and 20% were used for testing.

The quality of the models was operationalized as Mean Squared Error (MSE), which is arguably the most widely used loss function for neural network models that perform regression tasks:

$$MSE = \frac{1}{n}\sum_{i=1}^{n}(y_i - \hat{y}_i)^2, \tag{1}$$

where $\hat{y}_i$ is the predicted value and y_i is the true value. The closer the MSE is to 0, the better the forecast of the model. Relative errors are a solid alternative, but in our case, the goal was not to build models fit for the actual prediction but to have a comparable quality parameter.

So, the independent variables in our study were:

- The neural network model architecture: *Architecture* {*ANN/CNN*},
- The subjective visual impression scale: *Scale* {*Complexity/Aesthetics/Orderliness*}.

The additional derived independent variable was the size of the training dataset, which varied between the domains: *N* (263–2154).

The intermediate dependent variables were the models, while the derived dependent variables actually used in the study were the models' MSEs and training times: MSE_{ANN} and MSE_{CNN}, $Time_{ANN}$ and $Time_{CNN}$.

Thus, we had the following null hypotheses in our experiment:

- H1: There is no difference in MSEs per the architectures.
- H2: There is no difference in the training time per the architectures.
- H3: The outcome of H1 and H2 is the same for any N.
- H4: The outcome of H1 and H2 is the same for any scale.

3.2 Material and the Input Data

The initial material in our study was screenshots of homepages of websites that belonged to one of 6 domains, as listed in Table 1. The screenshots were automatically collected using our dedicated script that followed the URIs provided by student volunteers and captured the rendered webpages as 1280 × 960 or 1280 × 900 pixels images. In the subsequent manual inspection, the screenshots that had technical problems, e.g., webpages that failed to load or had a pop-up covering a significant portion of the screen, or that did not belong to the specified domain were removed (see [3] for more detail).

The resulting 2932 screenshots were submitted to our WUI Measurement Integration Platform in "batch" mode, to calculate the 32 metrics acting as the input for the ANN models. For 240 (8.19%) of the screenshots, the VA and AIM services failed to produce some or all of the metrics, so we had to exclude the screenshots from the datasets for both ANN and CNN models. This dropout was not random, but it was approximately evenly distributed across the domains, with the exception of the *Games* domain (see in Table 1), probably due to more the complex structure and more robust graphics of the corresponding websites.

3.3 Subjects and the Output Data

The 3 visual perception dimensions were represented as Likert scales ranging from 1 (the lowest degree of the characteristic) to 7 (the highest degree). The subjective assessments of the websites per the scales were performed in a dedicated survey by 137 participants (67 females, 70 males), whose ages ranged from 17 to 46 (mean 21.18, SD = 2.68).

Table 1. The screenshots collected from the 6 domains and used for the ANN and CNN models.

Domain name	Description	Number of the screenshots	
		Collected	Used for the models
Culture	Websites of museums, libraries, exhibition centers, other cultural institutions	807	746 (92.4%)
Food	Websites dedicated to food, cooking, healthy eating, etc	388	369 (95.1%)
Games	Websites dedicated to computer games	455	362 (79.6%)
Gov	E-government, non-governmental organizations' and foundations' websites	370	346 (93.5%)
Health	Websites dedicated to health, hospitals, pharmacies, medicaments	565	541 (95.8%)
News	Online and offline news editions' websites, news portals	347	328 (94.5%)
Total:		**2932**	**2692 (91.8%)**

Most of them were Bachelor's and Master's students of Novosibirsk State Technical University (NSTU), but there were also students and staff of some other universities, and specialists working in the IT industry. The majority of participants were Russians (89.1%), the rest being from Bulgaria, Germany, South Africa, etc. The subjects took part in the experiment voluntarily and no random selection was performed. All the participants had normal or corrected to normal vision and reasonable experience with websites. In total, we collected 35265 assessments for the 2692 screenshots from the 6 domains, and the descriptive statistics per the 3 scales can be found in [3, Table 4].

3.4 The Models: ANN and CNN

To increase the number of models for the sake of a more robust comparison between the NN architectures, for each scale we used all possible combinations of the 6 domain datasets (e.g., Culture + News, Food + News + Gov, etc.). This resulted in $3 \cdot (2^6 - 1) = 189$ ANN and 189 CNN models.

To construct and train the ANN models, we used the `Colab` service freely offered by Google (TensorFlow 2.5 environment with Keras 2.4, etc.).The feedforward ANN models were built with the `Keras Tuner` library that helps select the best models with different combinations of various layers and hyperparameters. The models were trained until the verification accuracy began to decrease for several epochs in a row, i.e., a stopping mechanism was employed. The ANN models' code is as follows:

```
def build_model(hp):
    model = keras.Sequential()
    activation_choice = hp.Choice('activation',
values=['relu', 'sigmoid', 'tanh', 'elu', 'selu'])
    model.add(Dense(units=hp.Int('units_input',
                                       min_value=512,
                                       max_value=1024,
                                       step=32),
                    activation=activation_choice))
    for i in range(2, 6):
        model.add(Dense(units=hp.Int('units_' + str(i),
                                          min_value=128,
                                          max_value=1024,
                                          step=32),
                        activation=activation_choice))
    model.add(Dense(1))
    model.compile(
        optimizer="adam",
        loss='mse',
        metrics=['mse', coeff_determination])
    return model
```

The CNN models were built using GoogLeNet architecture, with the output layer being replaced with a single neuron layer to accommodate the regression task. The GoogLeNet CNN architecture consists of the following types of layers [24]:

- **Convolutional Layer**. The layer is used to extract features from the input image, in this layer the input image is convolved using convolutional filters. At the output of this layer, new images appear, called feature maps.
- **Concatenate Layer**. This layer returns a tensor containing the concatenation of all inputs, provided they have the same dimension.
- **MaxPooling, AveragePooling2D**. Union layers are usually used after convolutional layers in order to simplify the information displayed by the convolutional layer. Thus, the layer prepares a compressed feature map from the feature map created in the previous step.
- **Dropout**. This layer is an overfitting prevention technique that randomly removes connections from earlier layers during neural network training [25].

The Adam optimization algorithm that is a gradient-based first-order stochastic function [26] was chosen as the optimization algorithm. This method is well suited for the implementation of models with a large set of data and parameters; it is also not memory-intensive and computationally efficient. The machine that we used to train the models had four i7-3930K CPUs @ 3.20 GHz, 16 GB of memory and NVIDIA Quadro RTX 5000.

4 Results

4.1 Descriptive Statistics

In total, we built 378 models and registered *MSE* and *Time* for each of them. Pearson correlation between MSE_{ANN} and MSE_{CNN} obtained for the datasets for the same combination of domains turned out to be moderate, but significant: $r_{189} = 0.341$, $p < 0.001$. The correlation between $Time_{ANN}$ and $Time_{CNN}$ was also highly significant: $r_{189} = 0.623$, $p < 0.001$.

The Shapiro-Wilk's tests suggest that the normality hypotheses had to be rejected for MSE_{CNN} ($W_{189} = 0.901$, $p < 0.001$), but not for MSE_{ANN} ($W_{189} = 0.989$, $p = 0.171$). The descriptive statistics (means and standard deviations) for the dependent variables are presented in Table 2.

Table 2. Descriptive statistics for *MSE* and *Time* per the architectures and scales.

Architecture	ANN		CNN	
Scale	MSE_{ANN}	$Time_{ANN}$	MSE_{CNN}	$Time_{CNN}$
Complexity	0.644 (0.081)	93.7 (17.4)	0.750 (0.127)	2165.4 (1440.7)
Aesthetics	0.772 (0.104)	107.2 (20.1)	0.968 (0.182)	2704.4 (1560.0)
Orderliness	0.769 (0.102)	101.3 (18.6)	0.859 (0.122)	2650.6 (1495.8)
All	0.739 (0.106)	100.7 (19.4)	0.859 (0.170)	2506.8 (1511.3)

4.2 The Models' Training Time

We found no significant correlations between $Time_{ANN}$ and MSE_{ANN} ($p = 0.140$) or $Time_{CNN}$ and MSE_{CNN} ($p = 0.104$). This suggests that the training stopping mechanism worked properly and training the models for longer would not yield better results. At the same time, Pearson correlations between the training datasets sizes (*N*) and the training times were highly significant for both ANN ($r_{189} = 0.812$, $p < 0.001$) and CNN ($r_{189} = 0.765$, $p < 0.001$) architectures. These positive correlations are also in line with the NN theory and practice.

On average, training a CNN model took 25 times longer than an ANN model. However, one must note that the feature extraction process in our study took about 43 h (57 s per one valid screenshot) with the dedicated WUI Measurement Platform. So, ANN involves a considerable initial "investment" of time but allows much quicker construction of the models afterward. Assuming the same number of screenshots and the same configuration of the machines that we had in the current study, ANN gets an advantage if **at least 64 models are constructed**; otherwise, the CNN approach results in lower overall time costs.

ANOVA found significant effects not only of *Architecture* ($F_{1,371} = 701.1$, $p < 0.001$), but also of *Scale* ($F_{2,371} = 3.71$, $p = 0.025$) on *Time*. The interaction of the two factors was also significant ($F_{2,371} = 3.41$, $p = 0.034$). In other words, constructing a model for Complexity took considerably less time than for the other two scales, particularly for the CNN architecture. So, the effect of different scales needs to be taken into account when constructing and studying the models.

4.3 Benchmarking the Models' MSEs

Despite MSE_{CNN} not being normally distributed, we used a t-test for paired samples (equal variances not assumed) to check the difference in the MSEs produced by the two architectures. The difference between MSE_{ANN} and MSE_{CNN} turned out to be highly significant: $t_{188} = -9.904$, $p < 0.001$. Figure 2 demonstrates the differences in the distributions of the MSEs for the two architectures.

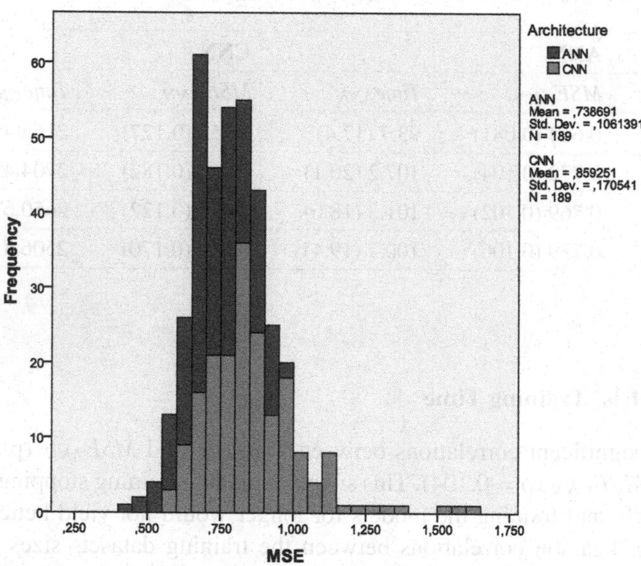

Fig. 2. The distributions of MSEs for the two NN architectures.

Further, we performed the analysis of the difference with all the factors in the study, to adhere to the effect of scales. ANOVA found significant effects of *Architecture* ($F_{1,371} = 90.5$, $p < 0.001$) and *Scale* ($F_{2,371} = 53.1$, $p < 0.001$) on *MSE*. The interaction between them was also significant ($F_{2,371} = 9.0$, $p < 0.001$). Post-hoc tests found significant differences (at $\alpha = 0.001$) between all three scales.

Interestingly, MSE_{CNN} did have a significant negative Pearson correlation with *N* ($r_{189} = -0.174$, $p = 0.017$), whereas MSE_{ANN} did not ($r_{189} = 0.033$, $p = 0.655$). So, we can conclude that the amount of data we have in the study was adequate for the ANN models, whereas the ones built with CNN architecture would benefit from more data.

4.4 Regression Analysis for MSE

To further explore the effect of N on MSE, we constructed a regression model for MSE_{CNN}, which had rather low $R^2 = 0.03$, but was significant ($F_{1,187} = 5.85$, $p = 0.017$):

$$MSE_{CNN} = 0.932 - 0.663 \cdot 10^{-4} N. \quad (2)$$

Stretching the model (2) beyond the interval used in our study ($N \leq 2153$), we can speculate that **at $N = 2912$, MSE_{CNN} would catch up** with the average $MSE_{ANN} = 0.739$ (the latter was not significantly affected by N, as we noted before).

Since previously we found a significant effect of the scales, we built regression models with N for the difference between the MSEs. The models were significant for Aesthetics ($F_{1,61} = 3.99$, $p = 0.050$, $R^2 = 0.06$) and Orderliness ($F_{1,61} = 5.34$, $p = 0.024$, $R^2 = 0.08$), but not for Complexity ($F_{1,61} = 0.42$, $p = 0.520$):

$$(MSE_{CNN} - MSE_{ANN})_{Aesthetics} = 0.315 - 1.082 \cdot 10^{-4} N. \quad (3)$$

$$(MSE_{CNN} - MSE_{ANN})_{Orderliness} = 0.188 - 0.900 \cdot 10^{-4} N. \quad (4)$$

From (3) it follows that for the Aesthetics models, MSE_{CNN} would become smaller than MSE_{ANN} when $N > 2908$. For the Orderliness models (4), the same would be achieved when $N > 2090$.

Finally, we constructed linear regression models for MSE with dummy variables (having the values {0/1}): $Scale_A$ (has the value of 1 if the current model predicts Aesthetics) and $Scale_O$ (has the value of 1 if the current model predicts Orderliness). Another dummy variable was A_{CNN} (which has the value of 1 if the current model was built using CNN architecture). The rational scale factor in the regression was N, the training dataset size for the current model. All the variables turned out to be significant (at $\alpha = 0.05$) in the resulting model, which had $R^2 = 0.341$ ($F_{4,373} = 48.2$, $p < 0.001$):

$$MSE = 0.684 + 0.121 A_{CNN} + 0.158 Scale_A + 0.102 Scale_O - 0.293 \cdot 10^{-4} N. \quad (5)$$

5 Discussion and Conclusion

In our work, we compared ML models constructed based on two different approaches: ANNs based on 32 pre-extracted features and deep learning CNNs working with raw UI images. In total, we constructed 378 models and trained them on subsets of the dataset consisting of about 3000 screenshots of web UIs. The models would predict subjective user impressions of Complexity, Aesthetics and Orderliness, whose 35265 assessments were provided by 137 participants. Our analysis of the experimental data suggests the following outcome for the formulated hypotheses:

- H1: There is significant difference ($p < 0.001$) in the models' MSEs per the architectures. The average MSE for the ANN architecture was 16.2% smaller than for the CNN architecture.

- H2: There is significant difference in the models' training time per the architectures, assuming that the features for the ANNs are pre-extracted. Training a single CNN model took 0.696 h, which is 25 times longer than for an ANN model. However, extracting the features for all the 2692 screenshots in our study took about 43 h.
- H3: The size of the training dataset naturally has significant effect on training time for both architectures. More interestingly, it did significantly affect MSE_{CNN} ($p = 0.017$), but not MSE_{ANN} ($p = 0.655$). So, at $N > 2912$, the former should become smaller than the latter, although we could not observe it in our study, due to limited size of the dataset.
- H4: For different subjective impressions scales, the outcome of the models' comparison varies. In our study, training an average Complexity model took 11.3% less time for ANNs and 23.6% less time for CNNs. Complexity models also on average had 19.6% smaller MSE_{ANN} and 21.8% smaller MSE_{CNN}. Moreover, N did not have significant effect on the errors for Complexity, unlike for the other two scales.

Since no existing work comparing different NN architectures for image-based UI analysis came to our attention, we are unable to compare our findings to a solid baseline. In [17], where the datasets comparably had 100s and 1000s of documents, they similarly found that feature-based approach with normalized difference measure had advantage over DL for text documents classification. In one of our own previous experiments [3], we obtained comparable MSEs for ANN models (on average, 0.928 for Complexity, 1.09 for Aesthetics, 1.119 for Orderliness), which though had simpler architecture and did not optimize hyperparameters. In [3], we also found that the effect of the training dataset size on the models' MSE was not significant.

We need to note that the absolute MSE values were still rather high in our study. The standard GoogLeNet convolutional network architecture, which we relied on, is primarily intended for image classification, not predicting subjective impressions. Moreover, the dataset in our study was much smaller than the ones generally used in computer vision DL projects. For instance, in [27] to predict the aesthetics of photographs with a fairly high accuracy they employed a set of 255,000 images. Among our research prospects is using pre-trained models and testing if they could significantly change the current findings. Particularly, DL models could be trained on ImageNet in general image recognition, and then be fine-trained to predict aesthetical and other subjective impressions.

As for ANNs, the nuance is that we did not perform feature engineering, but relied on the 32 features output by the VA and AIM services. The services would fail on 8.19% of the screenshots, thus introducing an additional argument against the feature-based approach, as well as a threat to the study validity. Still, since the goal of our study was not to create production-use ML models, but to compare the different NN architectures on HCI-realistic dataset sizes, we believe the obtained MSEs are still fit for benchmarking based on statistical methods.

We consider our study having the following main contributions:

- We demonstrated that feature-based NNs are more accurate in predicting the subjective impressions with datasets of several hundred websites.
- We estimated at which training dataset size (about 3000 websites) the DL approach should start having an advantage.

- We explored the time costs of the feature extraction and the training. Extracting features is a considerable initial investment, but it allows better subsequent flexibility in exploring the models. However, if one plans to only build several dozens of models with the dataset, the DL approach working with raw data would require less total time.
- We found that the results may vary depending on the concrete subjective dimension being predicted. So, research and practical ML models engineering should consider this.
- We built a regression model (5) for foretelling MSEs in similar ML experiments, which might be useful for AI-HCI researchers and practitioners.

Acknowledgment. The reported study was funded by RFBR according to the research project No. 19–29-01017. The research was partially funded by the Deutsche Forschungsgemeinschaft (DFG, German Research Foundation)—Project-ID 416228727—SFB 1410.

References

1. Oulasvirta, A., et al.: Aalto interface metrics (AIM): a service and codebase for computational GUI evaluation. In: The 31st Annual ACM Symposium on User Interface Software and Technology Adjunct Proceedings, pp. 16–19. ACM (2018)
2. Bakaev, M., Heil, S., Khvorostov, V., Gaedke, M.: Auto-extraction and integration of metrics for web user interfaces. J. Web Eng. **17**(6), 561–590 (2018)
3. Bakaev, M., Speicher, M., Heil, S., Gaedke, M.: I Don't Have That Much Data! Reusing User Behavior Models for Websites from Different Domains. In: Bielikova, M., Mikkonen, T., Pautasso, C. (eds.) ICWE 2020. LNCS, vol. 12128, pp. 146–162. Springer, Cham (2020). https://doi.org/10.1007/978-3-030-50578-3_11
4. Lima, A.L.D.S., Gresse von Wangenheim, C.: Assessing the visual esthetics of user interfaces: a ten-year systematic mapping. Int. J. Hum. Comput. Interact. **38**(2), 144–164 (2022)
5. Dou, Q., Zheng, X.S., Sun, T., Heng, P.A.: Webthetics: quantifying webpage aesthetics with deep learning. Int. J. Hum Comput Stud. **124**, 56–66 (2019)
6. Deka, B., et al.: Rico: A mobile app dataset for building data-driven design applications. In: Proceedings of the 30th Annual ACM Symposium on User Interface Software and Technology, pp. 845–854 (2017)
7. Bakaev M., Heil, S., Hamgushkeeva, G., Gaedke, M.: The effect of input data quality in feature-based modeling of user behavior. In: ESK International Symposium (2021) (In Print)
8. Ciołkosz-Styk, A., Styk, A.: Advanced image processing for maps graphical complexity estimation. In: Proceedings of the 26th International Cartographic Conference, Dresden, Germany, pp. 25–30 (2013)
9. Carballal, A., Santos, A., Romero, J., Machado, P., Correia, J., Castro, L.: Distinguishing paintings from photographs by complexity estimates. Neural Comput. Appl. **30**(6), 1957–1969 (2016). https://doi.org/10.1007/s00521-016-2787-5
10. López-Rubio, J.M., Molina-Cabello, M.A., Ramos-Jiménez, G., López-Rubio, E.: Classification of Images as Photographs or Paintings by Using Convolutional Neural Networks. In: Rojas, I., Joya, G., Català, A. (eds.) IWANN 2021. LNCS, vol. 12861, pp. 432–442. Springer, Cham (2021). https://doi.org/10.1007/978-3-030-85030-2_36

11. Kreinovich, V.: From traditional neural networks to deep learning: towards mathematical foundations of empirical successes. In: Shahbazova, S.N., Kacprzyk, J., Balas, V.E., Kreinovich, V. (eds.) Recent Developments and the New Direction in Soft-Computing Foundations and Applications. SFSC, vol. 393, pp. 387–397. Springer, Cham (2021). https://doi.org/10.1007/978-3-030-47124-8_31
12. Khan, A., Sohail, A., Zahoora, U., Qureshi, A.S.: A survey of the recent architectures of deep convolutional neural networks. Artif. Intell. Rev. **53**(8), 5455–5516 (2020). https://doi.org/10.1007/s10462-020-09825-6
13. Talebi, H., Milanfar, P.: NIMA: Neural image assessment. IEEE Trans. Image Process. **27**(8), 3998–4011 (2018)
14. Xing, B., Si, H., Chen, J., Ye, M., Shi, L.: Computational model for predicting user aesthetic preference for GUI using DCNNs. CCF Trans. Pervasive Comput. Interact. **3**(2), 147–169 (2021). https://doi.org/10.1007/s42486-021-00064-4
15. Chen, J., et al.: Object detection for graphical user interface: old fashioned or deep learning or a combination? In: proceedings of the 28th ACM joint meeting on European Software Engineering Conference and Symposium on the Foundations of Software Engineering, pp. 1202–1214 (2020)
16. Kamath, C.N., Bukhari, S.S., Dengel, A.: Comparative study between traditional machine learning and deep learning approaches for text classification. In: Proceedings of the ACM Symposium on Document Engineering 2018, pp. 1–11 (2018)
17. Asim, M.N., Ghani, M.U., Ibrahim, M.A., Mahmood, W., Dengel, A., Ahmed, S.: Benchmarking performance of machine and deep learning-based methodologies for Urdu text document classification. Neural Comput. Appl. **33**(11), 5437–5469 (2020)
18. de Oliveira T. Souza, J., de Souza, A.D., Vasconcelos, L.G., Baldochi, L.A.: Usability Smells: A Systematic Review. In: Latifi, S. (ed.) ITNG 2021 18th International Conference on Information Technology-New Generations. AISC, vol. 1346, pp. 281–288. Springer, Cham (2021). https://doi.org/10.1007/978-3-030-70416-2_36
19. Zen, M., Vanderdonckt, J.: Towards an evaluation of graphical user interfaces aesthetics based on metrics. In: 2014 IEEE Eighth International Conference on Research Challenges in Information Science, RCIS, pp. 1–12. IEEE (2014)
20. Yang, B. et al.: Don't Do That! Hunting down visual design smells in complex UIs against design guidelines. In: 2021 IEEE/ACM 43rd International Conference on Software Engineering, ICSE, pp. 761–772. IEEE (2021)
21. Michailidou, E., Eraslan, S., Yesilada, Y., Harper, S.: Automated prediction of visual complexity of web pages: Tools and evaluations. International Journal of Human-Computer Studies **145**, 102523 (2021)
22. Bakaev, M., Heil, S., Khvorostov, V., Gaedke, M.: HCI vision for automated analysis and mining of web user interfaces. In: Mikkonen, T., Klamma, R., Hernández, J. (eds.) ICWE 2018. LNCS, vol. 10845, pp. 136–144. Springer, Cham (2018). https://doi.org/10.1007/978-3-319-91662-0_10
23. Boychuk, E., Bakaev, M.: Entropy and compression based analysis of web user interfaces. In: Bakaev, M., Frasincar, F., Ko, I.-Y. (eds.) ICWE 2019. LNCS, vol. 11496, pp. 253–261. Springer, Cham (2019). https://doi.org/10.1007/978-3-030-19274-7_19
24. Elngar, A.A., et al.: Image classification based on CNN: a survey. J. Cybersecurity Inf. Manag. (JCIM) **6**(1), 18–50 (2021)
25. Özgür, A., Nar, F.: Effect of dropout layer on classical regression problems. In: 2020 28th Signal Processing and Communications Applications Conference, SIU, pp. 1–4. IEEE (2020)

26. Kingma, D.P., Ba, J.: Adam: A method for stochastic optimization. arXiv preprint arXiv:1412.6980 (2014)
27. Bianco, S., Celona, L., Napoletano, P., Schettini, R.: Predicting image aesthetics with deep learning. In: Blanc-Talon, J., Distante, C., Philips, W., Popescu, D., Scheunders, P. (eds.) ACIVS 2016. LNCS, vol. 10016, pp. 117–125. Springer, Cham (2016). https://doi.org/10.1007/978-3-319-48680-2_11

My Tutor is an AI: The Effects of Involvement and Tutor Type on Perceived Quality, Perceived Credibility, and Use Intention

Mo Chen(✉), Fanjue Liu, and Yu-Hao Lee

College of Journalism and Communications, University of Florida, Gainesville, FL, USA
{chenmo0825,fanjueliu,leeyuhao}@ufl.edu

Abstract. With the advancement of AI technology, AI tutors are already being utilized in classrooms throughout the world as teaching aides, tutors, and peer learning specialists. AI tutors are good at facilitating various teaching-learning practices within and outside the classroom, and support students 24/7. However, little is known whether AI tutors can be as effective in learning languages as human tutors, and what factors would cause student learning outcome differences between human tutors and AI tutors, especially for those students who are not engaged in learning. The current study sought to address these questions by discovering the combination of two factors: involvement (high vs. low) and tutor type (human tutor vs. AI tutor) under two conditions: weak and high writing quality. The findings indicate that there is an interaction effect between user involvement and tutor type. When user involvement is low, the AI tutor is perceived to have a higher writing quality than the human tutor; when user involvement was high, tutor type did not affect the perceived writing quality of the tutor, no matter the tutor was a human or an AI. The reason that the human tutor is preferred is that the human tutor is perceived to have a higher level of controllability than the AI tutor. The writing quality of tutors affects the credibility of tutors as well.

Keywords: AI tutor · CASA · ELM · Controllability · Credibility · Human-machine communication

1 Introduction

The application of artificial intelligence (AI) tutors in educational institutions has fundamentally changed the traditional learning process from teacher-student interaction to AI tutor-student interaction. AI tutors enhance learning outcomes such as facilitating various teaching-learning practices (e.g., generating questions, checking homework, monitoring learning progress) within and outside the classroom, and supporting students 24/7. AI tutors have been used in K-12 schools and higher education institutions helping students with various subjects, such as Julian at Walden University [1], Jill Watson at Georgia Tech [2], Duolingo Bots, Thinkster, Squirrel AI, etc. AI tutors are great tools to achieve equality in education. AI tutors can provide students from economically disadvantaged areas access to all kinds of learning materials without being in the same geographical

H. Degen and S. Ntoa (Eds.): HCII 2022, LNAI 13336, pp. 232–244, 2022.
https://doi.org/10.1007/978-3-031-05643-7_15

location. AI tutors are often more patient than humans, can give each student individualized attention, and offer adaptive learning based on machine learning technology. Although many types of AI tutors are currently in use, many students, teachers, and parents remain hesitant to accept AI tutors. They believe that compared to AI tutors, human tutors are more effective at helping students with language learning such as creative wring and language conversations [3].

Some studies have shown that AI tutors are effective in helping students with language learning in increasing learning involvement [4, 5] and language fluency [5], offering diverse conversational contexts [6, 7], and promoting positive behaviors and attitudes toward technology [4–8]. However, those studies did not compare if the learning outcomes are different or not when students acquire knowledge from AI tutors and human tutors. Moreover, students may have different levels of initial learning involvement. Little is known whether AI tutors can be as effective in learning languages as human tutors, and what factors would cause student learning outcome differences between human tutors and AI tutors, especially for those students who are not engaged in learning.

The current study seeks to address these questions by discovering the combination of two factors: involvement (high vs. low) and tutor type (human tutor vs. AI tutor) under two conditions: weak and high writing quality. We focus on how involvement and tutor type affect users' perception toward tutors through the theoretical framework of attribution theory and the Elaboration Likelihood Model (ELM). The findings of this study advance the theoretical knowledge of the mind perception of AI agents in the ELM and provide practical guidelines for designing AI educational systems.

2 Related Work

2.1 AI Tutors

With the advancement of AI technology, AI tutors are already being utilized in classrooms throughout the world as teaching aides, tutors, and peer learning specialists. AI tutors are algorithm-based technology that "play a meaningful role during an interaction with humans in helping them engage in affective, cognitive, and behavior learning through various ways" [9]. For example, in language acquisition, AI tutors can measure and visualize learning outcomes to encourage self-learning, replace pricey private teachers, provide personalized educational services, keep track of the learner's educational levels and status, and make recommendations for educational goals and content [10, 11].

AI tutors have different forms such as embodied and disembodied. Embodied AI tutors have physical bodies. For example, telepresence robots in London's Saatchi gallery give remote teaching sessions concerning the exhibited paintings and sculptures [12], a robot avatar went to school and interacted with teachers and classmates for a sick boy in Germany [13], or social robots aid teachers teaching at preschools and elementary schools [14–16]. Disembodied AI tutors are software-based and do not have physical bodies, such as the Duolingo bot that facilitates second language learners to practice language [17] and Squirrel AI, an AI-based platform that offers adaptive online after-school tutoring for K-12 students.

As a result of the growth of AI agents in education, researchers began to compare the effectiveness of AI tutors and human tutors. Some studies have found that although students rated both a human teacher and a robot teacher as credible instructors, the human teacher (including telepresence human teachers) was rated more credible than a robot teacher [18, 19]. In the human-robot co-teaching context, students rated the human as lead teacher team more credible and more appealing than the robot as lead teacher team [20]. Moreover, other factors such as the perceived similarity also affect the perceived credibility of AI agents. Students who identified themselves as "older" perceived the older AI voice instructor as more credible than the younger AI voice instructor and vice versa [21]. Other studies showed that a social robot or a virtual assistant with a human voice was perceived as more credible than the same social robot or the virtual assistant with a synthetic voice [22, 23]. These studies suggest that AI tutors could be customized to meet the demands of students with various features and needs. Overall, despite the fact that AI tutors are new, the idea of bringing AI tutors, whether they are embodied or disembodied, into educational environments has gotten a lot of interest from both industry and academics.

2.2 The Elaboration Likelihood Model (ELM) and Computers are Social Actors (CASA)

The CASA paradigm proposed that individuals apply social roles and social norms to machines in interpersonal communications as if machines are humans [24, 25]. Early research in the CASA paradigm has revealed that when interacting with computers, individuals exhibit the same social responses as they interact with humans. For example, individuals applied politeness and social norms to computers [24, 26], affiliated with computers as teammates [25], and interacted with computers that have a similar personality to themselves [27]. The dominant explanation of CASA is mindlessness. Nass and Moon attributed the mindless responses of humans to evolution that individuals have not evolved a "new" brain to differentiate the mediated and non-mediated experience [26]. They proposed that individuals are more sensitive to social cues and ignore the asocial cues of machines because social cues can easily trigger social expectations and responses in human-human interactions. When social cues are observed, humans mindlessly apply interaction norms to the entity as if they were human.

Although the CASA paradigm argues that when social cues are detected, people mindlessly treat machines as if they were humans, some studies showed that people may apply different communication strategies when communicating with machines. For example, individuals who could not differentiate between Twitter bots and human bots in the perceived credibility, communication competence, and use intention [28]. In the news writing context, participants had higher perceived credibility, when the news was written by a tandem (half human and half machine) than the news written by a human or an AI software [29]. When purchasing a flight ticket, participants were more likely to disclose their personal information to a machine than a human agent [30]. The question that "when and why mindless behavior will occur" still need to be explored [26].

The ELM model may explain that question. The model posits that people use two routes when processing information: the peripheral route and the central route [31–33]. When people use the peripheral route to make decisions, they look for simple cues to help them make a quick decision, such as an attractive source or specific features of a product, without carefully scrutinizing issue-relevant information [33]. When people use the central route to make decisions, they carefully and thoughtfully consider the true merits of the information.

Issue involvement is a key factor in determining whether the individual uses the central route or the peripheral route of cognition to process information. For example, when purchasing a product, the involvement level of consumers determines which route they process information. When consumers are highly involved in assessing the product, the argument quality of a product description is more important in forming attitudes toward the product than a well-known celebrity endorser in the product advertising [32]. In this case, consumers process information through the central route. On the contrary, when consumers are not involved in assessing the product, a well-known celebrity endorser in the product advertising is more important in forming a positive attitude toward the product than the argument quality of the product description, which means consumers process information through the peripheral route [32]. While, in the educational context, student involvement is a key motivation for them to acquire knowledge and interact with teachers. When students are involved in learning, they are more likely to assess the tutor's writing quality rather than who is their tutor. However, when students are not involved in learning, they will take the peripheral route and look for heuristics to decide if the tutor's writing quality is high or low. In this condition, tutor type is a heuristic cue that triggers the peripheral route of cognition. The information generated by a machine is perceived as free of bias, which is known as machine heuristic [34]. A previous study found that compared to a human agent, users were more likely to give their personal information to a machine agent [30]. Thus, we propose that:

H1: There is an interaction effect between involvement and tutor type. Only when user involvement is low, users will perceive the AI tutor has a higher writing quality than the human tutor.

2.3 Attribution Theory

Although AI tutors have a lot of benefits in facilitating online learning, human tutors are still preferred. To understand why this happens, attribution theory provides one alternative explanation. Attribution theory posits people try to figure out what causes a particular event in order to comprehend why things happen [34]. When people have bad luck, they instinctively hunt for the cause of the bad luck and attribute who or what was responsible for it. Attribution processes influence students' perceptions of the service quality of tutors. In general, perceived controllability is the factor that influences people to place responsibility toward the service of AI agents [35]. Students form the initial impression of tutors' service quality is mediated by the perceived controllability [34], which refers to a student's perception of the extent to which the writing quality was under the tutor's control. According to a meta-analysis study, the controllability attribution has a stronger effect mediating consumers' satisfaction toward a specific service [36]. Humans are perceived to have a higher level of controllability than robots when doing service work [35, 37, 38]. Thus, human tutors may be perceived to have a higher level of controllability. Based on the Modality-Agency-Interactivity-Navigability (MAIN) model the perceived quality of information influences the credibility judgment

[39] and therefore, people are more likely to use the product in the future. Therefore, we propose:

H2: Compared to the AI tutor, participants will perceive the human tutor has more controllability than the AI tutor.

H3: The perceived writing quality will positively influence the perceived credibility of the tutor and the future use intention.

3 Method

We designed a mixed experiment: 2 (involvement: high vs. low) × 2 (tutor type: human tutor vs. AI tutor) between-subjects and with 1 within-subject (writing quality: week and strong). To test the hypothesis, test-based writing essays were created for this study.

3.1 Participants

We recruited participants from Prolific in 2021 March. In total, 330 participants completed the experiment. Four of the participants who did not pass the attentions checks were removed from the final dataset. In total, 326 participants' responses were included in the final dataset for our analysis. This study was approved by the university IRB. Each participant was paid $1.44. The average completion time was 13.01 min. The average age of participants was 33.89 years old ($SD = 12.60$), ranging from 18 years old to 71 years old. Among them, 49.4% were male ($n = 161$), and 48.8% were female ($n = 159$). Among all participants, 43.8% of them have a bachelor's degree or above ($n = 143$). Majority of them were White (68.9%, $n = 199$), followed by Asian (15.9%, $n = 46$), African American (7.6%, $n = 22$), and others (7.6%).

3.2 Procedure

When recruiting participants from Prolific, the participants were informed that they were going to participate in a study that explore people's perceptions toward a tutor that helps students with their essays. They were asked to read a short description of the tutor and then read two pieces of writing samples that were edited by the tutor. After finishing reading each piece of the writing sample, participants were asked to evaluate the quality and credibility of the tutor's writing. After finishing evaluating the two pieces of essays, participants were asked to report their future use intention, issue importance, educational level, and demographic information.

3.3 Stimuli

Participants were randomly assigned to one of the four conditions. In the high involvement condition, participants were informed that they had to read the information carefully, and if they could not answer the message description question correctly, they would not get paid. In the low involvement condition, participants were not informed that they would not get paid. In the human tutor condition, participants were told that the information was written by an English major doctoral student. In the AI tutor condition, participants were told that the information was written by an AI-powered algorithm. All participants were asked to read two pieces of essays (see Fig. 1). One has a high writing quality, and the other one has a low writing quality in random order. Both essays were based on the same topic, which was selected from the TOEFL test writing sample questions (ets.org/toefl/).

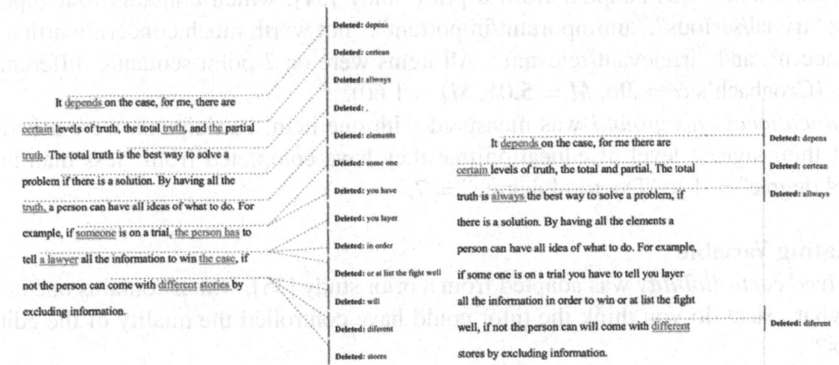

Fig. 1. Essay topic: "Always telling the truth is the most important consideration in any relationship". The left one has high writing quality and the right one has low writing quality.

3.4 Measurement

Manipulation Check

Involvement was measured with one item, "To me, overall, being a participant in this task to evaluate a writing assistant was ___". Participants were asked to rate their involvement in a seven-point semantic differential scale, from "involving" to "uninvolving" [31, 32].

Tutor type was measured with one item, "The writing assistant is ___". Participants were asked to choose the type of the writing assistant in a seven-point semantic differential scale, from "AI-powered algorithm" to "human".

Dependent Variables

Perceived credibility was adapted from a prior study [39]. Participants were asked to rate their perceived credibility of the tutor in 7-point semantic differential scales, which contains six bipolar items: "intelligent/unintelligent", "untrained/trained", "inexpert/expert", "informed/uninformed", "incompetent/competent", "bright/stupid" (Cronbach's $\alpha = .91$, $M = 3.92$, $SD = 1.23$).

Perceived writing quality was measured with one item on a seven-point Likert scale, "How would you rate the editing quality of the tutor compared to the original essay", from "extremely unclear" = 1 to "extremely clear" = 7.

Future use intention was adapted from a prior study [32], which contains three items: "I intend to use the writing tutor in the future", "I expect that I would use writing tutor in the future", "I plan to use the writing tutor in the future". The items were measured by 7-point-Likert scales, from "strongly disagree" = 1 to "strongly agree" = 7 (Cronbach's $\alpha = .97, M = 3.32, SD = 1.85$).

Control Variables

Issue importance was adapted from a prior study [31], which contains four bipolar items: "trivial/serious", "unimportant/important", "not worth much concern/worth a lot of concern", and "irrelevant/relevant". All items were on 7-point semantic differential scales (Cronbach's $\alpha = .96, M = 5.01, SD = 1.60$).

Educational background was measured with one item. Participants were asked to report their highest level of education that they have completed from "less than high school degree" = 1 to "Doctoral degree" = 7.

Mediating Variable

Perceived controllability was adapted from a prior study [35], which contains one item: "To what extent do you think the tutor could have controlled the quality of the edited essays?".

4 Results

To test the manipulations, two t-test analyses were conducted. The results revealed that there was a significant difference between high and low involvement conditions, $t(324) = 18.38, p < .0001, d = 0.54$; There was a significant difference between the human tutor and the AI tutor conditions, $t(324) = 25.41, p < .0001, d = 0.90$.

To test H1, a MANOVA analysis was conducted controlling for educational background and issue importance. The independent variables were involvement and tutor type. The dependent variables were 1) perceived writing quality, 2) perceived credibility, 3) use intention. The results showed that the effect of involvement on 1) perceived quality ($F(1, 288) = 0.2, p = .655$, partial $\eta^2 = .001$), 2) perceived credibility ($F(1, 288) = .37, p = .543$, partial $\eta^2 = .001$), 3) use intention ($F(1, 288) = .79, p = .376$, partial $\eta^2 = .003$.) were not statistically significant. The effect of tutor type on perceived quality ($F(1, 288) = 1.81, p = .179$, partial $\eta^2 = .006$) and perceived credibility ($F(1, 288) = 2.01, p = .157$, partial $\eta^2 = .007$) were not statistically significant. However, the effect of tutor type on future use intention was statistically significant ($F(1, 288) = 9.34, p = .002$, partial $\eta^2 = .032$). There was an interaction effect between involvement and tutor type on perceived quality, F (1, 283) = 4.47, $p = .035$, partial $\eta^2 =. 016$. Under the low involvement condition, the AI-powered tutor ($M = 5.07, SE = .16, p = .015$) was perceived to have a higher quality than the human tutor ($M = 4.50, SE = .17$). Under the high involvement condition, there was no statistically significant difference between the AI tutor ($M = 4.77, SE = .17, p = .557$) and the human tutor ($M = 4.90, SE = .15$) on perceived quality (see Fig. 2). Therefore, H1 was supported.

To test H2 if perceived controllability would mediate the relationship between tutor type and the perceived quality. A mediation analysis was run with the PROCESS macro

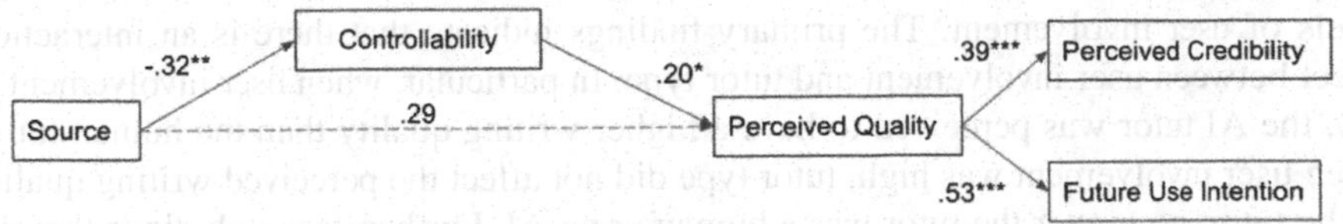

Fig. 2. The predicted relationships (H2 and H3). $^{***}p < .001$, $^{**}p < .01$, $^{*}p < .05$.

3.4 using 5,000 bootstrapped samples and 95% bias-adjusted confidence intervals controlling for the education level and the issue importance of participants. The indirect effect of tutor type on the perceived quality through the pathway of controllability was statistically significant, $\beta = -.06$, 95% CI [−.16, −.001]. As shown in Fig. 3, compared to AI-generated, human-generated information had a greater controllability ($\beta = -.32, p = .005$), and a higher controllability led to higher the perceived quality ($\beta = .20, p = .017$). The direct effect of tutor type and perceived quality was not statistically significant ($\beta = .29, p = .105$). The indirect effect of tutor type on use intention through the pathway of expectation violation was not statistically significant, $\beta = .26, p = .110$, 95% CI [−.06, .58]. Therefore, H2 was supported.

To test H3, two linear regression analyses were conducted to test the relationship between perceived quality and 1) perceived credibility and 2) use intention. The results revealed that the perceived quality was a significant predictor of 1) perceived credibility ($\beta = .39, t(324) = 8.65, p < .0001$) and 2) use intention ($\beta = .53, t(324) = 7.65, p < .0001$). Therefore, H3 was supported.

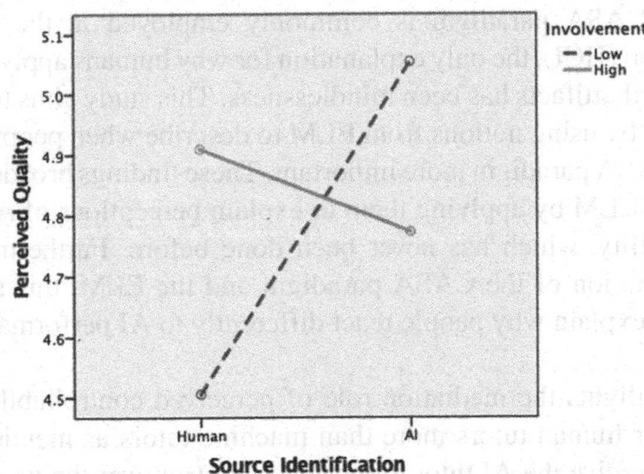

Fig. 3. The interaction effect between tutor type and involvement on perceived quality.

5 Discussion

The present research examined user involvement and tutor type on users' perceptions toward the tutor's writing quality and credibility and future use intention. We compared the perception differences between a human tutor and an AI tutor with two different levels of user involvement. The primary findings indicate that there is an interaction effect between user involvement and tutor type. In particular, when user involvement is low, the AI tutor was perceived to have a higher writing quality than the human tutor; when user involvement was high, tutor type did not affect the perceived writing quality of the tutor, no matter the tutor was a human or an AI. Further, the study finds that the reason that the human tutor is preferred is that the human tutor had a higher level of controllability than the AI tutor. Tutors' writing quality affects the credibility of tutors as well.

5.1 Contributions and Implications

The findings advanced the theoretical knowledge of the attribution of AI agents in the ELM and also provided practical guidelines. The findings show that user involvement moderates the effect of tutor type on perceived writing quality. The findings are in accordance with the ELM framework. The high involvement triggered the central route of cognition, and there was no significant difference between the perceived assignment quality of the AI tutor and the human tutor. In the low involvement condition, tutor type triggered the peripheral route of cognition, and people mindlessly process the AI tutor's writing assignment quality was better than the human tutor. These outcomes support the ELM and the concept of mindlessness in the CASA paradigm depending on if the information is processed through the central route or the peripheral route. The findings suggest that the ELM can help explain the CASA paradigm on "when and why mindless behavior will occur" [26]. The result shows that user involvement can be a factor that determines when mindless behavior occurs.

Although the CASA paradigm is commonly employed in the field of human-computer interaction (HCI), the only explanation for why humans apply social behaviors to new technological artifacts has been mindlessness. This study aims to provide a theoretical contribution by using notions from ELM to describe when people become mindless, making the CASA paradigm more important. These findings broaden the usefulness of both CASA and ELM by applying them to explain perceptions of AI tutors' writing quality and credibility, which has never been done before. Furthermore, by demonstrating the combination of the CASA paradigm and the ELM, this study provides a new application to explain why people react differently to AI performances in different scenarios.

This study highlights the mediation role of perceived controllability that explains why students prefer human tutors more than machine tutors as mentioned earlier. We found that users perceive the AI tutor to have less control over the writing quality than the human tutor, which leads users to attribute more credibility and be more willing to use the tutor in the future. This finding is consistent with studies that test the attribution of responsibility when an AI and a human both experience service failures [35, 40–42]. They found that people are more likely to blame humans than AI because humans have higher control over their service and should be more responsible for the service failure. This finding also supports a meta-analysis study that perceived controllability has a strong effect in predicting people's emotional responses [36].

This study has practical implications. Even if many pedagogists are skeptical about the performance of AI tutors in classrooms, the current study brings user involvement into AI education, which serves as a foundation for instructors and product designers to better understand how students perceive AI tutors and human tutors. Given the abundance of data demonstrating the value of AI in educational settings in terms of cognitive and behavioral learning outcomes, perhaps addressing different student attitudes about AI in education in the future could persuade doubters and those who may currently be skeptical. Although AI tutors are perceived as less controllable than human tutors, AI tutors still could facilitate educational equality in a cost-effective way, especially in those financially disadvantaged areas where human teachers are limited.

We found that perceived controllability was important in influencing users' perceptions, which indicates that the identity of the agent (as human or AI) served as interface cues that could trigger the machine heuristic [30, 43] and perceived controllability. In order to improve the controllability of the identity of agents, interfaces could signal to users that the software/system is based on algorithms, by employing AI or technology-related interfaces or icons that urge people to assume AI is error-free and makes fewer errors than humans. Even when users do not comprehend or engaged in the internal meaning of algorithms, triggering the machine heuristic will generate increased affinity and credibility of algorithms. Human interface cues, on the other hand, may improve perceived controllability. For example, emphasizing that the service's overall quality is assessed by human specialists or emphasizing anthropomorphic interface cues could enhance the perceived controllability.

5.2 Limitations

Our study has some limitations. First, the study employed a short description to inform participants about an AI or a human tutor. Participants only revied single, restricted information about the idea of the writing tutor. Although the chosen writing essays were written objectively, it might be possible that some participants misinterpreted the essays and perceive the essays as positive or negative. Moreover, reading the edited essays rather than directly interacting with the writing tutor may have reduced participants' perceptions of the writing tutor. Participants' perceptions may shift if they have more direct and ongoing experiences with the writing tutor in the actual world. Future studies should examine the perception differences toward a real tutor and an AI tutor when interacting directly. Second, this study only tested users' perceptions toward a writing tutor in a short term. A longitudinal study would be helpful to see if users' perceptions change over time. Last, the age range in this study is relatively big, and the mean age of the participants in this study is much older than the mean age of undergraduate students. It might be possible that students enrolled in universes are more likely to accept and use new technology, so their perceptions toward AI tutors may be different. Future research should consider this issue, collecting data from undergraduate students to examine the differences.

6 Conclusion

With the advancement of AI technology, AI tutors are already being utilized in classrooms throughout the world as teaching aides, tutors, and peer learning specialists. User involvement of online learners moderates the effect of tutor type on perceived quality. When user involvement was low, the AI tutor was perceived to have a higher writing quality than the human tutor; when user involvement was high, tutor type did not affect the perceived writing quality of the tutor, no matter the tutor was a human or an AI. The reason that the human tutor is preferred is that the human tutor had a higher level of controllability than the AI tutor. Tutors' writing quality affects the credibility of tutors and their future use intention. These findings expand on the literature that applied the ELM to the CASA paradigm to explain when and why people have mindless behaviors. The practical implication for AI product designers is that interface cues may be beneficial in triggering the machine heuristic, therefore, increasing the perceived controllability of the system, and promoting greater affinity and credibility of algorithms.

References

1. Kelly, R.: AI-powered tutor uses google cloud to generate learning activities. https://campustechnology.com/articles/2021/09/07/ai-powered-tutor-uses-google-cloud-to-generate-learning-activities.aspx
2. Preston, J.: Jill Watson, an AI Pioneer in Education, Turns 4. https://ic.gatech.edu/news/631545/jill-watson-ai-pioneer-education-turns-4
3. Hao, K.: China has started a grand experiment in AI education. It could reshape how the world learns. https://www.technologyreview.com/2019/08/02/131198/china-squirrel-has-started-a-grand-experiment-in-ai-education-it-could-reshape-how-the/
4. Nazari, N., Shabbir, M.S., Setiawan, R.: Application of artificial intelligence powered digital writing assistant in higher education: randomized controlled trial. Heliyon **7** (2021). https://doi.org/10.1016/j.heliyon.2021.e07014
5. Ruan, S., et al.: EnglishBot: an AI-powered conversational system for second language learning. In: 26th International Conference on Intelligent User Interfaces, pp. 434–444. ACM, College Station TX USA (2021)
6. Tu, J.: Learn to speak like a native: AI-powered chatbot simulating natural conversation for language tutoring. J. Phys. Conf. Ser. **1693**, 012216 (2020). https://doi.org/10.1088/1742-6596/1693/1/012216
7. Pokrivcakova, S.: Preparing teachers for the application of AI-powered technologies in foreign language education. J. Lang. Cult. Educ. **7**, 135–153 (2019). https://doi.org/10.2478/jolace-2019-0025
8. Ahmad, M.I., Mubin, O., Orlando, J.: Understanding behaviours and roles for social and adaptive robots in education: teacher's perspective. In: Proceedings of the Fourth International Conference on Human Agent Interaction, pp. 297–304. Association for Computing Machinery, New York, NY, USA (2016)
9. Kim, J., Merrill, K., Xu, K., Sellnow, D.D.: My teacher is a machine: understanding students' perceptions of AI teaching assistants in online education. Int. J. Hum. Comput. Interact. **36**, 1902–1911 (2020). https://doi.org/10.1080/10447318.2020.1801227
10. Hsu, C.-K., Hwang, G.-J., Chang, C.-K.: A personalized recommendation-based mobile learning approach to improving the reading performance of EFL students. Comput. Educ. **63**, 327–336 (2013). https://doi.org/10.1016/j.compedu.2012.12.004
11. Bradac, V., Walek, B.: A comprehensive adaptive system for e-learning of foreign languages. Expert Syst. Appl. **90**, 414–426 (2017). https://doi.org/10.1016/j.eswa.2017.08.019
12. McDill, S.: Robots get private view of major pop art show (2020). https://www.reuters.com/article/us-health-coronavirus-art-robots-idUKKBN27E1ZZ

13. Szymanska, Z.: Avatar robot goes to school for ill German boy (2022). https://www.reuters.com/technology/avatar-robot-goes-school-ill-german-boy-2022-01-14/
14. Kohli, D.: An Andover preschool hired an unusual teacher's aide: a robot–The Boston Globe. https://www.bostonglobe.com/2021/12/06/business/an-andover-preschool-teacher-is-robot/
15. Hams, M.: Robot teacher introduced in Gaza classroom. https://www.i24news.tv/en/news/middle-east/palestinian-territories/1639688788-robot-teacher-introduced-in-gaza-classroom
16. McDonagh, M.: Sligo schoolchildren's new teacher will be Nao–a robot. https://www.irishtimes.com/news/education/sligo-schoolchildren-s-new-teacher-will-be-nao-a-robot-1.4659247
17. Wolhuter, S.: AI in education: how chatbots are transforming learning (2019). https://wearebrain.com/blog/ai-data-science/top-5-chatbots-in-education/
18. Edwards, A., Edwards, C., Spence, P.R., Harris, C., Gambino, A.: Robots in the classroom: differences in students' perceptions of credibility and learning between teacher as robot and robot as teacher. Comput. Hum. Behav. **65**, 627–634 (2016). https://doi.org/10.1016/j.chb.2016.06.005
19. Edwards, C., Edwards, A., Albrehi, F., Spence, P.: Interpersonal impressions of a social robot versus human in the context of performance evaluations. Commun. Educ. **70**, 165–182 (2021). https://doi.org/10.1080/03634523.2020.1802495
20. Abendschein, B., Edwards, C., Edwards, A., Rijhwani, V., Stahl, J.: Human-Robot teaming configurations: a study of interpersonal communication perceptions and affective learning in higher education. J. Commun. Pedagog. **4**, 123–132 (2021). https://doi.org/10.3316/INFORMIT.105941407010443
21. Edwards, C., Edwards, A., Stoll, B., Lin, X., Massey, N.: Evaluations of an artificial intelligence instructor's voice: social identity theory in human-robot interactions. Comput. Hum. Behav. **90**, 357–362 (2019). https://doi.org/10.1016/j.chb.2018.08.027
22. Xu, K.: First encounter with robot alpha: how individual differences interact with vocal and kinetic cues in users' social responses. New Media Soc. **21**, 2522–2547 (2019)
23. Chérif, E., Lemoine, J.-F.: Anthropomorphic virtual assistants and the reactions of internet users: an experiment on the assistant's voice. Recherche et Appl. en Mark. (Engl. Ed.) **34**, 28–47 (2019). https://doi.org/10.1177/2051570719829432
24. Nass, C., Steuer, J., Tauber, E.R.: Computers are social actors. In: Proceedings of the SIGCHI Conference on Human Factors in Computing Systems, pp. 72–78 (1994)
25. Nass, C., Fogg, B.J., Moon, Y.: Can computers be teammates? Int. J. Hum Comput Stud. **45**, 669–678 (1996). https://doi.org/10.1006/ijhc.1996.0073
26. Nass, C., Moon, Y.: Machines and mindlessness: social responses to computers. J. Soc. Issues **56**, 81–103 (2000). https://doi.org/10.1111/0022-4537.00153
27. Nass, C., Lee, K.M.: Does computer-synthesized speech manifest personality? Experimental tests of recognition, similarity-attraction, and consistency-attraction. J. Exp. Psychol. Appl. **7**, 171–181 (2001). https://doi.org/10.1037/1076-898X.7.3.171
28. Edwards, C., Edwards, A., Spence, P.R., Shelton, A.K.: Is that a bot running the social media feed? Testing the differences in perceptions of communication quality for a human agent and a bot agent on Twitter. Comput. Hum. Behav. **33**, 372–376 (2014). https://doi.org/10.1016/j.chb.2013.08.013
29. Waddell, T.F.: Can an algorithm reduce the perceived bias of news? Testing the effect of machine attribution on news readers' evaluations of bias, anthropomorphism, and credibility. Journal. Mass Commun. Q. **96**, 82–100 (2019). https://doi.org/10.1177/1077699018815891
30. Sundar, S.S., Kim, J.: Machine heuristic: when we trust computers more than humans with our personal information. In: Proceedings of the 2019 CHI Conference on Human Factors in Computing Systems, pp. 538:1–538:9. ACM, New York, NY, USA (2019)

31. Petty, R.E., Cacioppo, J.T., Goldman, R.: Personal involvement as a determinant of argument-based persuasion. J. Pers. Soc. Psychol. **41**, 847–855 (1981). https://doi.org/10.1037/0022-3514.41.5.847
32. Petty, R.E., Cacioppo, J.T., Schumann, D.: Central and peripheral routes to advertising effectiveness: the moderating role of involvement. J. Consum. Res. **10**, 135–146 (1983). https://doi.org/10.1086/208954
33. Petty, R.E., Cacioppo, J.T.: The elaboration likelihood model of persuasion. In: Communication and Persuasion. Springer Series in Social Psychology. Springer, New York, NY (1986). https://doi.org/10.1007/978-1-4612-4964-1_1
34. Weiner, B.: Attribution, emotion, and action. In: Handbook of Motivation and Cognition: Foundations of Social Behavior, pp. 281–312. Guilford Press, New York, NY, US (1986)
35. Leo, X., Huh, Y.E.: Who gets the blame for service failures? Attribution of responsibility toward robot versus human service providers and service firms. Comput. Hum. Behav. **113**, 106520 (2020). https://doi.org/10.1016/j.chb.2020.106520
36. Van Vaerenbergh, Y., Orsingher, C., Vermeir, I., Larivière, B.: A meta-analysis of relationships linking service failure attributions to customer outcomes. J. Serv. Res. **17**, 381–398 (2014). https://doi.org/10.1177/1094670514538321
37. Gray, H., Gray, K., Wegner, D.: Dimensions of mind perception. Science **315**, 619 (2007). https://doi.org/10.1126/science.1134475
38. Gray, K., Wegner, D.M.: Feeling robots and human zombies: mind perception and the uncanny valley. Cognition **125**, 125–130 (2012). https://doi.org/10.1016/j.cognition.2012.06.007
39. McCroskey, J.C., Teven, J.J.: Goodwill: a reexamination of the construct and its measurement. Commun. Monogr. **66**, 90–103 (1999). https://doi.org/10.1080/03637759909376464
40. Hong, J.W.: Why is artificial intelligence blamed more? Analysis of faulting artificial intelligence for self-driving car accidents in experimental settings. Int. J. Hum. Comput. Interact. **36**, 1768–1774 (2020). https://doi.org/10.1080/10447318.2020.1785693
41. Hong, J.-W., Williams, D.: Racism, responsibility and autonomy in HCI: testing perceptions of an AI agent. Comput. Hum. Behav. **100**, 79–84 (2019). https://doi.org/10.1016/j.chb.2019.06.012
42. Hong, J.-W., Choi, S., Williams, D.: Sexist AI: an experiment integrating CASA and ELM. Int. J. Hum. Comput. Interact. 1–14 (2020). https://doi.org/10.1080/10447318.2020.1801226
43. Sundar, S.: The MAIN model: a heuristic approach to understanding technology effects on credibility. In: MacArthur Foundation Digital Media and Learning Initiative. The MIT Press, Cambridge (2008)

Design of AI-Enabled Application to Detect Ayurvedic Nutritional Values of Edible Items and Suggest a Diet

Kousik Dutta(✉), Aditya Rajput, Shreya Srivastava, Annamalai Chidambaram, and Anmol Srivastava

Department of Interaction Design, School of Design, University of Petroleum and Energy Studies, Bidholi, via, Prem Nagar, Dehradun 248007, Uttarakhand, India
{500075098,500077259,500076844,500074999}@stu.upes.ac.in, asrivastava@ddn.upes.ac.in

Abstract. People these days primarily focus on having a well-measured calorific diet which results in a healthy body but lacks mindfulness. The Ayurvedic diet system, which is more than thousands of years old, focuses on balancing different energies in the body which in turn promotes wellness of both body and mind. Due to lack of information available, most of the youth is unaware of its benefits and hence struggles to follow a proper dietary system. From the initial interviews with N = 16 participants, it was identified that many people are interested to know more about the Ayurvedic dietary system but lack the means to do so. The findings indicate a need to design an AI-based mobile application that presents information about the Ayurvedic dietary system in an actionable way, giving users the ability to track and compare diet with their peers and identify what to consume consciously according to their body type, life-situation & season. Users can scan any food item using their phone's camera to understand the ayurvedic dietary & nutritional values associated with it. Using an Artificial Intelligence, their app will suggest alternatives and recipes related to that food item based upon the user's needs like weight loss/gain, immunity improvement, taste preference, etc. This research is interdisciplinary utilizing the knowledge from fields of Ayurveda, Human Food Interaction, Quantified Self, Artificial Intelligence to make young Indians aware of traditional ayurvedic diet system. Lastly, gamification elements have been used to provide intrinsic and extrinsic motivation to the users to follow the diet system.

Keywords: Artificial intelligence · Ayurvedic dietary system · Food and nutrition · Quantified self

1 Introduction

In such a rapidly changing world where every day new body ailments are arising people are eager to find out the best ways to improve their body metabolism and live a disease-free healthy life. They have inherited many dietary practices from time to time to live healthy life. Humans have relied on a calorie based system for a very long time but

H. Degen and S. Ntoa (Eds.): HCII 2022, LNAI 13336, pp. 245–256, 2022.
https://doi.org/10.1007/978-3-031-05643-7_16

now they are observing a shift towards the traditional Indian Ayurveda based system for diets and lifestyle since it only measures the quantified value of food which is unable to judge the effect of a particular food based on its values on a particular person with a specific body type [2–6]. Ayurveda is one of the ancient healthcare systems in the world, has quite generic & simplistic concepts but their sophistication is evident from their contemporariness and universality of applications. In modern times most human beings monitor their daily activities, habits, behaviour, food consumption, etc. through digital mediums like smartwatches, habit trackers among many others, and old-school physical means like a diary or maybe a piece of paper. Now, with the easy availability of data, they must monitor the right values. Many people get lost in the number of calories burnt and steps taken every day as a result of which they are always in an anxious state. This paper explores the various ways in which the authors can promote healthy living and better nutrition to the young generation by combining the areas of the ayurvedic dietary system, quantified self, human food motivation & gamification.

2 Literature Review and Related Works

2.1 Understanding Ayurveda

The origin of Ayurveda dates back to the Vedic Era period where most materials related to health and diseases were available in Atharva Veda. The word Ayurveda has been derived from the two words 'Ayu' and 'Veda' where 'Ayu' means 'life' and 'Veda' means 'knowledge or science' [1]. Ayurveda refers to' the knowledge or the science of life. Ayurveda comprises all living things, human and non-human. It is divided into three main branches which are: Nara Ayurveda- it deals with human life, Sattva Ayurveda- it is the science which deals with animal lives and it's disease and the third is Vriksha Ayurveda- it is the science that deals with the science of plant life, its growth and diseases. It is very clear that Ayurveda is not only a system of medicine but also a way of life for having a complete positive health and spiritual attainments [2]. Going to the diet, the Ayurvedic diet is not that kind of 'diet' which as per the modern senses focuses only on foods one consumes instead, it offers a much broader approach that comprises not only what we eat but also how we eat and when we eat it, including our state of mind to have ultimate support of a vibrant state of health [3]. Ayurveda believes that positive health is the basis for attaining all four cherished goals of life (Chaturvidha purushartha) that are Dharma, Artha, Karma, Moksha. All these four goals cannot be achieved without a person having a sound positive health. Positive health comprises: Mannah (mind), Prasanna Atma (Happy state of soul), Indriya (Senses) and Dosha Dhatu Samya (Balanced metabolism). Senses here means the five organs of perception Gyanendriya which is: smell, taste, sight, touch and hearing coupled with the organs of action- Karmendriya which are: mouth, hands, foot and organs of excretion and reproduction [4–7].

2.2 Understanding Ayurvedic Diet System

The Ayurvedic Diet is an eating pattern that has been around for more than thousands of years. It is based on the principles of Ayurveda which focuses on balancing different energies within your body, which leads to good health. It not only focuses on giving you a healthy body but also a happy, refreshed, and energetic mind. The first step is to discover your Ayurvedic body type [5, 6]. At a glance, there are three main categories– Sattvic, Rajasic, and Tamasic. The food that humans eat affects their physical and cognitive well-being. A Sattvic Diet, simply, means light and healthy food, which does not go to any taste extremes. Sattvic food has body purification and mind-calming properties. A Sattvic diet comprises of pure unprocessed food with lighter potency and is abundant in prana (life force). This energizes the body and mind. Food, which is cooked and consumed within 3–4 h, is Sattvic. The consumption of Sattvic food helps enhance the consciousness by improving the cognitive health and energy of an individual. It helps restore the harmony and balance of the body and mind. Formation and rebuilding of high-quality body tissues could be facilitated by consuming a Sattvic diet regularly. A Rajasic or Tamasic food comprises all foods produced by harming living beings (such as meat and fish) and should, therefore, be avoided. A Rajasic diet can exaggerate Pitta and Vata doshas levels in one's body. Consuming such foods results in rising in the levels of physiological or nervous activities in the body and mind. If consumed in an excessive amount it can cause restlessness, anger, sleeplessness, hyperactivity, and irritability. When Sattvic food is prepared in a Tamasic or toxic environment, it becomes Tamasic and should not be consumed. Tamasic foods are those which dull the mind and bring inertia, confusion, and disorientation. Consumables that are super oily or feel heavy on the stomach when consumed can also be stale, reheated, or artificial foods such items come under the Tamasic category [8, 9]. Such foods can also increase the aggressive quality of Rajas towards violence. According to Ayurveda, the five elements make up the universe- Vayu (air), Jal (water), Akash (Space), Teja (fire), and Prithvi (Earth). These elements are believed to form three different doshas which are defined as the types of energies which articulate into your body [10–12]. Every dosha is responsible for a specific physiological function happening in the body. The Ayurvedic diet is based on determining your dominant Dosha and eating specific foods to maintain a balance between all three doshas [2–6]. Ayurveda teaches us to eat meals at consistent times each day with lunch as the largest meal and avoiding snacks in between. The Ayurvedic diet for Vata dosha brings balance to Vata by favouring warm, grounding, hydrated foods with a soft and smooth texture. It incorporates a variety of spices and emphasizes proteins and fats. The Ayurvedic diet for Pitta dosha brings balance to pitta by incorporating food that is cooling, energizing, somewhat dry, and high in carbohydrates. It encourages eating fresh, whole foods, both cooked and raw, decreasing internal heat. The Ayurvedic diet for Kapha dosha brings balance to kaph by including easy-to-digest whole foods that are light, dry, warming, and well spiced. The best-suggested meals for Kapha are generally freshly cooked and served warm or hot. For all diet types, a supportive herbal formula like Vata Digest, Pitta Digest, or Kapha Digest can help your digestive fire. It accumulates new types of foods and transforms them into nutrients. The Ayurvedic diet sets guidelines for when, how, and what to eat depending on your body's doshas. Some of the main characteristics for each dosha to determine which type matches you best: Pitta (fire + water) intelligent, hard-working, and decisive. This dosha generally has a medium physical build, short temper, and may suffer from conditions like indigestion, heart disease, or high blood pressure. Vata (air + space) is creative, energetic, and lively.

People having Vata dosha are usually thin with a light frame and may have digestive issues, anxiety, or fatigue when out of balance. Kapha (earth + water) is naturally calm, grounded, and loyal. Those with a Kapha dosha often have a sturdy frame and may have issues with weight gain, asthma, depression, or diabetes [10–13]. The diet also minimises processed foods, which often lack fibre and important vitamins and minerals. Mindfulness is a practice that involves paying close attention to how you feel in the present.

2.3 Understanding Quantified Self

The term quantified self refers to a proactive individual or a community of proactive individuals monitoring various physical, behavioural & cognitive parameters while performing various activities, often with the goal of physical, cognitive & emotional enhancement [14]. Health and diet are one of the most important focus areas in this field, where objectives may range from general monitoring & analysis to pathobiological resolution to physical and cognitive performance improvement [15]. Applications of quantified self are also being used to improve productivity & efficiency in offices by monitoring how much time is being spent on various projects, meeting timings, etc. In Education it's being used to educate students & make them more conscious of their daily activities related to studies and time management. In some sense everyone is already utilizing a self-monitor since most humans measure various things about themselves like the amount of food they are consuming, the increase in their weight, how many hours they are sleeping & many others This is because of innate curiosity, tinkering, and problem-solving capabilities present in Human beings. One of the earliest recorded examples of quantified self-monitoring in history is that of "Sanctorius of Padua" in the 16th century [15–17]. It was related to a study of energy expenditure in living systems by monitoring his body weight in food intake and elimination for a period of 30 years. Fitness bands, watches and trackers from companies like Apple, Fitbit & Samsung to name a few have made quantified self-monitoring technology accessible to a large population. While the concept of the quantified self may have begun for individual self-monitoring, it's also being used for aggregated data from a group of individuals who are doing the same activity and want to compare the results with each other. In recent times, a sub-movement of Gamification combined with Quantified Self is being adopted & loved by much of the user base [16]. This involves using game mechanics and elements to turn everyday activities into games to motivate users to push harder in their respective areas via extrinsic motivations like awards, money, etc. as well as intrinsic motivations like autonomy, mastery, and purpose. The authors have also used gamification combined with Quantified Self in their concept prototype which they will explain in the coming sections.

2.4 Understanding Major Determinants of Food Choice

Biological Determinants of Food Choice. The physiological needs are the basic determinants of food choice. Humans need enough energy from food for their survival to continue proper functioning. They respond to the feelings of hunger. Their central nervous system controls the balance between hunger, appetite stimulation, and food intake to fulfil body requirements [20–22]. Macronutrients such as carbohydrates, proteins, and fats generate satiety signals of different intensities. The evidence found in research suggests that fat has the lowest satiating power, while carbohydrates have an intermediate effect and protein has been the most satiating [23]. Palatability is proportional to the pleasure a person experiences when eating a particular food. It depends on the sensory properties of the food, which are taste, smell, texture, and visual appeal. Sweet and other high-fat foods have an exceptional sensory appeal. So, it is not surprising, then, that food is not solely regarded as a source of nourishment but is more often consumed by the pleasure value it imparts. The effects of palatability on the appetite and food intake of humans have been researched in several studies. There is an increase in a person's appetite proportionally as palatability increases, but the effect of palatability on appetite in the period after consumption is still not clear. Growing food variety can also grow food and energy intake and, in the short term, alter the energy balance. 'Taste' is described as a major effect on Human food behaviour. In reality, 'taste' is the sum of all sensory stimulation that is produced by the consumption of food. Which includes the taste, smell, appearance, and texture of the food. All these sensory aspects influence, in particular, spontaneous food choice. From a very young age, taste and familiarity influence behaviour towards food. Taste choices and food aversions develop through life experiences and are influenced by the attitudes, beliefs, and expectations of individuals.

Economic and Physical Determinants of Food Choice. Low-income groups have a higher tendency to consume unbalanced diets and, in particular, have lower intakes of fruit and vegetables. However, access to more money does not automatically equate to a superior diet, but the range of foods from which a person can choose should increase. Accessibility to shops is an important physical factor influencing food choice. It depends on resources, such as transport and geographical location. Healthy food is often more expensive when available within towns and cities compared to supermarkets. Research indicates that the level of education can influence dietary behaviour during adulthood [24]. Dissimilarly, nutrition knowledge and good dietary habits are not strongly correlated. This is because information disseminated on nutrition comes from a variety of sources and is viewed as conflicting or is mistrusted, which discourages motivation to change.

Social Determinants of Food Choice. Population studies show there are obvious differences in social classes about food and nutrient intakes. Poor diets can cause under- and overnutrition; problems that face different sectors of society, requiring various levels of expertise and methods of intervention. Cultural influences lead to the difference in the habitual consumption of some foods and traditions of preparation and certain cases can cause restrictions such as the exclusion of meat and milk from the diet. Cultural influences are, however, compliant with change. Social influences on food intake refer to the impact that one or more persons have on the eating behaviour of others, either directly (buying food) or indirectly (learn from peer behaviour), either conscious (transfer of beliefs) or subconscious. However, quantifying the social influences on food intake is difficult because the influences that people have on the eating behaviour of others are not limited to one specific type and people are not necessarily conscious of the social influences that are exerted on their eating behaviour. Social support can have a beneficial effect on food choices and nutritious dietary changes. Social support from the household and co-workers was positively associated with improvements in fruit and vegetable consumption and with the preparation stage of enhancing eating habits, respectively. Social support may enhance health promotion by fostering a sense of group belonging and helping us to be more competent and self-efficacious. The place in which food is eaten can affect food choice, particularly in terms of what food choices are on offer. This is true for people with irregular hours or with particular requirements, e.g. vegetarian. With most adults, women, and men in employment, the influence of work on health behaviours such as food choices is an important area of investigation [23–25].

Psychological Factors. The effect of stress on food choice is complex, not least because of the various stress one can experience. The effect of stress on food intake depends highly on the individual, the stressor, and the circumstances. Some people eat more and some eat less than normal when experiencing stress or other psychological disorders. Dieters, the people with high restraint and some women report feeling guilty because of not eating what they think they should. Consumer attitudes, beliefs, knowledge and optimistic bias also affect. Better understanding of how the public perceives their diets would help in the design and implementation of healthy eating initiatives [23–26].

3 Research Approach

With regards to the field of Human Food Interaction, Ayurvedic Dietary System, and Quantified Self, our work is situated in the area of food nutrition and diet. We integrated machine learning-based image classification functionality to evaluate the food type according to the Ayurvedic dietary system and nutritional value. We designed a mobile app prototype that would allow us to test and derive an in-depth analysis of the user's dietary cycle. To gain insight into the field of the Ayurvedic Dietary System, the Quantified Self, and to develop a better understanding of human food interaction and motivation, we chose a five-step methodological approach. First, we conducted a semi-structured interview Study with N = 16 participants from various cities of India. Secondly, we did a Literature review on the related topics to support our research. Next, with all our primary and secondary research data and insights, we started ideating on the solution and designed a clickable prototype for a mobile application. This mobile application provides information about the Ayurvedic dietary system in an actionable way, giving users the ability to track and compare diet with their peers and identify what to consume consciously according to their body type, life situation & season. Lastly, we did task-based usability testing with 16 users where we gave them three tasks and took their feedback on the same.

4 Interview Study

4.1 Study Setup and Method

The objective of our interview study was to gain a rudimentary insight into the food habits, food purchase behaviour, and diet cycles, followed by our prospective users. Our main objective was to gain inspiration and find possible starting points for the design. Our interview study was conducted with 16 participants who were students between the age of 18 to 27. Initially, our participants were recruited using phone calls to establish rapport with them, and then the final interviews were conducted on Google Meet. We conducted a semi-structured interview that had the following questions: "Can you tell me what all food items you had last week?", "Where did you purchase them/raw materials for them?", "Do you plan what all food items you are going to consume in a week?", "If yes, then on what basis do you select these food items?", "How do you get to know if something is healthy or not?", "Do you know how the Indian traditional food cycle works?", "Are you interested in knowing how the traditional Indian food cycle works?", "Do you think food habits affect human behaviour?", "In such a fast-changing world, how are you planning to maintain/improve your immunity?", "Are you interested in changing your food habits to the traditional food cycle?", "Do you track/monitor what all food items do you eat in a week?", "From the following three words, choose the one which describes your weekly food cycle; Monotonous, Varied, Somewhere in between.", "When was the last time you had a craving for some food item?", "What do you think triggered that craving?" and "What is your favourite dish and why?". All the interviewee responses were recorded and transcribed in English. We recruited the participants from 7 cities (Delhi, Dehradun, Bangalore, Indore, Chennai, Guwahati, Ahmedabad).

4.2 Results of Initial Interview Study

Initially, there were mixed reactions to the questions regarding the diet and food intake by the participants. Some participants (6) eat home-cooked food and have a repetitive diet local to their state. They assumed and were quite sure that the food they consume is healthy as they have been consuming the same type of food since they were born as P8 responded by saying, "If the food is home-cooked, it should be healthy". Many of the participants (10) receive their food from their respective hostel mess or buy food from outside tiffin services as they are living on their own. They knew that the food they have is quite unhealthy because of the poor food quality (oily, adulterated masalas, unhygienic food preparation, etc.) like P5 responded by saying, "I know that the food I consume is mostly unhealthy". They are forced to eat this kind of food as they feel that they have no better option. Some of the participants (6) stated that they are health-conscious and plan their own diet routine irrespective of their living conditions. 6/16 participants read about the nutrient values before purchasing food items. 12/16 participants stated that their diet depended upon the season of fruits and vegetables available. 7/16 participants were unsure if diet affects one's daily behaviour & mood. 4/16 participants stated that they believe the type of diet they have affects their mood & behaviour directly, like P1responded by saying, "Yes. Because eating a lot of fast food can make you lazy". The rest (5/16) of the participants said that it doesn't affect one's behaviour. In addition, 6/16 participants stated that they track their food consumption & items in some way or another often with the goal of reducing weight, maintaining muscle mass & immunity. Other participants (10/16) stated that they do not track their food intake and diet. Besides this, 6 participants stated that they have a monotonous diet, 4 of them stated they have a varied food diet and the rest have their food diet somewhere in between monotonous and varied. Most of the participants responded that they have a craving for food like pizza, burgers, etc. which was triggered mostly when they see any related advertisement, leftover sauces or toppings, etc. Some participants (4/16) believed that having home-cooked food will improve or maintain immunity, as P5 responded by saying, "I maintain my immunity by eating fruits and once in a while eat healthy food". 4/16 participants state that having fruits and following the diet will improve and maintain their immunity. The most common response was "no" for the basic knowledge of the Indian traditional food cycle. Only 4/16 participants had an idea of the traditional Indian food cycle. Most of the participants (10/16) were ready to shift towards the traditional food cycle because they wanted to maintain and improve a good diet if they could get information & prompts in an easy-to-understand way. We noticed that all the participants will shift towards the Ayurvedic food diet provided if they are educated about them.

5 Design and Implementation

Fig. 1. Four main prototype screens from the mobile application

Based on the insights we got from our interviews we came up with various solutions and narrowed them down to the most practical ones. As students complained about the monotony of their diet we came up with an ML-based image recognition model that scans various raw materials and suggests new sattvic recipes of the same. Many students were extremely sure that their home-cooked food was healthy. When we enquired more about it by asking them where the ingredients of those foods were, we came to know that many of them were consuming Rajasic and Tamasic food filled with unnecessary masalas. Hence, we came up with a concept where when a user scans a food item the app tells them the proportion of rajas, sattva, and tamas in it. Many participants stated that they don't know about the Indian ayurvedic dietary system as they were unaware of any information source for the same. For that reason, the onboarding of the app is designed to educate a novice user about the benefits of the Ayurvedic diet system in an easy-to-understand manner. During our interview, we got to know that different users expected to accomplish various goals using our app hence we created a quiz to get to know the user's ayurvedic body type, goals, and other demographic factors to suggest diets tailored according to their needs. Students complain about having no idea how to maintain immunity necessary in the current scenario. The app suggests diet plans which are not only healthier options but also good for improving their immunity. It also provides different ways to monitor user progress in a diet plan. Users are prompted to enter their mood data in a visual 5 option Likert scale with smiles ranging from very sad to very happy. We have implemented gamification in the app to motivate users to follow their diet and compete with their friends. When a user successfully completes one full week of diet, they will be awarded badges that they can share on their social media. When a user collects four badges, we will send a gift hamper with immunity-boosting ayurvedic herbs (Fig. 1).

5.1 Determination of Nutritional Values and Ayurvedic Gunas for Food Items

The user is made to scan the food item through the app's camera. The application then uses machine learning-based image classification models to determine the kind of food item. This is done by analysing the image and matching it to the closest possible image from a diverse dataset of food item images (like Calorie Mama Food Image Recognition API). In an event where the app is not able to determine the kind of food product, the user is prompted to specify the food product name and ingredients. The application image classification model will become more accurate with the increasing number of food item images uploaded there.

5.2 Diet Suggestions Based on Body Type

The users are made to answer a short MCQs-based quiz of 30 questions to determine their ayurvedic body type, diet goals, existing sleeping and eating habits. This is done by matching their responses with various pre-built ayurvedic & nutritional models.

6 Usability Testing

The objective of our usability testing was to determine the usability of our app, capture the reaction of users towards the overall idea & get more ideas for improvement in the future. The evaluation was done using a clickable prototype prepared in Figma. It was shown to 16 participants between the age of 18–27 who were from 7 different cities of India. The testing took 4 days. They were asked to use the prototype through screen sharing on Google meet and their responses, reaction change, and attitude towards the application were recorded. The participants were given 3 tasks.

6.1 Task 1: Determine Your Body Type in the Application Using Quiz

During the first task, 14 out of 16 participants were able to complete the task with no error. They felt the onboarding was quick and easy to understand the app's functions and uses. P5 stated, "Landing on the home page was easy, the quiz was simple, so were the few questions". Users rated their task completion experience with an average score of 3.9 out of 5. Most questions were straight forward but few (2) felt the need to google terms.

6.2 Task 2: Scan Any Food Item and Determine Its Ayurvedic Nutritional Information

During the second task, 15 out of 16 users were able to complete the task within 2 trials with no errors. They felt scanning the food items to find their ayurvedic nutritional information quite simple. P1 stated, "With the scan feature, I can now know the Ayurvedic guna of my food and make diet decisions according to suggestions easily. This makes it convenient to follow our traditional ayurvedic diet". Users rated their task completion experience with an average rating of 3.8 out of 5. Users found the "similar food suggestions" feature very useful and also suggested that the app should recommend alternatives that are easily available in the user's locality during a particular season. They also loved the overall infographic presentation of numerical data and stated (P8, P9, P11) that it makes the numerical data efficient to understand.

6.3 Task 3: Track Your Diet and Mood in the Application

During the third task, 13 out of 16 users were able to complete the task with no errors. They felt that the tracking of their diet was easy and accessible. P10 stated, "All the features help track the diet and mood". Users rated their task completion experience with an average rating of 4.0 out of 5. The users were pleased with the features and information layout of the app. They also reported that trackers are very easy to understand and use.

6.4 Gamification

The users were excited about collecting badges and sharing them across social media. P2 stated, "Competing with my friends through this app motivated me more the follow this diet system". They were also excited about the rewards that they get from collecting badges and said that it was a very good initiative.

7 Conclusion

This is an initial study that was conducted to understand how ayurvedic diet system could be combined with modern fields like quantified self, human food interaction & gamification to spread awareness & motivate youth to lead a healthier lifestyle. The participants have shown much interest into the prototype and overall idea. This is a work in progress and more work shall be done in this area.

References

1. Jaiswal, Y.S., Williams, L.L.: A glimpse of Ayurveda–the forgotten history and principles of Indian traditional medicine. J. Tradit. Complement. Med. **7**(1), 50–53 (2016). Published 28 Feb 2016. https://doi.org/10.1016/j.jtcme.2016.02.002
2. Srour, B., et al.: Ultra-processed food intake and risk of cardiovascular disease: prospective cohort study (NutriNet-Santé). BMJ **365**, 11451 (2019). Published 29 May 2019. https://doi.org/10.1136/bmj.l1451
3. Fiolet, T., et al.: Consumption of ultra-processed foods and cancer risk: results from NutriNet-Santé prospective cohort. BMJ. **360**, k322 (2018). Published 14 Feb 2018. https://doi.org/10.1136/bmj.k322
4. Schnabel, L., Kesse-Guyot, E., Allès, B., et al.: Association between ultraprocessed food consumption and risk of mortality among middle-aged adults in France. JAMA Intern. Med. **179**(4), 490–498 (2019). https://doi.org/10.1001/jamainternmed.2018.7289
5. Sharma, S., Puri, S., Agarwal, T., Sharma, V.: Diets based on ayurvedic constitution–potential for weight management. Altern. Ther. Health Med. **15**(1), 44–47 (2009)
6. Rioux, J., Thomson, C., Howerter, A.: A pilot feasibility study of whole-systems ayurvedic medicine and yoga therapy for weight loss. Glob. Adv. Health Med. **3**(1), 28–35 (2014). https://doi.org/10.7453/gahmj.2013.084
7. Dalen, J., Smith, B.W., Shelley, B.M., Sloan, A.L., Leahigh, L., Begay, D.: Pilot study: mindful eating and living (MEAL): weight, eating behavior, and psychological outcomes associated with a mindfulness-based intervention for people with obesity. Complement. Ther. Med. **18**(6), 260–264 (2010). https://doi.org/10.1016/j.ctim.2010.09.008
8. Kristeller, J.L., Jordan, K.D.: Mindful eating: connecting with the wise self, the spiritual self. Front. Psychol. **9**, 1271 (2018). Published 14 Aug 2018. https://doi.org/10.3389/fpsyg.2018.01271
9. Payyappallimana, U., Venkatasubramanian, P.: Exploring ayurvedic knowledge on food and health for providing innovative solutions to contemporary healthcare. Front. Public Health **4**, 57 (2016). Published 31 Mar 2016. https://doi.org/10.3389/fpubh.2016.00057
10. Lanou, A.J., Svenson, B.: Reduced cancer risk in vegetarians: an analysis of recent reports. Cancer Manag Res. **3**, 1–8 (2010). Published 20 Dec 2010. https://doi.org/10.2147/CMR.S6910
11. McMacken, M., Shah, S.: A plant-based diet for the prevention and treatment of type 2 diabetess. J. Geriatr. Cardiol. **14**(5), 342–354 (2017). https://doi.org/10.11909/j.issn.1671-5411.2017.05.009
12. Olfert, M.D., Wattick, R.A.: Vegetarian diets and the risk of diabetes. Curr. Diab. Rep. **18**(11), 1–6 (2018). https://doi.org/10.1007/s11892-018-1070-9
13. Patwardhan, B.: Bridging Ayurveda with evidence-based scientific approaches in medicine. EPMA J. **5**, 19 (2014). https://doi.org/10.1186/1878-5085-5-19
14. Swan, M.: Big Data, pp. 85–99, Jun 2013. https://doi.org/10.1089/big.2012.0002
15. Feng, S., Mäntymäki, M., Dhir, A., Salmela, H.: How self-tracking and the quantified self promote health and well-being: systematic review. J. Med. Internet Res. **23**(9), e25171 (2021). Published 21 Sep 2021. https://doi.org/10.2196/25171
16. Lupton, D.: The Quantified Self. John Wiley & Sons, Hoboken (2016)
17. Whitson, J.R.: Gaming the quantified self. Surveill. Soc. **11**(1/2), 163–176 (2013)
18. Barcena, M.B., Wueest, C., Lau, H.: How safe is your quantified self, p. 16. Symantech: Mountain View, CA, USA (2014)
19. Lee, V.R.: What's happening in the quantified self movement? In: ICLS 2014 Proceedings, p. 1032 (2014)

20. Anderson, A., et al.: The development of and evaluation of a novel school based intervention to increase fruit and vegetable intake in children (Five a Day The Bash Street Way), N09003. Report for the FSA, London (2003)
21. Anderson, A., Cox, D.: Five a day–challenges and achievements. Nutr. Food Sci. **30**(1), 30–34 (2000)
22. Baranowski, T., et al.: Squire's quest! Dietary outcome evaluation of a multimedia game. Am. J. Prev. Med. **24**, 52–61 (2003)
23. De Irala-Estevez, J., et al.: A systematic review of socioeconomic differences in food habits in Europe: consumption of fruit and vegetables. Eur. J. Clin. Nutr. **54**, 706–714 (2000)
24. Devine, C.M., et al.: Sandwiching it in: spillover of work onto food choices and family roles in low- and moderate-income urban households. Soc. Sci. Med. **56**, 617–630 ((2003))
25. Dibsdall, L.A., et al.: Low-income consumers' attitudes and behaviour towards access, availability and motivation to eat fruit and vegetables. Public Health Nutr. **6**(2), 159–168 (2003)
26. Donkin, A.J., et al.: Mapping access to food in a deprived area: the development of price and availability indices. Public Health Nutr. **3**(1), 31–38 (2000)

An AI-Based Decision Support System for Quality Control Applied to the Use Case Donor Cornea

Gian-Luca Kiefer[1](✉), Tarek Safi[2], Matthias Nadig[1], Mansi Sharma[1], Muhammad Moiz Sakha[1], Alassane Ndiaye[1], Matthieu Deru[1], Loay Daas[2], Katja Schulz[2], Marvin Schwarz[2], Berthold Seitz[2], and Jan Alexandersson[1]

[1] Department of Cognitive Assistants, DFKI - German Research Center for Artificial Intelligence, Saarbrücken, Germany
gian-luca.kiefer@dfki.de

[2] Department of Ophthalmology, Saarland University Medical Center, Homburg, Germany

Abstract. In recent years, more and more AI models and algorithms get used in previously uncharted domains. The medical domain is one of them and already shows a significant usage of AI methods, for example computer vision algorithms for the analysis of medical imagery. The field of ophthalmology studies medical conditions relating to the eye. One of those conditions, Cornea guttata, can be identified by analysing post mortem microscope images of the donor's cornea endothelium, which needs to be done manually by a skilled professional. To help facilitate this analysis, this paper proposes a hybrid Decision Support System that combines computer vision methods and AI classifiers to guide the decision of the clinicians. By conducting a UX-driven study with professionals from an eye bank, we show that our Decision Support System is able to help users with the classification of Cornea guttata in microscope images. Moreover, the system was able to boost the agreement between two professionals classifying the same cases. The implemented classifiers showed a higher performance compared to the human baseline and the combination of human expertise and AI classifiers detected most of the guttata cases.

Keywords: Decsion support systems · Cornea guttata · Artificial Intelligence · Case-Based Reasoning

1 Introduction

In Germany, approximately 9,000 corneal transplantations - keratoplasty - are performed annually of which roughly 15% show Cornea guttae (CG) after transplantation [1,2]. CG is typically classified from "0" (healthy, no signs of CG) to "4" (severe signs of CG). The endothelial layer in healthy individuals is responsible for actively pumping fluids out of the cornea to maintain corneal clarity.

H. Degen and S. Ntoa (Eds.): HCII 2022, LNAI 13336, pp. 257–274, 2022.
https://doi.org/10.1007/978-3-031-05643-7_17

Corneas affected with CG become edematous and cannot maintain their transparency anymore leading to irreversible visual impairment. Therefore, the only treatment option for this disease is corneal transplantation [3–6]. Nevertheless, CG is present in around 11% in the older population [7,8]. Therefore, during every keratoplasty there is a risk of transplanting a diseased donor cornea. Although donor corneas go through an extensive screening process in the eye banks, the detection of CG in the donor cornea is currently a challenging process that is not yet standardized. To determine whether a cornea is suitable for transplantation, the clinicians examine various properties, such as cell density in the endothelia layer, cell shapes, and obvious visual signs of blebs (bulges of the cell membrane), etc. To improve the accuracy in screening for CG on donor corneas before transplantation, we aim to find ex ante signs of morphological deformations in the endothelial cells associated with the postoperative appearance of guttae. We do so by a transparent and explainable decision support system based on the case-based reasoning scheme that combines additional information including machine learning estimations and computer vision tools aiming at increasing the decision accuracy.

To describe our approach in detail, we first present an excerpt of related research work about CG classification and medical decision support systems. Then, the methodology of the proposed decision support system with its various AI components is explained. Afterwards, the structure of the conducted study is elaborated and the results are discussed. Finally, a conclusion of the presented work is given alongside further possibilities for future work.

2 Related Work

There are many works which concentrate on the segmentation of cells in microscope imagery as a tool for extracting semantic insights. Vigueras-Guillén et al. infer cell segmentations of the corneal endothelium by first using a watershed algorithm to do the initial segmentation which is followed by a merging of oversegmented cells [9]. Their method achieves good results on in vivo images. Moreover, Vigueras-Guillén et al. proposed a method for detecting the region of interest in cornea images with the utilization of convolutional neural networks [10]. This is a crucial step in analysing the images since a strongly curved endothelium causes contrast and focus differences which make the cell segmentation difficult. In the case of CG classification, it is not only important to segment each cell but also to detect pathological cells or areas which show signs of guttata. Sierra et al. create a segmentation dataset of in vivo cornea images where an ophthalmologist not only annotates healthy cells, but also regions with guttata [11]. Based on the dataset, they train a U-Net architecture to provide a reliable feature segmentation. This enables accurate cell density estimations for deciding the current state of the cornea. In our case of donor corneas, the microscope images are taken after they are extracted from the deceased donor. As a result, the images of donor corneas are significantly different from the in vivo images of the discussed related work.

Another important part of research focuses on the conception of medical Decision Support Systems (DSSs) using AI predictions to facilitate diagnoses in various fields of medicine. In their review of recent AI-supported DSSs, the authors Suzuki et al. show that many intelligent algorithms have become successfully integrated into daily clinical processes [12]. After Braun et al. [13], the AI-powered DSSs can be categorized into 3 classes: Conventional AI-driven decision support systems that only influence the clinicians decision with a simple recommendation, integrative AI-driven decision support systems that classify some criteria autonomously but leave the main decision to the clinician, and fully automated AI-driven decision support systems that make a decision without any clinician's support or monitoring. The DSS of this paper can be classified as a conventional AI-DSS since it only aims to give a reasonable suggestion about the guttata status and does not make any decision on its own.

3 Decision Support System

In general, diagnosing a medical condition is a very sensitive decision which should only be performed by trained clinicians. Therefore, our approach of a AI-driven DSS supports only with additionally inferred knowledge. The decision-making responsibility remains with the expert. The following sections about the proposed system's structure clarify this purpose in more details. We propose a hybrid approach combining a series of Graphical Analytic Tools (GATs), Machine Learning Classifiers (MLCs) along with a Case-Based Reasoning (CBR) component [14].

3.1 Data

Compared to the previously discussed related works that focused on in vivo images of the corneal endothelium, in this paper, we classify a condition by analysing the post mortem images. The collected dataset of post mortem images consists of 948 corneas transplanted between 2017 and 2021. All corneas have been assessed 6 weeks after transplantation. We categorize corneas having a CG level of at most 1 as healthy (class *ok*) and all other corneas, that developed severe CG levels 2, 3 or 4, as CG positive (class *not ok*). 894 corneas fall into the category *ok* and 54 corneas where found to be *not ok*. This results in an imbalanced binary classification problem, since there are significantly more cases of a cornea being *ok* than there are for the class *not ok*. Each cornea is defined by 5–6 instances (in sum 5460), whereby each instance consists of an image and corresponding features like cell density and cell shapes. These features were extracted using the software system Robin Endothelium Analyzer (REA) [15]. Additionally, for each image the clinicians assessed semiquantitative criteria that correlate with the development of CG [1]. These include the quantity of occurring bleb in the cell membranes, the general average shape of the cells, and how complete the average cell membranes are. Since the dataset does not contain any ground truth annotation for the segmentation of the cells, it was necessary to use traditional computer vision algorithms that do not rely on a large set of ground truth annotations, which is normally needed for modern machine learning segmentation.

3.2 Graphical Analytic Tools

A series of Graphical Analytic Tools (GATs) was designed to help the clinicians identify irregular patterns inside the microscope images. To achieve this, it is crucial to detect the singular cells of the cornea in a robust way. A common image recognition procedure for regular pattern segmentation is the watershed transform algorithm [16], which already proved suitable for the segmentation of cornea endothelium cells [9]. In advance to applying the watershed transform to the microscope images, a few pre-processing steps are required:

1. **Invert**. Inverting the pixel values of the grayscale image.
2. **Otsu thresholding**. Converts the grayscale image to a boolean mask, which is positive for pixels belonging to the inside of the cell.
3. **Erosion**. Erosion is a fundamental morphological image processing operation which can be used to reduce the positive regions of a mask. This helps us to retain and emphasize thin parts of the cell membranes.

In general, the watershed transform is a region-based segmentation algorithm that uses local minima/maxima in the image and their surrounding gradients to segment local shapes. The resulting list of local contours then represents the individual cells. To extract as much information from the image as possible, additional information is computed on each detected cell contour. This includes, among others, the cell area, the cell radius, and the cell center. The latter is calculated by generating a minimum enclosing circle around the contour and using the circle's center point as the cell center. Moreover, the raw complex cell contours are approximated by simple polygons described by 4 to 7 corners. This is later used to create a global statistic on the occurring cell shapes in the image. Besides the cell shapes, some other statistics are calculated, containing cell count, cell density, and average cell areas and radii. For the professionals in the eye bank, uncommonly large cells and bigger areas without cells can be important signs for a cornea developing CG later on. To embed this criteria inside the GATs, we use thresholding to identify large areas. Therefore, the average cell area size of an image is calculated. Then, all areas with a size that exceeds the computed average by a constant *scalar* s are marked as large areas (see Eq. 1). In the end, s was defined to be 2.0 after testing multiple values with the clinicians.

$$a_i \mathrel{\widehat{=}} \begin{cases} \textit{large cell area} & \text{if } a_i > \frac{s}{N}\sum_{n=1}^{N} a_n \\ \textit{normal cell area} & \text{otherwise} \end{cases} \tag{1}$$

In the final output image of the cell detection (see Fig. 1), cell shapes with large areas are highlighted in red.

Another approach to identify problematic areas in the image was introduced by connecting all cell centers to their 6 nearest surrounding centers. This creates

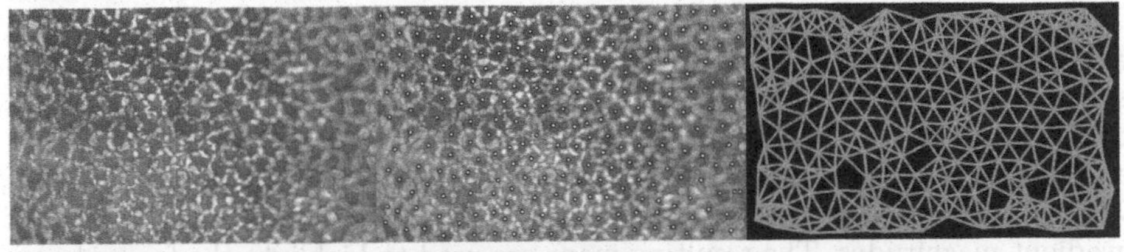

(a) An example image of a healthy cornea.

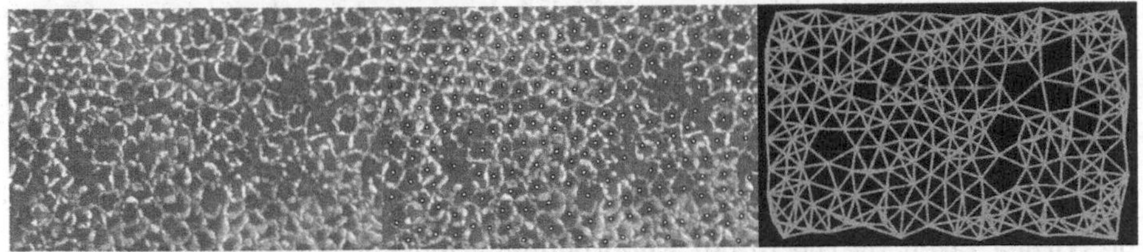

(b) An example image of cornea with severe cornea guttata (level 4).

Fig. 1. Examples for the GATs results showing the microscope image, the cell detection image, and the honeycomb image.

"honeycomb"-like structures which show regular triangular structures for evenly occurring cells (see Fig. 1a), but large and irregular connections for black spots and extremely large cells (see Fig. 1b). Figure 1 shows the results of the graphical analysis of two sample images. Here, Fig. 1a shows an image of a healthy cornea. A few large cells are spotted and some irregular areas can be recognized in the honeycomb, but the image has mostly regular structures. The second example, depicted in Fig. 1b, shows the same analysis, but for a cornea that has later developed level 4 (severe) guttata. Please note the higher amount of uncommonly large cells and the increased occurrence of large black areas in the honeycomb detection. In the DSS, these implemented GATs can be used to indicate a possible future condition of the cornea by analysing image-level features.

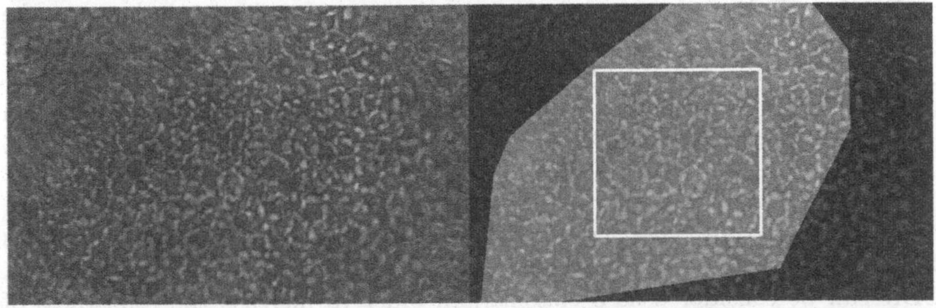

Fig. 2. Automatic detection of the focused image area and extraction of a fixed image frame used for training the machine learning classifiers.

A common problem with the explored cornea samples is that only a certain region per image is in focus while the rest appears blurry. For the graphical analysis as well as for the professionals, it would be preferable to know which area of the image is accurately captured and which is not. Therefore, we integrated a focus detection for the images based on the work of Golestaneh et al. [17] which calculates blur detection maps based on a high-frequency transform of gradient magnitudes. The resulting maps are used to highlight the focused area as seen in Fig. 2. Moreover, the GATs extract a frame of fixed size (the white quad) from the detected focus area which is later used for the training of some of the implemented machine learning classifiers. This combination of GATs help to analyse the cornea images more thoroughly and is, therefore, an essential part of the DSS.

In the next sections we describe the classification and decision support backend. A cornea is specified by a set of instances corresponding to the images of the cornea taken by the Robin Endothelium Analyzer and enhanced with the extracted annotations like cell density, cell shapes, bleb status, cell membrane completeness, etc. as well as the global features like donor's age and lens status.

3.3 Case-Based Reasoning as a Tool for Explainability

The clinical process for donor cornea screening is as follows: after the extraction, images taken by a Zeiss Primovert microscope are analysed by the Robin Endothelium Analyzer (REA) [15] providing features like cell density and percentage of cell shape types. In combination with additional characteristics like endothelial blebs, completeness of the cell membrane, donors' age, and lens status, a CBR retrieve function is built. CBR follows a 4R (retrieve, reuse, revise and retain) paradigm [14] which we implemented by using pycbr [18], a python micro-framework for implement Case-Based Reasoning systems.

- **Retrieve**: First, the system determines if the new case can already be solved with an existing solution. Concretely, the previously-added corneas, that are most similar to the present one, are identified.
- **Reuse**: In our scenario, in principle, the postoperative guttata classification of the selected (most similar) corneas are considered.
- **Revise**: Before the transplantation, the corresponding solutions to the retrieved cases are considered for assessing and giving a raw prediction of the cornea (e.g. based on the average voting).
- **Retain**: The final solution will be actually determined at a later examination 6 weeks after transplantation and then stored as the solution of the new case. This complete case is then part of the case basis and available for later use.

CBR has two outcomes: a guttata prediction and a list of most similar corneas which are presented to the clinician in the DSS. According to the first outcome, CBR can be considered as a classifier. In order to increase the robustness of the solution proposed by the CBR, the system is backed by other ML-based classification methods, which will be described in the next subsection.

3.4 Machine Learning Classifiers

Supervised machine learning methods allow for predictions based on annotated data. To increase the robustness of the CBR predictions, we developed several Machine Learning Classifiers (MLCs) which are implemented in Python using the TensorFlow and scikit-learn frameworks [19,20]. At the first step, data preprocessing takes place where we filter out corrupted samples and transform usable samples into valid features. Before training some of the models, we apply a random under-sampling strategy to handle the data imbalance.

- **Feed Forward Neural Network**: We built a neural network model with two hidden layers, each layer being fully connected with the successive one. The input layer contains as many neurons as the size of the input space corresponding to the extracted annotations per image, and the output layer contains a single neuron for the guttata prediction value.
- **Support Vector Classifier**: A Support Vector Machine [21,22] is a supervised learning algorithm that is very suitable for binary classification with a limited set of data, which fits our case where the amount of non-guttata cases outnumber the guttata cases. The idea is to find a hyperplane separating the two classes; the majority class is then penalized to compensate misclassification of the minority class. We use the scikit-learn implementation of the SVM classifier that also balances the skewed class distribution.
- **Random Forest Classifier**: Random Forest [23] realizes an ensemble learning approach which is based on the wisdom of crowd assumption. It uses multiple decision trees (considered as weak learners) on different subsets of the dataset and on different parts of the feature set. The results of the weak learners then vote for the final result.
- **Visual similarity**: We applied a pretrained version of the VGG16 model [24] on the images taken through the REA software for feature extraction. On top of this feature extraction follows a fully connected layer to build the final classifier that computes the similarities between the images to predict their class.

3.5 Aggregation

The central idea is to fuse the discussed machine learning approaches and the CBR to predict the overall guttata status of the current cornea. The fusion is based on the average votes at the instance level of all the single image classifications belonging to a cornea. Using this technique of combining a small set of heterogeneous learners generally performs better compared to single models, as it helps to overcome the limitations of the individual learners by "averaging out" the various errors of the respective models [25].

Table 1 shows the results of the single classifiers and their fusion. A high precision is important for a DSS since it should mark a cornea as bad only if the probability of CG is high. Our classifiers achieve relatively high precision, as can be seen in Table 1. As expected, this comes at the cost of low recall. Here it

Table 1. Average performance of the different classifiers and the fusion over all folds as **Precision**, **Recall/Sensitivity**, **Specificity** and **F1** score respectively.

Classifiers	Prec	Rec/Sens	Spec	F1
Fusion	**0.68**	0.28	0.92	0.60
Case-based Reasoning	0.60	0.42	0.76	0.60
Neural network	0.65	**0.45**	0.82	**0.64**
Support Vector Classifier	0.66	0.23	0.92	0.57
Random Forest Classifier	0.65	0.18	**0.94**	0.54
Vision similarity	0.59	0.30	0.83	0.56

is important to consider that the dataset used to train the models has already passed through a first filter, namely the examination by the clinicians. Thus, only those corneas with no visible signs of CG are part of our dataset, making severe cases of CG rare and hard to detect.

3.6 Graphical User Interface

A client-server architecture was implemented in Node.js [26], which serves the DSS's User-Interface to the user and acts as a proxy server for requesting the GAT, MLC, and CBR services. Those services are mainly implemented as Flask micro-services [27] and offer on-the-fly computation of new input images and data. The micro-services are requested via a REST API [28] provided by the Node.js proxy. Since these AI micro-services are encapsulated, it is possible to refine and update them without modifying the Node.js server, the main communication interface of the GUI. Figures 3, 4, and 5 show the components of the client GUI which implements the decision process outlined in Fig. 6. The design is based on a series of joint workshops with the clinicians and is kept clean and simple to not overload the user with too much options and information. An important feature of the DSS is the ability to compare the images of one cornea to another. This special view is triggered by clicking the image of any cornea container, either one from the similar corneas (see Fig. 4) or one from the canonical examples (see Fig. 5). The appearing view shows the clicked cornea's images and GAT analyses side by side with the currently analysed cornea's. This way, a clinician can compare, for example, the current case with its most similar cornea case returned by the CBR.

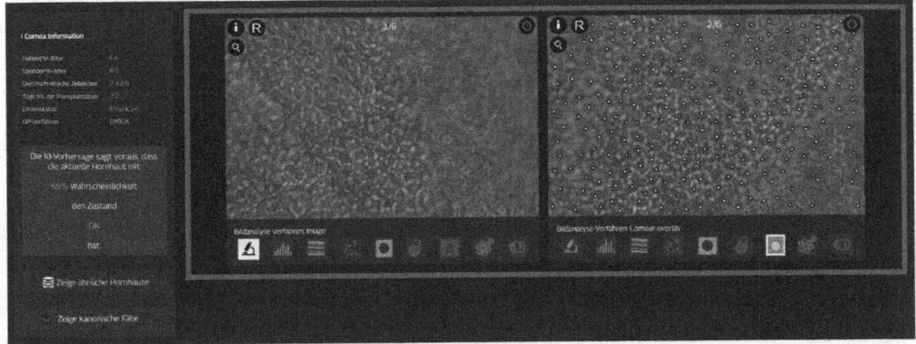

Fig. 3. Information and GAT results of the currently selected cornea. The left side shows general information of the current corneal endothelium including the age of both donor and receiver, average cell density and surgical procedure. Right underneath, the user can find a short summary of the MLC's prediction with its associated confidence. The right part shows the corresponding microscope images. For each of the images, the user has the option to show image-level information including cell count, cell shapes, and the semi-quantitative criteria assessed by the clinicians [1]. All the different steps and results of the GATs can be shown by pressing the buttons underneath the image container. It is also possible to activate the inferred focus area of the image in combination with the detection images.

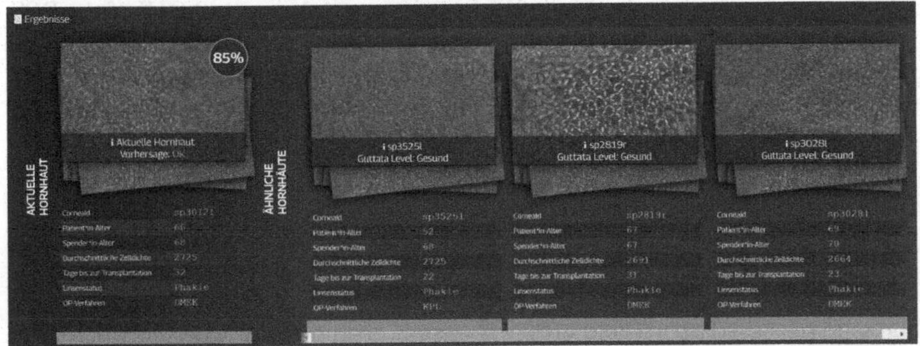

Fig. 4. MLC prediciton and CBR results. The first cornea container on the left side shows the currently selected cornea with an image and its general information. The result of the fusion AI prediction is indicated by the coloring of the bottom field. While the green color suggests a healthy cornea, an orange color is used for a cornea developing guttata. The percentage in the top-right corner of the left cornea displays the confidence of the AI prediction. The other cornea containers on the right are the similar corneas returned by the CBR ordered by decreasing similarity. (Color figure online)

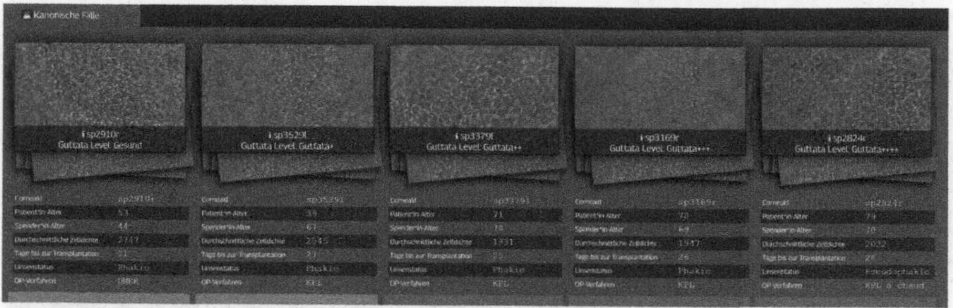

Fig. 5. Canonical examples of corneas. Here, the five displayed cornea containers show an example cornea case for each CG level (from healthy to CG level 4).

4 Evaluation

In the proposed decision support system, the prediction of unsuitable corneas consists of a multi-step decision procedure including the previously discussed AI methods. To explore the effectiveness of this system, a virtual study was set-up which allowed the users to participate remotely. Its main goal is to find evidence that the presented DSS increases the performance of the clinicians decisions. The general structure of the study process is depicted in Fig. 6. The study's user interface features two separate modes, the supported mode (Mode S) and the default, unsupported mode (Mode D). In contrast to the general GUI of the DSS, both study modes have some study-specific UI. As can be seen in Fig. 7, these include a display of the current mode (top-left), a progress counter (top-right), and the decision functionality for the currently analysed cornea (bottom). The latter offers a simple button layout with the option between *ok* and *not ok*. After pressing one of them, the participant is prompted with a pop-up modal to verify the decision.

4.1 Study Set-Up

The study is based on a 4-fold cross validation, within-subject design where each participant tests all possible configurations. Firstly, we split the database of 948 into 894 healthy and 54 guttata corneas. We separately and randomly split these two sets into four sets which are randomly conjoined into 4 folds, each containing 237 (223 healthy and 14 guttata). For each of the 4 test folds, we created separate instances of the MLCs and CBR models based on the remaining three train folds. For the evaluation, we selected for each fold randomly a sub-set containing 12 corneas. Due to the highly skewed distribution, the set was composed of $\frac{2}{3}$ healthy and $\frac{1}{3}$ guttata corneas. Each cornea of the set is classified with both modes. Hence, in total, we obtain $12 + 12 = 24$ classification decisions per fold yielding $4 * 24 = 96$ CG decisions per participant.

We invited 7 participants of which all are experienced clinicians within the Department of Ophthalmology in Homburg. The participants were split-up in

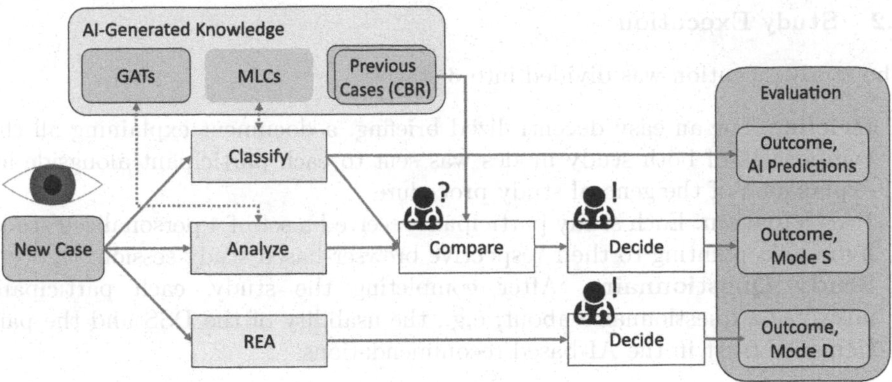

Fig. 6. The decision processes for the different modes. Given a new cornea, the cornea is analysed (GATs), classified (MLCs), and the CBR retrieves relevant previous cases from the case base. These predictions result in the AI prediction outcome during the evaluation. In the middle row, the clinician uses the additional AI-generated knowledge to compare the cornea with retrieved cases before the decision is taken. This defines the outcome of the supported mode (Mode S). The last row describes the default mode (Mode D) which should recreate the current decision practice in the cornea bank. In this case the clinicians solely rely on the images and the detection results of the REA software.

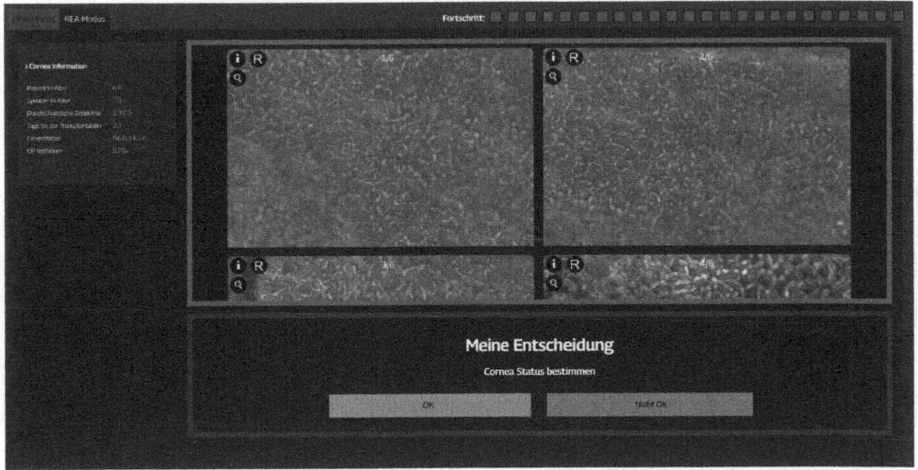

Fig. 7. Example of the study interface in *Mode D* including the study-specific User Interface elements.

groups of two/three where participants of the same group received the same study sets. In this way, we can compute the pairwise inter-annotator agreement κ [29,30].

4.2 Study Execution

The study execution was divided into 3 stages:

1. **Briefing**. For an easy decentralized briefing, a document explaining all the components of both study modes was sent to each participant alongside an explanation of the general study procedure.
2. **Participation**. Each study participant received a set of 4 personalized study hyperlinks pointing to their respective browser-based study session.
3. **Study Questionnaire**. After completing the study, each participant answered a questionnaire about, e.g., the usability of the DSS and the participants' trust in the AI-based recommendations.

The evaluation was performed over a period of two weeks and anonymously stored on a secure server.

4.3 Study Results

The first step is to analyse the average classification results of all participants for the different modes. The respective confusion matrices (CFs) are displayed in Fig. 8. Here, the false-positive rate is interesting: For both decision modes it is significantly higher than the respective rate of the AI predictions shown in Fig. 8c.

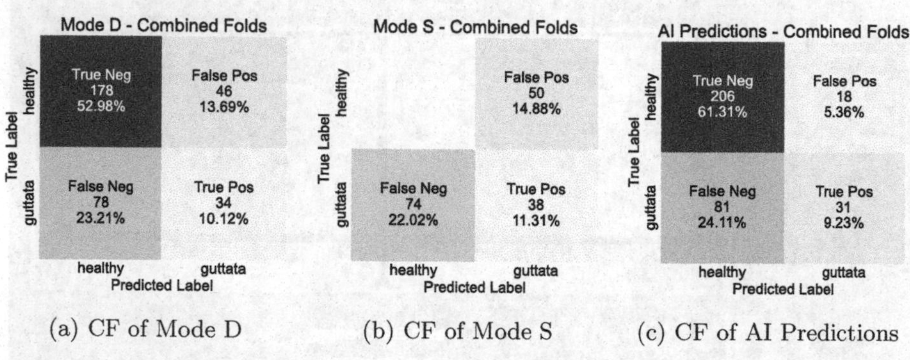

(a) CF of Mode D (b) CF of Mode S (c) CF of AI Predictions

Fig. 8. Confusion matrices (CF) for different modes averaged over all respective folds.

We indicate performance by precision, recall, specificity, and the F1 score, see Table 2. The AI predictions perform better in terms of the F1 score and precision, but the recall is highest in Mode S. Conclusively, the combination of AI tools with the expertise of the clinicians yields the best rate for detecting corneas developing CG.

Table 2. Average performance of the different modes and the AI prediction over all folds as **Prec**ision, **Rec**all/**Sens**itivity, **Spec**ificity and **F1** score respectively.

	Prec	Rec/Sens	Spec	F1
Mode D	0.42	0.30	0.79	0.35
Mode S	0.43	**0.34**	0.78	0.38
AI prediction	**0.63**	0.28	**0.92**	**0.39**

The individual decision times of the clinicians were measured during the study execution, see Fig. 9. Even though they show a similar shape, a shift from the high frequency of 10 s decisions of Mode D to the 20 s range in Mode S is visible.

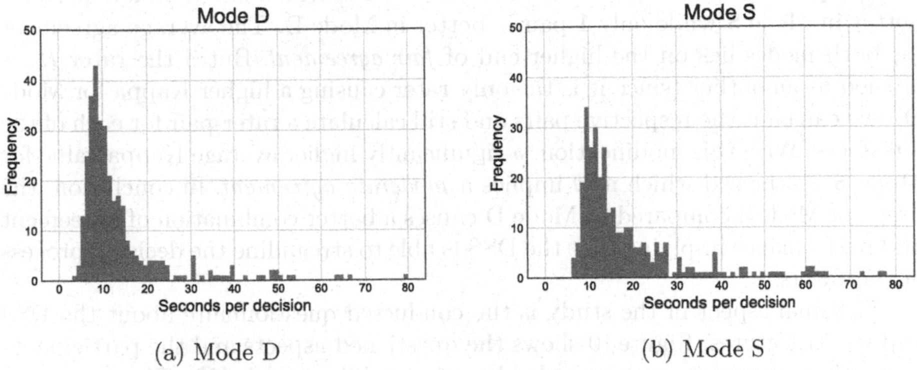

(a) Mode D

(b) Mode S

Fig. 9. Distributions of decision duration for both modes.

This is also mirrored in the median and average decision times depicted in Table 3. Naturally, the AI-enhanced Mode S has higher mean and medium times than the default mode since it features more additional information and UI elements. Nevertheless, the difference is still in an acceptable range which indicates that the use of our DSS is very time-efficient.

As described earlier, we use Cohen's Kappa to examine the interrater reliability of the study participants. A Kappa value of less than 0 means that the agreement of two participants is mere random chance. The greater a value is than 0, the better is the agreement.

Table 3. Average decision times (in seconds) for both study modes.

	Minimum	Maximum	Mean	Median
Mode D	3	91	14	10
Mode S	6	116	20	13

Moreover, these values can be categorized into the following semantic descriptions [31]:

- **0.01–0.20**: none to slight agreement
- **0.21–0.40**: fair agreement
- **0.41–0.60**: moderate agreement
- **0.61–0.80**: substantial agreement
- **0.81–1.00**: almost perfect agreement

Since this metric does not incorporate the correctness of the decisions, we present the Kappa values alongside the averaged F1 scores of the rater-pair in Table 4. When both the Kappa and F1 scores are better in one mode, it signals that the agreement is not only better, but also that this agreement in the respective mode is tied to a better performance. Looking at the individual rater-pairs, especially with regard to the associated F1 scores, 3 out of 5 pairs perform better in Mode S while only 1 pair is better in Mode D. The average agreement for both modes lies on the higher end of *fair agreement*. But if the rater R_3 is labeled as an outlier (since it is the only rater causing a higher Kappa for Mode D), we can omit the respective pairs and still calculate a rater-pair for each of the 3 testsets. With this modification, a significantly higher average Kappa value for Mode S is achieved which now implies a *moderate agreement*. In conclusion, the usage of Mode S compared to Mode D causes a better combination of agreement and performance implying that the DSS is able to streamline the decision process of the raters.

The final aspect of the study is the conducted questionnaire about the DSS and its AI features. Figure 10 shows the questioned aspects and the participants respective agreement, each recorded by a 5-step Likert Scale [32]. The user interface is almost consistently rated as being easy to use and its components as being intuitive. This indicates that the general design of the system is comprehensible and satisfying. At least for some participants, the different AI tools (CBR, MLCs, GATs) seemed to help with the decision which correlates with the overall improved performance when using the DSS. Subjectively, the familiar cornea information still helped the decision process the most. This can also be due to its new and improved presentation inside the DSS. Concerning the trust in the AI predictions and its influence on the participant's decision, the votes are rather indecisive. Additionally, some find that the AI predictions unsettle them in their decision process, but the majority does not have this feeling. Some participants would use the system on a daily basis, while others are rather indecisive.

Table 4. Interrater reliability: The Kappa and averaged F1 scores for the rater-pairs in both study modes, the averages over all raters, and the averages excluding the pairs containing the possible outlier R_3.

Rater-pair	Mode D Kappa	Mode D F1	Mode S Kappa	Mode S F1
R_{12}	0.09	0.47	**0.42**	**0.52**
R_{13}	**0.27**	0.49	0.16	**0.52**
R_{23}	**0.52**	**0.52**	0.00	0.51
R_{45}	0.33	0.17	**0.37**	**0.27**
R_{67}	0.52	0.24	**0.60**	**0.25**
ϕR	**0.35**	0.38	0.31	**0.41**
$\phi R \setminus \{R_{13}, R_{23}\}$	0.31	0.29	**0.46**	**0.35**

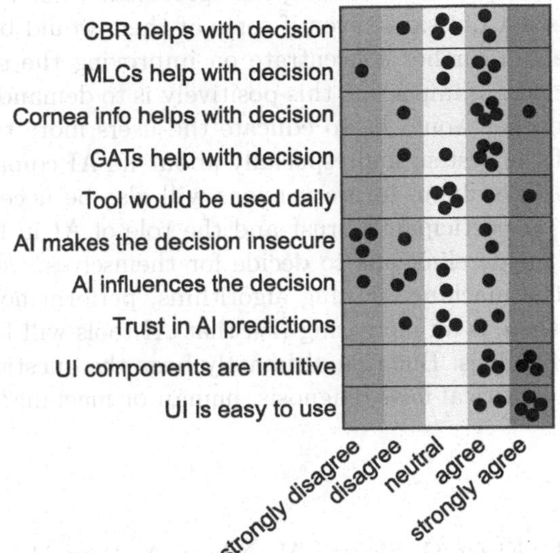

Fig. 10. Answers for the questionnaire. The answer of each participant to each question is marked by a dot. For better clarity, the original questions were abbreviated.

5 Summary and Future Work

The correct classification of the CG status in the corneal endothelium prior to its transplantation can be challenging since CG symptoms can still develop weeks after the transplantation. Clinicians and professionals are not always able to filter out all the donor corneas developing CG, which leads to postoperative complications or even to a repeat keratoplasty in severe cases. In this paper, we proposed a Decision Support System which works with post mortem corneal images from the eye banks. The tool offers a combination of analytical and machine learning algorithms as well as Case-Based Reasoning. The analytical algorithms provide visual feedback, the machine learning algorithms compute a score for how likely the cornea will develop guttata in the future, and the Case-Based Reasoning features a retrieval method that allows for comparison with similar corneas. We conducted a 4-fold evaluation study with 7 professionals. Overall, our DSS leads to improvements in the participations' decision accuracy. Except for one outlier, the average pairwise interrater reliability measured with $\kappa = 0.46$, peaking at 0.60, demonstrating promising results. The participants rated the UI of the DSS as very easy to use and understood the single UI components well. While they were indecisive if the AI predictions unsettle their decision or should be trusted, they generally found the separate tools useful.

Future work includes using the newly gained information about the effectiveness of the DSS to rework and optimize its UI and the integrated machine learning algorithms. Algorithm improvement will be crucial which is why we will instantly collect more data as well as reassessing previously discarded corneas. Initially, focus will be put on increasing the agreement value κ since it is desirable to take consistent decisions, even if some of them would be wrong. Having achieved that, we can further concentrate on improving the system's decision performance. One way of impacting this positively is to demand users to explain their decisions, another would be to educate the users more thoroughly about the functioning of the system and especially about its AI components. Inviting more participants to evaluate future versions will also be necessary. Particular focus will be put on participant's trust and the role of AI in the decision process: how can we nugde clinicians to decide for themselves even if the system, and particularly the machine learning algorithms, perform nearly perfect? As discussed in [33], there is an increasing risk that AI tools will begin to compensate for missing clinicians. But this ultimately begs the question of who would be responsible for a critical false diagnosis, human or machine?

References

1. Safi, T., Daas, L., Kiefer, G., Sharma, M., Ndiaye, A., Deru, M., et al.: Semiquantitative criteria in the eye bank that correlate with cornea guttata in donor corneas. Klin. Monatsbl. Augenheilkd. **6**, 680–687 (2021)
2. Lisch, W., Seitz, B.: Corneal dystrophies. Dev. Ophthalmol. **48**, 155–160 (2011)
3. Giasson, C.J., Solomon, L.D., Polse, K.A.: Morphometry of corneal endothelium in patients with corneal guttata. Ophthalmology **114**(8), 1469–1475 (2007)
4. Waring III, G.O., Rodrigues, M.M., Laibson, P.R.: Corneal dystrophies. ii. endothelial dystrophies. Surv. Ophthalmol. **23**(3), 147–168 (1978)
5. Adamis, A., Filatov, V., Tripathi, B., Tripathi, R.: Fuchs' endothelial dystrophy of the cornea. Surv. Ophthalmol. **38**(2), 149–168 (1993)
6. Weiss, J.S.: IC3D classification of corneal dystrophies-edition 2. Cornea **34**(2), 117–159 (2015)
7. Zoega, G.M.: Prevalence and risk factors for cornea guttata in the reykjavik eye study. Ophthalmology **113**(4), 565–569 (2006)
8. Eghrari, A.O., Gottsch, J.D.: Fuchs' corneal dystrophy. Expert Rev. Ophthalmol. **5**(2), 147–159 (2010)

9. Vigueras-Guillén, J.P.: Corneal endothelial cell segmentation by classifier-driven merging of oversegmented images. IEEE Trans. Med. Imaging **37**(10), 2278–2289 (2018). https://doi.org/10.1109/TMI.2018.2841910
10. Vigueras-Guillén, J.P., Lemij, H.G., Van Rooij, J., Vermeer, K.A., Van Vliet, L.J.: Automatic detection of the region of interest in corneal endothelium images using dense convolutional neural networks. In: Medical Imaging 2019: Image Processing, vol. 10949, pp. 779–789. SPIE (2019)
11. Sierra, J.S., et al.: Automated corneal endothelium image segmentation in the presence of cornea guttata via convolutional neural networks. In: Applications of Machine Learning 2020, vol. 11511, pp. 59–64. SPIE (2020)
12. Suzuki, K., Chen, Y. (eds.): Artificial Intelligence in Decision Support Systems for Diagnosis in Medical Imaging. ISRL, vol. 140. Springer, Cham (2018). https://doi.org/10.1007/978-3-319-68843-5
13. Braun, M., Hummel, P., Beck, S., Dabrock, P.: Primer on an ethics of AI-based decision support systems in the clinic. J. Med. Ethics **47**(12), e3–e3 (2021)
14. Richter, M.M., Weber, R.O.: Case-Based Reasoning. Springer (2016)
15. Langstrof, G., Klein, S., Rottkamp, L.: Robin endothelium analyzer. https://robin-solutions.com/rea-xdl/
16. Roerdink, J.B., Meijster, A.: The watershed transform: definitions, algorithms and parallelization strategies. Fund. Inform. **41**(1, 2), 187–228 (2000)
17. Golestaneh, S.A., Karam, L.J.: Spatially-varying blur detection based on multiscale fused and sorted transform coefficients of gradient magnitudes. In: CVPR, pp. 596–605 (2017)
18. Hernández, G.: Pycbr. https://github.com/dih5/pycbr
19. Abadi, M., et al.: TensorFlow: large-scale machine learning on heterogeneous systems (2015). https://www.tensorflow.org/, software available from tensorflow.org
20. Pedregosa, F., et al.: Scikit-learn: machine learning in Python. J. Mach. Learn. Res. **12**, 2825–2830 (2011)
21. Akbani, R., Kwek, S., Japkowicz, N.: Applying support vector machines to imbalanced datasets. In: Boulicaut, J.-F., Esposito, F., Giannotti, F., Pedreschi, D. (eds.) ECML 2004. LNCS (LNAI), vol. 3201, pp. 39–50. Springer, Heidelberg (2004). https://doi.org/10.1007/978-3-540-30115-8_7
22. Walsh, P.: Support vector machine learning for ECG classification. In: CERC, pp. 195–204 (2019)
23. Chen, C., Liaw, A., Breiman, L.: Using random forest to learn imbalanced data. Technical Report 666, Department of Statistics, UC Berkley (2004). http://xtf.lib.berkeley.edu/reports/SDTRWebData/accessPages/666.html
24. Simonyan, K., Zisserman, A.: Very deep convolutional networks for large-scale image recognition. arXiv preprint arXiv:1409.1556 (2014)
25. Gashler, M., Giraud-Carrier, C., Martinez, T.: Decision tree ensemble: small heterogeneous is better than large homogeneous. In: Decision Tree Ensemble: Small Heterogeneous is Better than Large Homogeneous, pp. 900–905, January 2008. https://doi.org/10.1109/ICMLA.2008.154
26. Dahl, R.: Node.js. https://nodejs.org
27. Ronacher, A., et al.: Flask. https://flask.palletsprojects.com/en/2.0.x/
28. Fielding, R.T.: Architectural Styles and the Design of Network-based Software Architectures. University of California, Irvine (2000)
29. Artstein, R.: Inter-annotator agreement. In: Ide, N., Pustejovsky, J. (eds.) Handbook of Linguistic Annotation, pp. 297–313. Springer, Dordrecht (2017). https://doi.org/10.1007/978-94-024-0881-2_11

30. Kvålseth, T.O.: Note on Cohen's kappa. Psychol. Rep. **65**(1), 223–226 (1989)
31. McHugh, M.L.: Interrater reliability: the kappa statistic. Biochem. Med. (Zagreb) **22**(3), 276–282 (2012)
32. Joshi, A., Kale, S., Chandel, S., Pal, D.K.: Likert scale: explored and explained. Br. J. Appli. Sci. Technol. **7**(4), 396 (2015)
33. Neri, E., Coppola, F., Miele, V., Bibbolino, C., Grassi, R.: Artificial intelligence: who is responsible for the diagnosis? Radiol. Med. (Torino) **125**(6), 517–521 (2020). https://doi.org/10.1007/s11547-020-01135-9

Design and Implementation of Platform Protocol and Client of Hakka Residential System Based on Artificial Intelligence

Hong Li[1,2] and Shengqing Huang[3(✉)]

[1] School of Education Science, Gannan Normal University, Ganzhou 341000, Jiangxi, China
[2] School of Psychology, Jiangxi Normal University, Nanchang 341000, Jiangxi, China
[3] School of Art Design and Media, East China University of Science and Technology, Shanghai 200237, China
hsq_0702@163.com

Abstract. Nowadays, with the rapid development of science and technology and the wide popularization and application of Internet and computer technology, many emerging technologies have emerged, among which AIT (Artificial Intelligence Technology) is one. With the increasing demand for high-quality life, a variety of smart home systems and platforms emerge in endlessly. In this paper, in order to explore the effect of the application of AIT in the design and implementation of Hakka residential system platform protocol and client, we select two companies specializing in Hakka residential system as the experimental research object. The results of the experimental research show that the application of AIT in the design and implementation of Hakka residential system platform protocol and client H company, which has developed AIT, has higher design efficiency and client utilization rate than G company due to traditional methods. The highest design efficiency and utilization rate of H company are 98.71% and 92.35% respectively, while the highest design efficiency and client utilization rate of G company are 84.39% and 72.36% respectively.

Keywords: Artificial intelligence technology · Hakka residence · Home system · Platform protocol

1 Introduction

In recent years, the development of AIT has exceeded our imagination, it is widely used in various fields. Smart home is emerging in recent years. It has brought about a qualitative change in people's lives, so that people are not only limited to the relationship between people and things, but also the relationship between things has become closer. It's not just a few smart home products that can build a smart home, it's a collection of smart systems [1, 2]. Through a number of intelligent products directly closely related to achieve home intelligent integration, common refrigerators, air conditioners, televisions, etc. will be unified by the network equipment integrated management, with technology to change people's lives. And it not only provides traditional home services, but also

H. Degen and S. Ntoa (Eds.): HCII 2022, LNAI 13336, pp. 275–283, 2022.
https://doi.org/10.1007/978-3-031-05643-7_18

takes into account information, networking, construction, monitoring and other aspects of the home. It can effectively optimize people's living environment, provide healthy and comfortable operation experience, and enhance the fun of home. The emergence of artificial intelligence provides great convenience and help for these [3, 4].

Science and technology are changing our lives. This is our main theme of development in the 21st century. Smart home is the product of the organic combination of science and technology and human living environment. It has a good development prospect and is favored by various fields at home and abroad. Therefore, many enterprises have given up the traditional enterprise policy and devoted to the research of a better intelligent ecosystem. With the development of smart home, more and more smart devices can be created and used. Through the connection of various intelligent devices, especially the unified intelligent interactive platform, unified scheduling and processing, and cooperation in various modules, to create a "living" home for users is the focus of many manufacturers in recent years [5, 6].

As a relatively new industry, smart home is at the rising point on the road of development. As far as the current market situation is concerned, its consumer market has not yet opened, but there is no doubt that with the popularity and development of smart home, it is bound to lead the development trend of the times [7, 8]. Throughout the current development of domestic intelligent platform, the potential of smart home is huge. Some leading enterprises have built their own smart brands, and the government is actively encouraging the development of these emerging products, which just complement each other. The combination of AIT and intelligent furniture system is also a starting point of innovative thinking, and we hope that the combination of the two can create greater surprise for us in the future [9, 10].

2 Method

2.1 Application Fields of Artificial Intelligence

In July 2017, the State Council issued the "New Generation Artificial Intelligence Development Plan". The "Planning" proposes six key tasks: first, to build an open collaborative artificial intelligence technology innovation system; second, to promote industrial intelligent upgrading, to create artificial intelligence innovation highland; third, to use artificial intelligence to improve public security capabilities; fourth, to strengthen labor The integration of military and civilian in the field of intelligence; the fifth is to build a ubiquitous and efficient intelligent infrastructure system; the sixth is to look forward to the layout of major scientific and technological projects, and to form an artificial intelligence project with a new generation of artificial intelligence major science and technology projects as the core and to coordinate the current and future R&D tasks. In the "Planning", by 2020, the overall technology and application of artificial intelligence will be synchronized with the world's advanced level, and the artificial intelligence industry will become a new important economic growth point. The core industry scale will exceed 150 billion yuan, driving the related industries to exceed 1 trillion yuan; by 2025, a new generation of artificial intelligence has been widely used in the fields of intelligent manufacturing, smart medical care, smart city, intelligent agriculture, and national defense construction. The core industry scale exceeds 400 billion yuan, and the scale of related industries exceeds

5 trillion yuan. By 2030, the theory, technology and application of artificial intelligence have reached the world's leading level, forming a complete industrial chain and high-end industrial cluster covering core technologies, key systems, support platforms and intelligent applications. The scale of artificial intelligence core industry exceeds 1 trillion yuan, driving the scale of related industries. More than 10 trillion yuan [11–13].

In recent years, more and more industries are developing by leaps and bounds under the influence of artificial intelligence. As the most eye-catching technology in the 21st century, there is no doubt that artificial intelligence has laid a solid foundation in people's lives and all walks of life. In terms of the current technical form, those processes with certain rules can be easily controlled by artificial intelligence. For example, our common intelligent assistant products, such as Xiaoai classmate and sweeping robot, patrol robot, intelligent monitoring and other security products, and pilotless aircraft, pilotless cars and other autonomous products, intelligent detector, intelligent medical and other medical products, intelligent shopping guide, artificial intelligent warehousing and other logistics products and intelligent customer service, investment consultant and other financial products. They are applied in various platforms: Jingdong, Taobao, Amazon, Alibaba, iFLYTEK, and learning ape. These enterprises cannot do without the support of artificial intelligence. All in all, in today's society, all aspects of our life are full of artificial intelligence crystallization, they are convenient for our life, but also in the rapid promotion of the scientific development of modern society.

2.2 Hakka Houses

As one of the classic styles of Hakka, it is known as the ancient Roman castle in the East, and the living fossil of Jinwu castle in China. There are many architectural styles of famous Hakka houses, such as Weiwu village, Tuwei, Shuiwei, etc. different styles have different humanistic flavor, which is the fundamental reason why its architectural characteristics enjoy a high reputation in the construction industry at home and abroad. Hakka dwellings are not only unique in architectural style, but also in their types, such as Weilong house, quadrangle building, square house and so on. According to reliable historical records, it began in the Tang and Song Dynasties, especially in the Ming and Qing Dynasties. It combines the ancient style of Central Plains and the regional characteristics of southern culture. Hakkas often live in concentrated areas, so traces of their houses can be seen in many places. They are mainly distributed near Shenzhen and other Hakka settlements at home and abroad. Its unique brick concrete structure combines water with special soil, supplemented by sticky materials such as glutinous rice, thus creating a unique enclosure.

Utilizing earth or mud as the basic building material, Hakka house contributed to the sustainability of the physical environment. Round walls of the yuan lou enclosed more floor space than square walls. Being cool in summer and warm in winter, they reduced usage of human and material energy to make the dwelling comfortable in all seasons. The semi-circular ponds were utilized according to a well-known protocol to raise fish for food. Utilizing earth or mud as the basic building material, Hakka house contributed to the sustainability of the physical environment. Round walls of the yuan lou enclosed more floor space than square walls. Being cool in summer and warm in winter, they reduced usage of human and material energy to make the dwelling comfortable in all seasons. The semi-circular ponds were utilized according to a well-known protocol to raise fish for food. Closed to the outside but open on the inside, the house created security and solidarity for the clan [14, 15].

Most of the besieged houses in southern Jiangxi, such as Wushi Wai, Yanyi Wai, Guanxi Wai, Dongsheng Wai and so on, originated from the Shang and Qin Dynasties. The layout structure of the WAI can be divided into outer and inner WAI. The periphery is mostly square, the four corners are built with a strong fort building. The outer wall is mostly made of hemp stone, cobblestone, blue brick and glutinous rice pulp into a solid closed body, more than two meters thick, the wall is distributed with rows of muzzle holes, majestic. The outer corridor is divided into two to four floors. The first floor is for kitchen and livestock, the second floor is for living and storing goods, the third floor is for living, and the fourth floor is for the passage when dealing with external attacks. The inner perimeter is built on one to three floors according to the size of the outer perimeter. However, no matter how big or small, a shrine or hall for ancestor worship must be built on the central axis of the enclosure. There are also hidden Wells, Wells, sewage channels, granaries, etc., which are closed in peacetime and saved in wartime. When the gates are closed, it is an "independent kingdom" isolated from the outside world.

2.3 Smart Home System

As a new life experience, smart home system relies on engineering technology to link all aspects related to home, and through network technology, computer technology, artificial intelligence and communication technology, it combines home monitoring, lighting control, health system, air conditioning remote control and other intelligent management, so as to bring people a new home experience new system. A smart home is an application of ubiquitous or pervasive computing or environment. It also has another name, we call it smart house, home automation, intelligent home, adaptive home, and aware house. In fact, there are many words with similar meaning, such as network home, electronic home and so on. In fact, the original intention is to make our home life more convenient, comfortable, safe and healthy through scientific means. With the popularization and development of intelligence, people's requirements in this field are constantly improving. Some simple intelligent scenes cannot meet the needs of people's life. Nowadays, the system configuration of smart home is increasingly perfect, which can be called "smart". Smart home is not only the requirement of intelligent residential, residential skew is also the case. Nowadays, smart home has been able to access security system, telemedicine system, heating system, online education system, online TV and many other external systems. The combination of these external systems and home is the broader sense of smart home [16, 17].

2.4 Function of Smart Home System

Smart home constitute a branch of ubiquitous computing that involves incorporating smartness into dwellings for comfort, healthcare, safety, security, and energy conservation. Nowadays, more and more families are willing to try smart home. In family life, smart home system takes residence as the platform to build a safe, healthy, environment-friendly and energy-saving living environment. People can hand things over to artificial intelligence to complete, remote control of home appliances, but also real-time monitoring of the situation at home. This greatly improves the convenience, comfort and safety of the home.

Smart homes offer a better quality of life by introducing automated appliance control and assistive services. They optimize user comfort by using context awareness and predefined constraints based on the conditions of the home environment. A user can control home appliances and devices remotely, which enables him or her to execute tasks before arriving home. Ambient intelligence systems, which monitor smart homes, sometimes optimize the household's electricity usage. Smart homes enhance traditional security and safety mechanisms by using intelligent monitoring and access control [18, 19].

2.5 Calculation Methods Used in the Experiment

When we do experimental research, we usually use some algorithm formulas to help us count and calculate the results of experimental data, and analyze the results of experimental data. The following are some algorithm formulas involved in this paper:

$$f(x) = a_0 + \sum_{n=1}^{\infty}\left(a_n \cos\frac{n\pi x}{L} + b_n \sin\frac{n\pi x}{L}\right) \tag{1}$$

$$x = \frac{-b \pm \sqrt{b^2 - 4ac}}{2a} \tag{2}$$

$$\sin\alpha \pm \sin\beta = 2\sin\frac{1}{2}(\alpha \pm \beta)\cos\frac{1}{2}(\alpha \mp \beta) \tag{3}$$

3 Experiment

3.1 Selection of Experimental Research Objects

In order to study the influence of AIT on the platform protocol and client design and implementation of Hakka residential home system, we specially selected two companies operating in this direction as the research object. Among them, H company applied AIT in the platform protocol and client design and implementation of Hakka residential home system, while company G The traditional technology method is still adopted.

3.2 Selection of Experimental Measurement Standards

We investigated the platform protocol of Hakka residential home system designed and implemented by the two companies, the design efficiency of the client and the utilization rate of the client. In order to ensure the accuracy of the experimental data results, we conducted five experimental tests on the two groups of experimental data scales of the two companies, and checked the data results several times to ensure the accuracy of the experimental data The objective and authenticity of experimental data are guaranteed, and then the experimental data results are analyzed statistically. Finally, the experimental data are recorded in the chart for reference.

4 Discussion

4.1 Investigation on Design Efficiency of the Two Companies

We conducted five groups of experimental data survey on the design efficiency of the two companies, and the results of the experimental data are as follows (both experimental data results are kept with two decimal places):

Table 1. Survey on design efficiency of two companies

	Design efficiency	
	H company	G company
Group one	87.69%	81.23%
Group two	88.91%	83.56%
Group three	93.56%	79.81%
Group four	95.66%	84.39%
Group five	98.71%	80.75%

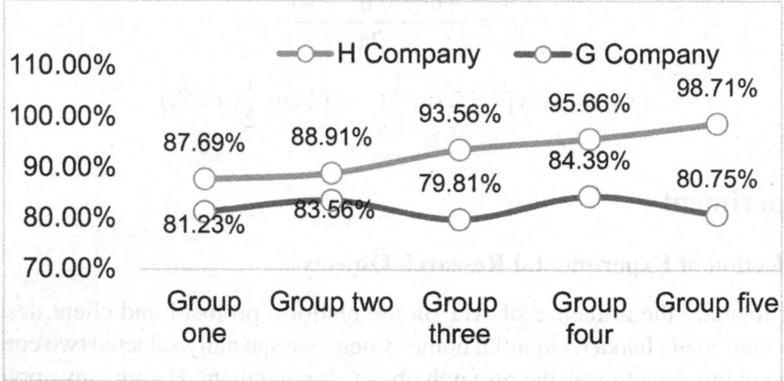

Fig. 1. Survey on design efficiency of two companies

From Table 1 and Fig. 1, we can clearly understand the design efficiency of Hakka residential system platform protocol and client of the two companies. As shown in the chart above, we can see that, The design efficiency of H company is 87.69% in the first group, 88.91% in the second group, 93.56% in the third group, 95.66% in the fourth group and 98.71% in the fifth group; while the design efficiency of G company is 81.23% in the first group, 83.56% in the second group, 79.81% in the third group, 84.39% in the fourth group and 80.75% in the fifth group. From these data and the curve trend of design efficiency of the two companies in Fig. 2, we can know that the design efficiency of H company is higher than that of G company, and the design efficiency of G company needs to be improved. The above data also shows that AIT can have a positive impact on the design efficiency of Hakka residential system platform protocol and client, and can help improve the design efficiency.

4.2 Client Utilization Survey Designed by Two Companies

We have also conducted five groups of experimental data investigation on the utilization rate of Hakka residential system clients designed by these two companies, and these experimental data are also recorded in the chart, as shown in Table 2 and Fig. 2 below (the experimental data results are reserved for two decimal places):

Table 2. Client utilization survey designed by two companies

	Investigation of client utilization	
	H company	G company
Group one	79.80%	60.58%
Group two	83.91%	67.91%
Group three	88.91%	63.79%
Group four	90.78%	72.36%
Group five	92.35%	68.33%

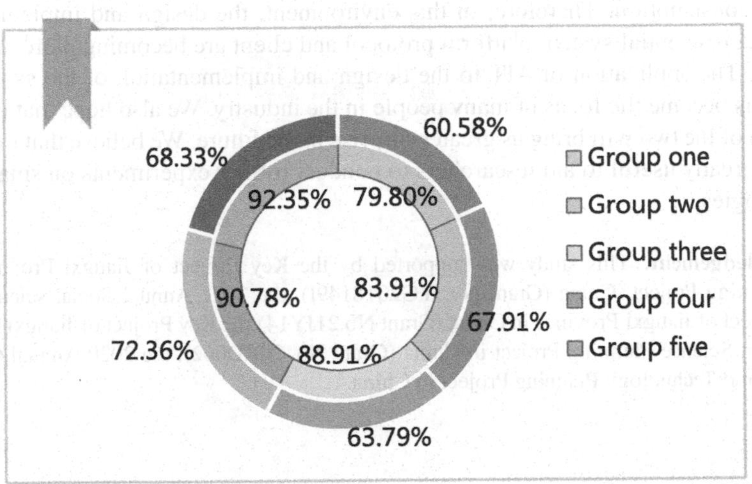

Fig. 2. Client utilization survey designed by two companies

By carefully observing Table 2 and Fig. 2, we can see that the utilization rate of Hakka residential system clients developed by H company is 79.80% for the first group, 80%–90% for the second group, and 83.91% for the specific utilization rate. The utilization rate of the third group is 88.91% higher than that of the second group, 90.78% for the fourth group, and 90.78% for the fifth group It is 92.35%. We can see that the data results of these five groups of experiments are progressive layer by layer, which indicates that the utilization rate of the client developed by H company has been increasing, and the number of uses of the client is more and more; while the utilization rate of the client developed by G company is 60.58% for the first group, 67.91% for the second group, and 67.91% for the third group. The experimental data is 63.79%, the utilization rate of the fourth group is 72.36%, and the utilization rate of the fifth group is lower than that of the fourth group, which is 68.33%. These data show that the utilization rate of clients developed by G company is relatively low compared with that of H company, and these utilization rates cannot be maintained in a stable state, and the utilization rate is good and bad.

5 Conclusions

The design of a smart home depends on user requirements and user living styles. Generally, smart homes offer comfort, safety, security, remote control, and energy conservation. Hakka house system presents a new challenge to smart home design. As AIT continues to mature and improve, our way of life will also be affected by the technology environment, and even the whole world will change greatly. It can be said that with its rapid development and wide application, our life will gradually develop in the direction of intelligence. Now, with the development of economy, many people have more and more demands for higher living standards. Smart homes will gain massive popularity in the future because current trends indicate that they are becoming the center of intelligent service consumption. Therefore, in this environment, the design and implementation of Hakka residential system platform protocol and client are becoming more and more popular. The application of AIT to the design and implementation of the system and client has become the focus of many people in the industry. We also hope that the combination of the two will bring us greater surprise in the future. We believe that this paper will be greatly useful to aid researchers to conduct further experiments on smart home technologies.

Acknowledgement. This study was supported by the Key Project of Jiangxi Province Culture Planning Project, China (Grant No. YG2018149I), the 2021 Annual Social science Planning project of Jiangxi Province in China (Grant No.21JY14),the Key Project of Jiangxi Province Education Science Planning Project in China (Grant No. 20ZD062), the 2020 Annual Ganzhou Science and Technology Planning Project in China.

References

1. Yihan, S.: Research and implementation of smart home system based on ZigBee. Commun. World **26**(05), 21–22 (2019)
2. Xia, P.: Design and implementation of smart home system based on machine learning. China's Strateg. Emerg. Ind. **44**(128), 158+160 (2017)
3. Liang, R., Huang, T.: Design and development of smart home control system based on Wechat platform. Inf. Comput. (Theor. Ed.) **408**(14), 77–78+82 (2018)

4. Liu, Y., Zhu, X., Hu, A.: Design and development of smart home embedded control system based on syn7318 speech recognition. Electron. Prod. **376**(12), 20–21 (2019)
5. Sun, W., Li, W., Wen, K., et al.: Design and implementation of smart home system based on automatic identification technology. TV Technol. **42**(508)(11), 98–102 (2018)
6. Wang, Y.: Research on smart home system design based on ZigBee and Wechat platform. J. Changchun Univ. **30**(248)(10), 31–34+49 (2020)
7. Qiuhuan, M., Na, L.: Research on Internet home control system based on AIT. Digital Technol. Appl. **037**(001), 17–18 (2019)
8. Yuexia, Q., Baohua, Y.: Design and implementation of household intelligent green cabinet system. Comput. Knowl. Technol. Acad. Exchange **014**(031), 78–79 (2018)
9. Ren, R.: Application of artificial intelligence in smart home system. Intell. Build. Urban Inf. (005), 89–90,94 (2019)
10. Xue, H., Wu, J., Wang, S.: Artificial intelligence, thinking of smart home system under the background of Internet of things. Netw. Secur. Technol. Appl. **228**(12), 157–158 (2019)
11. Li, L.-C.: Research on the development of artificial intelligence industry from the perspective of modern economic system. China Bus. Trade **4**, 15–16 (2018)
12. Zhang, S., Xu, H., Huang, R.: Research on the development of artificial intelligence industry in China. J. Changchun Univ. Sci. Technol. **31**(5), 1–6 (2018)
13. Mao, X.-F.: A comparative study on application modes of artificial intelligence technology at home and abroad. Econ. Res. Guide **36**, 130–132 (2018)
14. Knapp, R.G.: Chinese Houses: The Architectural Heritage of a Nation. Tuttle Publishing, North Clarendon (2005)
15. Lowe, K.D.: Heaven and earth—sustaining elements in Hakka Tulou. Sustainability **4**, 2795–2802 (2012)
16. Chan, M., Esteve, D., Escriba, C., Campo, E.: A review of smart homes-present state and future challenges. Comput. Methods Prog. Biomed. **91**, 55–81 (2008)
17. Robles, R.J., Kim, T.-H.: Review: context aware tools for smart home development. Int. J. Smart Home **4**, 1–12 (2010)
18. Alam, M.R., Bin Ibne Reaz, M., Ali, M.A.M.: A review of Smart Homes—past, present, and future. IEEE Trans. Syst. Man Cybern. **6**, 1190–1203 (2012)
19. Lutolf, R.: Smart Home concept and the integration of energy meters into a home based system. In: Proceedings of 7th International Conference on Metering Apparatus Tariffs Electric Supply, pp. 277–278 (1992)

Framework for User Experience Evaluation in MOOC Platforms

Ana Poma Gallegos, Germania Rodríguez Morales(✉), Pablo V. Torres-Carrión, and Samanta Cueva Carrión

Computer Science and Electronic Department, Universidad Técnica Particular de Loja, Loja, Ecuador
{alpomax,grrodriguez,pvtorres,spcuenva}@utpl.edu.ec

Abstract. User Experience (UX) from the simplest perspective is defined in how people feel when using a product or service, which is fundamental to the success or failure of any product in the market. On the other hand, Massive Open Online Courses (MOOCs) have become one of the most popular trends in the field of education, reaching great popularity among several universities, which offer MOOCs through prestigious platforms, however, most of them do not meet the expectations and satisfaction of users, and mechanisms have not yet been designed to comprehensively measure the UX in these platforms. Therefore, the objective of this paper is to develop a comprehensive framework for the evaluation of UX in MOOC platforms from a technological point of view, after a systematic review of the literature to identify the most frequently applied and/or important evaluation approaches, which are analyzed and organized according to the following components: technological criteria and MOOC indicators, type of users, UX dimensions and UX factors. Through this approach it is possible to evaluate the UX in individual components, compare it between similar products and measure it over time.

Keywords: Massive Open Online Courses · User Experience · Usability

1 Introduction

User Experience (UX) from the simplest perspective is defined as how do people feel when they use a product or service? [1], which is fundamental to the success or failure of any product in the market [2]. On the other hand, Massive Open Online Courses (MOOCs) have become one of the most popular trends in online education, attracting millions of students every year, achieving great popularity among various universities [3], which offer MOOCs through prestigious platforms.

However, not all students manage to complete MOOCs; in fact, the completion rate is usually below 10% [4–6]. The main factors that contribute to student attrition on MOOC platforms according to [7–11] are the quality of the content and the technical aspects of the platform. Regarding the second factor [12–15] mentioned that the main problems contributing to attrition in MOOCs are poor usability and User Interface Design (UID).

H. Degen and S. Ntoa (Eds.): HCII 2022, LNAI 13336, pp. 284–304, 2022.
https://doi.org/10.1007/978-3-031-05643-7_19

Research on UX assessment in MOOC platforms is essential to successful online learning and teaching [9, 16, 17]. However, this research is limited and mainly focused on usability studies or other specific UX factors (satisfaction, accessibility, etc.), but mechanisms that comprehensively measure UX in such platforms have not yet been designed.

Therefore, the objective of the present study is to develop a comprehensive and iterative framework called FUXE-MOOC (Framework for UX Evaluation in MOOC) focused on the technical aspects of the MOOC platform. For this purpose, a Systematic Literature Review (SLR) is carried out [18] to identify the evaluation methods, techniques and tools that have been proposed or used to evaluate the UX in MOOC platforms, the results of which refer to the evaluation of UX in prototypes and in the implementation of MOOC platforms in operation. Such evaluation approaches are analyzed and selected according to the frequency of publication in the base articles and/or according to their relevance, then organized according to the following components: technological criteria and MOOC indicators, type of users, UX dimensions and UX factors.

The development of FUXE-MOOC provides a comprehensive and useful evaluation tool for MOOC providers, researchers, developers and Higher Education Institutions (HEIs), allowing them to identify and choose the UX evaluation methods, techniques and tools that best suit their evaluation needs and available resources.

To make explicit the work done, this article has been structured in the following sections: Sect. 2 describes the theoretical framework, Sect. 3 describes the proposal, Sect. 4 presents the limitations and future research and finally, Sect. 5 the conclusions and recommendations.

2 Introduction

2.1 Massive and Open Online Courses

Massive Open Online Courses (MOOCs) have become one of the most popular trends in online education, attracting millions of students every year, achieving great popularity among various universities [3], which offer MOOCs through various prestigious platforms such as Coursera, Udacity, edX, among others.

There are different types of MOOCs with certain common characteristics, but based on different structures and methodologies [10], the best known being cMOOCs and xMOOCs [10, 19–21]: Connectivist MOOCs (cMOOCs), commercial MOOCs or also called extended MOOCs (xMOOCs), task-based MOOCs or hybrid MOOCs (hMOOCs), localized MOOCs.

There are also several learning platforms that host a large number of MOOCs from different universities around the world. These platforms choose their course lists carefully, as they only accept courses with a specific structure and proposed by competent and qualified faculty members [10].

2.2 Classification of MOOC Criteria

Many determining elements are required for a MOOC platform to be effective and widely used by students: quality of the content, types of materials and other elements related to the technical aspects of the platform [10]. In this sense, MOOCs must be designed through a set of educational and technological requirements, also considering the concepts and methodologies of HCI [22], taking into account the fact that the audience cannot be predicted in advance [23].

In Fahmy et al. [24] an empirical study is conducted on the specific criteria to be taken into account when designing and implementing MOOCs to ensure the quality of MOOC design, based on the Technology-Enhanced Learning (TEL) approach in higher education. Seventy-four indicators classified into two main dimensions of pedagogical and technological criteria distributed in six categories are identified as shown in Fig. 1.

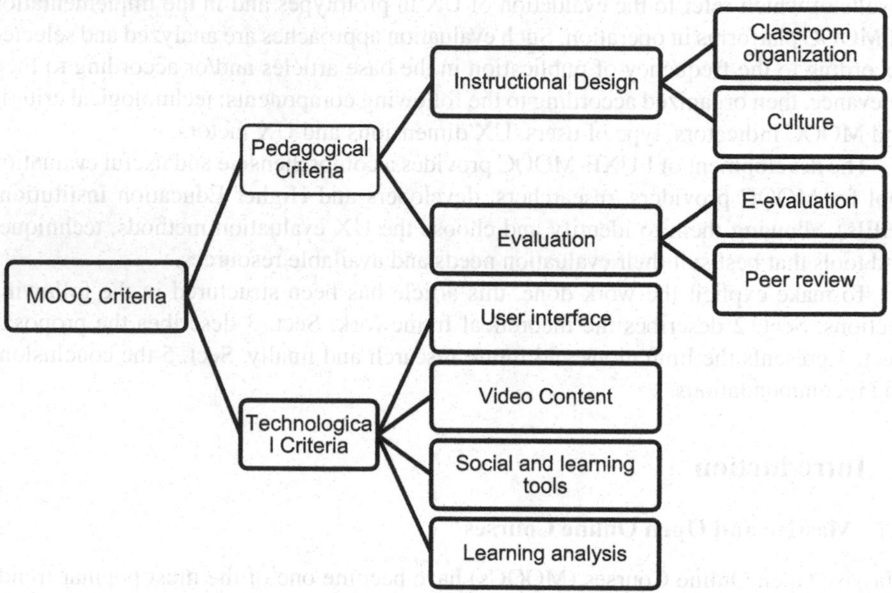

Fig. 1. Classification of MOOC criteria. Based on [24].

MOOCs not only provide the opportunity for easy access to learning resources, but also include several technological features that support different activities important for successful learning such as interaction, collaboration, assessment and self-reflection [24].

2.3 User Experience

The term UX was first introduced by Donald Norman to cover some of the critical aspects of human interface research and application at Apple or [25] and became popular in the field of Human-Computer Interaction (HCI) [26], mainly in the professional web development environment - which refers to UX as a new approach to interactive product development [27]. However, UX is a broader set of considerations than HCI, since in addition to aggregating and contextualizing human-computer interaction, it incorporates concerns of end users and organizations. In other words: UX consists of all the factors that influence the relationship between the end user and an organization, especially when a product is involved in that relationship [28]. Garrett [29] mentions that UX is not about the inner workings of a product or service, it is about how it works on the outside, where a person comes in contact with that product or service. Therefore, UX is critical to the success or failure of any product in the marketplace [2].

There are currently several definitions of UX, such as those provided by [1, 30–33]. ISO 9241-11:2018 defines UX as follows: "the UX refers to user perceptions and responses resulting from the use and/or anticipated use of a system, product, or service" [34].

2.4 Categories and Factors that Make Up the UX

Although ISO 9241-11:2018 mentions different UX factors, such as emotions, behaviors, attitudes, etc., however, it does not provide a complete set of established factors to measure UX in interactive systems. Therefore, below are several UX models that have been developed to describe the different categories and factors that make up UX, among which the following are the most important.

The model proposed by Arhippainen and Tähti [31] describes a comprehensive model that decomposes UX into five distinct categories of factors: user-specific, social, cultural, context-of-use and product-specific factors. This model indicates that UX is formed in the user's interaction with the product in the particular context of use, including social and cultural factors.

Morville [35] created a model called the Web-focused UX Honeycomb, outlining seven factors of overall UX: useful, usable, findable, credible, desirable, accessible and valuable. This model is a great tool to move beyond usability and to help people understand the need to define priorities: Is it more important for your website to be desirable or accessible? Usable or credible? It all depends on the unique balance of context, content and users [35].

Roto et al. [33] mentions that, although a wide range of factors can influence a person's UX with a system, the factors can be classified into three main categories: context, user and system. The context around the user and the system, the state of the user and the properties of the system. In addition, Roto et al. [33] mentions that while UX itself cannot be described by describing UX factors, but UX factors and their main categories can be used to describe the situation in which a person felt a particular UX. UX factors also help to identify the reasons for a particular experience.

Figure 2 presents a global perspective of UX according to the ISO 9241-11:2018 definition of UX [34] and the combination of the categories and factors presented in [31, 33, 35], understanding by category the components: context, user and system; and UX factors such as perceptions, motivations, usability, etc.

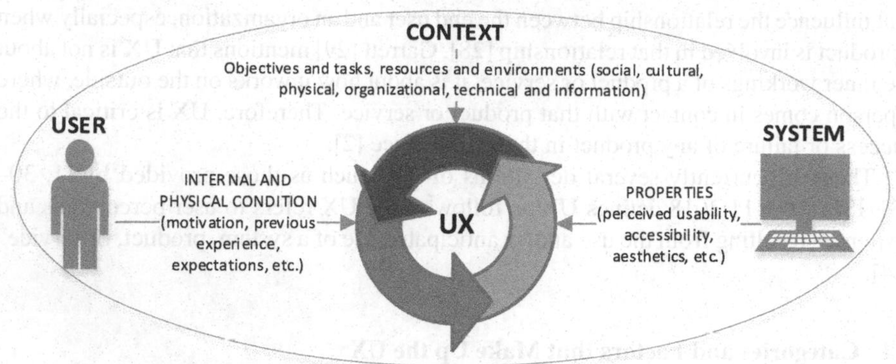

Fig. 2. Categories and factors that make up the UX. Based on [31, 33–35].

2.5 UX Dimensions

UX evaluation can be based on tasks or general impressions. Task-based UX can be rated by participants at the end of each task or scenario, which aims to improve the specific part of the interface design. Overall UX is usually evaluated immediately after participants complete all interactions with the platform, with the goal of comparing different platform designs with similar functions [36].

UX evaluation should be performed with the aim of discovering areas for improvement (formative evaluation) or determining the quality of UX (summative evaluation), with the objective of satisfying user needs and achieving system objectives [37].

UX becomes a temporal phenomenon, oriented to the present and changing over time, bearing in mind that orientation to the present does not exclude summary retrospective or prospective judgments about experiences [32]. Therefore, it is important to clarify the UX time span, i.e., the period of UX study in which Roto et al. [37] describes four facets of UX: Anticipated UX (AUX) which is the experience prior to use, through expectations formed from existing experience with related technologies, branding, advertisements, presentations, demonstrations or other people's opinions. According to [38] AUX allows designers the ability to gather the aspirations, assumptions and needs of users in the initial development phase of an artifact. Momentary UX (MUX) specific change in sentiment during interaction, pragmatic qualities. Focusing on the moment can give insight into a person's emotional responses to UI details. Episodic UX (EUX) is the evaluation of a specific episode after use, collects user reactions after interacting with a specific scenario. Cumulative UX (CUX) is the views on a system as a whole, after having used it for some time. Focusing on longer periods can reveal the eventual impact of momentary experiences on cumulative UX. For example, the importance of strong negative feedback during use may diminish after successful results and the feedback may be remembered differently.

Roto et al. [37] clarifies that the phases of the experience overlap and interleave in different orders, there is no fixed sequence from anticipation to cumulative UX. In addition, periods are essential because user responses may be different, for example, when measuring UX, a visceral user response may occur at that time, however, it may change after some time. Thus, a study that considers more than one period could be more enriching.

In this regard, Sanchez et al. [38] mentions that it is vital to evaluate all aspects that have been taken into account for the evaluation of a certain period of time (e.g. AUX), and to reapply it, this time for another period of time (e.g. EUX), taking care to measure similar parts or functionalities between both stages. This is done in order to check the UX changes that user have experienced over time.

3 Proposal

Several studies indicate that research on UX assessment in MOOC platforms is essential to the success of online learning and teaching [9, 16, 17]. However, these investigations are limited and focus on specific UX factors (among which usability and satisfaction stand out), which evaluate specific MOOC criteria through the application of certain evaluation approaches as evidenced in the previous chapter.

However, mechanisms have not yet been designed to evaluate the UX in these platforms in a comprehensive and iterative manner. Therefore, this chapter proposes the creation of an integrated framework for UX evaluation in MOOC platforms called FUXE-MOOC, which is adaptable to the period of study of UX, the changing environment of people (their internal and emotional state) and the context of use, depending on the evaluation needs and available resources. Whose objectives are the following:

Evaluate the design of MOOC platforms by expert evaluation through the application of heuristics and accessibility guidelines provided.

Evaluate user perceptions of MOOC platform properties (technological criteria and MOOC indicators), applying the most common UX factors and evaluation approaches.

Provide a comprehensive evaluation tool. That is, evaluate the UX in individual components, compare it between similar products, and measure it over time periods.

Evaluate the fulfillment of the objectives of users and organizations (MOOC providers and HEIs).

Provide feedback to continuously improve the quality of MOOCs and thus the quality of online learning.

3.1 FUXE-MOOC Design

Based on the evaluation approaches (evaluation methods, techniques and tools) obtained through the SLR process developed in the previous chapter, FUXE-MOOC is conceptualized and built, which integrates several components as described below:

MOOC platform/s to be evaluated in general, as well as their technological criteria and MOOC indicators; the type of users who will perform the evaluation (users/experts); the UX dimensions (AUX, MUX, EUX, CUX, task-based UX, general UX); system-specific and user-specific UX factors; the most frequently applied evaluation approaches in the base articles. Figure 3 presents the FUXE-MOOC design, the components of which are described below.

When selecting an evaluation approach, it is important to consider the availability of resources. Resources to consider according to [39] are equipment, time, money, participants, evaluator experience and context.

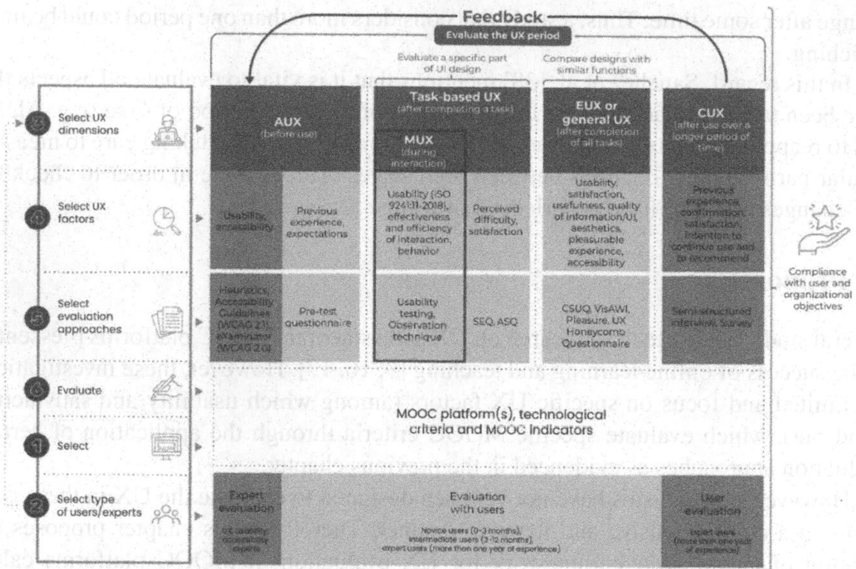

Fig. 3. Design of the proposed FUXE-MOOC framework.

3.2 FUXE-MOOC Components

There are five distinct components that make up our model for UX evaluation in MOOC platforms, as follows.

Component of Technological Criteria and MOOC Indicators. The technological criteria and MOOC indicators applied for the evaluation of the UX in FUXE-MOOC are as follows:

Technological criterion 1 (TC1): UI of the MOOC platform.
Technological criterion 2 (TC2): video interface and content.
I2.1. Control of video functions.
I2.2. Transcription of the video conference.
I2.3. Clear sound.
Technology criterion 3 (TC3): social and learning tools.
Technological criterion 4 (CT4): learning analysis.

It should be emphasized that only the indicators that have been evaluated in one of the base articles are taken into account.

Component of the Types of Users Who Perform the Assessment. According to Dix et al. [39] and Granollers [40], There are two types of users performing the evaluation: the evaluation performed by an expert in usability, accessibility and UI design, without the direct participation of users; and the evaluation that studies the actual use of the system through the participation of users. The former is especially useful for evaluating early designs and prototypes; the latter usually requires a working prototype or implementation. However, this is a broad distinction and, in practice, the user can be involved in the evaluation of early design ideas (e.g., through focus groups), and expert-based analysis can be performed on finished systems, as an inexpensive and quick usability evaluation [39]. Therefore, the evaluation techniques are considered under two groups of users: evaluation with experts and evaluation with users.

On the other hand, according to the time that users have been participating in MOOCs, we consider novice users (from 0 to 3 months), intermediate users (from 3 to 12 months) and expert users (more than one year of experience in MOOC [41].

Component of UX Dimensions. According to the reviewed literature there are two groups that correspond to the UX dimensions: 1. Task-based UX and general UX described in [36]; and 2. The period of the UX described in [37]. Regarding the first group:

Task-based UX: evaluated after completing a task, it is useful to evaluate a specific part of the UI design.

General UX: based on general impressions, it is evaluated after completing all tasks, it is useful to compare MOOC platform designs with similar functions.

Since UX is mainly dynamic, it is necessary to evaluate it before, during and after the user's interaction with the platform, as well as over longer periods of time, the UX period (anticipatory, momentary, episodic and cumulative) as described in Roto et al. [37]. A study that considers more than one period could be more enriching, because user responses may change over time. In addition, evaluating UX periods is critical for decision making according to the factors that contribute to the intended, actual and repeated usage decision on a given MOOC platform.

Anticipated UX (AUX): pre-use experience and performance expectations (pragmatic aspects-desirable features with respect to the MOOC platform).

Momentary UX (MUX): specific change in sentiment during interaction (pragmatic qualities). MUX focuses on evaluating users' feelings and emotions (behaviors).

Episodic UX (EUX): evaluation of a specific episode after use, collects user reactions after interacting with a specific scenario.

Cumulative UX (CUX): the views on the MOOC platform as a whole, after having used it for some time.

It should be noted that the different UX periods overlap and interleave in different orders, there is no fixed sequence from anticipated UX to cumulative UX.

In addition, MUX measures changes in sentiment during the interaction that also includes emotions, i.e., it measures user behavior, while task-based UX measures the usability, effectiveness and efficiency of the interaction, as well as the perceived difficulty of the task. Likewise, EUX and general UX refer to the same thing, i.e. to evaluate the UX after completing all tasks in a specific scenario.

Component of UX Factors. The present proposal focuses on the evaluation of system-specific and user-specific UX factors. On the one hand, it evaluates the design of MOOC platforms through evaluation with expert users, measuring usability and accessibility from heuristics and accessibility guidelines respectively. On the other hand, it evaluates user perceptions regarding MOOC platform properties, these are: previous experience (experience with similar products or with the same product), expectations, usability, effectiveness and efficiency of interaction, perceived difficulty, usefulness, quality of information and quality of the UI, satisfaction, aesthetics, pleasant experience, accessibility, confirmation, intention to continue use and intention to recommend. These last three factors were taken from the research model based on the theory of confirmation of expectations (TEC) applied in [42], in which confirmation refers to the fulfillment of user expectations and positively influences user satisfaction. Satisfaction, in turn, influences user behavior through intention to continue use and intention to recommend.

Component of the Evaluation Approaches. This component integrates the UX evaluation approaches most frequently applied in the base articles (See Tables 1, 2, 3 and 4), with the exception of the standardized SUS questionnaire, because SUS and CSUQ measure the same thing, i.e., perceived usability, but CSUQ is a multidimensional instrument that also measures satisfaction, perceived usefulness, information quality and UI quality, for such reason, CSUQ is selected to be applied in the framework. Likewise, the VisAWI questionnaire is replaced by its short version, i.e. VisAWI-S, described in [43] to reduce evaluation time. VisAWI-S can be an accurate substitute for the full VisAWI and can be used to measure the perceived visual aesthetics of websites when evaluation times must be kept to a minimum [43]. Therefore, the evaluation approaches are classified according to each UX dimension. Another aspect to take into account is that the different standardized questionnaires have a Likert scale of 5 or 7 points, therefore, all the questionnaires are modified to the same 5-point scale so that there is coherence at the time of the respective analysis.

With respect to the methods, the inquiry method, the user test method, the experimental method and certain research models are applied as indicated below.

Inquiry method: it is reflected through the application of questionnaires, observation and interviews, which are specified below.

User testing method: through usability tests and the observation technique. The field observation technique is applied (real environment), individual or group (according to the resources), non-participant (so as not to cause distraction to the user at the time of interaction with the MOOC platform).

Research models: certain items of the survey of the research model proposed by [42] which correspond to confirmation, satisfaction, intention to continue and intention to recommend. Confirmation occurs when users' expectations are met and positively influences users' overall satisfaction with the platform; satisfaction in turn influences the intention to continue use and the intention to recommend.

Experimental method: in the experimental method, hypotheses are formulated according to user behavior to be evaluated [39]. The proposal of [44], in which the independent variable is the MOOC platforms to be evaluated and its level depends on the number of platforms to be evaluated, while the dependent variable includes the UX and its dimensions.

AUX is applied for both expert evaluation or evaluation with novice (0–3 months), intermediate (3–12 months) or expert (more than one year of experience) users. MUX, EUX, task-based UX and general UX is applicable to novice (0–3 months), intermediate (3–12 months) or expert (more than one year of experience) users; while CUX evaluation should be performed only with expert users who have more than one year of MOOC experience.

Appendix 1 presents in detail the relationship between technological criteria and MOOC indicators, type of users/experts, UX factors, evaluation approaches and UX dimensions that make up MEUX-MOOC.

Appendix 2 specifies the UX evaluation techniques and tools that have been selected to be part of MEUX-MOOC according to the technological criteria and MOOC indicators, type of users/experts, UX dimensions and UX factors.

Therefore, FUXE-MOOC constitutes a comprehensive and iterative UX framework for MOOC platforms, which can be applied from different perspectives: task-based UX evaluation, general UX evaluation, and evaluation according to the UX period.

4 Limitations and Future Research

Currently there are few studies that evaluate the emotions of users in MOOC platforms through the observation of facial expressions, sentiment analysis, among others, so it is important to promote research in these areas.

Likewise, there are few studies that focus on evaluating the social, collaborative and communication tools applied in MOOC environments, however, studies indicate that this is a very important aspect to motivate users to continue using MOOCs and avoid a sense of isolation.

Learning analytics tools is another technological criterion that needs to be evaluated and improved to keep users active and focused.

In the present work, the study of MOOC criteria was conducted from the technological point of view, so in future research MOOC criteria can be evaluated from the pedagogical point of view whose main components are instructional design and evaluation.

5 Conclusions

The proposed creation of FUXE-MOOC allows to evaluate user perceptions of MOOC platform properties (technological criteria and MOOC indicators) by applying evaluation approaches most frequently applied in the literature to assess certain system-specific UX factors.

Using FUXE-MOOC, the internal state of the user can be evaluated by applying evaluation approaches to assess certain user-specific UX factors.

The proposed creation of FUXE-MOOC offers an integrated framework, adaptable to the UX study period, to the changing environment of people (their internal and emotional state) and to the context of use, depending on the evaluation needs and available resources.

Through the application of FUXE-MOOC it is possible to evaluate the UX in individual components, compare it between similar products and measure it over time periods.

Through the application of FUXE-MOOC it is possible to evaluate the fulfillment of the objectives of users and organizations (MOOC providers and HEIs), as well as to provide feedback to continuously improve the quality of MOOCs and thus the quality of online learning.

Appendix

Appendix 1. Components of the proposed framework for UX evaluation in MOOC platforms (FUXE-MOOC).

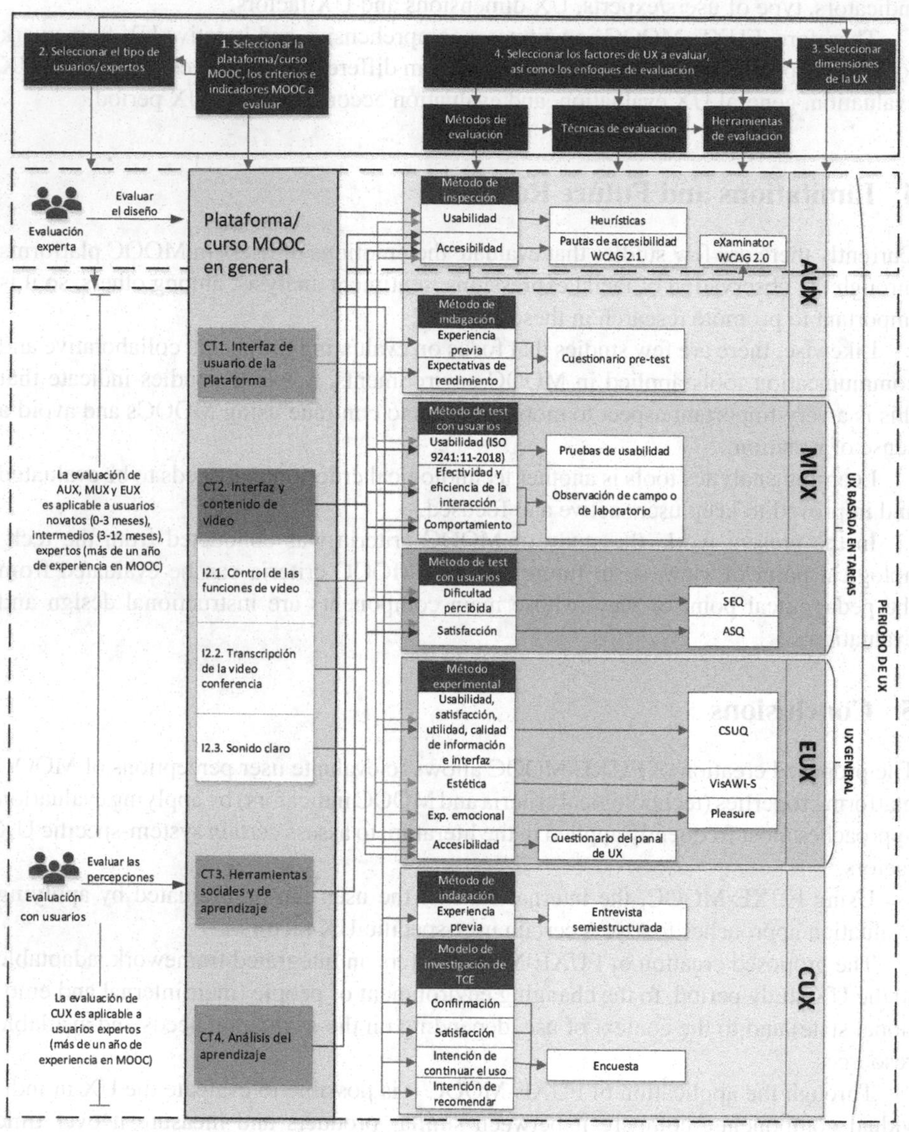

Appendix 2. Description of the UX evaluation approaches that make up FUXE-MOOC.

Table 1. Description of anticipated UX evaluation approaches.

Approach	UX factor(s) evaluated	Application	Procedure	Source of information
Heuristics	Usability	MOOC platform in general, UI of the MOOC platform	To improve the usability of an application it is important to have a well-designed interface. Shneiderman's "Eight Golden Rules of Interface Design" are a guide to good interaction design	[16, 45]
Heuristics	Usability	MOOC platform/course in general, MOOC platform UI, social and learning tools, learning analytics	A non-exhaustive set of heuristics is applied to evaluate the user-interface interaction. Such evaluation is to be performed by a usability expert	[46]
Accessibility guidelines	Accessibility	Interface and video content	Certain accessibility principles and guidelines are evaluated according to WCAG 2.1 with respect to interface and video content. Such evaluation is to be performed by an accessibility expert	[47]
eXaminator	Usability, accessibility	MOOC platform UI and video UI	The MOOC platform UI and video UI are evaluated according to the accessibility principles and guidelines according to WCAG 2.0. It is recommended that such evaluation be performed by an accessibility expert	[48, 49]

(*continued*)

Table 1. (*continued*)

Approach	UX factor(s) evaluated	Application	Procedure	Source of information
Pre-test questionnaire	Previous experience with the use of MOOCs	MOOC platform in general	Pre-course questionnaire which is emailed immediately after registering for the MOOC. Collects demographic data and basic MOOC usage information	[50]
Pre-test questionnaire	Expectations	MOOC platform in general	Pre-course questionnaire which is sent by email immediately after registering for the MOOC. Expectations are assessed	[51]

Table 2. Description of task-based UX evaluation approaches.

Approach	UX factor(s) evaluated	Application	Procedure	Source of information
Usability testing	Usability	MOOC platform UI and MOOC video UI	Usability tests are performed using certain tasks in order to evaluate the usability of the UI and collect qualitative data	[50, 52]
Observation technique	Effectiveness and efficiency of interaction	MOOC platform UI and MOOC video UI	Field or laboratory observation technique is applied, individual or group, participant or non-participant. The experiment is monitored and camera recordings are made to observe the actions of the users. Measures of task performance through participant-platform interaction are: a) task success rate, b) time on task, c) errors made by users while performing tasks	[50]

(*continued*)

Table 2. (*continued*)

Approach	UX factor(s) evaluated	Application	Procedure	Source of information
SEQ (Single Ease Question)	Perceived difficulty of the task	UI of the MOOC platform and of the MOOC video UI	UI of the MOOC platform and of the MOOC video UI Procedure: used as a measure of perceived task difficulty. For each of the following statements, circle the rating of your choice, with a 5-point response scale: 1 very difficult to 5 very easy	[50]
ASQ (After-Scenario Questionnaire)	Satisfaction	UI of the MOOC platform and the UI of the MOOC video	Used as a measure of task satisfaction. The questionnaire is given to a participant after he/she has completed a task during a usability evaluation. The three item scores (effectiveness, efficiency, and satisfaction) are averaged (with the arithmetic mean) to obtain the ASQ score for a participant's satisfaction with the system for a given task. If a participant does not respond to an item or marks N / A, average the remaining items to obtain the ASQ score. For each of the following statements, circle the rating of your choice, with a 5-point response scale: 1 strongly disagree to 5 strongly agree	[44]

Table 3. Description of general EUX or UX evaluation approaches.

Approach	UX factor(s) evaluated	Application	Procedure	Source of information
Pre-test questionnaire	Previous experience with the use of MOOCs	MOOC platform in general	Demographic data questionnaire administered in [50] and interview questions applied in [44] which includes basic MOOC usage conditions, such as platform name and frequency of use Note: This questionnaire is performed if only the overall UX is evaluated	[44, 50]
CSUQ (The Computer System Usability Questionnaire)	Overall satisfaction, perceived usefulness, information quality and interface quality	MOOC platform in general, MOOC platform UI	A total of 19 items are incorporated in the four dimensions of this scale: overall satisfaction score (OVERALL 1–19), system usefulness (SYSUSE 1–8), information quality (INFOQUAL 9–15) and interface quality (INTERQUAL 16–18) For each of the following statements, circle the rating of your choice, with a 5-point response scale: 1 strongly disagree to 5 strongly agree	[44]
VisAWI (Visual Aesthetics of Website Inventory)	Aesthetics	MOOC platform UI	VisAWI-S is applied to measure the perceived visual aesthetics of the MOOC platform UI. For each of the following statements, circle the rating of your choice, with a 5-point response scale: 1 strongly disagree to 5 strongly agree	[43]

(*continued*)

Table 3. (*continued*)

Approach	UX factor(s) evaluated	Application	Procedure	Source of information
Pleasure	Pleasure (pleasurable experience)	Evaluates the UI of the MOOC platform	The Pleasure questionnaire is applied which uses a 5-point scale with a single dimension and includes three items: attractive, entertaining, enjoyable. This questionnaire is used to rate the pleasurable experience of the overall UX	[52]
Post-test Questionnaire	Accessibility	MOOC platform UI, UI and video content	The accessibility factor of the UX honeycomb questionnaire is applied in [52], where items 1 and 2 evaluate the UI of the MOOC platform, item 3 evaluates the sound indicator, item 4 evaluates the video conference transcript indicator. In addition, item 2 of the usability factor of the same questionnaire is added as part of the accessibility factor to evaluate the UI of the MOOC video	[52]

Table 4. Description of cumulative UX evaluation approaches.

Approach	UX factor(s) evaluated	Application	Procedure	Source of information
Semi-structured interview	Previous experience	MOOC platform in general	MOOC platform UX is evaluated in a general way, over a longer period of time (expert users with more than one year of MOOC experience)	[41]

(*continued*)

Table 4. (*continued*)

Approach	UX factor(s) evaluated	Application	Procedure	Source of information
Survey	Confirmation	MOOC platform in general	The MOOC platform is evaluated over a longer period of time with respect to confirmation (fulfillment of intent or fulfillment of expectations)	[42, 53]
Survey	Satisfaction	MOOC platform in general	The MOOC platform is evaluated over a longer period of time with respect to satisfaction, which is produced through confirmation	[42, 51]
Survey	Intention to continue use (behavior)	MOOC platform in general	The MOOC platform is evaluated over a longer period of time with respect to the intention to continue use, which is influenced through user satisfaction	[42, 51]
Survey	Intention to recommend (behavior)	MOOC courses in general	The MOOC platform is evaluated over a longer period of time with respect to the intention to recommend, which is influenced through user satisfaction	[42]

References

1. Soegaard, M.: The Basics of User Experience Design: A UX Design Book by the Interaction Design Foundation (2002)
2. Morville, P.: The 7 Factors that Influence User Experience, Interaction Design Foundation (2018). https://www.interaction-design.org/literature/article/the-7-factors-that-influence-user-experience
3. Rabahallah, K., Mahdaoui, L., Azouaou, F.: MOOCs recommender system using ontology and memory-based collaborative filtering. In: ICEIS 2018 - 20th International Conference on Enterprise Information Systems, vol. 1, ICEIS, pp. 635–641 (2018)
4. Foon, K., Sum, W.: Students' and Instructors' use of Massive Open Online Courses (MOOCs): motivations and challenges. Educ. Res. Rev. **12**, 45–58 (2014). https://doi.org/10.1016/j.edurev.2014.05.001
5. Jordan, K.: Massive open online course completion rates revisited: assessment, length and attrition. Int. Rev. Res. Open Distrib. Learn. **16**(3), 341–358 (2015)
6. Luján, S.: "¿Qué son los MOOCs?" (2012). http://desarrolloweb.dlsi.ua.es/cursos/2012/que-son-los-moocs/preguntas-respuestas#que-es-un-mooc. Accessed 30 Jan 2020
7. Cruz, J., Borras, O., Garcia, F., Blanco, A., Theron, R.: Learning communities in social networks and their relationship with the MOOCs. Rev. Iberoam. Tecnol. del Aprendiz. **12**(1), 24–36 (2017). https://doi.org/10.1109/RITA.2017.2655218
8. Frolov, I., Johansson, S.: An adaptable usability checklist for MOOCs A usability evaluation instrument for Massive Open Online Courses (2014)
9. Hakami, N., White, S., Chakaveh, S.: Motivational factors that influence the use of MOOCs: learners' perspectives a systematic literature review. In: CSEDU 2017 – Proceedings of 9th International Conference on Computer Supporting Education, vol. 2, CSEDU, pp. 323–331 (2017). https://doi.org/10.5220/0006259503230331
10. Pascual, J., Castillo, C., García, V., González, R.: Method for analysing the user experience in MOOC platforms. In: 2014 International Symposium Computing Education, SIIE 2014, pp. 157–162 (2014). https://doi.org/10.1109/SIIE.2014.7017722
11. Wautelet, Y., Heng, S., Kolp, M., Penserini, L., Poelmans, S.: Designing an MOOC as an agent-platform aggregating heterogeneous virtual learning environments. Behav. Inf. Technol. **35**(11), 980–997 (2016). https://doi.org/10.1080/0144929X.2016.1212095
12. Korableva, O., Durand, T., Kalimullina, O., Stepanova, I.: Studying user satisfaction with the MOOC platform interfaces using the example of coursera and open education platforms. In: ACM International Conference Proceeding Series, pp. 26–30 (2019). https://doi.org/10.1145/3322134.3322139
13. Korableva, O., Durand, T., Kalimullina, O., Stepanova, I.: Usability testing of MOOC: Identifying user interface problems. In: ICEIS 2019 – 21st International Conference on Enterprise Information Systems, vol. 2, ICEIS, pp. 468–475 (2019). https://doi.org/10.5220/0007800004680475
14. Xiao, J., Jiang, B., Xu, Z., Wang, M.: The usability research of learning resource design for MOOCs. In: 2014 IEEE International Conference on Teaching, Assessment and Learning for Engineering (TALE), pp. 277–282 (2014). https://doi.org/10.1109/TALE.2014.7062640
15. Zaharias, P., Poylymenakou, A.: Developing a usability evaluation method for e-learning applications: beyond functional usability. Int. J. Hum. Comput. Interact. **25**(1), 75–98 (2009). https://doi.org/10.1080/10447310802546716
16. Azhar, T., Kasiyah, H.S.: Evaluation of instructional and user interface design for MOOC: short and free futurelearn courses. In: 2019 International Conference on Advanced Computer Science Information System, ICACSIS 2019, pp. 425–434 (2019). https://doi.org/10.1109/ICACSIS47736.2019.8979754

17. Veletsianos, G., Collier, A., Schneider, E.: Digging deeper into learners' experiences in MOOCs: Participation in social networks outside of MOOCs, notetaking and contexts surrounding content consumption. Br. J. Educ. Technol. **46**(3), 570–587 (2015). https://doi.org/10.1111/bjet.12297
18. Poma, A., Rodríguez, G., Torres, P.: User experience evaluation in MOOC platforms: a hybrid approach human-computer interaction. In: Ruiz, P.H., Agredo-Delgado, V., Kawamoto, A.L.S. (eds.) Human-Computer Interaction: 7th Iberoamerican Workshop, HCI-COLLAB 2021, pp. 208–224. Springer, Cham (2021). https://doi.org/10.1007/978-3-030-92325-9_16
19. Jacoby, J.: The disruptive potential of the Massive Open Online Course: a literature review. J. Open Flexible Distance Learn. **18**, 73–85 (2018). http://journals.akoaotearoa.ac.nz/index.php/JOFDL/article/viewFile/214/168%5Cnhttps://ezproxy.royalroads.ca/login?url=http://search.proquest.com/docview/1749263827?accountid=8056%5Cnhttp://wp6eu6tz5x.search.serialssolutions.com/?ctx_ver=Z39.88-2004&ctx_en
20. McAvinia, C.: Lessons for the Future – The VLE and the MOOC. In: Online Learning and its Users, pp. 207–228 (2016)
21. Peco, P.P., Mora, S.L.: Los MOOC: orígenes, historia y tipos, Centro de Comunicación y Pedagogía Facebook Twitter Pinterest (2013). http://www.centrocp.com/los-mooc-origenes-historia-y-tipos/. Accessed 27 Jan 2020
22. Casanova, A., Espinoza, A.: Experiencia De Usuario En Entornos Virtuales De Aprendizaje (2015)
23. Kopp, M., Lackner, E.: Do MooCs need a special instructional design? In: EDULEARN 2014 Proceedings, July 2014, pp. 7138–7147 (2014). http://library.iated.org/view/KOPP2014DOM
24. Fahmy, Y., Chatti, M., Schroeder, U., Wosnitza, M.: What drives a successful MOOC? An empirical examination of criteria to assure design quality of MOOCs. In: 2014 IEEE 14th International Conference on Advanced Learning Technologies, ICALT 2014, 2014, pp. 44–48, July 2014. https://doi.org/10.1109/ICALT.2014.23
25. Norman, D.A., Henderson, A., Nonnan, D., Miller, J., Henderson, A.: What you see, some of what's in the future, and how we go about doing it: HI at Apple computer. In: Conference Companion Human Factors Computing Systems - CHI 1995, January 1995, pp. 4–5 (1995). https://doi.org/10.1145/223355.223477
26. Hassenzahl, M., Tractinsky, N.: User experience - a research agenda. Behav. Inf. Technol. **25**(2), 91–97 (2006). https://doi.org/10.1080/01449290500330331
27. Hassan, Y., Martín, F.: La Experiencia del Usuario (2005). http://www.nosolousabilidad.com/articulos/experiencia_del_usuario.htm. Accessed 11 Mar 2020
28. Kuniavsky, M.: User Experience and HCI. In: The Human-Computer Interaction Handbook Fundamentals, Evolving Technologies, and Emerging Applications, 2nd edn., pp. 897–916 (2009)
29. Garrett, J.J.: The Elements of User Experience: User Centered Design for the Web and Beyond, Second, Berkeley (2011)
30. Norman, D., Nielsen, J.: The Definition of User Experience (UX) (2003). https://www.nngroup.com/articles/definition-user-experience/. Accessed 11 Mar 2020
31. Arhippainen, L., Tähti, M.: Empirical evaluation of user experience in two adaptive mobile application prototypes. In: Proceedings of 2nd International Conference on Mobile and Ubiquitous Multimedia, pp. 27–34 (2003). http://www.ep.liu.se/ecp/011/007/ecp011007.pdf
32. Hassenzahl, M.: User experience (UX): towards an experiential perspective on product quality. In: ACM International Conference Proceeding Series, September 2008, pp. 11–15 (2008). https://doi.org/10.1145/1512714.1512717
33. Roto, V., Law, E., Vermeeren, A., Hoonhout, J.: Abstracts collection demarcating user experience. In: Dagstuhl Semin. Proceedings, pp. 1–26 (2011)

34. ISO 9241-11: 2018(en), Ergonomics of human-system interaction — Part 11: Usability: Definitions and concepts (2018). https://www.iso.org/obp/ui/#iso:std:iso:9241:-11:ed-2:v1:en. Accessed 25 July 2020
35. Morville, P.: User Experience Design (2004). http://semanticstudios.com/user_experience_design/. Accessed 29 July 2020
36. Tullis, T., Albert, B.: Measuring the User Experience: Collecting, Analyzing, and Presenting Usability Metrics, 2nd edn., London, UK (2013)
37. Roto, V., et al.: All UX evaluation methods, ALL ABOUT UX (2011). https://www.allaboutux.org/all-methods. Accessed 14 June 2020
38. Sánchez, L., Urquiza, J., Mendoza, S.: Measuring anticipated and episodic UX of tasks in social networks. Appl. Sci. **10**(22), 1–17 (2020). https://doi.org/10.3390/app10228199
39. Dix, A., Finlay, J., Abowd, G.D., Beale, R.: Human-Computer Interaction Chapter 9: Evaluation Techniques (2004)
40. Granollers, T.: MPIu+a. Una metodología que integra la Ingeniería del Software, la Interacción Persona-Ordenador y la Accesibilidad en el contexto de equipos de desarrollo multidisciplinares, Universitat de Lleida (2004)
41. Nurhudatiana, A., Anggraeni, A., Putra, S.: An exploratory study of MOOC adoption in Indonesia. In: ACM International Conference Proceeding Series, pp. 97–101 (2019). https://doi.org/10.1145/3337682.3337690
42. Lu, Y., Wang, B., Lu, Y.: Understanding key drivers of MOOC satisfaction and continuance intention to use. J. Electron. Commer. Res. **20**(2), 105–117 (2019)
43. Moshagen, M., Thielsch, M.T.: A short version of the visual aesthetics of websites inventory. Behav. Inf. Technol. **32**(12), 1305–1311 (2013). https://doi.org/10.1080/0144929X.2012.694910
44. Liu, S., Liang, T., Shao, S., Kong, J.: Evaluating localized MOOCs: the role of culture on interface design and user experience. IEEE Access **8**, 107927–107940 (2020). https://doi.org/10.1109/ACCESS.2020.2986036
45. Hanifa, M.R., Santoso, H.B., Kasiyah: Evaluation and recommendations for the instructional design and user interface design of Coursera MOOC platform. In: 2019 International Conference on Advanced Computer Science and information Systems (ICACSIS) ICACSIS 2019, vol. 2014, pp. 417–424 (2019). https://doi.org/10.1109/ICACSIS47736.2019.8979689
46. Jiménez, S., et al.: Heuristic approach to evaluate basic types of interactions-communications in MOOCs (2016)
47. Acosta, T., Zambrano, J., Luján, S.: Analysis of the accessibility of educational videos in Massive Open Online Courses. In: EDULEARN 2019 Proceedings, vol. 1, pp. 8321–8331, July 2019. https://doi.org/10.21125/edulearn.2019.2076
48. Iniesto, F., Covadonga, R.: Accessibility assessment of MOOC platforms in Spanish: UNED COMA, COLMENIA and Miriada X, pp. 169–172 (2014). https://doi.org/10.1109/SIIE.2014.7017724
49. Calle, T., Sánchez, S., Luján, S.: Web accessibility evaluation of massive open online courses on Geographical Information Systems. In: IEEE Global Engineering Education Conference EDUCON, pp. 680–686, April 2014. https://doi.org/10.1109/EDUCON.2014.6826167
50. Tsironis, A., Katsanos, C., Xenos, M.: Comparative usability evaluation of three popular MOOC platforms. In: IEEE Global Engineering Education Conference EDUCON, pp. 608–612 (2016). https://doi.org/10.1109/EDUCON.2016.7474613
51. Chen, C., Lee, C., Hsiao, K., Chen, C., Lee, C., Hsiao, K.: Comparing the determinants of non-MOOC and MOOC continuance intention in Taiwan effects of interactivity and openness (2018). https://doi.org/10.1108/LHT-11-2016-0129

52. Nurhudatiana, A., Caesarion, A.S.: Exploring user experience of massive open online courses (MOOCs), pp. 44–49 (2020). https://doi.org/10.1145/3383923.3383968
53. Rabin, E., Kalman, Y.M., Kalz, M.: An empirical investigation of the antecedents of learner-centered outcome measures in MOOCs. Int. J. Educ. Technol. High. Educ. **16**(1), 1–20 (2019). https://doi.org/10.1186/s41239-019-0144-3

Evaluation on Comfortable Arousal in Autonomous Driving Using Physiological Indexes

Naoki Sakashita, Narumon Jadram(✉), Peeraya Sripian(✉), Tipporn Laohakangvalvit(✉), and Midori Sugaya(✉)

Shibaura Institute of Technology, 3-7-5 Toyosu, Koto-ku 135-8548, Tokyo, Japan
{al18051,ma21067,peeraya,tipporn,doly}@shibaura-it.ac.jp

Abstract. At level 3 of autonomous driving, the driver has to take over driving when the system requires. In automatic driving, the arousal level tends to decrease. Drowsiness or less arousal is the leading cause of car accidents. For safety, it is necessary to increase the arousal level before driving. Moreover, due to the emotional state effect on the driving performance, it is important to consider comfort while improving the driver's arousal level. Previous studies proposed the comfortable arousal model based on physiological signals to evaluate arousal and comfort during autonomous driving. However, the accuracy evaluation using this model has not been sufficiently performed. This study aims to construct a more accurate and reliable comfortable arousal model. We explore various physiological indexes and calculate feature importance using the random forest method to achieve our goal. Then we compare and validate the evaluation accuracy with the subjective evaluation score against the previous comfortable model proposed. The result shows that the proposed method has more accurate than the methods of the previous method. However, the improved accuracy is still not very high, so we need to consider creating a comfortable arousal model.

Keywords: Physiological signals · Arousal · Comfort · Autonomous driving

1 Introduction

In recent years, much attention has focused on developing autonomous driving for practical use. There are different levels of autonomous driving, depending on the degree of driving operations carried out by people and vehicles. The Society of Automotive Engineers (SAE) [1] defines the autonomous driving level into 6 levels as follows,

- Level 0: No driving automation
- Level 1: Driving automation assistance
- Level 2: Partial driving automation
- Level 3: Conditional driving automation
- Level 4: High driving automation
- Level 5: Full driving automation

H. Degen and S. Ntoa (Eds.): HCII 2022, LNAI 13336, pp. 305–316, 2022.
https://doi.org/10.1007/978-3-031-05643-7_20

From these categorizations, humans will be the primary driver for autonomous driving levels 0 to 2, and the system will be the primary driver for levels 3 to 5. In level 3, although the system performs all of the driving tasks, the driver will have to take over the control of the vehicle in a moment's notice when the system reaches its operational limits. However, drivers could be in the drowsiness and less aroused state during automated driving because they are relieved from the driving tasks [2], this cause taking over difficult in a highly automated vehicle [3]. Therefore, taking over driving in a state of low arousal may lead to accidents. It is necessary to maintain a high level of arousal and to ensure that drivers are in a state suitable for driving.

Safe driving also requires a consideration of the driver's emotional state at that time. Research indicates that emotional state affects driving performance. H. Cai described that lane control capability directly relates to driving safety. When drivers were in anger and excitation state, they tend to have poorer lane control capability, than when they were in the calm state [4]. Jeon explored the effects of specific emotions on subjective judgment on driving performance. The results showed that the effects of specific emotions were diverse beyond the valence and arousal dimensions. They showed that anger and happiness degraded driving performance compared to the fear and neutral [5]. Thus, it is important to consider comfort while improving the driver's arousal level to achieve driving safety as different comfort levels lead to a different emotional state.

There are many physiological signals index that can be used to detect drowsiness, such as the electrocardiogram (ECG) [6], the electromyogram (EMG) [7], the electroencephalogram (EEG) [8], and the electroretinogram (EOG) [9]. By analyzing changes in arousal, which can be detected using physiological signals, it is possible to objectively detect drowsiness instantly. Although many studies used physiological signals to evaluate arousal while driving, only a few evaluate comfort with arousal.

Jadram et al. proposed the comfortable arousal model based on physiological signals to objectively evaluate arousal and comfort during autonomous driving [10]. They conducted a principal component analysis (PCA) using multiple arousal and comfort indexes calculated by EEG and heart rate variability to create a comfortable arousal model. Each multiple comforts and arousal index are analyzed and reduced into one dimension. Only the first principal component was employed. Comfort and arousal were calculated using the equation of each first principal component. The comfort value was placed on the x-axis and the arousal value on the y-axis in the two-dimensional coordinates, making it possible to simply visualize and evaluate comfort together with arousal. However, the physiological indexes were arbitrarily selected in their work [10]. They have not explored other indexes to create the comfortable arousal model. Hence, the model's accuracy was not validated using more optimal indexes.

2 Research Objective

This study aims to construct a comfortable arousal model with higher accuracy and reliability by using optimal physiological indexes. To achieve our goal, we explore various physiological indexes and calculate feature importance using random forest method. Then we compare and validate the evaluation accuracy of the comfortable arousal models. For the evaluation, we will compare the subjective evaluation score with our comfortable arousal model against the previous comfortable model proposed by Jadram [10].

3 Research Method

3.1 Physiological Indexes Based on Feature Importance

Jadram et al. selected physiological indexes suitable for evaluating arousal and comfort from previous studies to create a comfortable arousal model [10]; arousal index was calculated by EEG; comfort index was calculated by heart rate variability. We show various EEG index in Table 1 and heart rate variability index in Table 2.

The selected arousal indexes included the content rate of theta wave (θ), alpha wave (α), beta wave (β), β/α wave, and Attention-Meditation. The calculation method for the content rate of theta, alpha, and beta wave are shown in indexes 11 to 13 in Table 1. Attention-Meditation is the difference between Attention and Meditation obtained from the EEG sensor (NeuroSky Inc.'s Mind Wave Mobile 2) [11]. The selected comfort indexes included pNN10, pNN20, pNN30, pNN40, pNN50. pNNx indexes are the proportion of successive RR intervals that differ by more than x ms (where x is 10, 20, 30, 40, 50).

These indexes can be used to evaluate comfort and arousal, but they were not yet evaluated to have the higher accuracy comparing to other indexes. The evaluation accuracy of the model may be better if we use indexes with higher evaluation accuracy than these indexes. Therefore, in this study, we will create a comfortable arousal model using more effective indexes to achieve a model with high evaluation accuracy.

Suzuki et al. calculated the feature importance of EEG and heart rate variability indexes using random forest [12]. The feature importance is an index that quantitatively evaluates how much an index can contribute to data classification and estimation. In this study, we select the index according to Suzuki et al.' feature selection results. In their work, they averaged the normalized feature importance. The results showed that the top five heart rate variability indexes were LF, LF/HF, HF, SDNN/RMSSD, and pNN20. On the other hand, the top five EEG indexes are MA15γ, MA15midγ, MA15θ, MA15δ, and MA15lowγ. The descriptions of these indexes are also shown in Table 1 and 2.

In this study, we select the index based on Suzuki et al.' result. For the arousal index, MA15γ, MA15 mid γ, MA15θ, MA15δ, and MA15lowγ were selected. For comfort indexes we select top five indexes exclude LF, LF/HF, and HF because they require a period to calculate. As a result, SDNN/RMSSD, pNN20, SDNN, CVNN, and pNN20 were selected as comfort indexes.

For subjective evaluation, we used SAM (self-assessment manikin) scale [13]. SAM scale is a non-verbal subjective evaluation method that consist of avatars with different facial expressions. The user can answer the level of arousal and valence that he/she was feeling by choosing the avatar regardless of language representation as shown in Fig. 1. There are nine level of avatar expression, with 1 being lowest and 9 being highest. From the selection, arousal and valence level can be directly derived.

Table 1. EEG indexes [10, 12]

	Index	Frequency band	Meaning/Computation method
1	δ	1–3	Deep sleep without dreaming, unconscious
2	θ	4–7	Fantasy, imaginary, dream
3	Low α	8–9	Relaxed, peaceful, conscious
4	High α	10–12	Relaxed but focus
5	Low β	13–17	Thinking, aware of self & surroundings
6	High β	18–30	Alertness, agitation, irritability
7	Low γ	31–40	Memory, higher mental activity
8	Mid γ	41–50	Visual information processing
9	Attention	–	Concentration
10	Meditation	–	Relaxation
11	α wave content rate	–	$\frac{(\text{Low}\,\alpha+\text{High}\,\alpha)}{(\text{Low}\,\alpha+\text{High}\,\alpha+\text{Low}\,\beta+\text{High}\,\beta+\theta)}$
12	β wave content rate	–	$\frac{(\text{Low}\,\beta+\text{High}\,\beta)}{(\text{Low}\,\alpha+\text{High}\,\alpha+\text{Low}\,\beta+\text{High}\,\beta+\theta)}$
13	θ wave content rate	–	$\frac{\theta}{(\text{Low}\,\alpha+\text{High}\,\alpha+\text{Low}\,\beta+\text{High}\,\beta+\theta)}$
14	β/α	–	$\frac{(\text{Low}\,\beta+\text{High}\,\beta)}{(\text{Low}\,\alpha+\text{High}\,\alpha)}$
15	MA15γ	–	Moving average of (Low γ + Mid γ) window size 15
16	MA15midγ	–	Moving average of Mid γ window size 15
17	MA15θ	–	Moving average of θ window size 15
18	MA15δ	–	Moving average of δ window size 15

Table 2. Heart rate variability indexes [10, 12]

	Index	Computation method
1	IBI	Heart Rate Interval
2	BPM	Number of beats per minute
3	pNNx (x = 10, 20, 30, 40, 50)	Percentage of adjacent IBIs with absolute values greater than x ms
4	SDNN	Standard deviation of IBI
5	RMSSD	Root mean square of the difference of IBIs
6	SDNN/RMSSD	SDNN/RMSSD
7	CVNN	Coefficient of variation of IBI
8	LF	Frequency-domain analysis of IBI power value of 0.04–0.15 Hz
9	HF	Frequency-domain analysis of IBI power value of 0.15–0.40 Hz
10	LF/HF	A ratio of Low Frequency to High Frequency

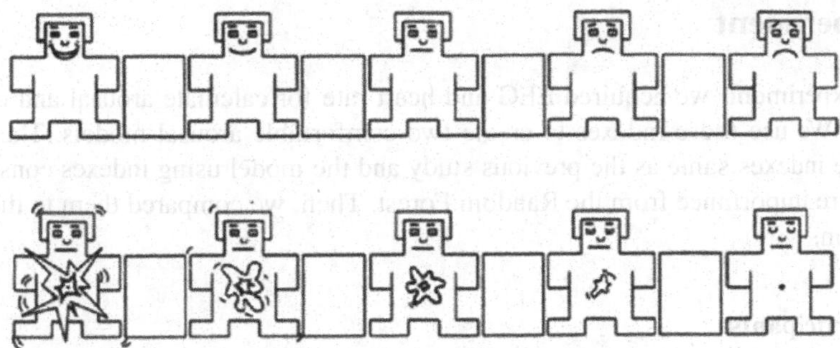

Fig. 1. SAM (self-assessment manikin) scale

3.2 Data Set and Model Creation

The comfortable arousal model is created based on the method proposed by Jadram et al. [10]. First, the analysis interval is decided by obtaining average values of indexes from the data in each interval, and collect them into a data set. From the index described in Sect. 3.1, we create a data set of EEG indexes (arousal indexes) and a data set of heart rate variability indexes (comfort indexes) separately. Next, we use PCA to reduce the dimensionality of the multiple indexes data set into one dimension (Fig. 2). PCA produces linear combinations of the original variables to generate the axes, also known as principal components. The first principal component (Z_1) is given by a linear combination of the variables $X_1 + X_2 + \ldots + X_n$ that accounts for the greatest possible variance in the data. In this study, we focus on only the first principal component. The first principal component (Z_1) is calculated by Eq. 1, when the variables $X_1 + X_2 + \ldots + X_n$ is indexes, $w_1 + w_2 + \ldots + w_n$ is the weight of each index in first principal component. We employed the first principal component from EEG indexes data set as arousal equation (new arousal index) and employed the first principal component from heart rate variability indexes data set as comfort equation (new comfort index). Finally, the obtained equation is used to plot two-dimensional coordinates. Comfort is the x-axis, and arousal is the y-axis.

$$Z_1 = w_1X_1 + w_2X_2 + \ldots + w_nX_n \tag{1}$$

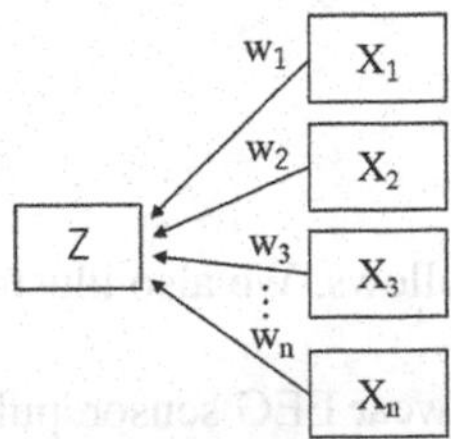

Fig. 2. PCA is doing to combine n measured (X) indexes into a single component

4 Experiment

In our experiment, we acquired EEG and heart rate for calculate arousal and comfort indexes. We use these indexes to create two comfortable arousal models. The model using the indexes same as the previous study and the model using indexes considering the feature importance from the Random Forest. Then, we compared them to the SAM evaluation.

4.1 Participants

Six adult males in their 20s cooperated in the experiment. Written consents had been obtained before the start of the experiments. Before the experiment, the participants will be asked to indicate how long they slept and how long they woke up that day. Participants who sleep less or wake up for a highly long time will be excluded.

4.2 Method

The experiment was conducted in a bright and quiet room. The experimental environment is shown in Fig. 3.

During the experiment, the participants wore EEG sensor and pulse sensor to acquire EEG and heart rate while they were watching the driving video. The SAM scale was output periodically while the subjects were watching the driving video to subjectively evaluate their emotional state at that particular moment.

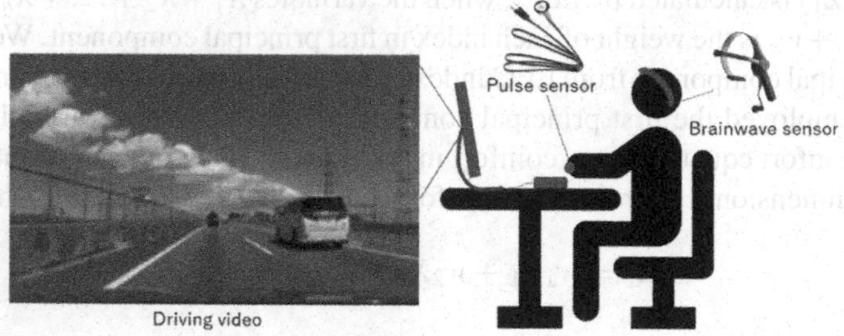

Fig. 3. Experimental environment.

4.3 Experimental Procedure

The experiment procedure is as follows. We also illustrate the procedure in Fig. 4.

1. Participants sit in a chair and wear EEG sensor, pulse sensors and earphones.
2. The participant will rest for 1 min for a baseline measurement.
3. The participant watches the driving video. The duration of the video is 12 min.
4. For every 3 min, the SAM subjective questionnaire will pop up on the screen to ask the participant to select what he/she was feeling at that moment.

5. End of the experiment.

During the resting period, a gray background image with a black cross in the center was displayed on the display in front of the participants to prevent afterimage. The participants were instructed to place their eyes on the cross in the center as much as possible.

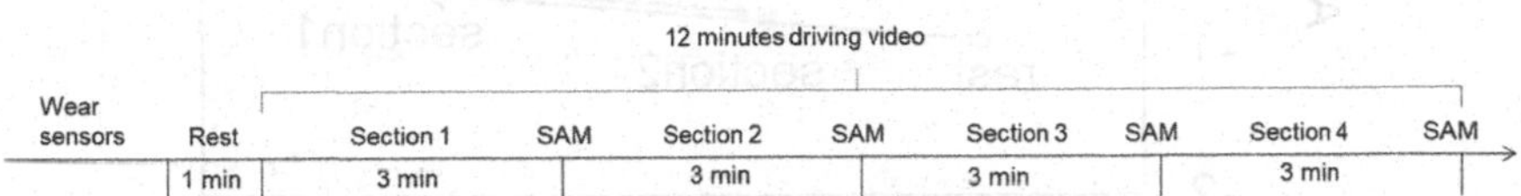

Fig. 4. Experimental procedure

5 Results and Discussion

During 12 min of watching the driving video, we continuously recorded the participant's physiological signals. We divided the driving time in four 3-min blocks: section 1, section 2, section 3 and section 4 as shown in Fig. 4. We also collected subjective evaluation of arousal and valence and acquired SAM scale every 3 min while watching driving video (at the end of each section).

The entire physiological signal data was divided into five sections; rest, section 1, section 2, section 3, and section 4. Then, we calculated the average of all EEG indexes and heart rate variability index for each section. In Jadram et al. [10], they employed pNN10, pNN20, pNN30, pNN40, and pNN50 index to represent comfort dataset and employed θ wave content rate, α wave content rate, β wave content rate, β/α wave, and Attention-Meditation to represent arousal dataset. However, in this study, we used SDNN/RMSSD, pNN20, SDNN, CVNN, and pNN20 to represent comfort dataset and used MA15γ, MA15midγ, MA15θ, MA15δ, and MA15lowγ to represent arousal dataset. We analyze each comfort and arousal dataset by PCA. The comfort and arousal equations were created using the loadings of PCA results. Finally, the values were substituted into the comfort and arousal equations and evaluated in two-dimensional coordinates, with comfort on the x-axis and arousal on the y-axis.

Figure 5 shows the comfortable arousal results using participant A's comfortable arousal model using the previous method. Figure 6 shows the comfortable arousal results using participant A's comfortable arousal model using the proposed method. In the figures, the comfort is represented on the x-axis and arousal on the y-axis. Changes to the right in the horizontal direction can be implied that the participant was feeling more comfort, while changes toward the top in the vertical direction can be implied that the participant was more aroused. From Figs. 5 and 6, directional changes from each section can be observed. Using the proposed method, it can be observed that the changes are positive for both arousal and comfort, comparing with the previous method.

For instant, the change from rest to section 1 for the previous method indicates lower arousal and higher comfort, while the change from rest to section 1 from our method indicates higher arousal and higher comfort.

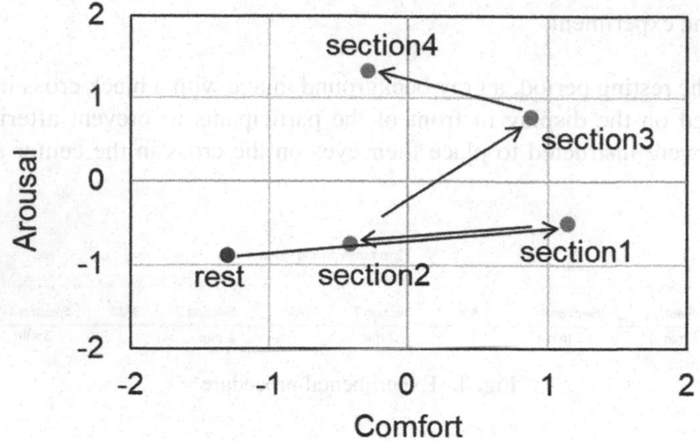

Fig. 5. Participant A's comfortable arousal model using our proposed method

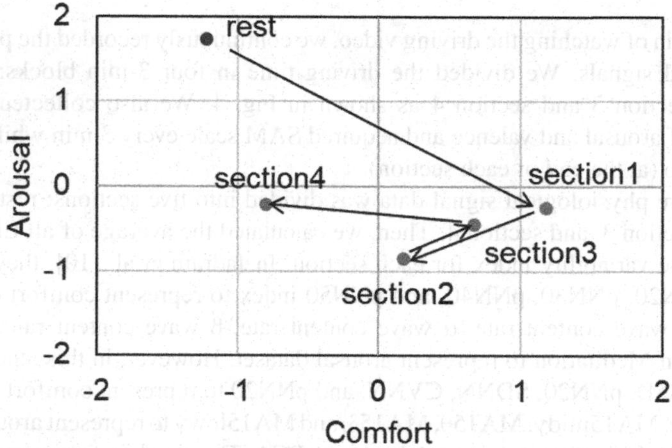

Fig. 6. Participant A's comfortable arousal model using the previous method [10]

To evaluate the performance of our proposed method and the previous method [10], we compare the changes in arousal and comfort observed from the physiological signals with the subjective evaluation for each section. The changes in arousal and comfort were calculated using our proposed method and the previous method, while the subjective evaluation results were derived from the experiment in this study. In this study, we are interested in the directional change only, i.e., increase, decrease, or no change.

In general, the physiological signals tend to vary over time, therefore, minimal changes in physiological signals should be regarded as "no change". In this work, we define the range for minimal change for arousal and comfort by first calculating the absolute difference of each index for all participants. Then, we calculate the 5th percentile of the entire difference. The difference that is within the 5th percentile is considered minimal change, therefore, it is defined as "no change".

Table 3 and 4 summarizes the results of change in arousal and comfort, calculated by our proposed method. Table 5 and 6 summarizes the results of change in arousal and comfort, calculated by the previous method [10]. Table 7 and 8 summarizes the change in arousal and comfort from the subjective evaluation obtained during the experiment.

Table 3. Arousal changes from proposed method results

Subject	Rest-Section 1	Section 1-Section 2	Section 2-Section 3	Section 3-Section 4
A	0.38454	−0.25084	1.53138	0.5591
B	0.01514	1.71482	−2.01563	−0.69941
C	−0.96064	−0.84464	0.1444	2.11893
D	−2.537	0.45843	1.15096	−0.17441
E	−2.04646	0.04771	−0.59689	1.29749

Table 4. Comfort changes from proposed method results

Subject	Rest-Section 1	Section 1-Section 2	Section 2-Section 3	Section 3-Section 4
A	2.43621	−1.54835	1.28743	−1.1635
B	−0.29936	0	1.59849	−0.00185
C	−0.75849	1.20753	−2.47808	0.67534
D	0.87299	−1.68854	0.097	0.96782
E	0.44996	−1.08248	−0.66832	−0.74907

Table 5. Arousal changes from previous method

Subject	Rest-Section 1	Section 1-Section 2	Section 2-Section 3	Section 3-Section 4
A	−1.9731	−0.60163	0.40879	0.22521
B	0.07332	2.08998	−1.66685	−0.89468
C	−1.08129	−0.02489	−1.57629	0.81246
D	1.18214	−0.48156	2.00194	−1.27287
E	−0.50357	−0.61454	0.38481	−1.90026

The comparison results between the changes in subjective evaluation and the comfort and arousal model derived from our proposed method and the previous method [10]. This study aims to construct a comfortable arousal model with higher accuracy and reliability by using optimal physiological indexes. To achieve our goal, we explore various physiological indexes and calculate feature importance using random forest method. Then we compare and validate the evaluation accuracy of the comfortable

Table 6. Comfort changes from previous method

Subject	Rest-Section 1	Section1-Section 2	Section 2-Section 3	Section 3-Section 4
A	2.39624	-0.99406	0.49058	−1.47419
B	−0.77779	1.82644	0.64612	−0.506
C	−1.51922	2.19179	−1.25692	1.55424
D	−2.55456	0.62183	0.42575	0.75891
E	0.76427	−0.94441	−1.51604	0.40848

Table 7. Arousal changes from SAM scale

Subject	Rest-Section 1	Section 1-Section 2	Section 2-Section 3	Section 3-Section 4
A	2	0	−1	−3
B	2	0	−3	1
C	−2	−1	−1	1
D	2	0	0	0
E	−1	−1	−1	3

Table 8. Comfort change from SAM scale

Subject	Rest-Section 1	Section1-Section 2	Section 2-Section 3	Section 3-Section 4
A	1	−1	1	1
B	1	−2	2	1
C	2	−1	1	0
D	−1	0	3	−1
E	2	−1	−1	−2

arousal models. For the evaluation, we will compare the subjective evaluation score with our comfortable arousal model against the previous comfortable model proposed by Jadram [10] are shown in Fig. 7. The figure shows the number of times that the physiological signal's results were changing in the same direction as the subjective evaluation's results. Although both methods could derive same result for changes in comfort (9 match for both method), but our proposed method clearly show that the change in arousal comply with the subjective evaluation result (8 matches) more than the previous method (6 matches). Therefore, it can be implied that the proposed method is more accurate than the methods of the previous method. The accuracy of the comfortable arousal model is slightly improved by choosing the index considering the importance of the features by Random Forests. It might be necessary to consider other dimensionality reduction methods to create a more accurate comfortable arousal model in the future.

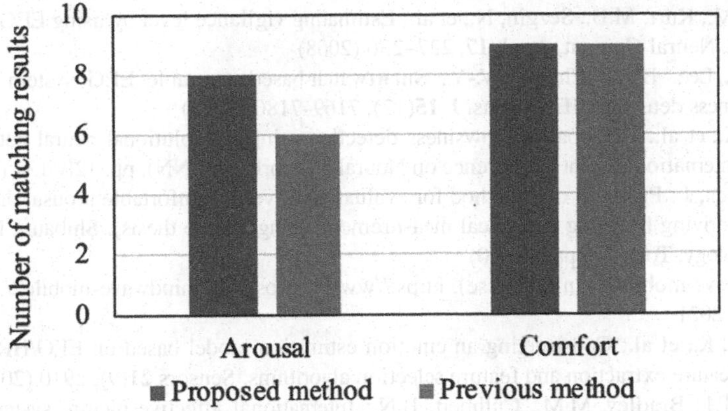

Fig. 7. The number of matching results between comfortable arousal model and SAM

6 Conclusions

In this paper, we compared two comfortable arousal models created from our proposed method and the previous method with subjective evaluation results. Our proposed method chooses an index by considering the feature importance computed by random forest. We performed the experiment to collect physiological signals and subjective evaluation. Then, we calculated the comfortable arousal value from physiological signals using our proposed method and the previous method. To evaluate the performance of each method, we compare the directional change derived from physiological signals with the subjective evaluation result. The results show that the index considering the importance of the features by random Forests could increase the accuracy of the comfortable arousal model. We will consider another method to create a high accuracy, comfortable arousal model in the future.

References

1. SAE: Taxonomy and Definitions for Terms Related to Driving Automation Systems for On-Road Motor Vehicle, J3016-201609 (2016)
2. Hirose, T., Kitabayashi, D., Kubota, H.: Driving characteristics of drivers in a state of low alertness when an autonomous system changes from autonomous driving to manual driving. SAE Technical Paper, 2015-01-1407 (2015)
3. Eriksson, A., Stanton, N.A.: Takeover time in highly automated vehicles: noncritical transitions to and from manual control. Human Factors **59**(4), 689–705 (2017)
4. Cai, H., Lin, Y., Mourant, R.: Study on driver emotion in driver-vehicle-environment systems using multiple networked driving simulators. In: Driving Simulation Conference, pp. 1–9 (2007)
5. Jeon, M., Walker, B.N., Yim, J.-B.: Effects of specific emotions on subjective judgment, driving performance, and perceived workload. Transp. Res. Part F Traffic Psychol. Behav. **24**, 197–209 (2014)
6. Chui, K.T., Tsang, K.F., Chi, H.R., Ling, B.W.K., Wu, C.K.: An accurate ECG-based transportation safety drowsiness detection scheme. IEEE Trans. Ind. Inform. **12**(4), 1438–1452 (2016)

7. Akin, M., Kurt, M.B., Sezgin, N., et al.: Estimating vigilance level by using EEG and EMG signals. Neural Comput. Appl. **17**, 227–236 (2008)
8. Li, G., Lee, B.-L., Chung, W.-Y.: Smartwatch-based wearable EEG system for driver drowsiness detection. IEEE Sens. J. **15**(12), 7169–7180 (2015)
9. Zhu, X., et al.: EOG-based drowsiness detection using convolutional neural networks. In: 2014 International Joint Conference on Neural Networks (IJCNN), pp. 128–134 (2014)
10. Narumon, J.: Proposal of a method for evaluating driver's comfortable arousal during automated driving by using biological measurements (Ungraduate thesis). Shibaura Institute of Technology, Tokyo, Japan (2020)
11. Mindwave mobile2. (in Japanese). https://www.neurosky.jp/mindwave-mobile2/. Accessed 18 Feb 2021
12. Suzuki, K., et al.: Constructing an emotion estimation model based on EEG/HRV indexes using feature extraction and feature selection algorithms. Sensors **21**(9), 2910 (2021)
13. Lang, P.J., Bradley, M.M., Cuthbert, B.N.: International affective picture system (IAPS): affective ratings of pictures and instruction manual. Technical report (1997)

Developing and Testing a New Reinforcement Learning Toolkit with Unreal Engine

Francesco Sapio(✉) and Riccardo Ratini

Sapienza University of Rome, Rome, Italy
sapio@diag.uniroma1.it, ratini.1656801@studenti.uniroma1.it
https://www.diag.uniroma1.it/

Abstract. In this work we tried to overcome the main limitations that can be found in current state-of-the-art development and benchmarking RL platforms, namely the lack of a user interface, a closed-box approach to scenarios, the lack of realistic environments and the difficulty in extending the obtained results in real applications, by introducing a new development framework for reinforcement learning built over the graphics engine Unreal Engine 4. *Unreal Reinforcement Learning Toolkit* (URLT) was developed with the idea of being modular, flexible, and easy to use even for non-expert users. To do this, we have developed flexible and modular APIs, through which it's possible to setup the major learning techniques. Using these APIs, users can define all the elements of a RL problem, such as agents, algorithms, tasks, and scenarios, and to combine them with each other to always have new solutions. By taking advantage of the editor's UI, users can select and execute existing scenarios and change the parameters of agents and tasks without to recompile the code. Users also have the possibility to create new scenarios from scratch using an intuitive level editor. Furthermore, task design is made accessible to non-expert users using a node-oriented visual programming system called Blueprint. To validate the tool, we produced a starter pack containing a suite of state-of-the-art RL algorithms, some example scenarios, a small library of props and a couple of trainable agents. Moreover, we ran an evaluation test with users in which the latter were required to try URLT and competing software (OpenAI Gym), then to evaluate both using a questionnaire. The obtained results showed a general preference for URLT in all key parameters of the test.

Keywords: Evaluation methods and techniques · Unreal Engine · Reinforcement Learning

1 Introduction

Reinforcement Learning is the branch of the AI that allows agents to learn strategies by interacting with the environment, observing the results and collecting rewards. The agent's aim is to learn an optimal strategy for the assigned

H. Degen and S. Ntoa (Eds.): HCII 2022, LNAI 13336, pp. 317–334, 2022.
https://doi.org/10.1007/978-3-031-05643-7_21

task. Over the years *Reinforcement Learning* has gained considerable popularity, so much that it has been studied in disciplines such as Game Theory, Control Theory, Research, Information Theory, Multi-Agent Systems, Swarm Robotics and Statistics. In all this fields RL state-of-the-art algorithms have achieved comparable performance to humans in numerous challenging problems.

Fundamental to the rapid growth of the field was the presence of research and benchmarking platforms that provided researchers with scenarios and simulations in which to test and study algorithms. Over time, indeed, numerous platforms have been developed and proposed for different application domains and task complexity. By analyzing existing frameworks, it is possible to find some shared and recurrent limitations which, although they did not prevent Reinforcement Learning from growing rapidly, if resolved, could favor further advancement and diffusion even outside the academic area. These limitations can be summarized in four fundamental categories, each of the platforms mentioned in this work share at least one of them:

- *Lack of UI.* Existing frameworks are mainly developed by researchers for researchers, so they often don't have a UI and the only way to use them is via programming. This discourages non-expert users from trying to use them, contributing to leave the field only in the academic area.
- *Closed-Box Approach.* For design needs, proposed scenarios are usually implemented following programming interfaces. On the one hand, this favors the reusability of the code, on the other hand, especially if not supported by an adequate user interface, it makes the scenarios similar to closed boxes. This makes the customization or the creation of scenarios a tedious and counter-intuitive process for non-expert users.
- *Lack of real-world application.* In most cases, proposed scenarios are too simple, such as small logical problems, or unrealistic, such as video game levels. If on the one hand this favors the benchmarking of algorithms, given that the computing complexity is reduced, on the other hand it means that the obtained results are of little relevance for the development of real applications.
- *Lack of interface uniformation.* Many frameworks have been developed using different programming interfaces, this means that implemented code often needs to be adapted to be used on different tools.

In this work we introduce *Unreal Reinforcement Learning Toolkit* (URLT), a brand new RL development and benchmarking framework designed with the idea of being modular, flexible and easy to use even for users with a less technical background. URLT is built upon *Unreal Engine 4*[1] and exploits it's features to overcome the limitations mentioned above. The contributions of this work are manifold:

1. We have provided a brand new general platform that allows researchers to test algorithms, design realistic scenarios, and develop real-world simulation quickly and easily;

[1] https://www.unrealengine.com.

2. We have developed a simple and intuitive user interface that can represent an access point to the AI even for non-expert users;
3. We have provided game developers with a tool that allows them to introduce intelligent elements into their gameplay.

This paper is structured as follows. In Sect. 2 the literature about the topics of this work will be presented, giving a wide overview of the most used and popular frameworks and tools. In Sect. 3 we will tackle every design aspect of *URLT*, discussing the general structure, the developed APIs and reporting the description of some example scenarios. In Sect. 4, a summary of an evaluation test with users made to validate the toolkit is reported, paying attention to the structure of the test, the sessions performed and the results obtained. Finally, in Sect. 5, conclusions are drawn.

2 Related Works

Over the years, numerous development and benchmarking platforms have been proposed; Borrowing the classification made in [11], we can divide them into three different categories:

2.1 Domain-Specific Frameworks

This includes platforms which allow the creation of sets of tasks within a specific domain such as locomotion, first-person navigation, games and so on.

A good starting point for this category is *VizDoom* [12,21,25], a light, fast and highly customizable platform based on the classic FPS videogame *Doom*. It allows users to train agents to play and learn various tasks such as completing the level, exploring maps, collecting items, and so on. The environments can be easily customized by inserting enemies, npc, obstacles or by changing the layout. It uses visual RGB Frames observations, while the action space is formed by the input keys accepted by the game. Still in FPS videogames, it is possible to cite the works in [16] and in [18]. In both cases the authors tried to apply RL in a shooting self-made small videogame, instead of using a commercial one, in order to have more control over the game loop.

Changing videogames category, it is possible to find other platforms capable of providing challenging scenarios for researchers. *Google Research Football* [13] for example, provides an environment where agents are trained to play football in an advanced 3D simulator. The engine implements a full football match and is capable of handling rules such as side fouls, corner kicks, penalties, cards and offsides. The framework provides a series of scenarios of increasing difficulty that allow users to manage numerous situations, from passing the ball to trying to score with or without defense. Also noteworthy is *MineRL* [9], a simulator based on the popular *Minecraft* videogame used to build and deliver a huge database of human demonstrations for Imitation Learning. MineRL is delivered via a client capable of assigning a specific task to the player and recording and uploading the player's gameplay to a dedicated repository. These sequences are then processed and annotated to expand a huge dataset (currently over 60 million annotations) containing samples for numerous tasks.

Another area of interest is Computer Vision, having realistic 3D scenarios is in fact of vital importance for the success of numerous visual applications.

A prime example worth reporting is *UnrealCV* [19]. It uses Unreal Engine 4 to allow users to create and use realistic and interactable virtual worlds. Unreal CV works using a client-server architecture, the engine containing the world and the agent is the server, which communicates with external python clients via TCP connection. Similar to UnrealCV is *CARLA* [6], an open simulator for autonomous driving. CARLA is implemented as an open source layer on Unreal Engine 4 and uses the engine to make a wide range of realistic urban scenarios available to users. The scenarios include numerous elements such as buildings, vegetation, road signs, pedestrians and other vehicles. It is possible to create new scenarios by designing layouts and placing elements and it is also possible to introduce new types of environments, as done for example in [10]. As for UnrealCV, CARLA has a client-server architecture where, Unreal Engine acts as a server, while clients communicate with it via socket. Another interesting platform is *AirSim* [20], a simulator for drones or other flying vehicles mainly, developed in Unreal Engine 4. As CARLA, AirSim provides users with realistic environments for indoor and outdoor scenarios and a very complex and realistic physical system. The platform is also easily extendable and over time numerous works based on it have been proposed [3,4,14]. It is also worth mentioning *Habitat* [15], an extremely realistic indoor 3D simulator developed using the C++ *Magnum* graphics engine.

2.2 Environment-Suite Frameworks

Platforms in this section consist of collections of scenarios and environments made available to users mainly to test and benchmark algorithms on different levels of difficulty and interest.

Proposed in [2], *Arcade Learning Environment* was one of the first environments based on videogames. It provides an interfacing framework that allow the design and training of agents playing Atari 2600 games. ALE is built on top of Stella, an open-source Atari 2600 emulator. It allows the user to interface with the atari by receiving inputs, sending screen or RAM informations and so on. It also provide a game-handling layer which transforms games into standard RL problems. Similar to ALE, *OpenAI Gym* [5,7], is a toolkit for reinforcement learning research. It's aim is to combine the elements of previous benchmark platforms in a unique software package which is easily accessible and usable. It provides many collections of tasks (called Environments) with a common interface, which are updated and expanded continuously. In addition to the software package Gym has a website where users are encouraged to submit their code and results in order to build scoreboards for each environment. OpenAI Gym contains several collections of POMDP environments like *Classic control*, *Algorithmic* task, *Atari* games using the ALE platform, *Board games*, *2D and 3D Robots* using MuJoCo as physics engine. It is also possible to create new scenarios by implementing its programming interface. Some examples can be found in [8,17,22,24].

Of particular interest are also the *DeepMind Suites*, different platforms, each oriented to a particular domain of interest. Here we report only DeepMind Control and DeepMind Lab as the largest and most used.

DeepMind Control [23] is a collection of python libraries and scenarios used to allow robots and agents with articulated bodies to solve continuous control tasks. It uses MuJoCo as physics engine and provides users a wrapper, an API for the creation of articulated bodies, an API to set RL problems, and a Composer to wrap-up everything. The proposed tasks vary in difficulty and domain; From Locomotion to Manipulation.

DeepMind Lab [1] is a first-person 3D gaming platform designed for research and development based on the popular *Quake Arena* videogame. It provides users with coverage for a wide range of problems, as navigation tasks, collection of items, traversing dangerous environments, platforming, laser tag, memory tasks and experiments inspired by neuroscience. The scenarios are treated as procedurally generated game levels or defined by hand through the use of layout files.

Finally, *Meta-World* [26], a multi-task and meta-RL benchmark platform for parametric continuous control problems, is also worth mentioning. It provides a wide range of parametric scenarios which can be used for Meta-Reinforcement Learning tasks. Tasks range from opening drawers or doors, to using a hammer with nails.

2.3 General Frameworks

These are generic frameworks able to create scenarios with different graphic and physical complexity, with social interactions and with different tasks.

At present, only *UnityML* [11] can be placed in this category. It was developed using the graphics engine *Unity 3D*, supports major learning techniques, such as Reinforcement Learning, Imitation Learning and Behavioral Cloning and provides users with a wide range of predefined scenarios. It also allows the construction of new scenarios by using the Engine's level editor which gives the users the possibility to compose environments by placing objects in the scene. The framework provides an initial set of agents, sensors, NPCs and static objects, and it is also possible to easily create new ones using the Unity class system. The framework also provides a python package containing APIs to communicate with the Unity server and to control environments via python. Communication takes place via the gRPC protocol.

3 URLT

3.1 Unreal Work Pipeline

By exploiting the structure of Unreal Engine, for the development of URLT we have tried to develop APIs that could be used by both programmers and non-programmers. In fact, Unreal provides some tools that make life easier for developers, above all the *Blueprint* system and the *exposing variables and functions* system. The Blueprint visual scripting system is a simple and flexible node-oriented scripting system that allows even non-programmers, such as designers or artists, to use programmable tools usually accessible only to programmers. The variable exposing system, on the other hand, is a mechanism that allows, through the use of C++ macros, to mark variables and functions as *exposed* to the blueprints. Variables and functions exposed can then be called and modified in the graphic editor of unreal without having to recompile the code. To balance the workload between blueprints and C++ and make the most of both systems, Unreal developers suggest the following work pipeline: To define abstract classes and core aspects of gameplay in C++ and expose to blueprints those elements that can be modified and customized by designers. For more details, refer to UE documentation.

3.2 Framework Structure

Figure 1 shows the block structure used in the development of URLT. The APIs consist of three core entities strongly connected with each others: Environment, UE Agent and RL Engine. Note that while the first two were written in C++ by subclassing the native unreal engine classes, the last block was defined in Pyhton, thus producing hybrid APIs capable of exploiting the strengths of both languages. Also note that, for the development of the C++ blocks, we have decided to follow the pipeline introduced previously, defining interfaces and abstract classes in C++ and leaving the designer the possibility to implement objects directly in Blueprints or in C++ and then exposing variables. For the example scenarios shown at the end of this section, however, we used the second approach.

- **Environment:** The scenario in which the training takes place; It is made up of obstacles, walls, interactive and programmable objects and bots. Each scenario can be easily designed using UE's level editor by simply picking and placing objects in the scene. As example we have provided in the starting pack different types of obstacles, walls, food and poison items, triggers volumes, cameras and target objects. This library can be easily extended by creating new objects via blueprints or C++.
- **UE Agent:** The main entity of the training, it can performs actions in the environment, observes information and it is the entity that must complete the task goal of the reinforcement learning problem. Objectives and specifications of the task are defined by implementing a programming interface, called *URLT Interface*, which allows users to define attributes such as action

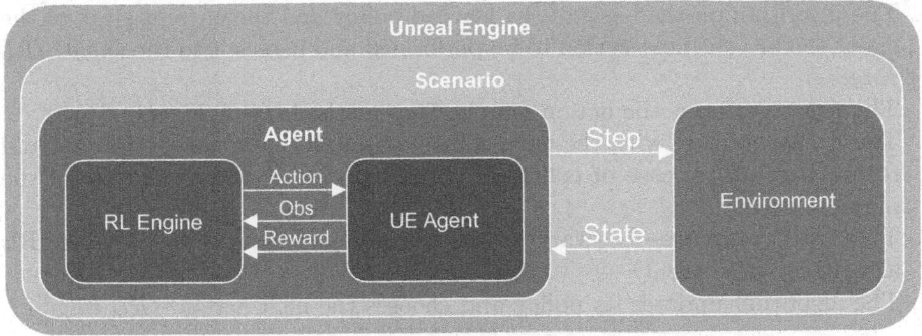

Fig. 1. URL Framework general schema

and observation spaces, or functions to perform actions, reset the environment and so on. It is also capable of loading the *RL Engine* block through the use of an external plugin called *UnrealEnginePython*, which allows some unreal classes to load and execute python scripts at runtime. It can also be equipped with tools such as weapons and sensors. At present, only one family of agents has been implemented in the starting pack, that is the HumanoidAgent, similarly only one category of RayCast type sensors is available. However, an expansion of the library of agents and tools is planned for the near future and users can also create their agents freely using the produced APIs.
- **RL Engine:** This block represents the AI logic of the agent. It consists in the implementation of an RL algorithm and communicates directly with the UE Agent. Usually in this block hyperparameters and network model are implemented, as well as methods for querying and updating the current policy. To make life easier for users, we have implemented a large collection of state-of-the-art RL algorithms in the starter pack already mentioned. These can be easily selected through the use of the user interface. More details on the algorithms implemented in the next paragraphs.

RL Engine and UE Agent together form the complete agent that interacts with the environment. Decomposing the system into three modular blocks allows for greater flexibility and customization, thus making the users able to try different combinations. For example, different agents can be tried in the same scenario (In a self-parking car scenario it's possible to implements different kind of cars and try all of them), or different algorithms can be tried with the same agent or even different tasks can be tried in the same map (Think of a map containing a car park, this can be used for a self-parking task with car agents or as a scenario for a shooter game between soldier agents). Furthermore, moving *action space*, *observation space* and *reward function* inside the UE Agent gives greater freedom to the designer, who can customize the agents according to the needs of the task. Below is reported the flow of the system training loop:

1. The algorithm on the basis of the learned policy and the current state of the agent chooses the next action to be performed and passes it to the agent. *(RL Engine)*
2. The agent performs the action via the Step method. *(UE Agent)*
3. The agent interacts with the environment through the action performed and receives reports in case of collisions with obstacles or other elements of the map. *(Environment)*
4. The agent computes observations and rewards and returns them to the RL algorithm. *(UE Agent)*
5. The algorithm updates its policy and chooses the next action. *(RL Engine)*

Also note that, since the agent has its own internal RL Logic and is, therefore, independent by the environment, several agents can be used simultaneously in the same scenario. This allows users to speed up the hyperparameters tuning phase, in fact it will be possible to run different instances of the same task at the same time, each with different parameters and see which combination obtains the best results. Also this allows a direct comparison between the agents.

Moreover, to make the platform as integrated and customizable as possible, we have exposed all the variables and parameters related to RL aspects. In this way, through the textbox and dropdown menus of the blueprint interface, it is possible to check and customize in a few clicks aspects of the training or scenario such as: the behavior of the agent (training, inference, heuristic), the algorithm used, training duration, update rate, policy save rate, hyperparameters, action space and observation space, multipliers of the reward function and so on.

Finally, another crucial aspect was the choice of the Machine Learning library. In our starter pack the proposed algorithms have been written using *PyTorch*, however implementations with other libraries, such as *Tensorflow* or *Keras* can be used as long as they implement the same programming interface.

Finally, pay also attention to the fact that reinforcement learning algorithms usually act in loop, however in UE4 the control of the game loop is left to the engine. Therefore, for the implementation of the algorithms the UE's *Tick* method can be exploited. The Tick method of a UE Class, if activated, is executed in every frame, for this reason, the idea is to implement in the update method of the RL block only the code of a single iteration of the algorithm, and to call it in Tick.

3.3 Starter Pack

As mentioned above, to demonstrate the validity of the tool, we produced a starter pack containing a suite of state-of-the-art RL algorithms, some example scenarios, a small library of meshes and programmable objects usable in the scenarios and a couple of trainable agents. For each of these scenarios, agents were trained using each of the proposed algorithms and performing hyperparameters tuning to find the best configuration. Subsequently, qualitative and quantitative analyzes were performed in order to extract considerations on the behavior of the algorithms and understand which of them was the most or least suitable for

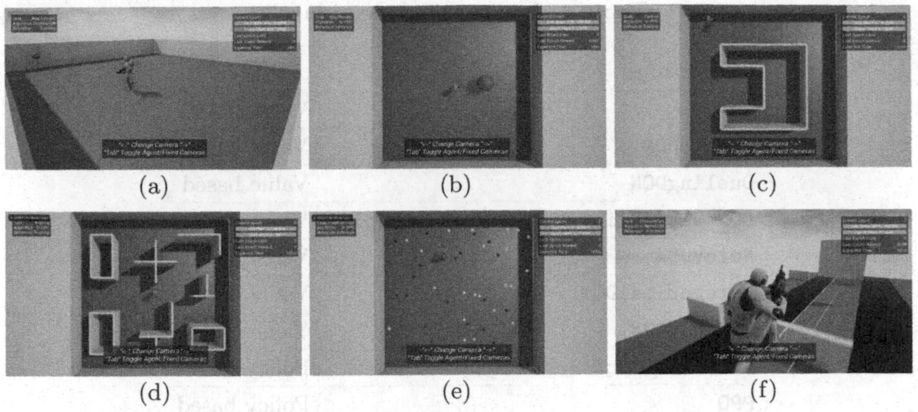

Fig. 2. FoodCollector scenario: *(a)* Reach Target; *(b)* Ring Shooter; *(c)* Explore - Ring Arena; *(c)* Explore - Maze Arena; *(c)* Food Collector; *(c)* Obstacle Run;

a particular type of scenario. This should demonstrate to the reader the effective ease of scenario design and algorithm benchmarking offered by URLT.

In the next paragraph the list of scenarios implemented is reported while in (Table 1) a list with all implemented algorithms is shown.

Example Scenarios

(a) *Reach Target* - A locomotion task in an empty arena where a target object is spawned randomly at the beginning of each epoch. Agent goal is to reach target's location.
(b) *Ring Shooter* - A simple *aim and shoot* task. A target object is spawned randomly in a circumference centered in the agent position. The agent can rotate left and right and shoot. Task goal is to shoot the target.
(c) *Explore* - Exploration task. Agent goal is to explore the environment while avoiding walls and obstacles. Two different environments have been designed for the task, a *ring arena* and a *maze.*
(d) *Food Collector* - A square arena environment where food and poison items are spawned randomly. Agent goal is to picks all the food items while avoiding the red ones.
(e) *Obstacle Run* - An obstacle race with high and low obstacles. The agent move forward by default so it has to learn to avoid obstacles by jumping or crouching.

Figure 2 shows some example images of the scenarios.

Table 1. Implemented algorithms

Algorithms	Family
`DQN`	Value based
`DoubleDQN`	Value based
`DuelingDQN`	Value based
`DQN With Prioritized Buffer Replay`	Value based
`NoisyDQN`	Value based
`CategoricalDQN`	Value based
`RainbowDQN`	Value based
`Actor-Critic`	Policy based
`PPO`	Policy based

4 User Validation

To validate the tool, a comparative assessment test with users was organized. This section will provide an overview of the test, the sessions performed, the users who took part in it and the obtained results.

4.1 Goal and Comparison Tool Choice

The objective of the test was to evaluate the functionalities and the user interface of *URLT* by comparing it with one of the existing frameworks and see if this actually led to improvements in terms of usability, learnability, ease of use and intuitiveness of the graphical interface. While it may seem natural to use another general framework such as *UnityML* as a comparison tool, the choice ultimately fell on *OpenAI Gym*. This choice is justified by the popularity of OpenAI Gym, at present the most used framework, which makes it a more interesting yardstick.

4.2 Test Structure and Questionnaire

The test had a duration of 90 min and was structured in three phases:

1. *Introduction*: In this phase, a brief introductory presentation of the test is made. This presentation includes a description of the test objective and structure, a small theoretical overview of reinforcement learning and a general introduction of both *OpenAI Gym* and *URLT*. Once the presentation is done, Users were showed tasks specifications and files to work with. Finally users were asked to fill a demographics and skills pre-questionnaire.
2. *First Tool test*: Users are assigned three tasks, of increasing difficulty, to be carried out with one of the two tools in a limited time (30 min). Once the tasks have been completed or time is up, they will have to fill in an evaluation

questionnaire on the use of the tool in aspects such as usability, learnability and user interface.
3. *Second Tool test*: As phase 2 but with the tool still not used.

Before starting, users were divided into two groups (A and B): group A was assigned Gym as the first tool and URLT as the second, while group B vice versa. The proposed questionnaire was Opinion-Based with a 5-point Likert scale. Users were presented with statements about some items of the tool or the tasks and should indicate their level of agreement on a scale from 1 (Strongly Agree) to 5 (Strongly Disagree). The questions were divided into four different categories, namely, Learnability, Usability, Task-Specific Questions and User Interface according to the items addressed by the statement. Also note that some questions have been negated to keep users' attention high and avoid biased answers. A summary of the breakdown of questions can be found in (Table 2).

Table 2. Questionnaire tasks

Phase	Category	Questions
`Introduction`	`Anagraphics and Skills`	10
`First Tool`	`Learnability`	10
	`Usability`	10
	`Tasks-Specific`	8
	`User-Interface`	8
`Second Tool`	`Learnability`	10
	`Usability`	10
	`Tasks-Specific`	8
	`User-Interface`	8
	`Total:`	82

4.3 Assigned Tasks

The reinforcement learning research pipeline is made of many common atomic tasks like algorithm and scenario choices, hyperparameters tuning and so on. By analyzing this pipeline we have extracted three tasks, of increasing difficulty, aimed at evaluating the ease of execution of these atomics action with both the frameworks. A summary of the three tasks is shown in (Table 3).

4.4 Performed Sessions and Data Processing

The sessions took place remotely via *Google Meet*. To ensure maximum transparency, users were asked to share their screen during the tests. A total of 33 users took part in the test in five different sessions. The users were chosen in

Table 3. Assigned tasks

#	Task	Difficulty
1	`Execute an existing scenario`	Easy
2	`Customize an existing scenario`	Medium
3	`Create a new scenario`	Hard

order to have an audience that shows a good variety of age, level of education, IT and AI skills, some statistics on users repartition are shown in (Table 4).

At the end of the testing sessions, obtained data were *normalized* by assigning a value from 1 (maximum) to 5 (minimum) to each item discussed in the sentences proposed in the questionnaire. More in detail: in case of a positive sentence the value assigned goes from 1 in case of *strongly agree* to 5 in case of *strongly disagree*. Vice versa in case of negative sentence. Once normalized, the data were averaged by framework and test sections and filtered by user's skills. We reported them in (Table 5).

4.5 Data Analysis and Considerations

The results obtained seem very encouraging, URLT obtained better values in all sections and in almost all users categories. It is interesting to note that the values obtained are almost always above the average demonstrating, in fact, a general appreciation for the tool.

Going more in detail in the analysis we notice, for the general results, the greater gap for the UI category and the smaller for Learnability, the gap for Usability and Tasks is a middle ground between the other two categories. These differences seem sensible and predictable, In fact the big gap that emerged in the UI section could be justified by the presence of the intuitive interface of Unreal Engine; changing parameters through the use of textbox and dropdown menus is in fact faster and more intuitive than doing it via code. Similar considerations can be made for Usability and Tasks, where again the UI, the level editor and URLT APIs, probably make it easier to design scenarios and customize parameters, the slight reduction in the gap could be due to the *dispersiveness* of a software like Unreal that could confuse users at first and the simplicity of the programming interface of the Gym scenarios that would make the differences less evident for more experienced users. For what concerns Learnability, probably the large amount of tools and information shown on the screen by Unreal Engine could be confusing and make learning more difficult for users who use it for the first time. In any case, URLT shows better values in each category, which would demonstrate real improvements in all evaluation criteria.

Other interesting observations can be made by filtering data by user categories. For example, looking at the *Computer Skills* category, there is a greater gap for users with medium and good skills and a lower gap for users at the extremes, this would lead to think that, for different reasons obviously, users

Table 4. User demographics and skills statistics. *The table reports the repartition of the users by demographics and skills categories.*

User repartition				
Age				
Under 18	**18–24**	**25–34**	**35–44**	**45+**
0	20	12	1	0
School				
Less than H.S.	**High School**	**Bachelor**	**Master**	**Doctoral**
0	5	23	5	0
Employement				
Student	**Employed 40-**	**Employed 40+**	**Not Employed**	**Retired**
20	5	5	3	0
Relevance of study/work with AI				
Str. Relevant	**Relevant**	**Neutral**	**Not Relevant**	**Str. Not Relevant**
3	5	9	8	8
Computer skills				
Excellent	**Good**	**Medium**	**Poor**	**None**
2	9	14	8	0
Coding skills				
Excellent	**Good**	**Medium**	**Poor**	**None**
3	4	9	7	10
AI knowledge				
Excellent	**Good**	**Medium**	**Poor**	**None**
2	7	3	8	13
UE4 knowledge				
Excellent	**Good**	**Medium**	**Poor**	**None**
2	5	7	14	5

with excellent or bad computer skills may find URLT features less useful. Indeed, users with excellent skills may not find it very difficult to perform the assigned tasks with both Gym and URLT, while users with no computer skills may have had many difficulties with both tools, not appreciating the differences between them. This analysis is partially confirmed in the *AI Knowledge* category, which shows a substantial breakeven for users with Excellent knowledge and clear gap for all the other bands.

The above can be justified by assuming that users with high knowledge and AI expertise (and perhaps of Gym) may not have found great difficulties in implementing tasks using both platforms; looking at the values of the singular sections in fact there is a slight preference for URLT in Usability and UI, however, balanced by a worse Learnability. This lead us to think that although these users have appreciated and recognized a greater ease of use in URLT, the excessive amount of elements introduced may have made their experience more confused and dispersed. However, since only two users are part of this category,

Table 5. Test Results. *In bold the best average between the two frameworks*

	OpenAI Gym					URLT				
	Learn.	Usab.	Tasks	UI	Avg	Learn.	Usab.	Tasks	UI	Avg
Degree										
High School	3,68	3,72	3,67	4,50	3,89	2,80	2,40	2,25	2,57	**2,51**
Bachelor degree	3,93	3,78	3,83	3,84	3,85	2,92	2,77	2,80	2,63	**2,78**
Master degree	3,20	3,00	3,37	3,87	3,36	3,00	2,58	2,20	2,32	**2,32**
Computer skills										
Excellent	3,15	3,15	3,37	3,93	3,40	3,30	2,50	2,50	2,94	**2,81**
Good	3,54	3,64	3,66	3,79	3,66	2,76	2,57	2,59	2,55	**2,62**
Medium	4,16	3,96	4,00	4,26	4,10	2,91	2,70	2,57	2,45	**2,66**
Poor	3,56	3,26	3,45	3,58	3,46	3,00	2,82	2,81	2,73	**2,84**
AI knowledge										
Excellent	2,90	3,05	3,18	3,81	3,24	3,35	2,75	3,25	3,05	**3,10**
Good	3,50	3,40	3,75	4,00	3,66	2,54	2,54	2,23	2,66	**2,49**
Medium	3,00	3,13	3,54	3,54	3,30	2,90	2,50	2,41	2,12	**2,48**
Poor	3,90	3,68	3,47	3,86	3,73	3,13	2,84	3,00	2,75	**2,93**
None	4,18	4,00	4,00	4,09	4,07	2,92	2,70	2,57	2,46	**2,66**
GameDev skills										
Excellent	3,26	3,40	3,41	3,75	3,46	3,20	2,76	2,87	2,87	**2,93**
Good	3,90	3,58	4,15	4,63	4,06	2,52	2,48	2,05	2,18	**2,31**
Medium	3,47	3,50	3,52	3,72	3,55	2,98	2,45	2,75	2,85	**2,76**
Poor	3,89	3,77	3,68	3,91	3,81	2,90	2,77	2,66	2,46	**2,70**
None	4,22	3,80	4,06	3,78	3,97	3,12	2,97	2,87	2,78	**2,94**
UE4 skills										
Excellent	3,10	2,90	2,82	3,50	3,08	2,70	2,50	2,06	2,56	**2,46**
Good	3,48	3,40	3,63	4,10	3,65	2,82	2,70	2,48	2,45	**2,61**
Medium	3,52	3,67	3,91	4,00	3,78	2,91	2,41	2,68	2,85	**2,71**
Poor	4,23	3,91	3,93	4,05	4,03	3,01	2,89	2,87	2,58	**2,84**
None	3,48	3,48	3,42	3,55	3,48	2,84	2,56	2,27	2,32	**2,50**
All	3,78	3,65	3,73	3,94	3,78	2,92	2,68	2,763	2,57	**2,70**

these considerations must be taken with caution, not excluding the possibility of outliers.

The considerations just made were also confirmed by the verbal feedback provided by users during and after the test. In particular, most users appreciated many features introduced such as level editor, the possibility to quickly vary parameters using the UI, the possibility to view the training status live and the possibility to use the Blueprint system for the programming part. On the other hand, however, the main criticisms and perplexities were directed at the excessive *complexity* of UE's interface which may results too *disorienting* for new users and make the learning curve steep.

In conclusion, the results obtained in the test can be considered very promising, both the visual and quantitative analysis seem to confirm the thesis proposed in this work, namely how the use of the tools made available by a modern graphic engine in combination with flexible and modular APIs can reduce or overcome the limitations mentioned in the introduction of this paper, providing an easier access point to RL for both expert and non-expert users. A second test cycle with a larger population of AI expert may be required to further validate the results obtained.

5 Conclusions and Future Work

In this work, we proposed Unreal Reinforcement Learning Toolkit (URLT), a new research and development framework for Reinforcement Learning algorithms developed in Unreal Engine 4 with the aim of overcoming some of the most frequent limitations in the most used RL platforms, namely the lack of a user interface, a closed-box approach to scenarios, the lack of realistic environments and the difficulty in extending the obtained results in real applications

Among the various features, URLT shows a responsive and intuitive user interface that allows the users to quickly select tasks and scenarios and to modify parameters and attributes without having to access the code; A modern physical and graphic engine with high computing capabilities ensuring support for extremely realistic and complex scenarios, the latter designed through a simple and easy-to-use editor; Structured and modular programming APIs that allow easy planning of agents and tasks.

These and other features make URLT a very flexible general platform oriented for both research and benchmarking of algorithms and for the development of real applications. Thanks to its ease of use, the software is aimed both at researchers and at users who are not experts in AI or programming, thus opening up new possibilities external to academic research.

To demonstrate the validity of the tool, we produced a starter pack containing a suite of state-of-the-art RL algorithms, some example scenarios, a small library of meshes and programmable objects usable in the scenarios and a couple of trainable agents. For each of these scenarios, agents were trained using each of the proposed algorithms and performing hyperparameters tuning to find the best configuration. Subsequently, qualitative (through visual inspection of the learned strategy) and quantitative (through tables and graphs of the trend of epochs, loss and rewards) analyzes were performed in order to extract considerations on the behavior of the algorithms and understand which of them was the most or least suitable for a particular type of scenario. This should demonstrate to the reader, and to the user, the effective ease of scenario design and algorithm benchmarking offered by URLT.

To further validate the platform, we carried out an evaluation test with users in which the latter are required to carry out some commonly used activities, such as executing or modifying scenarios, using URLT and competing software (OpenAI Gym) and to evaluate both using a questionnaire. In particular, users had to carry out three tasks for each of the two tools in a limited time and then evaluate them in aspects such as learnability, usability and user interface. The results obtained showed a general preference and appreciation for the features proposed by URLT in all the comparison parameters of the test.

Among the possible future developments we report:

- *Concurrent system and Parallel training APIs.* Although it is conceptually supported and some experiments have already been carried out successfully, setting up parallel or concurrent training is still cumbersome and complicated, the implementation of ad hoc APIs would allow a faster setting of these techniques.
- *Implementation of Imitation Learning algorithm and tools.* Imitation Learning is a learning technique in which an agent tries to learn a policy by observing samples taken from human demonstrations. To make the algorithms library more complete, we could implement state of the art IL algorithms and a companion system that allows users to take control of the agent and record his actions as demonstration.
- *Implementation of Curriculum Learning algorithm.* Curriculum Learning is a learning technique in which an agent is made to learn a complex task, starting from a very simple subtask and gradually increasing the complexity of the task to be learned as the previous ones are learned. As for the previous point, it could be interesting to expand the library of algorithms with the main state of the art CL algorithms and with an ad hoc companion system.
- *Expansion of proposed scenarios collection.* As in the case of other frameworks, it could be useful to expand the list of scenarios proposed with new tasks of different complexity, environments, type of action space, observations space and agents.
- *Expansion of scenario's objects library.* To help users design new environments or scenarios, it may be useful to expand the library of usable objects, introducing new obstacles, sensors, bots and interactable objects.
- *A second test cycle with a larger AI experts population.* To verify the results obtained in the excellent group of the AI Knowledge category, it might make sense to carry out a new test cycle with a greater number of expert AI users.
- *Try to simplify Unreal Engine UI.* Listening to the feedback provided by users, it might be worth studying and modifying the source code of Unreal Engine to try to make the user interface cleaner and lighter by eliminating or hiding elements that are not necessary for the tool.

In conclusion, we have proposed a new reinforcement learning platform that allows users to develop new applications and to benchmark algorithms easily. The framework has an intuitive and easy-to-use user interface, guaranteeing an access point to Reinforcement Learning and AI even for less experienced users.

References

1. Beattie, C., et al.: Deepmind lab. CoRR abs/1612.03801 (2016). http://arxiv.org/abs/1612.03801

2. Bellemare, M.G., Naddaf, Y., Veness, J., Bowling, M.: The arcade learning environment: an evaluation platform for general agents. J. Artif. Intell. Res. **47**, 253–279 (2013)
3. Bondi, E., et al.: A simulation environment for wildlife conservation with UAVs. In: Proceedings of the 1st ACM SIGCAS Conference on Computing and Sustainable Societies. COMPASS 2018. Association for Computing Machinery, New York, NY, USA (2018). https://doi.org/10.1145/3209811.3209880
4. Bondi, E., et al.: Near real-time detection of poachers from drones in AirSim, pp. 5814–5816, July 2018. https://doi.org/10.24963/ijcai.2018/847
5. Brockman, G., et al.: OpenAI Gym. arXiv preprint arXiv:1606.01540 (2016)
6. Dosovitskiy, A., Ros, G., Codevilla, F., Lopez, A., Koltun, V.: CARLA: an open urban driving simulator, vol. 78, pp. 1–16, 13–15 November 2017. https://proceedings.mlr.press/v78/dosovitskiy17a.html
7. Duan, Y., Chen, X., Houthooft, R., Schulman, J., Abbeel, P.: Benchmarking deep reinforcement learning for continuous control. In: International Conference on Machine Learning, pp. 1329–1338. PMLR (2016)
8. Gawlowicz, P., Zubow, A.: NS3-Gym: extending OpenAI gym for networking research. CoRR abs/1810.03943 (2018). http://arxiv.org/abs/1810.03943
9. Guss, W.H., et al.: MineRL: a large-scale dataset of minecraft demonstrations. CoRR abs/1907.13440 (2019). http://arxiv.org/abs/1907.13440
10. Han, I., Park, D.H., Kim, K.J.: A new open-source off-road environment for benchmark generalization of autonomous driving. IEEE Access **9**, 136071–136082 (2021). https://doi.org/10.1109/ACCESS.2021.3116710
11. Juliani, A., et al.: Unity: a general platform for intelligent agents. CoRR abs/1809.02627 (2018). http://arxiv.org/abs/1809.02627
12. Kempka, M., Wydmuch, M., Runc, G., Toczek, J., Jaśkowski, W.: ViZDoom: a doom-based AI research platform for visual reinforcement learning. In: 2016 IEEE Conference on Computational Intelligence and Games (CIG), pp. 1–8. IEEE (2016)
13. Kurach, K., et al.: Google research football: a novel reinforcement learning environment. CoRR abs/1907.11180 (2019). http://arxiv.org/abs/1907.11180
14. Madaan, R., et al.: AirSim drone racing lab. In: Escalante, H.J., Hadsell, R. (eds.) Proceedings of the NeurIPS 2019 Competition and Demonstration Track. Proceedings of Machine Learning Research, vol. 123, pp. 177–191. PMLR, 8–14 December 2020. https://proceedings.mlr.press/v123/madaan20a.html
15. Savva, M., et al.: Habitat: a platform for embodied AI research. In: Proceedings of the IEEE/CVF International Conference on Computer Vision (ICCV) (2019)
16. McPartland, M., Gallagher, M.: Reinforcement learning in first person shooter games. IEEE Trans. Comput. Intell. AI Games **3**(1), 43–56 (2010)
17. Nichol, A., Pfau, V., Hesse, C., Klimov, O., Schulman, J.: Gotta learn fast: a new benchmark for generalization in RL. arXiv preprint arXiv:1804.03720 (2018)
18. Piergigli, D., Ripamonti, L.A., Maggiorini, D., Gadia, D.: Deep reinforcement learning to train agents in a multiplayer first person shooter: some preliminary results. In: 2019 IEEE Conference on Games (CoG), pp. 1–8. IEEE (2019)
19. Qiu, W., et al.: UnrealCV: virtual worlds for computer vision, pp. 1221–1224 (2017). https://doi.org/10.1145/3123266.3129396
20. Shah, S., Dey, D., Lovett, C., Kapoor, A.: AirSim: high-fidelity visual and physical simulation for autonomous vehicles, pp. 621–635 (2018)
21. Song, S., Weng, J., Su, H., Yan, D., Zou, H., Zhu, J.: Playing FPS games with environment-aware hierarchical reinforcement learning. In: IJCAI, pp. 3475–3482 (2019)

22. Spangher, L., et al.: OfficeLearn: an OpenAI Gym environment for building level energy demand response. In: NeurIPS 2020 Workshop on Tackling Climate Change with Machine Learning (2020). https://www.climatechange.ai/papers/neurips2020/56
23. Tassa, Y., et al.: dm_control: software and tasks for continuous control. CoRR abs/2006.12983 (2020). https://arxiv.org/abs/2006.12983
24. Vázquez-Canteli, J.R., Kämpf, J., Henze, G., Nagy, Z.: CityLearn v1.0: an OpenAI gym environment for demand response with deep reinforcement learning. In: Proceedings of the 6th ACM International Conference on Systems for Energy-Efficient Buildings, Cities, and Transportation, pp. 356–357. BuildSys 2019. Association for Computing Machinery, New York, NY, USA (2019). https://doi.org/10.1145/3360322.3360998
25. Wu, Y., Tian, Y.: Training agent for first-person shooter game with actor-critic curriculum learning (2016)
26. Yu, T., et al.: Meta-world: a benchmark and evaluation for multi-task and meta reinforcement learning. CoRR abs/1910.10897 (2019). http://arxiv.org/abs/1910.10897

AI Applications in HCI

Evaluation of Webcam-Based Eye Tracking for a Job Interview Training Platform: Preliminary Results

Deeksha Adiani[1(✉)], Chang Qu[1], Timothy Gass[2], Sneha Gurram[2], Dylan LeMay[2], Ankit Bhusal[2], Medha Sarkar[2], and Nilanjan Sarkar[1]

[1] Vanderbilt University, Nashville, TN 37235, USA
deeksha.m.adiani@vanderbilt.edu

[2] Middle Tennessee State University, Murfreesboro, TN 37132, USA

Abstract. In job interviews, eye gaze towards the interviewer is an important non-verbal behavior that is considered a trait for hirability of a candidate. Several virtual job interview training platforms include eye trackers to measure eye gaze to provide feedback on performance. Though useful, these eye tracking devices are often pricey and not always accessible. In this article, we explore several camera-based eye tracking methods and implement a webcam-based eye tracking algorithm to determine its suitability for potential integration in virtual job interview simulation platforms. We further use the gaze predictions for interview relevant regions of interest detection. Our study with 12 participants, 7 with eyeglasses and 5 without, shows that during calibration, eyeglasses play no significant role in the differences in mean calibration error. Results from the ROI detection, however, show a limitation that it is important to maintain the same head position and distance during multiple tasks after calibration. Overall, webcam-based eye-tracking has potential, to be integrated in virtual job interview training environments.

Keywords: Webcam-based eye tracking · Human-computer interaction · Job interview simulator · Accessible computing

1 Introduction

The face-to-face job interview is an integral step in the process of obtaining employment [13]. Several factors are considered for a candidate's hirability, and an important non-verbal behavioral trait that is considered in several studies is a candidate's eye gaze towards the interviewer, including appropriate levels of eye contact [10,12,13,20]. Eye contact has been linked to the perception of competence, where a candidate's gaze towards an interviewer is perceived favorably [10]. Studies show that candidates who exhibited less eye contact were not favored by interviewers compared to those who showed more [15], and percentage of time for which an interviewee gazes at the interviewer has played a role in hirability [17]. Several career advisors also link eye contact to trust and active

H. Degen and S. Ntoa (Eds.): HCII 2022, LNAI 13336, pp. 337–352, 2022.
https://doi.org/10.1007/978-3-031-05643-7_22

listening [7,16], as well as presence of eye contact and interview outcomes [12]. Hence eye tracking is a useful mode of data collection in virtual interview training environments and in recent years, several virtual job interview platforms have emerged for practicing and training verbal as well as non-verbal interview skills to help potential candidates perform well in job interviews. Baur et al. [11] created a job interview simulation for training of interview related social skills, that automatically identifies non-verbal social cues, using input from a Microsoft Kinect camera, from hands (e.g., gesticulating), eyes (e.g., looking away), face (e.g., smile), and posture (e.g., leaning forward). Their social cue recognizer allows the virtual interviewer to the adapt to the user's behavior and emotions and provide end-of-session feedback on non-verbal behaviors. Virtual Speech [6] is a commercially available virtual public speaking and job interview simulation platform that provides real-time feedback on verbal responses and post-session feedback on the level of eye contact during a simulation when using a Virtual Reality (VR) headset. Xu et al. [27] created an augmented reality Google Glass application to assist with providing real-time feedback on speech volume as well as capture visual attention via head pose. Ahmed et al. [9] created a mixed reality job interview simulation that uses a VR head-mounted display (HMD) such as the Oculus Rift or HTC Vive with integrated eye trackers, to track the duration of breaking of eye gaze towards the virtual interviewer. Tian et al.'s simulator [23] captures eye movements of the interviewee via a VR HMD to predict social traits and interview performance via eye gaze.

Although the aforementioned tools provide useful feedback on gaze, they require the use of eye trackers and/or equipment (e.g., VR HMDs and Kinect cameras) that are not very accessible due to their cost, and oftentimes their need for technical assistance for setup. Recently, as more human-centered research is being conducted remotely, the use of cost-effective webcam-based eye tracking methods are being explored, where webcams used are the ones already present in personal devices such as laptops and tablets. In this article, we discuss methods of eye tracking explored that include video/image acquisition, feature extraction, and gaze mapping to determine the gaze point on the screen in the form of *(x, y)* coordinates. We expand the use of a webcam-based gaze prediction algorithm [18], an extension of [19] without pupil detection which has been benchmarked and has shown sufficient accuracy [22], to accurately measure gaze on regions of interest (ROI), and to determine if the eye tracking method is suitable for interview relevant ROI detection on a virtual interview environment. We conducted a study with 12 participants (7 with eye-glasses and 5 without) to determine whether the webcam-based eye tracking method is suitable for future integration in virtual job interview environments. Furthermore, we determine any significant difference in results between those who wore eyeglasses and those who did not. Our results show that we could detect eye gaze on relevant regions of interest (ROI) with this method, with a limitation of maintaining head position and distance throughout the experiment. Our findings also suggest that presence of eyeglasses solely does not play a role in hindering eye tracking, but rather the quality of eye images that can be taken in their presence (e.g., the more reflective the eyeglasses, the more obscure are the eye images that lead to higher mean prediction error). We further discuss some findings on this phenomenon in Sect. 5.

In Sect. 1.1, we discuss related work on camera-based eye tracking. Section 2 discusses the system architecture including a tool to create ROI experiments, and to conduct calibration and testing, which includes implementation of the gaze mapping and prediction algorithm. Section 3 discusses the experiment design with participants, calibration, and ROI detection, and Sect. 4 discusses the results from the experiment. Section 5 discusses some further interesting findings from the results, where we finally conclude this article with current limitations and future work.

1.1 Related Work

A literature survey was conducted to determine which method of camera-based eye tracking would be suitable for future integration in virtual job interview environments. Our search led to the discovery of articles and tools, that are summarized in Table 1. Zhu et al. [30] proposed a novel eye tracking method using dual cameras with infrared LEDs to capture a user's eye images and pupils. The gaze point, *(x, y)* coordinate on the screen, was determined by using the relative position of the pupil and the "glint" or speck of infrared (IR) light that is reflected from the eyes. They developed a nonlinear gaze mapping function using Support Vector Regression that achieves sufficient accuracy in gaze prediction under natural head movements. The authors further improved the method by introducing a 3D gaze estimation technique that models the cornea of the eyeball as a convex mirror and uses its properties to determine 3D gaze direction [29]. Yang et al. [28] developed a dual camera-based gaze mapping system to monitor a driver's non-driving activities whilst in a car. They extracted features from two cameras, where one was placed in front of the driver and above the dashboard to extract location and orientation of the face, and the second was placed across the top of the driver's head that was used to capture eye features for gaze estimation. Their gaze mapping function was able to identify non-driving activities such as watching a movie on a tablet, using the gaze prediction to detect marked ROI. Vargas-Cuentas et al. [24], developed an eye tracking algorithm which extracts facial features from frames of a video captured by an external webcam using the Viola-Jones object detection framework [25] and Haar features classifiers, and then extracts the left and right eye images as features for gaze prediction. They used the radius between the brightest pixels that belonged to left and right regions of the sclera to determine in which direction a participant was gazing-left, right, or center. If the left sclera region was less than or equal to the threshold value, the participant was gazing left. The authors showed that their algorithm using their tablet-based system, was able to predict gaze direction with sufficient accuracy. TurkerGaze by Xu et al. [26], is a webcam-based eye tracking tool that was developed to help collect large scale gaze data, which extracts left and right eye images from full facial images taken from a webcam (Logitech HD C720) using facial landmarking, where they map the features of each pair of eye images to a gaze point on the screen using Ridge Regression. Their method was compared against a commercial eye tracker, with 9-point calibration and validation performed at the start of the experiment, and their results show consistent mean error of 9.1 pixels every two blocks of calibration and validation. They achieved varying accuracy among participants since accuracy primarily depends on calibration, as well as maintaining head pose during experiments. The methods used in the aforementioned literature have been shown to estimate gaze points with relatively less errors, they use external cameras, often with infrared LEDs, which deviates from our aim of using integrated cameras.

Papoutsaki et al.'s [19] WebGazer, built on the concept of TurkerGaze [26], is a self-calibrating webcam-based eye tracking method for online browser-based studies, which uses pupil detections to estimate gaze linearly while also treating the left and right eye images as features. Since the tool is built for integration in web applications, the click coordinates, i.e., user interactions on a web browser, are used as ground truth for training, based on the assumption that where a person clicks, they look. The gaze is predicted using regularized linear regression, and their online study showed a mean error of 104 pixels. Semmelmann and Weigelt [22] expanded the use of WebGazer for online eye tracking studies in the context of cognitive psychology, where their in-lab and online studies gave a mean error of 172px and 207px, respectively, in a fixation task. Papoutsaki et el. [18], further adapted their own work, now called SearchGazer, for use in remote studies using integrated webcams. SearchGazer self-calibrates (or retrains) in real-time using user interactions and uses a regression model to map pixels from videos captured from the webcam for gaze predictions, using images of eyes only while excluding the pupil detection as was done previously. Their model achieved a mean error of 128.9px (1.6 in.), and although higher than the predecessor, it is sufficient when considering the study was conducted using integrated webcams.

Among the aforementioned literature and tools, the algorithm developed in [18] was most suited for our aim and was reproducible as a web-independent standalone application to which any client application could make API calls, in order to get gaze predictions. We further used the gaze predictions to identify marked ROI.

2 Method

To ease the process of creating ROI experiments for different tasks, we built a web application using the React framework [5] with three components: 1) the 9-point calibration interface (see Fig. 1.a); 2) an ROI experiment generator that allows a user to upload a screenshot of the virtual interview interface and select boxes that represent the areas or regions of interest that are stored as coordinates (see Fig. 1.b); and 3) a validation screen to test the accuracy of the ROI detection after calibration; The three components comprise the front-end of the application.

Table 1. Summaries of eye tracking related literature.

Literature	Aim	Equipment	Features	Results
Zhu et al. [30]	Novel eye tracking method that allows natural head movement	Dual infrared (IR) cameras	Images of eyes captured with "glint" reflected from IR light. Non-linear mapping function generated using Support Vector Machine	Approximately 1.5-degree higher gaze accuracy achieved under natural head movement
Zhu et al. [29]	Use eye anatomy to get gaze predictions. Propose two novel solutions to allow natural head movement and minimize calibration	Dual IR stereo cameras	Modelling the cornea of the eye as a convex mirror to develop 3D gaze tracking technique proposing a 2D gaze mapping function	Eye gaze estimation with higher accuracy, allowing natural head movement while minimizing the number of calibration procedures
Yang et al. [28]	Propose a low-cost and non-intrusive dual-cameras-based gaze tracking system for detection of a driver's non-driving activities	Two external video cameras	Head orientation, facial features, action units, eye direction	For the in-vehicle experiment, the mean square error for (x, y) coordinates is $(7.8 \pm 5.99, 4.64 \pm 3.47)$px with image resolution of 1440×1080 pixels
Vargas-Cuentas et al. [24]	To estimate gaze preference of children using an eye tracking algorithm for potential use in early screening of autism spectrum disorder	External webcam while looking at a tablet screen	No calibration required. Extracts eye images from facial images from a video and calculates the sclera pixels on the left and right of the iris, to estimate gaze preference	Spearman correlation of manual and automatic classification of frames as being left gaze or right gaze was 73.24%
Xu et al. [26]	TurkerGaze, a webcam-based gaze tracking system which supports large-scale crowdsourced eye tracking deployed on Amazon Mechanical Turk	Logitech HD C720 webcam	Facial landmark tracking (adjusted for accuracy using a Kalman Filter), eye region extraction, user task specific model training for calibration and gaze prediction using Ridge Regression	Mean error for every two blocks of testing (9-point calibration and validation) is 9.1px when compared with the predictions from a commercial eye tracking device (EyeLink 1000)
Papoutsaki et al. [19]	WebGazer, a tool for online eye tracking that uses common webcams integrated in laptops to infer gaze locations on a webpage in real-time	Integrated webcam	Extracts left and right eye images and pupil coordinates and uses it to generate feature vector for each gaze prediction using a Ridge Regression. User interactions (mouse clicks) are ground truth for training of the model	Mean error is 104px when compared with a commercial eye tracker (Tobii EyeX) in a remote online study
Papoutsaki et al. [18]	SearchGazer, an extension of WebGazer that performs eye tracking in real-time and self-calibrated in real-time using gaze-cursor user interactions	Integrated webcam	Extends the algorithm used by WebGazer, however, removes reliance on pupils for gaze tracking. Can evaluate page elements on web browsers for remote online studies	Mean error is 128.9px with an average visual angle of 4.17° or 1.6 in. when compared with the Tobii EyeX

A face detection library from OpenCV [3] was used to capture images of the face. For eye features extraction, we used the Dlib [1] facial landmarks library that marks the features of the face on the facial image as shown in Fig. 2. Using the markings around the eyes, we extracted left and right eye images that were preprocessed into a 120-dimension feature vector that would act as the input to the prediction algorithm. The gaze prediction algorithm from [18] was implemented in Python and served locally on a Flask [2] application running in the background to which the front-end web application (the client) sends API calls. The mouse click coordinates/cursor position were captured using PyAutoGUI [4], as we wanted to capture the actual screen coordinates and not the web browser coordinates, for offline as well as online use.

3 Experiment Design

3.1 Participants

$N = 12$ (age $M = 24.08$, $SD = 3.75$) participants were recruited for the study and signed consent were obtained from all participants before interacting with the application. Out of the 12, 7 wore prescription eyeglasses and 5 did not. A Surface Pro 7 with 4GB RAM and 128 GB SSD, with a 5.0MP front-facing camera that has 1080p full HD video and a screen resolution size (as detected by PyAutoGUI) of 2736 × 1824-pixel resolution, was used to run the experiment. The back-end and front-end applications were served locally, and the user interacted with the interface using a mouse. The user was seated at 63 cm from the front-facing camera and was requested to sit still. The seat was lowered to have their eyes to be roughly at level with the front-facing camera, and the device's kickstand was placed on the lowest setting to have it stand close to perpendicular to the table. We also kept a lit floor lamp in front of the user to provide ambient lighting for best results. A fixed image of a virtual environment from our previous work [8] was used for the experiment. The image had ROI

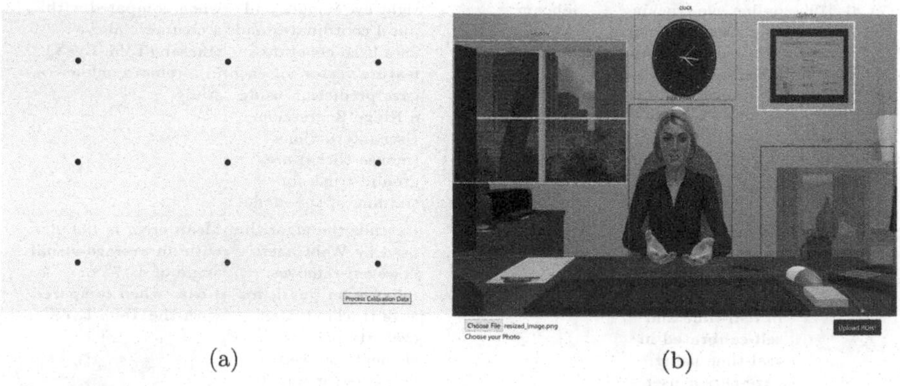

Fig. 1. a) 9-point calibration component; b) ROI selection component

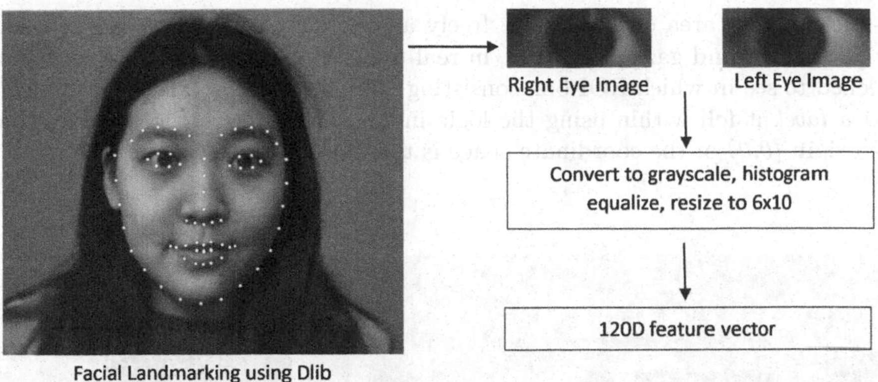

Fig. 2. The Dlib facial feature landmarks library is used to extract left and right eye images that are preprocessed, resized, and concatenated to form a 120D input vector.

marked and stored using Component 2 of the front-end interface, with a label (e.g., clock) and the top, bottom, left, and right coordinates of the ROI box. Below we discuss the method of collecting data from calibration, and how that is used for gaze prediction in ROI detection.

3.2 Calibration

The algorithm in [18] self-trains in real-time using the click coordinates from user interactions on a web browser. This was not relevant for the purpose of a job interview simulation as the user will be sitting idle while interacting with a virtual interviewer verbally, without mouse click interactions. Hence, the self-calibration feature was removed, and we chose the 9-point calibration method as was used in [26]. The user was asked to click on each dot 5 times, and 6 frames (images) per click were captured along with the *(x, y)* coordinates of the clicks/cursor position at the time. A total of 270 images were captured per calibration task, however, some images were discarded in the event where eye features were not detected from extracted images such as when the user blinked. The images were then preprocessed to fit in the gaze mapping algorithm from [18] to compute the weights for the x and y coordinates to be used for gaze prediction. The calibration error for each frame/feature vector was computed by predicting the gaze points *(x',y')* using the weight vector, and then calculating the Euclidean distance of the predicted point from the ground truth *(x,y)* in coordinate space. The average of all the errors were taken to be the final mean calibration error for each participant.

3.3 ROI Detection

To test the gaze predictions to see if they fall within the correct ROI box, the validation component of the front-end interface was used. The user was asked to click on any area on the image freely and 6 images of the face were taken for processing and gaze prediction, in real-time. The click coordinate *(x,y)* was checked to see in which ROI box consisting of lines (*top*, *bottom*, *left*, and *right*) and a *label*, it fell within using the logic in Algorithm 1 (see Fig. 3). Note that the origin *(0,0)* of the coordinate space is the top-left corner of the screen.

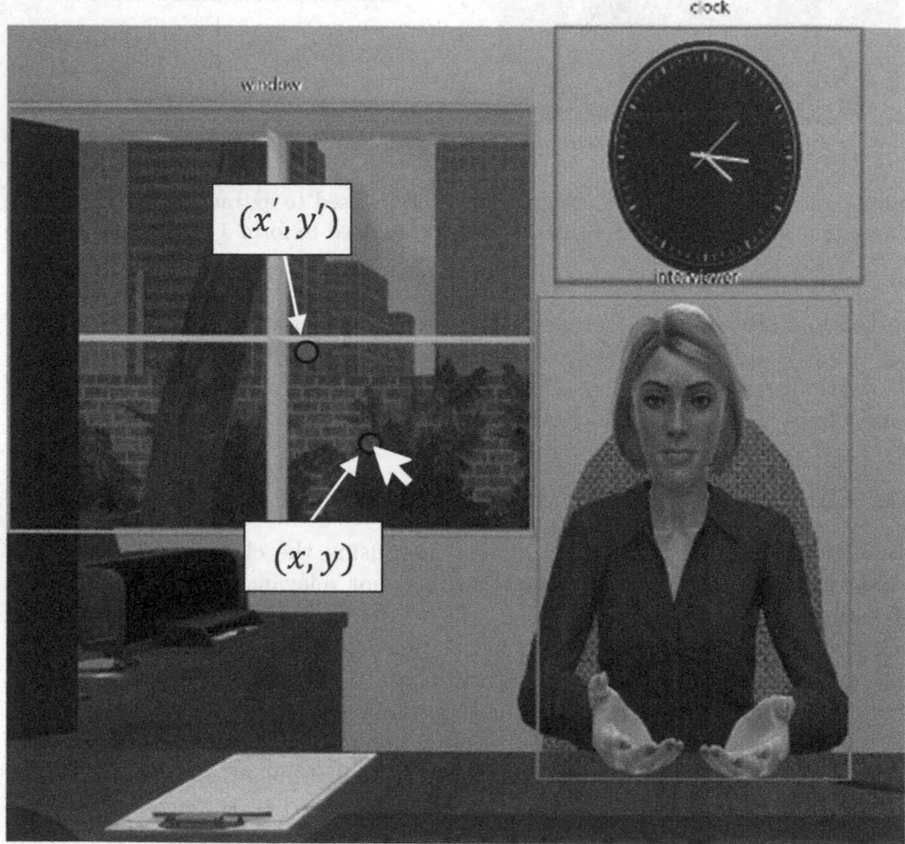

Fig. 3. If the predicted gaze point *(x', y')* is within the same ROI box that is labelled (e.g., window), as the click coordinate *(x, y)* then the ROI detected using Algorithm 1, is correct.

Algorithm 1. ROI detection code to check whether gaze point hits ROI

if $x \leq right$ and $x \geq left$ and $y \geq top$ and $y \leq bottom$ **then**
  $roi = label$
else
  $roi = "N/A"$
end if

4 Results

4.1 Calibration Task

The mean calibration error for all participants was 169.4 (SD = 76.4) pixels. The calibration results for each participant are shown in Table 2. The mean calibration error of participants with eyeglasses was found to be 195.7 (SD = 81.9) pixels and without glasses was 132.6 (SD = 48.1) pixels. We observe that the presence of eyeglasses does affect mean calibration error. However, there are some unusual results. Participants 4 and 6 have similar calibration errors, despite the fact that Participant 4 had eyeglasses on. Same can be observed in Participants 7 and 12 where the results are similar. Based on these observations, we hypothesized that presence of eyeglasses has no effect on calibration error and gaze prediction results because as long as clear eye images are detected for extracting eye features, the final gaze prediction should have sufficient accuracy. We conducted a two-sample, unpaired t-test on the results in Table 2 and found that there is no significant difference between the mean calibration errors of the group that wore eyeglasses and the group that did not ($t(10) = 1.532$, $p = 0.078$, where $p > 0.05$).

Table 2. Mean calibration error (in pixels) for all participants.

Type	Participants							
Eyeglasses	1	2	3	4	7	9	11	M(SD)
N = 7	325.5	127.6	285.0	72.4	205.8	149.7	204.2	195.7(81.9)
No eyeglasses	5	6	8	10	12			M(SD)
N=5	111.7	74.7	112.8	146.6	217.4			132.6(48.1)

Separating the mean calibration errors for each group per calibration point, however, we can see the difference in the distribution of mean errors per region or per calibration point (see Table 3 for results). Figure 4.a and 4.b show the difference in mean calibration error between each calibration region, and visually we can see that the error in pixels is less for the participants without eyeglasses. However, based on the results from Table 2, we know that the overall difference is not significant. This indicates that the mean calibration error is dependent on the quality of eye images taken, regardless of the presence of eyeglasses. Some further interesting findings are discussed in Sect. 5.

4.2 ROI Task

The pre-defined ROI were labelled using Component 2 of the tool and the areas were defined by the lines on the x-axis and y-axis. The x and y lines for the top, bottom, left, and right margins of each ROI box are given in Table 4. The ROI were erroneously stored with an offset, as the selected region on the ROI

Table 3. Mean calibration error (in pixels) for each calibration error, between two groups.

Region	Mean error (in pixels)	
	Eyeglasses N = 7	No eyeglasses N = 5
1	197.0	150.1
2	175.3	133.0
3	188.8	139.1
4	190.1	118.7
5	194.1	112.9
6	216.1	127.6
7	198.4	133.6
8	203.4	144.7
9	201.9	134.0

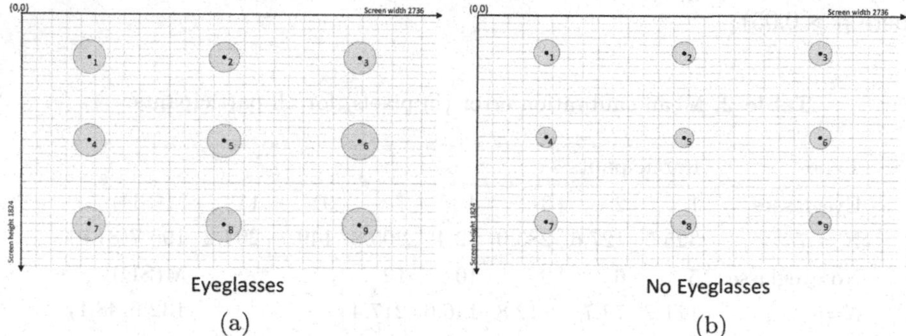

Fig. 4. Difference in distribution of mean calibration errors per region between groups; a) with eyeglasses (left); b) without eyeglasses (right).

generation tool had to be converted to the coordinates returned by PyAutoGUI for eye tracking to be performed on screen coordinates rather than webpage coordinates. Since that did not affect the task, we went with the stored ROI displayed in Fig. 5. Visually we can see that the overall predicted gaze points are scattered with a few gaze coordinates hitting the defined ROI boxes.

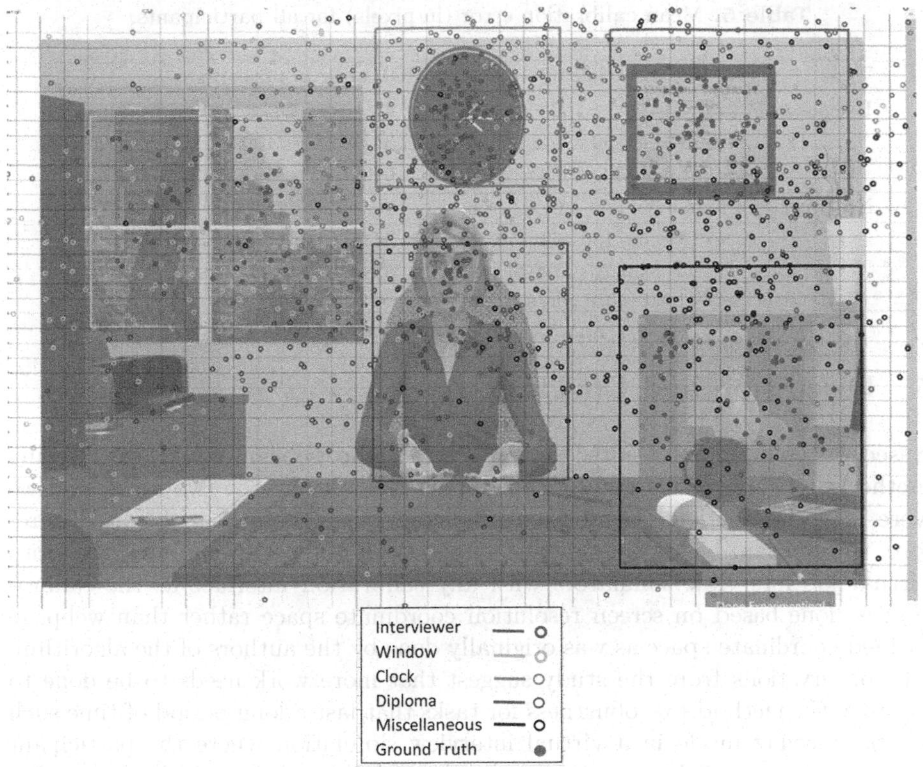

Fig. 5. Scatter plot on the experiment view with ROI boxes marked.

Table 5 shows the overall results from the two groups-with and without eyeglasses. We can see that the participant with the highest number of gaze predictions (out of 150 images) that led to correctly detected ROI when compared with ground truth click coordinates was the participant wearing eyeglasses, and the participant with the lowest calibration error in both groups had varying ROI scores. The results have been discussed further in the section below.

Table 4. ROI labels and their markers in coordinate space.

Label	Top(y1=)	Bottom(y2=)	Left(x1=)	Right(x2=)
Interviewer	771	1418	1112	1700
Window	323	957	271	1088
Clock	61	539	1123	1679
Diploma	68	577	1828	2540
Miscellaneous	782	1680	1852	2574

Table 5. Mean calibration error (in pixels) for all participants.

Type	Participants (detected ROI; error in pixels)						
Eyeglasses N = 7	1	2	3	4	7	9	11
	5/150	6/150	57/150	34/162[a]	6/150	78/150	32/150
	1539.6	1053.2	418.6	549.9	1359.1	428.2	669.9
No Eyeglasses N = 5	5	6	8	10	12		
	53/150	62/150	11/150	34/150	64/150		
	433.6	749.8	900.7	628.2	428.8		

[a] Participant performed more clicks in one region.

5 Discussion and Conclusion

Based on preliminary results, we can see that the webcam-based eye tracking method was able to successfully capture eye gaze during the two tasks, and we were also able to detect ROI from predicted gaze points in real-time. Therefore, the webcam-based eye tracking method can potentially be integrated into virtual job interview simulators with any calibration interface as the calibration is done based on screen resolution coordinate space rather than webpage defined coordinate space as was originally done by the authors of the algorithm. Our observations from the study suggest that more work needs to be done to improve the method for robustness for tasks that last a long period of time such as free viewing mode in a virtual interview simulation where the participant views the screen with no accompanying mouse interactions, and gaze predictions occur in real-time under natural head movement. Our study revealed some interesting findings from the individual tasks. The calibration results in Sect. 4 visually look different between the two groups of participants, however, the *t*-test suggested that the overall difference is not significant and the high mean calibration errors (>150 px) present in both groups indicate that the presence of eyeglasses does not have a significant effect on the mean calibration error for a participant. The mean calibration error for participants 4 and 6 were similar, and among the eyeglasses group, the mean calibration error varied. We further investigated this phenomenon. Figure 6 shows images focused on the eyes of Participants 1, 3, and 4 with their corresponding mean calibration errors. We can see that each of the participants are wearing eyeglasses that reflect light differently. For Participant 1, the lamp was turned on, and their eyeglasses were very reflective, therefore proper feature extraction was not possible. Participant 1's left eye image shows some indication of the iris, which is why the feature extraction algorithm accepted it as a valid image, but it is obscured, hence, the error was high. For Participant 3, the lamp was turned off and the eye images were extracted, however, they were dark and lacked the presence of the "glint". The image of Participant 3 also shows the presence of the reflection of the screen, however that did not affect eye image extraction. Participant 4 had the lowest mean calibration error among all seven participants wearing eyeglasses. The lamp was on for Participant 4, and their eye features were captured clearly as the eyeglasses were least reflective. This implies that the quality of eyeglasses plays a role, i.e., how reflective they are. Another observation shows that participants' eye sizes vary across the images where Participant 3 appears to have smaller eyes than Participant 4, which implies that height of the person and distance of 1–2 in. on either side of 63 cm may cause differences in the size of eye images captured which, in turn, may affect calibration error.

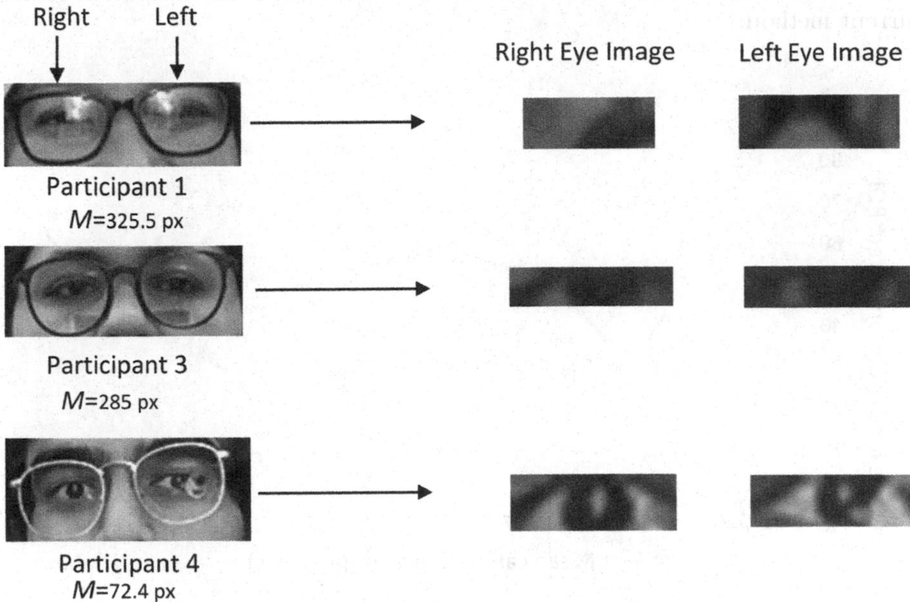

Fig. 6. Eye images from three participants showing how reflection affects feature extraction.

From the ROI task results, we note some observations. Participant 9, who wore prescription eyeglasses, had the highest ROI detection score from gaze predictions (78/150), and their mean calibration error was 149.7px. Their results support the conclusion from the calibration task that presence of eyeglasses has no effect on gaze predictions, and ultimately ROI detection. Participant 4, on the other hand, had the lowest calibration error of 72.4px. However, during the ROI task, their score was a low 34/162. Further, Participant 7 had a mean calibration error of 205.7px, but their ROI score was 6/150. This may be because the participant got up to leave thinking the experiment was over. We reseated them at the same distance, however, by then the potential of better gaze prediction was lost. Participant 4 had also moved back after the calibration. We plotted the results of the mean calibration error verses the number of predictions (see Fig. 7) and we can see that the mean calibration errors do not always correlate to higher ROI scores. Participants 12 and 6 had the next highest ROI scores where the mean calibration errors were 217.4px and 74.7px respectively. This was perhaps because Participant 12 and Participant 6 had maintained their position throughout the two blocks (calibration task and ROI task). Hence, in order for this version of eye tracking to provide predictions with sufficient accuracy, the participant needs to maintain the same position throughout the study, and in the future, in a virtual practice job interview. Since in reality, while an interviewee speaks to virtual interviewer, they may move their head around and will often not be conscious of their level of movement. Hence, this is one limitation of the current method.

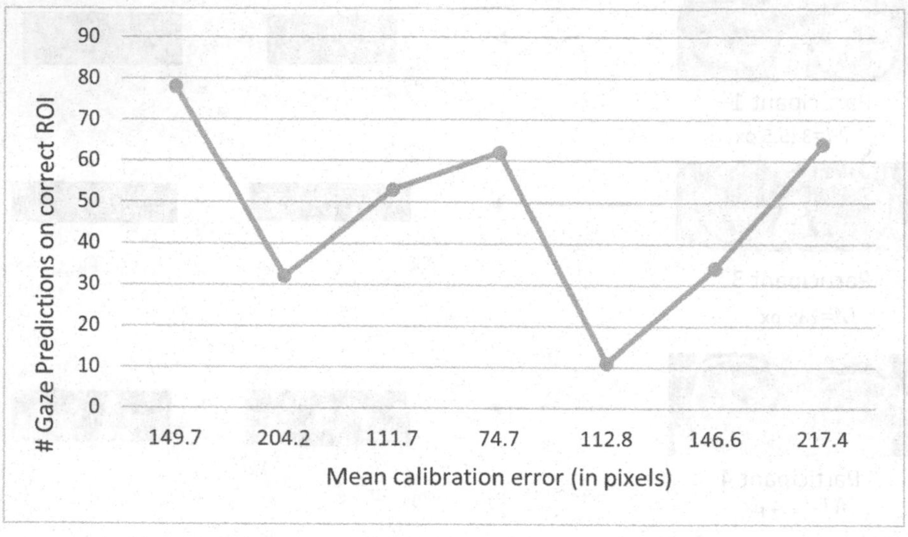

Fig. 7. Line chart of the mean calibration error verses the number of gaze predictions that fall with-in correct ROI

Despite the aforementioned limitations and observations, webcam-based eye tracking has potential in the area of virtual job interview simulators in providing gaze information and having an accessible method such as cost-effective integrated webcam-based eye tracking can make that possible. The results reported in this article are with a small sample size and are preliminary. Future work includes testing the method with an actual virtual interview simulation using our novel tool CIRVR [8] to understand the performance of this eye tracking method under natural head movement while the participant speaks. Additional calibration on ROI using the ROI task, before free viewing of the interview interface may lead to improved ROI detection, and this investigation will be part of the above-mentioned study. We will explore several error correction methods such as Kalman Filter [14] and Extended Kalman Filter [21] on the gaze prediction value, in order to improve the gaze prediction results. We will also explore higher frame rates (>6 images per click) to see for variation in prediction results.

Overall, this preliminary study has provided us with insights on how to proceed with future work.

References

1. Dlib. https://pypi.org/project/dlib/. Accessed 1 Mar 2022
2. Flask. https://flask.palletsprojects.com/en/2.0.x/. Accessed 1 Mar 2022
3. OpenCV on Wheels. https://pypi.org/project/opencv-python/. Accessed 1 Mar 2022
4. PyAutoGUI. https://pyautogui.readthedocs.io/en/latest/. Accessed 1 Mar 2022
5. React - a javascript library for building user interfaces. https://reactjs.org/. Accessed 1 Mar 2022
6. Virtual Speech. https://virtualspeech.com/. Accessed 1 Mar 2022
7. How to improve your eye contact (2021). https://www.indeed.com/career-advice/career-development/eye-contact. Accessed 1 Mar 2022
8. Adiani, D., et al.: Career interview readiness in virtual reality (CIRVR): a platform for simulated interview training for autistic individuals and their employers. ACM Trans. Accessible Comput. **15**, 1–28 (2022)
9. Ahmed, S., et al.: InterViewR: a mixed-reality based interview training simulation platform for individuals with autism. In: 2020 IEEE 44th Annual Computers, Software, and Applications Conference (COMPSAC), pp. 439–448 (2020). https://doi.org/10.1109/COMPSAC48688.2020.0-211
10. Anderson, N.R.: Decision making in the graduate selection interview: an experimental investigation. Human Relat. **44**(4), 403–417 (1991). https://doi.org/10.1177/001872679104400407
11. Baur, T., Damian, I., Gebhard, P., Porayska-Pomsta, K., André, E.: A job interview simulation: social cue-based interaction with a virtual character. In: 2013 International Conference on Social Computing, pp. 220–227 (2013). https://doi.org/10.1109/SocialCom.2013.39
12. Forbes, R.J., Jackson, P.R.: Non-verbal behaviour and the outcome of selection interviews. J. Occup. Psychol. **53**, 65–72 (1980). https://doi.org/10.1111/j.2044-8325.1980.tb00007.x
13. Gifford, R., Ng, C.F., Wilkinson, M.: Nonverbal cues in the employment interview: links between applicant qualities and interviewer judgments. J. Appl. Psychol. **70**(4), 729–736 (1985). https://psycnet.apa.org/doi/10.1037/0021-9010.70.4.729
14. Kalman, R.E.: A new approach to linear filtering and prediction problems. Trans. ASME-J. Basic Eng. **82**(Ser. D), 35–45 (1960). https://doi.org/10.1115/1.3662552
15. McGovern, T.V., Tinsley, H.E.: Interviewer evaluations of interviewee nonverbal behavior. J. Vocat. Behav. **13**(2), 163–171 (1978). https://doi.org/10.1016/0001-8791(78)90041-6
16. McKeever, V.: How much eye contact is too much in a job interview? (2020). https://www.cnbc.com/2020/03/11/how-much-eye-contact-is-too-much-in-a-job-interview.html. Accessed 1 Mar 2022
17. Nguyen, L.S., Frauendorfer, D., Mast, M.S., Gática-Pérez, D.: Hire me: computational inference of hirability in employment interviews based on nonverbal behavior. IEEE Trans. Multimedia **16**(4), 1018–1031 (2014). https://doi.org/10.1109/TMM.2014.2307169

18. Papoutsaki, A., Laskey, J., Huang, J.: SearchGazer: webcam eye tracking for remote studies of web search. In: CHIIR 2017, pp. 17–26. Association for Computing Machinery, New York, NY, USA (2017). https://doi.org/10.1145/3020165.3020170
19. Papoutsaki, A., Sangkloy, P., Laskey, J., Daskalova, N., Huang, J., Hays, J.: WebGazer: scalable webcam eye tracking using user interactions. In: Proceedings of the 25th International Joint Conference on Artificial Intelligence (IJCAI), pp. 3839–3845. AAAI (2016)
20. Parsons, C.K., Liden, R.C.: Interviewer perceptions of applicant qualifications: a multivariate field study of demographic characteristics and nonverbal cues. J. Appl. Psychol. **69**(4), 557–568 (1984). https://doi.org/10.1037/0021-9010.69.4.557
21. Ribeiro, M.I.: Kalman and extended Kalman filters: concept, derivation and properties. Inst. Syst. Robot. **43**, 46 (2004)
22. Semmelmann, K., Weigelt, S.: Online webcam-based eye tracking in cognitive science: a first look. Behav. Res. Methods **50**(2), 451–465 (2017). https://doi.org/10.3758/s13428-017-0913-7
23. Tian, F., Okada, S., Nitta, K.: Analyzing eye movements in interview communication with virtual reality agents. In: Proceedings of the 7th International Conference on Human-Agent Interaction, pp. 3–10, HAI 2019. Association for Computing Machinery, New York, NY, USA (2019). https://doi.org/10.1145/3349537.3351889
24. Vargas-Cuentas, N.I., et al.: Developing an eye-tracking algorithm as a potential tool for early diagnosis of autism spectrum disorder in children. PLOS ONE **12**(11), e0188826 (2017). https://doi.org/10.1371/journal.pone.0188826
25. Viola, P., Jones, M.: Rapid object detection using a boosted cascade of simple features. In: Proceedings of the 2001 IEEE Computer Society Conference on Computer Vision and Pattern Recognition, CVPR 2001, vol. 1, p. I-511 (2001). https://doi.org/10.1109/CVPR.2001.990517
26. Xu, P., Ehinger, K.A., Zhang, Y., Finkelstein, A., Kulkarni, S.R., Xiao, J.: TurkerGaze: crowdsourcing saliency with webcam based eye tracking. CoRR abs/1504.06755 (2015). http://arxiv.org/abs/1504.06755
27. Xu, Q., Cheung, S.C.S., Soares, N.: LittleHelper: an augmented reality glass application to assist individuals with autism in job interview. In: 2015 Asia-Pacific Signal and Information Processing Association Annual Summit and Conference (APSIPA), pp. 1276–1279 (2015). https://doi.org/10.1109/APSIPA.2015.7415480
28. Yang, L., Dong, K., Dmitruk, A.J., Brighton, J., Zhao, Y.: A dual-cameras-based driver gaze mapping system with an application on non-driving activities monitoring. IEEE Trans. Intell. Transp. Syst. **21**(10), 4318–4327 (2020). https://doi.org/10.1109/TITS.2019.2939676
29. Zhu, Z., Ji, Q.: Novel eye gaze tracking techniques under natural head movement. IEEE Trans. Biomed. Eng. **54**(12), 2246–2260 (2007). https://doi.org/10.1109/TBME.2007.895750
30. Zhu, Z., Ji, Q., Bennett, K.: Nonlinear eye gaze mapping function estimation via support vector regression. In: 18th International Conference on Pattern Recognition (ICPR 2006), vol. 1, pp. 1132–1135 (2006). https://doi.org/10.1109/ICPR.2006.864

A Systematic Review of Artificial Intelligence and Mental Health in the Context of Social Media

Xing Chen and Yegin Genc(✉)

Pace University, New York, NY 10038, USA
{xc86008n,ygenc}@pace.edu

Abstract. Objective: We conducted a systematic review on the use of Artificial Intelligence (AI) in the psychology domain within the context of social media's role on mental health. We identified the types of mental health studies that AI has supported, reviewed the machine learning methods in these studies, and reported on the different approaches for data collection. We provided a critical review of the applicability of these methods in real-world settings. Finally, we discussed the challenges faced in this area of study and provided advice for other researchers interested in solving these issues in the future.

Methods: We collected our data from three outlets: ACM, JMIR, and CLPsych. We focused on the studies on the application of AI in clinical psychology in the past six years (2016 to 2021).

Results: A total of 37 articles were included in our study for further review. The number of publications increased over time. While CLPsych has the highest number of articles, Reddit was the commonly used social media site for data collection. Suicide was the most mentioned mental disorder mentioned in the studies. SVM was the most frequently used approach when applying AI in mental health studies.

Conclusion: Our review of the existing literature identified three issues on the topic. First, social media is underutilized for mental health care. Second, there is a lack of collaboration between seemingly disconnected research communities: i.e., machine learning experts and clinicians. Third, little attention is paid to humans when conducting the research.

Keywords: Artificial intelligence · Social media · Mental health · Psychology · Machine learning · Clinical

1 Introduction

46.4% of all adults worldwide have been reported to experience mental health issues at a certain point in their lives [1]. 18.5% of the adults in the US have mental health issues [1], and 14.3% of deaths worldwide are attributable to such illness [2]. Although such dire statistics reveal the prevalence of mental health issues, the existing mental health support remains inefficient [3]. Since mental health can have a substantial influence on

H. Degen and S. Ntoa (Eds.): HCII 2022, LNAI 13336, pp. 353–368, 2022.
https://doi.org/10.1007/978-3-031-05643-7_23

matters, such as education access and poverty alleviation, it has been included in the agenda of the United Nations Sustainable Development Goals along with efforts from the World Bank, International Monetary Fund, and World Health Organization (WHO) [2].

The recent advancement of AI has led researchers to explore its potential in supporting mental health [4]. Notably, there is a growing interest in the field of Human-Computer Interaction (HCI) to utilize AI for comprehending and predicting how individuals express mental illness in online settings [2], study the experiences of the vulnerable population [5], and design clinical interventions [2]. Different machine learning algorithms are currently being applied to or even replace the traditional analytic procedures in many domains, including health care [6].

The studies on AI applications in healthcare generally rely on electronic healthcare data collected through doctors, patients, and pharmacists [7]. While the same can be used in mental health-related initiatives, social media has gained considerable attention to model mental well-being [8], partly because new computational methods have successfully detected behavioral and linguistic cues from social media [9]. In fact, compared to the traditional on-site meetings with clinicians, social media serves as a highly accessible and efficient communication tool for people with mental illness [10]. Some clinicians would review relevant insights from the patient's social media activities, such as the number of depression-indicative posts while interviewing a patient [7]. Still, given the heavy usage of the Internet worldwide, social media, despite its potential, is arguably highly underutilized [6] when it comes to medical concerns [11].

This research aims to conduct a systematic review on the use of Artificial Intelligence (AI) in the psychology domain within the context of social media's role on mental health. Our paper is organized as follows: we continue with the reporting on the methodology used to conduct this systematic review. Next, we explain the findings of our study. Finally, we discuss the issues on this topic and provide guidelines for future research in this area of study.

2 Method

2.1 Data Selection

We used the Association for Computing Machinery (ACM), Journal of Medical Internet Research (JMIR), and Workshop on Computational Linguistics and Clinical Psychology (CLPsych) as search engines to retrieve relevant literature.

Since AI in mental health is of interest to various communities – i.e., computer scientists and clinical psychologists, we decided to include results from three different outlets that focus on computational, clinical, and interdisciplinary aspects of AI in mental health. Relevant HCI work primarily emphasize issues around technical issues or issues around the use of such technology. Clinical studies, on the other hand, focus on health-related outcomes. Therefore, we believe these three outlet types provide significant coverage of studies on the topic. Mainly, we selected the Association for Computing Machinery database that stores the publications from the leading conferences on computer scientists and machine learning; Journal of Medical Internet Research which serves as one of the largest digital libraries for health researchers; and the Workshop on Computational

Linguistics and Clinical Psychology which is considered as a critical interdisciplinary resource for machine learning, natural language processing, and mental health.

The articles included in our study were characterized by: 1) artificial intelligence or machine learning techniques, 2) mental health studies, 3) the use of social media data. In addition, due to the rapid development and change of machine learning applications, we decided to focus on the latest studies. We restricted the research to the period from the year 2016 to 2021. Note that the search results below were conducted and finalized by January 2, 2022.

2.2 Query Selection

We derived a list of keywords to describe the topic of our study and combined them into a query:

"Artificial intelligence" OR "AI" OR "machine learning" AND "mental health" OR "mental disorder" OR "mental illness" OR "mental wellness" OR "mental disease" OR "psychology" OR "psychiatry" AND "social media" OR "social network"

However, after trying different combinations of search terms, we decided to narrow it down into three keywords: "artificial intelligence," "social media," and "mental health" because this combination gave us the closest search result to our study. Finally, we used the query "artificial intelligence" AND "social media" AND "mental health" for ACM, JMIR, and CLPsych to retrieve relevant studies.

2.3 Articles Selection

The entire process of our database searching was done through 3 stages (see Fig. 1 for details). This flowchart also shows the number of articles screened, reviewed, included, and excluded during each step, along with the reasons for exclusion.

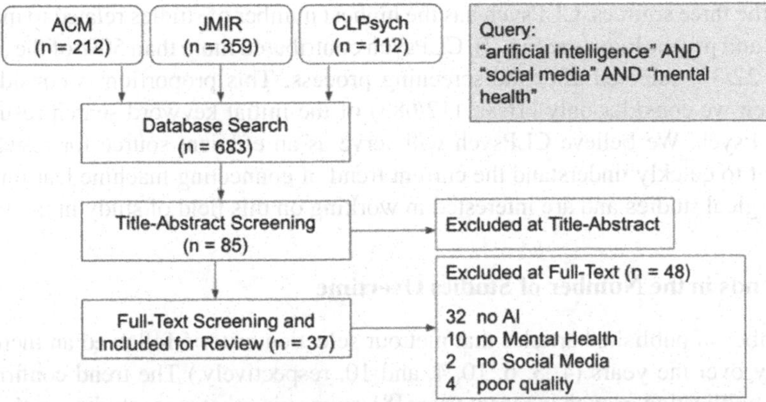

Fig. 1. A flowchart for screening articles with the query from three databases and the reasons for exclusion

Stage 1: Keyword Search. From running the query separately in three databases, we identified 683 articles in total, from which 212 papers were from ACM, 359 pieces were from JMIR, and 112 articles were from CLPsych.

Stage 2: Title-Abstract Screening. We screened the relevance of articles identified by reviewing the titles and abstracts. First, the two authors reviewed randomly selected 20 papers separately and compared their findings to evaluate the inter-rater reliability. After confirming high inter-rater reliability (Cronbach's alpha = 0.82), the first author completed the screening process. Of the 683 articles, 85 articles were selected for full-text screening: 22 from ACM, 24 from JMIR, and 39 from CLPsych.

Stage 3: Full-Text Screening. We reviewed the full text for the 85 articles selected in stage 2 based on the abovementioned criteria (see Sect. 2.1). Thirty-two articles did not mention the application of machine learning techniques. Since our goal was to review the most recent and novel machine learning techniques created by field experts, we eliminated these studies on plain discussion and review of machine learning theories. We focused on the studies tested on machine learning methods in practice. There were two articles that did not include the use of social media data. Due to the wide range of utilizing AI in mental health treatment, we decided to solely focus on social media settings. We ruled out the data collected from other sources, such as clinical interviews, questionnaires, etc. Ten articles did not specifically focus on the analysis of mental health treatment. Also, there were four articles that were of poor quality due to the lack of deep analysis. As a result, we derived 37 papers that were used to conduct our final study.

3 Results

3.1 Sources in Which the Studies Were Published

Among the three sources, CLPsych has the highest number of studies related to machine learning and psychology (see Fig. 2). CLPsych contributed more than 50% of the articles (59.5%, 22/37) selected after the screening process. This proportion is considerably high when we consider only (16%, 112/683) of the initial keyword search results are from CLPsych. We believe CLPsych will serve as an efficient source for researchers who want to quickly understand the current trend of connecting machine learning with psychological studies and are interested in working on this field of study in the future.

3.2 Trends in the Number of Studies Overtime

The number of published articles that met our selection criteria followed an increasing trajectory over the years (4, 3, 6, 10, 4, and 10, respectively.) The trend confirms the reported publication growth in recent years [8], suggesting that more studies on this topic can be published in the following years. Figure 3 shows the overall trend in the number of publications per outlet during the past six years, from 2016 to 2021. The breakdown by outlet suggests the increasing tendency to be steeper in CLPsych.

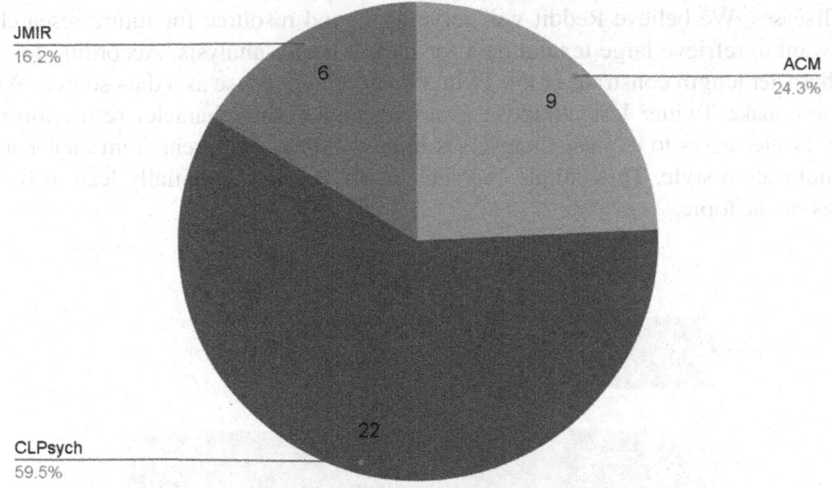

Fig. 2. The number of articles in each search engine and its corresponding percentage

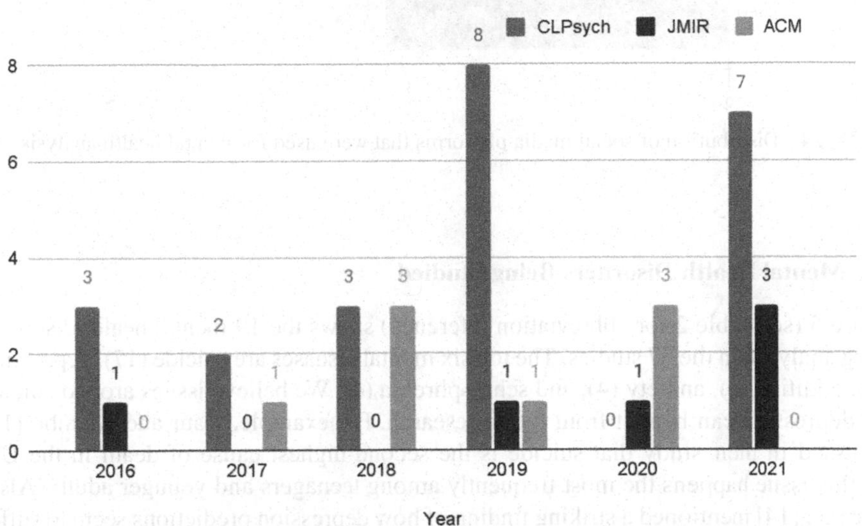

Fig. 3. The trend in the number of studies per outlet over six years

3.3 Social Media Platforms Being Analyzed

Three social media platforms were being studied in the 37 articles that met our selection criteria (see Sect. 2.1). Figure 4 is mainly based on the number of times each platform was being analyzed and used to retrieve data for further study. In 19 articles, Reddit was the data source for mental health studies, followed by Twitter (11) and mental health forums (4). In their research, Glaser and Morain [12] mentioned that Reddit is the 6th most visited platform in the US. The entire platform is made by subreddits based on topics ranging from news and politics to personal issues, such as relationships, finances, and diseases. We believe Reddit will serve as a good resource for future researchers who want to retrieve large textual data for mental health analysis. According to [13], the character length constrain of the Twitter space limits its use as a data source. While this may make Twitter less attractive as a data source, this character restriction may cause Twitter users to express themselves in a way that is different from their natural communication style. This unique character of Twitter can potentially lead to further studies on the topic.

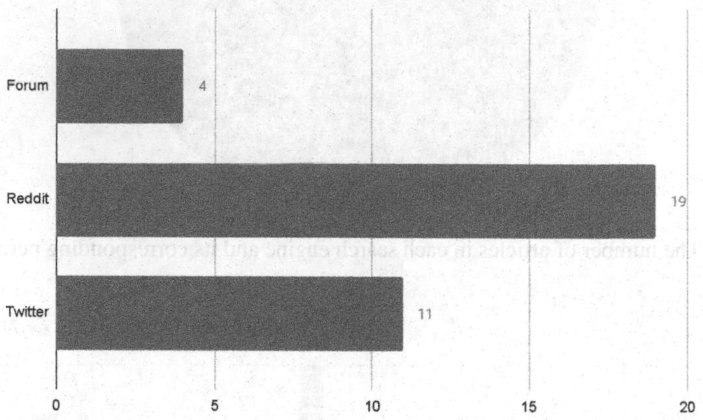

Fig. 4. Distribution of social media platforms that were used for mental health analysis

3.4 Mental Health Disorders Being Studied

Figure 5 (see Table 2 for abbreviation reference) shows the 19 mental health disorders being analyzed in the 37 studies. The top six mental diseases are suicide (17), depression (10), addition (4), anxiety (4), and schizophrenia (4). We believe issues around suicide and depression can benefit from future research. For example, Gaur and Alambo [14] discussed in their study that suicide is the second-highest cause of death in the US, and this issue happens the most frequently among teenagers and younger adults. Also, Sherman [14] mentioned a striking finding of how depression predictions seem to suffer from gender biases. For instance, women were overdiagnosed with depression because the key features that identify depression are more tuned for one gender, not the other. We hope future researchers are aware of those issues when conducting their studies.

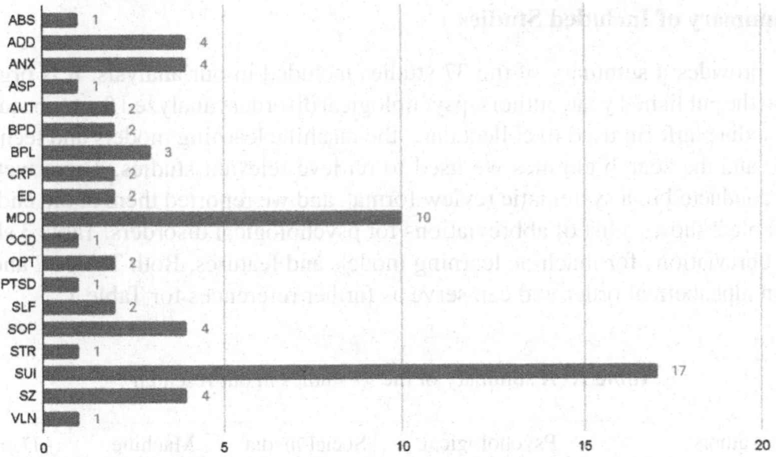

Fig. 5. The number of times each mental health disorder shown in the studies

3.5 Machine Learning Models and Features Being Applied

Notably, as shown in Fig. 6 (see Table 3 for abbreviation reference), the top five frequent approaches utilized when applying machine learning in the mental health domain are SVM (20), RF (12), CNN (9), LIWC (9) and LSTM (8). In the next section, we further discuss the trends on the models, social media sites, and the psychological disorder being studied from each article.

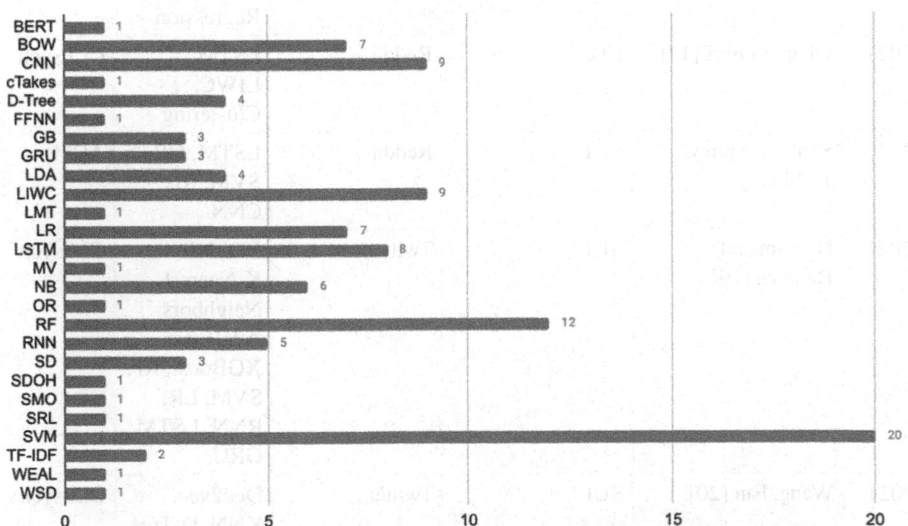

Fig. 6. The number of times each model and feature used in the study

3.6 Summary of Included Studies

Table 1 provides a summary of the 37 studies included in our analysis. It is organized based on the published year, authors, psychological disorders analyzed for each study, the social media platform used to collect data, the machine learning models and techniques applied, and the search engines we used to retrieve relevant studies. There were four studies conducted in a systematic review format, and we reported them at the end of the table. Table 2 shows a list of abbreviations for psychological disorders. Table 3 shows a list of abbreviations for machine learning models and features. Both Tables 2 and 3 are sorted in alphabetical order and can serve as further references for Table 1.

Table 1. A summary of the 37 studies in our research

Year	Authors	Psychological disorders	Social media platform	Machine learning models and features	Database
2021	Jiang, Zomick [15]	OCD, SZ, BPD, PTSD, ED, MDD, ANX, BPL	Reddit	N-Grams, LIWC, NB	CLPsych
2021	Sherman, Harrigian [16]	MDD	Reddit	BOW, N-Grams, LIWC, TF-IDF, Regression	CLPsych
2021	Uban, Chulvi [17]	ED	Reddit	LSTM, LIWC, Clustering	CLPsych
2021	Shah, Sawhney, Joshi [18]	SUI	Reddit	LSTM, OR, SVM, RF, CNN	ACM
2021	Bayram and Benhiba [19]	SUI	Twitter	MV, NB, K-Nearest Neighbors, AdaBoost, XGBoost, RF, SVM, LR, RNN, LSTM, GRU	CLPsych
2021	Wang, Fan [20]	SUI	Twitter	Doc2vec, KNN, D-Tree, RF, LR, SVM	CLPsych

(*continued*)

Table 1. *(continued)*

Year	Authors	Psychological disorders	Social media platform	Machine learning models and features	Database
2021	Gollapalli, Zagatti [21]	SUI	Twitter	GloVE, LDA, LSTM	CLPsych
2020	Glaser, Morain [12]	SUI	Reddit	Word2Vec, Clustering, BOW, N-Grams	ACM
2020	Xue, Chen [22]	VLN, ABS, SUI	Twitter	LDA	JMIR
2020	Skaik and Inkpen [23]	MDD	Twitter	LIWC, SVM, LR, RF, GB, XGBoost	ACM
2019	Cacheda, Fernandez [24]	MDD	Reddit	RF	JMIR
2019	Mohammadi, Amini [25]	SUI	Reddit	GloVe, ELMo, CNN, RNN, LSTM, GRU, SVM	CLPsych
2019	Ruiz, Shi [26]	SUI	Reddit	cTakes, SDOH, WEAL, spaCy, SRL, NB, GB, RF, SVM, CNN, LSTM	CLPsych
2019	Allen, Bagroy [27]	SUI	Reddit	CNN, GloVe, LIWC	CLPsych
2019	Zomick, Levitan [13]	SZ	Reddit	LIWC	CLPsych
2019	Bitew, Bekoulis [28]	SUI	Reddit	N-Grams, LR, Ensemble, SVM	CLPsych
2019	Chen, Aldayel [29]	SUI	Reddit	LIWC, Clustering, RF, SVM	CLPsych
2019	Ríssola, Ramírez-Cifuentes [30]	SUI	Reddit	BOW, N-Grams, GloVe, LR, SVM, RF	CLPsych
2019	Ambalavanan, Jagtap [31]	SUI	Reddit	BERT, Word2Vec, LSTM, RNN, CNN	CLPsych

(continued)

Table 1. *(continued)*

Year	Authors	Psychological disorders	Social media platform	Machine learning models and features	Database
2019	Gaur, Alambo [14]	SUI, MDD	Reddit	SVM, RF, FFNN, CNN	ACM
2018	Altszyler, Berenstein [32]	SOP	Mental Health Forum ReachOut.com	Word2Vec, N-Grams, SVM	CLPsych
2018	Ive, Gkotsis [33]	BPD, BPL, SZ, ANX, MDD, SLF, SUI, ADD, CRP, OPT, AUT	Reddit	CNN, RNN	CLPsych
2018	Gaur, Kursuncu [34]	ADD, CRP, ANX, OPT, ASP, OPT, AUT, SZ, SLF, BPL, SUI	Reddit	N-Grams, RF, Ensemble, TF-IDF	ACM
2018	Sadeque, Xu [35]	MDD	Reddit	SVM, BOW, GRU	ACM
2018	Husseini Orabi, Buddhitha [36]	MDD	Twitter	CNN, RNN, Word2Vec, N-Gram, BOW, LSTM, SVM	CLPsych
2018	Pillai, Thelwall [37]	STR	Twitter	WSD, AdaBoost, NB, D-Tree, LR, SVM	ACM
2017	Shen and Rudzicz [38]	ANX	Reddit, Twitter	Word2Vec, Doc2Vec, BOW, SVM, CNN, LR, LDA, LIWC, N-Gram	CLPsych
2017	Jamil, Inkpen [39]	MDD	Twitter	BOW, SVM	CLPsych
2017	Yazdavar, Al-Olimat [40]	MDD	Twitter	LDA, NB, SVM, Clustering	ACM
2016	Almeida, Queudot [41]	SOP	Mental Health Forum ReachOut.com	N-Grams, POS tags, SD, NB, SMO, SVM, LMT	CLPsych
2016	Malmasi, Zampieri [42]	SOP	Mental Health Forum ReachOut.com	N-Grams, SVM, RF, D-Tree,	CLPsych

(continued)

Table 1. (*continued*)

Year	Authors	Psychological disorders	Social media platform	Machine learning models and features	Database
2016	Asgari, Nasiriany [43]	SOP	Mental Health Forum ReachOut.com	RF, SVM	CLPsych
2016	Braithwaite, Giraud-Carrier [10]	SUI	Twitter	LIWC, D-Tree	JMIR
2021	Yoo, Ernala [7]	–	–	Review	JMIR
2021	Le Glaz, Haralambous [4]	–	–	Review	JMIR
2021	Kim, Lee [8]	–	–	Review	JMIR
2020	Skaik and Inkpen [5]	–	–	Review	ACM

Table 2. A list of abbreviations for psychological disorders

Abbreviation	Description
ABS	Abuse
ADD	Addiction
ANX	Anxiety
ASP	Asperger
AUT	Autism
BPD	Borderline Personality Disorder
CRP	Crippling Alcoholism
ED	Eating Disorder
MDD	Major Depressive Disorder
OCD	Obsessive-Compulsive Disorder
OPT	Opiates
PTSD	Post-Traumatic Stress Disorder
SLF	Self-Harm
SOP	Severity of Posts
STR	Stress
SUI	Suicide
SZ	Schizophrenia
VLN	Violence

Table 3. A list of abbreviations for the machine learning models and techniques

Abbreviation	Description
BERT	Bidirectional Encoder Representations from Transformers
BOW	Bag of Words
CNN	Convolutional Neural Network
cTakes	Clinical Text Analysis and Knowledge Extraction System
D-Tree	Decision Tree
FFNN	Feed-Forward Neural Network
GB	Gradient Boosting
GRU	Gated Recurrent Unit
LDA	Latent Dirichlet allocation
LIWC	Linguistic Inquiry and Word Count
LMT	Logistic Model Tree
LR	logistic regression
LSTM	Long Short-Term Memory Network
MV	Majority Voting
NB	Naive Bayes
OR	Ordinal Regression
RF	Random Forest
RNN	Recurrent Neural Network
SD	Sentiment Dictionary
SDOH	Social Determinants of Health
SMO	Sequential Minimal Optimization
SRL	Semantic Role Labeling
SVM	Support Vector Machine
TF-IDF	Term Frequency and Inverse Document Frequency
WEAL	Word-Emotion Association Lexicon
WSD	Word Sense Disambiguation

4 Discussion

Our review of the existing literature identified three major issues on the topic.

4.1 The Use of Social Media Data is Underutilized for Mental Care

Our study confirms the increasing interest in utilizing social media data on mental care (Fig. 3). These studies commonly explore the use of social media platforms to examine an individual's mental health status, understand health outcomes [11] and provide adequate support for users with mental health issues [3]. In this emerging area, researchers combine the use of machine learning techniques (e.g., natural language processing) with clinical psychology for various predictive tasks (e.g., categorizing individuals' moods and detecting perceived well-being from social media data [11]). The benefit of combining computational strategies and those newly available Internet data could be profound for improving mental health prediction, preventing and advancing mental health globally [6]. For example, by extracting the behavior and linguistic features from social media data, some researchers in computer science can predict the presence of specific psychological disorders and symptoms, such as depression, suicidality, eating disorder, anxiety, schizophrenia, etc. with an accuracy rate of around 80–90% [11].

Moreover, studies show that 81% of young Americans, ages 18–24, engage with social media daily. These are the typical ages that suffer many mental health conditions, such as anxiety and mood disorders [3]. Therefore, an accurate prediction and timely intervention at this critical period of age may have a tremendous impact on the younger generations and save the future of our society.

4.2 The Lack of Collaboration Between Seemingly Disconnected Research Communities

With the fast pace of artificial intelligence research, the community leaves little room for providing valid results and a lack of reflection in the methods applied to identify psychological states; therefore, clinicians may not adopt those predictive models for their patients [11]. Among the 37 articles included in our study, only two articles [34, 44] mentioned that the evaluations were matched with the clinical standards. [34] introduced a novel method that followed the DSM-5 (Diagnostic and Statistical Manual of Mental Disorders – 5th Edition) guidelines and used a multi-class classifier to match subreddits with DSM-5 categories. Yazdavar, Al-Olimat [44] showed a potential for detecting the symptoms of depression, which emulates the PHQ-9 questionnaire used by clinicians nowadays. Their semi-supervised statistical model evaluated the duration and expression of those depression symptoms from Twitter and matched them with the medical findings from the PHQ-9. However, the rest of the 35 articles did not mention the medical community's involvement when evaluating their results. Therefore, we recommend that future research on this subject consider involving subject matter expertise for their model validity. Like many socio-technical issues of AI (i.e., explainable AI) [7], the practical implications of AI in mental health can be decoupled from their technical operationalizations and be evaluated by healthcare experts. Such efforts, however, require the collaboration between machine learning experts and clinicians.

4.3 The Lack of Attention to the Human Factors When Conducting the Research

Only eight articles [4, 5, 7, 8, 13, 16–18] mentioned the ethical considerations for AI and mental health. We highlight the lack of attention to human factors as ethical issues may have cascading effects. For example, skipping treatment, one of the significant concerns in mental health treatment, is attributed to the negative social stigma received from disclosing patients' mental conditions [3]. Due to the high sensitivity of this field of study, we believe future researchers should be required to handle the task carefully and not harm the research participants during the process. Additionally, machine learning experts may fail to consider the patients' needs; instead, the patients are often treated as inputs for training data which is used for building model and result optimization [9]. We want to remind future researchers that patients have the right to fair and sensitive treatment. In their study, Chancellor, Baumer [9] mentioned that it is critical to remember that a human is both a data provider, the object of machine learning techniques, and a beneficiary who should be centered and prioritized during the research.

5 Conclusions

We have reported our review of the literature on AI and mental in the context of social media. Our study found 37 relevant articles after a manual review of 683 articles. Our analysis shows an increasing trend in the number of studies on the topic. Our findings suggest three potential areas that research can grow. First, we see evidence that social media data, a popular data source in AI, is under-utilized in the context of mental health. Second, there is room for more collaboration between the machine learning community and practitioners. And third, the human factors in data collection, which is deemed a technical issue, are often overlooked. We think further research on any of these topics can advance the use of AI in mental wellness. Finally, our study is not without limitations. Although we think the selected outlets represent the existing research, it is not exhaustive. Therefore, our finding, although valid, may not be complete. If a wider net is cast for outlet selection, other issues and trends may emerge from the analysis.

References

1. Calvo, R.A., et al.: Computing in mental health. In: Proceedings of the 2016 CHI Conference Extended Abstracts on Human Factors in Computing Systems, pp. 3438–3445. Association for Computing Machinery, San Jose (2016)
2. Pendse, S.R., et al.: Mental health in the global south: challenges and opportunities in HCI for development. In: Proceedings of the 2nd ACM SIGCAS Conference on Computing and Sustainable Societies, pp. 22–36. Association for Computing Machinery, Accra (2019)
3. Blair, J., Abdullah, S.: Supporting constructive mental health discourse in social media. In: Proceedings of the 12th EAI International Conference on Pervasive Computing Technologies for Healthcare, pp. 299–303. Association for Computing Machinery, New York (2018)
4. Le Glaz, A., et al.: Machine learning and natural language processing in mental health: systematic review. J. Med. Internet Res. **23**(5), e15708 (2021)
5. Skaik, R., Inkpen, D.: Using social media for mental health surveillance: a review. ACM Comput. Surv. (CSUR) **53**(6), 1–31 (2020)
6. Haines-Delmont, A., et al.: Testing suicide risk prediction algorithms using phone measurements with patients in acute mental health settings: feasibility study. JMIR Mhealth Uhealth **8**(6), e15901 (2020)

7. Yoo, D.W., et al.: Clinician perspectives on using computational mental health insights from patients' social media activities: design and qualitative evaluation of a prototype. JMIR Mental Health **8**(11), e25455 (2021)
8. Kim, J., Lee, D., Park, E.: Machine learning for mental health in social media: bibliometric study. J. Med. Internet Res. **23**(3), e24870 (2021)
9. Chancellor, S., Baumer, E.P., De Choudhury, M.: Who is the "human" in human-centered machine learning: the case of predicting mental health from social media. In: Proceedings of the ACM on Human-Computer Interaction, vol. 3 (CSCW), pp. 1–32 (2019)
10. Braithwaite, S.R., et al.: Validating machine learning algorithms for twitter data against established measures of suicidality. JMIR Mental Health **3**(2), e21 (2016)
11. Chancellor, S., De Choudhury, M.: Methods in predictive techniques for mental health status on social media: a critical review. NPJ Digit. Med. **3**(1), 1–11 (2020)
12. Glaser, E., et al.: Comparing automatically extracted topics from online suicidal ideation and the responses they invoke. In: Proceedings of the 35th Annual ACM Symposium on Applied Computing, pp. 1818–1825. Association for Computing Machinery (2020)
13. Zomick, J., Levitan, S.I., Serper, M.: Linguistic Analysis of Schizophrenia in Reddit Posts. Association for Computational Linguistics, Minneapolis (2019)
14. Gaur, M., et al.: Knowledge-aware assessment of severity of suicide risk for early intervention. In: The World Wide Web Conference (2019)
15. Jiang, Z., et al.: Automatic Detection and Prediction of Psychiatric Hospitalizations from Social Media Posts. Association for Computational Linguistics (2021)
16. Sherman, E., et al.: Towards Understanding the Role of Gender in Deploying Social Media-Based Mental Health Surveillance Models. Association for Computational Linguistics (2021)
17. Uban, A.S., Chulvi, B., Rosso, P.: Understanding Patterns of Anorexia Manifestations in Social Media Data with Deep Learning. Association for Computational Linguistics (2021)
18. Sawhney, R., et al.: Towards ordinal suicide ideation detection on social media. In: Proceedings of the 14th ACM International Conference on Web Search and Data Mining (2021)
19. Bayram, U., Benhiba, L.: Determining a Person's Suicide Risk by Voting on the Short-Term History of Tweets for the CLPsych 2021 Shared Task. Association for Computational Linguistics (2021)
20. Wang, N., et al.: Learning Models for Suicide Prediction from Social Media Posts. Association for Computational Linguistics (2021)
21. Gollapalli, S.D., Zagatti, G.A., Ng, S.-K.: Suicide Risk Prediction by Tracking Self-Harm Aspects in Tweets: NUS-IDS at the CLPsych 2021 Shared Task. Association for Computational Linguistics (2021)
22. Xue, J., et al.: The hidden pandemic of family violence during COVID-19: unsupervised learning of tweets. J. Med. Internet Res. **22**(11), e24361 (2020)
23. Skaik, R., Inkpen, D.: Using twitter social media for depression detection in the Canadian population. In: 2020 3rd Artificial Intelligence and Cloud Computing Conference (2020)
24. Cacheda, F., et al.: Early detection of depression: social network analysis and random forest techniques. J. Med. Internet Res. **21**(6), e12554 (2019)
25. Mohammadi, E., Amini, H., Kosseim, L.: CLaC at CLPsych 2019: Fusion of Neural Features and Predicted Class Probabilities for Suicide Risk Assessment Based on Online Posts. Association for Computational Linguistics, Minneapolis (2019)
26. Ruiz, V., et al.: CLPsych2019 Shared Task: Predicting Suicide Risk Level from Reddit Posts on Multiple Forums. Association for Computational Linguistics, Minneapolis (2019)
27. Allen, K., et al.: ConvSent at CLPsych 2019 Task A: Using Post-level Sentiment Features for Suicide Risk Prediction on Reddit. Association for Computational Linguistics, Minneapolis (2019)

28. Bitew, S.K., et al.: Predicting Suicide Risk from Online Postings in Reddit the UGent-IDLab Submission to the CLPysch 2019 Shared Task A. Association for Computational Linguistics, Minneapolis (2019)
29. Chen, L., et al.: Similar Minds Post Alike: Assessment of Suicide Risk Using a Hybrid Model. Association for Computational Linguistics, Minneapolis (2019)
30. Ríssola, E., et al.: Suicide Risk Assessment on Social Media: USI-UPF at the CLPsych 2019 Shared Task. Association for Computational Linguistics, Minneapolis (2019)
31. Ambalavanan, A.K., et al.: Using Contextual Representations for Suicide Risk Assessment from Internet Forums. Association for Computational Linguistics, Minneapolis (2019)
32. Altszyler, E., et al.: Using Contextual Information for Automatic Triage of Posts in a Peer-Support Forum. Association for Computational Linguistics, New Orleans (2018)
33. Ive, J., et al.: Hierarchical Neural Model with Attention Mechanisms for the Classification of Social Media Text Related to Mental Health. Association for Computational Linguistics, New Orleans (2018)
34. Gaur, M., et al.: Let me tell you about your mental health!: contextualized classification of Reddit posts to DSM-5 for web-based intervention. In: Proceedings of the 27th ACM International Conference on Information and Knowledge Management, pp. 753–762. Association for Computing Machinery, Torino (2018)
35. Sadeque, F., Xu, D., Bethard, S.: Measuring the latency of depression detection in social media. In: Proceedings of the Eleventh ACM International Conference on Web Search and Data Mining (2018)
36. Husseini Orabi, A., et al.: Deep Learning for Depression Detection of Twitter Users. Association for Computational Linguistics, New Orleans (2018)
37. Pillai, R.G., Thelwall, M., Orasan, C.: Detection of Stress and Relaxation Magnitudes for Tweets. In: Companion Proceedings of the Web Conference 2018, pp. 1677–1684. International World Wide Web Conferences Steering Committee, Lyon (2018)
38. Shen, J.H., Rudzicz, F.: Detecting Anxiety Through Reddit. Association for Computational Linguistics, Vancouver (2017)
39. Jamil, Z., et al.: Monitoring Tweets for Depression to Detect At-risk Users. Association for Computational Linguistics, Vancouver (2017)
40. Yazdavar, A.H., et al.: Semi-supervised approach to monitoring clinical depressive symptoms in social media. In: Proceedings of the 2017 IEEE/ACM International Conference on Advances in Social Networks Analysis and Mining 2017 (2017)
41. Almeida, H., Queudot, M., Meurs, M.-J.: Automatic Triage of Mental Health Online Forum Posts: CLPsych 2016 System Description. Association for Computational Linguistics, San Diego (2016)
42. Malmasi, S., Zampieri, M., Dras, M.: Predicting Post Severity in Mental Health Forums. Association for Computational Linguistics, San Diego (2016)
43. Asgari, E., Nasiriany, S., Mofrad, M.R.K.: Text Analysis and Automatic Triage of Posts in a Mental Health Forum. Association for Computational Linguistics, San Diego (2016)
44. Yazdavar, A.H., et al.: Semi-supervised approach to monitoring clinical depressive symptoms in social media. In: Proceedings of the 2017 IEEE/ACM International Conference on Advances in Social Networks Analysis and Mining 2017, pp. 1191–1198. Association for Computing Machinery, Sydney (2017)

Object Size Prediction from Hand Movement Using a Single RGB Sensor

Maria Dagioglou[1(✉)], Nikolaos Soulounias[1,2], and Theodoros Giannakopoulos[1]

[1] National Centre for Scientific Research 'Demokritos', Neapoleos 27 and Patriarchou Grigoriou E, 153 41 Ag. Paraskevi, Attica, Greece
mdagiogl@iit.demokritos.gr

[2] National and Kapodistrian University of Athens, Panepistimiopolis, 157 72 Ilissia, Attica, Greece

Abstract. Human intention prediction is essential, among others, for safe and fluent human-robot collaboration. Prediction of the intention from human movement offers the advantage of a context-free paradigm. Naturally, such robot capabilities require high spatial and temporal resolution. While certain sensing devices, such as the motion capture systems, satisfy these requirements, in many applications visual sensors might be preferable. However, the information regarding human movement from RGB-D cameras is noisy and of lower frequency. In the present work, we study if it is possible to predict human intentions from hand movements observed by a single RGB-D sensor. We collected data from eight participants as they were grasping objects of three different sizes. OpenPose was used to extract the 2D hand and arm joint pixel coordinates that were then processed to extract human movement kinematic information and engineer appropriate features. Traditional machine learning methods were applied to evaluate the usability of our dataset. Overall, the results were significantly above chance level and showed that it is possible to predict the size of the object a human intents to grasp using hand kinematics extracted from a single visual sensor. Finally, it is feasible, under certain conditions, to use this prediction in real-time human-robot collaboration.

Keywords: Human action prediction · Human intention recognition · User studies · Datasets · Machine learning · Robot vision · Human-robot interaction · Human-robot collaboration

1 Introduction

Human movement prediction can considerably boost the behaviour of intelligent agents in many human-computer interaction applications. For example, in virtual

This work was partially supported by the 'Stavros Niarchos Foundation' Industrial Post-Doc Fellowship of NCSR 'Demokritos' on *HRC: Human Collaborator Representation for Robot Autonomous Decisions.*

H. Degen and S. Ntoa (Eds.): HCII 2022, LNAI 13336, pp. 369–386, 2022.
https://doi.org/10.1007/978-3-031-05643-7_24

reality environments the prediction of future interactions can compensate for computational delays and improve user experience [9]. In the case of human-robot interaction, robots need to be able to anticipate human behaviour in order to plan and act without jeopardizing the safety of the interaction [14]. Especially during human-robot collaboration (HRC), the prediction of human behaviour is crucial not only for safety reasons but also for enabling fluency of actions and efficiency [2]. Human motion prediction can allow robots to timely perform motion re-planning [18], select their actions [19], etc.

The problem of prediction is undoubtedly a popular one; a recent survey on human motion trajectory prediction lists over 200 methods [22], focusing on the prediction of ground-level 2D trajectories alone. This number is indicative of the challenges related to the problem. Firstly, people behave in variable ways within unstructured environments. This makes the generalization of the methods to other people, tasks and environments very demanding. Moreover, the methods used for prediction are constrained by real-time operation requirements.

In the context of HRC, where a human and a robotic arm collaborate in a common workspace, short-time predictions are needed in real-time. Although task information and scene understanding are essential to support robot prediction capabilities, information regarding the movement kinematics can also be exploited. Models that describe biological movement, like the minimum-jerk or the two-thirds power law [28] have been used to this end. For example, in [19] a minimum-jerk-based prediction of reaching movements was used for proactive robot decision making.

The models mentioned above, work well with end-point reaching movements but fail with more complicated ones [23]. Moreover, many prediction methods are bound to the tasks studied and cannot be generalized. To tackle this issue, [15] present a system that includes a velocity-based position projection, time series classification and a sequence prediction in order to predict human motion without making any assumptions about the type of the tasks or the motions.

The scenarios in the previous studies comprise goal-oriented movements, where the task of prediction is focused on anticipating future trajectories. However, recent neuroscientific behavioural research shows that movement kinematics are affected over time by the intrinsic properties of the objects [1], as well as from action intention; one can reach to grasp a bottle with the intention to drink from it or pour its content to a glass [4]. Recognizing the *intention from movement* [32] can not only complement motion trajectory prediction but also higher-lever robot cognitive capabilities.

Having accurate short-time predictions in real-time depends on both the spatial and temporal resolution of the available data. At many experimental set-ups, human movement is tracked via motion capture systems [1,15,18]. However, at a HRC environment the installation of such a system might not be a choice. Instead, a single camera is preferable; the set-up is easier, the human movement is not obstructed by any wearable components and the related cost is considerably lower. However, visual information, 2D and especially 3D, lacks the accuracy of the information collected with a motion capture system. Moreover, the frames per second are usually lower when using a camera and they can drop further if a library like OpenPose [3] is used in real-time to extract skeletal data.

The goal of the present work was to study whether it is possible to predict human intention from movements described by noisy skeletal data, which were extracted from visual information. Moreover, we wanted to assess the feasibility of integrating this information in a real-time robotics system. The paper is structured as follows: Sect. 2 reviews the related work and Sect. 3 summarizes our contributions. In Sect. 4 we present our methods. The results are reported in Sect. 5. We discuss our findings in Sect. 6 and conclude in Sect. 7.

2 Related Work

Object Size Prediction from Hand Kinematics. Our work is based on the paradigm presented in [1]. In this work participants reached to grasp two objects of different sizes. Their movements were recorded using a motion capture system at 100fps. A set of kinematic variables was used as features in a Support Vector Machine model. The results showed that the target size was correctly classified shortly after the movement onset, while a 100% accuracy was achieved from the 60% of the movement completion onward.

OpenPose Data for Prediction. As mentioned in the introduction, the use of a single camera can be a requirement in many HRC environments. One way to exploit visual data would be to develop computer vision methods based directly on the raw information [26,32]. Alternatively, visual information can be used to extract skeletal data and use these to approximate movement kinematic variables. OpenPose (OP) [3] is a state-of-the-art *open and real-time* library to detect the pixel positions of the human joints using a single camera, and several robot operating system (ROS) wrappers are also available[1]. OP has been exploited in many different human-robot interaction applications recently, including its use for robot teleoperation [21], for learning from demonstration [8], in robotic-assisted and rehabilitation environments [11], for user detection in the field of social robotics [10] and in a real-time human robot competitive game of reaching objects [27].

Skeleton Human-Action Datasets. NTU RGB-D 60 [24] is a human-action dataset, which provides 3D skeletal data and contains 60 action classes. The dataset was further extended to NTU RGB-D 120 [16] with 60 extra action classes added. Some of the action classes involve the interaction of the subject with an object (e.g. put on a hat/cap, tear up paper) and some do not (e.g. make victory sign, hand waiving). The video samples of the datasets were captured by three Microsoft Kinect V2 cameras concurrently and the 3D locations of 25 full body joints are provided for each frame of the videos. Similarly to NTU RGB-D, Kinetics-400 [13] is another large-scale human-action dataset, which contains 400 distinct action classes, a percentage of which are characterized as Person-Object Actions (e.g. opening present, mowing lawn, washing dishes). In [30] the

[1] https://github.com/firephinx/openpose_ros.

2D skeletal data of 18 full body joints were extracted using OP [3] and made publicly available in the Kinetics-Skeleton dataset. Skeleton-based approaches [5–7,17,25] on these datasets focus on the task of action recognition, where the full information of the video is available. While the task of early action prediction is also explored [12,29], multiple data modalities are fused together (RGB, depth, skeletal data).

3 Contribution

In the present work we used a *single RGB-D sensor* to record participants while grasping objects of different size based on [1]. The OpenPose library was used to extract the 2D hand and arm joint pixel coordinates that were further processed to calculate human movement kinematic information and engineer appropriate features. The usability and the quality of our dataset for human action prediction was evaluated by applying traditional machine learning methods. Our contributions are summarized below:

- We present a publicly available dataset[2] that contains the OpenPose 2D pixel coordinates of the upper body joints (torso, arms and hands) of *eight* participants during 715 grasping movements towards three objects of different sizes. We also report the processing of the dataset in order to evaluate relevant kinematic variables and to engineer machine learning (ML) features. The pre-processing code is also available (see footnote 2).
- We evaluate the suitability of our dataset for human movement prediction by using traditional ML methods. We consider two different feature sets (workspace-dependent or not) and two dataset split strategies at different movement completion percentages.
- We evaluate the feasibility of applying the methods in real-time considering the motion capabilities of a UR3 collaborative robot (cobot).

4 Methods

4.1 Raw Data Collection

Eight participants took part in the data collection (age range = 23–44 years old; 5 females). They were all right-handed, with normal or corrected-to-normal vision, and with no history of either psychiatric or neurological disorders. All participants provided a written consent after being informed about the procedures of the data collection and the data management.

Participants were seated on a height-adjustable stool so that their elbow and wrist rested on a black table (width: 120 cm, depth: 80 cm). The tips of the right thumb and index were held together on a marked point (see Fig. 1). Starting always from this point, participants were instructed to move in a natural way and reach, grasp, pick up, and move a cubic object to a pre-defined point.

[2] https://github.com/Roboskel-Manipulation/object_size_prediction.

Figure 2 demonstrates the entire movement of a participant; the frames of the first row belong to the reach-to-grasp (R-t-G) part of the movement, while the frames in the second row show the pick-up-and-move (P-n-M) the object part of the executed movement. The object was placed 42 cm away form the fingers' starting point and its final location was 30 cm to the left of its initial position. Three different cubic objects were used with different edge size es: a) a 'large cube' (es = 7.5 cm), b) a 'medium cube' (es = 5.5 cm) and c) a 'small cube' (es = 2.5 cm) (Fig. 1). Each participant completed 9 separate blocks of 10 trials, grasping each cube 30 times in total. The order of the blocks was randomly chosen by the experimenter. Each participant was also given a few practice trials to each object.

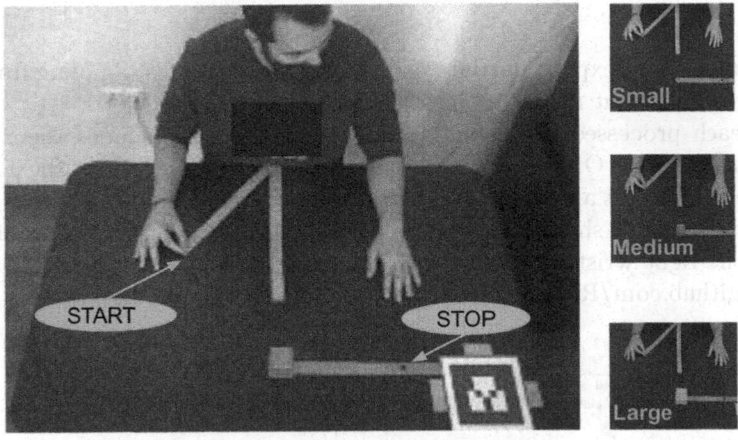

Fig. 1. The data collection set-up as captured by the data collection camera and the three objects used.

An ASUS Xtion pro was used to collect raw visual information (sampling frequency: 60 fps, resolution: 640 × 480). The camera was placed at a height of around 138 cm from the table's surface and it was maximally tilted to approximate a bird's eye view of the table. Figure 1 shows the data collection set-up from the point of view of the camera. Each movement was recorded in a separate rosbag for further processing. The augmented reality (AR) marker depicted in Figs. 1 and 2 is not exploited in the context of the present work. The visual information was used to track the human joint positions via OpenPose [3][3]. The output of OP comprises the 2D joint pixels and a related probability. Depending on the GPU used, the joint information becomes available at a considerably lower frequency compared to the camera's sampling frequency. For example, OP output is available at 22 Hz when a Quadro RTX 4000 is used [8]. To overcome

[3] https://github.com/Roboskel-Manipulation/openpose_3D_localization.

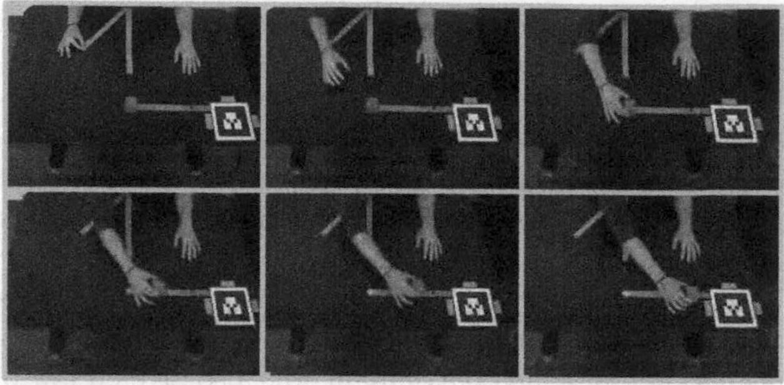

Fig. 2. Each movement of the dataset consists of two major parts: the *reach-to-grasp* part (1st row) and the *pick-up-and-move* the object part (2nd row).

this limitation and exploit the data collected at the camera's sampling frequency, a rosbag service that reads one message at a time was used[4].

For each processed movement (rosbag) our dataset includes the 2D pixel information of the OP library and the related probabilities for the following joints: left and right arms (wrist, elbow, shoulder), neck, mid hip, and right and left hands. Figure 3 shows an example of the 2D pixel information produced by OP for the right wrist during an entire movement. The dataset is available at: https://github.com/Roboskel-Manipulation/object_size_prediction.

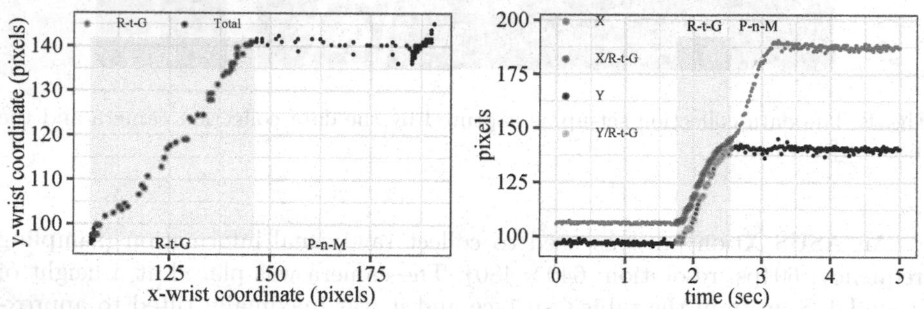

Fig. 3. A right wrist movement (OpenPose pixel coordinates): in space (left) and across time (right). The reach-to-grasp (R-t-G) and pick-up-and-move (P-n-M) parts of the movement are shown approximately within the green and yellow shaded areas, respectively. The points outside the shaded areas correspond to the resting hand periods at the beginning and end of the movement. (Color figure online)

4 https://github.com/Roboskel-Manipulation/bag_read_service.

4.2 Data Processing and Movement Kinematics Variables

The 2D OP information of the arm and the hand joints was used to compute a number of movement kinematic variables that were then exploited to engineer appropriate features as inputs for the ML methods. Two main pre-processing steps were applied to the dataset before computing any kinematic variable; a) filtering of the OP pixel noise and b) isolation of the pixels that corresponded to the R-t-G part of movement.

Two noise filtering criteria were applied initially only to the y-coordinate pixels of the right wrist joint. The reason for treating initially only the y-pixel wrist information was related to the use of this variable for the isolation of the movement of interest (see below). Firstly, any OP keypoint that had an associated probability $p_w < 0.6$ was removed. Moreover, the keypoints that were 10 pixels apart from their previous and next point were also filtered. The information for the rest of the joints in the frames that satisfied the above criteria was also discarded. In total, 0.9% of the frames were filtered and 97.7% of them corresponded to the periods before and after the R-t-G movement. Both criteria were defined after inspecting and observing our dataset.

As discussed earlier, each movement comprises two main parts: the reach-to-grasp (R-t-G) part and the pick-up-and-move (P-n-M) part (Figs. 1 and 3). Moreover, each movement recording includes two resting periods, at the beginning and the end of the action (Fig. 3). However, for the purposes of the present work we only needed the R-t-G part after movement onset.

To isolate the R-t-G part of the movement we initially considered the velocity of the *right wrist* [1] (both the x- and y- component, as well as the speed). However, these data were quite noisy (Fig. 4). Instead, we considered, as an approximation of the velocity, the standard deviation of the right wrist y-coordinate keypoints (Fig. 3, black points in the right plot), in a sliding window of ten points std_{10}. The std_{10} of the movement in Fig. 3 is shown in the right plot of Fig. 4.

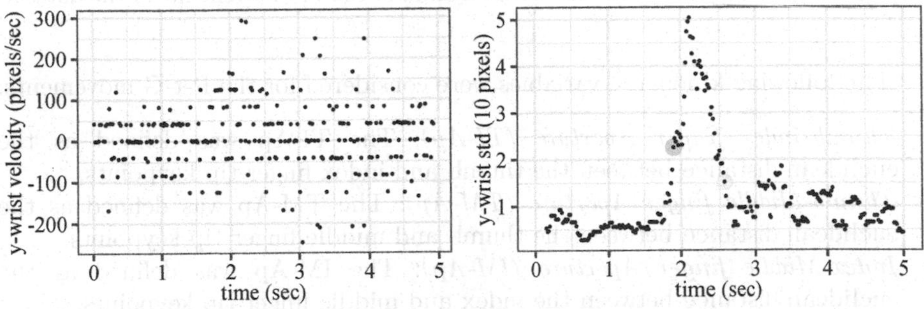

Fig. 4. The velocity in y-axis (left) and the std_{10} of the y-coordinate pixels (right) of the movement presented in Fig. 3. The highlighted points in the std_{10} plot correspond to the points where the onset (red) and end (blue) of movement criteria are activated. (Color figure online)

The following rules were defined after experimentation and were applied for extracting the R-t-G part of the movement:

- *R-t-G movement onset*: The first frame was defined as the last frame of the 10 frames window for which the std_{10} was greater than 2 pixels (for the first time).
- *R-t-G movement end*: The last frame (just before grasping) was defined as the penultimate frame of the 10 frames window for which the std_{10} dropped below 1.5 pixels (for the first time) after the occurrence of the std_{10} global maximum.

The red highlighted points in all the plots of Fig. 3 are the points of the R-t-G part of the movement as resulted after applying the criteria above in the std_{10} of the right wrist (Fig. 4). Five movements were completely removed after applying these steps due to faulty recorded rosbags. Figure 5 shows the distribution of the number of frames in the 715 movements of the dataset. On average there are 34 frames in each R-t-G movement. This means that a R-t-G movement lasts on average approximately 570 ms (given the frame rate of 60 fps).

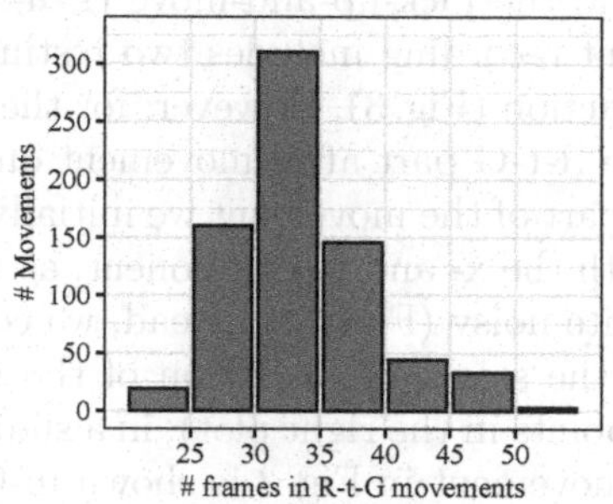

Fig. 5. The distribution of the number of frames in the 715 movements of the dataset.

The following kinematic variables were considered for the R-t-G movements:

- *Thumb-Index finger Aperture (TI-Ap)*: The TI-Ap was defined as the euclidean distance between the thumb and index finger tip keypoints.
- *Thumb-Middle finger Aperture (TM-Ap)*: The TM-Ap was defined as the euclidean distance between the thumb and middle finger tip keypoints.
- *Index-Middle finger Aperture (IM-Ap)*: The IM-Ap was defined as the euclidean distance between the index and middle finger tip keypoints.
- *Wrist x- and y- pixel coordinates.*

Figure 6 shows the average and the standard deviation of all the data points of the kinematic variables at the 20%, 40%, 60%, 80% and 100% of the R-t-G movements.

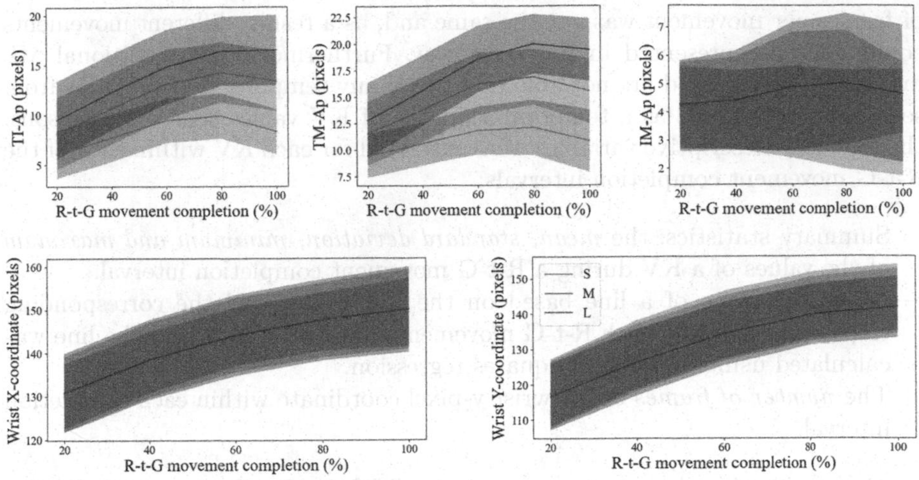

Fig. 6. The kinematic variables used for feature engineering averaged across all data points at five R-t-G movement instants, for the small (red), medium (green) and large (blue) object. The shaded areas represent the standard deviation. (Color figure online)

Before constructing the features of the three apertures presented above, the related keypoints were filtered similarly to the pre-processing of the wrist keypoints. In this case, in addition to the related probability ($p < 0.6$) and the distance of the y-coordinate keypoint to its neighbours ($distance < 10\ pixels$), we also required that each x-coordinate keypoint was at most 10 pixels apart from its previous and next point. Naturally, if one of the two fingers' keypoints were missing the aperture was not calculated for that particular frame. Movements with less than two variable values were not taken into consideration. Consequently, out of the total 715 movements of the dataset the following number of movements was considered for each of the aperture features: 704 for the TI-Ap, 603 for the TM-Ap and 579 for the IM-Ap.

4.3 Feature Engineering and Classifiers

Movement Completion Intervals. The ML models were trained and evaluated at the: 20%, 40%, 60%, 80% and 100% of the R-t-G movement completion intervals. In order to identify the frames of an interval, the normalized time of each frame f $(1 \leq f \leq F)$ was calculated in the following way:

$$t_{norm}(f) = \frac{t(f) - t(1)}{t(F) - t(1)} 100\%$$

where $t(f)$ is the timestamp of frame f and F is the total number of frames of a R-t-G movement.

Feature Engineering. The values of the kinematic variables (KV) values were calculated for all the frames of the R-t-G movements. As expected, the number of frames per movement was not the same and, as a result, different movements could not be represented in the same way. Furthermore, the traditional ML models that were used are not able to capture any temporal dependencies from sequential data, such as a temporal sequence of KV values. For these reasons, the following descriptive variables were extracted for each KV within each of the R-t-G movement completion intervals:

- Summary statistics: the *mean, standard deviation, minimum and maximum* of the values of a KV during a R-t-G movement completion interval.
- *Slope*: the slope of a line based on the KV values and the corresponding elapsed time during each R-t-G movement completion interval. The line was calculated using linear least-squares regression.
- The *number of frames* of the wrist y-pixel coordinate within each completion interval.

Due to filtering, in some cases an interval of the R-t-G movement did not have any valid values of an aperture kinematic variable. In this case, all the descriptive variables of this particular kinematic variable were set to 0. Similarly, if the movement contained only one valid value of a kinematic variable, the slope could not be defined and was set to 0.

After the extraction of all the descriptive variables, each movement was represented as a set of $1 + (|KV| \times 5)$ features, given that the summary statistics and the slope were calculated for each KV, while the number of frames was calculated only once. This representation captures information regarding the magnitude and the temporal evolution of the kinematic variables during the intervals of the R-t-G movement (*mean*, *standard deviation*, *slope*, *number of frames*), but also provides a snapshot description of the KVs' peaks (*max*, *min*).

Workspace Dependency. As mentioned in the previous Section, the kinematic variables that were taken into account were the finger apertures (TI-Ap, TM-Ap, IM-Ap) and the wrist pixel coordinates. While the aperture kinematic variables do not depend on the spatial configuration of the workspace and on the data collection set-up, this is not the case for the wrist pixel coordinates. Therefore, two feature sets were taken into account:

- a *workspace-dependent* (Ws-D) feature set, which considers both the apertures and the wrist pixel coordinates. The performance of a model that is trained using this feature set would drop if the objects to be grasped were placed in different positions of the workspace.
- a *workspace-independent* (Ws-I) feature set, which considers only the aperture kinematic variables. The results of a ML model that uses these features could potentially be generalized to other workspace configurations without additional training data.

Data Splits. In order to evaluate the performance of a ML model, two data split strategies were considered:

- *All-subjects-in* (all-in): Both the training set and the test set contained movements of all eight participants towards the three objects. Approximately 10% of the movements of a participant towards each object were randomly chosen for the test set and the rest 90% were used for training. In this strategy, a model can pick up a movement pattern of a specific individual during training and this favours the prediction during testing.
- *One-subject-out* (one-out): The training set contained all the movements of seven participants. The movements of the remaining participant comprised the test set. In this strategy, the model during testing makes predictions without being previously trained on the movements of a participant. This strategy is a much more challenging task compared to the all-in strategy and tests the ability of a model to generalize to unseen participants and behaviours, which is closer to real-world scenarios.

In both cases, a k-fold evaluation scheme was used to obtain a less biased estimate of the ML model's performance on unseen data. The value of k was chosen to be 10 and 8 for the 'all-in' and the 'one-out' data splits, respectively. Each movement was included in the test set once.

ML Models. The following ML models were evaluated: Random Forest, Extra Trees, Gradient Boosting, Support Vector Machine, Gaussian Process. To this end, the Scikit-learn Machine Learning framework [20] was used. In the next section, the results of only the top-performing ML models are reported for each case of feature set and data split.

Real-Time Feasibility. To explore whether the results for the prediction could be used in a real-time set-up, previously collected robot motion data [27] with a UR3 collaborative robot were used. Specifically, given a viable robot movement profile and speed (0.9 m/s), the UR3 can travel 5, 10 and 20 cm in $t_5 = 112$ ms, $t_{10} = 159$ ms and $t_{20} = 256$ ms, respectively. These durations are used to evaluate in which cases the UR3 cobot would have the information about the prediction early enough to decide on an appropriate action.

5 Results

Classifier Performance. In order to measure the performance of the trained ML models on unseen data, the mean and the standard deviation of the accuracy rates is reported for each of the movement completion intervals (Fig. 7).

For the 'all-in' data split strategy the Extra Trees model yielded the best results both for the Ws-D and the Ws-I feature sets. In the first case, an average accuracy of above 80.0% was already achieved when only 40% of the R-t-G movement was completed. As expected, in the case of the Ws-I feature set an average accuracy of above 80.0% was achieved at a later stage, when 60% of the R-t-G movement was completed. For both feature sets, the standard deviation was less than 6.0% for each of the movement completion intervals.

For the 'one-out' data split strategy, the Support Vector Machine model was the top performing model for both the Ws-D and the Ws-I feature sets.

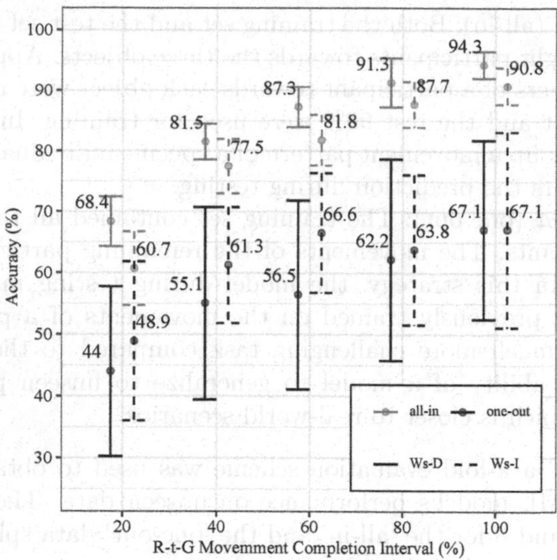

Fig. 7. The errorbars (mean and standard deviation) of the accuracy across the k-fold evaluation for both data split strategies (all-in (blue) and one-out (black)) and for both feature sets (workspace dependent (Ws-D - solid line) and workspace independent (Ws-I - dashed line). (Color figure online)

In this case the achieved accuracy is considerably worse compared to the 'all-in' strategy. A mean accuracy of less than 70.0% was achieved for both feature sets after seeing the entire movement (100% completion of the movement). The standard deviations of the accuracy in this strategy were more than twice as large as the corresponding standard deviations in the 'all-in' strategy, ranging from 8.9% to 15.4%.

The confusion matrices of the models at the 60% R-t-G movement completion interval are presented in Fig. 8. In all conditions of split strategies and feature sets, the accuracy rates of the small object predictions were the highest compared to the other two objects. The suboptimal performance of the models appears to be driven mainly by the misclassification of the large object as medium and vice versa. Nevertheless, in the case of the 'one-out' data split, the small object is also often misclassified as medium and vice versa. The confusion matrices for the rest of the completion intervals are comparable[5].

To evaluate the contribution of each feature to the results, within each feature set, the impurity-based (Gini) feature importances of the Extra Trees models were calculated for the all-in strategy (Fig. 9). The TI-Ap and TM-Ap appear to be the most important KVs. The slight improvement of the accuracy in the Ws-D feature set (Fig. 7) seems to be driven by the y-coordinate KV and not by the x-coordinate, which was expected given that the R-t-G movements were

[5] Available at: https://github.com/Roboskel-Manipulation/object_size_prediction/tree/main/supplementary_material.

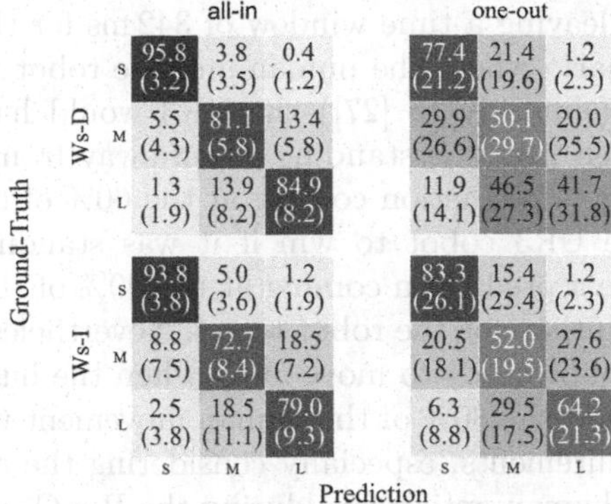

Fig. 8. The confusion matrices of the models at the 60% of the R-t-G movement completion for the 'all-in' (left column) and the 'one-out' (right column) split strategies and for the Ws-D (first row) and Ws-I (second row) feature sets.

principally executed in the y-direction. Note that the *number of frames* feature was only calculated once based on y-wrist movement and it was not calculated for each KV, as the number of frames within each KV was quite variable and dependent on the data collection noise rather than actual characteristics of a KV.

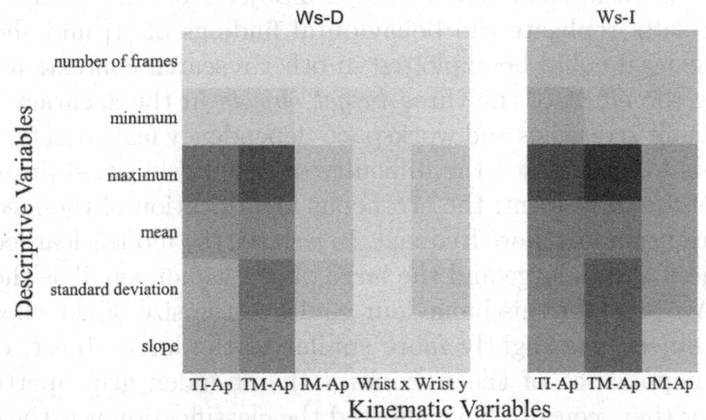

Fig. 9. The importance of the features at the 80% of the R-t-G movement completion for both feature sets: the workspace dependent (Ws-D, on the left) and the worskspace independent (Ws-I, on the right), for the 'all-in' data split strategy.

Real-Time Feasibility Evaluation. As described in Sect. 4.2, the average R-t-G movement lasted approximately 570 ms (Fig. 5) and the distance covered was set at 42 cm. Based on the results presented above, a satisfactory accuracy in the human action prediction is achieved already by the 40% of the R-t-G movement completion (in the 'all-in'/Ws-D case); this would be approximately 228 ms after the movement onset, leaving a time window of 342 ms for the robot to act. In a competitive HRI scenario where the human and the robot were trying to reach for the same object (similarly to [27]) the UR3 would have good chances at wining the human even if it was standing 20 cm away from the object or a bit farther away. However, a prediction coming at the 60% of the R-t-G movement would only allow the UR3 cobot to win if it was standing 5 or 10 cm away from the object, while a prediction coming at the 80% of the human movement would not give enough time for the robot to act. Nevertheless, in a safety-driven scenario, where the robot needs to move away when the human is approaching, a prediction as late as at the 80% of the human movement would most probably satisfy the safety requirements, especially considering the accuracy achieved in the prediction of the human action late during the R-t-G movement.

6 Discussion

The results reported above show that it is possible to predict the size of the object a human intends to grasp when using OpenPose skeletal information extracted from visual information collected with a single RGB camera at 60 fps, similarly to using a motion caption system that provides information at 100 fps [1]. However, due to both the data collection frequency and the data noise, even in the best scenario, the achieved accuracy is lower compared to [1]. Yet, it is above chance in all cases. Also, in the present work, three objects were included in the prediction task, compared to the two objects of [1]. Finally, to a certain extent, our results replicate the behavioural findings of [1] and show that the vision pipeline used could be exploited in other research contexts as well.

Regarding the effect of the three *target objects* in the accuracy rates, in all conditions of split strategies and workspace-dependency feature sets, the medium object appears to have raised the difficulty of the classification problem. At the later stages of the movement, the erroneous identification of the medium object as large or vice-versa was more frequent. In a sense, the models learned to identify the small object as non-large and the large object as non-small as the movement progressed. A reason for this behaviour could be the size of the chosen objects; the medium object was slightly more similar to the large object, especially in light of the importance of the maximum thumb-index grip aperture feature. Another factor that seems to have affected the classification was the use (or not) of the middle finger during grasping; this is again supported by the importance of the TM-Ap kinematic variable. Note that participants were not given any instructions regarding how to use their finger to grasp the objects.

The effect of different behaviours in the prediction accuracy and the ability of the methods to generalise to *unseen human behaviours*, was studied through two dataset split strategies. The performance of the 'all-subjects-in' strategy was superior compared to the 'one-subject-out' strategy. This was expected, considering the variable human behaviour. If a participant had a distinct movement pattern, a model not trained with his data would not be able to generalise in the 'one-out' strategy. On the other hand, in the 'all-in' strategy all behaviours are captured. The impact of the different behaviours in the case of the 'one-out' strategy is also manifested by the higher variability of the achieved accuracy during the k-fold evaluation. Note that the lower accuracy in the 'one-out' case is not driven by the behavior of one or more outliers[6]. In any case, the 'one-out' strategy, although more challenging, is perhaps the only realistic solution in applications that involve a large number of users. On the other hand, in a scenario where only a few people interact with a robot a personalised model training approach could be pursued [31].

Another factor that affects the generalisation of the methods to *unseen environments* is the extent to which the features used are specific to the set-up of the data collection. In our case, we used two feature sets; a workspacc-dependent and a workspace-independent. The Ws-D feature set resulted in a higher prediction accuracy for the 'all-in' data split strategy case but did not have an impact in the case of the 'one-out' data split strategy. Based on the importance of the features, the aperture ones, which are workspace independent were more important compared to the set-up dependent movement coordinates.

To evaluate the applicability of the present findings in a HRI scenario, we used robot motion data previously collected in [27]. Regarding the accuracy and time of the predictions, it is realistic to actually use the data in a real-time HRC system. However, certain issues need to be addressed. Firstly, the GPU used should support the processing of all camera frames. In our case, given the GPU available, the information in real-time would only be the one third of the information used in the present work; this is why the frames of the camera were analysed in an on-demand way. The higher obstacle though, towards a real-time HRC system, is the fact that the present work exploits the knowledge of the entire movement duration to identify specific movement completion instants and predict the human intention in these moments. An approach similar to [27] or the use of complementary knowledge regarding the environment, the task or the behaviour of the human might be necessary for developing a real-time system.

7 Conclusions

In the present work we studied if it is possible to predict the size of an object from hand kinematics observed using a single RGB-D sensor. Towards this, a dataset of eight participants grasping objects of three different sizes was collected. The dataset is open. RGB visual data were used to extract the 2D OpenPose hand and arm joint pixel coordinates. This information was then used to calculate appropriate human movement kinematic information and engineer suitable ML features. Traditional ML methods were used to evaluate the usability of our dataset for human action prediction. The results were significantly above chance level and showed that it is possible to predict the size of the object using hand kinematics extracted from a single RGB-D sensor. Moreover, the achieved

[6] See boxplots at: https://github.com/Roboskel-Manipulation/object_size_prediction/tree/main/supplementary_material.

accuracy and the timing of the predictions are viable given the performance requirements of a HRC system.

Acknowledgments. M.D. designed the study and the data collection. All authors contributed to the design of the pre-processing of the dataset. N.S. designed the ML features, developed all the necessary code and run all the analysis. All authors contributed to the manuscript. M.D. supervised the HRI aspects of the work. T.G supervised the ML aspects of the work. The authors want to thank G. Mpazakos for assisting with the data collection and A.C. Tsitos for processing the raw dataset and producing the OpenPose 2D dataset, as well as providing the robot data.

References

1. Ansuini, C., Cavallo, A., Koul, A., Jacono, M., Yang, Y., Becchio, C.: Predicting object size from hand kinematics: a temporal perspective. PLoS One **10**(3), e0120432 (2015)
2. Bütepage, J., Kragic, D.: Human-robot collaboration: from psychology to social robotics. arXiv preprint arXiv:1705.10146 (2017)
3. Cao, Z., Hidalgo Martinez, G., Simon, T., Wei, S., Sheikh, Y.A.: OpenPose: realtime multi-person 2D pose estimation using part affinity fields. IEEE Trans. Pattern Anal. Mach. Intell. (2019)
4. Cavallo, A., Koul, A., Ansuini, C., Capozzi, F., Becchio, C.: Decoding intentions from movement kinematics. Sci. Rep. **6**(1), 1–8 (2016)
5. Chen, Y., Zhang, Z., Yuan, C., Li, B., Deng, Y., Hu, W.: Channel-wise topology refinement graph convolution for skeleton-based action recognition (2021)
6. Cheng, K., Zhang, Y., Cao, C., Shi, L., Cheng, J., Lu, H.: Decoupling GCN with dropgraph module for skeleton-based action recognition. In: Vedaldi, A., Bischof, H., Brox, T., Frahm, J.-M. (eds.) ECCV 2020. LNCS, vol. 12369, pp. 536–553. Springer, Cham (2020). https://doi.org/10.1007/978-3-030-58586-0_32
7. Cheng, K., Zhang, Y., He, X., Chen, W., Cheng, J., Lu, H.: Skeleton-based action recognition with shift graph convolutional network. In: 2020 IEEE/CVF Conference on Computer Vision and Pattern Recognition (CVPR), pp. 180–189 (2020)
8. Dagioglou, M., Tsitos, A.C., Smarnakis, A., Karkaletsis, V.: Smoothing of human movements recorded by a single RGB-D camera for robot demonstrations. In: The 14th PErvasive Technologies Related to Assistive Environments Conference (2021)
9. Gamage, N.M., Ishtaweera, D., Weigel, M., Withana, A.: So predictable! continuous 3D hand trajectory prediction in virtual reality. In: The 34th Annual ACM Symposium on User Interface Software and Technology, pp. 332–343 (2021)
10. Garcia-Salguero, M., Gonzalez-Jimenez, J., Moreno, F.A.: Human 3D pose estimation with a tilting camera for social mobile robot interaction. Sensors **19**(22), 4943 (2019)
11. Hernández, Ó.G., Morell, V., Ramon, J.L., Jara, C.A.: Human pose detection for robotic-assisted and rehabilitation environments. Appl. Sci. **11**(9), 4183 (2021)
12. Hu, J.F., Zheng, W.S., Ma, L., Wang, G., Lai, J., Zhang, J.: Early action prediction by soft regression. IEEE Trans. Pattern Anal. Mach. Intell. **41**(11), 2568–2583 (2019)
13. Kay, W., et al.: The kinetics human action video dataset (2017)

14. Lasota, P.A., Fong, T., Shah, J.A., et al.: A Survey of Methods for Safe Human-Robot Interaction, vol. 104. Now Publishers Delft, Delft (2017)
15. Lasota, P.A., Shah, J.A.: A multiple-predictor approach to human motion prediction. In: IEEE International Conference on Robotics and Automation (ICRA) (2017)
16. Liu, J., Shahroudy, A., Perez, M., Wang, G., Duan, L.Y., Kot, A.C.: NTU RGB+D 120: a large-scale benchmark for 3D human activity understanding. IEEE Trans. Pattern Anal. Mach. Intell. **42**(10), 2684–2701 (2020)
17. Liu, Z., Zhang, H., Chen, Z., Wang, Z., Ouyang, W.: Disentangling and unifying graph convolutions for skeleton-based action recognition. In: Proceedings of the IEEE/CVF Conference on Computer Vision and Pattern Recognition (2020)
18. Mainprice, J., Hayne, R., Berenson, D.: Predicting human reaching motion in collaborative tasks using inverse optimal control and iterative re-planning. In: IEEE International Conference on Robotics and Automation (ICRA) (2015)
19. Oguz, O.S., Gabler, V., Huber, G., Zhou, Z., Wollherr, D.: Hybrid human motion prediction for action selection within human-robot collaboration. In: Kulić, D., Nakamura, Y., Khatib, O., Venture, G. (eds.) ISER 2016. SPAR, vol. 1, pp. 289–298. Springer, Cham (2017). https://doi.org/10.1007/978-3-319-50115-4_26
20. Pedregosa, F., et al.: Scikit-learn: machine learning in python. J. Mach. Learn. Res. **12** (2011)
21. Rolley-Parnell, E.J., et al.: Bi-manual articulated robot teleoperation using an external RGB-D range sensor. In: 2018 15th International Conference on Control, Automation, Robotics and Vision (ICARCV), pp. 298–304. IEEE (2018)
22. Rudenko, A., Palmieri, L., Herman, M., Kitani, K.M., Gavrila, D.M., Arras, K.O.: Human motion trajectory prediction: a survey. Int. J. Robot. Res. **39**(8), 895–935 (2020)
23. Schaal, S., Sternad, D.: Origins and violations of the 2/3 power law in rhythmic three-dimensional arm movements. Exp. Brain Res. **136**(1), 60–72 (2001). https://doi.org/10.1007/s002210000505
24. Shahroudy, A., Liu, J., Ng, T.T., Wang, G.: NTU RGB+D: A large scale dataset for 3D human activity analysis (2016)
25. Song, Y.F., Zhang, Z., Shan, C., Wang, L.: Constructing stronger and faster baselines for skeleton-based action recognition (2021)
26. Tenbrink, L., Feldotto, B., Röhrbein, F., Knoll, A.: Motion prediction of virtual patterns, human hand motions, and a simplified hand manipulation task with hierarchical temporal memory. In: 2019 IEEE International Conference on Cyborg and Bionic Systems (CBS), pp. 305–309. IEEE (2019)
27. Tsitos, A.C., Dagioglou, M., Giannakopoulos, T.: Real-time feasibility of a human intention method evaluated through a competitive human-robot reaching game. In: 17th ACM/IEEE International Conference on Human-Robot Interaction (HRI) (2022)
28. Viviani, P., Flash, T.: Minimum-jerk, two-thirds power law, and isochrony: converging approaches to movement planning. J. Exp. Psychol. Hum. Percept. Perform. **21**(1), 32 (1995)
29. Wang, X., Hu, J.F., Lai, J.H., Zhang, J., Zheng, W.S.: Progressive teacher-student learning for early action prediction. In: 2019 IEEE/CVF Conference on Computer Vision and Pattern Recognition (CVPR), pp. 3551–3560 (2019)
30. Yan, S., Xiong, Y., Lin, D.: Spatial temporal graph convolutional networks for skeleton-based action recognition (2018)

31. Zunino, A., Cavazza, J., Murino, V.: Revisiting human action recognition: personalization vs. generalization. In: Battiato, S., Gallo, G., Schettini, R., Stanco, F. (eds.) ICIAP 2017. LNCS, vol. 10484, pp. 469–480. Springer, Cham (2017). https://doi.org/10.1007/978-3-319-68560-1_42
32. Zunino, A., et al.: Predicting intentions from motion: the subject-adversarial adaptation approach. Int. J. Comput. Vis. **128**(1), 220–239 (2020)

Replacing Human Input in Spam Email Detection Using Deep Learning

Mathew Nicho[1(✉)], Farzan Majdani[2], and Christopher D. McDermott[2]

[1] College of Technology Innovation, Zayed University, Dubai, UAE
mathew.nicho@zu.ac.ae

[2] School of Computing, Robert Gordon University, Aberdeen, UK
{farzan.majdani,c.d.mcdermott}@rgu.ac.uk

Abstract. The Covid-19 pandemic has been a driving force for a substantial increase in online activity and transactions across the globe. As a consequence, cyber-attacks, particularly those leveraging email as the preferred attack vector, have also increased exponentially since Q1 2020. Despite this, email remains a popular communication tool. Previously, in an effort to reduce the amount of spam entering a users inbox, many email providers started to incorporate spam filters into their products. However, many commercial spam filters rely on a human to train the filter, leaving a margin of risk if sufficient training has not occurred. In addition, knowing this, hackers employ more targeted and nuanced obfuscation methods to bypass in-built spam filters. In response to this continued problem, there is a growing body of research on the use of machine learning techniques for spam filtering. In many cases, detection results have shown great promise, but often still rely on human input to classify training datasets. In this study, we explore specifically the use of deep learning as a method of reducing human input required for spam detection. First, we evaluate the efficacy of popular spam detection methods/tools/techniques (freeware). Next, we narrow down machine learning techniques to select the appropriate method for our dataset. This was then compared with the accuracy of freeware spam detection tools to present our results. Our results showed that our deep learning model, based on simple word embedding and global max pooling (SWEM-max) had higher accuracy (98.41%) than both Thunderbird (95%) and Mailwasher (92%) which are based on Bayesian spam filtering. Finally, we postulate whether this improvement is enough to accept the removal of human input in spam email detection.

Keywords: Spam detection · Phishing emails · Simple word embedding · Global max pooling · Deep learning

1 Introduction

Email has become a de facto standard of communication across the globe. The number of global email users, which was 3.8 billion in 2018, is set to grow to

H. Degen and S. Ntoa (Eds.): HCII 2022, LNAI 13336, pp. 387–404, 2022.
https://doi.org/10.1007/978-3-031-05643-7_25

4.48 billion by the year 2024 [67]. As the popularity of the internet continued to grow, email followed suit, resulting in users getting substantially more unsolicited emails, some of which has malicious intent and carries payloads in 'genuine' looking attachments. In this respect, spam has produced considerable economic damage [5] and is still a preferred attack vector for attackers.

While attacks vectors take multiple methods, one of the most common ways of data breach is via spam or phishing emails. Research undertaken by Verizon found that almost a quarter (22%) of data breaches were caused by impersonation, where an attacker acted as though they belonged to the company [36]. Here, the attacker leveraged email to gain the trust of a user and gather information, specially financial information. Once successful, the information was either used to commit a fraud, request further information through exploitation, or it was sold onto a third party.

By definition, spam email, also known as junk email, is any kind of unwanted, unsolicited, digital communication. Often, the email is sent out en-mass, resulting in a in reduction of Internet quality of service, and incurring considerable direct and indirect costs associated with the management of such spam [33]. Alternatively, phishing is an advanced type of spam email where the attacker spoofs genuine email and creates fraudulent websites to steal sensitive data such usernames, passwords, credit cards, and bank account details [62]. In these type of attacks, the email identity and header information are not normally verified or authenticated, such that it purports to originate from a legitimate company or bank.

Given the considerable rise in email use it is now estimated that an average person spends around 28% of a regular workweek interacting with emails. However, of the emails received, only 38% are considered relevant and important, with the rest categorised as spam [27]. In an attempt to reduce the amount of time spent on unnecessary emails many users have adopted software-based spam filters such as (*Mailwasher*[1] and *Thunderbird*[2]) which are based on bayesian statisical analysis and rely heavily upon human interaction to train the spam filter. While these bayesian-based classifiers return good accuracy, that can be further improved as more messages are classified [48], they are wholly dependent on a human completing the training task on a regular basis to remain resistant to new forms of spam.

Since the start of the Covid-19 pandemic, the rate of spam has increased, with 96% of phishing attacks now arriving by email, and a further 3% carried out through malicious websites or telephone communications (1%) [60]. The pandemic has been the driving force for a substantial increase in online meetings, activities and transactions across the globe. Armed with this knowledge, attackers have sought to explore this event circulating messages relating to Covid-19, capitalising on fear and uncertainty as the world reacted to the virus's initial outbreak progression [35]. In this respect, Covid-19-themed attacks exploded in

[1] https://www.firetrust.com/products/mailwasher-pro.
[2] https://support.mozilla.org/en-US/kb/thunderbird-and-junk-spam-messages/.

mid to late March 2020, linked to the Covid-19 news cycle, utilising multiple attack vectors and techniques [35].

The aim of this research is to evaluate the current state of spam detection, explore human input in the process, and evaluate the use of deep learning in this context. In doing, we seek to answer the research question: *Does the use of deep learning remove the need for human input in spam email detection?*. In this respect, first, the research evaluates popular spam and phishing detection applications (freeware software) available to the research, and used by the wider community. Second, we explore and analyse current machine learning techniques proposed for spam detection, leading to the selection of an appropriate machine learning technique for use in our study. Here, the selected machine learning technique is compared to the freeware spam filters and evaluated for accuracy and loss. Finally, we explore the use of human input during the detection process to determine whether this can be replaced by deep learning.

2 Email as an Attack Vector

Since threats to email security can come from multiple sources, it is essential to establish a comprehensive threat model based on the risk posed to a company. For example, attackers could use Traffic Distribution Systems (TDS) to effectively serve up different types of spam, and even malware, to a varying range of machines in different locations [7]. A number of protocols are used for the delivery of email, each with its own associated advantages and disadvantages. SMTP servers alone often struggle to distinguish between genuine (*ham*) and unsolicited (*spam*) email. In addition, the main drawback of sending through an SMTP server is the anonymity of a sender's identity [22]. Alternatively, IMAP can be difficult to maintain, leading to the less support and use of the protocol. Copies of messages are also stored in the server space, requiring larger amounts of mailbox space resulting in increased costs [47]. POP3 is another popular email protocol, but can consume considerable resources of a system because since messages are downloaded and saved on the local device. This introduces additional risks since if the device crashes or is stolen, data could be lost. As such, legacy email protocols like SMTP, POP3 and IMAP, are often targeted by hackers and spammers [59].

Covid-19 Related Attack Vector: As internet-worked users become more dependent on online services, they also become vulnerable to online fraud. As discussed, these threats have been accelerated since the start of the Covid-19 pandemic [1]. In this respect, the top 10 cyber security threats amid the Covid-19 pandemic were found to be DDoS attack, malicious domains, malicious websites, malware, ransomware, spam emails, malicious social media messaging, business email compromise, mobile apps, and browsing apps [39]. Of these, spam email served as a direct attack vector for malware, ransomware, business email compromise, and a supporting vector for malicious domains, and malicious websites. As such, spam was considered one of the most potent threats in the ream of online communication. Consequently, spam emails exploiting the Covid-19 pandemic have become rampant where the most common technique deployed by spammers was *snowshoe*. This is where an attacker uses multiple IPs and domains for spam campaigns in an effort to avoid detection, where as much as 85% of emails sent were considered spam [17]. Using automated tools, the cost to reward ratio is very low, with countless emails flooding the web at negligible cost. In this respect, the FBI recently indicated that phishing campaigns had become the most common type of cybercrime in 2020, where phishing incidents nearly doubled in frequency, from 114,702 incidents in 2019, to 241,324 incidents in 2020 [68]. Close inspection showed that many were related to Covid, where the phishing attack used titles, messages contents and attachments targeted for the pandemic. These included zoom meeting requests (spoofed hyperlink), leverage of heuristic and cognitive biases such as fear to trick a user into downloaded malware embedded in remote working tools. [68]. As such the attack vector moved beyond simple spam to very specific and targeted phishing attempts [1]. Here, phishing can be considered an advanced type of spam email where phishers use spoofed emails and fraudulent websites to steal sensitive data like usernames, passwords, credit cards, and bank account details [62]. Ultimately, in this kind of targeted attack the end user has become an integral part of the overall vector leading to many researchers labelling the end user as the 'weakest link' in the security chain [28,52]. Furthermore, beyond spam or phishing attacks, end users remain one of the most persistent vulnerabilities in many computer systems [70]. For these, and many more reasons, hackers continue to exploit human vulnerabilities rather than breaking into systems directly, ensuring spam and phishing attacks remain a real threat [29].

2.1 Spam Detection Approaches

While spam detection cannot protect a user completely, there are techniques developed by researchers and practitioners to enhance the spam detection rate. Here, we categorise the detection methods into two approaches namely: *machine learning* and *non-machine learning* approaches, with further subcategories.

Non-machine Learning Approaches: Non-machine learning methods have historically been used in spam email detection. Often, they simply include a list of email addresses or words on which the filter determines whether the given mail is spam or not [44]. Various methods have been used successfully including content based, heuristic, signature based, challenge/response and DNS blacklist. For example, content-based filtering involves automatic filtering rules to classify emails. The occurrence and distribution of words and phrases in an email are evaluated and matched against predefined rules to filter the incoming spam emails [19]. Heuristic or rule based spam filtering technique have prior rules or heuristics to assess enormous patterns which are usually regular expressions against a chosen message. The score of the message increases with similar patterns and it deducts from the score if the patterns didn't match. When the message's score outpace a specific threshold, it is spam; else it is counted as valid [16].

Usually spammers send a replica of their spam message to all the possible email accounts they can find. When the site receives a message, it generates a signature for it and stores it in the database. To determine if the received message is spam, the anti-spam software simply checks to see if the signature for the incoming message matches with any of the signatures in the spam signature database. If it does, then the message is considered as spam [41]. Alternatively, DNS blacklisting filtering technique uses a centralised database to block all email from a specific host attempting to send the spam messages. The blacklists are static lists and require to be maintained manually by adding entries in the database for new hosts that are considered to be spamming. The blacklist is stored and served in conjunction with the DNS system serving queries [56]. Challenge/response filtering systems send an automated reply to an email, enquiring the authenticity of the original sender in a reply, prior to delivery of the original email. The basic idea is not to block unsolicited bulk email (UBE), but rather to allow emails from humans only, who can assert that a response to challenge is needed [6].

Every spam filtering method has weaknesses that spammers can exploit and launch attacks. The limitations of main spam detection methods are summarised in Table 1.

Machine Learning Approaches: Machine learning approaches have grown in popularity and include algorithms such as support vector machine (SVM), naive bayes, k nearest neighbour and artificial neural networks. In many cases of supervised learning a set of emails which are pre-classsified (by a human) and used to train the associated ML model. This approach is more efficient to detect and tackle spams because of the machine learning system's ability to evolve itself over the time reducing the concept drift [46]. The most commonly used machine learning spam filtering is bayesian filter. Bayesian filter learns the difference between ham (non spam) and spam by looking at two categories of email message. One category is comprised of spam messages received by a site, and the other one contains ham messages received by the same site. A comparison is undertaken about how frequently a given word appears in both ham and spam messages, after which the filter determines the probability that a message containing the given word is spam [34]. Similarly, artificial neural networks perform spam filtering by either computing the rate of occurrence of keywords or patterns in the email messages. Neural network algorithms for email filtering usually attain moderate classification performance [30]. SVM filters are supervised learning models that are very potent for the identification of spam patterns and classifying them into a specific class or group. SVM is a good classifier due to its sparse data format, satisfactory recall, precision value and high classification accuracy [54].

This section demonstrates a comparison of selected Machine Learning Techniques (MLT) for identifying spam and malicious phishing emails. Studies have compared the predictive accuracy of several machine learning methods namely Logistic Regression (LR), Classification and Regression Trees (CART), Bayesian Additive Regression Trees (BART), Support Vector Machines (SVM), Random

Table 1. Spam detection methods and weaknesses

Method	Refences	Critique
Signature matching	A. Kolcz et al. [40]	The spam catching rate is low. The spammer can easily avoid it. Requires frequent access to anti-spam vendor systems. Methods react to the spammer, instead of proactively rejecting spam messages
Heuristic	Dudley et al. [23]	The system has a high false-positive rate if the rules are poorly written
Bayesian	Heron et al. [34]	The system needs extremely high resource requirements. The method takes training to learn the difference between spam and ham messages
DNS blacklisting	Hao et al. [31]	The system has a comparatively low spam catch rate
Challenge/response	Alkahtani et al. [6]	It has a weakness in the authentication. Wireless network security issues. If both sending and receiving mail servers implement them, dead lock will result as both servers will wait for the other to respond to their challenges
Rule-based system	Najadat et al. [49]	The detection speed is extremely limited
Statistical content filter	M.T Banday [10]	The detection speed is extremely limited

Forests (RF), and Neural Networks (NNet) for predicting phishing emails [2]. S.Baadel et al. considered phishing as a classification problem and outlined some of the recent intelligent machine learning techniques (associative classifications, dynamic self-structuring neural network, dynamic rule-induction, etc.) in the literature that is used as anti-phishing models [9]. Meanwhile, G.H.Lokesh et al. designed a phishing classification system with the comparative study of classical machine learning techniques such as Random Forest, K nearest neighbours, Decision Tree, Linear SVC classifier, One class SVM classifier and wrapper-based features selection, which contains the metadata of URLs and use the information to determine if a website is legitimate or not [32]. Table 2 illustrates the anti-phishing tools based on machine learning algorithms.

Table 2. Anti-phishing tools based on machine learning algorithms

Tool	Machine Learning models	Authors
PHISH-SAFE	SVM and Naïve Bayes classifiers	A.K. Jain et al. [37]
PhishBlock	Neural networks based SVM	M.A. Fahmy [24]
PhishMon	K Nearest Neighbors (KNN), AdaBoost, Random Forest (RF)	A. Niakanlahiji [50]
PILFER	Random Forest (RF)	I. Fette et al. [26]
PhishStack	Random Forest (RF)	S.S.M. Rahman et al. [55]
MailTrout	Bidirectional Long Short-Term Memory (BLSTM) networks	P. Boyle et al. [12]
SpamAssassin	Bayesian Additive Regression Trees (BART)	A.K Seewald et al. [61]
Automated Individual Whitelist (AIWL)	Naïve Bayesian classifier	Y. Cao et al. [14]
MMSPhiD	Machine learning approach (NNet), typosquatting-based approach, phoneme-based approach	G. Sonowal et al. [65]
CBR-PDS	K nearest neighbours (kNN)	H. Abutair et al. [3]

3 Methodology

To promote reproducibility of this paper, a detailed description of the test environment and algorithm implementation is presented.

In this paper, we explore the use of a deep learning method to remove the need for human interaction during the training phase. Specifically, the first contribution of this paper is the performance analysis of two popular bayesian-based software spam filtering solutions, and the novel application of a model based on *simple word embedding* and *global max pooling* referred to hereafter as (SWEM-*max*). The proposed method can more efficiently analyse topics within email messages since relationships between words are captured and the statistical structure of the language is mapped within a geometric space to improve accuracy. Previous research has shown this combination of techniques to outperform other forms of neural networks such *RNN*, *CNN* during training [64].

3.1 Data Sources

To evaluate the detection methods in this study the publicly available *Spam Assassin Dataset*[1] was used. The collection consisted of 6046 emails classified as either *ham:0* or *spam:1*. Following preprocessing the collection was reduced to 5293 (*ham:3915, spam:1378*) before being split using an 80:20 training/test ratio.

Before the dataset could be used we needed to address the imbalanced nature of the data. This was important because our proposed deep neural network would be comprised of multiple non-linear hidden layers, to form a sophisticated model able of learning very complex relationships. However, in most cases these relationships are likely to be a result of the sampling noise that exists in the training data, but not the test data. Therefore, even if a models test and training data are from the same dataset, there is a risk of overfitting the model. This risk is further increased when the imbalanced dataset is used for training. Since our dataset was imbalanced (74% ham to 26% spam) and would be used to train our deep learning model we first needed to select an appropriate technique to address this challenge. A number of such techniques exist in the literature, namely: reweight, weight sharing [57] and Deep synthetic minority oversampling technique (SMOTE) [18]. To avoid overfitting our model we selected to use a technique called Dropout [66]. In this method a unit (hidden and visible) of the neural network, along with its incoming and outgoing connections, is temporarily removed to prevent it from co-adapting too much. This dropout happens randomly during the training phase and can drastically reduce overfitting of the model. To increase accuracy and avoid overfitting the model we used multiple drop out layers as shown in Algorithm 1.

3.2 Deep Learning Spam Detection Method (SWEM-max)

The second contribution of this paper is the application of *Deep Learning* to the problem domain to remove the need for human input during the training phase. To implement the model we first converted the dataset into a multidimensional dataset, using a technique called *simple word embedding.* Unlike other methods such as *one-hot encoding* where relationship information between words is missed, the words were represented as dense word vectors and the statistical structure of the language was mapped within a geometric space called an *embedding space.* Thus, the embedding layer formed the first layer within the neural network. Next, we down sampled the incoming feature vectors using *global max pooling* operation by only taking the maximum value of the time dimension. Models such as those presented in this paper can be prone to overfitting, therefore, the model was passed through a dropout layer where input units were frequently set to *0* at each step during the training phase to prevent overfitting. Next, to reduce the dimensionality of the data the model was passed through a number of dense layers. Here, the output layer was a dense layer with the

[1] https://www.kaggle.com/.

dimension of *1* and the *sigmoid activation* function was used to narrow the output value between [0,1]. Finally, the formed neural network was compiled with *Adam optimiser* and *Binary Cross Entropy* loss function, and trained over 20 epochs (See Algorithm 1).

Algorithm 1. SWEM-max Spam Detection Algorithm

```
TrainAndValidate (training data, test data)
model ← sequential()
loss ← binary cross entropy
optimizer ← adam
epochs ← 20
Get input shape from training data
Add Embedding layer as the input layer
Add global max pooling operation for 1D layer
Add a drop out layer
Add new Dense Layer with relu activation
Add a drop out layer
Add Dense layer with sigmoid activation
Compile model using Optimiser and Loss
repeat
    /*Fit Model*/
    for i ← 1, epochs do
        Evaluate Loss
        Evaluate Validation Loss
        Evaluate Accuracy
        Evaluate Validation Accuracy
    end for
until All epochs completed
Return (Loss, ValLoss, Acc, ValAcc)
```

4 Results and Discussion

To test the performance of the two bayesian-based software software spam filters a local *email server*[1] was configured with default settings and training emails (*ham:3132*, *spam:1102*) sent from the dataset to the spam filters using the python *smtplib* module. Once received, each email was manually classified as either *ham/spam* to train the filters. Next, the same method was used to send the test emails (*ham:783*, *spam:276*) to each filter and performance was recorded.

To evaluate the performance of the methods in this study we measured the *tp*: true positive, *fp*: false positive, *tn*: true negative and *fn*: false negative rates and used these to calculate the classification accuracy as specified below.

[1] https://www.hmailserver.com/.

1. **True positive (*tp*):** spam that is successfully detected
2. **False positive (*fp*):** ham email that is incorrectly classified as spam
3. **True Negative (*tn*):** ham email that is successfully classified as ham
4. **False Negative (*fn*):** spam email that is missed and classified as ham

While accuracy is a key performance indicator found within the literature other metrics derived from information retrieval and decision theory can help gain better insights into the obtained results [27]. Therefore, the following metrics were also calculated using the equations below where the Detection Rate *(DR)* signifies the ratio of spam instances detected by the model. The False Alarm Rate *FAR* signifies a ratio of misclassified email instances.

Detection Rate (DR): Defined as the % ratio of the number of true positive (*tp*) emails divided by the sum of true positive (*tp*) and false negative (*fn*) classified emails.

$$DR = \frac{tp}{tp + fn}, detection\, rate \in [0, 1]$$

False Alarm Rate (FAR): Defined as the % ratio of the number of false positive (*tp*) emails divided by the sum of true negative (*tn*) and false positive (*fp*) classified emails.

$$FAR = \frac{fp}{tn + fp}, false\ alarm\ rate \in [0, 1]$$

Precision (P): Defined as the % ratio of the number of true positive (*tp*) records divided by the sum of true positive (*tp*) and false positive (*fp*) classified records.

$$P = \frac{tp}{tp + fp}, precision \in [0, 1]$$

Recall (R): Defined as the % ratio of number of true positive records divided by the sum of true positive and false negative (*fn*) classified records.

$$R = \frac{tp}{tp + fn}, recall \in [0, 1]$$

F Measure ($\mathbf{F_1}$) : Defined as the harmonic mean of precision and recall and represents a balance between them. It is often used to measure the performance of a system when a single number is preferred [69].

$$F_1 = 2 * \frac{P * R}{P + R}, F\, Measure \in [0, 1]$$

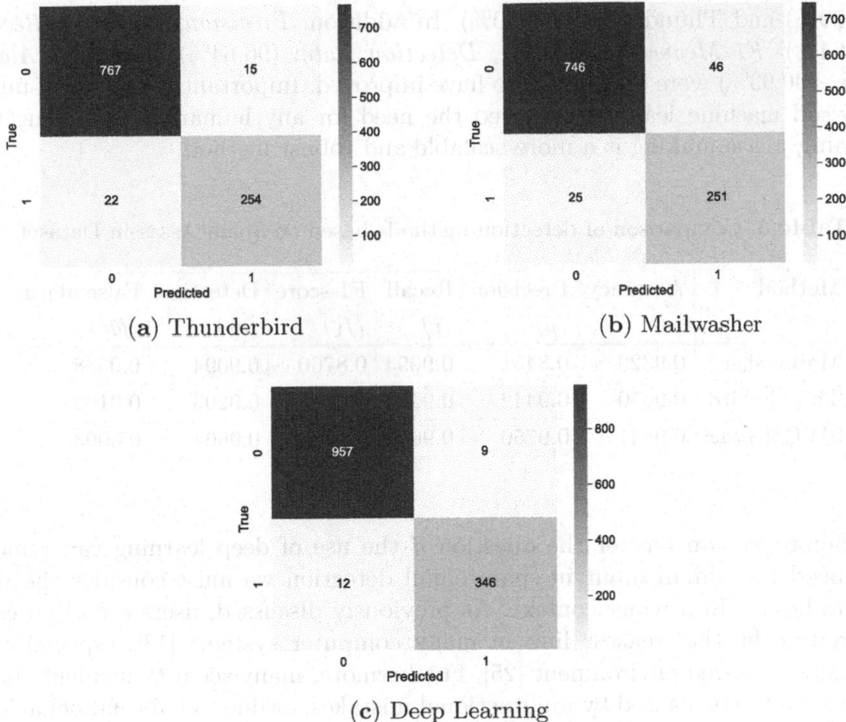

(a) Thunderbird (b) Mailwasher

(c) Deep Learning

Fig. 1. Confusion matrices for detection of spam email

Figure 1 shows the calculated confusion matrices based on the metrics described above. Figure 2 shows the accuracy and loss values for the implemented SWEM-*max* model. Finally, Table 3 shows a performance comparison between the two bayesian-based software spam filtering solutions and the deep learning approach. It can be clearly seen that classification accuracy is improved using the Deep Learning approach (98.41%) when compared to both Mailwasher

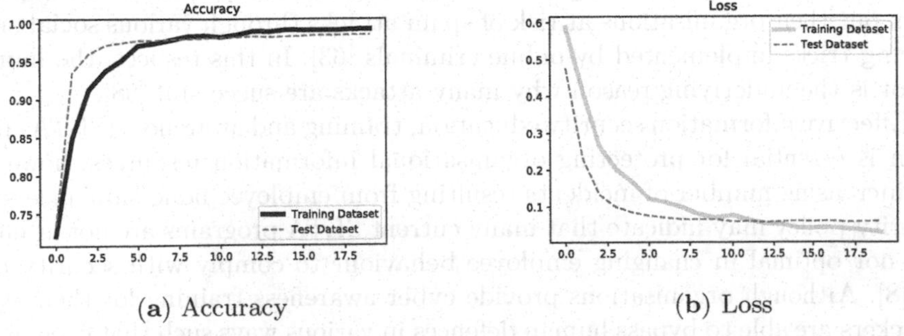

(a) Accuracy (b) Loss

Fig. 2. Accuracy and Loss of SWEM-*max* model

(93.29%) and Thunderbird (96.50%). In addition, *Precision*: (97.50%), *Recall*: (96.64%), *F1 Measure*: (97.05%), *Detection Rate*: (96.64%) and *False Alarm Rate*: (00.93%) were also shown to have improved. Importantly, the use of unsupervised machine learning removed the need for any human input during the training phase making it a more scalable and robust method.

Table 3. Comparison of detection methods based on Spam Assassin Dataset

Method	Accuracy *(a)*	Precision *(p)*	Recall *(r)*	F1-score (f_1)	Detection *(dr)*	False alarm *(far)*
Mailwasher	0.9329	0.8451	0.9094	0.8760	0.9094	0.0588
Thunderbird	0.9650	0.9442	0.9203	0.9321	0.9203	0.0192
SWEM-*max*	0.9841	0.9750	0.9664	0.9705	0.9664	0.0093

Before we can answer the question if the use of deep learning can remove the need for human input in spam email detection we must consider the role of the human in a wider context. As previously discussed, users are often considered to be the weakest link in many computer systems [13], especially in a human-centered environment [25]. Furthermore, many security incidents have been found to be caused by unintentional mistakes, or due to habitual behaviour that promotes an automatic response, rather than malicious acts by an attacker [72] In this respect, users' lack of understanding of how computer systems work, a lack of attention to security and the high quality visual deception deployed by phishers can weaken human defences [21]. From a spear phishing perspective, the human factor is especially inherent and can pose great danger to employees and organisations due to the inherent weakness of humans to identify every threat from spear phishing cues [51]. This can result in spam filtering software, such as those evaluated in this study, not being adequately trained. Additionally, this situation presupposes that the end user has taken time to train and retrain the filter in the first place, which may not be the case. Research on the human factor in cyber-enabled and cyber-dependent crime indicated that individuals' online behaviours facilitate cyber-dependent crime victimisation [4]. Hence, computer users put their organisations at risk of spam attacks through various social engineering tricks implemented by online criminals [63]. In this respect, the human factor is the underlying reason why many attacks are successful [58].

Effective information security education, training and awareness (SETA) program is essential for protecting organisational information resources, however, the increasing number of incidents resulting from employee noncompliance with security policy may indicate that many current SETA programs are not as effective nor optimal in changing employee behaviour to comply with security policy [8]. Although organisations provide cyber awareness training for their staff, attackers are able to bypass human defences in various ways such that even experienced staff make mistakes and can be deceived [11]. Since a secure system relies on humans making good decisions, human factors may create weaknesses in a system that an attacker could exploit [20]. In response, organisations often use rule-based training to teach individuals to identify threats in order to mitigate phishing's impact, however, even regular repetition of rule-based training may not yield increasing resistance to attacks [38].

Machine learning algorithms have been applied by researchers to automatically detect spam [15]. A bottleneck in developing such machine learning techniques is the lack of high quality labelled training data where human labelling to obtain high quality labelled data is expensive and not scalable [45]. Additionally, manually classifying spam can be time consuming. To be done effectively users are required to spend considerable time reading email messages and deciding whether it is spam or not. As such, some e-mail service providers prefer to automate spam detection using server based spam detectors and filters that can classify e-mails as spam automatically [53]. While normal spam filters has proven very useful by focusing on the content of email, they do not prevent the bandwidth from being wasted and is ineffective against the clever manipulation of the spam content by spammers [43]. Furthermore, spam filtering methods usually compare the contents of emails against specific keywords, which are not robust as the spammers frequently change the terms used in emails [71]. In this respect, automatic email filtering using machine learning may be the most effective method of detecting spam as spammers can easily bypass common spam filtering methods (text analysis, white and blacklisting of domain names, and community-primarily based techniques) easily [42].

The final area of consideration is the ever-changing landscape of spam email detection. As shown in Sect. 2 the methods and techniques used by attackers are becoming increasingly more sophisticated and targeted. This was clearly demonstrated in [1,35,68] where the methods used by attackers during the current covid-19 pandemic became very specific, exploiting vulnerabilities in human psychology to leverage the fear surrounding the pandemic and generate phishing emails unique to this context. Here, it is unclear whether automated spam filtering, including the use of deep learning, can sufficiently understand the context in order to accurately detect spam email. A lack of available datasets based on this context prevented us from exploring this further, however, it was accepted that given the timely context, human input in the form of manual training would be advantageous. As such, the question of contextualisation in spam email detection remains unanswered.

5 Conclusions and Future Work

In this study, we evaluated the current state of spam detection and sought to explore the question: *Does the use of deep learning remove the need for human input in spam email detection?*. In doing so, we demonstrated an improvement in accuracy through the use of deep learning. The results in Sect. 4 showed that our deep learning model, based on simple word embedding and global max pooling (SWEM-max), returned higher detection accuracy (98.41%) than both the bayesian-based software spam filters: Thunderbird (95%) and Mailwasher(92%). However, while we demonstrated that replacing human input with machine learning during the training phase can improve accuracy, we postulated that this may not paint a full picture of the current state of affairs. We demonstrated that new attacks may target the same heuristics and cognitive biases (e.g. fear), but in new and unique ways, and in the context of a specific event. This was demonstrated in [59] where phishing attacks specifically targeted an increase in Zoom usage, and other remote working tools, due to the Covid-19 pandemic. As such, good research is often said to raise more questions than it answers. By that standard, this study raises new questions relating to the role of human input in spam detection. Future avenues of research could be motivated by follow-up questions such as:

1. What is the role and impact of context in spam detection?
2. Does using a dataset out of context affect detection performance?
3. Are new metrics beyond those used on Sect. 4 needed for spam detection?

References

1. Abroshan, H., Devos, J., Poels, G., Laermans, E.: Phishing happens beyond technology: the effects of human behaviors and demographics on each step of a phishing process. IEEE Access **9**, 44928–44949 (2021)
2. Abu-Nimeh, S., Nappa, D., Wang, X., Nair, S.: A comparison of machine learning techniques for phishing detection. In: Proceedings of the Anti-Phishing Working Groups 2nd Annual eCrime Researchers Summit, pp. 60–69 (2007)
3. Abutair, H., Belghith, A., AlAhmadi, S.: CBR-PDS: a case-based reasoning phishing detection system. J. Ambient. Intell. Humaniz. Comput. **10**(7), 2593–2606 (2019)
4. Akdemir, N., Lawless, C.J.: Exploring the human factor in cyber-enabled and cyber-dependent crime victimisation: a lifestyle routine activities approach. Internet Res. (2020)
5. Alghoul, A., Al Ajrami, S., Al Jarousha, G., Harb, G., Abu-Naser, S.S.: Email classification using artificial neural network. Int. J. Acad. Eng. Res. (IJAER) **2**(11), 8–14 (2018)
6. Alkahtani, H.S., Gardner-Stephen, P., Goodwin, R.: A taxonomy of email spam filters. In: Proceedings of the 12th International Arab Conference on Information Technology (ACIT 2011), pp. 351–356 (2011)
7. Alrwais, S., Yuan, K., Alowaisheq, E., Li, Z., Wang, X.: Understanding the dark side of domain parking. In: 23rd {USENIX} Security Symposium ({USENIX} Security 14), pp. 207–222 (2014)
8. Alshaikh, M., Naseer, H., Ahmad, A., Maynard, S.B.: Toward sustainable behaviour change: an approach for cyber security education training and awareness (2019)
9. Baadel, S., Lu, J.: Data analytics: intelligent anti-phishing techniques based on machine learning. J. Inf. Knowl. Manage. **18**(01), 1950005 (2019)
10. Banday, M.T., Jan, T.R.: Effectiveness and limitations of statistical spam filters. arXiv preprint arXiv:0910.2540 (2009)

11. Bhardwaj, A., Sapra, V., Kumar, A., Kumar, N., Arthi, S.: Why is phishing still successful? Comput. Fraud Secur. **2020**(9), 15–19 (2020)
12. Boyle, P., Shepherd, L.A.: Mailtrout: a machine learning browser extension for detecting phishing emails. In: 33rd British Human Computer Interaction Conference: Post-Pandemic HCI-Living digitally. Association for Computing Machinery (ACM) (2021)
13. Caldwell, T.: Training-the weakest link. Comput. Fraud Secur. **2012**(9), 8–14 (2012)
14. Cao, Y., Han, W., Le, Y.: Anti-phishing based on automated individual white-list. In: Proceedings of the 4th ACM Workshop on Digital Identity Management, pp. 51–60 (2008)
15. Chen, C., et al.: A performance evaluation of machine learning-based streaming spam tweets detection. IEEE Trans. Comput. Social Syst. **2**(3), 65–76 (2015)
16. Christina, V., Karpagavalli, S., Suganya, G.: Email spam filtering using supervised machine learning techniques. Int. J. Comput. Sci. Eng. (IJCSE) **2**(09), 3126–3129 (2010)
17. Cveticanin, N.: (2021). https://dataprot.net/
18. Dablain, D., Krawczyk, B., Chawla, N.V.: Deepsmote: fusing deep learning and smote for imbalanced data. IEEE Trans. Neural Netw. Learn. Syst., 1–15 (2022)
19. Dada, E.G., Bassi, J.S., Chiroma, H., Adetunmbi, A.O., Ajibuwa, O.E., et al.: Machine learning for email spam filtering: review, approaches and open research problems. Heliyon **5**(6), e01802 (2019)
20. Desolda, G., Ferro, L.S., Marrella, A., Catarci, T., Costabile, M.F.: Human factors in phishing attacks: a systematic literature review. ACM Comput. Surv. (CSUR) **54**(8), 1–35 (2021)
21. Dhamija, R., Tygar, D.: Hearst. m. 2006. why phishing works. In: Proceedings of the SIGCHI conference on Human Factors in Computing Systems, pp. 22–27 (2006)
22. Dhanaraj, S., Karthikeyani, V.: A study on e-mail image spam filtering techniques. In: 2013 International Conference on Pattern Recognition, Informatics and Mobile Engineering, pp. 49–55. IEEE (2013)
23. Dudley, J.: Improving the performance of heuristic spam detection using a multi-objective genetic algorithm. The University of Western Australia, School of Computer Science and Software Engineering (2007)
24. Fahmy, H.M., Ghoneim, S.A.: Phishblock: A hybrid anti-phishing tool. In: 2011 International Conference on Communications, Computing and Control Applications (CCCA), pp. 1–5. IEEE (2011)
25. Fan, W., Kevin, L., Rong, R.: Social engineering: IE based model of human weakness for attack and defense investigations. IJ Comput. Netw. Inf. Secur. **9**(1), 1–11 (2017)
26. Fette, I., Sadeh, N., Tomasic, A.: Learning to detect phishing emails. In: Proceedings of the 16th international conference on World Wide Web, pp. 649–656 (2007)
27. Gangavarapu, T., Jaidhar, C.D., Chanduka, B.: Applicability of machine learning in spam and phishing email filtering: review and approaches. Artif. Intell. Rev. **53**(7), 5019–5081 (2020). https://doi.org/10.1007/s10462-020-09814-9
28. Guo, K.H., Yuan, Y., Archer, N.P., Connelly, C.E.: Understanding nonmalicious security violations in the workplace: a composite behavior model. J. Manag. Inf. Syst. **28**(2), 203–236 (2011)
29. Gupta, B.B., Arachchilage, N.A.G., Psannis, K.E.: Defending against phishing attacks: taxonomy of methods, current issues and future directions. Telecommun. Syst. **67**(2), 247–267 (2017). https://doi.org/10.1007/s11235-017-0334-z

30. Han, J., Pei, J., Kamber, M.: Data Mining: Concepts and Techniques. Elsevier, Amsterdam (2011)
31. Hao, S., Syed, N.A., Feamster, N., Gray, A.G., Krasser, S.: Detecting spammers with snare: spatio-temporal network-level automatic reputation engine. In: USENIX security symposium, vol. 9 (2009)
32. Harinahalli Lokesh, G., BoreGowda, G.: Phishing website detection based on effective machine learning approach. J. Cyber Secur. Technol. **5**(1), 1–14 (2021)
33. Hayati, P., Potdar, V., Talevski, A., Firoozeh, N., Sarencheh, S., Yeganeh, E.: Definition of spam 2.0: new spamming boom, pp. 580–584 (2010). https://doi.org/10.1109/DEST.2010.5610590
34. Heron, S.: Technologies for spam detection. Netw. Secur. **2009**(1), 11–15 (2009)
35. Hill, J.: (2021). https://abnormalsecurity.com/blog/how-to-stop-email-spoofing
36. Irwin, L.: (2020). https://www.itgovernance.eu/blog/en/the-5-most-common-types-of-phishing-attack
37. Jain, A.K., Gupta, B.B.: PHISH-SAFE: URL features-based phishing detection system using machine learning. In: Bokhari, M.U., Agrawal, N., Saini, D. (eds.) Cyber Security. AISC, vol. 729, pp. 467–474. Springer, Singapore (2018). https://doi.org/10.1007/978-981-10-8536-9_44
38. Jensen, M.L., Dinger, M., Wright, R.T., Thatcher, J.B.: Training to mitigate phishing attacks using mindfulness techniques. J. Manag. Inf. Syst. **34**(2), 597–626 (2017)
39. Khan, S.A., Khan, W., Hussain, A.: Phishing attacks and websites classification using machine learning and multiple datasets (a comparative analysis). In: Huang, D.-S., Premaratne, P. (eds.) ICIC 2020. LNCS (LNAI), vol. 12465, pp. 301–313. Springer, Cham (2020). https://doi.org/10.1007/978-3-030-60796-8_26
40. Kołcz, A., Chowdhury, A.: Hardening fingerprinting by context. In: CEAS 2007 (2007)
41. Kołcz, A., Chowdhury, A., Alspector, J.: The impact of feature selection on signature-driven spam detection. In: Proceedings of the 1st Conference on Email and Anti-Spam (CEAS-2004) (2004)
42. Kumar, N., Sonowal, S., et al.: Email spam detection using machine learning algorithms. In: 2020 Second International Conference on Inventive Research in Computing Applications (ICIRCA), pp. 108–113. IEEE (2020)
43. Lam, H.Y., Yeung, D.Y.: A learning approach to spam detection based on social networks. Ph.D. thesis, Hong Kong University of Science and Technology (2007)
44. Liu, X., et al.: CPSFS: a credible personalized spam filtering scheme by crowdsourcing. Wireless Communications and Mobile Computing 2017 (2017)
45. Luo, C., Xia, C., Shao, H.: Training high quality spam-detection models using weak labels (2020)
46. Mansoor, R., Jayasinghe, N.D., Muslam, M.M.A.: A comprehensive review on email spam classification using machine learning algorithms. In: 2021 International Conference on Information Networking (ICOIN), pp. 327–332. IEEE (2021)
47. Mohamed, S.A.E.: Efficient spam filtering system based on smart cooperative subjective and objective methods (2013)
48. Mozilla Support: Thunderbird and junk/spam messages (2021). https://support.mozilla.org/en-US/kb/thunderbird-and-junk-spam-messages. Accessed on 19 Jan 2021
49. Najadat, H., Hmeidi, I.: Web spam detection using machine learningin specific domain features (2008)

50. Niakanlahiji, A., Chu, B.T., Al-Shaer, E.: Phishmon: a machine learning framework for detecting phishing webpages. In: 2018 IEEE International Conference on Intelligence and Security Informatics (ISI), pp. 220–225. IEEE (2018)
51. Nicho, M., Fakhry, H., Egbue, U.: Evaluating user vulnerabilities vs phisher skills in spear phishing. Int. J. Comput. Sci. Inform. Syst. **13**, 93–108 (2018)
52. Paans, R., Herschberg, I.: Computer security: the long road ahead. Comput. Secur. **6**(5), 403–416 (1987)
53. Patidar, V., Singh, D., Singh, A.: A novel technique of email classification for spam detection. Int. J. Appl. Inf. Syst. **5**(10), 15–19 (2013)
54. Patil, R.C., Patil, D.: Web spam detection using SVM classifier. In: 2015 IEEE 9th International Conference on Intelligent Systems and Control (ISCO), pp. 1–4. IEEE (2015)
55. Rahman, S.S.M.M., Islam, T., Jabiullah, M.I.: Phishstack: evaluation of stacked generalization in phishing URLs detection. Proc. Comput. Sci. **167**, 2410–2418 (2020)
56. Ramachandran, A., Dagon, D., Feamster, N.: Can DNS-based blacklists keep up with bots? In: CEAS (2006)
57. Ren, M., Zeng, W., Yang, B., Urtasun, R.: Learning to reweight examples for robust deep learning. In: International Conference on Machine Learning, pp. 4334–4343. PMLR (2018)
58. Richardson, M.D., Lemoine, P.A., Stephens, W.E., Waller, R.E.: Planning for cyber security in schools: the human factor. Educat. Plann. **27**(2), 23–39 (2020)
59. Roman, R., Zhou, J., Lopez, J.: An anti-spam scheme using pre-challenges. Comput. Commun. **29**(15), 2739–2749 (2006)
60. Rosenthal, M.: (2021). https://www.tessian.com/blog/phishing-statistics-2020/
61. Seewald, A.K.: Combining Bayesian and rule score learning: automated tuning for spam as sassin. Intelligent Data Analysis. Technical report, TR-2004-11 Austrian Research Institute for Artificial Intelligence, Vienna, Austria (2004)
62. Sendpulse: (2020). https://sendpulse.com/support/glossary/phishing
63. Shakela, V., Jazri, H.: Assessment of spear phishing user experience and awareness: an evaluation framework model of spear phishing exposure level (SPEL) in the Namibian financial industry. In: 2019 international conference on advances in big data, computing and data communication systems (icABCD), pp. 1–5. IEEE (2019)
64. Shen, D., et al.: Baseline needs more love: On simple word-embedding-based models and associated pooling mechanisms (2018). https://doi.org/10.18653/v1/P18-1041
65. Sonowal, G., Kuppusamy, K.: Mmsphid: a phoneme based phishing verification model for persons with visual impairments. Inf. Comput Secur. **26**(5), 613–636 (2018)
66. Srivastava, N., Hinton, G., Krizhevsky, A., Sutskever, I., Salakhutdinov, R.: Dropout: a simple way to prevent neural networks from overfitting. J. Mach. Learn. Res. **15**(1), 1929–1958 (2014)
67. Statista (2021). https://www.statista.com/statistics/255080/number-of-e-mail-users-worldwide
68. Tessian (2021). https://www.tessian.com/blog/covid-19-real-life-examples-of-opportunistic-phishing-emails-2/
69. Tong, Z., Weiss, S.M.: The Handbook of Data Mining. Lawrence Erlbaum Associates, New Jersey (2003)
70. Wash, R., Cooper, M.M.: Who provides phishing training? facts, stories, and people like me. In: Proceedings of the 2018 Chi Conference on Human Factors in Computing Systems, pp. 1–12 (2018)

71. Wu, C.H.: Behavior-based spam detection using a hybrid method of rule-based techniques and neural networks. Expert Syst. Appl. **36**(3), 4321–4330 (2009)
72. Zafar, H., Randolph, A., Gupta, S., Hollingsworth, C.: Traditional seta no more: investigating the intersection between cybersecurity and cognitive neuroscience. In: Proceedings of the 52nd Hawaii International Conference on System Sciences (2019)

Scene Change Captioning in Real Scenarios

Yue Qiu[(✉)], Kodai Nakashima, Yutaka Satoh, Ryota Suzuki, Kenji Iwata, and Hirokatsu Kataoka

National Institute of Advanced Industrial Science and Technology (AIST), Tsukuba 305-8560, Japan
{qiu.yue,nakashima.kodai,yu.satou,ryota.suzuki, kenji.iwata,hirokatsu.kataoka}@aist.go.jp

Abstract. This paper discusses the scene change captioning task that describes scene changes using natural language for real scenarios. Most current three-dimensional understanding tasks focus on recognizing static scenes. Despite its importance in a variety of real environment applications, scene change understanding remains less discussed. Existing change understanding methods discussed in robotics focus on change detection and lack the ability to perform detailed recognition of scene changes. Most previous experiments on change captioning methods were conducted on simulation datasets with limited visual complexity, limiting their availability for real scenarios. To solve the above issues, we propose a scene change captioning dataset with scenes photographed using RGB-D cameras. We also propose an automatic simulation dataset generation process, aiming for training models transferring to real scenarios. We conducted experiments with various input modalities and proposed a method that integrates different input modalities using an attention mechanism over modalities and dynamic attention to select related information during the sentence generation process. The experimental results show that models trained on the proposed simulation dataset obtained promising results on real scenario dataset, indicating the proposed dataset generation process's practicality in real scenarios. The proposed multimodality integrating method can generate change captions with high change type and object attribute accuracy while showing robustness in real scenarios. We hope our work can open a door for future research on scene change understanding in real scenarios.

Keywords: Computer vision · Deep learning · Natural language processing

1 Introduction

Scene change recognition is essential for a variety of real environment applications. For home robots, knowledge of scene changes is useful for managing and updating room information needed for executing household tasks efficiently.

H. Degen and S. Ntoa (Eds.): HCII 2022, LNAI 13336, pp. 405–419, 2022.
https://doi.org/10.1007/978-3-031-05643-7_26

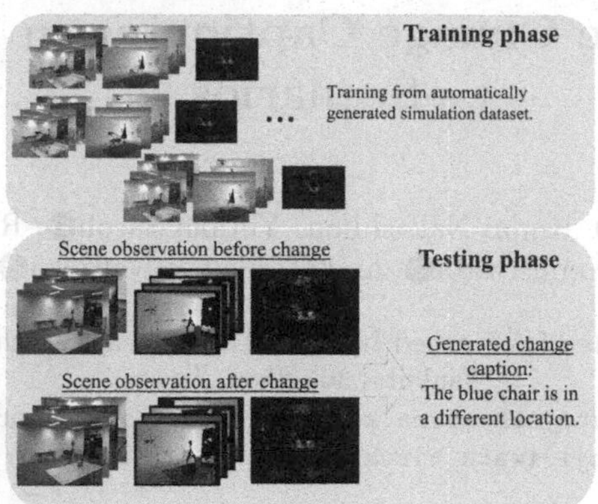

Fig. 1. We generate scene change captions under real scenarios with multiview RGB-D images and the point clouds observed before and after a scene change. We propose an automatic simulation generation process for generating datasets for training models.

Existing scene change recognition methods [1–3] applied in robotics mainly focus on detecting changed regions of a scene and lack the ability to perform detailed semantic recognition of changes, such as change type and attribute recognition of changed objects.

Natural language can be an alternative to convey information to human operators for providing effective human-robot interaction. Image captioning is one of the most discussed vision and language tasks [4–7]. Conventional image captioning methods describe the content of a given image through natural language text. More recently, researchers have adapted image captioning to change recognition that generates change content from two observations of a scene. Jhamtani et al. [8] and Park et al. [9] propose scene change captioning methods from single-view images of scenes. Due to object occlusion and camera position change occurring in real scenarios, change recognition from single-view images could be problematic. Qiu et al. [10] proposed a method for scene change understanding from multiview RGB-D images. However, they only conducted experiments under simulated environments and object models with larger scales than their normal sizes, limiting the practicality in real scenarios.

To address the above issues, as shown in Fig. 1, we propose a scene change captioning dataset with images photographed using RGB-D cameras in real office environments. We created the dataset by rearranging objects in scenes manually. Due to the high labor costs of constructing real photographed scene change captioning datasets, we further propose an automatic simulation dataset generation process, which generates RGB-D images with high similarity to real scenarios for training models. We trained models on a simulated dataset and evaluated the models on both simulation and real datasets. We conducted extensive experiments on different input modalities, including RGB images, depth images, and point clouds.

In order to integrate information of different input modalities, we introduce a modality-attention module that determines the importance of modality based on the visual features of different modalities. We also adopted a dynamic attention module to further determine the importance of different modalities in the sentence generation process.

The experimental results indicate that models trained on our proposed simulation dataset exhibit promising performance when transferred to test set with real photographed scenes. The single-modality model with RGB images input achieved high accuracy on predicting object color, while the model with point cloud input obtained high accuracy on change type and object class prediction. We also found that the modality-attention mechanism helps to improve the robustness in real scenarios. The dynamic attention mechanism tends to keep the strengths of different input modalities, achieving high object color, class, and change type accuracy.

We found that there is still a performance gap between real scenarios and simulated environments through experiments on simulated and real photographed datasets on different modalities. Our dataset can be a benchmark for future discussion of the scene change captioning for real-world scenarios, such as indoor environments.

2 Related Work

2.1 Change Detection

Change detection from scenes captured from different moments has been studied in various real-world scenarios. [1,2,11] have discussed change detection from indoor scenes. Herbst et al. [1] propose a method for determining the movable parts from two aligned 3-D maps using a probabilistic model. In [2], Ambrus et al. proposed a rule-based method that separates the static and dynamic parts of a room scene from multiple observations. Halber et al. [11] proposed a temporal model of indoor scenes for representing semantic information of scenes across different times.

Various existing studies discuss change detection for disaster management [12,13], resource monitoring [14,15], and vehicle navigation [16,17]. Fujita et al. [12] proposed a dataset consisting of pre- and post-tsunami images to detect washed-away buildings. Sakurada et al. [13] proposed a method that integrates CNN structure with superpixel segmentation for detecting changes of tsunami-damaged areas. Khan et al. [14] proposed a spatiotemporal inpainting mechanism to recover the missing surfaces between forest images. Saha et al. [15] proposed an unsupervised framework for change detection that utilizes deep features for enhancing the robustness to images with various appearances. Alcantarilla et al. [16] and Daudt et al. [17] introduced deep deconvolutional networks to detect pixel-wise change region of street view images. Different from change detection, we address the problem of localizing and describing change information with language text.

2.2 3D Scene Understanding

A series of methods handle multiview images [18–20]. The author of MVCNN [18] proposed a view-pooling method that adopts a max or average pooling operation over separately extracted image features to integrate the information of multiview images. Their method achieved strong performance in object recognition. Qi et al. proposed PointNet [21] and PointNet++ [22], which can learn representation for downstream tasks such as recognition and segmentation. In the present work, we handle the input of multiview RGB-D images of scenes. We adapt MVCNN to obtain an integrated scene representation from multiview images and PointNet as an encoder for point clouds.

2.3 Image Captioning

Recently, a range of image captioning methods has been proposed. Xu et al. [4] proposed a method that first extracts feature maps from input images and generates image captioning using an RNN with attention structure, which dynamically determines the image attention during decoding steps. Anderson et al. [5] proposed incorporating bottom-up attention into image captioning models for extracting salient objects. Biten et al. [6] adapted image captioning to illustrate articles by generating a news caption from an image and news article. Yoshida et al. [7] proposed a humorous image captioning model that can generate image captions with high humor scores.

Some recent work has been on generating change captions from two observations of a scene [8–10]. Jhamtani et al. [8] proposed a method for describing object-level differences from two RGB images. They cluster pixel differences in two images to determine change content. Park et al. [9] proposed a method that computes image feature differences of two RGB images of a scene and adopted an attention mechanism to determine important image regions for change understanding. Both of these methods handle change understanding based on single-view RGB images, making them vulnerable to occlusion and camera movements. Qiu et al. [10] proposed a change captioning method that incorporates multimodality multiview observation. They combined multimodality image features by concatenation and obtained high accuracy in a simulation dataset. However, they did not conduct experiments under real scenario setups, limiting the availability in real scenarios. In contrast, we conduct experiments under both simulation and real dataset setups and introduce an attention mechanism for integrating multimodality input.

2.4 Change Captioning Datasets

Jhamtani et al. [8] proposed the spot-the-diff dataset for describing differences between image pairs sampled from surveillance videos. However, their dataset does not contain camera viewpoint change, lacking the ability to evaluate models' robustness to camera changes. Park et al. [9] proposed a simulated change captioning dataset CLEVR_Change based on the CLEVR Engine proposed by

Johnson et al. [23]. However, the CLEVR_Change dataset consists of preliminary geometric objects and thus has limited the visual complexity.

Recently, a range of large-scale scene dataset has been proposed [24–26]. Matterport3D dataset [24] consists of textured meshes and semantic labels of 90 buildings photographed from real indoor scenes. Qiu et al. [10] proposed a simulation scene change captioning dataset built upon Matterport3D datasets by arranging objects in different rooms. In contrast, in this paper, we propose a change captioning dataset consisting of scenes and objects photographed using RGB-D cameras to evaluate models under real scenarios.

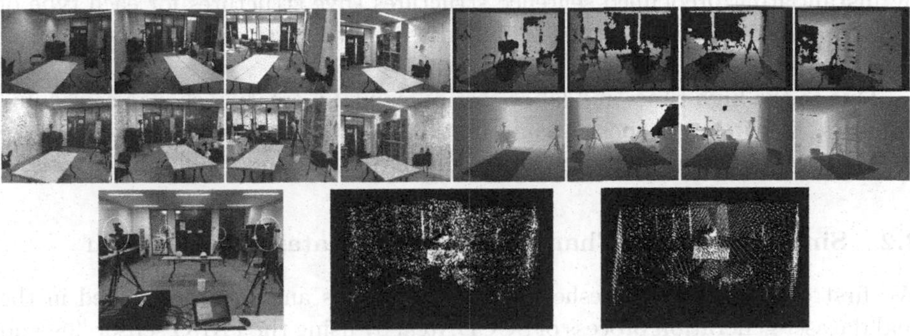

Fig. 2. Camera setups and examples of SCCD_Real and SCCD_Sim dataset. Top row: RGB and depth images photographed from four viewpoints of SCCD_Real. Second row: RGB and depth images of SCCD_Sim (generated using the proposed automatic simulated dataset generation process). Bottom row (from left to right): RGB-D camera setups where the cameras are highlighted by yellow ovals; point cloud generated from the images of the top row; point cloud generated from the images of the second row. (Color figure online)

Table 1. Dataset statistics of sccd_sim and sccd_real.

Dataset	Scenes (train/test)	Captions (train/test)	Change types	Viewpoints	No. of rooms	Object classes (Instances)	Objects per scene
SCCD_Real	(0/479)	(0/2,395)	5	4	5	4 (17)	3–7
SCCD_Sim	(30,000/10,000)	(150,000/50,000)	5	4	5	4 (17)	3–7

3 Dataset

3.1 Real Scene Change Captioning Dataset: SCCD_Real

In order to capture multiview RGB-D images of indoor scenes, as shown in Fig. 2 (bottom row, left), we placed four ASUS Xtion PRO LIVE cameras [27] and completed internal and external camera calibration for each scene. We shot

RGB and depth images from four viewpoints and reconstructed a point cloud for each scene.

After capturing the original observation data of a scene, we create four types of change: add (add an object), delete (delete an object), move (relocate an object), and replace (replace an object with a new one) by manually rearranging objects of the original scene. In our dataset generation, we used five office rooms as scenes and randomly placed four to six objects in each original scene from four object classes: ball (four instances), box (five instances), ashcan (three instances), and chair (five instances). Each instance of a class has a different color. We recorded scene changes and generated five change captions for each scene change by instantiating predefined sentence structures (five structures for each type of change). We show the statistics of the dataset in the first row of Table 1 and an example in Fig. 2.

Due to the high time- and labor cost of manually creating change captioning datasets, we further propose an automatic dataset generation process to create RGB-D scene change caption pairs to enable training and evaluating models.

3.2 Simulated Scene Change Captioning Dataset: SCCD_Sim

We first create textured meshes for the five rooms and 17 objects used in the real dataset generation process of SCCD_Real by using the FARO sensor [28] and FARO's mesh generation program. Next, we import textured meshes of rooms in the AI Habitat simulator [29], which can render RGB and depths images simultaneously. We set four virtual cameras for each scene and adjusted camera positions and rotations to obtain observations similar to those under the real dataset setup.

We generated scene changes by placing object models at tables or floors of each scene randomly. We generated four types of changes (one instance for each change type) and one distractor (no change) with only camera movement for each scene. We added a random camera movement ([−0.015 m, 0.015 m] for each of the three dimensions) to the scenes of each of the four types of changes and the distractor. We generated point clouds from RGB and depth images observed from four viewpoints and randomly sampled each point cloud to 5,000 points. The caption generation process is the same as that of the real dataset generation. The statistics of the dataset that we used in experiments are shown in the second row of Table 1 and an example is shown in Fig. 2.

4 Approach

4.1 Overall Framework

In this work, we generate change captioning from two observations of a scene with a scene change. Each observation contains RGB and depth images observed from multiple viewpoints and a registered point cloud. As shown in Fig. 3, our overall framework consists of two components: a scene encoder that encodes the

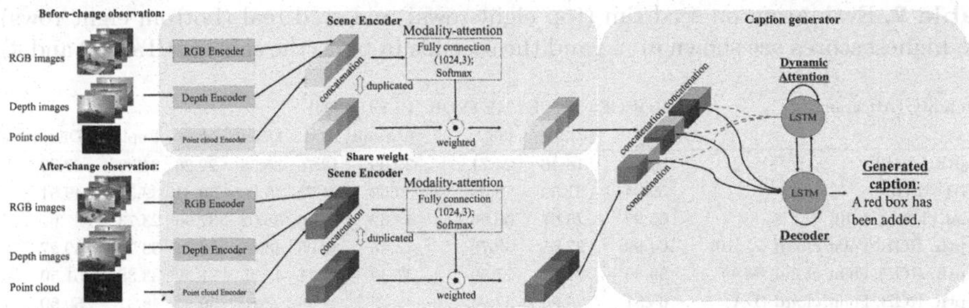

Fig. 3. Illustration of the proposed network. The overall framework encodes before- and after-change scene observation using two scene encoders with shared weight. The caption generator generates a change caption based on the output of the scene encoders.

multimodality input of before- and after-change scenes; and a caption generator that generates a natural language text change caption based on the output of the scene encoder.

4.2 Scene Encoder

The scene encoder encodes multimodality input into a scene representation. We first encode input modality with different encoders. For RGB and depth images, we adapted the MVCNN models to obtain an integrated image feature from multiview images. We used PointNet to extract features from input point clouds. In our implementation, we used the RGB/depth and point cloud encoder proposed in [10]. For details of the network structures, please refer to [10].

Due to occlusion and sensor accuracy, the information obtained in the three modalities differs for different scenes. To enable determination of the importance of the three modalities, we introduce a modality-attention (MA) module. As shown in Fig. 3, we first concatenate three obtained features and use a fully connection and softmax layer to compute weights over those three modalities. The weighted features are inputted to the caption generator. We use the same network to extract scene representations of both before- and after-change scene observations and concatenate before- and after-change features of three modalities.

4.3 Caption Generator

The caption generator describes scene change through text from the output of the scene encoder. We deployed a two-layered LSTM [30] structure for caption generation. Since different modalities can exhibit different strengths in change type and object attributes prediction, we adopted the dynamic attention mechanism (DA) proposed in Park et al. [9] for dynamically determining the importance of different modalities during the caption generation process. For details of the network structures, please refer to [9].

Table 2. Evaluation on sccd_sim (top eight rows) and sccd_real (bottom eight rows). the highest scores are shown in red and the seconds in blue (the same for Table 3 and 4).

Modality (Attention)	ROUGE	SPICE	METEOR	BLEU-4 [34]					
	[31]	[32]	[33]	Overall	Add	Delete	Move	Replace	Distractor
Depth (-) [10]	54.60	18.46	24.71	32.99	12.76	35.53	22.26	24.30	63.39
RGB (-) [10]	59.34	21.59	29.45	39.59	21.74	45.26	39.84	39.54	49.51
Point cloud (-) [10]	65.96	25.67	30.96	46.62	21.46	38.02	37.90	23.73	91.07
Depth, RGB, Point cloud (-) [10]	64.99	22.95	30.79	42.48	32.06	48.05	46.74	33.76	49.27
Depth, RGB, Point cloud (MA)	59.90	21.33	27.50	37.60	21.11	45.45	31.99	33.88	51.50
Depth, RGB, Point cloud (DA)	65.51	25.80	32.93	49.73	39.08	53.60	50.84	48.31	50.90
Depth, RGB, Point cloud (MA, DA)	66.13	27.29	33.12	47.31	34.95	44.83	52.27	42.83	54.37
Random	44.16	9.72	15.38	14.31	8.22	11.86	15.40	14.61	19.95
Depth (-) [10]	52.98	17.76	24.67	35.17	9.71	16.25	30.14	17.30	74.14
RGB (-) [10]	64.21	23.55	32.26	46.79	27.04	31.97	33.77	32.39	90.43
Point cloud (-) [10]	58.84	19.82	27.59	42.45	10.89	24.72	25.83	13.35	90.87
Depth, RGB, Point cloud (-) [10]	61.53	16.57	25.72	34.94	16.77	26.54	28.66	21.11	84.06
Depth, RGB, Point cloud (MA)	63.93	16.98	26.55	36.13	17.46	19.57	34.95	24.96	100.00
Depth, RGB, Point cloud (DA)	64.97	21.52	30.39	41.76	17.29	23.83	36.89	31.70	100.00
Depth, RGB, Point cloud (MA, DA)	66.01	20.55	29.86	43.88	36.03	30.30	37.84	28.40	91.56
Random	45.41	10.31	16.53	17.76	7.31	15.42	17.26	13.41	12.21

Notably, the number of input modalities can be arbitrary, ranging from a single-modality. For single-modality input, we remove both the MA and DA modules.

5 Experiments

5.1 Experimental Setups

We evaluated the models' performance on datasets SCCD_Sim and SCCD_Real. We implemented the proposed models with attention mechanisms introduced in Sect. 3. And the models without attention originally proposed in [10] on different input modalities.

We evaluated each model using image caption evaluation metrics ROUGE [31], SPICE [32], METEOR [33], and BLEU-4 [34]. Those evaluation metrics evaluate the similarity between generated caption sentences and ground truth cations. We also introduced caption correctness evaluation, which extracts change type-related words, category-related words, color-related words, and objects (color and class, e.g., red box) from generated captions and calculates the accuracy by referring to those words in ground truth captions. We also conducted a per-class-BLEU-4 evaluation to evaluate model performance for changes related to different object classes.

We implemented the RGB/depth and point cloud encoder as RGB/Depth Encoder (MVCNN based structures) and PCD Encoder (PointNet based structure) as implemented in [10], setting the input image size for the RGB and depth images to 256 × 256. We used the Adam optimizer [35] in all implementations and set the learning rate for the RGB/depth encoder and caption generator to

Table 3. Change caption correctness evaluation on sccd_sim (top eight rows) and sccd_real (bottom eight rows) dataset.

Modality (Attention)	Accuracy (%)			
	Change type	Object	Color	Class
Depth (-) [10]	38.97	14.47	21.72	51.60
RGB (-) [10]	40.45	35.32	46.00	49.43
Point cloud (-) [10]	60.78	13.61	24.05	55.23
Depth,RGB,Point cloud (-) [10]	54.32	24.09	33.99	50.25
Depth,RGB,Point cloud (MA)	44.10	25.45	35.73	48.60
Depth,RGB,Point cloud (DA)	52.50	34.01	43.32	56.87
Depth,RGB,Point cloud (MA,DA)	44.65	39.48	50.01	55.03
Random	19.72	5.97	14.84	25.31
Depth (-) [10]	35.49	6.94	18.82	30.27
RGB (-) [10]	47.80	34.02	53.79	49.55
Point cloud (-) [10]	43.78	7.56	23.57	23.16
Depth, RGB, Point cloud (-) [10]	46.58	10.42	22.31	32.00
Depth, RGB, Point cloud (MA)	48.85	18.61	35.06	37.50
Depth, RGB, Point cloud (DA)	50.93	19.70	35.93	42.14
Depth, RGB, Point cloud (MA, DA)	49.26	34.79	51.98	51.09
Random	21.61	4.15	11.55	21.50

10^{-4} and that for the point cloud encoder to 10^{-3}. We trained each model using the training set of SCCD_Sim for 20 epochs.

5.2 Experiments on SCCD_Sim

We show the results for the test set of SCCD_Sim in the top half of Table 2. We provide overall performance on ROUGE, SPICE, METEOR, BLEU-4, and per-change-type accuracy on BLEU-4. We report the accuracy for three single-modality and four ensembles (without attention [10], with MA, with DA, with MA and DA). For comparison, we randomly picked one sentence from the training set for each test instance and report the results in the eighth and sixteenth row of Table 2 (Random).

Among single-modality models, the model with RGB images input performs better for changes (e.g., add, delete, and replace), and the model with point cloud input performs better for distractors, which only contain camera movements. The model with depth images input obtained the lowest performance. We used real-scale objects in SCCD_Sim and the object sizes could be small, making it extremely challenging to obtain useful information from point clouds. We found that the model with only the MA module obtained relatively poor performance among the ensembles. The two ensembles with the DA module obtained the best performance in terms of overall accuracy and achieved a relatively high performance for each of the four change types. The results indicate that the DA module, which aims to adjust the importance of different modalities during the sentence generation process, can help improve performance under this dataset setup.

We show the evaluation results for captioning correctness in Table 3 (top). From the results of the single-modality models, we found that the RGB input helps better determine the color and objects, and the depth and point cloud inputs can improve the accuracy in class prediction. The model with point cloud input obtains the highest accuracy for change type prediction. Under this dataset setup, object shapes differ between classes. Therefore, the geometric information in depth images and point clouds could be beneficial in class prediction. The ensemble with only the DA module obtains relatively high accuracy on both change type and object prediction, which might indicate that the DA module can help maintain different input modalities' strengths. Since some instances of a class have slightly different shapes, the color can possibly be inferred from object shapes (refer to the results of point cloud and depth images).

Table 4. Per-class-bleu-4 evaluation on sccd_sim (top eight rows) and sccd_real (bottom eight rows) dataset.

Modality (Attention)	Per-class-BLEU-4 [34]			
	Ball	Box	Ashcan	Chair
Depth (-) [10]	25.32	24.93	27.44	32.61
RGB (-) [10]	37.15	35.82	34.31	43.10
Point cloud (-) [10]	33.02	26.02	45.22	52.61
Depth,RGB,Point cloud (-) [10]	41.16	42.82	46.59	56.21
Depth,RGB,Point cloud (MA)	34.32	33.86	30.26	42.65
Depth,RGB,Point cloud (DA)	42.84	44.03	45.65	51.68
Depth,RGB,Point cloud (MA,DA)	46.47	37.62	37.56	48.99
Random	12.75	12.53	11.40	12.55
Depth (-) [10]	14.30	15.64	20.63	28.06
RGB (-) [10]	24.33	32.79	26.59	38.83
Point cloud (-) [10]	13.96	20.74	23.13	25.87
Depth,RGB,Point cloud (-) [10]	19.29	20.78	19.72	36.94
Depth,RGB,Point cloud (MA)	16.80	24.49	26.69	32.75
Depth,RGB,Point cloud (DA)	16.40	24.02	24.26	41.34
Depth,RGB,Point cloud (MA,DA)	37.67	34.99	27.55	37.85
Random	11.33	14.93	9.89	11.57

As shown in Table 4 (top), we computed BLEU-4 scores for different classes. All models obtained the highest BLEU-4 score for the chair class, which is the class with the biggest objects. The results indicate that incorporating active perception technology to obtain viewpoints with large object sizes might enhance the current models.

We show one example result in Fig. 4 (left). Our model with both of the MA and DA modules correctly predicted the caption, while the single-modality model with RGB input gave the correct object prediction but wrong change type. The single-modality with point cloud input, ensemble without attention, and ensemble with the DA module correctly predicted the change type but gave the wrong object attributes, while the remaining models gave incorrect predictions for both objects and change type. The RGB input is beneficial for predicting the objects, whereas the point cloud input contributes to change type prediction.

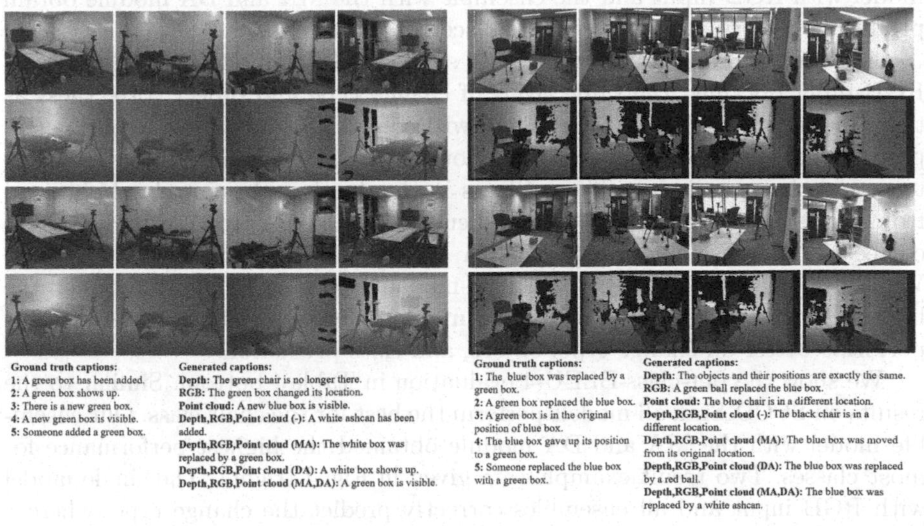

Fig. 4. Result examples for SCCD_Sim (left) and SCCD_Real (right). Top and second rows: RGB and depth images of the before-change scenes. Third and Fourth rows: RGB and depth images of the after-change scenes. For generated captons - green: correct; blue: incorrect object attributes; cyan: incorrect caption type; red: incorrect caption type and object attributes. (Color figure online)

5.3 Experiments on SCCD_Real

We evaluated the models' performance on SCCD_Real trained on the training set of SCCD_Sim (Table 2, bottom). We also report the results for Random, where each test captions is randomly picked from the training set. We found that most models obtained degraded performance for the four types of change but tended to perform better on the distractor. In the SCCD_Real, we used the original scene as the distractor, making it less challenging to specify distractors. Among the single-modality models, the model with RGB input is the most robust, whereas the model with point cloud input exhibits a large performance gap compared with the results on SCCD_Sim. The depth images and point clouds obtained from RGB-D sensors contain artifacts due to the sensors' precision, making them more vulnerable to variations in real scenarios. From the results with the ensembles, we found that models with the MA module exhibit relatively slight performance degradation. The MA module can adjust the importance of different modality features based on the ensemble features, making it possible to suppress a modality's importance if the features are less informative. Although the ensembles used depth and point cloud data with relatively low quality, they exhibited better performance than the single-modality model with RGB input for part of the evaluation metrics. Also, the single-modality model with RGB input and the ensemble with the MA and DA module obtain promising performance under the real scenario setup.

As shown in Table 3 bottom, among single-modality models, the model with RGB input obtained the same levels of change type and object correctness as the results on SCCD_Sim. The model with depth input was degraded on class prediction, and the model with point cloud input was degraded on both change type and class prediction. The artifacts in the depth and point cloud obtained from RGB-D sensors might make it difficult to predict the geometric information correctly. The ensembles with the MA module were relatively less degraded. We also found that although the single-modality with RGB input obtained the highest accuracy for color prediction, our ensemble model with the MA and DA performs better on change type, object, and class prediction.

We show the per-class-BLEU-4 evaluation in Table 4 bottom. Similar to the results on SCCD_Sim, all models perform the best for the chair class. Our ensemble model with the MA and DA module obtained the highest performance for most classes. Two result examples are given in Fig. 4 (right). The single model with RGB input and all ensembles correctly predict the change type, whereas the remaining models gave incorrect change type and object attributes.

6 Conclusions

Scene change understanding is essential in various real-world applications. However, most existing methods have been discussed only for a simulation setup, limiting their availability for real scenarios. Therefore, we proposed a scene change captioning dataset generated using RGB-D cameras along with a simulation dataset generation process. We conducted extensive experiments on input modalities and attention mechanisms for integrating modalities under both simulation and real dataset setups. The experimental results show that models trained on the simulation dataset exhibit promising performance on real scenario setup.

However, there is still a performance gap between the simulation and real dataset setups. We plan to introduce domain adaptation methods and conduct experiments on other simulated and real scenarios that are captured in different buildings to enhance the models' robustness to real scenarios.

Acknowledgements. We want to thank Hikaru Ishitsuka, and Tomomi Satoh for their helpful comments during research discussions and their help in constructing the experimental environment used in this research. Computational resource of AI Bridging Cloud Infrastructure (ABCI) provided by National Institute of Advanced Industrial Science and Technology (AIST) was used.

References

1. Herbst, E., Henry, P., Ren, X., Fox, D.: Toward object discovery and modeling via 3-D scene comparison. In: 2011 IEEE International Conference on Robotics and Automation, pp. 2623–2629 (2011)
2. Ambruş, R., Bore, N., Folkesson, J., Jensfelt, P.: Meta-rooms: building and maintaining long term spatial models in a dynamic world. In: Proceedings of the 2014 IEEE/RSJ International Conference on Intelligent Robots and Systems, pp. 1854–1861 (2014)
3. Langer, E., Ridder, B., Cashmore, M., Magazzeni, D., Zillich, M., Vincze, M.: On-the-fly detection of novel objects in indoor environments. In: 2017 IEEE International Conference on Robotics and Biomimetics, pp. 900–907 (2017)
4. Xu, K., Ba, J., Kiros, R., et al.: Show, attend and tell: neural image caption generation with visual attention. In: International Conference on Machine Learning, pp. 2048–2057 (2015)
5. Anderson, P., et al.: Bottom-up and top-down attention for image captioning and visual question answering. In: Proceedings of the IEEE Conference on Computer Vision and Pattern Recognition, pp. 6077–6086 (2018)
6. Biten, A.F., Gomez, L., Rusinol, M., Karatzas, D.: Good news, everyone! context driven entity-aware captioning for news images. In Proceedings of the IEEE Conference on Computer Vision and Pattern Recognition, pp. 12466–12475 (2019)
7. Yoshida, K., Minoguchi, M., Wani, K., Nakamura, A., Kataoka, H.: Neural joking machine: humorous image captioning. arXiv preprint arXiv:1805.11850
8. Jhamtani, H., Berg-Kirkpatrick, T.: Learning to describe differences between pairs of similar images. In: Proceedings of the 2018 Conference on Empirical Methods in Natural Language Processing, pp. 4024–4034 (2018)
9. Park, D.H., Darrell, T., Rohrbach, A.: Robust change captioning. In: Proceedings of the IEEE International Conference on Computer Vision, pp. 4624–4633 (2019)
10. Qiu, Y., Satoh, Y., Suzuki, R., Iwata, K., Kataoka, H.: Indoor scene change captioning based on multimodality data. Sensors **20**(17), 4761 (2020)
11. Halber, M., Shi, Y., Xu, K., Funkhouser, T.: Rescan: inductive instance segmentation for indoor RGBD Scans. In: Proceedings of the IEEE International Conference on Computer Vision, pp. 2541–2550 (2019)
12. Fujita, A., Sakurada, K., Imaizumi, T., Ito, R., Hikosaka, S., Nakamura, R.: Damage detection from aerial images via convolutional neural networks. In: 2017 Fifteenth IAPR International Conference on Machine Vision Applications, pp. 5–8 (2017)
13. Sakurada, K., Okatani, T.: Change detection from a street image pair using CNN features and superpixel segmentation. In: British Machine Vision Conference, vol. 61, pp. 1–12 (2015)
14. Khan, S.H., He, X., Porikli, F., Bennamoun, M.: Forest change detection in incomplete satellite images with deep neural networks. IEEE Trans. Geosci. Remote Sens. **55**(9), 5407–5423 (2017)

15. Saha, S., Bovolo, F., Bruzzone, L.: Unsupervised deep change vector analysis for multiple-change detection in VHR images. IEEE Trans. Geosci. Remote Sens. **57**(6), 3677–3693 (2019)
16. Alcantarilla, P.F., Stent, S., Ros, G., Arroyo, R., Gherardi, R.: Street-view change detection with deconvolutional networks. Auton. Robot. **42**(7), 1301–1322 (2018). https://doi.org/10.1007/s10514-018-9734-5
17. Daudt, R.C., Le Saux, B., Boulch, A.: Fully convolutional Siamese networks for change detection. In: 2018 25th IEEE International Conference on Image Processing, pp. 4063–4067 (2018)
18. Su, H., Maji, S., Kalogerakis, E., Learned-Miller, E.: Multi-view convolutional neural networks for 3D shape recognition. In: Proceedings of the IEEE International Conference on Computer Vision, Santiago, Chile 7–13, pp. 945–953 (2015)
19. Kanezaki, A., Matsushita, Y., Nishida, Y.: Rotationnet: joint object categorization and pose estimation using multiviews from unsupervised viewpoints. In: Proceedings of the IEEE Conference on Computer Vision and Pattern Recognition, pp. 5010–5019 (2018)
20. Esteves, C., Xu, Y., Allen-Blanchette, C., Daniilidis, K.: Equivariant multi-view networks. In: Proceedings of the IEEE International Conference on Computer Vision, pp. 1568–1577 (2019)
21. Qi, C.R., Su, H., Mo, K., et al.: Pointnet: deep learning on point sets for 3D classification and segmentation. In: Proceedings of the IEEE Conference on Computer Vision and Pattern Recognition, pp. 652–660 (2017)
22. Qi, C.R., Yi, L., Su, H., Guibas, L.J.: Pointnet++: deep hierarchical feature learning on point sets in a metric space. In: Advances in Neural Information Processing Systems (2017)
23. Johnson, J., Hariharan, B., Van Der Maaten, L., Fei-Fei, L., Lawrence Zitnick, C., Girshick, R.: Clevr: a diagnostic dataset for compositional language and elementary visual reasoning. In: Proceedings of the IEEE Conference on Computer Vision and Pattern Recognition, pp. 2901–2910 (2017)
24. Chang, A., et al.: Matterport3D: learning from RGB-D data in indoor environments. In: Proceedings of the 2017 International Conference on 3D Vision, pp. 667–676 (2017)
25. Xia, F., Zamir, A.R., He, Z., Sax, A., Malik, J., Savarese, S.: Gibson ENV: real-world perception for embodied agents. In: Proceedings of the IEEE Conference on Computer Vision and Pattern Recognition, pp. 9068–9079 (2018)
26. Straub, J., et al.: The Replica dataset: a digital replica of indoor spaces. arXiv 2019, arXiv:1906.05797
27. Xtion Site. https://www.asus.com/jp/3D-Sensor/Xtion_PRO_LIVE/. Accessed on 1 Jan 2022
28. FARO Site. https://www.faro.com/ja-jp/. Accessed on 1 Jan 2022
29. Savva, M., et al.: A platform for embodied AI research. In: Proceedings of the IEEE/CVF International Conference on Computer Vision, pp. 9339–9347 (2019)
30. Gers, F.A., Schmidhuber, J., Cummins, F.: Learning to forget: continual prediction with LSTM. Neural Comput. **12**, 2451–2471 (2000)
31. Lin, C.-Y.: ROUGE: a package for automatic evaluation of summaries. Association for Computational Linguistics, pp. 74–81 (2004)
32. Anderson, P., Fernando, B., Johnson, M., Gould, S.: SPICE: semantic propositional image caption evaluation. In: Leibe, B., Matas, J., Sebe, N., Welling, M. (eds.) ECCV 2016. LNCS, vol. 9909, pp. 382–398. Springer, Cham (2016). https://doi.org/10.1007/978-3-319-46454-1_24

33. Denkowski, M.,, Lavie A.: Meteor universal: language specific translation evaluation for any target language. In: Proceedings of the Ninth Workshop on Statistical Machine Translation, pp. 376–380 (2014)
34. Papineni, K., Roukos, S., Ward, T., et al.: BLEU: a method for automatic evaluation of machine translation. In: Proceedings of the 40th Annual Meeting on Association for Computational Linguistics. Association for Computational Linguistics, pp. 311–318 (2002)
35. Kingma, D.P., Ba, J.: Adam: a method for stochastic optimization. arXiv preprint arXiv:1412.6980

The Impact of Artificial Intelligence on the Investment Decision Process in Venture Capital Firms

Sarah Röhm[1], Markus Bick[1](✉), and Martin Boeckle[2]

[1] ESCP Business School, Heubnerweg 8-10, 14059 Berlin, Germany
mbick@escp.eu

[2] BCG Platinion, Revaler Straße 30, 10245 Berlin, Germany

Abstract. Investments are influenced by the cognitive biases and heuristics of investors in the face of a hyper-competitive market caused by capital overabundance pushing deal sizes, startup valuations, and deal activity. This exploratory study outlines the challenges, opportunities, current methods, and future potential of AI adoption in line with the VC investment funnel. A qualitative analysis was conducted based on 17 expert interviews with early-stage VC investors and academic researchers. The findings reveal that most firms do not yet leverage AI, even though they already adopt data-driven decision support, due to resource scarcity in terms of people, time, and budget. Those VC firms that already apply AI predominantly aim at making their sourcing and screening processes more efficient and increasing their portfolio diversity. The interviews also reveal that the number of VCs adopting AI will significantly increase in the next few years—independently of firm size and resource availability. The catalyst for this will be emerging third-party software providers offering affordable AI tools developed primarily to enhance the VC investment decision process.

Keywords: Venture capital industry · Decision-making process · Artificial intelligence · Cognitive biases · Technology

1 Introduction

Although investors are experts in identifying promising startups that operate at the forefront of technological disruption and innovation, their own investment decision-making methods have scarcely changed since the invention of the VC asset class 80 years ago [1]. Scholars and practitioners concur that VC processes are still highly manual, time-consuming, subjective, and hard to scale [1–3].

In the past years, the rise of artificial intelligence (AI) has transformed the processing of information, making it faster and more accurate than human abilities alone could achieve [4, 5]. Recent advancements in machine learning (ML) have enabled humans to process larger volumes of rapidly changing and unstructured data from an almost indefinite number of sources. Such technologies allow unbiased predictions to be made about future events [6] and are already applied to enhance decision-making in financial

H. Degen and S. Ntoa (Eds.): HCII 2022, LNAI 13336, pp. 420–435, 2022.
https://doi.org/10.1007/978-3-031-05643-7_27

markets, such as hedge funds operating in public markets [7]. Thus, AI algorithms represent a promising path in private markets, thus opening a new era of early-stage VC investment [8] and allowing VC firms to differentiate themselves beyond money. Despite the rising attention paid to AI and its ability to enhance business processes, little research has been conducted to assess its potential impact in an entrepreneurship context [9, 10].

Previous research conducted on VC investment decision-making primarily explains how these decisions are taken [11, 12] and which set of criteria investors apply to evaluate potential investment opportunities [13, 14]. However, solutions that could enhance the processes along the investment funnel have scarcely been investigated [15–17], and little is known about the current state of AI adoption in VC. Hence, our study aims to bridge this gap by providing guidance for VC firms wishing to unlock the potential of AI but which are unsure about how to do so, by describing the approaches other VC companies have taken. Our findings will increase the knowledge of investors and other relevant stakeholders involved in the investment decision-making process, such as startups or limited partners (LPs), as their strategies will most likely align in this regard.

The remainder of this paper is structured as follows. After providing an overview of the VC industry and its essential characteristics, we focus on the decision-making process by outlining how organizations approach it in times of uncertainty and highlighting the human limitations involved, thus answering the following question: What cognitive biases limit human decision-making? Subsequently, we take a closer look at the decision-making process within VC firms, responding to the next question: What steps do investors take along the investment funnel? Process-related limitations are then discussed accordingly. Next, we explain the difference between data-driven and AI-driven decision-making. Our qualitative approach follows and describes the research design, data collection via semi-structured interviews, and the corresponding structure of the data analysis. We conducted 17 expert interviews with early-stage VC investors and academic researchers.

2 Venture Capital

In the context of this study, VC is defined as a sub-segment of the private equity (PE) asset class, whereby investors provide equity financing to (often newly founded) unlisted companies in exchange for minority shareholdings [18–20]. To understand a VC firm's methods of working and its underlying business model, we outline the five key characteristics of venture capital according to Metrick and Yasuda [21].

VC firms are financial intermediaries that aggregate the capital of various investors and pool it in a fund, in order to reallocate it further by investing in startups. Venture capital investors are sometimes confused with business angels (BAs), but even though there are certain parallels in their investment processes, BAs follow different economics in their investment decisions, as they deploy their own private capital in ventures. At the same time, VCs reallocate money from their LPs and correspondingly face a higher cost of capital.

As VCs invest in private companies, the ventures' equity stakes cannot be traded on public markets at the time of funding. While publicly listed companies must regularly publish their financial reports and other statements, privately held companies do not have such an obligation. Thus, public access to information about private companies is relatively rare.

VC firms typically, but not necessarily, provide resources beyond capital, such as the recruitment of startups, thereby ensuring the quality and availability of the firm's most important asset, human capital. Moreover, they support the startups' operations by enhancing accounting, legal, administrative, and technological capabilities. Beyond that, investors also help build the correct skillset necessary for guiding the startup through its growth and lifecycle, e.g., by identifying target groups and measuring and reporting on performance. Furthermore, when working with VC firms, startups can leverage their networks [22].

Fourth, startups go through a particular investment timeline during their lifetime. While family, friends, and BAs usually focus on deploying capital in the early stages of the startup lifecycle, being pre-seed and seed, VCs invest at all stages, from the early seed round through multiple follow-on funding rounds. There are often no clear boundaries between the funding preferences of the different investor types. While some BAs might participate in later-stage rounds, certain VC firms mainly specialize in pre-seed investing and do not back the later stages.

Fifth, the primary goal of a VC is being able to withdraw the initial investment made in their portfolio companies, as this is the point at which the return on investments materializes and thus can be returned to the LPs. The typical timeframe between initial funding and exit is 10 to 12 years [23]. In general, there are several exit options that VC-backed startups can consider. Three of the most common strategies are [24]: mergers and acquisitions (M&As), an initial public offering (IPO), and special-purpose acquisition companies (SPAC).

3 The Decision-Making Process

In the following we provide a deeper understanding of the human decision-making process in organizations during times of uncertainty and highlight a number of related human limitations. We then focus on the VC investment funnel and the different decision-making steps investors take, before closing with an explanation of the process-related limitations investors face along the investment funnel.

3.1 Decision-Making in Organizations Under Uncertainty

Due to VC firm's organizational structure, the final investment decision to enter a deal is undertaken collectively by the fund's investment committee. The committee consists of the firm's partners, each holding a voting right [25]. These decision-makers iteratively need to assess external factors and make future predictions in the presence of uncertainty. As early-stage investors frequently accompany their portfolio companies for up to 12 years, the development of their ventures is difficult to predict [8, 23].

To reduce the complexity of information-processing, investors draw on heuristics ("rule of thumb"), which can be helpful in some cases, but they can also lead to cognitive biases, i.e., deviations from rational thinking, and often arise when decision-makers are challenged by high environmental uncertainty [26]. Cognitive biases provoke inaccurate judgments and faulty logic, resulting in systematic and severe decision errors that negatively affect organizational performance [27–31]. Moreover, investors are often not aware that they are prone to cognitive biases when it comes to interpreting soft information [32, 33].

3.2 Human-Related Limitations in Decision-Making

Different types of biases have been highlighted in the entrepreneurial finance literature and the field of strategic decision-making:

Overconfidence bias, or hubris, refers to investors' tendency to overestimate their know-how and investment skills and the likelihood of certain events. This negatively affects their decision accuracy [34]. The more available data the investor has at their disposal, the higher their overconfidence and the worse their decisions.

Similarity bias refers to VCs who tend to favor working with and investing in founders who have certain similarities to themselves. One example of this bias is when the entrepreneur has a similar behavioral trait or educational or professional background to the investors [35].

Availability bias is defined as the overweighting of certain memorable information that investors often use and thus comes to mind more readily than information that might be equally important but is less exciting or spectacular—and is thus underweighted [36].

The Halo effect refers to VCs who prefer investments in startups similar to one or more successful portfolio companies the investor has already invested in or supervised. The evaluation of potential targets tends to be prejudiced by previous experience.

Local bias describes VC firms' preference for investment targets in the same nation or region as the investor. The root cause for this bias is that investors do not like sourcing startups beyond a certain geographical distance [37, 38].

Implicit gender bias describes the tendency to prefer a specific gender and is a form of an unconscious bias. It occurs when an individual unconsciously connects certain stereotypes and attitudes to a group of people or another individual.

3.3 The Decision-Making Process in Venture Capital

The following explanation is based on the six-stage model developed by Fried and Hisrich [11]. As there is broad evidence that post-investment activities have a decisive impact on the growth and cash-out potential of ventures [39–41], the model is complemented with phases 8 and 9, based on Bruno and Tyebjee [12] and Wells [42], to propose a more holistic view on the decision-making process (Fig. 1).

1. *Deal Origination:* VC firms establish a pipeline by sourcing investment opportunities. The deal flow quantity depends very much on the VC firm's investment thesis, uncertainty, and competition in the market [11]. Several researchers have emphasized the importance of finding as many potential targets as early as possible at the beginning of the investment funnel. VC firms source their deals mainly through three channels: referrals, direct outreach, and cold calls [1, 43].

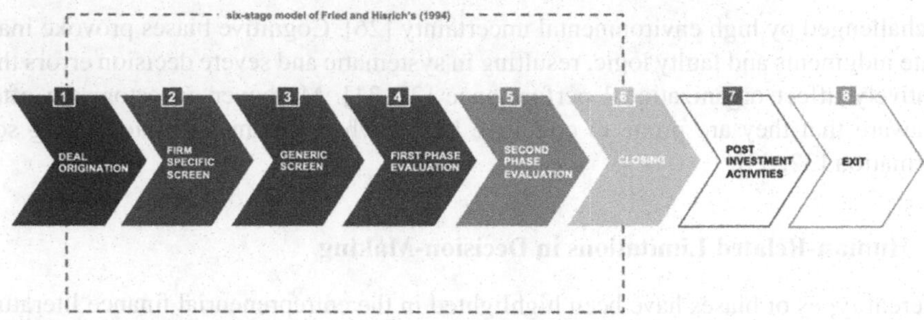

Fig. 1. VC investment funnel based on [11, 12, 42]

2. *Firm Specific Screen:* the investor narrows down the overabundance of investment opportunities to a manageable quantity, as a high-quality pipeline is essential to gaining strong returns [44, 45]. By applying hard selection criteria (SC), VC firms can further prioritize targets they view as most valuable. Exemplar hard SCs are the ventures industry, investment stage, ticket size, or geography, as well as the developed product, service, or technology behind it [11].
3. *Generic Screen:* the VC applies additional SCs, which are often softer and more generic than the hard SCs, to reduce the deal flow further. Examples include team composition or the founders' previous professional experience and academic background. This evaluation provides significant scope for a more subjective interpretation of the investment potential [46].
4. *First-Phase Evaluation:* This is the decisive phase, whereby the VC firm decides whether it wants to invest in the startup or not [45]. VCs frequently evaluate the venture's business plan with the help of benchmark analyses based on information provided by external and internal resources [11]. The market attractiveness, managerial capabilities, environmental threat resistance, cash-out potential, and the venture's competitive advantage are evaluated by conducting several analyses [12]. The investors meet the founder(s) to establish an understanding of the operating industry, to validate the business idea and skill set of the venture's management based on references from clients and relevant stakeholders, to conduct and analyze technical studies and pilot projects relating to the venture's product or service, and to consult subject matter experts [11].
5. *Second-Phase Evaluation:* When an investment opportunity reaches the second-phase evaluation, the VC firm has decided that the deal is attractive and now examines potential challenges and roadblocks, as well as mitigation strategies for overcoming them [11].
6. *Closing:* During the closing phase, several negotiations occur to decide upon the structure of the investment. The primary documents determining the terms and conditions are the term sheet and definitive agreements. Term sheets are mostly non-binding agreements between the venture and the investor and act formalize negotiations and outline the key terms to be incorporated in the definitive agreements. They are the legally binding final contracts for the transaction between the venture and the investor [47].

7. *Post-investment activities:* The literature concludes that it is critical for investors to provide their portfolio companies with resources that go beyond capital [39, 41, 44, 48]. According to a survey by Gompers et al. [44], conducted with almost 900 VC firms, 87% of investors assist their ventures after they have invested in them. Intensive advisory activities are the primary mechanisms venture capitalists use to add value to their portfolio companies [44].
8. *Exit:* In this phase, the VC firm traditionally returns the main investment made by its LPs and the fund [42]. The journey to grow a venture successfully and then exit it with a high return is often very long and uncertain, especially for firms that focus on early-stage investments [44].

3.4 Process-Related Limitations in VC Firms' Decision-Making

It is not only cognitive biases that affect the quality of decision-making in VC firms, but also process-related limitations. Investment decision-making by VC firms is slow, expensive, labor-intensive, and hard to scale, not only because of its manual nature, but also due to the imperfect databases investors use [2, 8]. Generally, investors have a hard time collecting relevant data from potential targets, as there is no obligation for the founder to make investment-decisive information publicly accessible. To give an example of this, in the upper part of the funnel, during the sourcing and screening stages, attractive investment opportunities may be absent due to the suboptimal use of data or its inaccessibility. Moreover, at the end of the funnel, due diligence processes are extremely lengthy and separate, and they still require physical presence (e.g., at the notary), which may even jeopardize the closing of the deal and incur high costs.

4 Research Methodology

To examine the status quo of VC firms' adoption of AI to enhance their investment decisions, qualitative research was conducted based on primary data collection. The primary data were collected during 13 semi-structured interviews complemented by a panel discussion between five experts (Table 1). The panel discussion "Do Algorithms Make Better—and Fairer—Investments Than Angel Investors?" took place on March 25th 2021 and was part of the START Summit program. Unlike structured interviews with their rigid format of set questions, semi-structured interviews are adaptable to the individual interview flow and expert answers. Thereby, it is possible to extract the beliefs, attitudes, and motivations behind the choices and behaviors of the interviewees [49]. The participants were identified and selected based on previous research in the field of data-driven VC firms [2] and [1]. The request for participation in this underlying study was made via LinkedIn, email, and personal contacts between November 2020 and February 2021. Before each interview, the participants received a briefing mail with a short overview of the interview structure and information about the recording and transcription of the conversation. Three interview guidelines were developed, one for each expert group [50].

For this study, we followed the inductive grounded theory method (GTM) which is suitable for our exploratory research design, as it aims to establish an understanding

Table 1. Expert interview overview.

No	Expert Cluster	Company/Institution	Expert Position	VC Venture Stage Focus	VC Industry Focus	Level of VC Tech-stack	Format of Data Collection
1	VC firm	Connetic Ventures	Principal	Early-stage I Seed	Agnostic	AI	Interview
2	VC firm	645 Ventures	Vice President	Early-stage I Seed - Series A	Agnostic	Data-driven	Interview
3	VC firm & Research	Earlybird VC	Principal	Early-stage	Agnostic	AI	Public Panel Discussion
4	VC firm	EQT Ventures	Investor	Early and Later stage	Agnostic	AI	Interview
5	VC firm	Speedinvest	Analyst	Early-stage I Pre-Seed - Seed	Agnostic	Data-driven	Interview
6	VC firm	IBB Ventures	Investment Director	Early-stage I Seed - Series A	Agnostic	Manual	Interview
7	VC firm & Research	Balderton Capital	Research Lead	Early-stage I Seed - Series A	Agnostic	Data-driven	Interview
8	VC firm	Backed VC	Head of Network & Communication	Early-stage I Seed - Series A	Agnostic	Data-driven	Interview
9	VC firm	btov Partners	Partner	Early-stage	Agnostic	N/A	Public Panel Discussion
10	VC firm	Atomico	Senior Investment Manager	Early and Later stage	Agnostic	Data-driven	Interview
11	VC firm	Global Founders Capital (GFC)	Investor	Early and Later stage	Agnostic	Data-driven	Interview
12	VC firm	EnerTech Capital	Partner	Early and Later-stage	Industry specific	Manual	Interview
13	Research	Gartner	Senior Director	-	-		Interview
14	Research	University of St. Gallen	Postdoctoral researcher at the University of St. Gallen	-	-		Public Panel Discussion
15	Research	University of St.Gallen	Director of the Institute for Technology Management	-	-		Public Panel Discussion
16	Research	University of St. Gallen	Assistant Professor for Data Science and Management	-	-		Interview
17	Technology firm	MorphAIs	Founder & CEO	Early-stage	Agnostic	AI	Interview and Public Panel Discussion

between the research objectives and the findings derived from expert interviews and the panel discussion. According to Strauss and Corbin [50, p. 16], understanding and analyzing complex data in grounded theory studies is "*Inductively derived from the study of the phenomenon it represents. That is, discovered, developed, and provisionally verified through systematic data collection and analysis of data pertaining to that phenomenon. Therefore, data collection, analysis, and theory should stand in a reciprocal relationship with each other. One does not begin with a theory, then prove it. Rather, one begins with an area of study, and what is relevant to that area is allowed to emerge.*" The requirement of this reciprocal relationship is a suspension of judgment and knowledge, which is crucial for conducting a GTM study [51].

To measure and validate quality in this qualitative research, we drew on Lincoln and Guba's [52] set of quality criteria to ensure trustworthiness: a) credibility, b) confirmability, c) transferability, and d) dependability. The credibility and confirmability of the underlying study were established through investigator triangulation. Thereby, possible perception gaps or biases from the gathered data during the interviews could be detected. In this way, it was possible to address the underlying research from different perspectives and thus expand the spectrum of findings [53]. Triangulation was achieved by interviewing experts from different professions and with different experiences of the examined topic. The three different expert clusters consisted of:

- *Industry- and geography-agnostic VC investors* (P1, P2, P3, P4, P5, P7, P8, P9, P10, P11, P17)
- *VC investors with a specific geographic or industry focus* (P6, P12)
- *Researchers and academics* (P13, P14, P15, P16)

To generate a global perspective, experts from the US and Europe were chosen. Moreover, P3 and P4—both currently employed as investors for VC firms—belong to cluster a) as well as cluster c). Both have published several academic papers and conducted their PhDs in this research field. The transferability of the findings was achieved by a comprehensive description of the research context and underlying assumptions [54], while dependability was achieved by outlining the GTM approach and capturing the process and results. Furthermore, the richness of the data was ensured by using open questions such as "Could you walk me through?" or "Could you please elaborate further on…?" to encourage storytelling and thereby gather as much information as possible [55].

5 Findings

The challenges mentioned by the experts during the interviews were mapped along the VC investment funnel (Fig. 2).

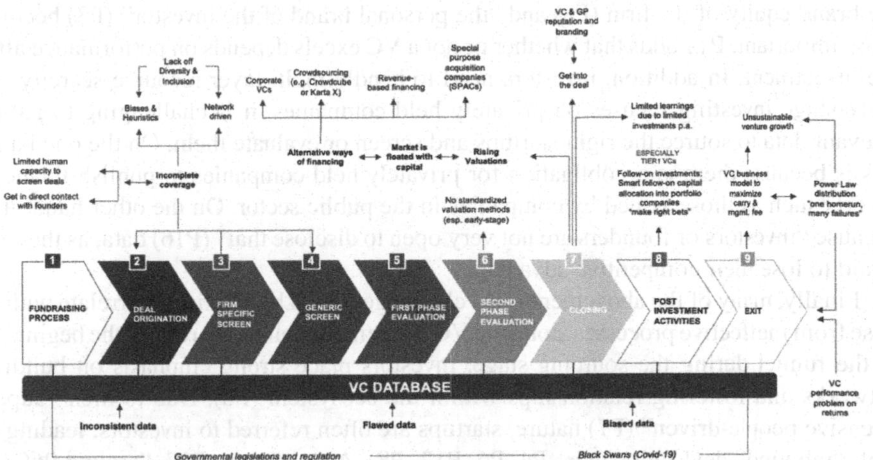

Fig. 2. Challenges along the VC investment funnel

VC firms have a limited ability to foresee macroeconomic uncertainties and how they might influence their portfolios, and they are also dependent on the willingness of founders to cooperate with them. Due to rapid and unpredictable market shifts such as those delivered by the COVID-19 pandemic or the financial crisis in 2008, investors are forced to make "decisions in an uncertain environment" (P6) and at high velocity (e.g., P10, P8, P4). In addition, they can decide in which startup they wish to invest, but they can only partly influence the decision of their counterpart, being the entrepreneurs themselves (e.g., P7, P5).

Moreover, investors need to deal with challenges related to the oversupply of capital in the market. Furthermore, VC firms "can't compete on price" (P2) any longer, as "there's so much capital in the market" (P2), thus creating hyper-competition among VCs and forcing "investors to differentiate in [ways] other" (P5) than capital. This challenges the attractiveness of VC firms for entrepreneurs (e.g., P9, P10, P12). In addition, there are also crowdsourcing platforms such as Crowdsmart.ai or Crowdsmart (P10, P13) and revenue-based VC firms that are not incentivized via a carry and management fee but rather with part of the startups' revenues. This is especially attractive for founders, as their shares are not diluted in the same way as they would be if working with traditional VC firms (P10). Such market shifts harm VC firms' returns and business models (P17). Although research has proven that "portfolio companies perform better if the investors work more on the downside than on the upside, meaning when they avoid bad investments instead of putting everything on the one potential homerun" (P15), investors still "want to find that needle in the haystack, that unicorn company[,]" to return the whole fund at once.

However, the compensation structure based on a carry and management fee incentivizes this kind of hubris, and investors see no need to change the ways in which they work (P8). VC firms also face challenges in terms of creating a sufficient value proposition and differentiating factors. As money and expert knowledge are currently abundant in the market, VC firms are no longer able to compete on money or value (P2). Thus, the brand equity of the firm (P8) and "the personal brand of the investor" (P3) become more important. P11 adds that whether or not a VC excels depends on performance after the investment. In addition, investors need to handle multi-layer resource scarcity. As early-stage investing focuses on privately held companies, it is challenging to gather relevant data to source the right startups and screen or evaluate them. On the one hand, this is because there is no obligation for privately held companies to publish financial reports such as those issued by companies in the public sector. On the other hand, it is because "investors or founders are not very open to disclose that" (P16) data, as they are afraid to lose their competitive advantage.

Finally, many of the abovementioned challenges faced by VC firms correlate with or arise from ineffective processes along the VC investment funnel. Starting at the beginning of the funnel during the sourcing stage, investors place strong emphasis on building networks and fostering relationships within the ecosystem (P8). Due to their "super-intensive people-driven" (P7) nature, startups are often referred to investors, leading to high "inbound" deal ratios (e.g., P4, P6, P12, P8). According to P17, "around 96% of VCs are overconfident" in their investment decisions, even though these are based on imperfect information (P8). Also, the lack of diversity and inclusion when VC firms make investments is perceived as a big issue in the industry (P1, P10, P11, P17).

During the interviews, it became clear that most VC firms are currently undergoing a transformation regarding their "tech-stack". In the context of this study, this comprises the whole technology infrastructure and data ecosystem consisting of different technology solutions and applications plugged into the firms' databases to enhance their processes (e.g., P13, P8, P4). Our results show that over 75% of all firms already leverage at least data-driven algorithms, and 31% apply AI models to their data, in order to make their processes more efficient. Two of the VC firms have neither AI nor data-driven approaches, and there was no information disclosed by one VC.

It is important to identify the stages of the investment funnel when VCs mainly adopt and apply their tools. Figure 3 reveals that this varies somewhat, because while some apply their AI models throughout all stages of the funnel—predominantly between the sourcing, screening, and evaluation phases—others focus on applying them during the sourcing stage and then again for post-investment or additional activities, but not during the screening, evaluation, and closing phases. The majority use their tools the most during the sourcing stage, and they are least applied during the closing stage. However, it is important to note that for confidentiality reasons, some firms might not have disclosed every feature or use-case of their tools, as they perceive that a sophisticated tech-stack contributes to their competitive advantage and thus want to protect it (e.g., P4, P8).

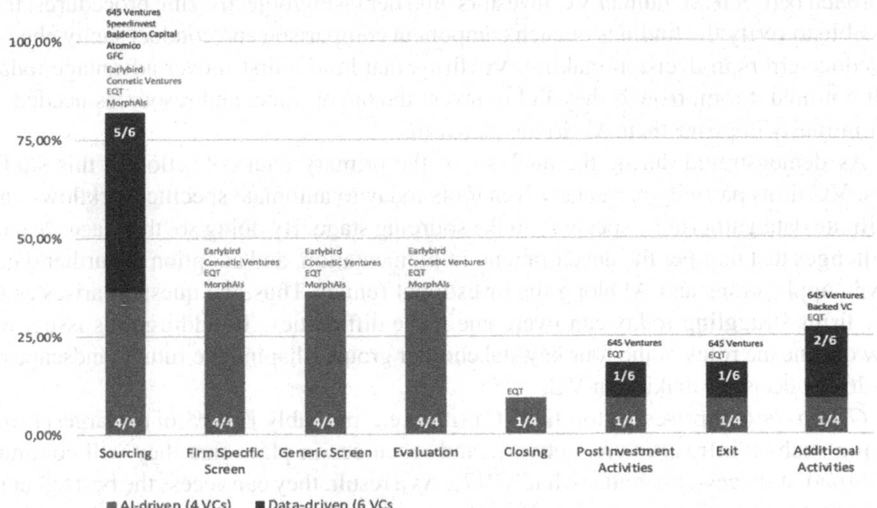

Fig. 3. Distribution of AI- and data-driven tools along the investment funnel

Our findings align with the results of other research, in that VC firms mainly leverage such tools during the sourcing processes [1, 2].

6 Discussion

It has been shown that ML algorithms can outperform human investors in selecting the most promising investment targets [1, 8]. AI can also provide significant help when considering a broader spectrum of deals, since it can collect more information in an automated manner and then "pre-select interesting startups by turning qualitative gathered data into quantitative facts" (P13). Hence, investors can shift their manual efforts to the target evaluation toward the end of the funnel. However, VCs will need to update the algorithms continuously and iteratively validate their effectiveness. The efficient interpretation and incorporation of outputs from AI tools are crucial. VC firms cannot be over-reliant on the early outputs if they are not tested. Due to the historic nature of the data, past trends are mirrored in the future. Consequently, debiasing and objectivizing AI is paramount. According to Retterath et al. [1], one way to mitigate biased AI models is by overruling ML in dimensions where it is particularly prone to biases. Deterministic AI can be leveraged, producing predefined outcomes based on a set of facts such as growth metrics or company and founder information, as well as a set of rules such as if/then statements. While deterministic AI is immutable and only requires a simple dataset, ML models such as the XG are probabilistic and not only constantly develop, evolve, and adapt, but also require a richer database [56]. Another way to objectivize AI is to derive from specific observations to a broader generalization leveraging inductive reasoning. During this process, data are gathered, patterns discerned, conclusions made, and explanations and theories built (P17). With the help of a continuous triangulation approach between AI, human VC investors, and debiasing/objectivizing procedures, it is possible to verify the findings of each component comparison and conduct sanity checks to reduce errors in decision-making. VC firms that hold a first-mover advantage today will not hold it tomorrow if they fail to invest the talent, time, and resources needed to continuously improve their AI-driven platforms.

As demonstrated during the analysis of the primary data collection in this study, most VC firms partially use data-driven tools today to automate specific workflows and facilitate data-gathering, especially in the sourcing stage. By doing so, they face various challenges that hamper the development, implementation, and adoption of further data-driven applications and AI along the investment funnel. Thus, the question arises as to how firms struggling today can overcome these difficulties. To address this issue, we now outline the roles of the four key stakeholder groups shaping the future landscape of AI-driven decision-making in VC:

Group one comprises the top-tier VC firms, i.e., "probably 1 or 2% of the largest firms having such an infrastructure, network, and resources in place that they will continue their road of success, no matter what" (P17). As a result, they can access the best talent in the industry and, resource-wise, will not have a problem incorporating new data-driven processes into their business.

Group two are data-driven VC firms that focus a crucial part of their resources on building an AI-driven decision-making approach. These attribute a significant part of the investment decision to this approach, especially at the beginning of the investment funnel. What further distinguishes these data-driven VC firms from their top-tier counterparts is that they usually have no human interaction with the startups prior to the in-depth evaluation process. Only when the AI decides that the venture is a potential investment opportunity is the data evaluated by human investors. If this is approached conscientiously, cognitive biases can be eliminated from the equation. Such tactics can be impartial to race or gender, unlike the gut instincts and established networks that have contributed to diversity issues in the industry. If implemented successfully, these models not only increase portfolio diversity, but they also—ultimately—have an impact on returns.

The third group consists of VC firms caught between groups 1 and 2. They do not see themselves turning into a data-driven VC to such an extent as Group 2, but they realize that they need to extract the value in their data if they want to remain competitive. While most are far from applying AI or ML to their databases, the majority leverage data-driven tools such as data-scraper or third-party tools, for example LinkedIn Sales Navigator (e.g., P5, P7, or P11). However, Group 3 does not want—or cannot deploy the time and resources—to design, build, maintain, and fix AI algorithms, and thus it does not make sense to create their own system. While self-build software applications can ensure competitive incremental advantages, buying them is more effective in 90% of cases [2]. Firms should be careful not to overestimate their ability to build such tools and fall victim to overconfidence biases, mainly because they and their teams dedicated to this undertaking are likely to outperform them in this aspect.

The fourth group consists of technology companies and startups that offer specific AI-driven tools and bridge the gap between the current 5% applying AI in investment decision-making and the 75% of VC firms expected to do so by 2025 [57]. Those solutions will become available at a comparatively low price and will be easily integrable into existing software solutions (P12). Group 4 firms are enablers for investors who lack the resources, talent, and time to leverage the benefits of AI-driven decision-support, thereby catering to their specific needs.

7 Conclusion

The rising adoption of data-driven decision-making reflects the constant transformation the VC industry has undergone. If applied appropriately, these tools have the potential to be remarkably powerful. Their impact will become more influential as training of the underlying algorithms advances, due to more experience and better feedback loops and because data quality and quantity will increase over time. However, VC firms should be cautious about becoming too reliant on technology, as the data gathered and fed to the algorithms mirrors human cognitive biases and heuristics. Unquantifiable factors will therefore remain, and there will be externalities whose impact can hardly be predicted. However, the human element of VC investment will remain a vital part of ventures' long-term success. Consequently, AI application along the investment funnel will be realized via an augmented approach between humans and algorithms, leveraging hybrid intelligence. An investment decision will always be made by two parties, namely, the investor and the founder.

As the VC business model continuously changes, it is necessary to discard the overconfidence associated with investors' gut feelings and consider the adoption of new processes. This will include a partial delegation of responsibility to technology, for example by delegating certain committee voting rights. Moreover, LPs must adapt to these forthcoming changes, as data-driven models will take on an increasing number of due diligence processes. Consequently, they should develop new skillsets pro-actively rather than reactively, as this will be rewarded in the long run. The ultimate impact of AI-driven decision-support will become evident when VC firms exit AI-sourced portfolio companies at the end of their lifecycle. Early-stage lifecycles usually range between 10 and 12 years between investment and exit.

Practitioners and scholars report a public misconception that AI in investing is the next unicorn, although it is leveraged to make investing smoother and more efficient when it comes to identifying, sourcing, and screening different opportunities. Using statistical models to discover statistical outliers is ironic in itself.

The biggest lever in the AI implementation movement in VC will be the rise of third-party software providers as catalysts, driving the availability and accessibility of

AI tools, especially for investors who do not have the time, resources, or talent to develop, integrate, and maintain them alone. Thereby, VC firms will have a realistic chance to increase diversity within the industry, efficiency along the investment funnel, decision quality, and ultimately ROI.

As with every empirical study, the underlying analyses and results come with several limitations. The timeframe in this study, for instance, was short, and the sample size of interviewees was too small to generalize findings across the industry. Moreover, the results relied on semi-structured interviews and are likely to suffer from post-hoc and recall rationalization bias. Zacharakis and Meyer [17] found that VC investors have difficulties in looking introspectively at their decision-making; nonetheless, this research method obtained insights into how data-driven and AI tools are already leveraged along the investment funnel—and which challenges and chances investors perceive in this context. However, to protect their competitive advantage, many investors fail to share detailed information about their internal processes. To measure whether AI adoption helps VC firms outcompete traditional processes, further investigation using more quantitative research methods must be conducted as soon as the necessary exit data on AI-sourced targets become available.

The findings of this study should encourage further research on the impact of AI on VC decision-making. First, as increasingly more VCs will leverage AI to enhance this skillset, it will become easier to conduct studies with larger sample sizes. Second, quantitative research on the return on investments recorded by AI-sourced targets should be conducted as soon as their exits materialize and respective data become available. Third, there needs to be a comparison of costs-to-outcome. Fourth, the software solutions of third-party software providers such as DealEngine or Crowdsmart should be further examined, and a comparison of the cost/impact ratio between third-party and in-house-built tools should be performed. Fifth, the adoption of NLP and psychometric profiling capabilities along the VC investment funnel should be further examined. This should consider not only VC firms, but also entrepreneurs, as they could trace and understand the external perceptions of their digital footprints and online presence.

References

1. Retterath, A., Braun, R.: Benchmarking venture capital databases. SSRN Electron. J. (2020). https://doi.org/10.2139/ssrn.3706108
2. Corea, F.: AI and venture capital. In: An Introduction to Data. SBD, vol. 50, pp. 101–110. Springer, Cham (2019). https://doi.org/10.1007/978-3-030-04468-8_15
3. Sheehan, P., Sheehan, A.: The paradox of experience. ETF Partners White Paper (2017)
4. Hastie, T., Tibshirani, R., Friedman, J.: Unsupervised learning. In: The Elements of Statistical Learning, pp. 485–585. Springer, New York (2009). https://doi.org/10.1007/978-3-540-28650-9_5
5. Jordan, M., Mitchell, T.: Machine learning: trends, perspectives, and prospects. Science **349**, 255–260 (2015). https://doi.org/10.1126/science.aaa8415
6. Agarwal, R., Dhar, V.: Editorial—Big data, data science, and analytics: the opportunity and challenge for IS research. Inf. Syst. Res. **25**, 443–448 (2014). https://doi.org/10.1287/isre.2014.0546
7. Blattberg, R.C., Hoch, S.J.: Database models and managerial intuition: 50% model + 50% manager. Manage. Sci. **36**, 887–899 (1990). https://doi.org/10.1142/9789814287067_0014

8. Blohm, I., Antretter, T., Sirén, C., Grichnik, D., Wincent, J.: It's a peoples game, isn't it?! A comparison between the investment returns of business angels and machine learning algorithms. Entrep. Theory Pract. (2020). https://doi.org/10.1177/1042258720945206
9. Obschonka, M., Audretsch, D.B.: Artificial intelligence and big data in entrepreneurship: a new era has begun. Small Bus. Econ. **55**(3), 529–539 (2019). https://doi.org/10.1007/s11187-019-00202-4
10. Schwab, A., Zhang, Z.: A new methodological frontier in entrepreneurship research: Big data studies. Entrep. Theory Pract. **43**, 843–854 (2019). https://doi.org/10.1177/1042258718760841
11. Fried, V., Hisrich, R.: Toward a model of venture capital investment decision making. Financ. Manage. **23**, 28–37 (1994)
12. Tyebjee, T.T., Bruno, A.: A model of venture capitalist investment activity. Manage. Sci. **30**, 1051–1066 (1984). https://doi.org/10.1287/mnsc.30.9.1051
13. Hisrich, R., Jankowicz, A.: Intuition in venture capital decisions: an exploratory study using a new technique. J. Bus. Ventur. **5**, 49–62 (1990). https://doi.org/10.1016/0883-9026(90)90026-P
14. Macmillan, I., Zemann, L., Subbanarasimha, P.: Criteria distinguishing successful from unsuccessful ventures in the venture screening process. J. Bus. Ventur. **2**, 123–137 (1987). https://doi.org/10.1016/0883-9026(87)90003-6
15. Khan, A.: Assessing venture capital investments with noncompensatory behavioral decision models. J. Bus. Ventur. **2**, 193–205 (1987). https://doi.org/10.1016/0883-9026(87)90008-5
16. Shepherd, D.A., Zacharakis, A., Baron, R.A.: VCs' decision processes: evidence suggesting more experience may not always be better. J. Bus. Ventur. **18**, 381–401 (2003). https://doi.org/10.1016/S0883-9026(02)00099-X
17. Zacharakis, A., Meyer, G.: A lack of insight: do venture capitalists really understand their own decision process? J. Bus. Ventur. **13**, 57–76 (1998). https://doi.org/10.1016/S0883-9026(02)00099-X
18. Achleitner, A.: Venture capital. In: Breuer, R.E. (ed.) Handbuch Finanzierung, pp. 513–529. Gabler Verlag, Wiesbaden (2001). https://doi.org/10.1007/978-3-322-89933-0_20
19. Bender, M.: Spatial Proximity in Venture Capital Financing: A Theoretical and Empirical Analysis of Germany. Gabler Verlag, Wiesbaden (2010). https://doi.org/10.1007/978-3-8349-6172-3
20. Kaserer, C., Achleitner, A., von Einem, C., Schiereck, D.: Private equity in Deutschland - Rahmenbedingungen, ökonomische Bedeutung und Handlungsempfehlungen. Books on Demand GmbH, Norderstedt (2007)
21. Metrick, A., Yasuda, A.: Venture Capital and the Finance of Innovation. Wiley, Hoboken (2021)
22. Hansen, D.: How VCs deploy operating talent to build better startups. https://www.forbes.com/sites/drewhansen/2012/12/26/how-vcs-deploy-operating-talent-to-build-better-startups/?sh=3822207836ef. Accessed 09 Feb 2022
23. Wagner, A.: The venture capital lifecycle. https://pitchbook.com/news/articles/the-venture-capital-lifecycle. Accessed 09 Feb 2022
24. Gompers, P., Lerner, J.: What drives venture capital fundraising? Nat. Bureau Econ. Res. (1999). https://doi.org/10.3386/w6906
25. Feld, B., Mendelson, J.: Venture Deals: Be Smarter Than your Lawyer and Venture Capitalist. Wiley, Hoboken (2019)
26. Hodgkinson, G., Bown, N., Maule, A., Glaister, W., Pearman, A.: Breaking the frame: an analysis of strategic cognition and decision making under uncertainty. Strateg. Manag. J. **20**, 977–985 (1999). https://doi.org/10.1002/(SICI)1097-0266(199910)20:10%3c977::AID-SMJ58%3e3.0.CO;2-X

27. Barber, B., Odean, T.: Boys will be boys: gender, overconfidence, and common stock investment. Q. J. Econ. **116**, 261–292 (2001). https://doi.org/10.1162/003355301556400
28. Milkman, K., Chugh, D., Bazerman, M.: How can decision making be improved? Perspect. Psychol. Sci. **4**, 379–383 (2009). https://doi.org/10.1111/j.1745-6924.2009.01142.x
29. Ritter, J.: To fly, to fall, to fly again. https://www.economist.com/briefing/2015/07/25/to-fly-to-fall-to-fly-again. Accessed 10 Feb 2022
30. Tversky, A., Kahneman, D.: Variants of uncertainty. Cognition **11**, 143–157 (1982). https://doi.org/10.1016/0010-0277(82)90023-3
31. Waweru, N., Munyoki, E., Uliana, E.: The effects of behavioural factors in investment decision-making: a survey of institutional investors operating at the Nairobi stock exchange. Int. J. Busi. Emerg. Markets. **1**, 24–41 (2008). https://doi.org/10.1504/IJBEM.2008.019243
32. Huang, L.: The role of investor gut feel in managing complexity and extreme risk. Acad. Manage. J. **61**, 1821–1847 (2018).https://doi.org/10.5465/amj.2016.1009
33. Huang, L., Pearce, J.: Managing the unknowable: the effectiveness of early-stage investor gut feel in entrepreneurial investment decisions. Adm. Sci. Q. **60**, 634–670 (2015). https://doi.org/10.1177/0001839215597270
34. Shepherd, D., Zacharakis, A.: Venture capitalists' expertise: a call for research into decision aids and cognitive feedback. J. Bus. Ventur. **17**, 1–20 (2002). https://doi.org/10.1016/S0883-9026(00)00051-3
35. Franke, N., Gruber, M., Harhoff, D., Henkel, J.: What you are is what you like— similarity biases in venture capitalists' evaluations of start-up teams. J. Bus. Ventur. **21**, 802–826 (2006). https://doi.org/10.1016/j.jbusvent.2005.07.001
36. Zacharakis, A., Meyer, G.: The potential of actuarial decision models: can they improve the venture capital investment decision? J. Bus. Ventur. **15**, 323–346 (2000). https://doi.org/10.1016/S0883-9026(98)00016-0
37. Cumming, D., Dai, N.: Local bias in venture capital investments. J. Empir. Financ. **17**, 362–380 (2010). https://doi.org/10.1016/j.jempfin.2009.11.001
38. Jääskeläinen, M., Maula, M.: Do networks of financial intermediaries help reduce local bias? Evidence from cross-border venture capital exits. J. Bus. Ventur. **29**, 704–721 (2014). https://doi.org/10.1016/j.jbusvent.2013.09.001
39. Amornsiripanitch, N., Gompers, P., Xuan, Y.: More than money: venture capitalists on boards. J. Law Econ. Organizat. **35**, 513–543 (2019). https://doi.org/10.1093/jleo/ewz010
40. de Clercq, D., Manigart, S.: The venture capital post-investment phase: opening the black box of involvement. In: Landström, H. (ed.) Handbook of Research on Venture Capital, pp. 193–218. Edward Elgar, Cheltenham (2007). https://doi.org/10.4337/9781847208781.00015
41. Elango, B., Fried, V., Hisrich, R., Polonchek, A.: How venture capital firms differ. J. Bus. Ventur. **10**, 157–179 (1995). https://doi.org/10.1016/0883-9026(94)00019-Q
42. Wells, W.: Venture capital decision-making (1974)
43. Sørensen, M.: How smart is smart money? A two-sided matching model of venture capital. J. Financ. **62**, 2725–2762 (2007). https://doi.org/10.1111/j.1540-6261.2007.01291.x
44. Gompers, P., Gornall, W., Kaplan, S., Strebulaev, I.: How venture capitalists make decisions. Harvard Business Review. March-April 2021
45. Kollmann, T., Kuckertz, A.: Evaluation uncertainty of venture capitalists' investment criteria. J. Bus. Res. **63**, 741–747 (2010). https://doi.org/10.1016/j.jbusres.2009.06.004
46. Gompers, P., Gornall, W., Kaplan, S., Strebulaev, I.: How do venture capitalists make decisions? J. Financ. Econ. **135**, 169–190 (2020). https://doi.org/10.1016/j.jfineco.2019.06.011
47. Brown, K.C., Wiles, K.W.: Opaque financial contracting and toxic term sheets in venture capital. J. Appl. Corp. Financ. **28**, 72–85 (2016). https://doi.org/10.1111/jacf.12160

48. Busenitz, L.W., Fiet, J.O., Moesel, D.D.: Reconsidering the venture capitalists' "value added" proposition: an interorganizational learning perspective. J. Bus. Ventur. **19**, 787–807 (2004). https://doi.org/10.1016/j.jbusvent.2003.06.005
49. Longhurst, R.: Semi-structured interviews and focus groups. In: Clifford, N., Cope, M., Gillespie, T., French, S. (eds.) Key Methods in Geography, pp. 143–156. SAGE, London (2010)
50. Niebert, K., Gropengießer, H.: Leitfadengestützte interviews. In: Krüger, D., Parchmann, I., Schecker, H. (eds.) Methoden in der naturwissenschaftsdidaktischen Forschung, pp. 121–132. Springer, Heidelberg (2014). https://doi.org/10.1007/978-3-642-37827-0_10
51. Strauss, A., Corbin, J.: Basics of Qualitative Research: Grounded Theory Procedures and Techniques. SAGE, London (1990)
52. Lincoln, Y.S., Guba, E.G.: Naturalistic Inquiry. SAGE, Newbury Park (1985)
53. Denzin, N.: Sociological Methods: A Sourcebook. McGraw Hill, New York (1978)
54. Trochim, W.M.K.: Qualitative validity. https://conjointly.com/kb/qualitative-validity/. Accessed 10 Feb 2022
55. Spradley, J.: The Ethnographic Interview. Thomson Wadsworth, Belmont (1979)
56. Smith, R.: The key differences between rule-based AI and machine learning, https://becominghuman.ai/the-key-differences-between-rule-based-ai-and-machine-learning-8792e545e6. Accessed 10 Feb 2022
57. Rimol, M., Costello, C.: Gartner says tech investors will prioritize data science and artificial intelligence above "gut feel" for investment decisions by 2025. https://www.gartner.com/en/newsroom/press-releases/2021-03-10-gartner-says-tech-investors-will-prioritize-data-science-and-artificial-intelligence-above-gut-feel-for-investment-decisions-by-20250. Accessed 10 Feb 2022

A New Human Factor Study in Developing Practical Vision-Based Applications with the Transformer-Based Deep Learning Model

Thitirat Siriborvornratanakul(✉)

Graduate School of Applied Statistics, National Institute of Development Administration (NIDA), 148 SeriThai Road, Bangkapi, Bangkok 10240, Thailand
thitirat@as.nida.ac.th

Abstract. The convolutional neural network is a deep learning architecture that has dominated most computer vision tasks for several years. But starting from 2020, Transformer architecture has turned to be a new challenger that has been expected to replace convolutional neural networks in the near future. Unlike researchers that prefer observing any new possibility in order to look for chances of improvement, achieving a new state-of-the-art model is not a goal for most practitioners. This paper observes in detail how the two types of architectures allow practitioners to easily use them in actual applications. Major models regarding each architecture in each computer vision task are described and summarized according to their task variety, availability, outputted performances, and computational resources. In conclusion, this paper discovers that the younger Transformer-based models are not inferior in terms of task variety, outputted performance, and computational resources. But it is the problem of availability that makes Transformer-based models more difficult to use at this moment.

Keywords: Human factor · Simplicity · Artificial intelligence · Deep learning · Convolutional neural network · Transformer

1 Introduction

It was back in 1943 when the term "neural network" was proposed by McCulloch and Pitts [17]. Nevertheless, it was not until 2012 that a deep neural network (a.k.a., deep learning) successfully made its world debut through AlexNet [14], a variant of deep neural networks called Convolutional Neural Network (CNN or ConvNet) and the winner of ImageNet challenge 2012. Because of the huge success of AlexNet, the year 2012 was marked as the "ImageNet moment" where the field of computer vision was disrupted by deep learning. After 2012, the global trend of deep learning has erupted together with the trend of artificial intelligence beyond academic and research laboratories. Since then, CNN-based deep

H. Degen and S. Ntoa (Eds.): HCII 2022, LNAI 13336, pp. 436–447, 2022.
https://doi.org/10.1007/978-3-031-05643-7_28

learning models have become a new standard and the major backbones in computer vision tasks for both researchers and practitioners. Apart from computer vision, natural language processing (NLP) is another field that has been greatly affected by deep learning. One of the major disruptions in natural language processing was inspired by Google's groundbreaking attention-based deep learning model named Transformer as presented in 2017 [25]. In the following year of 2018, Google proposed another Transformer-based language model named BERT (Bidirectional Encoder Representations from Transformers) [5] which allowed finetuning to specific tasks with fewer resources and smaller datasets. BERT is well-known as a major trigger that the year 2018 is called the year of ImagetNet moment in natural language processing.

Up to this point, there are two paths separating from each other—CNN for computer vision tasks and Transformer for natural language processing tasks. But in 2020, these two paths have been merged with the proposal of Vision Transformer (ViT) from Google, German Research Centre for Artificial Intelligence, and University of Cambridge [6,7]. Borrowing most concepts from BERT, ViT shows that an input image can be simply divided into non-overlapping patches of size 16×16 pixels. Then, these image patches are projected and used as if they are word inputs in common tasks of natural language processing. While ViT involves no convolutional operation at all, ViT's performances are comparable to and even better than some CNN-based state-of-the-art models in computer vision benchmarks. Since 2020, it has been widely discussed that Transformer-based models will eventually surpass and replace CNN models in computer vision tasks.

According to our own research experiences in computer vision, we have noticed that, despite the increasing popularity of Transformer-based models in computer vision research, many artificial intelligence practitioners still prefer using CNN-based deep learning models whenever their goal is a practical vision-based artificial intelligence solution for real-life applications. This hypothesis of us is confirmed when inspecting the numbers of publications regarding CNN-based and Transformer-based models shown in Fig. 1 (left); it is obvious that the numbers of publications regarding CNN are much more than those of Transformer at this moment. Inspiring by this difference we recognized between researchers and practitioners, this paper will make a close comparison between the two model architectures upon computer vision tasks. Instead of advanced technical issues for serious deep learning researchers, our comparison will focus on usability and user experience issues towards deep learning practitioners. This is in order to find out which architecture better aligns with human behaviors and is suitable for general developers and practitioners.

The rest of this paper is organized as following. Section 2 frames the study of this paper and explains issues to be inspected. Then, Sect. 3 and 4 explore each model architecture separately. After that, Sect. 5 compares the two architectures from the human factor aspect according to Fogg's six simplicity factors [8]. Finally, Sect. 6 concludes this paper.

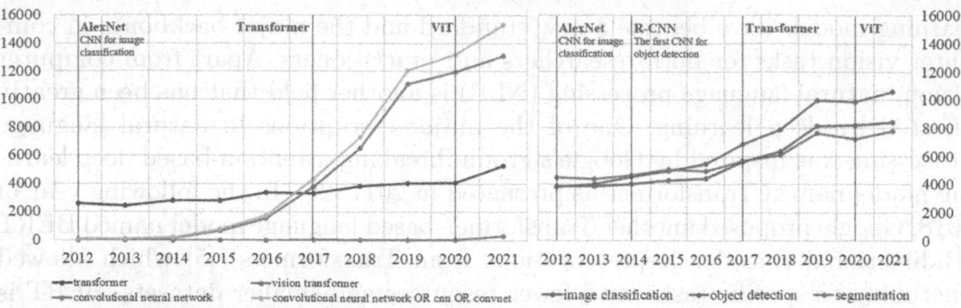

Fig. 1. Publication trends in two architectures (left) and in three computer vision tasks (right) respectively. The numbers of search results are shown in the vertical axis according to each publication year (horizontal axis) based on different search keywords. Data shown in this figure were retrieved from IEEE Xplore on February 10, 2022.

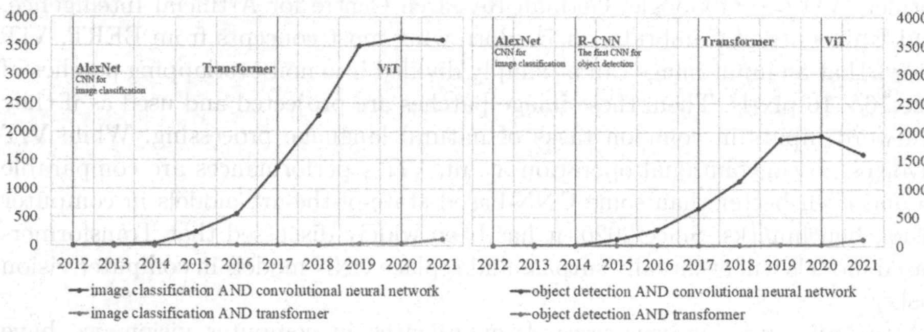

Fig. 2. Publication trends in image classification (left) and in object detection (right) regarding the two architectures. The numbers of search results are shown in the vertical axis according to each publication year (horizontal axis) based on different search keywords. Data in this figure were retrieved from IEEE Xplore on February 10, 2022.

2 Scope of Study

Our exploration in Sect. 3 and 4 will focus on four main issues that are important when a practitioner plans to start a new deep learning project. The four issues include task variety, availability in major deep learning platforms, outputted performances, and computational resources.

Speaking of major deep learning platforms, there is the survey of Kaggle in 2020 [18]. According to the survey, the numbers of respondents regarding five deep learning frameworks listed under the "most common machine learning frameworks" question are TensorFlow 49%, Keras 43.8%, PyTorch 29.6%, Fast.ai 5.2% and MXNet 1.5%. Consequently, the major deep learning platforms in this paper will mainly refer to the latest and stable releases of Google's TensorFlow (including its official high-level APIs—Keras) and Facebook's PyTorch (torchvision). At the time of writing this paper, our primary considerations are ranged from TensorFlow 2.7.0 Keras, low-level TensorFlow, and PyTorch. The reason for choosing TensorFlow Keras primarily is because it is a popular and mature alternative that allows beginners and practitioners to quickly create a deep learning model with few lines of code.

In the part of computational resources, deep learning involves three types of computational units—CPU (Central Processing Unit), GPU (Graphics Processing Unit), and TPU (Tensor Processing Unit); the latter two are accelerators that are quite important for training and using a deep learning model. While most GPUs for deep learning rely on Nvidia, TPU is proprietary to Google and is computational hardware specially designed for neural networks. According to Google [12], TPU-v1 was about 80x faster than CPU and 30x faster than GPU at neural network inference. However, as heavy use of TPU is currently available as a paid service on cloud only, researchers and practitioners outside Google tend to use non-TPU accelerators. This is reflected in the Kaggle survey conducted in 2020 [18] where 71.8% of respondents (using either machine learning or deep learning, or both) had never used TPUs; the most common accelerator types were GPUs 49.2%, none 46.7%, TPUs 5.7%, and other 3.9%.

3 CNN Walk-Through

Being a major backbone in the field of computer vision for several years, CNN-based models have strongly dominated most computer vision tasks in a way that any computer vision researcher can give a name of the model for each task immediately if being asked. Generally, deep learning models can be divided into two main categories—discriminative and generative models. Discriminative models are like judges as they are responsible for figuring out decision boundaries from training samples; the decision is basically classification and/or regression. Generative models are like artists as they first learn the underlying data distribution from training samples and then create whole new data by themselves according to the learned knowledge.

For CNN-based models, discriminative tasks are quite mature as they exist in computer vision since the very beginning of AlexNet in 2012, whereas generative tasks have just become popular since the proposal of GAN (Generative Adversarial Network) in 2014 [10,11] and the DeepFake viral in 2017. The following subsections will walk through some foundation and classic CNN-based discriminative models, focusing on the two most popular vision-based discriminative tasks according to Fig. 1 (right)—image classification and object detection. Tasks of image segmentation are not included as these tasks are still new for Transformer and there is not much information to conclude their representative trends. Also, the study in this paper does not include a discussion about generative models as well as tasks relating to video analysis (e.g., object tracking, action recognition) due to page limit.

3.1 Image Classification

For image classification tasks, practitioners may choose to design the whole CNN architecture and train them all from scratch. But the most popular alternative is to rely on pretrained CNN models as backbone models and continue training them to fit our custom image dataset. This pretraining technique is extremely useful and is a mainstream solution for both researchers and practitioners in computer vision. Using pretrained models significantly jumps start our model to the point that only a slight model extension, a few training data, and a normal computer are enough to train a good CNN-based image classifier. Among many available image datasets, ImageNet-1k is perhaps the most popular dataset that is used to supervisely train CNN-based backbone models. Famous CNN-based backbone models that are pretrained on ImageNet-1k and available in TensorFlow Keras, include Xception, VGG, ResNet, Inception, MobileNet, DenseNet, NASNet and EfficientNet. For PyTorch's torchvision, available image classifiers pretrained on ImageNet-1k are AlexNet, VGG, ResNet, SqueezeNet, DenseNet, Inception, GoogLeNet, ShuffleNet, MobileNet, ResNeXt, WideResNet, MNASNet, EfficientNet and RegNet.

Among all ready-to-use CNN backbone models available in TensorFlow Keras, EfficientNet-B7 (66 million parameters) from Google yields the maximum accuracy of 84.3% top-1 accuracy and 97.0% top-5 accuracy using 1578.90 and 61.62 ms per inference step[1] on CPU and GPU respectively. Nevertheless, training these CNN architectures from scratch on ImageNet-1k until reaching such performance is not cheap. According to [26], training EfficientNet-B0 (the smallest variant of EfficientNet) took 23 h on 8 cores of TPU-v2; but with careful optimizations, the larger EfficientNet-B2 and EfficientNet-B5 models got trained in 18 min and 1 h respectively on 1024 cores of TPU-v3.

Among ready-to-use image classifiers in PyTorch's torchvision, Facebook's RegNet [19] claimed to outperform EfficientNet using 5x less GPU resources. RegNetY-8.0GF (39.2 million parameters, 20.1 top-1 error) took 28.1 training hours and 113 ms inference time whereas EfficientNet-B5 (30 million parameters, 21.5 top-1 error) took 135.1 training hours and 504 ms inference time. From this side-by-side comparison, it can be seen that RegNetY-8.0GF is bigger in size but more accurate and has less GPU computation than EfficientNet-B5.

3.2 Object Detection

Once CNN-based models showed major success in image classification tasks, researchers started exploring the next-level task of CNN-based object detection where a model must both classify and localize an unknown number of objects in an input image via axis-aligned bounding boxes. R-CNN (Regions with CNN features) [9] is the first deep learning-based object detection model that was proposed in 2014 by UC Berkeley; R-CNN utilizes the pretrained AlexNet

[1] Times per inference step were obtained from https://keras.io/api/applications/ on December 28, 2021.

(a pretrained image classifier) as their internal image-based feature extractor so it is considered a CNN-based object detector. Figure 2 shows comparative trends between image classification and object detection tasks; it is obvious that image classification is more common and mature than object detection.

After the introduction of R-CNN, other deep learning-based object detectors have been proposed, for example, Faster R-CNN, YOLO, SSD, RetinaNet, CornerNet, CenterNet, Grid R-CNN and EfficientDet. Among these, Faster R-CNN, YOLO, and SSD are perhaps the most repeatedly used models with several proposed variants and updates for different usage purposes; for example, Faster R-CNN for higher accuracy and YOLO or SSD for faster speed. Unfortunately, these CNN-based object detection models are not officially available in TensorFlow Keras but some pretrained variants (on the MS COCO 2017) are available in TensorFlow 2 Object Detection APIs, including Faster R-CNN, SSD, and CenterNet.[2] For the popular YOLO family, the models are not available in TensorFlow 2 Object Detection APIs but in other deep learning platforms, for example, YOLOv1 to YOLOv4 in DarkNet, and YOLOv5 in PyTorch.

Nevertheless, training these CNN-based object detection models is also not cheap and it often involves using a pretrained image classifier backbone inside. Because of the network's complexity that is higher than image classification models, it is difficult to precisely measure and report the train-from-scratch training resources regarding object detection models. According to [20], the original Faster R-CNN trained on 8 unspecified GPUs has a frame rate of 5 fps and 17 fps at run time on VGG and ZF backbones respectively, using one Nvidia Tesla K40 GPU. Another report in the official GitHub of YOLOv5[3] states that training times for YOLOv5s/m/l/x are 2/4/6/8 days on a single Nvidia V100 GPU; a family of YOLOv5 models (whose numbers of parameters range from 1.9 to 141 million) yields the MS COCO val2017 dataset's mAP@0.5 (the average AP with IoU = 0.5) between 46–72%, and inference times from 45–3136 ms and 6.3–26.2 ms on a CPU and on a Nvidia V100 GPU respectively.

4 Transformer Walk-Through

Speaking of Google's Transformer [25], it is the concept of multi-head self-attention that helps discover the long-range relationship among tokens of a very long sequence in a non-sequential computation manner; Transformer is well-known for powering non-trivial tasks like machine translation in natural language processing. After the proposal of Vision Transformer (ViT) [6,7], the concept of multi-head self-attention was generalized into finding a non-local relationship among non-overlapping patches in an input image. Although there is a multi-head attention layer of `tf.keras.layers.MultiHeadAttention` available in TensorFlow Keras, there seems to be no proper API that refers to ready-for-

[2] This information refers to https://github.com/tensorflow/models/tree/master/research/object_detection/models on February 10, 2022.

[3] https://github.com/ultralytics/yolov5 accessed on December 30, 2021.

inference Transformer-based models for computer vision tasks. This is the same for PyTorch's torchvision where most ready-to-use models are CNN-based.

Fortunately, there is the well-known HuggingFace library[4] that has built and maintained most cutting-edge Transformer-based models, allowing practitioners and researchers to get pretrained Transformer-based models with a few lines of code. At the time of writing this paper, HuggingFace provides models for both natural language and computer vision tasks, and in both TensorFlow and PyTorch implementations (if available). In the part of computer vision, HuggingFace currently includes Transformer-based models for image classification, object detection, panoptic segmentation, and text-to-image. Note that panoptic segmentation refers to a model with hybrid image segmentation ability as it can segment instance objects like instance segmentation as well as non-instance objects like semantic segmentation.

The following subsections will discuss Transformer-based models for vision-based discriminative tasks. Because ViT was first introduced in 2020, these subsections will only focus on related works during 2020–2021.

4.1 Image Classification

Back in 2020, it is the task of image classification that the original ViT chose to tackle. Borrowing most concepts from BERT [4,5], only the Transformer's encoder and an additional prediction head were required. State-of-the-art ViT models were designed to be pretrained first on large datasets and later finetuned to smaller downstream tasks. Pretraining ViT variants took 2500 TPUv3-core-days for ViT-H/14 and 680 TPUv3-core-days for ViT-L/16 on the JFT-300M dataset; also it took 230 TPUv3-core-days for pretraining ViT-L/16 on the ImageNet-21k dataset. With these huge pretraining datasets, ViT yielded the state-of-the-art accuracy of 88.55% on ImageNet, 90.72% on ImageNet-ReaL, 94.55% on CIFAR-100, and 77.63% on VTAB. It was also reported that by using a TPUv3 accelerator, ViT had inference speed comparable to ResNet but was more memory-efficient.

To yield the state-of-the-art accuracy of ViT, very huge computational resources are required at pretraining, so it is not easy for other researchers and practitioners to replicate similar success. However, it is not so difficult to apply the pretrained ViT as our backbone model for feature extraction and later tune it to match our own dataset, just like what CNN-based backbones in Sect. 3.1 do. For example, the work of [13] finetuned the pretrained ViT-B/32 backbone on their downstream task that classified COVID-19 chest X-ray images. Their model with ViT backbone was trained for 10 min (for 10 epochs) on a single Nvidia RTX 2060 mobile GPU but still yielded better results compared to other experimental models with CNN-based backbones (i.e., InceptionV3, DenseNet, and WideResNet101) that were trained for 35 min (for 25 epochs) on Google Colab.

[4] https://huggingface.co/.

There are several attempts to replicate ViT's success using less computational resources. DeiT (Data-efficient image Transformers) [24] from Facebook AI and Sorbonne University is another high-performance Transformer-based image classification model that utilizes the concept of knowledge distillation to reduce the number of pretraining data. DeiT was trained by 1.2 million training images with a single 8-GPU server for 3 days, a lot less training resources compared to ViT, but still yielded 84.2% top-1 accuracy on ImageNet (a bit less accurate than Transformer-based ViT but more accurate than CNN-based EfficientNet). Another outstanding work is Microsoft BEiT (Bidirectional Encoder representation from Image Transformers) [1] that proposed self-supervised pretraining of ViT. Like ViT, BEiT was first pretrained on the large dataset of ImageNet-21k and then finetuned on the smaller dataset like ImageNet-1k; training BEiT took 5 days for 500k training steps using 16 Nvidia Tesla V100 GPUs. As a result, the large-size BEiT obtained 86.3% accuracy on ImageNet-1k, surpassing 85.3% accuracy of ViT-L pretrained on the same ImageNet-21k dataset.

Despite the impressive performances of Transformer-based models mentioned in the above paragraphs, these models share the same limitations of producing single-resolution feature maps and having quadratic complexity to image size. Hence, they are not suitable to become a new standard of general-purpose backbone for computer vision, particularly for tasks that require dense recognition like semantic segmentation. In 2021, Microsoft proposed Swin Transformer [15], the hierarchical vision transformer that can serve as a general-purpose backbone for several computer vision tasks (e.g., classification, object detection, segmentation) with linear complexity. Swin Transformer is able to surpass or offer better trade-offs compared to both old and new state-of-the-art CNN-based models as well as previously mentioned Transformer-based models. At this point, it seems very convincing that Transformer will surely surpass CNN in computer vision tasks.

Because ViT, DeiT, BEiT, and Swin Transformer are cutting-edge works in Transformer-based image classification models, their pretrained models have been included in HuggingFace's image classification pool. At the time of writing this paper, ViT has both TensorFlow and PyTorch implementations whereas only PyTorch implementations for DeiT, BEiT, and Swin Transformer are available in HuggingFace.

4.2 Object Detection

Facebook's DETR (DEtection TRansformer) [3] is a cutting-edge Transformer alternative for vision-based object detection. While CNN-based object detection models in Sect. 3.2 explicitly embed several human knowledge into models' design and architecture, DETR replaces these handcrafted pipelines with a Transformer by viewing a problem of object detection as a problem of direct set prediction. DETR includes three simple steps—(1) a pretrained CNN backbone (i.e., ResNet) for generating 2048 lower-resolution 2D activation maps from an input image, (2) a standard encoder-decoder Transformer, and (3) a feed-forward network for the final detection prediction. Here the standard Transformer [25] is used with some modification so that the decoder can decode N objects in parallel, allowing fast and efficient prediction. Training the baseline model of DETR for 300 epochs on 16 Nvidia V100 GPUs takes 3 days with 4 images per GPU. In terms of performance, the authors conclude that DETR uses half the computation power compared to Faster R-CNN with the same number of parameters, and it is competitive to Faster R-CNN with ResNet-50 backbone, resulting in 42 AP on the COCO validation dataset. At the time of writing this paper, HuggingFace only provides PyTorch implementations regarding DETR variants for object detection.

As DETR is quite new comparing to CNN-based models in Sect. 3.2, applying DETR in applications is not mainstream yet but there exists some works like [22] and [2] that use DETR for detecting road accident and diabetic feet respectively. Also, the work of [21] makes comparison on the YouTube video object dataset among four deep learning-based object detection models—three CNN-based models (i.e., SSD, YOLOv3, and CenterNet) and one Transformer-based model (i.e., DETR); reported mAPs are 63.57%, 57.85%, 55.37% and 32.20% for SSD, YOLOv3, DETR and CenterNet respectively. Another way of involving Transformer into an object detection model is to replace CNN-based backbones in existing CNN-based object detection models with Transformer, for example, ViT-YOLO [27] integrates the multi-head self-attention into YOLOv4-P7.

5 Comparative Human Factor Analysis

This section compares CNN-based models and Transformer-based models according to Fogg's six simplicity factors [8]—money, time, physical effort, brain cycles, social deviance, and non-routine. Only the first 3 factors will be discussed in detail as the other three are difficult to evaluate. For brain cycles, most cutting-edge deep learning models are quite complicated and there is no proper indicator to compare models' difficulty from a human perspective. For social deviance and non-routine, it is unfair to compare Transformer-based models introduced in 2020 with CNN-based models that have been popular since 2012.

Regarding less physical effort for practitioners to start utilizing models, CNN-based models are clear winners for several reasons. First, CNN-based models for all tasks in this paper are available as ready-for-inference APIs in one or more major deep learning platforms whereas these APIs are not available yet for Transformer-based models. Using Transformer-based models at this moment requires us to refer to separated libraries, GitHub, or unstable releases of major deep learning platforms. Second, CNN-based models often have at least one implementation to choose (TensorFlow, PyTorch, or both) whereas most Transformer-based models are still available only in PyTorch. Third, there are plenty of previous researches, reports, and tutorials about CNN-based models to help us initiate or troubleshoot our works whereas there are few for the younger Transformer-based models. Nevertheless, as Transformer-based models for vision tasks are still at their early ages, it is not surprising that their availability, resource, and material are still lacking behind CNN-based models at this moment.

Regarding time and money, although all major models mentioned in this paper are available for public use, training these state-of-the-art or cutting-edge models from scratch requires high computational resources that cost huge data, time, money, and environmental effects. The state-of-the-art ViT model is perhaps the one with the highest computational resource in this paper as it has to be trained on 300 million training images using 2500 TPUv3-core-days. Nevertheless, DeiT and BEiT, the successors of ViT, get improved so that they use training resources approximately the same as CNN-based models. Nevertheless, for practitioners that do not need to dub state-of-the-art success, using these pretrained models and tuning them to their works are not much expensive and can even be done with free Google Colab. Therefore, there is no clear winner whether which architecture is easier in terms of time and money.

In conclusion, we find that Transformer-based models are currently inferior in terms of simplicity for practitioners. This is because Transformer-based models are younger with obviously fewer model alternatives, reference works, tutorials, example codes, implementation alternatives, and easy-to-use APIs. In terms of technical performances, although the newer Transformer-based models outperform previous state-of-the-art CNN-based models in many computer vision benchmarks, some works report that Transformer-based models are inferior when applying them in actual applications. Nevertheless, the battleground of deep learning architectures on state-of-the-art performances is not over yet. In 2021, Google's MLP-Mixer [23] proposed that neither convolution nor attention is necessary as the multi-layer perceptron (MLP) architecture alone can yield similar results compared to existing state-of-the-art Transformer-based methods in image classification and object detection. In 2022, the latest work named ConvNeXt [16] from Facebook AI Research and UC Berkeley shows that state-of-the-art results of Transformer-based models can also be dubbed with pure CNN-based models that are carefully tuned and modernized.

At last, we think that it is not technical aspects but human factor aspects that make Transformer-based models not as popular as CNN-based models for practitioners at this moment. As learning a new thing is not easy for the human brain, there is no reason to convince practitioners to learn the newer Transformer-based models in order to get comparable results as the easier CNN-based models. However, as Transformer-based models get more mature in the future, they may surpass and eventually replace CNN-based models. This is because CNN has an inductive bias towards an image input whereas the concept of self-attention in Transformer is more scalable, generalized, and can be applied to both image and text inputs. Hence, for the long-term goal of developing an artificial general intelligent model, Transformer has been said to be more promising as one Transformer-based model has the potential to cope with several input types.

6 Conclusion

This paper compares two alternative deep learning architectures in computer vision tasks—the mature CNN-based models and the emerging Transformer-based models. Instead of discussing deep technical detail for serious researchers, our discussion is on issues about human factors that portray how easily practitioners can start using each model architecture in their works. After observing each architecture separately, we conclude that both architectures are more-or-less even in terms of task variety, outputted performances, and resources used in training and inference. But CNN-based models are easier to start with as they are quite mature and have plenty of example resources and lessons to follow. Nevertheless, in the long run, Transformer-based models will certainly become more mature and easier for practitioners. At last, Transformer-based models may surpass CNN-based models, particularly for multimodal tasks that require better generalization among various types of inputs.

References

1. Bao, H., Dong, L., Wei, F.: BEiT: BERT pre-training of image transformers. arXiv:2106.08254 (2021)
2. Brüngel, R., Friedrich, C.M.: DETR and YOLOv5: exploring performance and self-training for diabetic foot ulcer detection. In: IEEE International Symposium on Computer-Based Medical Systems (CBMS) (2021)
3. Carion, N., Massa, F., Synnaeve, G., Usunier, N., Kirillov, A., Zagoruyko, S.: End-to-end object detection with transformers. In: Vedaldi, A., Bischof, H., Brox, T., Frahm, J.-M. (eds.) ECCV 2020. LNCS, vol. 12346, pp. 213–229. Springer, Cham (2020). https://doi.org/10.1007/978-3-030-58452-8_13
4. Devlin, J., Chang, M.W., Lee, K., Toutanova, K.: BERT: pre-training of deep bidirectional transformers for language understanding. arXiv:1810.04805v1 [cs.CL] (2018)
5. Devlin, J., Chang, M.W., Lee, K., Toutanova, K.: BERT: pre-training of deep bidirectional transformers for language understanding. In: Conference of the North American Chapter of the Association for Computational Linguistics: Human Language Technologies (NAACL), pp. 4171–4186 (2019)
6. Dosovitskiy, A., et al.: An image is worth 16x16 words: transformers for image recognition at scale. arXiv:2010.11929v1 [cs.CV] (2020)
7. Dosovitskiy, A., et al.: An image is worth 16x16 words: transformers for image recognition at scale. In: International Conference on Learning Representations (ICLR) (2021)
8. Fogg, B.: A behavior model for persuasive design. In: International Conference on Persuasive Technology (Persuasive), pp. 1–7 (2009)
9. Girshick, R., Donahue, J., Darrell, T., Malik, J.: Rich feature hierarchies for accurate object detection and semantic segmentation. In: IEEE International Conference on Computer Vision and Pattern Recognition (CVPR) (2014)
10. Goodfellow, I.J., et al.: Generative adversarial nets. In: International Conference on Neural Information Processing Systems (NIPS), vol. 2, pp. 2672–2680 (2014)
11. Goodfellow, I.J., et al.: Generative adversarial networks. arXiv:1406.2661v1 [stat.ML] (2014)
12. Jouppi, N.: Quantifying the performance of the TPU, our first machine learning chip. Google Cloud, AI & Machine Learning (2017). https://cloud.google.com/blog/products/gcp/quantifying-the-performance-of-the-tpu-our-first-machine-learning-chip. Accessed 28 Dec 2021

13. Krishnan, K.S., Krishnan, K.S.: Vision transformer based COVID-19 detection using chest X-rays. In: IEEE International Conference on Signal Processing, Computing and Control (ISPCC), pp. 644–648 (2021)
14. Krizhevsky, A., Sutskever, I., Hinton, G.E.: ImageNet classification with deep convolutional neural networks. In: International Conference on Neural Information Processing Systems (NIPS 2012), vol. 1, pp. 1097–1105 (2012)
15. Liu, Z., et al.: Swin transformer: hierarchical vision transformer using shifted windows. In: IEEE/CVF International Conference on Computer Vision (ICCV), pp. 10012–10022 (2021)
16. Liu, Z., Mao, H., Wu, C.Y., Feichtenhofer, C., Darrell, T., Xie, S.: A ConvNet for the 2020s. arXiv:2201.03545 (2022)
17. McCulloch, W.S., Pitts, W.: A logical calculus of the ideas immanent in nervous activity. Bull. Math. Biophys. **5**, 115–133 (1943). https://doi.org/10.1007/BF02478259
18. Mooney, P.: 2020 Kaggle Data Science & Machine Learning Survey. Kaggle (2020). https://www.kaggle.com/paultimothymooney/2020-kaggle-data-science-machine-learning-survey. Accessed 28 Dec 2021
19. Radosavovic, I., Kosaraju, R.P., Girshick, R., He, K., Dollár, P.: Designing network design spaces. In: IEEE/CVF Conference on Computer Vision and Pattern Recognition (CVPR), pp. 10425–10433 (2020)
20. Ren, S., He, K., Girshick, R., Sun, J.: Faster R-CNN: towards real-time object detection with region proposal networks. In: International Conference on Neural Information Processing Systems (NIPS), vol. 1, pp. 91–99 (2015)
21. Sharma, C., Singh, S., Poornalatha, G., Ajitha Shenoy, K.B.: Performance analysis of object detection algorithms on YouTube video object dataset. Eng. Lett. **29**(2), 813–817 (2021)
22. Srinivasan, A., Srikanth, A., Indrajit, H., Narasimhan, V.: A novel approach for road accident detection using DETR algorithm. In: IEEE International Conference on Intelligent Data Science Technologies and Applications (IDSTA) (2020)
23. Tolstikhin, I., et al.: MLP-mixer: an all-MLP architecture for vision. In: Beygelzimer, A., Dauphin, Y., Liang, P., Vaughan, J.W. (eds.) Advances in Neural Information Processing Systems (NeurIPS) (2021)
24. Touvron, H., Cord, M., Douze, M., Massa, F., Sablayrolles, A., Jegou, H.: Training data-efficient image transformers & distillation through attention. In: International Conference on Machine Learning (ICML), vol. 139, pp. 10347–10357 (2021)
25. Vaswani, A., et al.: Attention is all you need. In: International Conference on Neural Information Processing Systems (NIPS), pp. 6000–6010 (2017)
26. Wongpanich, A., et al.: Training EfficientNets at supercomputer scale: 83% ImageNet top-1 accuracy in one hour. arXiv:2011.00071v2 [cs.LG] (2020)
27. Zhang, Z., Lu, X., Cao, G., Yang, Y., Jiao, L., Liu, F.: ViT-YOLO: transformer-based YOLO for object detection. In: IEEE/CVF International Conference on Computer Vision Workshops (ICCVW) (2021)

Attention-Based CNN Capturing EEG Recording's Average Voltage and Local Change

Long Yi[1(✉)] and Xiaodong Qu[2]

[1] Brandeis University, Waltham, MA 02453, USA
longyi@brandeis.edu
[2] Swarthmore College, Swarthmore, PA 19081, USA
xqu1@swarthmore.edu

Abstract. The attention mechanism is one of the most popular deep learning techniques in recent years and it is arguably able to produce human-interpretable results. In this research, we developed a classification model combining two self-attention modules and a convolutional neural network. This model achieved benchmark or superior performance on two electroencephalography (EEG) recording datasets. Moreover, we demonstrated that the self-attention modules were able to capture features, including average voltage of signal features and instant voltage change of the EEG signals, by visualizing the attention maps they produced.

Keywords: Self-attention · CNN · EEG classification · Brain-machine interface

1 Introduction

Brain-machine interface (BMI) aims to recover or enhance human abilities. BMI has benefited from the recent development of machine learning and deep learning [11]. For example, BMI enabled a paralyzed man to "type" 90 characters per minute in recent research [28]. BMI can also identify a variety of cognitive tasks in healthy subjects such as learning programming language [18,19,21]. Most research used the convolutional neural network (CNN), a type of deep neural network (DNN), as the model of choice [9,15]. Despite its general superior performance, CNN is notorious for its black-box nature. In other words, researchers are unable to understand the inner mechanism of the neural network or connect the latent features CNN learns to meaningful and human-understandable neural patterns [31]. More and more researchers are considering interpretability as equally, if not more, important than prediction performance in current BMI research, as it could enable researchers to: 1. verify the reliability of the neural networks, 2. discuss and improve the neural networks, 3. even gain insight into complex neurobiological patterns that human experts can not interpret [2,16,31].

H. Degen and S. Ntoa (Eds.): HCII 2022, LNAI 13336, pp. 448–459, 2022.
https://doi.org/10.1007/978-3-031-05643-7_29

Attention has been one of the most impactful machine learning techniques in recent years, and researchers have used it to achieve a number of breakthroughs since its invention, especially in the field of natural language processing. Self-attention is one of the attention mechanisms and it gains its name from the analogy to the human cognitive attention. As its name suggests, self-attention assigns weights (i.e., paying different levels of attention) to every element within a sequence or collection based on their degrees of importance. Therefore, human researchers can easily gain insights into self-attention models' inner operations. Moreover, Zhang et al. [31] stated that a general BMI framework requires the ability to both focus on and capture the most informative features of input data under different sizes and conditions, and the attention mechanism and CNN are respectively the ideal deep learning techniques for these two jobs. Based on this philosophy, we implemented a lightweight model combining two self-attention modules and a CNN classifier in this work. We experimented with the model on two electroencephalography (EEG) classification datasets, and it achieved comparable results to another type of state-of-the-art attention-based CNN model on both datasets. The two self-attention modules work on the temporal and spectral dimensions, respectively. We visualized the outputs from the two self-attention modules and demonstrated that they were able to capture global statistics and local changes of the EEG signals.

2 Related Work

The attention-like mechanism was first proposed in the 1960s [4], yet it was not until 2014 that this concept was successfully implemented as a machine learning module that reached meaningful results on real-world problems [1]. Since then, researchers have created different variations of the attention mechanism and incorporated them into traditionally powerful models. The self-attention mechanism was introduced in 2016 as a way to learn semantic correlations between words in a sentence [6]. Shortly after that, Vaswani et al. [26] created the Transformer model that is solely built on the attention mechanism.

Regarding the attention-based CNN (i.e., combination models of the attention mechanism and CNN) that this work focuses on, researchers have devised various configurations of them, and they excelled in performance on different tasks, including computer vision [29], natural language processing [30], and so on [5].

Within the scope of BMI research, researchers have recently used the attention modules or Transformer models to achieve high performance as well, on the grounds that there are correlations between time steps and signal sources of EEG recordings [13,25]. There were also a few studies that combined the attention mechanism with CNN and achieved state-of-the-art level prediction accuracy on EEG classification tasks [7,14,25]. However, to the best of the authors' knowledge, the incorporation of the attention mechanism into CNN in previous research can be categorized in two ways: 1. attention modules operate within the convolution layers and help capture latent features [7,14], 2. Transformer models receive inputs from CNN and generate predictions [25]. Different from these two approaches, we used the self-attention modules to learn important features and used the CNN to capture them. In other words, we used the self-attention modules to generate attention maps and fed them into the CNN as a classifier to make the classification predictions.

Regarding the work that wrestled with the interpretability problem in BMI, there were two teams of researchers who combined the interpretable Layer-wise Relevance Propagation modules with the powerful but black-box DNNs to enhance the model interpretability [2,24]. We incorporated the self-attention mechanism and CNN in a similar fashion, that the two parts of the model worked complementarily and were respectively designated to achieve high accuracy and enhance interpretability. Besides, there were other research groups who used the attention mechanism to visualize the correlation maps of subjects' brain activities on different motor imagery tasks (i.e., imagining in head but not performing a movement or task) [7,14,25]. Different from their work, we managed to interpret the model operation and distinguish distinct neurobiological features the model learned in our work.

Previous researches have used the attention-mechanism to capture features from the temporal, spectral, and spatial dimensions [13]. Based on the condition of the datasets we used, we employed two self-attention modules to capture features on the temporal and spectral dimensions [14,25]. We will call them Temporal Attention and Spectral Attention in this paper.

3 Experiment

Dataset. We experimented with our proposed model on two EEG datasets that differed in various conditions to show the validity and generalization power of our model.

The first dataset consists of 14 subjects' EEG recordings. Each subject performed five cognitive tasks during the recording in random order—reading, copying, answering, writing, and typing. Subjects were recorded using the Muse headbands with four data acquisition nodes, and the signal transmission rate 10 Hz. Each recording node's signal was decomposed into the five classic bands of brainwaves (i.e., α, β, γ, δ, and θ), thus producing 20 channels. The absolute Band Powers (BP) features were computed and used as our model inputs. We used non-overlapping 500-millisecond-long EEG recordings to feed into the model. In other words, the model inputs were 5 by 20 matrices. For more detail about the dataset, please refer to the original work that collected and analyzed the dataset [20].

The second dataset we used was the publicly available BCI competition III dataset V [3]. During recording, subjects performed three different motor imagery tasks—left-hand movement, right-hand movement, and word generation. The dataset contained three subjects' recordings, but we only used the first subject's. We used the power spectral density (PSD) features, and each PSD sample was a vector of 96 values (8 channels $\times$ 12 frequency components). Similarly, we used non-overlapping 500-millisecond-long recordings to feed into the model. The model inputs were 8 by 96 matrices.

We will refer to the first dataset as RWT in this paper. We used 90% randomly-split data to train the model and the remaining 10% to test it. We will refer to the second dataset using the abbreviation of BCI III, and we used 75% of the data for training and 25% for testing. A summary and comparison of the two datasets can be found in Table 1. Please refer to the original papers for more details.

Table 1. Summary of datasets

	RWT	BCI III
Recording signal	EEG	EEG
Category of task	Cognitive	Motor imagery
Number of subjects	14	1
Recording device	Muse headband	Biosemi system
Artifact removal	Muscle movement	None
Signal feature	BP	PSD
Data size for each subject	10528 × 96	2022 × 20
Recording length for each Input	500 ms	500 ms

Model and Training. Figure 1 A depicts the model's architecture. The EEG inputs will first be fed in parallel into the two self-attention modules, which operate on the temporal and spectral dimensions, respectively. Within each self-attention module, a position encoding is first concatenated to the inputs, then the dot-product computation is performed, as: $Output = Softmax(Q \cdot K^T) \cdot V$ [17]. Both of the self-attention modules produce outputs of the same size as the input. Each of the original inputs is added to its corresponding two attention outputs with weights to produce an attention maps as a residual connection [12]. The attention maps are then fed into the CNN. The CNN has three convolution layers; each layer contains a convolution kernel sequentially followed by a ReLU activation function, a Dropout layer, a Batchnorm layer, and a pooling layer. Two fully connected layers are appended to the end of the convolution layers and form the classifier, where the final predictions are generated. We used the Adam optimizer and Cross-entropy loss for all training and testing. The model structure and training method were the same for both datasets, except for necessary adjustment on the convolution kernel size to accommodate the input sizes. We varied the learning rates between 5e−4 and 5e−5 based on the model sizes. More hyperparameters and training processing can be found in our publicly available code[1].

[1] https://github.com/longyi1207/Attention_Based_CNN/blob/main/Attention_Based_CNN.py.

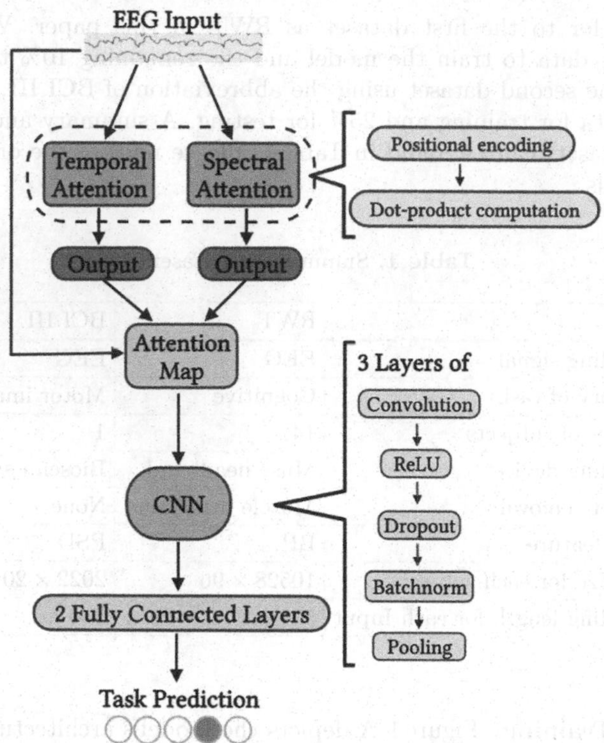

Fig. 1. Model architecture. Every EEG input is fed into the Temporal and Spectral Attention modules. The two outputs of the self-attention modules are added to the original input with weights and produce an attention map, which is then sent into the three-layers CNN. Two fully connected layers form the end of the CNN and make the task prediction (one of three classes for the BCI III dataset or one of five classes for the RWT dataset).

4 Result

Performance. We used prediction accuracy as our performance evaluation metric, as both datasets were well-balanced over classes of tasks. On the BCI III dataset, the chance of randomly guessing the true class was 33%, and our proposed model reached 79% prediction accuracy, which was comparable to the benchmark result (79%) [3]. On the RWT dataset, the random guessing chance was 20%, and our model reached 46%. The difference between the two performances was presumably caused by the different baseline random guessing accuracy as well as the non-stationarity of EEG signals suffered in the cross-subject setting [9]. The original paper collected RWT did not report a benchmark performance on the cross-subject setting. Therefore, we propose the performance we obtained as a benchmark for future comparison. To verify the effectiveness of the self-attention modules, we did ablation experiments on both datasets, where we compared the performance of our full model (i.e., CNN + Temporal Attention + Spectral Attention) to those of CNN alone, Temporal Attention alone, Spectral Attention alone, Temporal Attention combining CNN, and lastly Spectral Attention combining CNN. Note that the self-attention modules in the original model generated outputs of the same size as the inputs. For the purpose of this experiment, we appended two fully connected layers to both of them to make them full classification models.

Table 2 summarizes the results of the ablation experiment. It shows that every component of the model helped boost the performance. Moreover, we can observe several general patterns on both datasets: 1. CNN alone performed better than either self-attention modules alone (except for the Spectral Attention on RWT), despite that the CNN had fewer parameters than either of the self-attention modules alone, proving the power of CNN; 2. the Spectral Attention performed better than the Temporal Attention, given the inputs from both datasets carried more information on the spectral dimension; 3. both self-attention modules and CNN gained in performance when being concatenated to each other. The combination of CNN with either self-attention module beat CNN alone or self-attention modules alone. The performance was further boosted in the full model.

Table 2. Ablation experiment

	Accuracy on RWT (%)	Accuracy on BCI III (%)
Full model	46	79
CNN	36	73
Temporal attention	33	69
Spectral attention	38	70
Temporal attention + CNN	39	75
Spectral attention + CNN	41	77

Furthermore, we also compared the performance of our model to that of a three-layers CNN built on the state-of-the-art Convolutional Block Attention Module (CBAM) [29]. Our proposed model had slightly more parameters, but the two models achieved comparable accuracy. Refer to Table 3 for the concrete values.

In sum, the two experiments above demonstrate the effectiveness and power of our model. We provided a lightweight implementation of this model structure, and it can be incorporated or upgraded with other techniques to achieve higher performance.

Interpretability. In this section, we extracted the two self-attention modules from the original model, visualized their outputs on instance data, and offered insights into their model operation.

Table 3. Comparison with CBAM CNN

	Our model	CBAM-based CNN
Performance on RWT (%)	46	46
Number of parameters on RWT	5155	2532
Performance on BCI III (%)	79	78
Number of parameters on BCI III	63011	53658

Figure 2A is a visualization of an instance input from RWT whose size is 5 by 20. The twenty colored lines represent the 20 features, and the x-axis indicates the five time steps. For visual clarity, the concrete values of the 20 features are not provided, and the 20 lines are partitioned into five subplots and plotted in four colors corresponding to the five brainwaves and four data acquisition nodes. Panel B shows the attention map for this instance input. We illustrated it as a heatmap and we used a blue and white color palette with blue indicating a larger value. The attention map has the same size as the input. We located where the most and least attention were paid to by the self-attention modules, mapped them on the input, and attempted to interpret the model behavior. Visually inspecting Panel B, there is a horizontal blue band on feature 15 across the five time steps (indicated by the red arrow), indicating that it was assigned the largest weight, while feature 3 (indicated by the blue arrow) was assigned the least. In other words, the model determined that feature 15 provided the most reliable information for class prediction, while feature 3 provided the least. The ground truth label for this instance input was the fifth task. We compared value of feature 15 of the fifth task with those of the four other tasks, on the premise that the self-attention modules learned to classify tasks by focusing on features that differentiated the five tasks. We will denote the fifth task as Task V in Roman numerals later, likewise for the other four tasks.

Panel C shows the average values as well as 95% confidence intervals (CI) of the five tasks in the RWT training set. We state that the reliance on feature 15 was reasonable since it was negative only for Task V and was non-negative for every other task (circled in red); the CI of task V does not overlap those of the other tasks.

To justify the least weight given to feature 3, we computed the average voltage and CI for all 20 features of Task V. We can observe in Panel D that feature 3 has the largest confidence interval among all the 20 features and therefore the least indicative power (circled in blue), explaining the least reliance given by the model.

Moreover, we observed that despite most inputs were temporally steady, the Temporal Attention module was able to catch distinguishable local voltage changes. Figure 3 shows another instance data from RWT (Panel A) and its corresponding attention map (Panel B). Pinpointed by the two red arrows on the input and attention map, we can see that time steps 2 and 3 were assigned the heaviest weight by the self-attention modules, when the EEG signal fluctuated

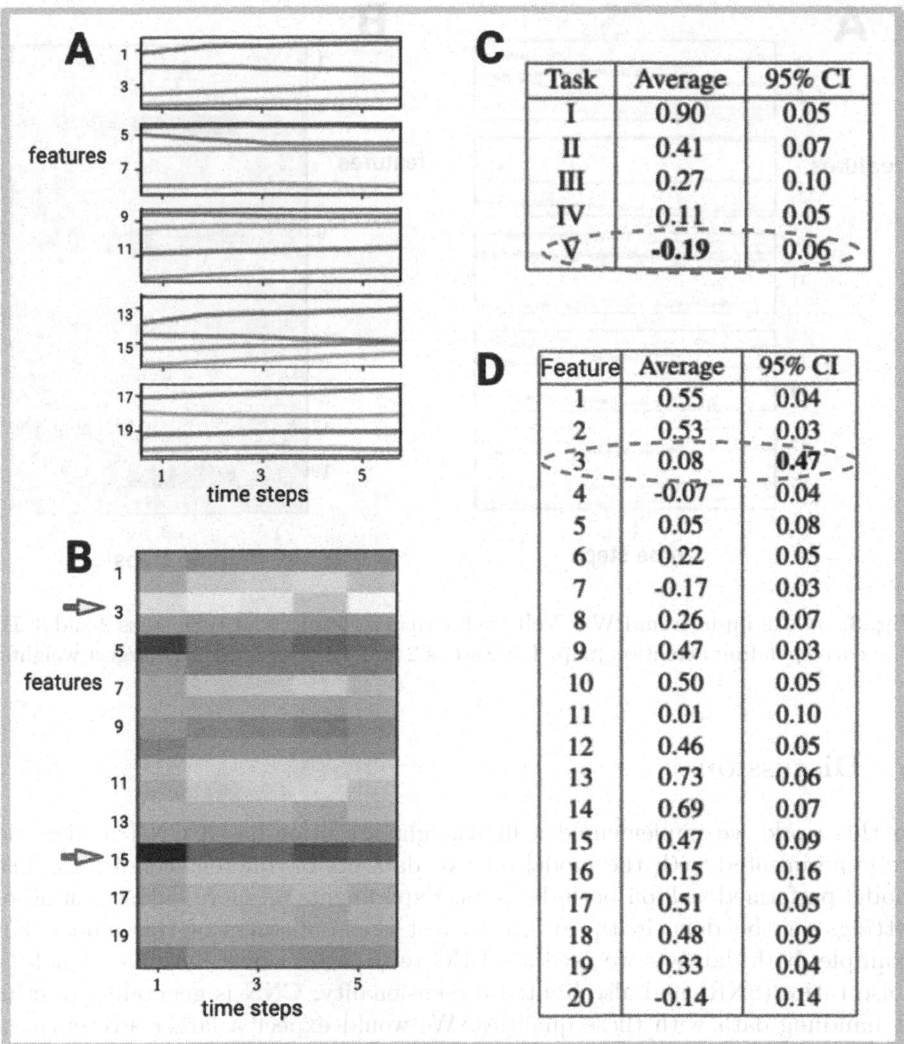

Task	Average	95% CI
I	0.90	0.05
II	0.41	0.07
III	0.27	0.10
IV	0.11	0.05
V	-0.19	0.06

Feature	Average	95% CI
1	0.55	0.04
2	0.53	0.03
3	0.08	0.47
4	-0.07	0.04
5	0.05	0.08
6	0.22	0.05
7	-0.17	0.03
8	0.26	0.07
9	0.47	0.03
10	0.50	0.05
11	0.01	0.10
12	0.46	0.05
13	0.73	0.06
14	0.69	0.07
15	0.47	0.09
16	0.15	0.16
17	0.51	0.05
18	0.48	0.09
19	0.33	0.04
20	-0.14	0.14

Fig. 2. A. An input from RWT whose label is task V. **B.** The corresponding attention map. Features 3 and 15 are assigned the largest and least weights, indicated by the blue and red arrows. **C.** All tasks' feature 15. Task V has a negative value; it does not overlap the 95% confidence interval (CI) of the four other tasks. **D.** Task V's all features. Feature 3 has the largest CI; it overlaps the CI of most of the other features. (Color figure online)

distinctly. Summarizing the two cases above, we state that the model behavior can be plausibly justified in hindsight. Specifically, the Spectral and Temporal Attention modules were able to learn the average voltage and distinct temporal variations, respectively.

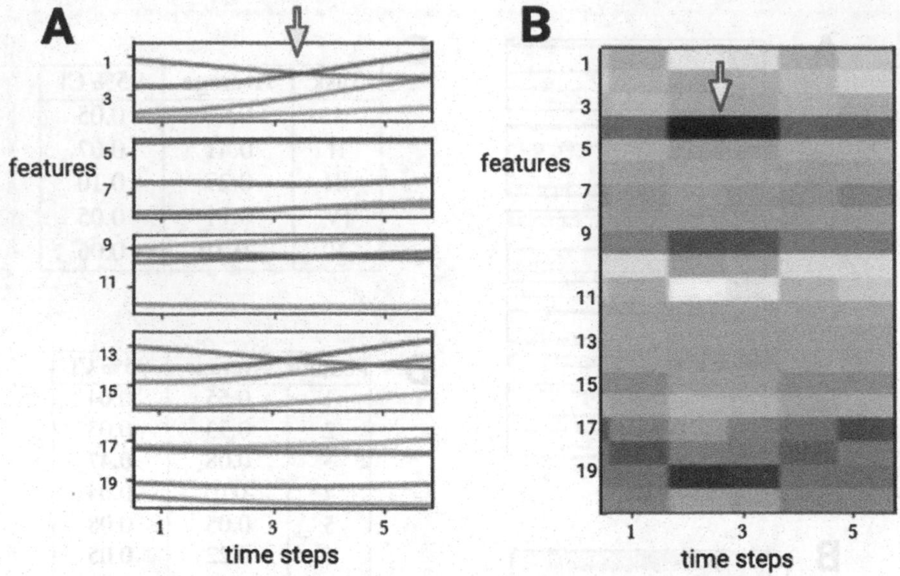

Fig. 3. **A.** An input from RWT. Voltage fluctuates distinctly at time steps 2 and 3. **B.** The corresponding attention map. Time steps 2 and 3 are assigned the largest weights.

5 Discussion

In this work, we implemented a lightweight attention-based CNN model and we experimented with the model on two datasets of different conditions. The model performed well on both datasets. Experiments on more datasets of other settings can be done in the future to test the robustness of this model. For example, both datasets we used are EEG recordings, which have low signal-to-noise ratios (SNR) and also limited dimensionality; CNN is generally powerful at handling data with these qualities. We would expect a larger advantage of the self-attention modules in our model on other types of recordings that have larger SNR and higher dimensionality, such as functional magnetic resonance imaging recordings. Incidentally, we aligned with previous study and used 500-milliseconds-recordings as model inputs [3], but long-range temporal correlations have been found in EEG recordings of MI tasks [27]. CNN is structurally enforced to extract local features and thus weak in capturing long-distance dependency, whereas the attention mechanism was invented to solve this problem. Therefore, we would also expect an advantage in performance if we lengthen the data inputs.

In addition to achieving satisfactory performance, we visualized our self-attention modules' outputs and gained insight into distinguishable neural characteristics underlying different cognitive tasks by interpreting the operation inside the two modules. However, we could only identify simple features such as average voltage of features and instant temporal oscillation and we were unable to recognize more complex neurobiological patterns. Moreover, we did not have prior knowledge of the neural patterns underlying the different MI and cognitive tasks in the datasets we used, namely what really differs in the EEG signals of different tasks, and thus we do not have an objective metric to evaluate how well the self-attention modules perform. One solution to this conundrum is to apply this model on types of EEG recordings that are well-studied and more recognizable by human experts (such as on epilepsy with its characteristic wave discharge [23]) and inspect model operation based on human knowledge.

Zhang et al. [31] proposed that CNN can work in complement with the attention mechanism and this model architecture would conceptually suffice a general BMI framework. However, there is currently no experimental framework that assesses the degree of compatibility of two model structures. Moreover, after researchers used attention models to achieve competitive performance on computer vision tasks, there were questions on the necessity of CNN or even arguments that CNN can be replaced by attention models based on experimental and theoretical evidence [8,10]. The nature of various model structures are yet to be determined, and deeper understandings into the model operation are required.

As the last word, BMI has benefited greatly from machine learning techniques, and researchers have developed advanced BMI applications in an engineering approach in recent years, such as the one described at the beginning of this paper. However, the future development of BMI is indispensable of and also currently hindered by the insufficiency of knowledge and understanding in neuroscience. In fact, the invention of CNN, the attention mechanism, and even the neural network are inspired by understanding of human organism or behavior. Fortunately, researchers can also and have been using computational models as a tool to gain more understanding in various neurobiological subjects, by interpreting the structure and parameters of models that fit well on recording data. For example, neuroscientists proved the existence of nonlinear computation in retinal bipolar cells in a recent study by using a linear-nonlinear model to prove that the previously assumed linear integration can not accurately define the intracellular recordings [22]. Equipped with stronger and stronger deep learning techniques and neural networks, we would like to encourage researchers to pursue interpretable as well as high-performance results in the future.

6 Conclusion

In this research, we developed a model combining two self-attention modules with a CNN, where the self-attention modules focus on the important features and the CNN captures them. This model achieves satisfactory prediction accuracy on two EEG datasets. We verified the effectiveness of our model structure by an ablation experiment; moreover, our model's performance is comparable with that of a CBAM-based CNN. Lastly, we visualized the self-attention modules' outputs as well as the attention maps and made attempts to interpret them. We demonstrated that the self-attention modules were able to learn meaningful features of the EEG signal, and this helped us to gain insight into the data, such as the relative importance of the features and time steps. This model can be future experimented on epilepsy EEG recordings and more datasets to assess its generalizing ability and practical values.

References

1. Bahdanau, D., Cho, K., Bengio, Y.: Neural machine translation by jointly learning to align and translate (2014). http://arxiv.org/abs/1409.0473, cite arxiv:1409.0473Comment. Accepted at ICLR 2015 as oral presentation
2. Bang, J.S., Lee, S.W.: Interpretable convolutional neural networks for subject-independent motor imagery classification (2021)
3. Blankertz, B., et al.: The BCI competition. III: validating alternative approaches to actual BCI problems. IEEE Trans. Neural Syst. Rehabil. Eng. **14**(2), 153–159 (2006). https://doi.org/10.1109/TNSRE.2006.875642
4. Chaudhari, S., Mithal, V., Polatkan, G., Ramanath, R.: An attentive survey of attention models (2021)
5. Chen, K., Wang, J., Chen, L.C., Gao, H., Xu, W., Nevatia, R.: ABC-CNN: an attention based convolutional neural network for visual question answering, November 2015
6. Cheng, J., Dong, L., Lapata, M.: Long short-term memory-networks for machine reading (2016)
7. Cisotto, G., Zanga, A., Chlebus, J., Zoppis, I., Manzoni, S., Markowska-Kaczmar, U.: Comparison of attention-based deep learning models for EEG classification (2020)
8. Cordonnier, J.B., Loukas, A., Jaggi, M.: On the relationship between self-attention and convolutional layers (2020)
9. Craik, A., He, Y., Contreras-Vidal, J.L.: Deep learning for electroencephalogram (EEG) classification tasks: a review. J. Neural Eng. **16**(3), 031001 (2019)
10. Dosovitskiy, A., et al.: An image is worth 16x16 words: transformers for image recognition at scale (2021)
11. Goodfellow, I., Bengio, Y., Courville, A.: Deep Learning. MIT Press, Cambridge (2016)
12. He, K., Zhang, X., Ren, S., Sun, J.: Deep residual learning for image recognition (2015)
13. Lee, Y.E., Lee, S.H.: EEG-transformer: self-attention from transformer architecture for decoding EEG of imagined speech (2021)
14. Liu, X., Shen, Y., Liu, J., Yang, J., Xiong, P., Lin, F.: Parallel spatial-temporal self-attention CNN-based motor imagery classification for BCI. Front. Neurosci. **14** (2020). https://doi.org/10.3389/fnins.2020.587520. https://www.frontiersin.org/article/10.3389/fnins.2020.587520
15. Lotte, F., et al.: A review of classification algorithms for EEG-based brain-computer interfaces: a 10 year update. J. Neural Eng. **15**(3), 031005 (2018)
16. Lotte, F., Lécuyer, A., Guan, C.: Towards a Fully Interpretable EEG-based BCI System, July 2010. https://hal.inria.fr/inria-00504658. Working paper or preprint
17. Luong, M.T., Pham, H., Manning, C.D.: Effective approaches to attention-based neural machine translation (2015)
18. Qu, X., Hall, M., Sun, Y., Sekuler, R., Hickey, T.J.: A personalized reading coach using wearable EEG sensors-a pilot study of brainwave learning analytics, pp. 501–507 (2018)

19. Qu, X., Liu, P., Li, Z., Hickey, T.: Multi-class time continuity voting for EEG classification. In: Frasson, C., Bamidis, P., Vlamos, P. (eds.) BFAL 2020. LNCS (LNAI), vol. 12462, pp. 24–33. Springer, Cham (2020). https://doi.org/10.1007/978-3-030-60735-7_3
20. Qu, X., Mei, Q., Liu, P., Hickey, T.: Using EEG to distinguish between writing and typing for the same cognitive task. In: Frasson, C., Bamidis, P., Vlamos, P. (eds.) BFAL 2020. LNCS (LNAI), vol. 12462, pp. 66–74. Springer, Cham (2020). https://doi.org/10.1007/978-3-030-60735-7_7
21. Qu, X., Sun, Y., Sekuler, R., Hickey, T.: EEG markers of stem learning, pp. 1–9 (2018). https://doi.org/10.1109/FIE.2018.8659031
22. Schreyer, H.M., Gollisch, T.: Nonlinear spatial integration in retinal bipolar cells shapes the encoding of artificial and natural stimuli. Neuron **109**(10), 1692–1706 (2021). https://doi.org/10.1016/j.neuron.2021.03.015
23. Smith, S.J.M.: EEG in the diagnosis, classification, and management of patients with epilepsy. J. Neurol. Neurosurg. Psychiatry **76**(suppl 2), ii2–ii7 (2005). https://doi.org/10.1136/jnnp.2005.069245. https://jnnp.bmj.com/content/76/suppl_2/ii2
24. Sturm, I., Bach, S., Samek, W., Müller, K.R.: Interpretable deep neural networks for single-trial EEG classification (2016)
25. Sun, J., Xie, J., Zhou, H.: EEG classification with transformer-based models. In: 2021 IEEE 3rd Global Conference on Life Sciences and Technologies (2021)
26. Vaswani, A., et al.: Attention is all you need 30 (2017). https://proceedings.neurips.cc/paper/2017/file/3f5ee243547dee91fbd053c1c4a845aa-Paper.pdf
27. Wairagkar, M., Hayashi, Y., Nasuto, S.J.: Dynamics of long-range temporal correlations in broadband EEG during different motor execution and imagery tasks. Front. Neurosci. **15** (2021). https://doi.org/10.3389/fnins.2021.660032. https://www.frontiersin.org/article/10.3389/fnins.2021.660032
28. Willett, F.R., Avansino, D.T., Hochberg, L.R., Henderson, J.M., Shenoy, K.V.: High-performance brain-to-text communication via imagined handwriting. Nature **593**, 249–254 (2021)
29. Woo, S., Park, J., Lee, J.-Y., Kweon, I.S.: CBAM: convolutional block attention module. In: Ferrari, V., Hebert, M., Sminchisescu, C., Weiss, Y. (eds.) ECCV 2018. LNCS, vol. 11211, pp. 3–19. Springer, Cham (2018). https://doi.org/10.1007/978-3-030-01234-2_1
30. Yin, W., Schütze, H., Xiang, B., Zhou, B.: ABCNN: attention-based convolutional neural network for modeling sentence pairs (2018)
31. Zhang, X., Yao, L., Wang, X., Monaghan, J., McAlpine, D., Zhang, Y.: A survey on deep learning-based non- invasive brain signals: recent advances and new frontiers. J. Neural Eng. **18**, 031002 (2021)

Human-AI Collaboration

Customizable Text-to-Image Modeling by Contrastive Learning on Adjustable Word-Visual Pairs

Jun-Li Lu[1,2(✉)] and Yoichi Ochiai[1,2]

[1] Research and Development Center for Digital Nature, University of Tsukuba, Tsukuba, Japan
lu@digitalnature.slis.tsukuba.ac.jp

[2] Faculty of Library, Information and Media Science, University of Tsukuba, Tsukuba, Japan

Abstract. Co-creation with AI is trending and AI-generation of images from textual descriptions has shown advanced and attractive capabilities. However, commonly trained machine-learning models or built AI-based systems may have deficient points to generate satisfied results for personal usage or novice users of painting or AI co-creation, maybe because of deficient understanding of personal textual expressions or low customization of trained text-to-image machine learning models. Therefore, we assist in creating flexible and diverse visual contents from textual descriptions, by developing neural-networks models with machine learning. In modeling, we generate synthesized images using word-visual co-occurrence by Transformer model and synthesize images by decoding visual tokens. To improve visual and textual expressions and their relevance with more diversities, we utilize contrastive learning applying on texts, images, or pairs of texts and images. In the experimental results of a dataset of birds, we showed that the rendering quality was required of models with some scale neural-networks, and necessary training process with fined training by applying relatively low learning rates until the end of training. We further showed contrastive learning was possible for improvement of visual and textual expressions and their relevance.

Keywords: AI visual content creation · Text-to-image model · Contrastive learning

1 Introduction

Co-creation with AI is trending and AI-generated images from textual descriptions has shown advanced and attractive capabilities. However, commonly trained machine-learning models or built AI-based systems may have deficient points to generate satisfied results for personal usage or novice users of painting or AI co-creation [3,6,8,12,16,18], which may be because of deficient understanding of personal textual expressions or low customization of trained text-to-image machine learning models. Therefore, we aim to assist in creating flexible

H. Degen and S. Ntoa (Eds.): HCII 2022, LNAI 13336, pp. 463–474, 2022.
https://doi.org/10.1007/978-3-031-05643-7_30

	This work: AI-supported interface of generating visual contents from text	Existing or past AI-based drawing capabilities[2]
Research issues	- How to generate images from text? - How to generate diverse images from various expressions of languages? - How to generate user-intended images? - How to infer user intents during creation? - How to effectively retrain text-to-image models, under huge dataset? - How to effective customization or personalization? • Novel and diverse generating visuals from text, diverse user-intended AI-visuals, effective and quality retraining of models	- How to revise or generate images by non-descriptive parameters (e.g., styles, sketch, parts or sub-objects) - How to model condition(style)-based image generation, with training data of limited categories - Limited generated visuals from limited parameters, models were biased on usages, limited customization or personalization
Methodologies (Technologies) required	- Text-to-image modeling with fine-grained words and visuals - Transformer-based neural network (NN) - Image reconstructor - Infer user's intended or diverse visuals from various expressions • Effective retraining by self-supervised learning	- Parameters-to-image NN modeling - Condition-based modeling - GAN-based NN modeling - Limited generation of models and retraining of machine learning
Contributions in Academics or Industries	- Development on human-AI visual content creation by descriptions, and related HCI and machine learning - AI-generated user-intended and diverse visual contents • Novel or accessible communication (e.g., by input of text descriptions) among normal and disabled users	- Leading to modeling or applications for AI-generated images (e.g., deepfakes of famous people) - Improved AI-generation on specific or non-user-intent parameters. - However, limited customization, user-centered creation, and retraining of machine learning

Fig. 1. Comparison of our proposal or modeling and existing GAN-based generation of rendering.

and diverse visual contents from textual description, by developing models using machine learning approaches.

Furthermore, once we have built machine-learning models of generating quality images from text, we can further improve the system in creating more customizable or personalized visual rendering from more meaningful or conditional textual expressions. Further, flexible user-centered input ways can be considered. Therefore, the inference of user intents by using the analysis or NLP tricks on user interests, behaviors, and profiles, or some of user feedbacks such as verbal or satisfaction degree, can be used to improve or increase users' experiences in creating visual rendering contents from their textual expressions.

In our modeling by machine learning and neural networks, there are three main modeling. Given text of words, we model co-occurrence of word-visual tokens by using neural-network Transformer. We then generate the synthesis of image, which is generated by a decoder of the relevant visual units of given words. Further, to increase visual expressions, textual expressions, and their relevance of matched texts and images, we utilize the approach of contrastive learning, and apply contrastive learning in three types of features or contexts. We apply contrastive learning on images, on texts, or on pairs of texts and images.

We evaluated the affect of our modeling and explored suitable machine-learning settings or modeling of neural networks, in a non-huge dataset of various birds. In adjusting rendering performance of models, we found that the rendering

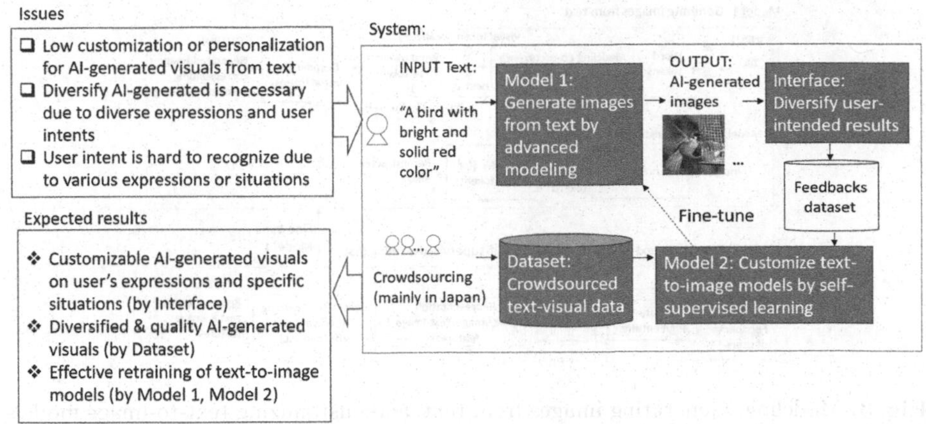

Fig. 2. System: Customizable AI-supported interface of text-based visual content creation.

quality was required some level of machine-learning computation power, i.e., the model size should be at some scale. More, the high rendering quality was required the long training process of detailed machine training by keeping using relative low learning rates, and at least, some extreme low learning rate seemed required at final training steps. Furthermore, in our experimental results, we found that contrastive learning might be possibly useful for improvement of visual and textual expressions, and their relevance or matching degrees. Throughout the paper, we also show the limitation or difficulties of current rendering technologies and show further development or applications in more user-centered factors of visual creations (Fig. 2).

2 Related Work: Limitation of GAN-Based Generation of Rendering and Further Development

As the current AI drawing capabilities might be limited on specific parameters or usages, we aim to create diverse AI-generated visual contents from the unlimited and interesting expressions, which can contribute or improve on valuable applications such as information visualization of user's written documents, creation tools for visual arts, novel ways of accessible communication between normal and disabilities, and even used to increase marketing effect by meaningful generated visual contents. Further, the effective customization or personalization on huge and various text-image data by advanced self-supervised learning will be studied since the current literature may be limited. In Fig. 1, we compare our proposals or modeling for generating flexible or diverse visual expressions from textual expressions, with limitation of existing GAN-based generation of rendering [3,6,8,12,16,18], and further showing applications or interfaces of human or social factors.

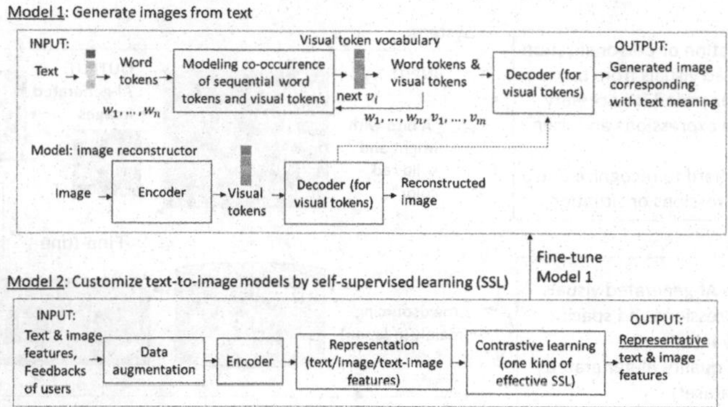

Fig. 3. Modeling: Generating images from text, and customizing text-to-image models by contrastive learning.

3 Generating Visual Images from Textual Descriptions

We introduce the modeling of generating images from textual descriptions. First, we model co-occurrence modeling of word-to-visual tokens by Transformer-based model. Second, we model image construction by GAN-based modeling with CNN and Transformer. Further, to generate more diverse images from more expressions of textual descriptions, in a give training dataset of text-image pairs, we customize text-to-image modeling of the above two models by proposing novel way of applying Contrastive Learning on adjustable Word-Visual pairs.

3.1 Co-occurrence Modeling of Sequential Words and Visual-Tokens

Word Tokens and Tokenizer. In the processing of words in sentences, we utilize word tokens and the tokenizer that process to word tokens from given words of sentences. We utilize the tokenizer based on Byte-Pair Encoding (BPE) [13]. The modeling of BPE tokenizer is as follows. In a set of documents, initially, a set of basic unique words and the frequency of each word are counted. Then, BPE tokenizer counts the frequency of each possible pair of words, and picks the pair of words occurring most frequently to be merged to form new unit of word. The merging of words for new unit of word is applied until the specified number of words is reached. In our experiments, we utilized around thirty thousands of word tokens in Japanese sentences, and utilized around five thousands of words in English sentences.

Visual Tokens. In modeling of the generation of images, we utilize the visual tokens, which are encoded by the decoder of CNN, to generate the image. Given a sequence of word tokens, the modeling of co-occurrence of word and visual tokens predicts a sequential output of visual tokens that are relevant to the word tokens. The list of visual tokens are input to the decoder of CNN for generating

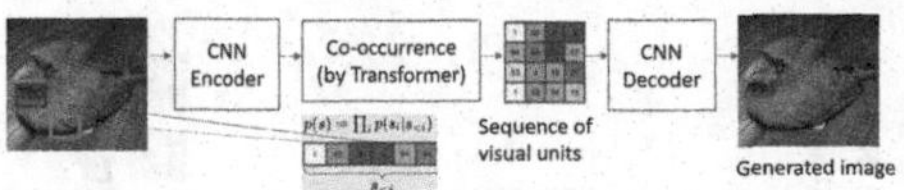

Fig. 4. Image-synthesis modeling.

the synthetic image. In our experiments, we use the size of visual units (i.e., size of codebook of VQGAN [4]) as about one thousand. Note that the size of visual units of VQGAN is less compared with the size of visual units of OpenAI's model, and the generated image quality is maintained and the training time of the whole models could be efficient than using OpenAI's visual model of large size.

Co-occurrence Modeling of Sequential Word and Visual Tokens by Transformer. For generating images from textual descriptions, we predict the relevant sequential visual units from the word tokens of description. In Fig. 3, the modeling of co-occurrence probabilities of sequential visual tokens $w_1, ..., w_n$ and sequential word tokens $v_1, ..., v_m$ is modeled by a Transformer model [11].

$$p(\{w_1, ..., w_n, v_1, ..., v_m\}) = \prod_i p(v_i | w_1, ..., w_n, v_{<i}).$$

3.2 Image Synthesis Using Visual Units by GAN Approaching

With the predicted sequential visual units $v_1, ..., v_m$, we generate the corresponding images by decoding the visual units. The corresponding models are shown in Fig. 4. In training, for each of a given set of images, a sequence of visual tokens $V_i = \{v_1, ..., v_m\}$ from visual codebook is trained from the image. In modeling, the co-occurrence of corresponding encoded visual tokens are predicted by probabilities modeled by a Transformer [4].

$$\arg\min_{V_i \in \mathbb{V}} ||\hat{V} - V_i||,$$

where V_i is the sequential visual units that are similar to the CNN encoded $\hat{V}$ of the given image.

4 Customize Text-to-Image Models with Contrastive Learning

To improve the quality or diversity of generated images by the modeling, we consider to customize or personalized the generation results, to increase the varieties of the generation results, and to efficiently the retraining of models in machine learning. Therefore, we utilize the approach of contrastive learning

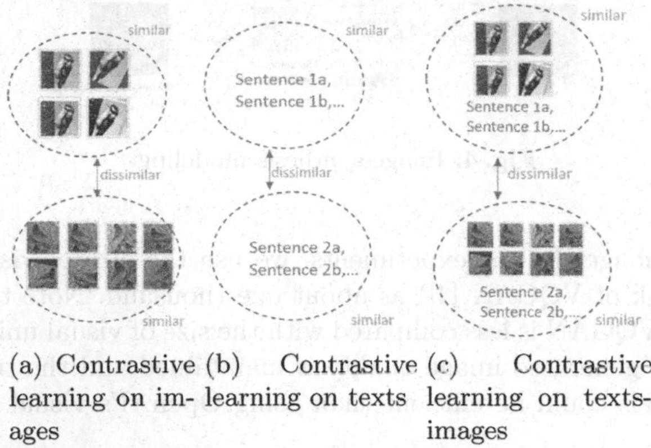

(a) Contrastive learning on images (b) Contrastive learning on texts (c) Contrastive learning on texts-images

Fig. 5. Contrastive learning on images, texts, or texts-images pairs, for improving visual expressions, textual expressions, and their relevance or diversities.

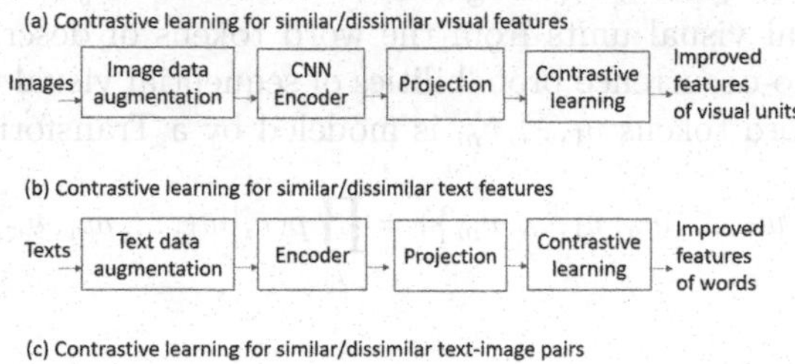

Fig. 6. Contrastive-learning modeling.

[1,2,9]. The approach of contrastive learning is effective to improve the models by using more kinds or variations of data or augmented or created data, and using the computations in machine learning or neural networks based on the viewpoints of comparisons (Figs. 5 and 6).

4.1 Benefits of Applying Contrastive Learning in Text-to-Image Generation Problems

The benefits of contrastive learning can be listed as follows. (a) Contrastive learning is a kind of unsupervised learning. Therefore, the training data can be used without labelling of data, thus making the cost of processing or labelling data can be reduced. (b) The approach of contrastive learning make those similar or similar-topic data to be encoded in the computational representations (e.g., vectors) that are close or with short distances. Inversely, those data, which are not similar, are encoded in representations to be far or with distances. Therefore, a more appropriate correlation or diversities among textual expressions and visual expressions of images, can be computed or explored.

4.2 Contrastive Learning on Increasing Visual Expressions of Images

The concepts and process of contrastive learning on visual expressions of images as follows.

Data Augmentation on Images. We increase the visual expressions or their varieties of a set of images by applying data augmentation on images. Given a set of images, we apply multiple operations on each of images to increase their visual expressions, including affine transformations, perspective transformations, contrast changes, gaussian noise, dropout of regions, hue/saturation changes, cropping/padding, blurring, etc. [17] Note that we apply tens of image augmentation and the image dataset for training becomes multiple times of the size of original dataset, proportional to the number of applied operations.

Data Augmentation on Variation of Detected Objects. Furthermore, to increase the visual expressions on the context of object region, we apply the operations of image augmentation around the area of objects. In a image, we detect and extract the area of objects by object detection [7], and we additionally apply image augmentation on the region of objects. Note that the augmented regions of objects are merged into the background (outside region of objects) of image.

Encoders and Training by Contrastive Loss. We use CNN encoder in the framework of image augmentation. Note that the CNN encoder is followed by simple projection (i.e., Fully Connected Layers). To train the encoder representing the values of similar visual expressions, visual expressions of similar objects, and the related, we utilize a common loss function for computation of contrastive loss, which is Normalized Temperature-scaled Cross Entropy Loss (NT-Xent) [15].

$$l_{i,j} = -log\frac{exp(sim(z_i, z_j)/\tau)}{\sum_{k=1}^{2N} 1_{k\neq i} exp(sim(z_i, z_k)/\tau)}.$$

4.3 Contrastive Learning on Increasing Textual Expressions

To improve or increase the textual expressions and their diversities, we also apply contrastive learning on textual data.

Data Augmentation on Text. As data augmentation in images, we apply data augmentation on text data as follows [5]. For each sentence in text data, we increase the variation of each sentence to create multiple sentences of similar but various expressions. For a sentence s, we probabilistically replace the terms in sentence s with relevant terms of similar meaning, including the terms in nouns, adjectives, or verbs. For example, in sentence "this is a small and yellow bird with wingbars", we can replace adjective "small" with the similar terms of "little", "tiny", "shallow", etc., and can replace noun "bird" with "sparrow" and "lentigo". In our experiments, we train the features or values of textual or word modeling by using the augmented text data with more and diverse textual expressions.

Training. In our experiments, since the probabilities of word tokens of text is computed based on the Transformer model, the text data is trained by Transformer with the image data. Therefore, the augmented data of textual expressions are used to train or retrain the Transformer model. For the loss, we use the loss function computed in the Transformer model in our experiments,

$$CrossEntropy_{text}(.) * w_{text} + CrossEntropy_{image}(.) * w_{image},$$

where $CrossEntropy_{text}$ and $CrossEntropy_{image}$ are computed of the cross-entropy loss on a sequence of word tokens and visual tokens, respectively.

4.4 Contrastive Learning for Improving Relevance of Text-Visual Pairs

Sometimes we may still observed some irrelevant or unsatisfied mapping among generated textual and visual pairs. Therefore, to further improve the relevance or mapping of textual and visual pairs, we apply the contrastive learning on the pairs of text-image.

Data Augmentation of Text-Image Pairs. As the approach of data augmentation in data of texts and images, here, we focus on pairs of texts and images and utilize the data of augmented texts and images and the links of their pairs.

Training on Text-Image Pairs. We use the same encoders and projections in augmentation of texts and images. Mainly, to improve the relevance of texts and images by using augmented data and their links of pairs, we modify the loss functions corresponding texts, images, and their pairs as:

$$\begin{aligned} CrossEntropy_{text}(.) * w_{text} + CrossEntropy_{image}(.) * w_{image} \\ + CrossEntropy_{pairs\ of\ text,image}(.) * w_{pairs}. \end{aligned}$$

Note that in $CrossEntropy_{pairs\ of\ text,image}(.)$, the cross-entropy loss of predicted sentence $\hat{S}$ is computed with other sentence S' belonging the same group of text-image pairs. The same computation is applied on the loss of images. Therefore, the relevance or matching among a group of text-image pairs can be computed.

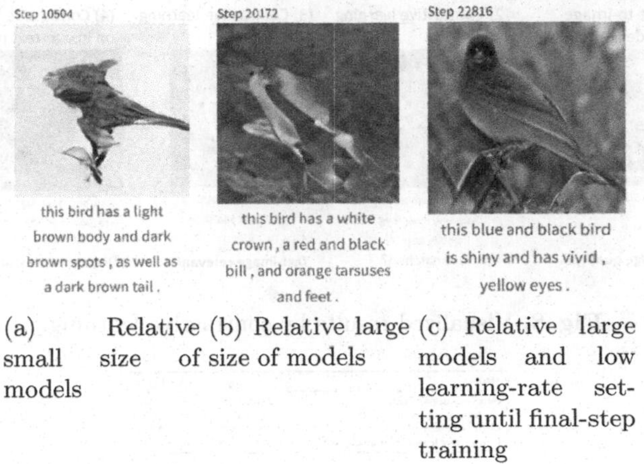

(a) Relative small size models (b) Relative large of size of models (c) Relative large models and low learning-rate setting until final-step training

Fig. 7. Experiments of suitable neural-networks and machine-learning settings. (Color figure online)

5 Experimental Results

In our experiments, we evaluated the performance of the models and contrastive learning.

5.1 Experiments of Suitable Neural-Network Models or Machine Learning

The dataset used in our experiments is a dataset consisting of various birds, which is Caltech-UCSD Birds 200 [14]. There were two hundreds of categories of birds in the total number of more than six thousands images, with the attached one or multiple textual expressions to describe about the birds of each image.

To generate visual images from textual expressions, we used the predictions of models and train the neural networks of models by machine learning. As there are multiple models, including co-occurrence word-visual modeling, image synthesis, and modeling for contrastive learning on image or text, we trained the transformers, encoders, decoders, or related neural networks and thus explored the suitable parameters in the size of models and parameters in machine learning.

The details of models will be showed in the program repository. Initially, we explored various machine-learning parameters and sizes of models, and found that quality of generated images might be affected by the size of neural networks of models. In Fig. 7, we found that the generation quality were not visually accepted (by human) as objects when relative small size of models were applied. Therefore, we augmented model sizes and found that the rendering quality of models could be improved but still was not reached satisfied rendering quality even after long time of machine training. With attempted trials and studying related machine-learning problems and experiences, we utilized the large setting

Fig. 8. Visualized results by contrastive learning.

Method	Top 1	Top 3	Top 5	Top 10
Generate images from text	0.220	0.163	0.126	0.084
Contrastive learning on images	0.241	0.181	0.140	0.094
Contrastive learning on texts	0.236	0.174	0.134	0.090
Contrastive learning on image-text pairs	**0.257**	0.189	0.146	0.098

Fig. 9. Results of contrastive learning settings on similarity of text-image.

of models and kept reducing setting the scale of learning rates until reaching a extremely low scale of learning rate. In the experiments, the final learning rate were required to be in $exp(-6)$ or even much below, for ensuring the rendering quality to be visually accepted as real-world objects, as shown in Fig. 7(c).

5.2 Experiments of Contrastive-Learning Modeling

We evaluated the performance of contrastive learning settings. The metrics used in the performance was the similarity of text and image, which is Contrastive Language-Image Pre-Training (CLIP) score [10]. The CLIP compute the similarity of text and image by the model trained by a set of pairs of image and text data.

In Figs. 8 and 9, we showed the possible effect of contrastive learning (CL) in our experiment settings and dataset. In analysis, the models without applying CL might not be reached the high quality of rendering. With applying contrastive learning, the models with CL applying on images might be reached quality rendering. The models with CL on texts might be maintained rendering quality and further improved the textual expressions and the relevance of text and generated image. Lastly, the CL applying on text-image pairs might be further improved visual quality and was possible to create more diverse visual expressions. In text-image similarity score, the results showed that contrastive learning on pairs of text-image were improved firstly, and followed by CL on texts or CL on images, and thus the models without CL.

Acknowledgement. This work was supported by Japan Science and Technology Agency (JST CREST: JPMJCR19F2, Research Representative: Prof. Yoichi Ochiai, University of Tsukuba, Japan), and by University of Tsukuba (Basic Research Support Program Type A).

References

1. Chang, Y., Subramanian, D., Pavuluri, R., Dinger, T.: Time series representation learning with contrastive triplet selection. In: Dasgupta, G., et al. (eds.) CODS-COMAD 2022: 5th Joint International Conference on Data Science & Management of Data (9th ACM IKDD CODS and 27th COMAD), Bangalore, India, 8–10 January 2022, pp. 46–53. ACM (2022)
2. Chen, T., Kornblith, S., Norouzi, M., Hinton, G.E.: A simple framework for contrastive learning of visual representations. In: Proceedings of the 37th International Conference on Machine Learning, ICML 2020, 13–18 July 2020, Virtual Event. Proceedings of Machine Learning Research, vol. 119, pp. 1597–1607. PMLR (2020)
3. Cherepkov, A., Voynov, A., Babenko, A.: Navigating the GAN parameter space for semantic image editing. In: IEEE Conference on Computer Vision and Pattern Recognition, CVPR 2021, virtual, 19–25 June 2021, pp. 3671–3680. Computer Vision Foundation/IEEE (2021)
4. Esser, P., Rombach, R., Ommer, B.: Taming transformers for high-resolution image synthesis. In: IEEE Conference on Computer Vision and Pattern Recognition, CVPR 2021, virtual, 19–25 June 2021, pp. 12873–12883. Computer Vision Foundation/IEEE (2021)
5. Haralabopoulos, G., Torres, M.T., Anagnostopoulos, I., McAuley, D.: Text data augmentations: permutation, antonyms and negation. Expert Syst. Appl. **177**, 114769 (2021)
6. Hong, Y., Niu, L., Zhang, J., Zhao, W., Fu, C., Zhang, L.: F2GAN: fusing-and-filling GAN for few-shot image generation. In: Chen, C.W., et al. (eds.) MM 2020: The 28th ACM International Conference on Multimedia, Virtual Event/Seattle, WA, USA, 12–16 October 2020, pp. 2535–2543. ACM (2020)
7. Ji, G., Zhu, L., Zhuge, M., Fu, K.: Fast camouflaged object detection via edge-based reversible re-calibration network. Pattern Recognit. **123**, 108414 (2022)
8. Liu, D., Nabail, M., Hertzmann, A., Kalogerakis, E.: Neural contours: learning to draw lines from 3d shapes. In: 2020 IEEE/CVF Conference on Computer Vision and Pattern Recognition, CVPR 2020, Seattle, WA, USA, 13–19 June 2020, pp. 5427–5435. Computer Vision Foundation/IEEE (2020)
9. Lo, Y., et al.: CLCC: contrastive learning for color constancy. In: IEEE Conference on Computer Vision and Pattern Recognition, CVPR 2021, virtual, 19–25 June 2021, pp. 8053–8063. Computer Vision Foundation/IEEE (2021)
10. Radford, A., et al.: Learning transferable visual models from natural language supervision. In: Meila, M., Zhang, T. (eds.) Proceedings of the 38th International Conference on Machine Learning, ICML 2021, 18–24 July 2021, Virtual Event. Proceedings of Machine Learning Research, vol. 139, pp. 8748–8763. PMLR (2021)
11. Ramesh, A., et al.: Zero-shot text-to-image generation. In: Meila, M., Zhang, T. (eds.) Proceedings of the 38th International Conference on Machine Learning, ICML 2021, 18–24 July 2021, Virtual Event. Proceedings of Machine Learning Research, vol. 139, pp. 8821–8831. PMLR (2021)
12. Richardson, E., et al.: Encoding in style: a styleGAN encoder for image-to-image translation. In: IEEE Conference on Computer Vision and Pattern Recognition, CVPR 2021, virtual, 19–25 June 2021, pp. 2287–2296. Computer Vision Foundation/IEEE (2021)
13. Sennrich, R., Haddow, B., Birch, A.: Neural machine translation of rare words with subword units. In: Proceedings of the 54th Annual Meeting of the Association for Computational Linguistics, ACL 2016, 7–12 August 2016, Berlin, Germany, Volume 1: Long Papers. The Association for Computer Linguistics (2016)

14. Welinder, P., et al.: Caltech-UCSD Birds 200. Technical report. CNS-TR-2010-001, California Institute of Technology (2010)
15. Weng, L., Elsawah, A.M., Fang, K.: Cross-entropy loss for recommending efficient fold-over technique. J. Syst. Sci. Complex. **34**(1), 402–439 (2021)
16. Ye, M., Shen, J., Lin, G., Xiang, T., Shao, L., Hoi, S.C.H.: Deep learning for person re-identification: a survey and outlook. CoRR abs/2001.04193 (2020)
17. Zhang, R., et al.: A progressive generative adversarial method for structurally inadequate medical image data augmentation. IEEE J. Biomed. Health Inform. **26**(1), 7–16 (2022)
18. Zheng, Z., Zheng, L., Yang, Y.: Unlabeled samples generated by GAN improve the person re-identification baseline in vitro. In: IEEE International Conference on Computer Vision, ICCV 2017, Venice, Italy, 22–29 October 2017, pp. 3774–3782. IEEE Computer Society (2017)

Trafne: A Training Framework for Non-expert Annotators with Auto Validation and Expert Feedback

Shugo Miyata, Chia-Ming Chang(✉), and Takeo Igarashi

The University of Tokyo, Tokyo, Japan
info@chiamingchang.con

Abstract. Large-scale datasets play an important role in the application of deep learning methods to various practical tasks. Many crowdsourcing tools have been proposed for annotation tasks; however, these tasks are relatively easy. Non-obvious annotation tasks require professional knowledge (e.g., medical image annotation) and non-expert annotators need to be trained to perform such tasks. In this paper, we propose *Trafne*, a framework for the effective training of non-expert annotators by combining feedback from the system (auto validation) and human experts (expert validation). Subsequently, we present a prototype implementation designed for brain tumor image annotation. We perform a user study to evaluate the effectiveness of our framework compared to a traditional training method. The results demonstrate that our proposed approach can help non-expert annotators to complete a non-obvious annotation more accurately than the traditional method. In addition, we discuss the requirements of non-expert training on a non-obvious annotation and potential applications of the framework.

Keywords: Medical image annotation · Non-expert training · Expert feedback · Interface design

1 Introduction

Recently, machine learning-based solutions have demonstrated breakthrough success in various fields; this success has resulted from the rapid increase of computation powers and the existence of large-scale datasets, such as ImageNet [4] or Labeled Faces in the Wild [13], which has led to early success in the field of image classification and face recognition. To apply machine learning methods to a new task, we need to prepare a sufficiently large dataset tailored for the task. Although significant efforts have been put to achieve higher performance with small datasets, such as one-shot learning and few-shot learning, or to extend the dataset scale by augmenting the original datasets, the dataset availability is still a prerequisite condition, especially if the target task is at an early attempt at learning-based approaches. However, it is difficult to create datasets for the abovementioned expert tasks by a manual annotation process. These tasks are often time-consuming and considerably difficult or almost impossible for non-expert annotators. Only a limited number of experts with task-specific knowledge and experience can

H. Degen and S. Ntoa (Eds.): HCII 2022, LNAI 13336, pp. 475–494, 2022.
https://doi.org/10.1007/978-3-031-05643-7_31

solve these tasks while their expertise is typically expensive. Owing to these challenges, previous approaches for efficient annotation, which rely on non-expert annotators, cannot be applied directly to expert tasks.

A possible solution for this problem is to train non-expert annotators to work on expert annotation tasks. In this paper, we propose a framework, Trafne, to facilitate the training process by combining feedback from the system and human experts. Figure 1 shows the concept of the proposed training framework. The key idea is to provide feedback to the non-expert annotators during training to improve the annotation quality. Our system provides not only feedback from human experts (expert validation), but also system-generated feedback (auto validation). This process aims to improve the capability of non-expert annotators to reduce the expert's workload, such as checking and modifying the annotation results. Herein, we present a prototype implementation designed for a brain tumor image annotation task to investigate the feasibility of the proposed framework.

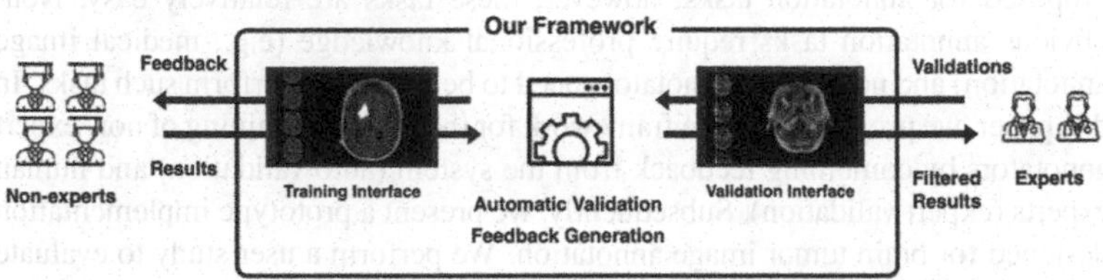

Fig. 1. *Trafne*: a training framework for non-expert annotators.

We ran a user study to evaluate the effectiveness of our proposed approach compared to a traditional training method without feedback. The results demonstrated that the label quality (Pixel-level Intersection of Unions) obtained using our method was higher than that of the traditional training method. The participants gave positive comments for the combined feedback (auto validation and expert validation) provided by our proposed method. In addition, the results indicated that feedback plays an important role in training non-expert annotators in expert annotation tasks. The main contributions of this study are:

- A non-expert training framework, *Trafne*, for improving annotation quality in expert image annotation.
- Identifying feedback is an important factor for training non-expert annotators.
- Demonstrating the benefits of feedback in a training process through a user study by comparing *Trafne* and a traditional method.

2 Related Work

2.1 Medical Image Annotation

Medical images are widely used to measure various aspects of human body [7, 16]. It becomes a common way to apply recent machine learning-based solutions [1, 8, 12] while they are still limited in some trials, owing to the insufficient task-specific dataset.

This problem arises due to various reasons, such as the difficulty of sharing with high-sensitivity data, and the time inefficiency of annotation; one of the most significant causes is that the limitation of expert annotators. Medical image annotation requires annotators to have a deep understanding and experience. Furthermore, even if some parts of the task may be done by non-expert annotators, it is still imperative to verify the quality of results using experts for applications that require good reliability. This tedious but necessary process wastes the limited and valuable resources of experts. In this study, we aim to address this issue by training non-expert annotators during annotation to reduce the demand for experts.

2.2 Efficient Annotation

One possible solution for this inefficiency is to reduce the cost of the annotation itself. For example, some studies used the concept of hierarchical classification in a data annotation to increase the labeling efficiency and label quality [26, 27]. Dong et al. [5] proposed an automatic annotation method for object instances. In addition, Chang et al. [30] investigated the effect of labeling styles in image annotation. In this study, a deep active curve network (DACN) was used, which was constructed from multi-scale ResNet as an encoder with edge detection and segmentation, and a graph convolutional network (GCN) was used as a decoder to refine the contours of objects. The results of automatic annotation and segmentation presented reasonable quality in some cases. Some of the papers also incorporated this approach in expert tasks. Philbrick et al. [17] proposed an interface for the voxel-level annotation of 3D slices. This system provides the optimized interface and various features to execute an efficient annotation while maintaining continuity through slices. It is also possible to extend the system by introducing recent learning-based models as plugins. These tools can satisfy the urgent need for experts who may be bored when performing the annotation task; however, the dataset creation speed is still limited largely by the number of experts.

2.3 Collaborative Crowdsourcing

Using a large-scale worker pool through crowdsourcing platforms is a reasonable way to scale the annotation task. It is possible to perform a large number of tasks in a relatively cheap and short time by using the crowd resources. In contrast, knowledge and experiences vary among workers, and it is sometimes difficult to complete if the task is complicated. Collaborative crowdsourcing is one solution to this problem. This idea involves collaboration between workers to complete the complex tasks and ensure the quality of results. A collaborative image labeling framework proposed by Chang et al. [2] is a good example. The proposed system provided three stages for the non-expert annotators to improve the results, maintaining the diversity in the image labeling task. Non-expert annotators vote on the category of images at the first vote stage, and explain the reason at the next explanation stage. The final categories are decided at the last categorize stage with the additional choices came from other annotators.

The more progressive way of dealing with the difficulty associated with expert tasks is the task division based on the idea of human computation [25]. Human perception is integrated into the system as one processing power, and an original difficult task is divided into a set of multiple sub-tasks. One good example is the collaborative three-dimensional (3D) modeling proposed by Suzuki et al. [21]. In this research, the 3D modeling task is divided into simpler sketch tasks and review tasks. Another example is a medical image annotation proposed by Heim et al. [10]. They converted 3D organ segmentation in CT images into a contour refinement task. The refined contours are then merged by pixel-wise majority voting. The system enables not only the quality to be harnessed, but also enables a higher quality to be achieved rather than using only non-expert resources. These approaches introduce the direct use of a large-scale non-expert worker pool; however, it is not clear about the potential for task division or conversion in other expert tasks, as mentioned in some papers [6, 14, 20]. In addition, the non-expert workers are not trained through all processes.

2.4 Training Non-expert Workers

An alternative way of accelerating expert dataset creation is to train non-expert annotators. A large number of workers for a specific expert task will be available after the training process is completed. A traditional training method is direct, synchronous teaching. The effectiveness of the training is strongly guaranteed by the presence of experts. However, it is quite inefficient because non-expert annotators and experts need to work simultaneously. Another traditional method is training with examples, to train non-expert annotators by showing correct examples in expectation of acquiring expertise from these static samples. This training method does not require any experts, and it is possible to train multiple non-expert annotators simultaneously. However, there is a limit to what one can learn from static samples, and it is often necessary and sometimes more efficient to know the reasons behind annotation; these are obtained only from human experts.

Recent training methods tackle this inefficiency by giving feedback to non-expert annotators to improve the annotation quality. Chang et al. [28] proposed a spatial layout labeling interface to improve label quality in non-expert image annotation. He et al. [9] converted a fish species recognition task into simplified visual similarity comparison tasks. Non-experts were trained in the simplified task with expert supervision and achieved higher scores, even in the original task. On the other hand, a limitation with their method is that experts have to check all of the results from non-expert annotators, which is a significant overhead. Wal et al. [24] also showed the potential of feedback through the observation of citizen scientist training in bumblebee identification. The study proposed a template-based feedback generation method, and the result score obtained in the user study was improved via generated feedback. On the contrary, the feedback variety was limited owing to the template-based generation.

Mathematical analyses of the training effect were also proposed. Singla et al. [19] described a non-expert as an agent who randomly walks through an assumption space based on the examples shown. With this model, the convergence of the error rate after training was guaranteed by theoretical analysis. Furthermore, the effectiveness of training based on this model was shown in a simultaneous experiment and a real-world study. However, this model hypothesized that workers can explore the entire assumption space with shown examples, while it is not obvious when the task is more complicated. These papers showed the possibility of feedback in non-expert training, but the exploration is still limited. We focused on another practical expert task that is not considered in previous work, and designed a non-expert training framework combining feedback from automatic validation and human experts.

3 Trafne: Proposed Workflow

We propose a novel training framework for non-expert image annotation (Fig. 2). This framework provides an expert supervised training process for non-expert annotators. The system contains two task-specific interfaces and data storage. For non-expert annotators, the system provides iterative training processes with feedback. Non-expert annotators complete an expert task and receive feedback from the system. Their annotation results were automatically validated by auto validation, and were then stored. The annotation results that have received scores higher than the baseline score in auto validation are then evaluated by human experts. Expert validations are stored in a reusable format, and used in subsequent training. However, it should be noted that our system is designed only for the training of non-expert annotators, and not for performing actual annotation tasks. Ground truth annotation is already given to all the data in the dataset, and results from non-expert annotators are not used for building the dataset.

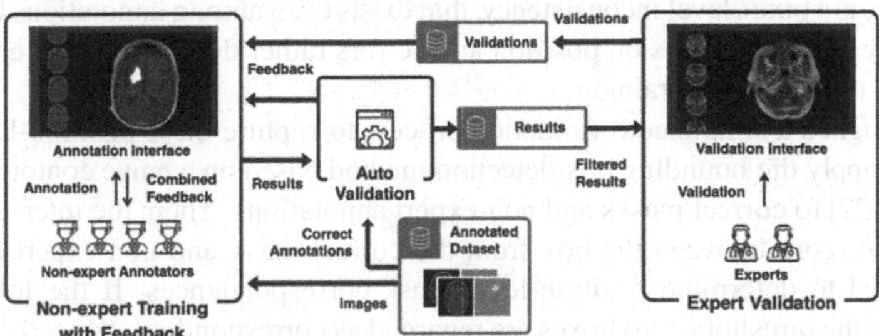

Fig. 2. An overview of our proposed workflow.

3.1 Brain Tumor Image Annotation

Our motivating problem is brain tumor image annotation, a type of pixel-level annotation, as shown in Fig. 3. Annotators give (b) tumor masks to (a) brain slices (the brackish images). Brain tumors are typically shown as white regions in brain slices (left), whereas it is sometimes even difficult for non-expert annotators to find tumors (right). These masks are practical enough for realistic use cases [3, 8]. It has the following two unique characteristics and our framework is designed to leverage these characteristics. Our framework can be applied to other problems with similar characteristics.

- **Need for Experts.** The problem is non-obvious for non-expert annotators and they need to learn from experts to complete the annotation appropriately.
- **Solvablility for Non-expert annotators.** The target task is but not impossible for non-expert annotators, who can provide appropriate annotations by learning from experts.

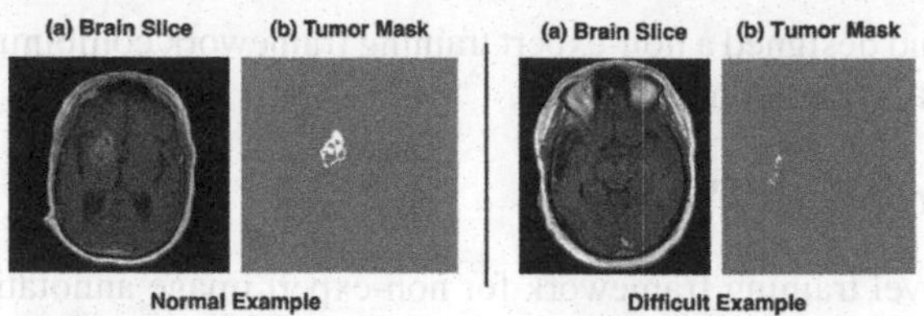

Fig. 3. Examples of brain tumor image annotation task.

3.2 Auto Validation

We introduce the concept of auto validation, which is a process to generate feedback by capturing typical failures that appeared in non-expert annotations. In our system, it is possible to filter the low-quality results compared with the previous feedback generation [24, 29]. In a pilot study, we observed two kinds of errors in non-expert annotation. One is a position-level error, where the overall location of annotations is clearly different from correct annotations. It also includes cases where the annotation is completely missing. We assume that experts do not make such errors. The other is a more subtle pixel-level error. There is a pixel-level inconsistency, that exists even among annotations by experts. For these reasons, we focus on position level errors rather than pixel-level errors in the early stage of non-expert training.

We designed a simple auto validation process to capture these position-level differences. We apply the bounding box detection method based on a naive contour detection algorithm [22] to correct masks and non-expert annotations. Then, the intersection over union (IoU) score between the box from the correct mask and non-expert annotation is calculated to determine position-level mask correspondences. If the IoU score is higher than the threshold, two boxes are regarded as corresponding. We categorize non-expert annotations into the following six categories based on these correspondences. We consider that false negatives (FNs) should the focus in non-expert training.

1. **Missed Slice:** If all boxes from a correct mask have no correspondences, we categorize the slice as a missed slice.
2. **Missed Area:** If there is a box from a correct mask with no correspondence, we calculate the area ratio of the box against the area of a slice. We categorize the slice as a missed area if the ratio is higher than the threshold.
3. **Extra Mask:** If there is a box from a non-expert annotation with no correspondence, we categorize the slice as an extra mask.
4. **Too Large:**/(5) **Too Small:** We consider it too Large or too Small if the slice does not satisfy the range of area ratio between two corresponding boxes.
5. **Wrong Edge:** The continuity of tumors through adjacent slices is also important for accurate brain tumor annotation. We consider it a wrong edge if non-expert annotations break this continuity.

After non-expert annotators are sufficiently trained so as not to make position-level errors, we present in detailed differences in the feedback to highlight pixel-level errors.

We show a diff image comparing the pixels of correct annotations and non-expert annotations. A diff image consists of pixels with three colors, red shows pixels that exist only in correct masks, blue pixels exist only in non-expert annotations, and green is matched. Figure 4 shows examples of auto validation results. The poor annotations are categorized by the failure types, and their pixel-level differences from the correct masks are shown by colorizing.

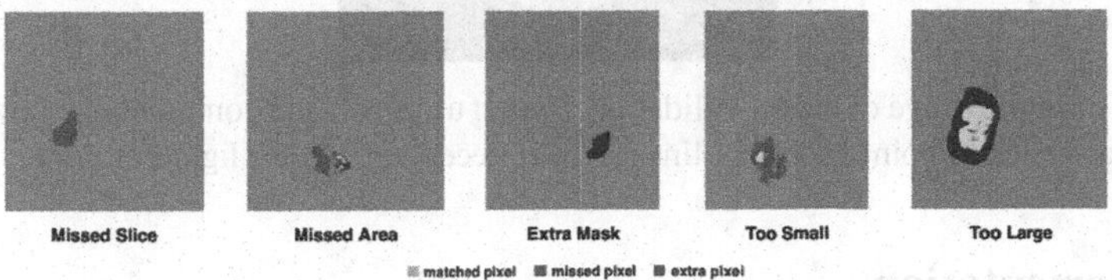

Fig. 4. Examples of auto validation results.

3.3 Expert Validation

In order to train non-expert annotators who cannot learn any more from auto validation, it is necessary to provide feedback from experts. Thus, we add an expert validation, which is a detailed validation process of non-expert annotations by experts. One of the most critical differences from traditional training methods is the reuse of expert validations. Once experts give validations to a specific non-expert annotation, these validations are also shown in other non-expert training with the same case. This concept is based on the idea that experts can provide general knowledge that is also effective for other non-expert annotators to enhance their knowledge.

To evaluate this assumption, we conducted another pilot study with experts. We asked two senior brain surgeons to give validations to non-expert annotations from the previous pilot study. In this study, some of the expert validations contained the general expertise, such as brain structures and tumor shapes. These validations were added to a specific annotation, but they could be understood even by other non-expert annotators. This result implies that it is possible to reuse these validations in the following training processes. Figure 5 shows an example usage of expert validation. We designed this process mainly using simple textual explanations. Flags are also provided to avoid the repetition of typing the same thing. In addition, the brush tool is available to illustrate something about shapes.

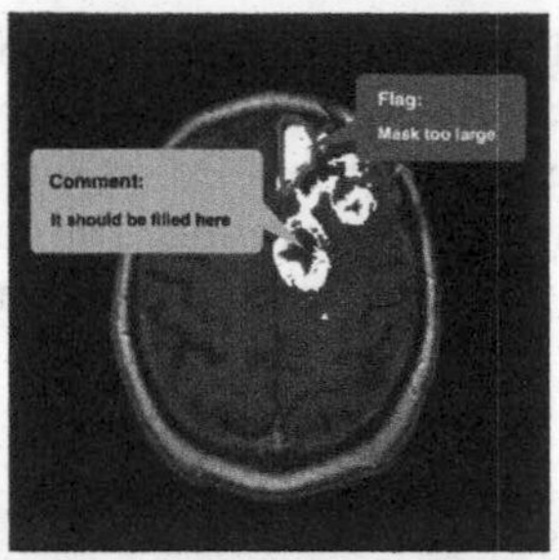

Fig. 5. An example usage of expert validation. Expert users can add comments (yellow) and flags (blue) on each clicked point and draw lines (red) if necessary. (Color figure online)

4 Implementation

We implemented user interfaces for both non-expert annotation and expert validation as browser-based applications using React and cornerstone.js. They are connected via a web API built with Node.js. We also used openCV to implement auto validation. Non-expert annotators first select a slice from the slice list shown on the left of the Fig. 6, and then annotations are given with basic drawing tools, such as a brush, eraser, and a filling tool. When all slices are annotated, the system shows the combined feedback for non-expert annotators, as shown in Fig. 7. The feedback contains results of both auto validation and expert validation. We show some examples of correct masks and slices before training.

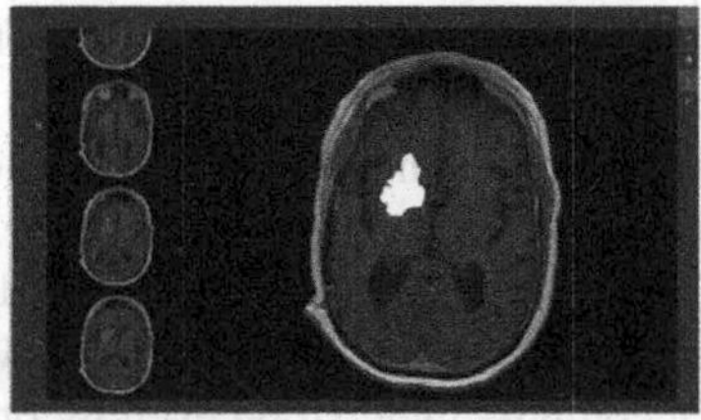

Fig. 6. An overview of our interface for non-expert annotation. Basic drawing tools are provided for pixel-level annotation.

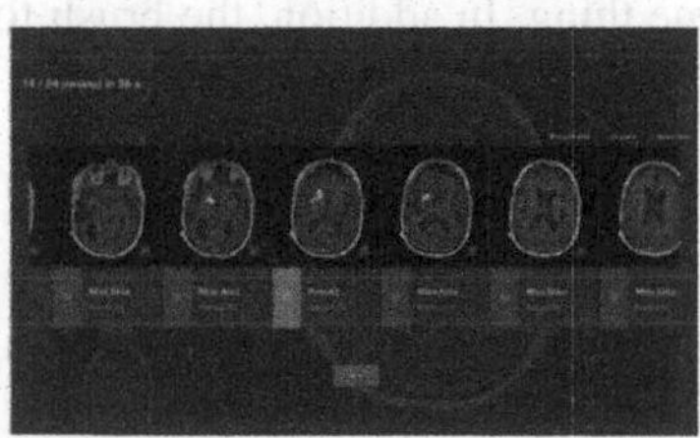

Fig. 7. An overview of the feedback after annotation. Non- experts receive feedback from both the system and experts.

The expert validation interface is shown in Fig. 8, and provides three types of validations, comment, flags, and a pen tool. Experts select the annotated slices and validate the clicked points.

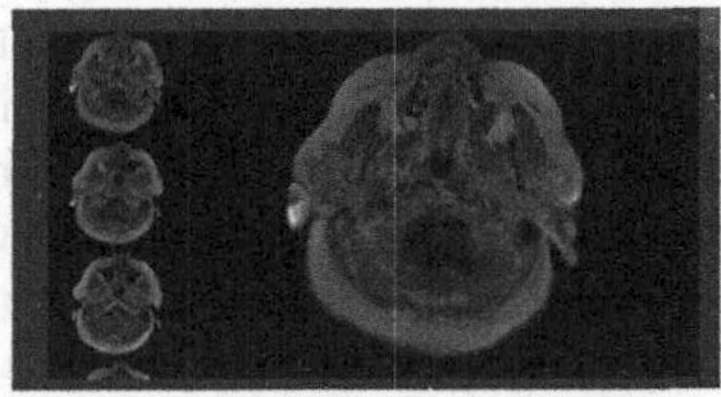

Fig. 8. An overview of our interface for expert validation. Expert users can add validation to the annotation results. Comments, flags, and pen are available for validation.

5 User Study

We conducted a user study to compare our proposed training approach with a traditional training method for the brain tumor image annotation task. We hypothesize that our proposed training framework is a more effective approach than the traditional method for training non-expert annotators as well as improving annotation quality by expert validation.

5.1 Data Preparation

We used a tumor image dataset from The Cancer Imaging Archive [18]. This dataset contains 40 cases, and each case consists of 20 to 27 slices in DICOM format [16]. These slices involved correct tumor masks created by expert brain surgeons. We randomly selected ten cases for our user study, two for static examples shown before training, and one for tool practice. We prepared the study dataset from the selected ten cases using the following procedures. We asked one non-expert annotator to provide annotations using our annotation interface. We also asked one senior brain surgeon with tumor annotation experience to validate these non-expert annotations.

5.2 Participants and Duration

We recruited eight participants with no expertise in a brain surgery and no prior experience in brain tumor annotation. They were divided into two groups, four participants were employed for our method, and the other was for the baseline method (between-subjects). Owing to the COVID-19 protocols, all studies were conducted in an online environment. We asked all participants to use a mouse as a pointing device during annotation training. In most cases, the training was completed within one hour.

5.3 Conditions

There are two conditions in the user evaluation. **(1) Training non-expert annotators without feedback.** This is the baseline method of the iterative training process without any feedback. Participants were asked to provide annotations through our interface. After every slice in one case is annotated, the system automatically shows a pair of correct masks and slices. This process is similar to a traditional training method: learning from samples mentioned in Sect. 3. **(2) Training non-expert annotators with feedback.** This is our proposed method of the iterative training process with feedback. Participants were asked to give annotations through our interface, and the system provided feedback from auto validation for non-expert annotators. In the meantime, expert validation was also shown if it existed.

5.4 Procedure

Almost all processes were completely the same for both conditions. Participants first read the instruction document with a brief explanation about the task objective and the tool usage, then checked two examples of correct masks and slices. After trying the interface with one case, the participants were asked to give annotations to all slices in the selected ten cases. During the training, it was not confirmed that all slices were annotated because our system considered the overlooking of slices to be an important failure. After participants thought the annotation was completed, only correct masks were shown on the original slices with the condition (a). The participants can toggle the visibility of masks to compare the masks and tumors. With condition (b), the complete feedback was shown in a similar layout as in (a).

5.5 Measurement

Annotation Quality. We used the Pixel-level Intersection of Unions (IoU) score between correct masks and non-expert annotations to make qualitative comparisons of the annotation quality. IoU was calculated using Eq. (1). TP is the number of pixels matched between correct masks and non-expert annotations, FP is shown only in annotations, and FN is shown only in correct masks.

$$\mathrm{IoU} = \frac{\mathrm{TP}}{\mathrm{TP} + \mathrm{FP} + \mathrm{FN}} \tag{1}$$

Questionnaire. We asked participants to answer the following questions after training. We used the Likert scale for Q1–Q3 and Q5.

Q1. Do you think the goal of the brain tumor image annotation task is clear through this study?

Q2. Do you think the examples and instructions contains sufficient details for understanding the goal of the brain tumor image annotation task?

Q3. Do you think you have a deeper understanding of the brain tumor image annotation task through this study?

Q4. Please write some comments if you have any difficulties or unclear points in the brain tumor image annotation task.
Q5. Do you think the interface has enough functions to support the brain tumor image annotation task?
Q6. Please point out the necessary functions if you think the interface was insufficient.
In addition, we asked the additional questions below to confirm the participants' understanding of the feedback contents.
q1. Please write the easiest or the most difficult points to understand about the feedback contents.
q2. Please write the easiest or the most difficult points to understand about the feedback styles.
q3. Please write about the situation if you have experienced that the feedback is useful in the task.
q4. Please write any other comments about feedback contents/styles.

6 Results

6.1 Annotation Quality

Figure 9 shows the box plot of pixel-level IoU averages per participant. The 10 data points shown in each box indicates the mean IoU scores in each case, and the horizontal line in boxes provides the median. The result showed that the mean IoU of 10 cases with our method was higher than the baseline method for all participants.

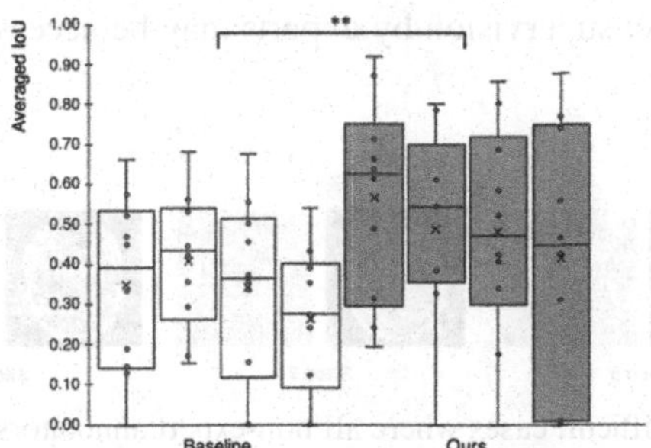

Fig. 9. Pixel-level mean IoU for each participants. Baseline: mean = 0.37, Ours: mean = 0.49.

We analyzed these 40 IoU scores from ten cases per participant using the one-sided t-test. The p-value was 0.0038, and this result showed that there was a significant difference ($p < 0.05$) between our method and the baseline method.

6.2 Annotation Results

Figure 10 shows examples of well-annotated cases from both the baseline and our proposed method. The four images illustrate the pixel-level differences between non-expert annotations and correct masks, and the IoU scores were 0.77, 0.83, 0.70, and 0.56. We assumed that even non-expert annotators could give accurate annotations to the tumors with clear borders, as shown on the left of the figure. As expected, annotators could recognize the tumor and give annotations representing the hollow shape of the tumor regardless of feedback. The differences of IoU scores between our proposed method and the baseline come from the more detailed divergences of annotations. Blue pixels that represent the false positives (FPs) were clearly shown only in the annotations without feedback. Furthermore, the more critical errors of false negatives (FNs) also appeared in wider regions without feedback.

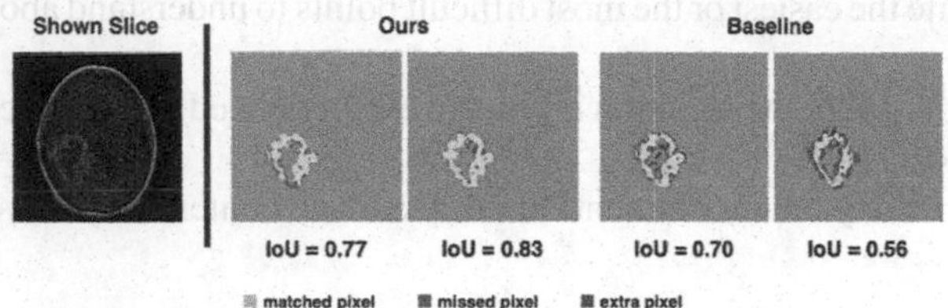

Fig. 10. Accurate annotation examples from non-experts. Both participants described the tumor shape in detail regardless of feedback.

In contrast, some tumors were completely overlooked by all non-expert annotators during training, nonetheless with feedback. Figure 11 shows an example of such difficult cases. These three slices are continuously positioned on the foot side in a case, and contain complicated structures such as eyes and throats. It is often difficult to find small tumors from such intricate slices for non-expert annotators. These results indicate the limitation of our method that direct supervision by experts may be necessary to learn from these cases.

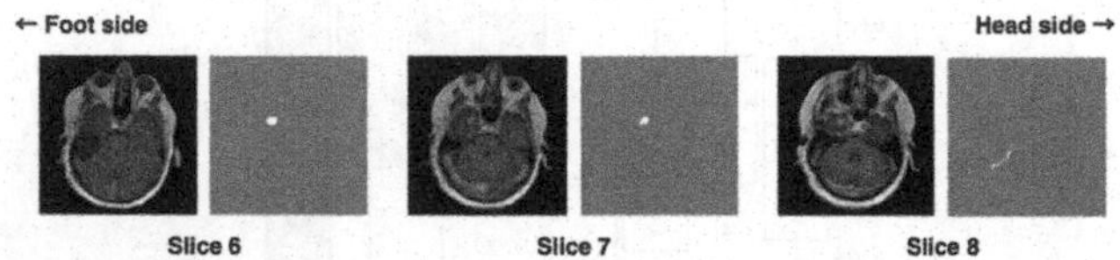

Fig. 11. An example of difficult cases where all non-expert annotators failed to give annotation. These slices are complicated and tumors are small.

6.3 Questionnaire

Figure 12 showed that almost all participants could understand the goal of the tumor annotation task. Only one non-expert annotator with the baseline method answered the neutral score. Figure 13 shows that the static examples provided before the training considerably sufficient or fairly sufficient for most participants. It should be noted that one participant with our proposed method felt that the example was poor. Although the cause is unclear owing to the limited number of participants, this may indicate that the feedback resulted in confusion for the task objective, while it was clear if only the static samples were shown. Figure 14 indicates that after the training, non-expert annotators earned a deeper understanding from their subjective. We did not observe any significant differences between our proposed method and the baseline method. Figure 15 displays the sufficiency of functions that our interface provided in the annotation training. All non-expert annotators with feedback answered the lower scores compared with the scores from the baseline.

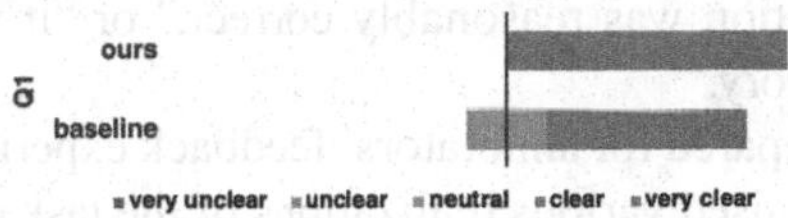

Fig. 12. Do you think the goal of the tumor annotation task is clear through this study?

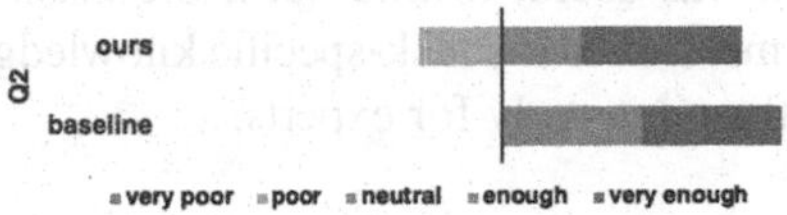

Fig. 13. Do you think the examples and instructions were sufficiently detailed to understand the goal of the tumor annotation task?

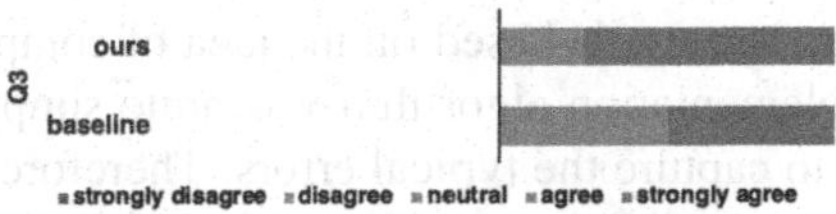

Fig. 14. Do you have a deeper understanding of the tumor annotation task through this study?

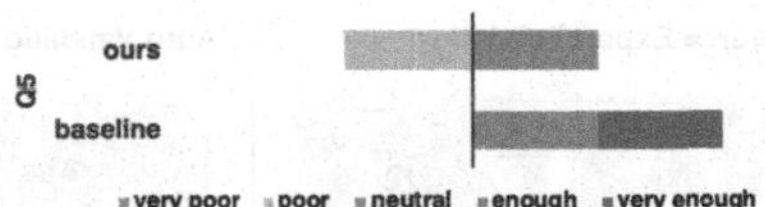

Fig. 15. Do you think the interface has enough functions to annotate tumors?

Furthermore, we obtained some comments regarding the difficulties of the brain tumor image annotation task asked in Q4. Five non-expert annotators mentioned the difficulty of tumor recognition if tumors had vague shapes. Three non-experts also answered that the unclear point in annotation came from the tumor structures. If the tumor had a hollow shape as in Fig. 10, it was initially not clear whether the inner regions should be annotated or not. Comments from Q5 were about the additional requests for interfaces. In this question, we observed the interesting differences between our method and the baseline. The difficulty or limitation related to using a mouse as a pointing device was only mentioned by three participants with feedback, such as "it is almost impossible to give accurate annotations with a mouse," while all non-experts for the baseline did not claim it. Some participants also gave useful comments for future improvements, such as "it would be more helpful if the examples can be seen all the time" or "it is helpful to show annotations given to the adjacent slices."

As mentioned in the previous section, we asked additional questions about the feedback contents and styles (q1, q2, and q4) to the non-expert annotators with our method. The positive comments especially argued the pixel-level differences shown on feedback like "colorized images were helpful to understand the mistakes" and "the accuracy of annotations was clear at a glance." In contrast, the negative comments were mostly about understanding the criteria of auto validation, for example "low coverage was often warned while the annotation was reasonably correct," or "it was unclear of the strict definitions for each category."

The answers to q3 prepared for annotators' feedback experience were obtained from three participants. They raised various realizations of the task objective from feedback, such as "I could learn that the black regions enclosed by white areas were not a tumor," "it was noticed that sometimes the tumor shadow was unclear at the top/bottom of tumor slices," and "the feedback was useful to find out if the mask was too small or large." Some of these comments mentioned the task-specific knowledge for accurate annotation that we also observed in the pilot study for experts.

7 Discussion

7.1 Auto Validation Compared with Expert Validation

The auto validation in our system is based on the idea of comparing the position-level differences, and the implementation algorithm was quite simple. It was not clear that whether it was possible to capture the typical errors. Therefore, we compared the auto validation results and expert validations, and we selected some cases shown in Fig. 16 to discuss the validity of auto validation.

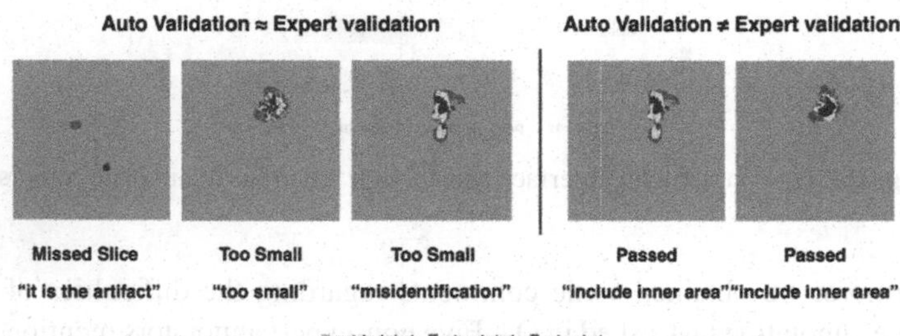

Fig. 16. Comparison of auto validation (upper line) and expert validation (bottom line).

The remaining three images show that the categories added in the auto validation were similar to the comments added in expert validation. The expert pointed out the failures that were also detected by auto validation. This result introduces the insight that even with the simple failure detection algorithm, it is possible to capture the typical failures and considerably reduce the number of results that have to be checked by experts. The right side of the figure shows examples of a mismatch between auto validation and expert validation. In these cases, auto validation judged the annotations pass while experts gave the comments for more detailed differences. However, these mismatches were within our expectation, because our starting point of auto validation is to reduce the expert burden by detecting typical failures, and not to completely imitate the experts. On the contrary, it can be argued that our assumption for the brain tumor image annotation task was reasonable to some extent, and it may be possible to improve the annotation quality by performing expert validation even after training with auto validation.

7.2 Effects of Annotation Feedback

One key idea of our proposed framework is to provide combined feedback from auto validation and expert validation during training. The results from this study also indicated the important viewpoints to discuss on the effect of this feedback on the annotation quality. Figure 17 shows the annotations from two non-expert annotators, one was with our method and the other was with the baseline. Both two non-expert annotators gave poor annotations with low IoU scores of 0.24 and 0.37 respectively at the early stage of training. They only used a brush tool that provides thin lines was not suitable for large area annotations. Since then, the participant without feedback continued to use the brush, and did not notice this improper annotation through the training, while the participant with feedback changed their annotation policy preferentially to use the fill tool. The pixel-level quality at the later stage reflects the difference that non-expert annotators for our method gave more accurate annotation with IoU = 0.64, whereas the other maintained a lower accuracy with IoU = 0.38. We considered this difference in tool usage as one clear sign that came from the task understanding of non-expert annotators during training. The annotators successfully learned the task objective and then tried to choose the proper tools for more accurate annotation. In these cases, feedback may provide the implicit guideline for a more effective task understanding compared with the static samples.

The answers from the questionnaire also reflected these differences. From a qualitative perspective, the comments for tool functions were more detailed in our method than in the baseline. For example, all participants without feedback gave similar comments,

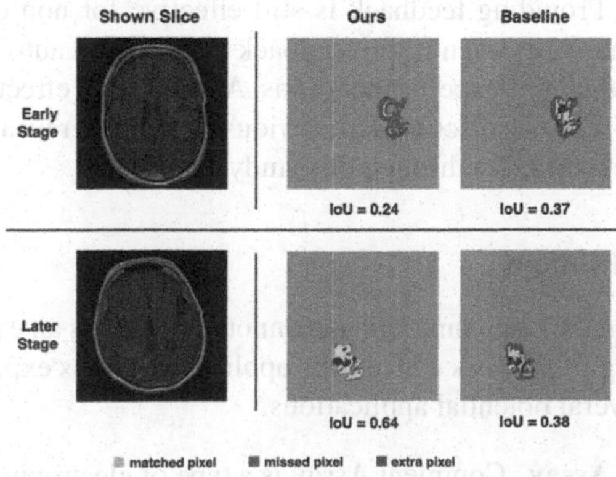

Fig. 17. The difference of annotation quality improvement with feedback.

such as "not insufficient in function, but it would be helpful if..." for Q6, while all participants with feedback claimed the insufficiency of functions. This tendency was also seen in the other scale question (Q5).

Figure 18 shows another example. These two participants were both "eager" annotators as shown in the upper row of the figure. They tried to give annotations that were as detailed as possible. However, this kind of enthusiasm sometimes caused more critical mistakes. The bottom row of the figure showed that the difficult case for non-expert annotators was similar to the previous example (see Fig. 11). In this case, the eager non-expert without feedback gave the much larger extra masks than the participant with feedback. We believe that these failures are caused by the wrong learning of annotation policy from the limited samples during training. It is difficult to correct such a misunderstanding without feedback, and to make matters worse, this incorrect annotation policy may be strengthened through the iterative training process. Hence, it is important to provide feedback during training in order to harness the learning, even in expert tasks.

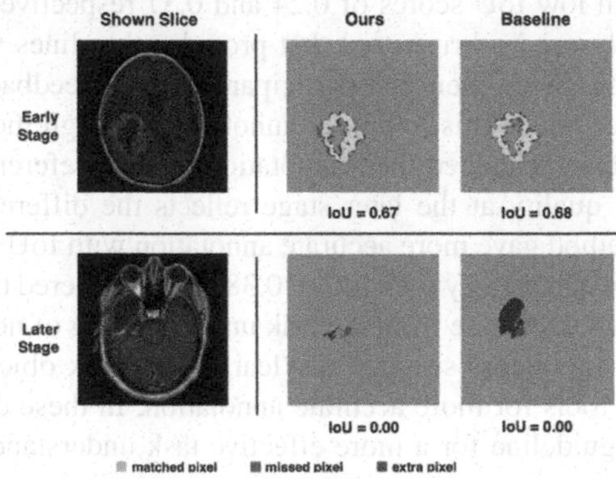

Fig. 18. An example of wrong learning of annotation policy during training. The participant without feedback made greater mistakes at the later stage.

These two examples introduce an important viewpoint for the role of feedback in non-expert training. Providing feedback is still effective for non-expert annotators to refine the annotation quality even if the feedback comes from auto validation or expert validation given to other non-expert annotations. Although the effectiveness of feedback during training itself was also discussed in previous studies, we revealed it in the different and more practical expert tasks through this study.

7.3 Potential Applications

This study focuses on the brain tumor image annotation task as an expert task. However, our proposed training framework can also be applied to various expert annotation tasks. Here, we discuss several potential applications.

Example 1: Comet Assay. Comment Assay is a type of electrophoresis method that is used to observe the DNA damage in the field of genotoxicity [15]. The DNA breakage is evaluated based on the length of the tail observed in the movement of dyed DNA, as shown in Fig. 19. In this case, it is sometimes difficult to recognize the boundary of the moving trajectory owing to the noisy background and different directions of tails, and extensive experience is required for accurate recognition. In addition, recent learning-based approaches [11] attempted to evaluate damages from input comet images.

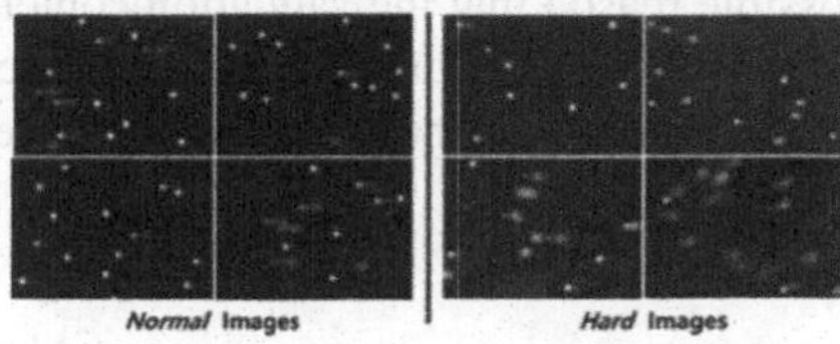

Fig. 19. Do you think the interface has enough functions to annotate tumors?

Example 2: Skin Disease Annotation/Segmentation. Figure 20 shows an another possible application, namely skin disease annotation/segmentation. Dermatologists commonly take clinical pictures that contain the disease regions such as the black spots or dried surfaces on the skin shown on the left of the figure. Recent end-to-end disease classification or segmentation [1] from these images still maintain a lower accuracy because the interesting areas are often shaded and their boundaries are certainly unclear and complicated. Thus, there remains the need for pixel-level annotation by experts as shown on the right, while the annotation process is the same or more difficult and time-consuming than the brain tumor image annotation. Of course, the careful observation of the task features is required for implementation, nevertheless, these examples show the potential of our framework for other expert tasks.

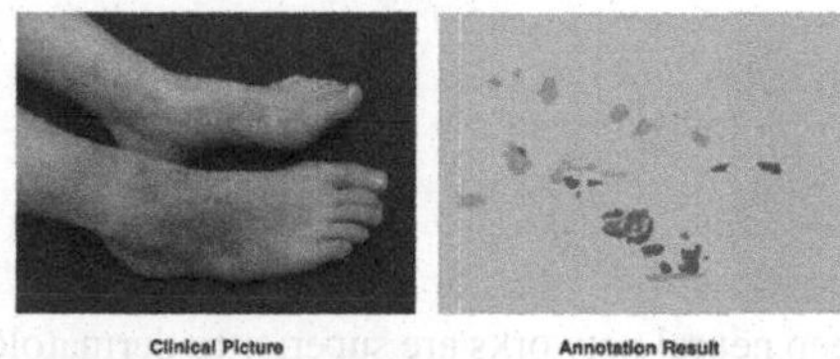

Fig. 20. Do you think the interface has enough functions to annotate tumors?

8 Limitation and Future Work

The user study results demonstrated that feedback resulted in some improvements in annotation quality even with a limited number of cases. However, it is still unclear how the quality changes with the longer training. Because it is difficult to simply increase the number of training sessions with considerable time, it is necessary to reduce the annotation time for each case. One solution may be to pick some important cases that are based on auto validation results. Comparisons with other traditional training methods, for example, direct teaching mentioned in Sect. 2.4, are also important to discuss the effect of feedback during training. It is possible to simultaneously run our workflow with non-expert annotators and experts in order to create a study condition that is similar to direct teaching. In addition, validation guidelines for experts may be required for more effective training. In this research, we did not provide any explicit guidelines in expert validation. This is the possible reason that the validation contents were limited against our expectations. The addition of more validation tools, such as extendable flags that can be added and shared between experts, may help to facilitate more expressive validations.

9 Conclusion

In this study, we proposed a new supervised training framework for non-expert image annotation. This framework enables the training of non-expert annotators with combined feedback from auto validation and expert validation. The worker pool for expert tasks with a limited number of experts can be extended by training non-expert annotators. We implemented a prototype of the framework and conducted a user study to compare our proposed framework with a traditional training method in a brain tumor image annotation task. The results showed that the annotation quality was improved more via the combined feedback of auto validation and expert validation from our proposed framework compared with the traditional method. In addition, the results showed that feedback plays an important role in non-expert training. In addition, this study showed that auto validation can reduce the expert workload even if it was implemented with a simple algorithm based on the task observation. We believe that this study has provided significant insights for the training of non-expert annotators in expert tasks.

Acknowledgements. This work was supported by JST CREST Grant Number JP- MJCR17A1, Japan.

References

1. Brinker, T.J., et al.: Deep neural networks are superior to dermatologists in melanoma image classification. Eur. J. Cancer **119**(2019), 11–17 (2019). https://doi.org/10.1016/j.ejca.2019.05.023
2. Chang, J.C., Amershi, S., Kamar, E.: Revolt: collaborative crowdsourcing for labeling machine learning datasets, pp. 2334–2346. Association for Computing Machinery, New York (2017). https://doi.org/10.1145/3025453.3026044
3. Clark, K., et al.: The Cancer Imaging Archive (TCIA): maintaining and operating a public information repository. J. Digit. Imaging **26**(6), 1045–1057 (2013). https://doi.org/10.1007/s10278-013-9622-7
4. Deng, J., Dong, W., Socher, R., Li, L.J., Li, K., Fei-Fei, L.: ImageNet: a large-scale hierarchical image database, pp. 248–255 (2009)
5. Dong, Z., Zhang, R., Shao, X.: Automatic annotation and segmentation of object instances with deep active curve network. IEEE Access **7**(2019), 147501–147512 (2019). https://doi.org/10.1109/ACCESS.2019.2946650

6. Eickhoff, C., de Vries, A.: How crowd sourcable is your task? Mathematical Structures in Computer Science - MSCS (2011)
7. Ferreira, R., et al.: The virtual microscope. In: Proceedings: A Conference of the American Medical Informatics Association. AMIA Fall Symposium, vol. 4, pp. 49–453 (1997). https://pubmed.ncbi.nlm.nih.gov/9357666
8. Havaei, M., et al.: Brain tumor segmentation with Deep Neural Networks. Med. Image Anal. **35**, 18–31 (2017). https://doi.org/10.1016/j.media.2016.05.004
9. He, J., Van Ossenbruggen, J., de Vries, A.: Do you need experts in the crowd?: a case study in image annotation for marine biology, pp. 57–60 (2013)
10. Heim, E., et al.: Large-scale medical image annotation with crowd-powered algorithms. J. Med. Imaging **5**(092018), 1 (2018). https://doi.org/10.1117/1.JMI.5.3.034002
11. Hong, Y., et al.: Deep learning method for comet segmentation and comet assay image analysis. Sci. Rep. **10**(1), 1–12 (2020)
12. Hu, E., Nosato, H., Sakanashi, H., Murakawa, M.: A modified anomaly detection method for capsule endoscopy images using non-linear color conversion and Higher-order Local Auto-Correlation (HLAC), pp. 5477–5480 (2013). https://doi.org/10.1109/EMBC.2013.6610789
13. Kae, A., Sohn, K., Lee, H., Learned-Miller, E.: Augmenting CRFs with Boltzmann machine shape priors for image labeling (2013)
14. Kittur, A., Smus, B., Khamkar, S., Kraut, R.: CrowdForge: crowdsourcing complex work. In: CHI 2011, pp. 43–52 (2011). https://doi.org/10.1145/2047196.2047202
15. Kumaravel, T.S., Vilhar, B., Faux, S., Jha, A.: Comet assay measurements: a perspective. Cell Biol. Toxicol. **25**, 53–64 (2007). https://doi.org/10.1007/s10565-007-9043-9
16. The Medical Imaging Technology Association (MITA): Standard Digital Imaging and Communications in Medicine (2020). https://www.dicomstandard.org/current
17. Philbrick, K.A., et al.: RIL-contour: a medical imaging dataset annotation tool for and with deep learning. J. Digit. Imaging **32**(4), 571–581 (2019). https://doi.org/10.1007/s10278-019-00232-0
18. Prah, M., Schmainda, K.M.: Data from brain-tumor-progression. Cancer Imaging Arch. (2018). https://doi.org/10.7937/K9/TCIA.2018.15quzvnb
19. Singla, A., Bogunovic, I., Bartók, G., Karbasi, A., Krause, A.: Near-optimally teaching the crowd to classify, pp. II-154–II-162 (2014)
20. Su, H., Deng, J., Fei-Fei, L.: Crowdsourcing annotations for visual object detection, pp. 40–46 (2012)
21. Suzuki, R., Igarashi, T.: Collaborative 3D modeling by the crowd, pp. 124–131 (2017)
22. Suzuki, S., Abe, K.: Topological structural analysis of digitized binary images by border following. Comput. Vis. Graph. Image Process. **30**(1), 32–46 (1985). https://doi.org/10.1016/0734-189X(85)90016-7
23. Tschandl, P., Rosendahl, C., Kittler, H.: The HAM10000 dataset, a large collection of multi-source dermatoscopic images of common pigmented skin lesions. Sci. Data **5**(2018), 180161 (2018)
24. van der Wal, R., Sharma, N., Mellish, C., Robinson, A., Siddharthan, A.: The role of automated feedback in training and retaining biological recorders for citizen science. Conserv. Biol. J. Soc. Conserv. Biol. **30**, 550–561 (2016). https://doi.org/10.1111/cobi.12705
25. von Ahn, L.: Human computation, pp. 1–2 (2008). https://doi.org/10.1109/ICDE.2008.4497403
26. Chang, C.M., Mishra, S.D., Igarashi, T.: A hierarchical task assignment for manual image labeling. In: 2019 IEEE Symposium on Visual Languages and Human-Centric Computing (VL/HCC), pp. 139–143 (2019). https://doi.org/10.1109/VLHCC.2019.8818828

27. Otani, N., Baba, Y., Kashima, H.: Quality control for crowdsourced hierarchical classification. In: 2015 IEEE International Conference on Data Mining, pp. 937–942 (2015). https://doi.org/10.1109/ICDM.2015.83
28. Chang, C.M., Lee, C.H., Igarashi, T.: Spatial labeling: leveraging spatial layout for improving label quality in non-expert image annotation. In: CHI Conference on Human Factors in Computing Systems (CHI 2021), Yokohama, Japan, 8–13 May 2021. ACM, New York (2021). https://doi.org/10.1145/3411764.3445165
29. Steven, D., Kulkarni, A., Bunge, B., Nguyen, T., Klemmer, S., Hartmann, B.: Shepherding the crowd: managing and providing feedback to crowd workers. In: Conference on Human Factors in Computing Systems – Proceedings, pp. 1669–1674 (2011). https://doi.org/10.1145/1979742.1979826
30. Chang, C.M., Yang, X., Igarashi, T.: An empirical study on the effect of quick and careful labeling styles in image annotation. In: The 48th International Conference on Graphics Interface and Human-Computer Interaction (GI 2022), Virtual Conference, 17–19 May 2022

Give Me a Hand: A Scene-Fit Hand Posture Drawing Aid

Xiaohua Sun, Juexiao Qin(✉), Weijian Xu, and Xibing Peng

Tongji University, Shanghai 200082, China
qinjuexiao2017@gmail.com

Abstract. Hand posture drawing is one of the greatest challenges for most people who are not experts in figure painting. The lack of professional knowledge and guidance limits their freedom of creation. This paper aims to explore the methods of using artificial intelligence technologies to assist people in drawing hand postures. We investigated the causes of frustrations in drawing hands and inferred the design requirements through a user study. Then we proposed a scene-fit hand posture drawing aid called "Give Me A Hand". The aid gives creators visual references that almost fully fit their ideation of hand postures and overall scenes in the form of 3D hand models. Unlike most existing studies on using artificial intelligence (AI) in the field of art creation, we pay more attention to the creative experience of humans during the intelligent collaboration between creators and AI. In the validation stage, we conducted a repeated-measures designed experiment to verify the effectiveness of the aid. The results of validation also provide us more inspirations on the relationship between human and AI in the artistic creation.

Keywords: Human-machine intelligent collaboration · Drawing · Co-create

1 Introduction

For most people who are not experts in figure painting, hand posture drawing is always a challenging mission [8,16]. However, not only artists but plenty of non-expert creators may also encounter requirements of drawing hands, such as designers or painting enthusiasts. The precise expression of hand postures stems from the sufficient understanding of hand joints and muscles, perspective principles, and substantial practices. The lack of professional guidance, knowledge or training of art leads to the plight that non-expert creators face in the process of self-study.

Currently, there is no practical approach to solve this issue. Although the great advance of deep learning algorithms in image processing and generation [15, 18] has stimulated the researches on using AI in artistic creation. Most studies have focused more on higher efficiency, image quality, or higher similarity with human artists. The problem of obtaining and understanding people's creative intentions is still rarely noticed.

H. Degen and S. Ntoa (Eds.): HCII 2022, LNAI 13336, pp. 495–512, 2022.
https://doi.org/10.1007/978-3-031-05643-7_32

In this paper, we attempt to explore the causes of people being unable to draw hand postures accurately and the methods to use AI as an aid in resolving their problems. We conducted two studies: (1) study1: user study, (2) study2: prototyping and validation.

In study1, we adopted the qualitative analysis including interviews, phenomenological observation, and questionnaires to inquire about the specific difficulties faced by non-expert creators. The results of the study1 revealed that a common problem for creators is the difficulty in acquiring appropriate visual references. Furthermore, we inferred the design requirements of the aid.

In study2, we proposed a scene-fit hand posture drawing aid, "Give Me A Hand". It could generate visual references that almost fully fit the creators' ideation of hand postures and the overall scenes in natural interactions. To evaluate its effectiveness, we built a prototype and conducted a repeated-measures designed experiment on 24 creators and the statistics mainly focus on the changes in the creative experiences of the participants. The results of study2 also provide us more inspirations on the relationship between human and AI in intelligent collaborative creation.

The main contributions of our work are as follows:

- We analyzed the reasons why people meet troubles with drawing hands, learned their requirements and the common process of creation. Based on this information, we positioned an appropriate entry point for AI to support creators.
- We designed a scene-fit hand posture drawing aid which could accurately understand people's creative intention in natural interactions and provide interactive visual references as creative support.
- We evaluated the prototype of the aid. The results showed our method improves user experiences of drawing hands, mainly reflected in more suitable references, more satisfactory works, and less difficulties.

2 Related Work

The related work was reviewed in two sections: (1) leading causes of difficulties in drawing hand postures, and (2) researches and applications of AI in the field of artistic creation.

2.1 Leading Causes of Difficulties in Drawing Hand Postures

People have plenty of opportunities to observe different hand postures from various perspectives every day, but most are unable to successfully draw these postures out. For a long time, researchers have tried to find the causes of these difficulties. They have given many slightly different definitions of drawing [7,16, 36]. By Summarizing these definitions, drawing is a procedure in which people translate their understandings of the world into lines, shapes, and colors on two-dimensional surfaces.

The expression of drawing is strongly influenced by people's understandings of the world. After a visual signal passing through the pupil to the brain, its routing is complicated [34]. In 1988, Cohen designed a program called AARON to investigate the cognitive principles underlying visual representation [9]. He found that the misperception of environment and objects is the main reason for the deviation of painting expression and conception [8]. The way that people use visual information exists in a highly adaptable and abstract form. When observing objects, people tend to extract the most representative features to construct the appearance of the world [16]. However, artists as experts develop the declarative knowledge of the visual world and the procedural knowledge of analyzing and depicting it. These make them cognitively different from non-artists [24]. The choice of visual information in the painting process affects the ability of painting a lot [28].

2.2 Researches and Applications of AI in the Field of Artistic Creation

For a long time, lots of researchers have attempted to explore the applications of AI in artistic creation. These previous researches can be divided into two types: autonomous generative systems and co-creative systems [10].

Autonomous Generative Systems. According to Lev Manovich, There is no real "AI arts" yet [26]. What researchers have done are teaching AI the skills of existing artists. It can be accomplished by training neural networks to generate sketches with human artworks. For instance, David Ha et al. present sketch-RNN to construct stroke-based drawings of common objects in 2017 [19]. Nan Cao et al. developed a deep generative model called AI-Sketcher to generate multi-class sketches according to a conditional vector [4]. Furthermore, they used the AI-Sketcher to build up an interactive system that generates line graph of human facial expressions for storyboard [32]. Meanwhile, methods of generating high-quality images were also noticed. In 2016, generative adversarial networks [18] and image style transfer [15] were proposed. Phillip Isola et al. used conditional adversarial nets to solve the problem of translating an input image into corresponding output images [22]. Taesung et al. proposed a method for synthesizing photorealistic images given an input semantic layout [29]. Some researchers also tried to teach machines to imitate the artist's brushstrokes and steps in painting [2,21]. AttnGAN allows attention-driven, multi-stage refinement for fine-grained text-to-image generation [38]. AI is also used much in colorization [14,35,39,41].

These works objectively played a role in inspiring creators. The main purpose of the automatic generation system is to replace people in a vast number of tedious and repetitive tasks. Therefore, it does not take people's creative experience into account or help them improve the creative abilities.

Co-creative Systems. A workshop to identify the need to create intelligent cognitive assistants was held in 2016. Its outcomes mentioned that AI assistants should enhance but not replace human capabilities [1]. Some researchers achieve this by stimulating people to get unexpected inspiration. Zhen Zeng et al. try to use machine learning to provide creative inspiration for font design with human-machine collaboration during multiple rounds of design iterations [40]. Yuyu Lin et al. designed an interactive creative aid system with physical entities that generates sketches based on the input and feedback from users [25]. Some other researchers try to build systems that allow AI and people to work together as colleagues. Nicholas et al. explored the paradigm of how humans and machines collaborate in creative processes based on a software called Drawing Apprentice [11,12]. Their work focused on giving enjoyable experiences to creators. In order to understand the user experience in user-AI collaboration, Changhoon Oh et al. designed a prototype DuetDraw which is an AI interface that allows users and the AI agents to draw pictures collaboratively [27].

These works inspired more possibilities in the field of co-creation between human and AI. However, most existing studies lack the understanding and research of scenes, contents and processes of creation. Thus the distinct plights and requirements of creators were still rarely noticed.

3 Study1: User Study

Drawing hand postures means creators need to express at least the hand shape and posture in perspective. Artists who can complete these tasks freely have undergone long-term training of observation and painting [24]. However, not only artists but also designers and people who are engaged in game art, animation, or are just interested in painting need to draw hand postures.

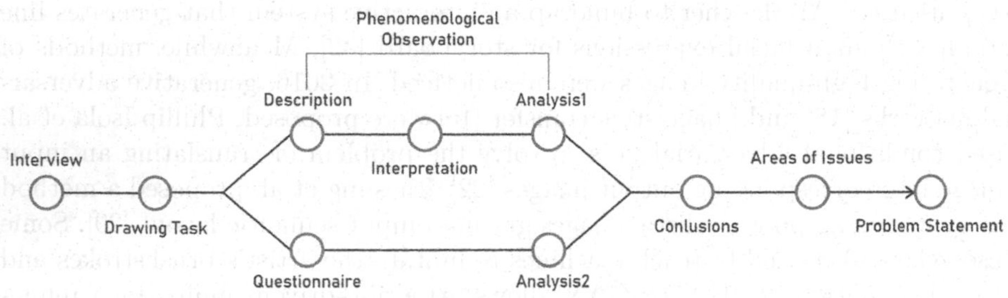

Fig. 1. The methodology of study1

In order to understand the common process people apply to draw hand postures and explore the causes of people being unable to draw hand postures accurately, as the Fig. 1 shown, we have conducted the interview, questionnaire, and phenomenological observation on 22 creators during the user study. We interviewed all participants about their background information, creative habits, and experiences of drawing hands. Then we gave them the same propositional drawing task with 2 sections. All participants need fill out a questionnaire after each section. We randomly selected 7 people from the 22 participants and adopted the phenomenological observation through their creative process during the whole process of the task.

3.1 Interview

In the stage of interview, we asked participants questions to learn some basic information related to drawing hands: (1) How old are you? (2) What is your job? (3) How long it has been since you started painting? (4) How often do you draw hands in your creations? (5) How do you draw hand postures and how is your feeling?

The results showed that most of our participants are from 20 to 30 years old. They are engaged in the design industry, game or animation industry, software industry, science and engineering, and financial industry. None of them are professional artists. The length of the time they started painting to now varies from 3 years to over 20 years. They all need to draw hand postures in creations more or less. However, all participants told us that they always feel troubled with drawing hands. They have rich and varied ideas about hand postures, but they cannot express them smoothly on the canvas. One thing in agreement is that suitable visual references of hands are useful. But searching for apposite references is also a time-wasting and tough mission which always exhaust them. Based on the information obtained from the interview, we set a propositional drawing task with 2 sections to compare the creative experiences with and without references and learn more details about the process of drawing hands.

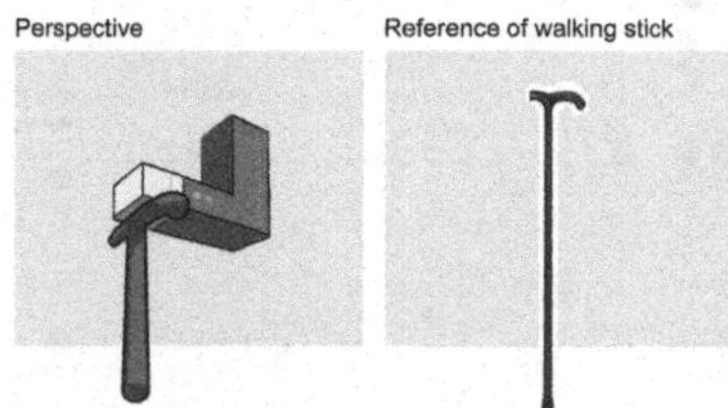

Fig. 2. The instruction image of the drawing task

3.2 Propositional Drawing Task

The content of the propositional task is drawing a hand holding a walking stick. We provided an instruction image (Fig. 2) which limits the perspective and the style of the walking stick. In order to avoid providing any addition hints to participants, we abstracted the arm and hand into square shapes. The hand structure and proportion should be reasonable, and participants need at least to draw the outline of the hand. Moreover, the way of grasping and the specific hand shape were up to participants. The task consists of 2 sections. In section1, participants need to complete the drawing independently from any references. In section2, they can find or produce references by any methods they are used to and finish the drawing with references. The reference here refers to the images, models or tutorials that creators obtain through various channels including internet, photography, etc. All participants need to fill out a questionnaire after each section to tell us the changes in their experiences.

Questionnaire. We asked participants to score from 10 to 0 for how difficult they feel about the drawing and another score from 0 to 10 for how satisfied they feel with the works completed in 2 sections. The different feelings of the difficulty of the same task can reflect the creator's drawing ability to a certain degree.

As Fig. 3(a) shown, the drawing ability of participants is not directly related to whether they are satisfied with their works. Among the participants who felt difficult, there were both satisfied and dissatisfied with the drawings and vice versa. Then we compared the scores of 2 sections. As shown in Fig. 3(b), most participants feel more satisfied with their works with the aid of references. Moreover, for some participants, references reduced the difficulty of the task. From these changes, we identified that the reference is an essential factor of creative experiences for non-experts creators in drawing hands.

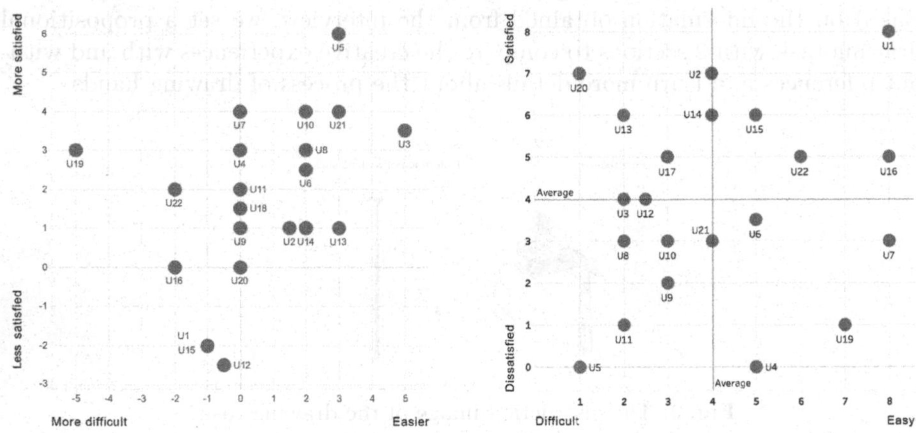

Fig. 3. (a) Subjective difficulty and satisfaction of section1 (b) Changes of subjective difficulty and satisfaction between two sections

Phenomenological Observation. We did the phenomenological observation [17,23] through the creative processes in both 2 sections on 7 people selected randomly from the 22 participants. We observed their screens with their consent during the process of 2 sections. Firstly, we described the behavior of participants from 3 aspects: the whole procedure of drawing, the interactions with their drawing tools, the actions in producing or finding references. Secondly, we interpreted participants' behavior through the description. Finally we summarized their difficulties and current solutions in each stage from different aspects as Table 1. Through the detailed observation, description, interpretation, and analysis of creators' behavior, it can be seen that the creators take actions related to the reference image with high frequency. Therefor we can further identify that the process of finding and using references affects the creative experiences of non-expert creators a lot.

Analysis. Based on a comprehensive analysis of the user study, we summarized five pain points and the corresponding user requirements in Table 2. The lack of knowledge about drawing hands and the inability to get practical help in time are main issues that influence the creative experiences. Appropriate visual references would help creators to understand the shape and movement of hands intuitively. However, hands as objects of creation are complex and changeable. It's hard to find references fully fit creators' ideation, for example the ideas are difficult to summarize into short keywords for image searching; the physical hand models with high mobility are expensive; the figure model software is difficult to operate; self-observation and photography are limited in terms of angle, the lens distortion may alter the perspective of the picture. Meanwhile an image can only display the shape of a hand posture at a single angle, two-dimensional information provides limited help in aspects of increasing people's understanding of hands and improving their creative abilities.

Therefore, we deduced four design requirements to help creators improve their creative experience:

- `Design Requirement1`: The help provided by the aid must fit the creators' ideation.
- `Design Requirement2`: The aid must be able to understand the intentions of creators naturally.
- `Design Requirement3`: The help provided by the aid should present multi-dimensional information of hand postures.
- `Design Requirement4`: The carrier and expression form of the help should be interactive.

4 Study2: Prototyping and Validation

4.1 Prototyping

We proposed the "Give Me A Hand", which is a scene-fit hand posture drawing aid. Creators can pose the hand posture they conceived in front of an ordinary

Table 1. Analysis of the phenomenological observation

Stage	Aspects	Difficulties	Solutions
Ideation	Conceive	It is hard to think of unique postures or imagine unusual hand postures	Search for reference images
Reference	Method	Search for images on different websites or search engines, manipulate physical or virtual hand models, take photos, observe their own hands. There are many methods, but not very effective	Collect more photos or painting works of different hand postures, ask someone else to help to take photos, or change the idea
	Type	Multiple kinds of references, including outlines, photos, etc., are needed. Hand models are always hard to manipulate. The lens distorts shooting	Reduce the expectation of references
	Amount	It is hard to find a precisely suitable one. Some creators have to find lots of references as supplements	Find references respectively for posture, perspective, color, etc.
	Time	Too long. Time wasting	Take photos if the posture was easy to pose or just give up
Drawing	Posture	It is hard to imagine unusual hand posture and the degree of movement of hand joints	Draw the posture in references instead of original ideas. Draw the posture within the scope of ability or give up drawing hands
	Structure	Creators do not understand the relationship between fingers and palms, muscles and bones well	Ignore the details of the structure
	Perspective	It is hard to draw out unusual or complex perspectives	Just give up
	Proportion	Creators do not understand the proportion of fingers and palm, the joints of fingers well	Analyze the references and modify the drawing repeatedly
	Occlusion	It is hard to determine which parts should be occluded or exposed	Occlude all the hands or change the idea to draw a posture without occlusion
	Style	The style of references influences drawings. It is hard to transfer styles and ensure an accurate structure at the same time	Abstract and refine the hand images in references, then transfer the style
Rendering	Light and Shadow	The accuracy of outline influences light and shadow effect, the references of light and shadow of hands are hard to find	Reluctantly draw it with the limited understanding of light and shadow, or draw a fuzzy shadow

Table 2. Analysis of pain points and user requirements

Pain point	User requirement
Poor understanding of hand	Provide multiple types and visual styles of references for different features of the hand
	Show the proportion of hand joints clearly
	Show the components of the hand that may be occluded
	Show the skeleton and muscle
Time-consuming in finding references	Get references quickly
Troublesome process of finding references	Meet all requirements on one platform or in one tool
Unsuitable references	References of unusual hand posture
	References can be viewed from multiple perspectives
	References can be highly in line with ideas
Transferring the style of references to personal style is difficult	Refining the references of hand posture without any style tendency
Complex light and shadow analysis	Adjustable lighting

RGB camera when blocked by drawing hands. The camera would take pictures of the creators' own hands. The aid will reconstruct a 3D hand model for every single image of the hand posture and adjust the model according to the perspective detection of the overall scene drawn by creators. If necessary, creators can also interact with the model to revise the perspective and size or observe the structure from a more comprehensive view. We will introduce the "Give Me A Hand" in detail from three aspects: creative intention understanding, creative assistance providing, and intelligent collaborative creative process.

Creative Intention Understanding. Corresponding to the design requirement1, the aid must quickly, conveniently and naturally understand people's creative intention. Hence, the aid should intervene the creative process in a suitable opportunity, the devices involved in must be popular among the majority and the interactions need conform to people's creative habits.

When creators draw hand postures, the actions they applied to obtain references could convey partial creative intention. But the traditional methods cannot meet the demands of creators and usually bring extra troubles.

Considering that creators can easily pose their own hands in the conceived action and observing their own hands is also one of the steps that most creators are accustomed to, we use the creator's self-observation as the intervention time for AI to capture the creative intention, and use the creators' hand movements and sketches as the input data. We choose the normal RGB camera as the input device to take photos of hand movements. With the method proposed by Adnane Boukhayma et al. [3], the aid will use openpose [5,6,33,37] to generate the 2D joint heat-maps of each single photo, then input the photo and the results of generation to the pre-trained model to obtain the spatial coordinates of 21 key points. At the same time, the aid will predict a reasonable perspective and rotation angle of the hand according to the overall sketch drawn by the creator [20,31,42].

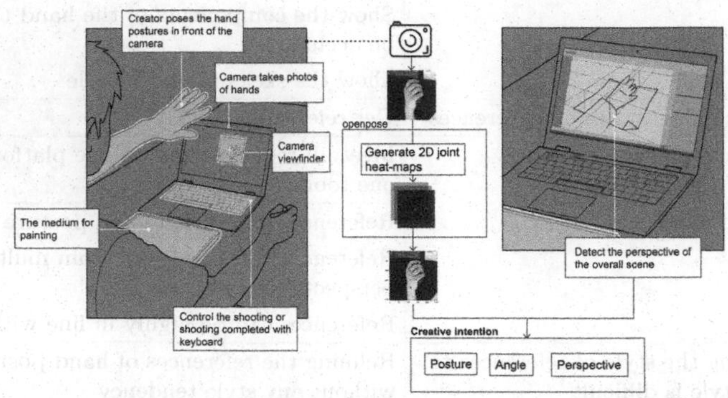

Fig. 4. The creative intention understanding

Creative Assistance Providing. According to the other design requirements, the assistance provided by the aid must fit the creators' ideation, present multi-dimensional information of hand postures, and be interactive. Therefore, we choose to reconstruct the 3D model of hand postures from creative intention as the expression form of the creative assistance.

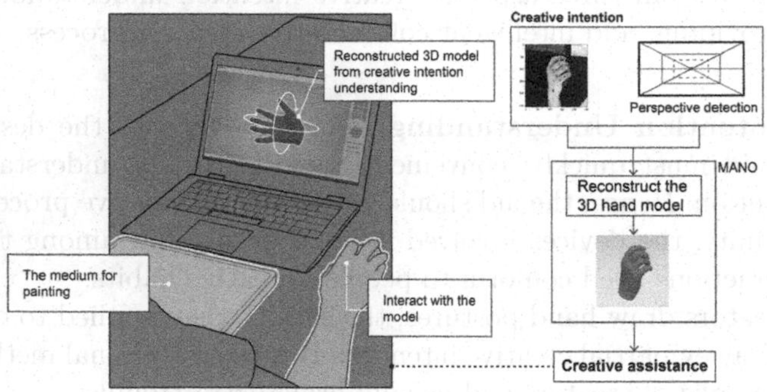

Fig. 5. The creative assistance providing

Based on the spatial coordinates and angles of the 21 key points of the hand posture obtained by creative intention understanding, we used the parametric model MANO [30] to reconstruct the 3D hand model for the corresponding action and perspective, then present it to the creator as output data in the 3D viewer. Compared with 2D images, 3D models are more interactive and observable. Models could provide comprehensive and detailed information about the structure of hands to creators. By manipulating and inspecting the reconstructed model, creators will not only be able to draw hand postures more smoothly, but they can also feedback the deficiencies of the aid.

The scene-fit methods for different paintings have not been developed yet. Since we gave the same propositional task to all participants, we conducted Wizard-of-OZ testing in the validation stage to let the participants experience the scene-fitting.

Intelligent Collaborative Creative Process. we designed three touchpoints in the interactive process between creators and the aid as the Fig. 6 shown.

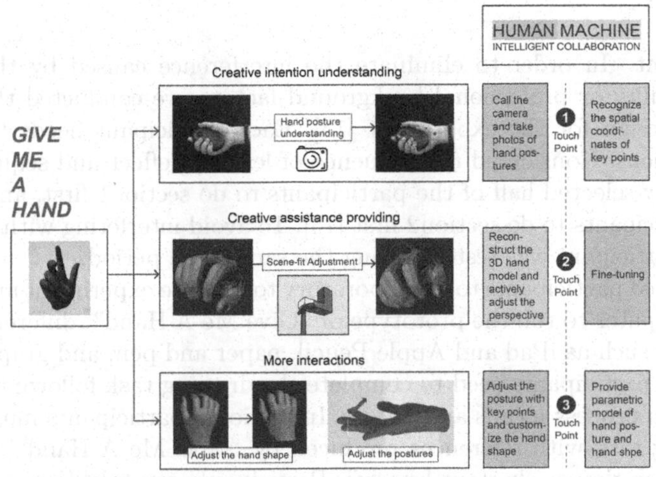

Fig. 6. The creative assistance providing

The first touchpoint is initiated by the creator. When the creator is drawing a character but does not know how to draw the hand posture, he or she can call the camera actively, then poses his or her hand in front of the camera without struggling to find the shooting angle.

The second touchpoint is initiated by the aid. It learns the perspective of the scene drawn by the creator, then adjusts the perspective of viewing the model, changes the model's size, and rotates the model to fit the creator's scene. If the creator is not satisfied with the scene-fit adjustment by the aid, he or she can also fine-tune the perspective, angle, and size of the model. Creators' fine-tuning on the aid's adjustment would also become a part of training data to improve the aid's performance in the future.

In the third touchpoint, the initiative will return to the creator. If the hand posture of the model does not accurately fit the creator's intention, the aid will show the key points of hand joints. The creator can revise the hand posture by adjusting the position of key points. If the creator needs more visual information of hands, some parameters of the handshape can be modified, such as the smoothness of the model surface and different genders.

4.2 Validation

To verify the effectiveness of our method, we invited 24 creators who have not taken part in Study1 to experience the prototype of "Give Me A Hand". During the test, we gave participants a two-section drawing task with the same proposition as in Study1. Participants need complete section1 with their original habits and complete section2 with the aid of "Give Me A Hand". They need to score the experiences of creation in 2 sections and answer a few questions. Finally, we did a quantitative and qualitative analysis of these data.

Experiment. In order to eliminate the interference caused by the creator's painting ability or professional background factors, we conducted the repeated measures design for the experiment [13]. Each participant needs to complete both 2 sections. Considered the influence of learning effect and sequence effect, we randomly selected half of the participants to do section1 first, and the other half of participants to do section2 first [13]. To avoid interfering with each other, only one participant was tested during the same time period.

We invited participants to the laboratory to join the experiment and provided them a computer to run the prototype of "Give Me A Hand", different mediums for painting such as iPad and Apple Pencil, paper and pen, and graphics tablet. In section1, participants need to complete the drawing task following their original creation process means and habits. In section2, participants must complete the drawing task with references produced by "Give Me A Hand". We set the shooting operation as shortcut key "x". Participants can take four photos of the hand posture. The aid will output the model reconstructed from the four photos. Because of the requirement of the drawing task, participants must draw the hand from the same perspective. So that we could conducted Wizard-of-Oz testing to simulate the scene-fitting. After the 3D hand model was reconstructed, we remotely adjusted the perspective, angle, and size of the model to fit the Fig. 2. Afterward, participants can fine-tune the adjustment and choose one model as the reference to use in drawing.

After each section, participants need to score from 0 to 10 for five questions. The five questions address different aspects of creative experiences, including the difficulty of the drawing task, the satisfaction with works, the degree of how the works fit the ideation, the fit of the references, and the usefulness of the references. In addition, after the end of both 2 sections, we asked an open-ended question for more thoughts or suggestions on "Give Me A Hand". At last, based on the comparison of two different creative processes, participants need to do a multiple-choice question to select the three most impressive features of the aid.

Data Analysis. We compared the participants' experiences of satisfaction, difficulty, and the fit of references in two sections and then graphed the results as the Fig. 7. The Fig. 7(a) shows that compared with section1, 10 participants were more satisfied with their works in section2, 5 participants were less satisfied with their works in section2. 12 participants felt easier with section2, and 7 participants felt easier with section1. We can see that the references provided by our aid make most participants feel more satisfied with their works and feel the task becomes easier in section2. At the same time, there is a negative correlation between the feeling of satisfaction and difficulty.

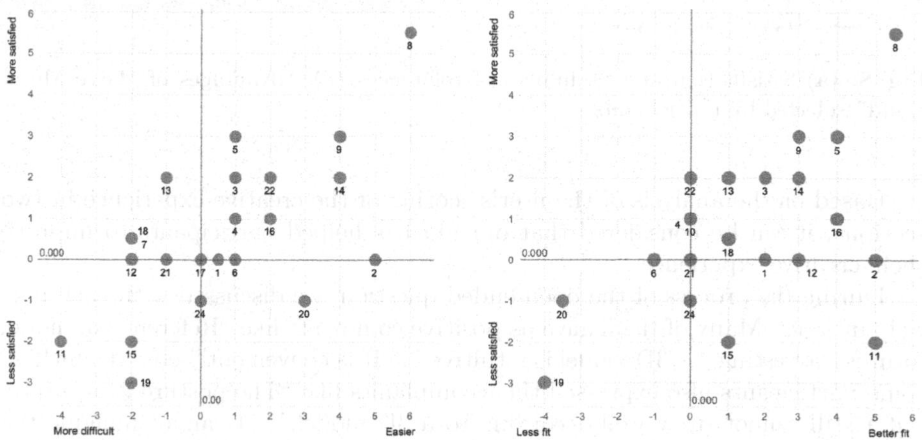

Fig. 7. (a) Changes of difficulty and satisfaction between 2 sections (b) Changes of fit and satisfaction between 2 sections

The Fig. 7(b) displays that not only the satisfaction with works changed, participants' perception of the suitability of references has also changed significantly. Compared to section1, 13 participants felt that the references are fit better in section2, 3 participants felt the references are fit less in section2. Most participants felt the references provided by our aid were more in line with their creative intention. There is a positive correlation between the suitability of references and the feeling of satisfaction. Further compared how the different references satisfied and helped participants, we calculated the average of the corresponding values in two sections and showed the result in Fig. 8(a). It can be seen that the references' usefulness in section2 is 0.416 higher than it in section1, the satisfaction of references in session2 is 1.062 higher than it in section1. The higher the fit of the reference, the more helpful it is to the creator.

The Fig. 8(b) shows that for participants, the most impressive feature of 'Give Me A Hand' is that the 3D hand model references highly fit their creative intention. Meanwhile, most participants think our method lets them intuitively observe the references from multiple perspectives, saves time, and gives better light and shadow references.

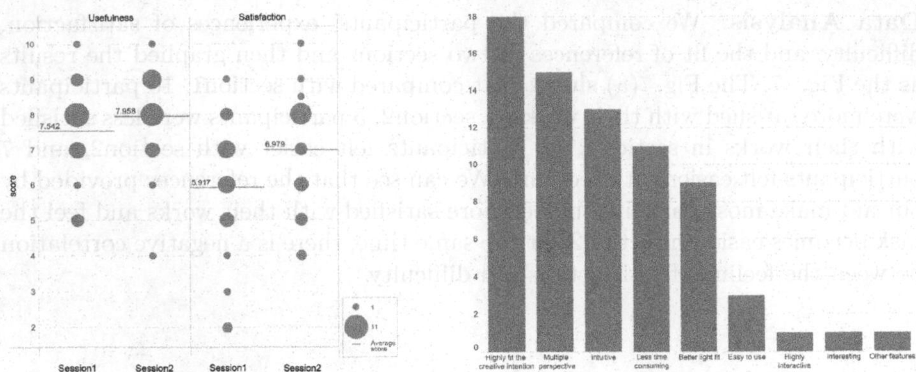

Fig. 8. (a) Satisfaction and usefulness of references (b) Advantages of "Give Me A Hand" selected by participants

Based on the analysis of the user's scoring of the creative experience in two sections, it can be considered that our aid has helped participants to improve their creative experience.

During the process of the open-ended question, we discussed with each participant a lot. Many of them gave us positive comments like "Reference in model form is interesting.", "3D model is intuitive.", "It is convenient!" etc. Meanwhile, some participants also expressed their complaints like "The posture is accurate, but I still cannot draw well according to a 3D model.", "I cannot imagine the occlusion relationship!" etc. We summarized their answers into:

- It would be better if the aid can present the 3D model references in more forms, such as outlines suitable for drawing, different skin textures nearly close to real hands, the model of objects they grasp, etc.
- The interactive experience of operating the model could be more friendly and smooth.
- It would be better if some model parameters could be customized, such as the hand shape, hand postures, etc.

Although we omitted the touch point3 of the prototype in the experiment, the feedback from participants proved that it is needed. Different creators prefer references with different shape and simplicity.

5 Discussion and Future Work

5.1 Discussion

In Study1, we came up with four design requirements. The method we used to understand creators' ideas aligns with creators' original habits and does not require any hard-to-obtain devices. Meanwhile, the 3D model can simultaneously convey hand posture, hand structure, proportions of hand joints, the relationship of light and shadow to creators. In addition, the 3D model can be observed and adjusted by rotating, changing the angle of view or perspective. Through the evaluation of the prototype, we verified its effectiveness in helping creators to draw hand postures and to improve their creative abilities. We believe that this approach has some degree of generality on the same type of drawing problems.

Although after using the prototype of "Give Me A Hand", the creative experiences of most participants have been improved, there are still some participants who are less satisfied with their drawings or feel that the task was still tricky. We compared the references participants used in section1, their drawings, and their answers to the open-ended question. We found that there is a diversity of creators. Therefore the references should be diverse as well.

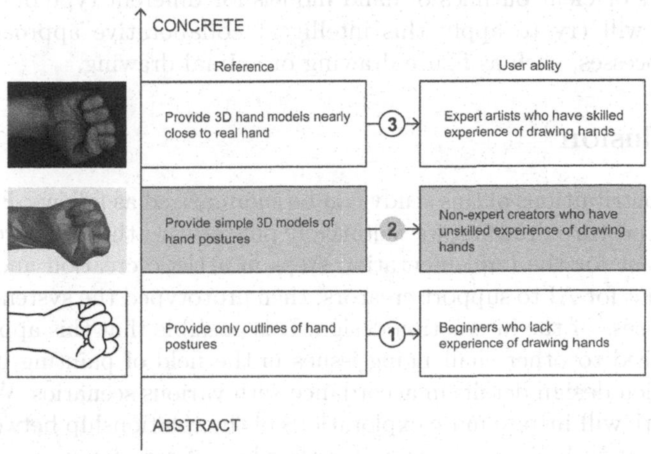

Fig. 9. Three stages of the reference and creative ability

As the Fig. 9 shown, creators can be divided into three stages according to their creative abilities: (1) Beginners who lack the experience of drawing hands. These creators prefer highly generalized references without trivial and complicated visual information, such as straightforward and clear outlines. (2) Non-expert creators who have unskilled experience in drawing hands. Those who have improved their creative experience in our experiments belong to this category of creators. They need an appropriately informative reference which means removing subtle folds, the shape of complex muscle and joints while retaining the basic hand posture and structure. (3) Expert artists who have skilled experience in drawing hands. They prefer references with more information, including the skin texture of different people, the shape of skin folds, muscles, and joints. They know how to select the valuable information from the references nearly close to real hands. It is worth mentioning that the expert artists refer to the creators with skilled experiences in figure drawing.

As a result, The prototype of "Give Me A Hand" mainly provides practical help for the second type of creators. Nevertheless, for the other two types of creators, the help provided by our method is insufficient.

5.2 Future Work

In the future, we will continue our work from the following four aspects: (1) Try to complete the scene understanding for artistic creation and expand the test sample to gather the fine-tuning data from creators to improve the performance of the aid. (2) Accomplish the function that allows users to customize the shape and posture of the hand model. (3) Based on the simple 3D model only retaining hand posture and structure, we will try to provide more options such as different skin textures or clear outlines of hand models for different type of creators. (4) Finally, we will try to apply this intelligent collaborative approach to other drawing processes, such as figure drawing or animal drawing.

6 Conclusion

The main contributions of this study can be summarized as follows: For the problem of hand posture drawing, we tentatively put forward the design requirements of AI assistant for the implementation steps in artistic creation and positioned an entry point for AI to support creators, then prototyped the system to validate the effectiveness of the interaction design. It is possible that this approach could also be applied to other challenging issues in the field of painting by adjusting the interaction design details in accordance with various scenarios. We also hope that our work will inspire more explorations of the relationship between creators and AI so that to help people gain more freedom of creation.

References

1. Intelligent cognitive assistants (2016)
2. Bidgoli, A., De Guevara, M.L., Hsiung, C., Oh, J., Kang, E.: Artistic style in robotic painting; a machine learning approach to learning brushstroke from human artists. In: 2020 29th IEEE International Conference on Robot and Human Interactive Communication (RO-MAN), pp. 412–418. IEEE (2020)
3. Boukhayma, A., Bem, R., Torr, P.H.: 3D hand shape and pose from images in the wild. In: Proceedings of the IEEE/CVF Conference on Computer Vision and Pattern Recognition, pp. 10843–10852 (2019)
4. Cao, N., Yan, X., Shi, Y., Chen, C.: AI-sketcher: a deep generative model for producing high-quality sketches. In: Proceedings of the AAAI Conference on Artificial Intelligence, vol. 33, pp. 2564–2571 (2019)
5. Cao, Z., Hidalgo, G., Simon, T., Wei, S.E., Sheikh, Y.: OpenPose: realtime multi-person 2D pose estimation using part affinity fields. IEEE Trans. Pattern Anal. Mach. Intell. **43**(1), 172–186 (2019)
6. Cao, Z., Simon, T., Wei, S.E., Sheikh, Y.: Realtime multi-person 2D pose estimation using part affinity fields. In: Proceedings of the IEEE Conference on Computer Vision and Pattern Recognition, pp. 7291–7299 (2017)

7. Cohen, D.J.: Look little, look often: the influence of gaze frequency on drawing accuracy. Percept. Psychophysics **67**(6), 997–1009 (2005)
8. Cohen, D.J., Bennett, S.: Why can't most people draw what they see? J. Exp. Psychol. Hum. Percept. Perform. **23**(3), 609 (1997)
9. Cohen, H.: How to draw three people in a botanical garden. In: AAAI, vol. 89, pp. 846–855 (1988)
10. Davis, N., Hsiao, C.-P., Popova, Y., Magerko, B.: An enactive model of creativity for computational collaboration and co-creation. In: Zagalo, N., Branco, P. (eds.) Creativity in the Digital Age. SSCC, pp. 109–133. Springer, London (2015). https://doi.org/10.1007/978-1-4471-6681-8_7
11. Davis, N., Hsiao, C.P., Yashraj Singh, K., Li, L., Magerko, B.: Empirically studying participatory sense-making in abstract drawing with a co-creative cognitive agent. In: Proceedings of the 21st International Conference on Intelligent User Interfaces, pp. 196–207 (2016)
12. Davis, N.M., Hsiao, C.P., Singh, K.Y., Magerko, B.: Co-creative drawing agent with object recognition. In: Twelfth Artificial Intelligence and Interactive Digital Entertainment Conference (2016)
13. Fox, M.T., Brathwaite, A.C., Sidani, S.: Evaluating the effectiveness of interventions: exploration of two statistical methods. Can. J. Nurs. Res. Arch. 20–30 (2004)
14. Frans, K.: Outline colorization through tandem adversarial networks. arXiv preprint arXiv:1704.08834 (2017)
15. Gatys, L.A., Ecker, A.S., Bethge, M.: Image style transfer using convolutional neural networks. In: Proceedings of the IEEE Conference on Computer Vision and Pattern Recognition, pp. 2414–2423 (2016)
16. Geer, T.: What we illustrate when we draw: normative visual processing in beginner drawings, and the capacity to observe detail. Thinking Drawing Pract. Knowl. 45 (2011)
17. Giorgi, A.: The theory, practice, and evaluation of the phenomenological method as a qualitative research procedure. J. Phenomenol. Psychol. **28**(2), 235–260 (1997)
18. Goodfellow, I.: Nips 2016 tutorial: Generative adversarial networks. arXiv preprint arXiv:1701.00160 (2016)
19. Ha, D., Eck, D.: A neural representation of sketch drawings. arXiv preprint arXiv:1704.03477 (2017)
20. Huang, S., Chen, Y., Yuan, T., Qi, S., Zhu, Y., Zhu, S.C.: Perspectivenet: 3D object detection from a single RGB image via perspective points. arXiv preprint arXiv:1912.07744 (2019)
21. Huang, Z., Heng, W., Zhou, S.: Learning to paint with model-based deep reinforcement learning. In: Proceedings of the IEEE/CVF International Conference on Computer Vision, pp. 8709–8718 (2019)
22. Isola, P., Zhu, J.Y., Zhou, T., Efros, A.A.: Image-to-image translation with conditional adversarial networks. In: Proceedings of the IEEE Conference on Computer Vision and Pattern Recognition, pp. 1125–1134 (2017)
23. Knaack, P.: Phenomenological research. West. J. Nurs. Res. **6**(1), 107–114 (1984)
24. Kozbelt, A.: Artists as experts in visual cognition. Vis. Cogn. **8**(6), 705–723 (2001)
25. Lin, Y., Guo, J., Chen, Y., Yao, C., Ying, F.: It is your turn: collaborative ideation with a co-creative robot through sketch. In: Proceedings of the 2020 CHI Conference on Human Factors in Computing Systems, pp. 1–14 (2020)
26. Manovich, L.: Defining AI arts: Three proposals. AI and dialog of cultures exhibition catalog. Hermitage Museum, Saint-Petersburg (2019)

27. Oh, C., Song, J., Choi, J., Kim, S., Lee, S., Suh, B.: I lead, you help but only with enough details: understanding user experience of co-creation with artificial intelligence. In: Proceedings of the 2018 CHI Conference on Human Factors in Computing Systems, pp. 1–13 (2018)
28. Ostrofsky, J., Kozbelt, A.: A multi-stage attention hypothesis of drawing ability. In: Thinking through Drawing: Practice into Knowledge. Proceedings of an Interdisciplinary Symposium on Drawing, Cognition and Education, pp. 61–66. Columbia University, New York, USA Teachers College (2011)
29. Park, T., Liu, M.Y., Wang, T.C., Zhu, J.Y.: Semantic image synthesis with spatially-adaptive normalization. In: Proceedings of the IEEE/CVF Conference on Computer Vision and Pattern Recognition, pp. 2337–2346 (2019)
30. Romero, J., Tzionas, D., Black, M.J.: Embodied hands: Modeling and capturing hands and bodies together. arXiv preprint arXiv:2201.02610 (2022)
31. Shaw, D., Barnes, N., et al.: Perspective rectangle detection. In: Proceedings of the Workshop of the Application of Computer Vision, in Conjunction with ECCV 2006, pp. 119–127 (2006)
32. Shi, Y., Cao, N., Ma, X., Chen, S., Liu, P.: EmoG: supporting the sketching of emotional expressions for storyboarding. In: Proceedings of the 2020 CHI Conference on Human Factors in Computing Systems, pp. 1–12 (2020)
33. Simon, T., Joo, H., Matthews, I., Sheikh, Y.: Hand keypoint detection in single images using multiview bootstrapping. In: Proceedings of the IEEE Conference on Computer Vision and Pattern Recognition, pp. 1145–1153 (2017)
34. Solso, R.L.: Cognition and the Visual Arts. MIT Press, Cambridge (1996)
35. Tan, J., Echevarria, J., Gingold, Y.: Palette-based image decomposition, harmonization, and color transfer. arXiv preprint arXiv:1804.01225 (2018)
36. Tchalenko, J.: Segmentation and accuracy in copying and drawing: experts and beginners. Vis. Res. **49**(8), 791–800 (2009)
37. Wei, S.E., Ramakrishna, V., Kanade, T., Sheikh, Y.: Convolutional pose machines. In: Proceedings of the IEEE Conference on Computer Vision and Pattern Recognition, pp. 4724–4732 (2016)
38. Xu, T., Zhang, P., Huang, Q., Zhang, H., Gan, Z., Huang, X., He, X.: AttnGAN: fine-grained text to image generation with attentional generative adversarial networks. In: Proceedings of the IEEE Conference on Computer Vision and Pattern Recognition, pp. 1316–1324 (2018)
39. You, S., You, N., Pan, M.: PI-REC: Progressive image reconstruction network with edge and color domain. arXiv preprint arXiv:1903.10146 (2019)
40. Zeng, Z., Sun, X., Liao, X.: Artificial intelligence augments design creativity: a typeface family design experiment. In: Marcus, A., Wang, W. (eds.) HCII 2019. LNCS, vol. 11584, pp. 400–411. Springer, Cham (2019). https://doi.org/10.1007/978-3-030-23541-3_29
41. Zhang, Q., Xiao, C., Sun, H., Tang, F.: Palette-based image recoloring using color decomposition optimization. IEEE Trans. Image Process. **26**(4), 1952–1964 (2017)
42. Zhou, Z., Farhat, F., Wang, J.Z.: Detecting dominant vanishing points in natural scenes with application to composition-sensitive image retrieval. IEEE Trans. Multimedia **19**(12), 2651–2665 (2017)

Emotional Communication Between Chatbots and Users: An Empirical Study on Online Customer Service System

Qianwen Xu[1], Jun Yan[2], and Cong Cao[1](✉)

[1] Zhejiang University of Technology, Hangzhou, China
congcao@zjut.edu.cn

[2] University of Wollongong, Wollongong, Australia

Abstract. In a digital environment, chatbots act as customer service agents to assist consumers in making decisions. Improving the service efficiency of chatbots has aroused widespread concern in the industry and academia. Based on the computer as a social actor (CASA) and emotional contagion theory, this study explores the influence mechanism of quality assessment in the process of communication between users and human-machine customer service, investigates the relationship between chatbot performance and user perception, and constructs an assessment model for the quality of communication process. It adopts partial least squares (PLS) structural equation modelling (SEM) to evaluate the research model and hypothesis. Based on 163 samples, the results show that, in the process of communication, users' perception of the robot's ability, especially the accuracy and effectiveness of the robot, will significantly affect users' evaluation of the quality of communication. At the same time, the language style of the chatbot has little impact on the evaluation of the quality of communication. The results of this study provide important insights into the rational use of human-computer interaction in e-commerce and lay a foundation for understanding the service mechanism and related theories of online service agents in artificial intelligence.

Keywords: Human – computer interaction · Chatbots · Communication quality · Emotional contagion · Quality of communication

1 Introduction

With advances in artificial intelligence (AI), chatbots are replacing human customer service, which companies used to solve problems such as "information overload" and "lack of human interaction" [1]. According to Insider (2021), the chatbot market is predicted to grow at 29.7% per year and is expected to reach $125 million by 2025[1]. The compound annual growth rate is 24.3% [2]. Brilliant customer service saves the considerable cost of human service and has a significant efficiency advantage in dealing with objective and procedural tasks [3, 4]. Based on these advantages, enterprises increasingly use intelligent customer service systems to communicate with human users [5].

[1] Insider, 2021, https://www.businessinsider.com/chatbot-market-stats-trends.

H. Degen and S. Ntoa (Eds.): HCII 2022, LNAI 13336, pp. 513–530, 2022.
https://doi.org/10.1007/978-3-031-05643-7_33

Chatbots use natural language to interact with users and answer their queries effectively. Due to its accessibility, flexibility and low cost, commercial companies widely use it. However, researchers suggest that they often fall short of consumer expectations despite the proliferation of chatbots due to their inability to understand users' needs entirely [6]. Consumer willingness to accept chatbots has been lower than industry expectations. A study of Facebook users suggests that more than 70% perceive their interactions with chatbots as failures, and there is thus still a strong demand for human interaction [7]. Given these results, it may be difficult for chatbots to completely replace humans, with some suggesting that human and AI-based agents will need to work together to provide better services [8].

Specifically, online chat agents lack humanity because their conversational style is often blunt, influenced by pre-existing programming scripts [9]. Online customer service system communicates with users employing text through manual customer service or machine customer service. It is a text-based computer-mediated communication (CMC) mediated by the computer. Due to the lack of audio-visual cues, expressing emotions in the text can be challenging [10]. Although the user's language skills can be easily transferred in human – computer communication, the perception and quality of the interaction could still differ significantly from human interaction [1]. Therefore, it becomes essential to clarify the impact of communication quality in human – computer interaction to improve the value of chatbot usage [6].

The wide application of chatbots has also attracted academic attention. Studies have noted the lack of humanity in technology intermediary services [11]. Two approaches are proposed to inject automated social presence (ASP) into e-services [12] and seek more emotional support [13]. In terms of consumer attitudes, studies have focused on consumer satisfaction [14], loyalty [15], and intention to continue using chatbots [7]. However, few studies have explored users' perception of the chatbot's performance and emotional state of the communication process from the perspective of human-computer interaction. There is still a gap in the research on the transmission mechanism of users' evaluation of the quality of the communication process.

Based on the social background in which chatbots are widely used and the above research gaps, this study raises the following questions: Which features will users evaluate services? Is there emotional contagion in the communication process, that is, is there emotional transmission in-text CMC? Will the user's performance perception and emotional perception in the process impact the user's perception process quality evaluation? How can we improve the perceptual communication quality of human-computer interaction to promote the high-quality development of chatbots?

Based on the computer as a social actor (CASA) and emotional contagion theory, this study takes the robot service agent of the online customer service system as the research object. It establishes the quality evaluation model of human-computer interaction users. We analyze 163 sample data collected by partial least squares structural equation modelling (PLS-SEM) and then test the research model and hypothesis proposed in this paper. The results show that the chatbot's accuracy and validity affect the users' judgment of the chatbot's performance and their perception of warmth during communication. Also, the users' perception of the chatbot's performance significantly affects the final quality evaluation. Then, the results showed that the style of language used by the chatbot, namely the use of "emotional words" and "emoticons", had no significant effect on the assessment of the whole process. These results will help explore the mechanism of users' response to the chatbot as a special service agent in e-commerce to help online service providers effectively improve the level of a bot service agent and provide some theoretical reference for future research.

This paper's research ideas and contents are as follows: First, the research ideas and results of human-computer interaction process quality evaluation are sorted and summarized. Secondly, based on CASA and emotional contagion theory of related literature, it puts forward the framework of this research and constructs the corresponding research hypothesis. Then the questionnaire is designed according to the scale of the existing literature. The relevant data are collected through online questionnaires, and the research model and hypothesis are evaluated and tested by PLS-SEM. Finally, the corresponding research conclusions and theoretical and practical significance are discussed. Of course, the limitations of this research and the direction of future research are also explained in this paper.

2 Theory and Model

2.1 CASA and Perceived Communication Quality

Social response theory, proposed by Nass, et al. [16], suggests that when a technology possesses a set of characteristics similar to people, a person's reaction to the technology will reflect as social behaviour and respond to it with social rules. Studies based on the computer as a social actor (CASA) paradigm show that people tend to make social responses to computers even when they are aware that they are interacting with machines [17].

CASA is often used to explain the human understanding of machines and attitudes held towards them in interactive contexts and has become a functional conceptual paradigm for the study of human's social cognition of computers [16]. With the rapid development of artificial intelligence, the application of CASA has been extended to human-computer interaction in different situations. Ho, et al. [18] found that the positive effects of emotion also apply to the perception of emotion when interacting with a chatbot. Lee and Liang [19] confirmed the effectiveness of human avoidance and the politeness strategy of robots seeking human help in human-machine communication [20]. Therefore, we choose the CASA paradigm to help us understand the specific human-computer interaction process.

Applying AI devices in different service industries requires communication between consumers and AI to provide the required services [21]. In human-computer interaction using chatbots, consumers expect AI to be considerate and have good communication skills similar to humans [22]. Chung, et al. [14] studied the impact of communication quality on customer satisfaction in the luxury retail environment and discussed accuracy, credibility, and communication ability as dimensions of communication quality. Xu and Lombard [23] argue that linguistic cues (e.g., language style) and agent names (e.g., human versus machine names) may influence human recognition of computer agents.

However, text-based computer-mediated communication (CMC) lacks audio-visual cues and limited communication methods during the interaction. Existing studies mainly focus on consumers' recognition of robot capabilities, such as accuracy and credibility, while few studies judge the communication quality from the perspective of emotion [14]. Whether there is emotional contagion in-text CMC, what clues contribute to emotional contagion in-text CMC, and the effect and mechanism of emotional contagion in human-computer interaction also need to be further discussed.

2.2 Emotional Contagion

Emotional contagion is considered a multi-stage mechanism involving imitation and incoming feedback. When a person perceives the emotional expression displayed by others, he will spontaneously imitate the expression, thus providing himself with incoming feedback and triggering others with the same emotions as those experienced in himself [10]. The process of emotional contagion includes three stages, namely imitation, feedback and contagion [24]. Once an emotion is (unconsciously) identified, people may begin to imitate, the concept of which is often spontaneous and helps humans empathize with others by mimicking their feelings [25].

It is important to note that interactions in contemporary service environments are no longer limited to humans. In the process of human-computer interaction, emotional contagion has been widely concerned by scholars. It has been shown that consumers show higher trust in robots that display positive emotions [18]. Similarly, Appel, et al. [26] points out that robots with emotions are more popular than neutral robots. Therefore, emotional contagion also exists in human-computer interaction, and the positive emotions conveyed by robots have a positive effect on customer satisfaction.

However, unlike face-to-face communication in real life, CMC is primarily based on plain text. When one participates in CMC, his ability to express emotions is limited due to the lack of audio-visual cues. A popular form of CMC communication is emoticons, namely text-based facial expressions, emotional states and feeling symbols [27]. Emoticons can help convey current emotions or provide information about the psychological state of the sender [28]. Therefore, this paper explores the effects of *emotive words* and *emoticons* on communication's emotional transmission and quality assessment.

Based on the CASA research paradigm [16] and emotional contagion theory [24], combined with the characteristics of text CMC, this paper takes the online customer service system as an example. It attempts to measure consumers' assessment of the quality of the communication process from the "Perceived warmth" and "Capability" of the communication process. Cuddy, et al. [29] points out that warmth is associated with perceived trustworthiness, empathy, and kindness, while competence is associated with perceived intelligence, power, efficacy, and skill. Combined with the characteristics of CMC and the particularity of human-computer interaction, this study considers that the accurate understanding, effective solution and use of language style of human-computer customer service will affect consumers' perception of warmth and ability to judge the communication process. Our research model is shown in Fig. 1.

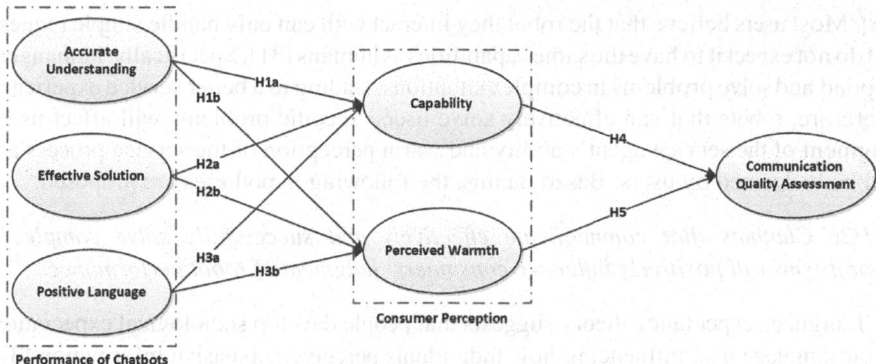

Fig. 1. Research framework

3 Hypotheses

3.1 Chatbot Capability Perception

Consumers' capability perception of chatbots refers to their perception of the ability to solve complex problems effectively [30]. Human beings can flexibly respond to and solve problems in complex situations. For example, in complex service scenarios, such as fraud, infringement, theft and other problems, human customer service can respond to problems by understanding users' needs and providing professional suggestions for solving problems. Similarly, as a more advanced and straightforward service agent, man-machine customer service should have the ability to solve complex problems efficiently. However, most users assume that the robot they interact with can only handle simple requests and do not expect it to have the same capabilities as humans [31]. Therefore, it is beneficial to understand the communication process of human-computer interaction better to explore the pre-factors of the user's perception of robot performance.

Accuracy is the ability to respond to users in a timely and accurate manner [32] and is considered the primary indicator for consumers to evaluate chatbot services [33]. Chatbots are equipped with advanced language processing systems to communicate and respond objectively to users without feeling frustrated or tired like humans [8]. When a customer establishes a good relationship with the communicator, they believe that information is credible and persuasive [34]. In other words, customers must realize that computer-mediated communicators will listen to their concerns, accurately diagnose their problems, and provide the required information to promote their trust in and choice of computers [30]. Therefore, in the use of service agents, timely and accurate responses from chatbots provide customers with more accurate performance perception and a greater likelihood of receiving a response within a short time, thus enhancing the willingness to adopt. Based on this, the following hypotheses are proposed:

H1: Timely and accurate responses from chatbots will positively affect consumers' judgment of robot performance.

Customers trust the reliability and integrity of accurate communication [35]. Correct processing often determines consumers' perceptions of retail services and service quality

[36]. Most users believe that the robot they interact with can only handle simple requests and do not expect it to have the same capabilities as humans [31]. Specifically, humans can respond and solve problems in complex situations, leading to a better service experience. Therefore, robots that can effectively solve users' specific problems will affect users' judgment of the service agent's ability and warm perception of the service process and will be welcomed by users. Based on this, the following hypotheses are proposed:

H2: Chatbots that communicate effectively and successfully solve complex problems will positively influence consumers' judgment of robot performance.

Language expectancy theory suggests that people develop sociological expectations about language use, influencing how individuals perceive persuasive information [37]. Compared to humans with cumbersome languages, chatbots can accurately respond to user needs with minimal text and symbols [38]. Previous studies have proved that recipients of information can recognize the social and emotional meanings of emoticons to a large extent, and emoticons can clarify text messages by emphasizing tone or meaning, thus helping users communicate more clearly [28]. At the same time, this paper defines words with apparent emotional and polite nature as "emotional words". Previous studies have shown that simple and straightforward literal language can increase the credibility of communicators compared with words with strong emotions [10]. Moreover, scholars have pointed out that the use of emoticons in for-mal business Settings can damage the credibility of the sender [9]. Because of this consensus, the senders' use of "emotional words" with emoticons may lead to negative perceptions of the senders' abilities by the recipients. Therefore, we assume:

H3: The language style of the chatbot will affect the user's judgment of the robot's performance, and the use of "emotional words" and positive emotions will have a negative impact on the robot's capability.

3.2 Warm Perception of Communication Process

Perceived warmth indicates that someone is perceived to have positive intentions for the recipient. In face-to-face communication, warm perception is associated with offline environments. Such environments often require more vital interpersonal skills such as friendliness, social perception, agreeableness, and positive listening and speaking skills. Under such circumstances, consumers will quickly make enthusiastic judgments, and such judgments will significantly influence others' opinions [39]. Thus, the hospitality of front-line employees [40], also known as politeness [41], has been proposed as an antecedent of service value. In a CMC context, a client may interpret the chatbot's emulative, reassuring words as positive intentions and thus assume that the agent is enthusiastic [42].

Currently, graphic emoticons are widely used in CMC to convey emotions, similar to non-verbal cues used in face-to-face interaction [43]. Therefore, we hypothesize that the language use of chatbots can affect emotional contagion in human-computer interaction and promote users' warm perception. In addition, previous studies have shown that warm capture is associated with the related characteristics of social objects, including trustworthiness and problem-solving effectiveness [13]. Therefore, this paper argues that the accuracy of chatbot responses and problem-solving effectiveness also affect users' perception of warmth during communication. Based on this, we make the following assumptions:

H4: Chatbots' timely and accurate responses will promote consumers' warm perception during communication.

H5: Chatbots that communicate effectively and successfully solve complex problems will promote the warm perception of consumers in the communication process.

H6: The language style of chatbot will affect consumers' perception of warmth during communication, and the use of "emotional words" and positive emoticons will promote consumers' perception of warmth.

3.3 Communication Process Quality Assessment

Perceived communication quality is a significant indicator of service effectiveness [6] and influences consumer attitudes [14]. Consumers expect AI to communicate like humans [22]. When users interact with human-machine customer service, the quality assessment of the communication process will affect users' choice of the durability of this service mode.

The term "Capability" is related to some of the benefits of using chatbots as service agents, such as problem-solving through service support and time-saving by receiving real-time information [7]. Araujo [21] pointed out that the message response is one of the many factors influencing consumers' first impression of a brand, so the capability of a chatbot is significant. Lin, et al. [44] believes that when users ask questions about shipping or return policies, they will be satisfied with the chatbot's capabilities if they receive a response that effectively solves the problem. However, if the user does not receive help from the chatbot, they may perceive the value of the interaction to be less than its cost. As a result, users become less satisfied and stop using it. Therefore, we assume:

H7: The user's perception of the robot's capability in human-computer interaction will affect the quality assessment of the communication process.

Unlike perceived brand competence, perceived brand warmth increases consumers' recognition of brands on social media, and perceived warmth may improve customer satisfaction [45]. Studies have proved that warm judgment is closely related to consumer satisfaction [46]. This is because perceived warmth is associated with positive intentions of front-line employees toward customers. In the online field, previous studies have shown that perceived warmth will affect customer outcomes at the attitude level, including brand attitude [47], loyalty intention [40], and willingness to interact with the provider again [48]. Regarding language style, it has been pointed out that consumers tend to think that service agents who use emoticons (as opposed to those who do not) are more enthusiastic [49]. Warm (as opposed to competent) messages used by retailers in responding to consumer complaints on online platforms are more likely to improve service perception and increase positive word of mouth for non-participating observers [50]. Therefore, we assume:

H8: Users' warm perception in human-computer interaction will affect their quality assessment of the communication process. Moreover, the higher the degree of perceived warmth is, the higher the quality evaluation of the communication process is.

4 Research Methodology

We designed a questionnaire based on a situational experiment to verify our research hypothesis. First, we built an online shopping environment dominated by digital products. We carried out human-computer interaction with robot service agents that could timely and accurately understand user requirements and effectively realize user requirements. To ensure that participants could relate to the overall scenario, we recruited participants who understood the online shopping scenario, had social experience and were able to experience the simulation fully, and answered the study questions. Furthermore, after completing the simulated scene experience, the success of independent variable manipulation was first tested by asking subjects what type of service agent they thought was depicted in the scene and then filling in the questionnaire. The scale design of this questionnaire takes mature scales in the relevant literature as a reference. It makes appropriate modifications and adjustments according to the characteristics of the online shopping environment and human-computer interaction. In the initial scale, Likert 5 subscale was used to measure all questions except the basic information of respondents. Specifically, the questions range from 1 to 5, with "1" meaning strongly disagree and "5" meaning strongly agree. After completing the initial questionnaire design, a small scale pre-test was carried out in related fields. A total of 15 questionnaires were collected to check whether the semantic and grammatical expressions of the options in the questionnaire were easy to understand and whether the reliability and validity met the requirements. At the same time, some expressions of the questionnaire were modified according to the interviewees' feedback, and the formal questionnaire was finally formed.

The questionnaires were mainly distributed online through the Qualtrics questionnaire tool. 250 questionnaires were collected for the experimental target, and 213 questionnaires were collected in total. 163 valid questionnaires were obtained after removing the questions with too short answer time or too centralized choice. According to the typical rule of PLS-SEM sample size, i.e., the principle of 10 times, the minimum sample number of this study is 60, so the data of 163 samples obtained in this study can effectively improve the accuracy of PLS evaluation. Since PLS-SEM has slight experimental data limitations, this study decided to adopt this method to evaluate the research model and verify relevant hypotheses. For example, PLS has good explanatory power even in the case of a small sample size. In addition, PLS does not require the normal distribution of data. In addition, the method can easily handle reflectance and formative measurement models without identification problems.

Demographically, women made up 56% of the total number of subjects, and men made up 44% of the total number of subjects, which was generally evenly distributed. In addition, combined with our interviews and observations in real life, women are more willing to try to communicate with robot service agents before and after the service, which is consistent with the current development of e-commerce. The average age of the subjects was mainly between 18 and 40 years old (69%), which is consistent with the current situation that the young and middle-aged are the primary consumers. In addition, since minors need permission from their guardians to participate in the experiment, and their shopping behaviours and habits are limited by their economic strength and influenced by their guardians, data samples under 18 are not collected in this experiment. In addition, most of the participants were highly educated, with about 88 per cent holding a bachelor's degree or higher. This is consistent with the basic situation of consumers' shopping in the e-commerce environment. In addition, the sample data of this experiment are not collected on the university campus but are recruited through social means, so our data are more representative (Table 1).

Table 1. Demographic profile of respondents, N = 163.

Measure	Category	N	Percent
Gender	Male	72	44%
	Female	91	56%
Age	18–30	83	51%
	31–40	29	18%
	41–50	37	23%
	51–60	10	6%
	Over 60	4	2%
Education	College	19	12%
	Undergraduate	105	64%
	Postgraduate	39	24%

4.1 Measurement Model

This study analyzed the measurement model approach to assess the constructs' reliability, composite reliability (CR), and average variance extracted (AVE). We have used Cronbach alpha (CA) and composite reliability to measure the reliability. The results for CA and CR are presented in Table 2 for Communication Quality Assessment (0.955, 0.968), Capability (0.897, 0.928), Perceived Warmth (0.926, 0.947), Accurate Understanding (0.924, 0.951), Effective Solution (0.972, 0.982) and Positive Language (0.947, 0.966) respectively. According to Hair, et al. [51], CA and CR values should be higher than 0.70, and this study found the values to be in an acceptable range. Additionally, we examined the convergent validity to obtain AVE values. All the values were greater than the 0.50 threshold (for entrepreneurial orientation, organizational commitment, innovation performance and transformational leadership, the AVE values were 0.882, 0.764, 0.818, 0.867,0.948 and 0.904, respectively), as suggested by Henseler, et al. [52] (see Table 2).

The construct validity of this study is mainly evaluated by content validity, convergent validity and discriminant validity. As the scales of this study are adapted from the existing literature, they feature content validity. As shown by Table 3, the standardized outer loadings of all indicators in their construct are larger than 0.820, and the AVE of different constructs is larger than 0.5 in Table 2 [53, 54]. Therefore, all constructs have good convergent validity. As shown by Table 4, the square root of the AVE of any construct in the model is greater than the corresponding correlation values with other constructs. Moreover, as shown by Table 3, the standardized outer loadings of all indicators in their belonging constructs are larger than their cross-loadings. Such indicates that this study's measurement of different con-structs has sufficient judgment validity [55, 56].

Table 2. Descriptive statistics for the constructs.

	CA	CR	AVE
Communication quality assessment (Quali)	0.955	0.968	0.882
Capability (Capab)	0.897	0.928	0.764
Perceived warmth (Warmt)	0.926	0.947	0.818
Accurate understanding (Under)	0.924	0.951	0.867
Effective solution (Solut)	0.972	0.982	0.948
Positive language (Langu)	0.947	0.966	0.904

Table 3. Correlations among constructs and the square root of the AVE.

	Quali	Capab	Warmt	Under	Solut	Langu
Quali	**0.939**					
Capab	0.871	**0.874**				
Warmt	0.742	0.805	**0.904**			
Under	0.015	0.116	0.306	**0.931**		
Solut	0.440	0.466	0.223	−0.255	**0.974**	
Langu	0.468	0.297	−0.024	−0.043	0.399	**0.951**

Note: Bold number represent the square roots of the AVEs.

4.2 Structural Model

In this study, the statistical significance of the t value of path coefficient in the research model was tested by the bootstrap method in SmartPLS 3.3.5. The original sample number was 163. Smart PLS software evaluated the structured equation model with 5000 guiding programs. The path coefficient and statistical significance test results are shown in Fig. 2. Five of the eight hypotheses presented in this paper passed the statistical

Table 4. Factor loadings and cross loadings.

	Quali	Capab	Warmt	Under	Solut	Langu
Quali.1	**0.929**	0.804	0.656	−0.007	0.405	0.466
Quali.2	**0.949**	0.827	0.702	0.026	0.443	0.462
Quali.3	**0.927**	0.804	0.721	0.044	0.409	0.387
Quali.4	**0.951**	0.837	0.708	−0.006	0.397	0.442
Capab.1	0.849	**0.924**	0.782	0.058	0.453	0.268
Capab.2	0.736	**0.852**	0.677	0.101	0.392	0.253
Capab.3	0.744	**0.879**	0.680	0.115	0.397	0.254
Capab.4	0.709	**0.840**	0.667	0.138	0.384	0.264
Warmt.1	0.730	0.766	**0.906**	0.227	0.208	0.043
Warmt.2	0.681	0.732	**0.905**	0.282	0.195	−0.061
Warmt.3	0.656	0.717	**0.914**	0.336	0.168	−0.011
Warmt.4	0.614	0.694	**0.892**	0.263	0.235	−0.061
Under.1	0.032	0.142	0.309	**0.952**	−0.269	−0.034
Under.2	−0.015	0.087	0.287	**0.926**	−0.226	−0.066
Under.3	0.023	0.089	0.253	**0.915**	−0.211	−0.018
Solut.1	0.432	0.451	0.210	−0.279	**0.974**	0.368
Solut.2	0.433	0.458	0.241	−0.233	**0.976**	0.391
Solut.3	0.421	0.453	0.197	−0.233	**0.971**	0.408
Langu.1	0.442	0.264	−0.048	−0.034	0.395	**0.954**
Langu.2	0.428	0.281	−0.008	0.001	0.335	**0.942**
Langu.3	0.463	0.300	−0.015	−0.085	0.408	**0.957**

Note: Bold number indicate outer loading on the assigned constructs.

significance test. The empirical results show that the accuracy of the response and the effectiveness of the problem solving have a significant impact on the user's perception of performance and warmth, and the stronger the user's perception of the performance of the chatbot, the higher the user's evaluation of the quality of the whole communication process.

In addition, this study points out that the language style of the chatbot has no significant effect on users' perception of chatbot performance and warmth during communication. Users' perception of warmth has no significant effect on final communication process quality evaluation. Finally, this study finds that different factors influence users' perception of chatbot performance and warmth during the chat, with accuracy and validity being the most influential ones, respectively.

The determination coefficient (R^2) is the most commonly used coefficient to evaluate the prediction ability of structural models [54]. R^2 is between 1 and 0. The higher the value, the greater the predictive power. Generally speaking, when R^2 is between 0.5–0.75, the explanatory ability is moderate. If R^2 is higher than 0.75, it has significant explanatory power [56]. In this study, R^2's willingness to trust consumers reached a relatively high level of 0.764, indicating that the model proposed has excellent explanatory ability.

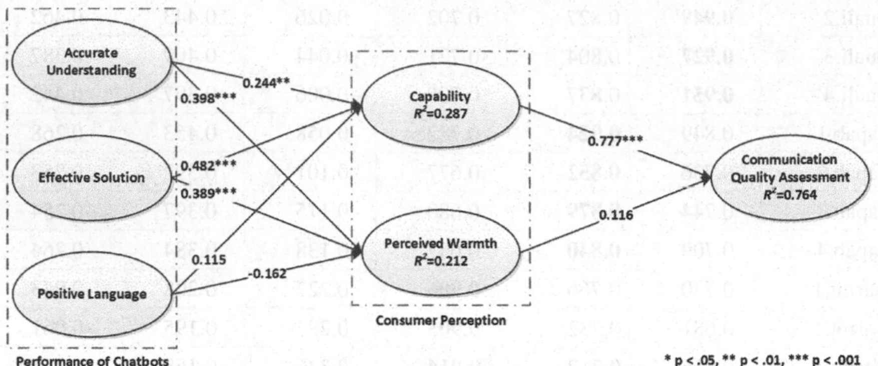

Fig. 2. PLS-SEM analysis results.

5 Results and Discussion

5.1 Summary of Results

This research through the scenario simulation and questionnaire design, the background in the existing e-commerce and under the background of the network shopping trend, with the auxiliary artificial customer-service chat robot as the research object, from the perspective of consumers, based on the speed and efficiency to solve the problem to chat robot, the use of language and the attitude of considering individual consumers, A perceptual communication quality model in human-computer interaction is constructed. This paper used PLS-SEM to evaluate its research model and hypothesis. Through the investigation of 163 samples, the results showed that the quality evaluation of users' communication with the chatbot was affected by multiple factors, including the performance perception of the chatbot and the warmth perception in the communication process. These perceptions are influenced by the specific performance of the chatbot, such as the accuracy of problem understanding and the effectiveness of problem-solving.

From the experimental results, the warmth felt by users in the process of communication has no significant impact on their quality evaluation. Through further interviews, we suspect that this may be related to the self-positioning of chatbots. Excessive anthropomorphism will blur the difference between human and human-machine customer service in users' minds, and users may prefer a chatbot that can only meet their needs efficiently. In addition, we investigated the influence of chatbot language style on users' perceptions. Specifically, emotion-loaded "emotional words" and "emoticons" did not promote users' perception of chatbot performance or warmth during communication. Some scholars have pointed out that happy emoticons have a negative effect on the recipient's first impression of the sender based on E-mail [4]. Combined with the experimental results of this paper, it can be further proposed that the language style of the chatbot has little impact on the overall communication quality of human-computer interaction and even has a negative effect.

In addition, in this paper, the experimental results show that the bot of accurate understanding of user needs, to meet the demand effectively can not only directly promote the user perception of the performance of the bot, which allows the user to the bot is intelligent. It also can promote warm user awareness in the process of communication. Through in-depth interviews with some users, we know that the user in the process of communicating with the bot perceived warm artificial customer service. Is there a difference in this enlightens us in the future should be focusing on the service broker, contrast artificial customer service and human customer service actual differences in problem-solving. Furthermore, explore the efficient human-computer customer service to the artificial transformation of the service time, in order to further improve the human-machine customer service to the whole online customer service system of the auxiliary role and ultimately achieve consumer perception communication quality and service satisfaction further improve.

5.2 Implication for Theory

Human-computer interaction research in the field of services is relatively new, but scholars have done much research on user perception and the use of service agents. These past works have helped scholars and practitioners grasp the role of service agents in online customer service. However, there are still valuable research gaps in understanding user perception communication evaluation mechanisms, human-machine interaction, and how collaboration between human-machine service agents improves service experience.

Based on CASA, this study comprehensively investigated the user's perception quality evaluation mechanism in human-computer interaction from the two dimensions of capability and perceived warmth and based on the chatbot's accuracy, effectiveness, and language style. This makes up for the lack of forgotten human-computer interaction research and provides a theoretical basis for realizing the maximum expected effect of human-computer collaboration in service delivery. Re-search based on the text of the CMC emotional transfer, based on exploring the bot language style, especially the specific function of "emotion words" and emoticons, trying to a more complete system structure analysis influence user perception communication quality evaluation mechanism for the bot with the actual user interaction provides a more comprehensive perspective. In addition, the empirical data of this study is based on social recruitment, which is more consistent with the current status of e-commerce consumers and is representative, helping researchers to understand further the internal mechanism of service efficiency improvement between chatbots and users.

5.3 Implication for Practice

The primary purpose of this study is to explore the influence mechanism of user perception communication quality during user interaction with chatbots. This is of great significance for finding a proper service balance between robot and human collaboration, rationally developing robot anthropomorphism, and improving robot service efficiency. With the popularization and development of e-commerce and online shopping, it has become an irresistible trend to apply chatbots to the online customer service system. To solve users' needs by combining human-machine customer service with manual customer service. Chatbots have high timeliness in solving problems and quickly respond to repetitive and straightforward problems to meet user needs and save labour costs. However, there are also some problems with the application of chatbots. How to avoid "artificial intelligence" becoming "artificial retarded" to achieve the actual improvement of user satisfaction has become an inevitable problem.

According to this empirical study, it is suggested that managers should pay attention to the improvement of chatbot's performance, and accurately understand and efficiently meeting the needs of chatbot is the essential property. In addition, friendly and polite "emoticons" and "emoticons" are not efficient. Managers should simplify the language style of chatbots, and straightforward language can promote users' choice. The bot must not only be regarded as a kind of artificial intelligence driver software tool but also a pivotal opportunity to build and manage the customer relationship. We need to pay attention to the user in the process of human-computer interaction design, cognitive-communication quality evaluation, the bot itself performance improvement. Establish an efficient online customer service system, and make the whole industry achieve long-term development.

5.4 Limitations and Future Research

Although this study makes a beneficial discussion on the factors affecting consumers perception and trust in the live streaming shopping environment, it suffers inherent limitations. Therefore, future studies must make further improvements. To begin with, the number of samples investigated in this study is 163. It satisfies the requirements of PLS-SEM on minimal sample size, but the larger sample size could enhance the accuracy of the study and evaluation by the model effectively [53, 54]. Moreover, although we use a social call to enhance data representation in the experimental sample collection, the large age span is difficult to accurately reflect consumers' shopping habits. In future studies, we need to refine the age span further to ensure further the universality, representation and accuracy of the data. In addition, this study only considers the impact of a chatbot as a single customer service agent on users. At the same time, the actual interaction process is usually the result of the interaction between human-machine customer service and human customer service. Switching and cooperation between the two service agents may change users' perception and evaluation of process quality. Therefore, future studies should use a relatively comprehensive and large sample size to analyze the interaction and cooperation mode between human-machine customer service and human customer service to expand this experiment's results further.

6 Conclusion

Communicating with customers through live chat interfaces has become an increasingly popular way to provide real-time customer service in an e-commerce environment. Customers use these chat services to obtain information (for example, product details) or help (for example, to solve technical problems), which provides much time and cost-saving opportunities for users and related industries. However, although users' language skills can be easily transferred in human-machine communication, the perception and quality of interaction may still be significantly different from human interaction [1]. Many users still encounter unsatisfied chatbots (for example, high failure rates), which can lead to scepticism and resistance to the technology, potentially discouraging users from complying with the suggestions and requests made by chatbots.

With the emergence and application of chatbots, problems and vulnerabilities also occur from time to time. Therefore, it is necessary to timely adjust the propagation path that affects consumer quality evaluation to promote the industry's high-quality development. At present, theoretical researches mainly focus on how humans and computers interact. However, few pieces of research focus on the types of service agents, emotional contagion and related influence mechanisms in human-computer interaction. Based on the empirical research method, this paper uses PLS-SEM to evaluate its research model and hypothesis. The results show that the user has perceived performance during communication, especially the chatbot's accurate understanding and effective solution of the problem, significantly affects the user's quality evaluation of the communication process. The research results of this paper suggest that a good, user-accepted chatbot should be able to understand and effectively solve the user's questions accurately. In addition, businesses should appropriately simplify the language when setting the language style of chatbot. Anthropomorphic elements such as "emotional vocabulary" and "emoticons" cannot promote the quality evaluation of users, and the perceived warmth of the communication process is not crucial to the process of human-computer interaction. This study explores the influence mechanism of user-perceived communication quality during the interaction between user and chatbot. It extends the theoretical knowledge of online customer service systems, especially human-machine customer service. We hope that this paper will provide the impetus for future research on harmonising human-machine customer service and human customer service. Also, it can improve AI-based capabilities in and outside the e-marketplace and customer self-service environment.

Acknowledgments. The work described in this paper was supported by grants from the Zhejiang University of Technology Humanities and Social Sciences Pre-Research Fund Project (GZ21731320013), the Zhejiang University of Technology Subject Reform Project (GZ21511320030) and the Zhejiang Province Undergraduate Innovation and Entrepreneurship Training Program (S202110337116).

References

1. Adam, M., Wessel, M., Benlian, A.: AI-based chatbots in customer service and their effects on user compliance. Electron. Mark. **31**(2), 427–445 (2020). https://doi.org/10.1007/s12525-020-00414-7

2. Pantano, E., Pizzi, G.: Forecasting artificial intelligence on online customer assistance: evidence from chatbot patents analysis. J. Retail. Consum. Serv. **55**, 102096 (2020)
3. Brandtzaeg, P.B., Følstad, A.: Chatbots: changing user needs and motivations. Interactions **25**(5), 38–43 (2018)
4. Castelo, N., Bos, M.W., Lehmann, D.R.: Task-dependent algorithm aversion. J. Mark. Res. **56**(5), 809–825 (2019)
5. Gnewuch, U., Morana, S., Maedche, A.: Towards designing cooperative and social conversational agents for customer service. In: The 38th International Conference on Information Systems, AIS eLibrary (AISeL), Seoul (2017)
6. Sheehan, B., Jin, H.S., Gottlieb, U.: Customer service chatbots: anthropomorphism and adoption. J. Bus. Res. **115**, 14–24 (2020)
7. Ashfaq, M., Yun, J., Yu, S., Loureiro, S.M.C.: I, Chatbot: modeling the determinants of users' satisfaction and continuance intention of AI-powered service agents. Telematics Inform. **54**, 101473 (2020)
8. Luo, X., Tong, S., Fang, Z., Qu, Z.: Frontiers: machines vs. humans: the impact of artificial intelligence chatbot disclosure on customer purchases. Mark. Sci. **38**(6), 937–947 (2019)
9. Krohn, F.B.: A generational approach to using emoticons as nonverbal communication. J. Tech. Writ. Commun. **34**(4), 321–328 (2004)
10. Hurwitz, S.D., Miron, M.S., Johnson, B.T.: Source credibility and the language of expert testimony1. J. Appl. Soc. Psychol. **22**(24), 1909–1939 (1992)
11. Rafaeli, A., et al.: The future of frontline research: invited commentaries. J. Serv. Res. **20**(1), 91–99 (2017)
12. van Doorn, J., et al.: Domo Arigato Mr. Roboto: emergence of automated social presence in organizational frontlines and customers' service experiences. J. Serv. Res. **20**(1), 43–58 (2017)
13. Gelbrich, K., Hagel, J., Orsingher, C.: Emotional support from a digital assistant in technology-mediated services: effects on customer satisfaction and behavioral persistence. Int. J. Res. Mark. **38**(1), 176–193 (2021)
14. Chung, M., Ko, E., Joung, H., Kim, S.J.: Chatbot e-service and customer satisfaction regarding luxury brands. J. Bus. Res. **117**, 587–595 (2020)
15. Følstad, A., Nordheim, C.B., Bjørkli, C.A.: What makes users trust a chatbot for customer service? an exploratory interview study. In: Bodrunova, S.S. (ed.) INSCI 2018. LNCS, vol. 11193, pp. 194–208. Springer, Cham (2018). https://doi.org/10.1007/978-3-030-01437-7_16
16. Nass, C., Fogg, B.J., Moon, Y.: Can computers be teammates? Int. J. Hum Comput Stud. **45**(6), 669–678 (1996)
17. Nass, C., Moon, Y.: Machines and mindlessness: social responses to computers. J. Soc. Issues **56**(1), 81–103 (2000)
18. Ho, A., Hancock, J., Miner, A.S.: Psychological, relational, and emotional effects of self-disclosure after conversations with a chatbot. J. Commun. **68**(4), 712–733 (2018)
19. Lee, S.A., Liang, Y.: Robotic foot-in-the-door: using sequential-request persuasive strategies in human-robot interaction. Comput. Hum. Behav. **90**, 351–356 (2019)
20. Srinivasan, V., Takayama, L.: Help me please: robot politeness strategies for soliciting help from humans. In: Proceedings of the 2016 CHI Conference on Human Factors in Computing Systems, pp. 4945–4955. Association for Computing Machinery, San Jose (2016)
21. Araujo, T.: Living up to the chatbot hype: the influence of anthropomorphic design cues and communicative agency framing on conversational agent and company perceptions. Comput. Hum. Behav. **85**, 183–189 (2018)
22. Pelau, C., Dabija, D.-C., Ene, I.: What makes an AI device human-like? the role of interaction quality, empathy and perceived psychological anthropomorphic characteristics in the acceptance of artificial intelligence in the service industry. Comput. Hum. Behav. **122**, 106855 (2021)

23. Xu, K., Lombard, M.: Persuasive computing: feeling peer pressure from multiple computer agents. Comput. Hum. Behav. **74**, 152–162 (2017)
24. Hatfield, E., Bensman, L., Thornton, P.D., Rapson, R.L.: New perspectives on emotional contagion: a review of classic and recent research on facial mimicry and contagion. Interpersona Int. J. Pers. Relationships **8**(2), 159–179 (2014)
25. Rymarczyk, K., Żurawski, Ł., Jankowiak-Siuda, K., Szatkowska, I.: Empathy in facial mimicry of fear and disgust: simultaneous EMG-fMRI recordings during observation of static and dynamic facial expressions. Front. Psychol. **10**, 701 (2019)
26. Appel, M., Izydorczyk, D., Weber, S., Mara, M., Lischetzke, T.: The uncanny of mind in a machine: humanoid robots as tools, agents, and experiencers. Comput. Hum. Behav. **102**, 274–286 (2020)
27. Skovholt, K., Grønning, A., Kankaanranta, A.: The communicative functions of emoticons in workplace E-Mails::-)*. J. Comput.-Mediat. Commun. **19**(4), 780–797 (2014)
28. Cherbonnier, A., Michinov, N.: The recognition of emotions beyond facial expressions: comparing emoticons specifically designed to convey basic emotions with other modes of expression. Comput. Hum. Behav. **118**, 106689 (2021)
29. Cuddy, A.J.C., Glick, P., Beninger, A.: The dynamics of warmth and competence judgments, and their outcomes in organizations. Res. Organ. Behav. **31**, 73–98 (2011)
30. Clokie, T.L., Fourie, E.: Graduate employability and communication competence: are undergraduates taught relevant skills? Bus. Prof. Commun. Q. **79**(4), 442–463 (2016)
31. Følstad, A., Skjuve, M.: Chatbots for customer service: user experience and motivation. In: Proceedings of the 1st International Conference on Conversational User Interfaces, pp. 1–9. Association for Computing Machinery, Dublin (2019)
32. Huang, D.-H., Chueh, H.-E.: Chatbot usage intention analysis: veterinary consultation. J. Innov. Knowl. **6**(3), 135–144 (2021)
33. Vos, M.: Communication quality and added value: a measurement instrument for municipalities. J. Commun. Manag. **13**(4), 362–377 (2009)
34. Yuan, C.L., Kim, J., Kim, S.J.: Parasocial relationship effects on customer equity in the social media context. J. Bus. Res. **69**(9), 3795–3803 (2016)
35. Mohr, J.J., Sohi, R.S.: Communication flows in distribution channels: impact on assessments of communication quality and satisfaction. J. Retail. **71**(4), 393–415 (1995)
36. Kim, S., Park, G., Lee, Y., Choi, S.: Customer emotions and their triggers in luxury retail: understanding the effects of customer emotions before and after entering a luxury shop. J. Bus. Res. **69**(12), 5809–5818 (2016)
37. Burgoon, M., Miller, G.R.: An expectancy interpretation of language and persuasion. In: Giles, H., Clair, R.N. (eds.) Recent Advances in Language, Communication, and Social Psychology, pp. 199–229. Routledge, London (2018)
38. Song, M., Xing, X., Duan, Y., Cohen, J., Mou, J.: Will artificial intelligence replace human customer service? the impact of communication quality and privacy risks on adoption intention. J. Retail. Consum. Serv. **66**, 102900 (2022)
39. Smith, N.A., Martinez, L.R., Sabat, I.E.: Weight and gender in service jobs: the importance of warmth in predicting customer satisfaction. Cornell Hosp. Q. **57**(3), 314–328 (2016)
40. Habel, J., Alavi, S., Pick, D.: When serving customers includes correcting them: understanding the ambivalent effects of enforcing service rules. Int. J. Res. Mark. **34**(4), 919–941 (2017)
41. Babbar, S., Koufteros, X.: The human element in airline service quality: contact personnel and the customer. Int. J. Oper. Prod. Manag. **28**(9), 804–830 (2008)
42. Čaić, M., Odekerken-Schröder, G., Mahr, D.: Service robots: value co-creation and co-destruction in elderly care networks. J. Serv. Manag. **29**(2), 178–205 (2018)

43. Saini, A.K., Khatri, P., Raina, K.: Towards understanding preference of use of emoticons for effective online communication and promotion: a study of national capital region of Delhi, India. In: Saini, A.K., Nayak, A.K., Vyas, R.K. (eds.) ICT Based Innovations. AISC, vol. 653, pp. 219–231. Springer, Singapore (2018). https://doi.org/10.1007/978-981-10-6602-3_22
44. Lin, X., Featherman, M., Sarker, S.: Understanding factors affecting users' social networking site continuance: a gender difference perspective. Inf. Manag. **54**(3), 383–395 (2017)
45. Bernritter, S.F., Verlegh, P.W.J., Smit, E.G.: Why nonprofits are easier to endorse on social media: the roles of warmth and brand symbolism. J. Interact. Mark. **33**, 27–42 (2016)
46. Gao, Y., Mattila, A.S.: Improving consumer satisfaction in green hotels: the roles of perceived warmth, perceived competence, and CSR motive. Int. J. Hosp. Manag. **42**, 20–31 (2014)
47. Lepthien, A., Papies, D., Clement, M., Melnyk, V.: The ugly side of customer management – consumer reactions to firm-initiated contract terminations. Int. J. Res. Mark. **34**(4), 829–850 (2017)
48. Li, X., Chan, K.W., Kim, S.: Service with emoticons: how customers interpret employee use of emoticons in online service encounters. J. Cons. Res. **45**(5), 973–987 (2018)
49. Li, H., Jain, S., Kannan, P.K.: Optimal design of free samples for digital products and services. J. Mark. Res. **56**(3), 419–438 (2019)
50. Huang, R., Ha, S.: The effects of warmth-oriented and competence-oriented service recovery messages on observers on online platforms. J. Bus. Res. **121**, 616–627 (2020)
51. Hair, J.F., Ringle, C.M., Sarstedt, M.: PLS-SEM: indeed a silver bullet. J. Mark. Theory Pract. **19**(2), 139–152 (2011)
52. Henseler, J., Hubona, G., Ray, P.A.: Using PLS path modeling in new technology research: updated guidelines. Ind. Manag. Data Syst. **116**(1), 2–20 (2016)
53. Barclay, D., Higgins, C., Thompson, R.: The partial least squares (PLS) approach to casual modeling: personal computer adoption and use as an illustration. Technol. Stud. Spec. Issues Res. Methodol. **2**(2), 285–309 (1995)
54. Chin, W.W., Newsted, P.R.: Structural equation modeling analysis with small samples using partial least squares. In: Hoyle, R. (ed.) Statistical strategies for small sample research, pp. 307–341. Sage Publication, Beverly Hills, CA (1999)
55. Fornell, C., Larcker, D.F.: Evaluating structural equation models with unobservable variables and measurement error. J. Mark. Res. **18**(1), 39–50 (1981)
56. Hair, J.F., Sarstedt, M., Ringle, C.M., Mena, J.A.: An assessment of the use of partial least squares structural equation modeling in marketing research. J. Acad. Mark. Sci. **40**(3), 414–433 (2012)

AI for Speech and Text Analysis

Misinformation in Machine Translation: Error Categories and Levels of Recognition Difficulty

Ka Wai Lee[1(✉)] and Ming Qian[2]

[1] University of Illinois at Urbana Champaign, Champaign, IL, USA
kawaiwl2@illinois.edu
[2] Peraton Labs, Basking Ridge, NJ, USA

Abstract. Extensive research has been done on typologies of machine translation(MT) errors, but one subset of mistranslation—misinformation—is relatively understudied. Unlike other types of mistranslation, misinformation does not necessarily affect the readability or coherence of the translation, but will inhibit target readers from accessing the accurate information presented in the source text. It is unreasonable to expect post-editors(PE) to devote the equivalent levels of time and effort on the MT pre-translated text as in traditional translation projects, given that PE tasks have relatively lower pay but identical, if not tighter, deadlines. To gain more understanding on the concept of misinformation with the aim to improve the efficiency and accuracy of post-editors' work, this study analyzed four English to Chinese MT texts to categorize the misinformation instances, observe distribution patterns of error types, and evaluate their levels of recognition difficulty. It was observed that the highest number of misinformation instances fell into the category of polysemy/named-entity errors, attributing to around half of all misinformation instances. The second most common misinformation category is the non-equivalent rhetoric/idiomatic expression. To help post-editors identify the hard-to-recognize misinformation, we propose three different approaches: (1) use interactive MT platforms or CAT tools that can provide alternative translation suggestions; (2) compare MT results generated by multiple MT tools, as the discrepancies in translations can alert post-editors of potential misinformation; (3) compare the original source text with the back translation result of MT to identify non-equivalent rhetorical/idiomatic expressions.

Keywords: Machine translation · Misinformation · Post-editing · Mistranslation · Product-based analysis · Machine translation platform · Back translation · Interactive platform · Human-machine collaboration · Human-machine interaction

1 Introduction

Mistranslation comes in various categories, it may affect the target text's readability, coherence, or accuracy. Machine translation (MT) researchers have been putting extensive efforts in categorizing and analyzing MT mistranslation errors in order to understand

H. Degen and S. Ntoa (Eds.): HCII 2022, LNAI 13336, pp. 533–545, 2022.
https://doi.org/10.1007/978-3-031-05643-7_34

how to further improve the quality of MT. Misinformation, on the other hand, is a subset of mistranslation that is less studied. In contrast to mistranslation, misinformation does not necessarily affect the readability or coherence of the translation. However, it presents inaccurate information regardless of translators' or post-editors' intent to mislead. It inhibits the target text (TT) readers from obtaining the same information as the source text (ST) readers. To clearly illustrate the difference between mistranslation and misinformation, below is an example from one of our analyzed MT texts.

ST: …the only tools we have that are as *big and powerful* as Mother Nature…
MT: …我们拥有的唯一与大自然一样强大而强大的工具…
(Back-translation: the only tool we have that is as *powerful and powerful* as nature).

English used a binomial pair "big and powerful" to describe the tools. In Chinese MT, "big" and "powerful" were each translated as "强大" (powerful, strong). This one word can sufficiently represent the full meaning of "big and powerful" of the source text. Thus, the duplication leads to a mistranslation problem in the MT. However, this mistranslation does not inhibit the target readers from obtaining the intended message of the ST. As a result, this is an example of mistranslation, but not misinformation.

In an ideal situation, a text will go through stages of translation, reviewing, and proofreading, ensuring the highest quality of the output. Traditionally, these stages were all performed by human translators. Yet with the advancement of technology, machine translation plus human post-editing has been gaining dominance due to lower cost and higher efficiency. Post-editor's role is to identify and correct the errors in the MT pre-translated text to produce a final target text. Unfortunately, when compared to traditional translation tasks, PE tasks have tighter time schedules and offer lower pay despite its growing demand. As a result, this may lead to lower incentives for the post-editors to devote the same level of cognitive effort and time on the MT pre-translated text. Consequently, the misinformation in MT could be overlooked and eventually mislead the target language readers.

To help strike a balance between project remuneration and quality, this study aims to enhance post-editor's efficiency and accuracy through analyzing the MT misinformation categories in English – Chinese translation. Product-based analyses were performed on four machine translated texts, focusing on the less studied topic of misinformation. The study categorized the observed misinformation errors, and graded them according to the level of recognition difficulty by post-editors.

2 Methodology

Google Translate and Youdao Translate were selected for analysis in this study because of their popularity among English-Simplified Chinese language pair users.

According to the Google AI Blog, Google has shifted the mechanism of their MT service in most language pairs, including English – Simplified Chinese, to Google Neural Machine Translation (GNMT) model [1]. It is a model trained using examples of translated sentences and documents typically collected on the public web [2]. The model will treat a complete sentence, instead of just pieces of it, as one unit for translation. This thus allows more in-text context to be considered for more accurate machine translation [3].

On the other hand, Youdao is one of the first, and most popular, companies providing MT services in the Chinese market. Like Google, Youdao Translate also uses the Neural Machine Translation model. The model is trained using parallel corpuses extracted from the Internet, open-sourced dataset, and crowd-sourced tagged data [4]. Youdao Translate was selected in addition to Google as Youdao serves mainly Chinese users as compared to Google, and therefore may have more abundant training data in Simplified Chinese.

Two English – Simplified Chinese bilingual articles were selected from The New York Times (NYT) for this study. The first article is "Want to Save the Earth? We Need a Lot More Elon Musks." (Article 1) with 1415 words, written by Thomas L. Friedman, and Simplified Chinese version translated by Qijiao Jin (晋其角) and Zhai Ming (明斋). The second article is "Welcome to the YOLO Economy" (Article 2) with 1,650 words, written by Kevin Roose, Simplified Chinese version translated by Qijiao Jin (晋其角) and Yan Deng (邓妍). NYT did not specify whether the simplified Chinese versions were fully human translated or if they were post-edited from machine translation.

In our study, the two articles were machine translated by the two selected MT tools – Google Translate and Youdao Translate on their web platforms, generating the four MT texts for our analysis. Due to the 5,000 character limit in both Google and Youdao Translate, the English source texts of the two articles were each split into half before inputting into the two MT tools. The resulting four machine translation outputs were then compared side-by-side with their respective source texts. Two translators analyzed the bi-texts for the search of misinformation instances in the MT, which were then categorized and graded according to their levels of recognition difficulty.

Although it is not certain whether NYT's Chinese translations were fully human-translated or MT post-edited, given the credibility of NYT, we assumed that the Chinese translations were professionally proofread and have the guaranteed standard of quality. Therefore they were still used as the references for machine translation quality comparison.

3 Results

3.1 Misinformation Categories

Category Definition. Extensive research has been done categorizing mistranslation errors with the aim to improve performance of MT. Popović has provided in his article a comprehensive overview of MT error typologies proposed by different researchers for different language pairs [5]. Zhao and Liu [6] have categorized common English-Chinese MT errors into seven categories, namely (1) Wrong choice of word, (2) Missing content word, (3) Incorrect word order, (4) Contradictory to ST, (5) Named entity error, (6) Quantifier and temporal word error, and (7) Other error, for their error analysis on ruled-based and statistic-based MT. Meanwhile, Hsu [7] has categorized the errors into a two-level hierarchy, with the main categories including orthographic, morphological, lexical, semantic, and syntactic errors, while each of these main categories further divided into more specific subcategories (See Fig. 1).

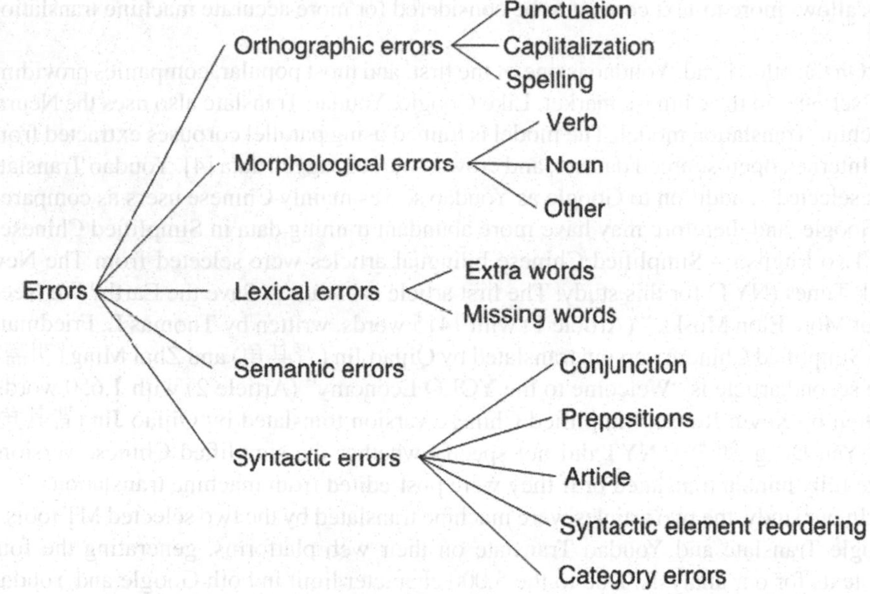

Fig. 1. Machine translation error classification by Hsu (2014). [7]

With reference to the MT mistranslation error categorization done by other researchers, we reformulated the categorization for misinformation in English - Chinese MT with three main categories and seven sub-categories (See Fig. 2).

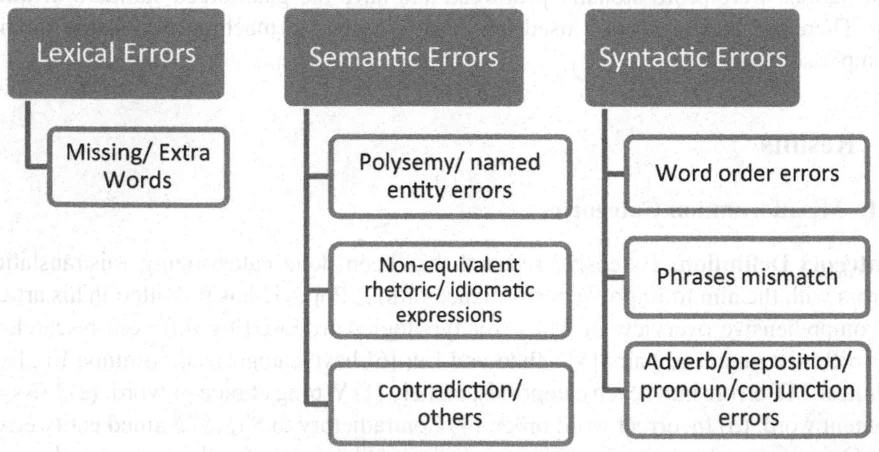

Fig. 2. Misinformation errors categorization.

Below listed are the examples found in the four MT texts illustrating each misinformation subcategory.

Lexical Error – Missing Words/Extra Words
ST: *It has become challenging to continue to work for companies who operate business as usual, without taking into account how* our lives have changed overnight.
MT: 我们的生活在一夜之间发生了变化。
(Back Translation: Our lives have changed overnight.)
Misinformation: The first part of the sentence is omitted by MT.

Semantic Error – Polysemy error
ST: "Capitalism has produced enormous wealth, but in part that's because it has been able to treat nature as self-replenishing, hyper-abundant and *free*,"…
MT: "资本主义创造了巨大的财富,但部分原因是它能够将自然视为自我补充、极度丰富和*自由*"…
Misinformation: MT mistranslated "*Free*" as in "not bound, confined, or detained by force", instead of "not costing or charging anything".

Semantic Error – Named entity error
ST: *Planet's* satellites plus AI, Marshall explained, can track a country's trees, farmlands, coral reefs, coastal mangroves and smokestack emissions…
MT:马歇尔解释说,*行星*的卫星+人工智能可以跟踪一个国家的树木、农田、珊瑚礁、沿海红树林和烟囱排放.
Misinformation: *Planet* in ST referred to "Planet.com", a named entity mentioned earlier in the article. MT misinterpreted it as common noun.

Semantic Error – Non-equivalent rhetoric/idiomatic expressions
ST:…*millions* of Americans are still grieving the loss of jobs and loved ones. (Article 2).
MT:…*数百万*美国人仍在为失去工作和亲人而悲痛。
(Back Translation: *Several millions of* Americans are still grieving the loss of jobs and loved ones).
Misinformation: English and Chinese have different numerical place value systems. "Million" in English covers numbers in the range of one million to hundred million, but the Chinese MT term "百万" back translates to cover numbers from one to nine million only. English "millions of" can also be the rhetorical way of saying "a large number of". The Chinese MT failed to provide an accurate translation. Due to non-equivalence in number system, Chinese translation of this expression does not necessarily have to provide any exact number, rather a metaphorical chengyu (Chinese idiom) "成千上万" which presents the meaning of "numerous, or a huge number" would be more appropriate.

Semantic Error – Contradiction/Misc
ST: …but that we can't *burden people* with a carbon tax or a gasoline tax to slow global warming.
MT:…但我们不能通过征收碳排放税或汽油税来*减轻人们的负担*来减缓全球变暖。
(Back Translation: …but that we can't impose a carbon tax or a gasoline tax to *lessen people's burden* to slow global warming.)

Misinformation: The goal of the tax is to burden people, so as to achieve the purpose of slowing global warming, but MT produced a contradictory translation -- "lessen people's burden."

Syntactic errors – Problematic word order
ST: …more than 40 percent of workers globally were considering leaving their jobs *this year*.
MT: …今年全球超过 40% 的员工正在考虑离职。
(Back Translation: …*this year* more than 40 percent of workers globally is considering leaving their jobs.)
Misinformation: The position of "今年" (this year) in the MT altered the meaning of the ST. In ST, "this year" is describing the action of "leaving their jobs"; Whereas in MT, "this year" describes the action "consider", but the workers' plan of quitting does not necessarily have to be within the current year.

Syntactic errors – Phrases mismatch
ST: …or it can stimulate foreign aid or investment in the country or community *protecting its natural resources*.
MT: …或者可以刺激外国援助或投资于该国或社区, *以保护其自然资源*。
(Back Translation: …or it can stimulate foreign aid or investment in the country or community, *to protect its natural resources*).
Misinformation: In ST "protecting its natural resources" is the verb phrase describing the "country or community" where foreign aid and investment may be stimulated. In MT, "protecting its natural resources" was misinterpreted as the purpose of the "foreign aid or investment".

Syntactic errors – Adverb, preposition, pronoun or conjunction errors
ST: …It feels like we've been so locked into careers for the past decade, and this is our opportunity to switch *it* up.
MT: …感觉过去 10 年我们一直被职业所束缚, 现在是我们改变职业的机会。
(Back translation: It feels like we have been locked into careers in the past 10 years, now is our opportunity to change our *career*.)
Misinformation: The pronoun "it" in "switch it up" in ST referred to the situation where the narrator felt being locked into careers. The narrator wanted to switch the situation up, instead of switching careers.

Category Distribution. There are in total 150 misinformation instances in the four MT texts. Among which 70 belong to the polysemy/named-entity error category, attributing to nearly half of all misinformation instances, ranking it the most common misinformation error category in our analysis. The second most common category is the non-equivalent rhetoric/idiomatic expressions with 28 errors found in the four MT texts. Third is the category of missing/extra words, with 17 errors (Table 1).

Table 1. Distribution summary of misinformation in all MT texts.

Main category	Sub-category	Number of errors
Lexical	Missing/Extra words	17
Semantic	Polysemy/Named entity	70
	Rhetoric/Idiomatic	28
	Contradiction	5
Syntactic	Word order	9
	Phrase dependency	8
	Adverb/Preposition/Pronoun/Conjunction	13
Total		**150**

Similar distribution patterns can be observed in each MT text. Around half of misinformation errors in each text belong to the category of polysemy/named entity, while the other half scatter across the remaining categories. In three of the MT texts, (i.e. Google translated article 1, Google translated article 2 and Youdao translated article 2), non-equivalent rhetoric/idiomatic expressions rank second, accounting for 1/5 of misinformation instances in respective texts.

When comparing between the two MT tools, texts translated by Google Translate have a total of 80 misinformation errors and that by Youdao Translate have 70. Among these misinformation instances, 21 are translated in the same way by the two MT tools and belong to the same misinformation category, all other misinformation instances are either occurring in different parts of the text, translated differently, or belonging to different misinformation categories (Table 2).

Table 2. Distribution of misinformation in the four MT texts.

		Article 1		Article 2	
Misinformation categories		Google	Youdao	Google	Youdao
Lexical	Missing/Extra words	3	7	5	2
Semantic	Polysemy/Named entity	13	18	24	15
	Rhetoric/Idiomatic	7	4	9	8
	Contradiction	0	1	2	2
Syntactic	Word order	3	0	4	2
	Phrase dependency	3	3	0	2
	Adverb/Preposition/Pronoun/Conjunction	4	5	3	1
Total		**33**	**38**	**47**	**32**

3.2 Levels of Difficulty in Misinformation Recognition

We have also evaluated the levels of difficulty in recognizing each instance of misinformation in the four MT articles. Based on the evaluation time, cognitive effort, cultural and linguistic awareness required of the post-editors, three levels of difficulties are defined.

A) *Easy* -- a post-editor can recognize the error by reading the MT alone.
B) *Moderate* -- a post-editor can recognize the error by comparing MT against the source text.
C) *Hard* -- a post-editor may not be able to detect the error by comparing MT against the source text. Extra-linguistics elements, for example, cultural or non-explicit meaning, is implied in the source text. Post-editors' extra efforts or awareness are required to recognize the misinformation error.

In all four MT texts, half of the misinformation instances have moderate level of recognition difficulty. Approximately 1/4 are easy to recognize, while the remaining 1/4 comparatively harder to recognize, requiring additional efforts or cultural and linguistic knowledge of post-editors. These harder-to-recognize misinformation errors usually belong to the categories of polysemy/named-entity and rhetoric/idiomatic expressions (Figs. 3, 4, 5 and 6).

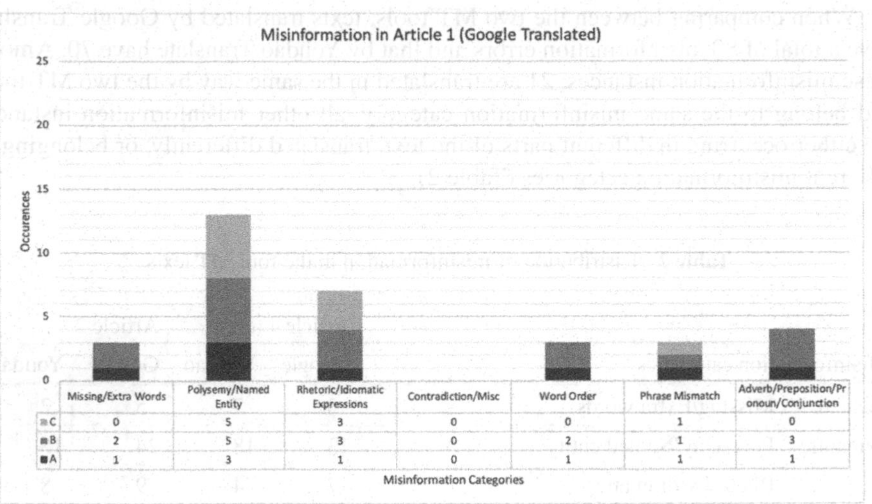

Fig. 3. Levels of difficulty in recognizing misinformation in Google translated Article 1

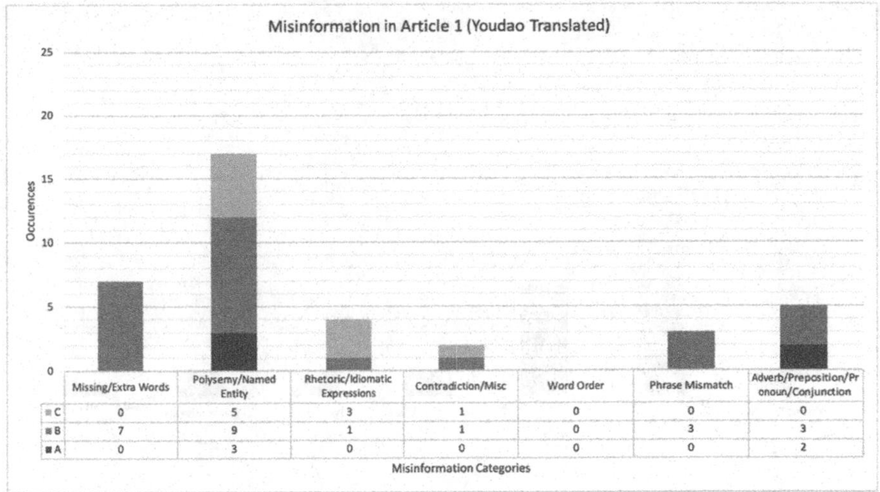

Fig. 4. Levels of difficulty in recognizing misinformation in Youdao translated Article 1

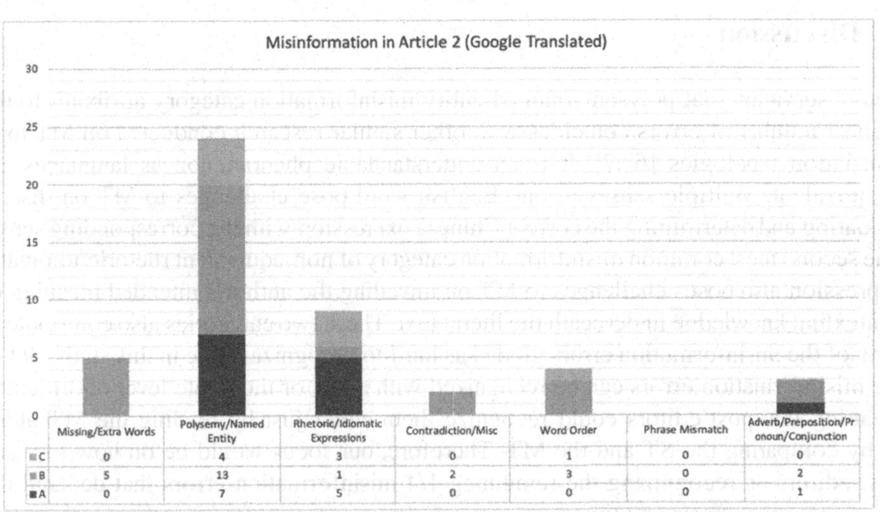

Fig. 5. Levels of difficulty in recognizing misinformation in Google translated Article 2

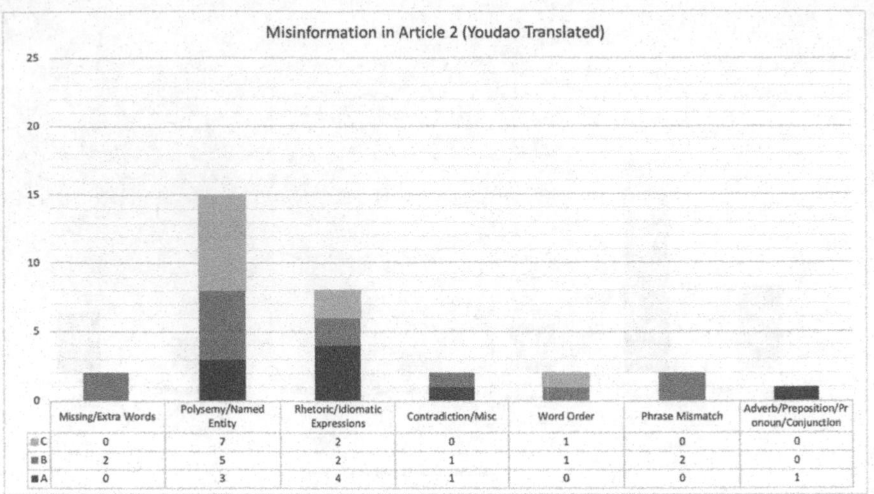

Fig. 6. Levels of difficulty in recognizing misinformation in Youdao translated Article 2

4 Discussion

The observation that polysemy/named-entity misinformation category attributes to the highest number of errors coincides with other similar research conducted on MT mistranslation typologies [6, 7]. It is an understandable phenomenon as languages are inequivalent. Multiple senses in one English word pose challenges to MT on disambiguating and determining the correct Chinese expression with the corresponding sense. The second most common misinformation category of non-equivalent rhetoric/idiomatic expression also poses challenges to MT on unveiling the author's intended meaning or contextual knowledge underneath the literal text. These two categories also contribute to 90% of the misinformation errors graded as hard-to-recognize. Here in this study, 3/4 of the misinformation errors can be recognized with a low or moderate level of difficulty, meaning that post-editors could recognize them either just by reading the MT alone or by comparing the ST and the MT. Therefore, our focus would be on how to assist post-editors on recognizing the remaining 1/4 misinformation errors that demand the most cognitive efforts and time.

If post-editors could use the help of an interactive MT platform providing alternative MT suggestions on the active segment, or words that tend to have ambiguous senses, post-editors can be alerted to evaluate the multiple senses of a polysemous word or proper noun, or the alternative meaning of a phrase (Fig. 7).

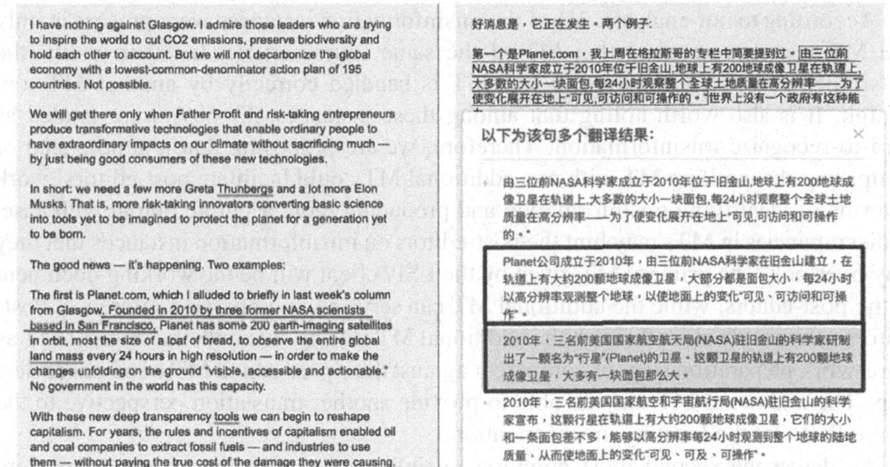
I have nothing against Glasgow. I admire those leaders who are trying to inspire the world to cut CO2 emissions, preserve biodiversity and hold each other to account. But we will not decarbonize the global economy with a lowest-common-denominator action plan of 195 countries. Not possible.
We will get there only when Father Profit and risk-taking entrepreneurs produce transformative technologies that enable ordinary people to have extraordinary impacts on our climate without sacrificing much — by just being good consumers of these new technologies.
In short: we need a few more Greta Thunbergs and a lot more Elon Musks. That is, more risk-taking innovators converting basic science into tools yet to be imagined to protect the planet for a generation yet to be born.
The good news — it's happening. Two examples:
The first is Planet.com, which I alluded to briefly in last week's column from Glasgow. Founded in 2010 by three former NASA scientists based in San Francisco, Planet has some 200 earth-imaging satellites in orbit, most the size of a loaf of bread, to observe the entire global land mass every 24 hours in high resolution — in order to make the changes unfolding on the ground "visible, accessible and actionable." No government in the world has this capacity.
With these new deep transparency tools we can begin to reshape capitalism. For years, the rules and incentives of capitalism enabled oil and coal companies to extract fossil fuels — and industries to use them — without paying the true cost of the damage they were causing.
好消息是，它正在发生。两个例子:
第一个是Planet.com，我上周在格拉斯哥的专栏中简要提到过。由三位前NASA科学家成立于2010年位于旧金山,地球上有200地球成像卫星在轨道上,大多数的大小一块面包,每24小时观察整个全球土地质量在高分辨率——为了使变化展开在地上"可见,可访问和可操作的。"世界上没有一个政府有这种能
以下为该句多个翻译结果:
由三位前NASA科学家成立于2010年位于旧金山,地球上有200地球成像卫星在轨道上,大多数的大小一块面包,每24小时观察整个全球土地质量在高分辨率——为了使变化展开在地上"可见,可访问和可操作的。"
Planet公司成立于2010年，由三位前NASA科学家在旧金山建立，在轨道上有大约200颗地球成像卫星，大部分都是面包大小，每24小时以高分辨率观测整个地球，以使地面上的变化"可见、可访问和可操作"。
2010年，三名前美国国家航空航天局(NASA)驻旧金山的科学家研制出了一颗名为"行星"(Planet)的卫星。这颗卫星的轨道上有200颗地球成像卫星，大多有一块面包那么大。
2010年，三名前美国国家航空和宇宙航行局(NASA)驻旧金山的科学家宣布，这颗行星在轨道上有大约200颗地球成像卫星，它们的大小和一条面包差不多，能够以高分辨率每24小时观测到整个地球的陆地质量，从而使地面上的变化"可见、可及、可操作"。

Fig. 7. Example of how alternative translation options can alert post-editors of possible misinformation (Screen captured from Youdao Translate).

In this example, alternative translation provided by the MT can hint post-editor on possible misinformation that could be overlooked.

ST: Founded in 2010 by three former NASA scientists *based in* San Francisco,...
MT-1: Planet公司成立于2010年, 由三位前NASA科学家*在旧金山建立*...
(Back-translation: Planet was established in 2010 *in San Francisco* by three former NASA scientists.)
MT-2: 2010年, 三名前美国国家航空航天局(NASA)*驻旧金山*的科学家研制出了一颗名为"行星"(Planet)的卫星。
(Back-translation: in 2010, three former NASA scientists *based in* San Francisco developed a satellite named "Planet".)

The source text stated that San Francisco is the location where the former NASA scientists were based in. The location of where the company was found was not specifically mentioned. Therefore MT-1 involves misinformation. Meanwhile, despite mistranslating other parts of the sentence, MT-2 correctly conveyed the information that the three scientists, instead of the company, were based in San Francisco. By offering these alternative MT suggestions for post-editors to review, there will be a higher chance that the post-editor can be alerted to possible misinformation. Then, by combining the MT suggestions, post-editors can achieve greater accuracy with minimal effort.

Meanwhile, other freelance post-editors may not have the option to work with such interactive MT platforms or CAT tools that can prompt them for alternative translation options as they post-edit. Instead, they may be handed the source text and a MT pretranslation in static documents. In such a case, we recommend post-editors to obtain additional MT generated by another MT tool, either from the language service providers (LSPs) or the client, or by using the online tools available on the market.

According to our analysis, 2/3 of the misinformation instances were present in only one MT text, but not the other MT of the same source article. In other words, the possibility that misinformation in one MT is handled correctly by another MT tool is high. It is also worth noting that among these instances, 33–60% were graded as hard-to-recognize misinformation. Therefore, we are proposing that a simple step of comparing the working MT with one additional MT could facilitate post-editors' work in terms of identifying misinformation and producing more accurate output with ease, as discrepancies in MTs may hint the post-editors on misinformation instances that they may overlook. The primary MT given by the LSP/ client will be the working document of the post-editors, while the additional MT can serve as a comparison reference. Post-editors can quickly skim through the additional MT side by side with the original MT as a pre-work preparation step, or compare it against their post-edited MT as a final review step. The additional MT may be able to provide another translation perspective to the post-editors for the locating misinformation.

To detect the second most common misinformation category of non-equivalent rhetoric/idiomatic expressions, good insight can be obtained by comparing the ST and the back-translated results. For example:

ST: Millions of Americans…
MT: 数百万美国人。。。。。。
Back-translation of MT: Several millions of Americans

Post-editors can then easily observe that semantic equivalence between the original and back-translated English text in the example is questionable. This could help identify the relatively hard-to-recognized misinformation in rhetorical/ idiomatic expressions when post-editors are in doubt.

5 Conclusion

As misinformation does not necessarily affect the readability or coherence of the text, post-editors reviewing the MT have a higher chance of overlooking misinformation errors when compared to other mistranslation types. Overlooked misinformation will then stay in the published text and become a barrier inhibiting the target readers from accessing the information in the source text. With more companies shifting to the workflow of machine translation plus human post-editing, it is crucial that we understand the categories and distribution of misinformation generated by MT to assist post-editors in accurately and efficiently recognizing and correcting these misinformation errors.

In our product-based analyses conducted on four MT texts, the most common misinformation category observed was the polysemy/named entity error, followed by the category of rhetoric/idiomatic expressions. We recommend several solutions: (1) use an interactive MT platform to provide alternative translation suggestions on selected segments; (2) compare the discrepant results generated by multiple MT tools to alert post-editors on potential misinformation instances. The fused approach should be effective in locating hard-to-recognize misinformation as most misinformation instances observed in our study are present in only one MT; (3) use back translation to clear doubts of post-editors when encountering misinformation involving rhetoric/idiomatic expressions.

While continuous efforts and resources have been devoted into research on perfecting word sense disambiguation for improving performance of machine translation, it is expected that in the immediate future, we will still be depending on human post-editors to locate polysemy/named entity and rhetoric/idiomatic expression misinformation instances, as well as to accurately disambiguate the word sense or underlying meaning of phrases using the context of the text. In the meantime, post-editors need to find an efficient way to locate these misinformation errors with justifiable time and cognitive efforts devoted into the project, when considering their relatively lower pay and tighter project deadlines compared to "traditional" translators. We hope this study will provide insights to post-editors and related stakeholders, as well as to invite further research for a deeper understanding of misinformation in MT.

References

1. Turovsky, B.: Found in translation: more accurate, fluent sentences in Google Translate. Google Blog the Keyword (2016). https://blog.google/products/translate/found-translation-more-accurate-fluent-sentences-google-translate/, Accessed 21 Jan 2022
2. Caswell, I., Liang, B.: Recent advances in google translate. google AI blog (2020). https://ai.googleblog.com/2020/06/recent-advances-in-google-translate.html, Accessed 21 Jan 2022
3. Le, Q.V., Schuster, M.: A neural network for machine translation, at production scale. Google AI Blog (2016). https://ai.googleblog.com/2016/09/a-neural-network-for-machine.html, Accessed 27 Jan 2022
4. 打败两款国际知名翻译引擎。解析网易有道神经机器翻译模型. https://www.jiqizhixin.com/articles/2018-12-25-22, Accessed 27 Jan 2022
5. Popović, M.: Error classification and analysis for machine translation quality assessment. In: Moorkens, J., Castilho, S., Gaspari, F., Doherty, S. (eds.) Translation Quality Assessment. MTTA, vol. 1, pp. 129–158. Springer, Cham (2018). https://doi.org/10.1007/978-3-319-91241-7_7
6. Zhao, H., Liu, Q.: Common error analysis of machine translation output (2016)
7. Hsu, J.: Error classification of machine translation a corpus-based study on Chinese-English patent translation. Stud. Interpretation Transl. **18**, 121–136 (2014)

Transformer-Based Multilingual G2P Converter for E-Learning System

Jueting Liu[1], Chang Ren[1], Yaoxuan Luan[1], Sicheng Li[1], Tianshi Xie[1], Cheryl Seals[1(✉)], and Marisha Speights Atkins[2]

[1] Auburn University, Auburn, AL 36849, USA
{jzl0122,czr0049,yzl0219,szl0072,tzx0019,sealscd}@auburn.edu
[2] Northwestern University, Evanston, IL 60208, USA
marisha.speights@northwestern.edu

Abstract. Phonetic transcription is an approach to represent speech sounds to specific symbols. The most common alphabet we used is the International Phonetic Alphabet (IPA), and the characters in the IPA are phonetic symbols. To support the phonetic transcription process in the phonetic exams of our linguistic E-learning system, we designed a machine translation tool that aims to translate English words to their phonetic formats. This progress can also be expressed as grapheme to phoneme (G2P). The Transformer model has been utilized to develop this G2P module. Also, to improve the functionality of the E-learning system, we trained multiple language models and generated a multilingual G2P translator. Moreover, we evaluated our G2P system by word error rate (WER) and phoneme error rate (PER) with edit distance.

Keywords: E-learning · International phonetic alphabet · Grapheme-to-phoneme · Transformer

1 Introduction

According to the data from UNESCO, nearly 1.6 billion students in more than 190 countries, 94% of the world's student population, were affected by the closure of educational institutions at the peak of the COVID-19 pandemic [1]. The global shift to E-learning or online learning is rapidly increasing in the Internet access area. E-learning is an approach that delivers knowledge or skills remotely and interactively by electrical devices such as smartphones, tablets and laptops. Compared with traditional classroom learning, E-learning can offer students flexible topics or subjects, the interactions with teachers or professors by email or platforms without the restrictions by the physical distance [2].

To support the students and faculty in the Department of Communication Disorders (CMDS), our human-computer interaction (HCI) group designed a linguistic E-learning system aims to provide interactive learning and testing to support the linguistic courses [3,4]. The system is named Automated Phonetic Transcription - the grading tool (APTgt), and this will focus on a critical field

H. Degen and S. Ntoa (Eds.): HCII 2022, LNAI 13336, pp. 546–556, 2022.
https://doi.org/10.1007/978-3-031-05643-7_35

in linguistics: phonetic transcription. The purpose of phonetic transcription is to represent the speech sounds by particular characters; for most languages, phonetic transcription shows the pronunciation as a one-to-one relationship between sounds and symbols more accurately than the language's orthography. The most commonly used character in this approach is the International Phonetic Alphabet (IPA) (see Fig. 1), and this is also what we used in our system.

APTgt supports teacher creation of interactive phonetic exams intended to train the students' phonetic transcription skills. Each question is a pronunciation of one word or phrase. The teacher uploads an audio file and needs to pre-store the correct answer. During the exam, students will spell the pronunciation as the answer by the specific IPA keyboard (see Fig. 1) [5]. The system will automatically compare the pre-stored teacher solution and the student submitted answer with the system calculating the difference between the by the Levenshtein distance [4].

Fig. 1. The IPA keyboard used for generating phonetic transcription exams

The teachers are required to pre-input the correct phonetic words corresponding to the question [4]. For example, if a teacher wants to utilize the phonetic format of word **relate** as a question, he/she needs to upload the audio file of the word **relate** and also input **rɪˈleɪt** as the answer. However, in general cogitation, the process of creating should be this (see Fig. 2).

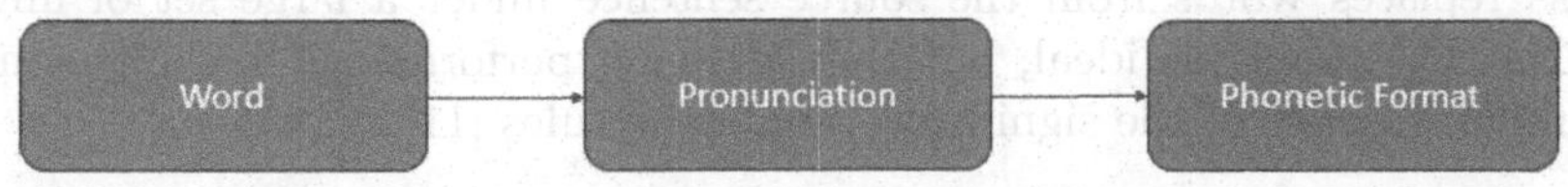

Fig. 2. The process of generating phonetic words from normal English words

For the majority of the teachers, generating the phonetic words in the APTgt exams needs to select English words and then translate these them into their phonetic format. To help teachers better formulate answers (phonetic words) from original English words, we proposed a neural machine translator (NMT) that aims to translate English words to their phonetic format [6]. This progress is called grapheme to phoneme (G2P) conversion [7]. G2P conversion is a letter-to-sound task, which converts a sequence of letters to their pronunciations. This paper selected the Transformer, a robust deep learning architecture for NLP problems, to build our G2P neural machine translator. To evaluate the transformer-based NMT, we used phoneme error rate (PER) and word error rate (WER) [8] to identify the accuracy. In past research, Hidden Markov Models had been used for G2P conversion, and this research reached 92.8% and 61.08% accuracy respectively for phoneme and word accuracy [9]. The Long Short Term Memory (LSTM) approach by Kanishka Rao increases the WER to 21.3% [10].

Multilingual conversion is also influential in linguistic courses, extending our E-learning system's functionality and enhancing system features. We also trained a Spanish model and French language models and combined them as a multilingual G2P converter.

2 Background

2.1 Grapheme-to-Phoneme

In linguistics, a grapheme is the smallest unit of a written language, while a phoneme is the smallest unit of speech sound. A grapheme-to-phoneme system is an implement that converts a spelled out word to its phonetic format (a sequence of IPA symbols). The process of G2P can be regarded as a procedure of machine translating from one language to another [7].

2.2 Machine Translation (MT)

Machine translation is a sub-subject of computational linguistics that uses computers to translate one natural language to another. It was first introduced in the 1950s and significantly developed in the past few decades [6].

Rule-Based Machine Translation. The rule-based machine translation is an MT system based on linguistic rules. The source and target languages are retrieved from enormous dictionaries with complex grammar. The translation process replaces words from the source sentence under a large set of linguistic rules. The theory is ideal, but the satisfying performance is challenging to implement because of the significant number of rules [11].

Statistical Machine Translation. Unlike the rule-based machine translation, statistical machine translation(SMT) utilizes the statistical translation models from the bilingual text corpus to build the system. Concretely, SMT finds the words with the same meanings from the corpus by statistics. It was the most widely used translation system before the introduction of neural machine translation (NMT). Compared with the rule-based machine translation, building a statistical model is simple, but the problem is that some minor languages do not have a text corpus [11].

Neural Machine Translation. With the development of Artificial Intelligence and Deep Learning in NLP problems. Neural Machine Translation (NMT) is a novel approach that applies a translation process by an artificial neural network predicting the likelihood of the sequence of words. The encoder and decoder are critical components of the NMT; the encoder will encode the input sequence into a fixed-length vector, while the decode aims to decode the vector and predict the output. There are three conventional encoders and decoders: convolutional neural network (CNN), recurrent neural network (RNN), and the Transformer [11].

3 Method

3.1 International Phonetic Alphabet

There are only 26 letters in the English language, but about 44 unique sounds. These speech sounds are also known as phonemes [5]. The International Phonetic Alphabet (IPA), derived from Latin script, is used by linguists, foreign language students, and Text-to-Speech (TTS) systems to represent these phonemes. Although CMU pronouncing dictionary (CMUDict) [12], an open-source pronouncing dictionary provides a mapping for English words in North American pronunciations is popular in multiply G2P systems. We desired to develop the phonetic exams based on the IPA keyboard and keep the potential to extend more languages. To support this effort, we built our GP2 system based upon the IPA dictionary instead of CMUDict to have broader language support, and Table 1 gives a comparison between the IPA symbols and CMUDict.

Table 1. CMUDict and IPA symbols

Written format	CMUDict	IPA symbols
eat	IY T	it
confirm	K AH N F ER M	kən'fɜrm
minute	M IH N AH T	'minət
quick	K W IH K	kwik
maker	M EY K ER	'meɪker
relate	R IH L EY T	rɪ'leɪt

3.2 Transformer

The neural machine translation is an end-to-end learning approach for automated translation, and it utilizes the artificial neural network to predict the likelihood of a sequence of words. In the NMT field, speech recognition field and G2P field, recurrent neural networks structures have played an essential role in the last few years. RNNs allow previous outputs to be used as inputs while having hidden states. In RNN, the information cycles through a loop. To make a decision, the network needs to consider the current input and what it learned from the input previously received.

There are still issues for RNN structures:

1) The RNN structure needs to process the data in sequence without hierarchy, the data from earlier layers may be eliminated by time. It can not remember anything that happened in the past layers.
2) The RNN structure is sequential; each hidden state requires the output of the previous layer. This will significantly reduce the efficiency of the GPU since the GPU has enormous computation power, but it has to wait for the data from the network.

To avoid the defects of RNN models, we applied the Transformer model to build the G2P converter in this work. In 2017, a novel paper, 'Attention Is All You Need' illustrates another encoder-decoder model [13], the Transformer with the attention mechanism. Without using any recurrent layers, the self-attention mechanism plays an important role in the Transformer model. The main idea for attention is that it allows the decoder to review the complete input and extract the necessary information for following the decoding.

The Transformer is organized by self-attention and a fully-connected layer for both encoder and decoder (See Fig. 3). Each encoder is composed of two major elements: the self-attention mechanism (Multi-head attention) and feed forward layer. The decoder generally consists of two multi-head attention mechanisms and one feed forward layer. The encoder maps input sequences into attention-based representations, while the decoder then takes the continuous representations and generates the output [13].

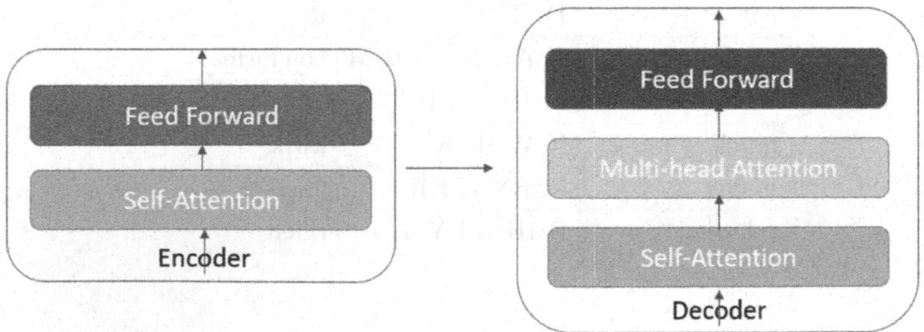

Fig. 3. Brief encoder and decoder structure in transformer

The attention adopted in the transformer is a scale dot-product attention mechanism. It is an attention mechanism where the dot products are scaled down by $\sqrt{d_k}$. **Query Q** represents a vector word, **keys K** are all other words in the sequence and **value V** represents the vector of the word [13] (Fig. 4).

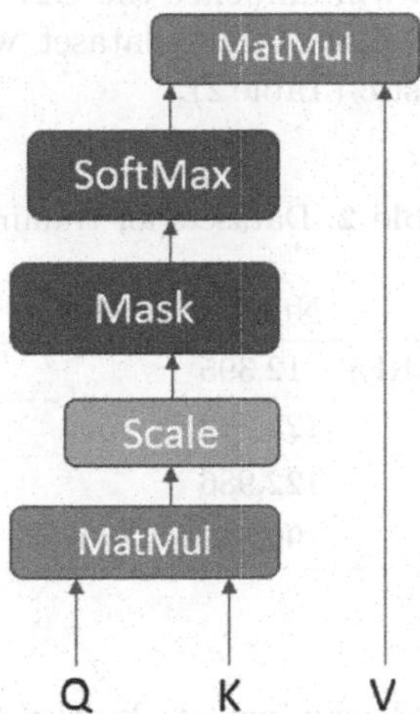

Fig. 4. Scaled dot-product attention

The attention function can be represented as:

$$Attention(Q, K, V) = softmax(\frac{QK^T}{\sqrt{d_k}})V$$

The multi-head attention mechanism is a linear projection of Q, K, V in h times. The idea of multi-head attention is to compute the scale dot-product attention h times in parallel, concatenate the results and project the concatenation to produce the result. Each head of the multi-head attention extracts the specific representation, which allows the whole system to receive information from different representation subspaces [13].

The multi-head attention function:

$$multihead(Q, K, V) = concat(head_1, ..., head_n)W^O$$

where

$$head_i = attention(QW_i^Q, KW_i^K, VW_i^V)$$

W_i^Q, W_i^K, W_i^V are the respective weight matrices calculated from Q, K and V.

4 Experiment

Data Preparation. In order to build a multilingual G2P system, we prepared four datasets for training: two English-IPA datasets, one French-IPA dataset, and one Spanish-IPA dataset. First two English-IPA datasets were used to investigate how the size of the data will influence the G2P systems' performance, and the French-IPA dataset and Spanish-IPA dataset were utilized to inspect the feasibility of the multi-linguistic (Table 2).

Table 2. Datasets for training

Dataset	Number of pairs of words	For validation
English-IPA (CET6+GRE)	12,395	20%
English-IPA (Full)	125,912	20%
French-IPA	122,986	20%
Spanish-IPA	99,315	20%

Experiment. We did several training sets by the NVDIA Tesla P100 graphic card with different parameters. We employed a six layers Transformer model and Adam optimizer in Keras with a learning rate of 0.0001. The batch size for the small English-IPA dictionary was 64 and 128 for the rest of the datasets.

5 Result and Evaluation

Since our system focuses on the single word or phrases conversion, we used phoneme error rate (PER) and word error rate (WER) to evaluate the result of our G2P system. The PER is the distance between two phonetic words calculated by the edit distance divided by the total number of phonemes, and the WER is a standard parameter for measuring the accuracy in the Automatic Speech Recognition(ASR) system [8]. The calculation of WER is

$$WER = \frac{S + D + I}{N}$$

where S is the number of Substitutions, D is the number of Deletions, I is the number of Insertions, and N is the number of words.

5.1 English-IPA (CET6+GRE) Vs English-IPA (Full)

For the English-IPA model, we applied two dictionaries. One dictionary is extracted from CET6 and GRE test, which contains a total of 12,395 pairs of words; another one is an entire English-IPA dictionary that includes 125,912 pairs of words (Figs. 5 and 6).

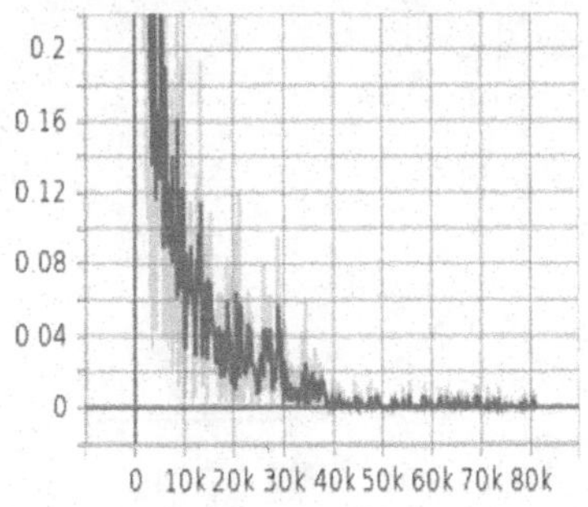

Fig. 5. Loss of English-IPA (CET6+GRE)

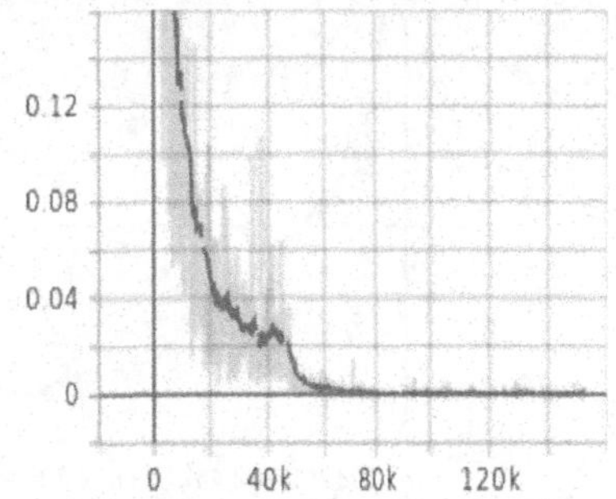

Fig. 6. Loss of English-IPA (Full)

It took 220 epochs training for English-IPA (CET6+GRE) with the batch size 64 and 190 epochs for English-IPA (Full) with the same batch size. The PER and WER for the smaller dataset is about 10.7% (see Fig. 7) and 38% (see Fig. 8). The PER for the full English-IPA dictionary is 2.6% (see Fig. 7) and WER is 11.43% (see Fig. 8).

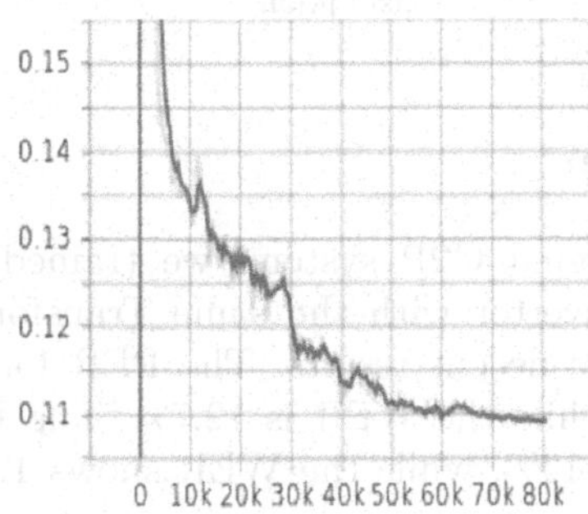

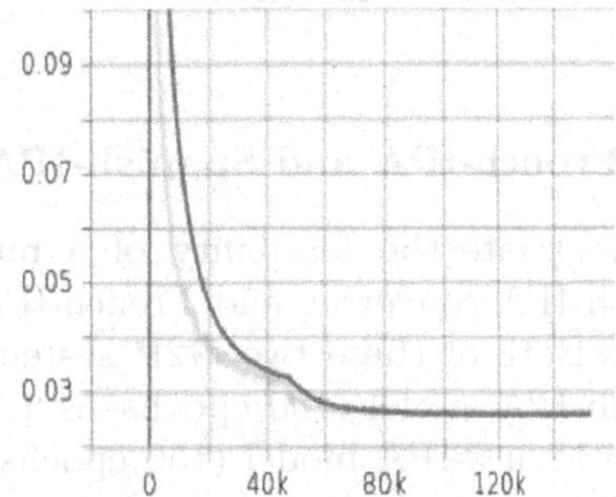

Fig. 7. The PER for two English-IPA dictionaries

The result shows that with the larger dataset, the model will give higher translation accuracy. The result of the English-IPA (full) model (11.4% WER) is acceptable in a G2P system. Table 3 illustrates some samples converted from English words to phoneme words.

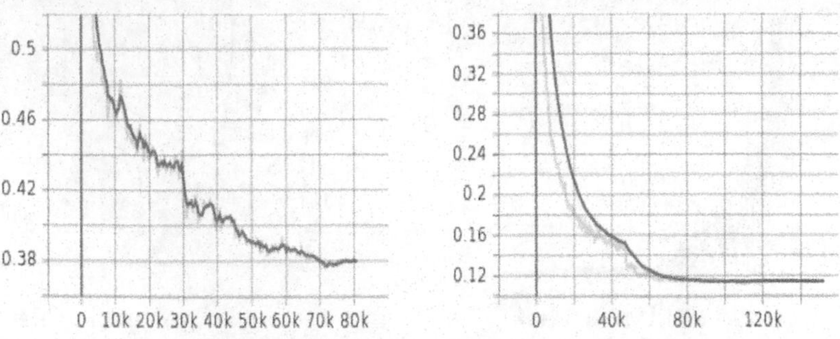

Fig. 8. The WER for two English-IPA dictionaries

Table 3. Samples for English G2P system

English words	Generated phoneme from G2P system	Correct Phoneme words
displeasure	dɪspl'ɛʒə	dɪspl'ʒə
buoyant	b'ɔɪənt	b'ɔɪənt
immortal	ɪm'ɔːtəl	ɪm'ɔːtəl
journeyman	dʒ'ːnɪmən	dʒ'ɜːnɪmən
phrasebook	fr'eɪzbʊk	fr'eɪzbʊk
distinction	dɪst'ɪŋkʃən	dɪst'ɪŋkʃən

5.2 French-IPA and Spanish-IPA G2P

To investigate the feasibility of a multilingual G2P system, we trained the Spanish-IPA converter and French-IPA converter with the same Transformer model. Both of these two G2P systems give decent results. The PER for the Spanish-IPA model (190 epochs) is 1.7%, while the WER is 12.7%. The PER for the French-IPA model (150 epochs) is 2.14%, while the WER shows 12.3% (Fig. 9).

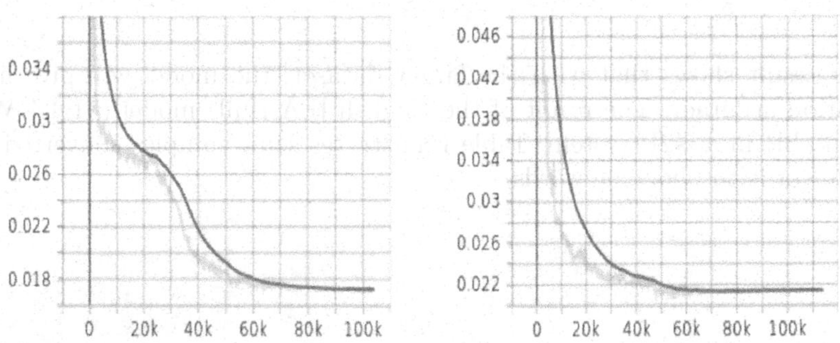

Fig. 9. The PER for Spanish-IPA (Left) and French-IPA (Right)

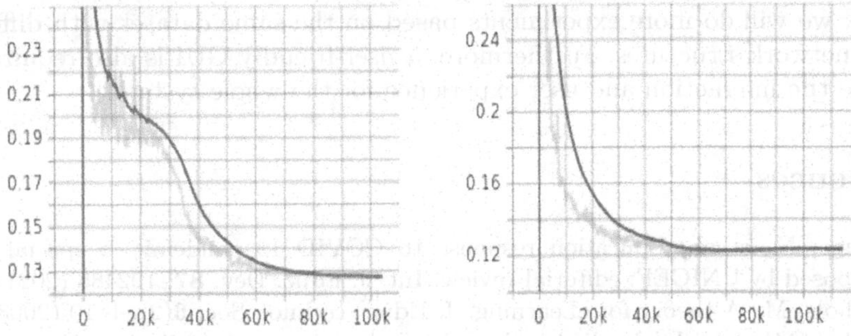

Fig. 10. The WER for Spanish-IPA (Left) and French-IPA (Right)

Table 4 and 5 illustrate some samples generated by Spanish-IPA G2P system and French-IPA G2P system (Fig. 10).

Table 4. Samples for Spanish G2P system

Spanish words	Generated phoneme from G2P system	Correct Phoneme words
ababillarais	aβaβiʎaɾis	aβaβiʎaɾis
cacofónicos	kakoˈfonikos	kakoˈfonikos
cadañega	kaðaeɣa	kaðaɲeɣa
inspirad	inspirað	inspirað
rascarla	raskaɾla	raskaɾla
silabeamos	silaβeamos	silaβeamos

Table 5. Samples for French G2P system

French words	Generated phoneme from G2P system	Correct Phoneme words
câlineriez	kalinəʁje	kalinəʁje
damasquiner	damaskine	damaskine
effrangé	efʁɑ̃ʒe	efʁɑ̃ʒe
discontinuâmes	diskɔ̃tinam	diskɔ̃tinɥam
mortifie	mɔʁtifj	mɔʁtifi
motivâmes	mɔtivam	mɔtivam

6 Conclusion

In this work, to enhance our phonetic exam E-learning system and help teachers more comfortable generating phonetic transcription exams, we built a Transformer-based multilingual Grapheme-to-Phoneme translation system with decent conversion accuracy. In the future, to find out the difference between models, we will do more experiments based on the same dataset with different neural network structures. Furthermore, a user-friendly GUI is also required to improve the interaction and user experience for the whole system.

References

1. Reuge, N., et al.: Education response to COVID 19 pandemic, a special issue proposed by UNICEF: editorial review. Int. J. Educ. Dev. **87**, 102485 (2021)
2. Nichols, M.: A theory for eLearning. J. Educ. Technol. Soc. **6**(2), 1–10 (2003)
3. Seals, C.D., et al.: Applied webservices platform supported through modified edit distance algorithm: automated phonetic transcription grading tool (APTgt). In: Zaphiris, P., Ioannou, A. (eds.) HCII 2020. LNCS, vol. 12205, pp. 380–398. Springer, Cham (2020). https://doi.org/10.1007/978-3-030-50513-4_29
4. Liu, J., et al.: Optimization to automated phonetic transcription grading tool (APTgt) – automatic exam generator. In: Zaphiris, P., Ioannou, A. (eds.) HCII 2021. LNCS, vol. 12784, pp. 80–91. Springer, Cham (2021). https://doi.org/10.1007/978-3-030-77889-7_6
5. Brown, A.: International Phonetic Alphabet. The Encyclopedia of Applied Linguistics (2012)
6. Bahdanau, D., Cho, K., Bengio, Y.: Neural machine translation by jointly learning to align and translate. arXiv preprint arXiv:1409.0473 (2014)
7. Bisani, M., Ney, H.: Joint-sequence models for grapheme-to-phoneme conversion. Speech Commun. **50**(5), 434–451 (2008)
8. Klakow, D., Peters, J.: Testing the correlation of word error rate and perplexity. Speech Commun. **38**(1–2), 19–28 (2002)
9. Taylor, P.: Hidden Markov models for grapheme to phoneme conversion. In: Ninth European Conference on Speech Communication and Technology (2005)
10. Rao, K., et al.: Grapheme-to-phoneme conversion using long short-term memory recurrent neural networks. In: 2015 IEEE International Conference on Acoustics, Speech and Signal Processing (ICASSP). IEEE (2015)
11. Yang, S., Wang, Y., Chu, X.: A survey of deep learning techniques for neural machine translation. arXiv preprint arXiv:2002.07526 (2020)
12. Kominek, J., Black, A.W.: The CMU arctic speech databases. In: Fifth ISCA Workshop on Speech Synthesis (2004)
13. Vaswani, A., et al.: Attention is all you need. In: Advances in Neural Information Processing Systems 30 (2017)

Speech Disorders Classification by CNN in Phonetic E-Learning System

Jueting Liu[1], Chang Ren[1], Yaoxuan Luan[1], Sicheng Li[1], Tianshi Xie[1], Cheryl Seals[1](✉), and Marisha Speights Atkins[2]

[1] Auburn University, Auburn, AL 36849, USA
{jzl0122,czr0049,yzl0219,szl0072,tzx0019,sealscd}@auburn.edu
[2] Northwestern University, Evanston, IL 60208, USA
marisha.speights@northwestern.edu

Abstract. Speech disorders may affect the process of phonetic transcriptions. In the Automated Phonetic Transcription-the grading tool (APTgt), a linguistic E-learning system, to reduce the influence of disordered speech in the phonetic exams, we proposed a speech disorders classification module that aims to classify disordered speech and non-disordered speech. The Mel-frequency cepstral coefficients (MFCCs) are utilized to represent the features of the speech sound files. With the two different formats of MFCCs, we adopted two approaches to classifying the MFCCs: calculating the similarity between MFCC values by dynamic time warping (DTW) algorithm and classifying the distances by support vector machine (SVM); directly image classification by the convolutional neural network (CNN). We will focus on the second approach in this paper.

Keywords: E-learning · Phonetic transcription · Speech disorders · Mel-frequency cepstral coefficients · Dynamic time warping · Convolutional neural network

1 Introduction

E-learning has become an essential requirement for educational institutions like colleges and universities around the world during the pandemic [1]. Compared with the traditional educational process in the classroom, E-learning enables students to access course information without time restrictions or geographical constraints. Automated Phonetic Transcription - the grading tool (APTgt) is an online E-learning system developed for students and faculties in the Department of Communication Disorders (CMDS) [2,3]. This system provides interactive phonetic exams to improve students' phonetic transcription skills and offers an auto-grading module.

Phonetic transcription is a process that represents speech sounds by visual characters or symbols. During the phonetic exams in our APTgt system, the audio files with speech disorders may significantly influence students. To avoid these influences from speech disorders, we proposed a classification function that can distinguish speech sounds from disordered speech and non-disordered speech.

H. Degen and S. Ntoa (Eds.): HCII 2022, LNAI 13336, pp. 557–566, 2022.
https://doi.org/10.1007/978-3-031-05643-7_36

The Mel-frequency Cepstral Coefficients (MFCCs) can appropriately represent and classify the sound signal. MFCCs are generated based on the human ear's bandwidth and widely represent human speech. In a speech recognition system, to calculate the similarity between audio files in time series, dynamic time warping (DTW) can be utilized. DTW is a classic dynamic programming algorithm for measuring similarity between two sequences that vary in speed or time [4,5].

The MFCCs values can be plotted as figures, and The Convolutional Neural Network (CNN) is a universal classification model for image classification. Therefore, we selected MFCC and CNN as an approach in our classification module [6]. This paper also compared the results generated from MFCC and CNN with the traditional method: MFCC with DTW.

2 System Design

2.1 APTgt System

The Automated Phonetic Transcription Grading Tool (APTgt) (see Fig. 1) is an interactive online Learning Management System (LMS) that facilitates the comparison of phonetic transcriptions for instruction and clinical training purposes [2]. Phonetic transcription exams are core adoptions in the APTgt system, and teachers can create and manage phonetic exams in varied difficulty levels. Phonetic transcription is a visual presentation of speech sounds by special characters or symbols. The International Phonetic Alphabet (IPA) is the core representation within the APTgt system [7].

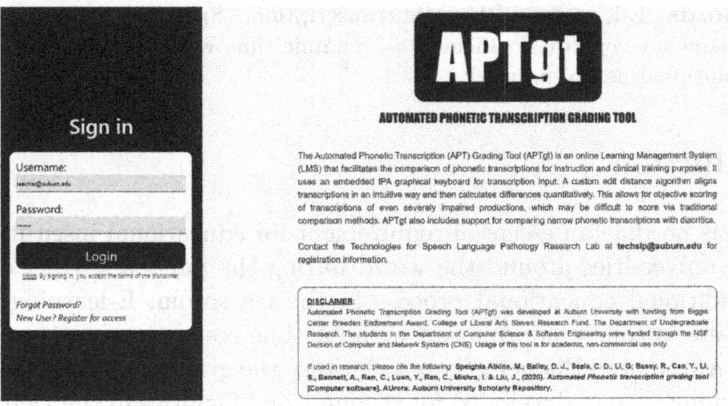

Fig. 1. The main page of the APTgt system.

During the exams, each question is a speech sound file of a word [2]. Students are required to listen to the question and spell the phonetic format of the words by the IPA keyboard. The submission will be calculated as the difference between the pre-stored correct answer versus student submission, and this provides the result of each question (see Fig. 2).

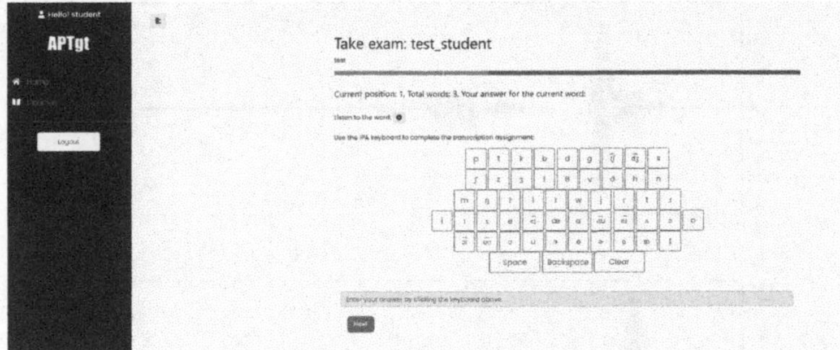

Fig. 2. Student exam page in APTgt system.

2.2 Speech Disorders Classification

A potential issue was discovered with the phonetic exam in our system. Since all the questions are speech sounds and recorded by different adults and children, some disordered speech sounds in the database may influence the results of the phonetic transcription. The speech disorder is a symptom of problems generating or creating speech sounds [8]. For example, here are two speech sounds with the same content but recorded by one disordered speaker and non-disordered speaker (see Fig. 3). From Fig. 3, speech disorders can significantly influence the speech quality; this situation inspires us to develop a classification module that can distinguish whether the speech sounds in the phonetic exams are disordered speech.

There are different types of speech disorders such as stuttering, apraxia, and dysarthria, all the disordered speech can be an obstacle in our phonetic exams [8]. To create a robust E-learning system, we proposed a general classification function to classify speech sounds. We proposed two approaches to access this classifier:

1. Calculate the difference between disordered speech and non-disorder speech. By comparing the different distances, we can find a parameter to classify disordered and non-disorder speech. This approach can be accomplished by MFCC and DTW.
2. Transform all the speech sounds files into figure format and calculate the similarity between figures. The result of image classification can illustrate the result of speech types. We utilized CNN to implement this classification function.

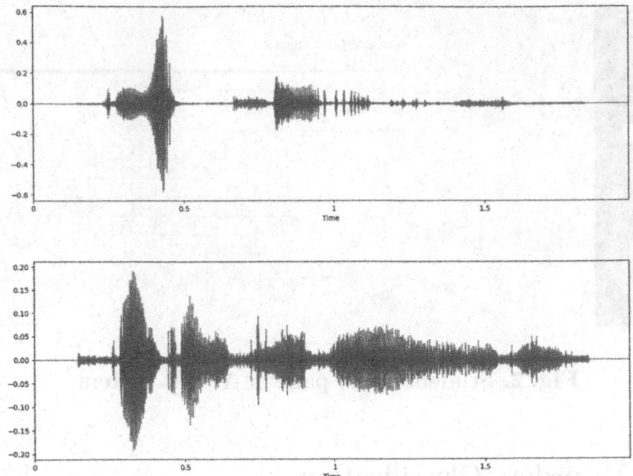

Fig. 3. Two speech sounds with the same content by different recorders.

3 Method

3.1 Mel-Frequency Cepstral Coefficients

From the approaches we proposed, a method that can calculate the similarity of sounds is required. To measure the closeness of speech sounds, we can not directly use the raw audio file for comparison since the speech sounds include not only linguistic content but also emotions and background noise. The Mel-frequency cepstral coefficients (MFCCs) are features that can represent the human sounds appropriately [9].

MFCCs are widely used in human speech recognition systems since MFCCs are based on human hearing perceptions that cannot perceive frequencies over 1Khz. In other words, MFCCs are derived from sets of experiments on human subjects [9]. Here is how we extract MFCCs from audio signals (see Fig. 4).

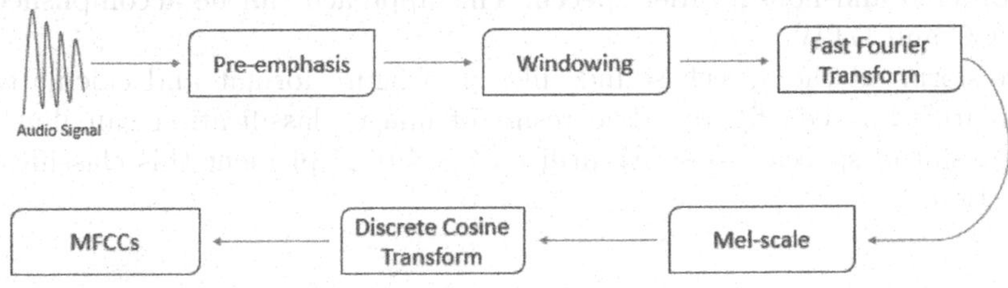

Fig. 4. The MFCCs extraction

1. **Pre-emphasis** Increase the energy of the audio signal in high frequency; for human speech audios, the energy in lower frequency is always much greater than the energy in high frequency. The pre-emphasis will promote phone detection accuracy [9].
2. **Windowing** MFCCs are features utilized for detecting phones in human speech, and audio signals are time-varying signals. Windowing indicates slicing the audio signal into different segments. These short segments will better represent the characteristics of speech audios [9].
3. **Fast Fourier Transform** FFT was used to converse the audio signal from the time-domain to the frequency-domain since analyzing the signal in the frequency-domain is much easier than the time-domain [9].
4. **Mel-scale** Compute the mel spectrum by passing the frequency-domain signal through the Mel-filter bank. The mel scale relates the perceived frequency of a tone to its actual measured frequency. It scales the frequency to match what a human ear can hear more closely. Here is the equation from Hertz scale to Mel scale:

$$Mel(f) = 2595 \log(1 + \frac{f}{700})$$

5. **Discrete Cosine Transform** The last step is taking the discrete cosine transform of the mel log signals. This process converts the log mel spectrum into the time domain and generates MFCCs [9].

By Python librosa library, we extracted MFCCs from speech audios in two formats: MFCC scale values (see Fig. 5) and MFCC images (see Fig. 6). In the following classification part, we employed DTW to handle the MFCC values and CNN to process the MFCC images.

```
[[-5.7929608e+02 -5.7353021e+02 -5.7313885e+02 ... -5.2029669e+02
  -5.4644800e+02 -5.5352570e+02]
 [ 1.4982168e+01  2.2076515e+01  2.2540791e+01 ...  4.3431477e+01
   5.3968311e+01  4.3773468e+01]
 [ 1.1683277e+01  1.6413883e+01  1.6874548e+01 ...  2.9499098e+01
   3.4336399e+01  2.4416019e+01]
 ...
 [ 8.2851470e-01  8.5813940e-01  2.8974738e+00 ...  9.8472804e-02
   5.7508678e+00  6.9667273e+00]
 [-1.1795038e-01  1.2469640e+00  4.2966623e+00 ...  5.2962589e+00
   5.1093683e+00  7.7527409e+00]
 [-5.1060808e-01  2.4376063e+00  5.3777962e+00 ...  3.3710027e+00
```

Fig. 5. MFCC value

Fig. 6. MFCC image

3.2 Dynamic Time Warping

Dynamic Time Warping (DTW) is an algorithm designed for measuring the similarity between two series in time-varying [4]. Suppose two time series A with the length of n and B with the length of m, where

$$A = a_1, a_2, \ldots, a_i, \ldots a_n$$

$$B = b_1, b_2, \ldots, b_j, \ldots b_m$$

$Distance(i, j)$ is the distance between a_i, b_j

$$Distance(i, j) = (a_i - b_j)^2$$

Assume $Dtw(i, j)$ is the distance between two series A and B:

$$Dtw(i, j) = Distance(i, j) + min \begin{cases} Dtw(i-1, j) \\ Dtw(i, j-1) \\ Dtw(i-1, j-1) \end{cases}$$

.

3.3 Convolutional Neural Network

Convolutional Neural Network (ConvNet/CNN) is a deep learning algorithm widely used for image classification and computer vision tasks. The CNN models are mainly composed of three types of layers [6]:

- **Convolutional Layer** The convolutional layer is the core build of the model. It takes convolution operations and converts the image into numerical values, allowing the neural network to interpret and extract relevant patterns.
- **Pooling Layer** The pooling layer aims to reduce the spatial dimensionality of the input. It decreases the number of parameters, reducing complexity and improving efficiency.
- **Fully-Connected Layer** The full-connected layer performs the classification function based on the features extracted through the previous layers (Fig. 7).

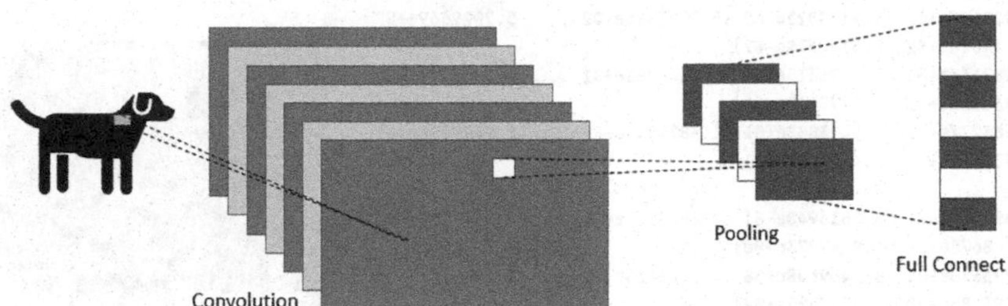

Fig. 7. Convolutional neural network

4 Implement and Analysis

4.1 Data Process

We utilized Speech exemplar and evaluation database (SEED) provided by Dr. Speights (see Table 1). The SEED project was designed to provide high-quality recordings of speech samples for researchers and instructors of phonetic transcription training courses. This library contains about 16,000 speech samples recorded by speakers aged 2 to 85 years. An important aspect of the SEED is that the speech sounds are recorded by speakers with speech disorders and speakers without speech disorders which means the speech files in SEED are labeled with disordered and non-disordered [10].

Table 1. Contents in SEED

Task list	List reference
Clinical assessment of articulation and phonology	Secord and Donohue (2014)
Sentences and phrases from Brown Bear, brown bear	Martin and Carle (1996)
Beginners intelligibility test	Osberger et al. (1994)
Phonetic contrasts from the dysarthria intelligibility test	Kent et al. (1989)
Multi-syllabic nouns	Young (1991), Masso et al. (2016)
...	...

We selected two of the lists from the SEED: **Beginner Intelligibility Test** and **Brown Bear, brown bear** as our data from training and validation. The total number of sound files is 1049. In this paper, we focused on the CNN approach and used MFCC with DTW approach as benchmark.

4.2 MFCC with DTW Implementation

For MFCC with the DTW approach, the similarity between the same speech content but recorded by different speakers is much larger than the similarity between different contents. To normalize the global parameter, we need to calculate the similarity from the speech content separately. (see Fig. 8).

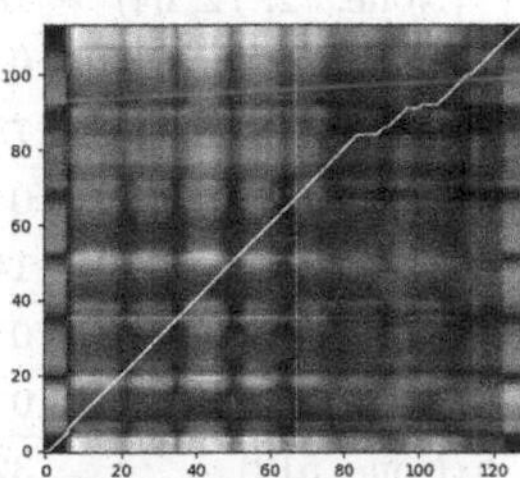

Fig. 8. DTW distance

We first computed the average distance between all the non-disordered speech for the same speech content and treated this average distance as a standard value. Then we calculated the similarity between every speech sound, including the disordered and non-disordered speech and the standard value. To normalize the rules, the difference should be represented by a percentage value. Here is an example of the result (see Fig. 9).

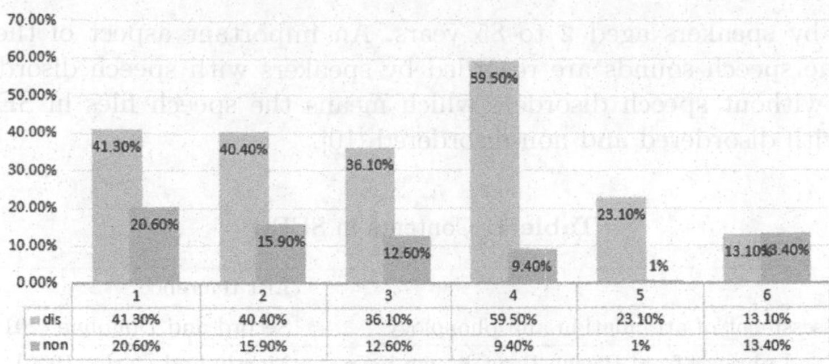

Fig. 9. Percentage results by MFCC and DTW

One hundred twenty speech sounds were utilized in the model. With an SVM classification algorithm, the accuracy of this approach is about 80.5% [11]. Since this approach is verbose and not general (each label of speech sounds needs to be calculated), we proposed the following classification method using a convolutional neural network (CNN).

4.3 CNN Implementation

Table 2. CNN model summary for BB database

Layer (Type)	Output shape	Param Number
conv2d	(None, 148, 148, 32)	896
max$_{p}ooling2d$	(None, 74, 74, 32)	0
conv2d_1	(None, 72, 72, 64)	18496
max$_{p}ooling2d_1$	(None, 36, 36, 64)	0
conv2d_2	(None, 34, 34, 128)	73856
max$_{p}ooling2d_2$	(None, 17, 17, 128)	0
conv2d_3	(None, 15, 15, 128)	147584
max$_{p}ooling2d_3$	(None, 7, 7, 128)	0
flatten	(None, 6272)	0
dense	(None, 512)	3211776
dense_1	(None, 1)	513

Table 2 is the model summary. We just placed all the disordered speech and non-disordered speech in the model without considering the contents of the speech files. We have 489 speech samples in **Beginner Intelligibility Test** dataset and 560 speech samples in **Brown Bear, brown bear** dataset. 80% of all the speech files were used for training, and the rest were used for validation. Each training takes 150 epochs. Here is the result of this classification approach (Figs. 10 and 11).

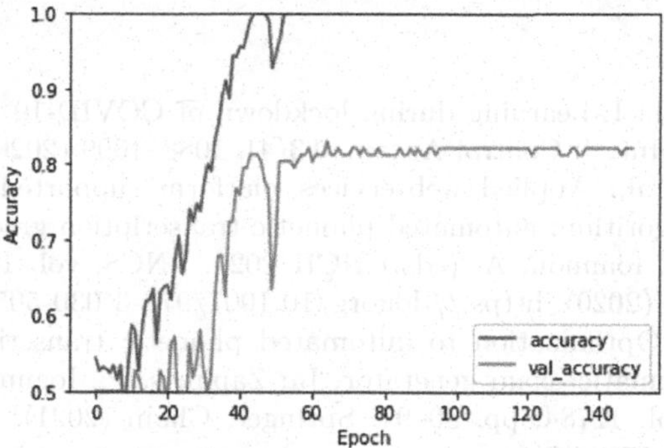

Fig. 10. Result for dataset BB

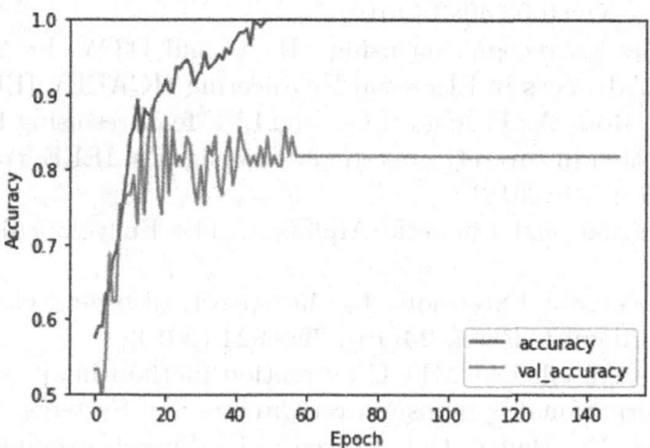

Fig. 11. Result for dataset BIT

The classification accuracy for **Brown Bear, brown bear** (BB) dataset is 82.4% and the classification accuracy for **Beginner Intelligibility Test** (BIT) is about 81.8%. Since this CNN classification approach can neglect the contents of the speech, it is more extensive and efficient with even a little bit higher accuracy than the traditional MFCC with DTW function.

5 Conclusion and Future Work

This paper proposed a classification module for the phonetic E-learning system to classify the speech sounds into disordered speech and non-disordered speech. MFCCs were extracted from audio files to represent the features of the speech sound, and DTW and CNN were employed as the classification algorithm. CNN provided a more comprehensive solution with higher classification accuracy than the traditional DTW algorithm. In the future, we will continue this work to improve the accuracy with more details according to the features of the speech sounds.

References

1. Radha, R., et al.: E-Learning during lockdown of COVID-19 pandemic: a global perspective. In: Int. J. Control Autom. **13**(4), 1088–1099 (2020)
2. Seals, C.D., et al.: Applied webservices platform supported through modified edit distance algorithm: automated phonetic transcription grading tool (APTgt). In: Zaphiris, P., Ioannou, A. (eds.) HCII 2020. LNCS, vol. 12205, pp. 380–398. Springer, Cham (2020). https://doi.org/10.1007/978-3-030-50513-4_29
3. Liu, J., et al.: Optimization to automated phonetic transcription grading tool (APTgt) – automatic exam generator. In: Zaphiris, P., Ioannou, A. (eds.) HCII 2021. LNCS, vol. 12784, pp. 80–91. Springer, Cham (2021). https://doi.org/10.1007/978-3-030-77889-7_6
4. Muda, L., Begam, M., Elamvazuthi, I.: Voice recognition algorithms using mel frequency cepstral coefficient (MFCC) and dynamic time warping (DTW) techniques. arXiv preprint arXiv:1003.4083 (2010)
5. Mohan, B.J.: Speech recognition using MFCC and DTW. In: 2014 International Conference on Advances in Electrical Engineering (ICAEE). IEEE (2014)
6. Chowdhury, A., Ross, A.: Fusing MFCC and LPC features using 1D triplet CNN for speaker recognition in severely degraded audio signals. IEEE Trans. Inf. Forensics Secur. **15**, 1616–1629 (2019)
7. Brown, A.: International Phonetic Alphabet. The Encyclopedia of Applied Linguistics (2012)
8. Shriberg, L.D., et al.: Extensions to the speech disorders classification system (SDCS). Clin. Linguist. Phon. **24**(10), 795–824 (2010)
9. Han, W., et al.: An efficient MFCC extraction method in speech recognition. In: 2006 IEEE International Symposium on Circuits and Systems. IEEE (2006)
10. Speights Atkins, M., Bailey, D.J., Boyce, S.E.: Speech exemplar and evaluation database (SEED) for clinical training in articulatory phonetics and speech science. Clin. Linguist. Phon. **34**(9), 878–886 (2020)
11. Mavroforakis, M.E., Theodoridis, S.: A geometric approach to support vector machine (SVM) classification. IEEE Trans. Neural Netw. **17**(3), 671–682 (2006)

Say It Right: AI Neural Machine Translation Empowers New Speakers to Revitalize Lemko

Petro Orynycz(✉)

LemkoTran.com, Edgewater, MD 21037, USA
p@orynycz.com

Abstract. Artificial-intelligence-powered neural machine translation might soon resuscitate endangered languages by empowering new speakers to communicate in real time using sentences quantifiably closer to the literary norm than those of native speakers, and starting from day one of their language reclamation journey. While Silicon Valley has been investing enormous resources into neural translation technology capable of superhuman speed and accuracy for the world's most widely used languages, 98% have been left behind, for want of corpora: neural machine translation models train on millions of words of bilingual text, which simply do not exist for most languages, and cost upwards of a hundred thousand United States dollars per tongue to assemble.

For low-resource languages, there is a more resourceful approach, if not a more effective one: transfer learning, which enables lower-resource languages to benefit from achievements among higher-resource ones. In this experiment, Google's English-Polish neural translation service was coupled with my classical, rule-based engine to translate from English into the endangered, low-resource, East Slavic language of Lemko. The system achieved a bilingual evaluation understudy (BLEU) quality score of 6.28, several times better than Google Translate's English to Standard Ukrainian (BLEU 2.17), Russian (BLEU 1.10), and Polish (BLEU 1.70) services. Finally, the fruit of this experiment, the world's first English to Lemko translation service, was made available at the web address www.LemkoTran.com to empower new speakers to revitalize their language.

New speakers are key to language revitalization, and the power to "say it right" in Lemko is now at their fingertips.

Keywords: Human-centered AI · Language revitalization · Lemko

1 Introduction

1.1 Problems

This experiment aims to contribute at the local level to the global challenge of language loss, which may be occurring at the rate of one per day, with as few as one tongue in ten set to survive [1, p. 1329]. At press time, SIL International's *Ethnologue* uses Lewis and Simons' 2010 Expanded Graded Intergenerational Disruption Scale to estimate that 3,018 languages are endangered [2], which is 43% of the 7,001 individual living ones

H. Degen and S. Ntoa (Eds.): HCII 2022, LNAI 13336, pp. 567–580, 2022.
https://doi.org/10.1007/978-3-031-05643-7_37

tallied at press time in International Organization for Standardization standard ISO 639-3 [3]. Meanwhile, Google Translate only serves 108 [4], and Facebook, 112 [5], which is a start. Nevertheless, one less language is now underserved, as the fruit of this experiment has been deployed to a web server as a public translation service.

New artificial intelligence technologies beckon with the promise of an aid that instantly compensates for language loss via human-computer interaction. In my previous experiment, next-generation neural engines achieved higher quality scores translating from Russian and Polish into English than the human control [6, p. 9]. Meanwhile, Facebook and Google[1] have invested enormous resources into delivering better-than-human automatic translation systems at zero cost to consumer.

Superhuman artificial intelligence does not come cheap: training neural language models requires bilingual corpora with wordcounts in the hundreds of thousands, and ideally, millions, which would cost hundreds of thousands of dollars to translate, sums beyond the means of most low-resource language communities. Fortunately, this experiment shows that there are more resourceful and effective ways to respond to the challenge of creating translation aids for revitalizing endangered languages in low-resource settings.

1.2 Work so Far

I built the world's first Lemko to English machine translation system and have made it available to the public. Its objective translation quality scores have been improving: the engine achieved a bilingual evaluation understudy (BLEU) score of 14.57 in the summer of 2021, as presented to professionals at the National Defense Industrial Association's Interservice/Industry Training, Simulation and Education Conference and published in its proceedings [6]. For reference, I scored BLEU 28.66 as a human translator working in field conditions, cut off from the outside world. By the autumn of 2021, the engine had reached BLEU 15.74, as reported to linguists, academics, and the wider community at an unveiling event hosted by the University of Pittsburgh.[2]

1.3 System Under Study

Lemko is a definitively to severely endangered [6, p. 3, 7, pp. 177–178], low-resource [8], officially recognized minority language [9] presumably indigenous to transborder highlands south of the Kraków, Tarnów, and Rzeszów metropolitan areas; historical demarcating isoglosses will hopefully be the topic of a future paper. Poland's census bureau tallied 6,279 residents for whom Lemko was a language "usually used at home" (even if in addition to Polish) in 2011 [10, p. 3], a 12% increase from the 5,605 for whom Lemko was a "language spoken most often at home" in 2002 [11, p. 6, 12, p. 7]. At press time, the results of a fresh count are being tabulated.

[1] Disclosure: I work as a paid Russian, Polish, and Ukrainian linguist and translation quality control specialist for the Google Translate project; headquarters are in San Francisco.

[2] Disclosure: the event was sponsored by the Carpatho-Rusyn Society (Pennsylvania), and I was paid by the University of Pittsburgh for my presentation.

Lemko is classifiable as an East Slavic language as it fits the customary genetic structural feature criteria, the most significant of which is pleophony [13, p. 20], whereby a vowel is assumed to have arisen in Proto-Slavic sequences of consonant *C* followed by mid or low vowel *V* (`*e`, or `*o`, with which `*a` had merged [14, p. 366]), followed by liquid R (that is, `*l` or `*r`), followed by another consonant *C*, that is, CVRC > CVRVC. To illustrate, compare the Old English word for "melt", *meltan* (CVRC) [15, p. 718], to its putative Lemko cognate mołódyj [16, p. 92, 17, p. 150] (CVRVC), meaning "young". Other East Slavic cognates include Ukrainian mołodýj and Russian mołodój [17], both exhibiting a vowel after the liquid (CVRVC). Meanwhile, West Slavic languages lack a vowel before the liquid; compare Polish *młody* and Slovak *mladý* (both CRVC) [17]. Further afield, kinship has been posited for other words translatable as "mild", including Sanskrit *mṛdú* (CRC) [18, p. 830] and Latin *mollis* (CVRC if from **moldvis*) [15, 17, 19, p. 323].

How well Lemko meets customary, modern Ukrainian genetic structural feature criteria was not evaluated in this experiment. However, similarity between Lemko and Standard Ukrainian was quantified, for the first time in print of which I am aware. Below, my Lemko engine scored BLEU 6.28, nearly three times the score of Google Translate's Ukrainian at BLEU 2.17. Further experiments could be performed for the purposes of quantification of similarity between Lemko, Standard Ukrainian, Polish, and Rusyn as codified in Slovakia, as well as a fresh take on the typological classification of Lemko.

The quantity and quality of resources have been improving, as has resourcefulness empowered by technology. All known bilingual corpora, comprising fewer than seventy thousand Lemko words, were mustered for this experiment. I have been cleaning a bilingual corpus of transcriptions of interviews conducted with native speakers in Poland and my translations into English, which a United States client paid me to perform and permitted me to use. I am also compiling monolingual corpora, which total 534,512 words at press time.

1.4 Hypothesis

Based on my subjective impression as a professional translator that Lemko native speakers interviewed in Poland were more likely to use words with obvious Polish cognates than Standard Ukrainian ones, I hypothesized that, all else being equal, a machine could be configured to translate into Lemko from English and achieve BLEU objective quality scores higher than those of Google Translate's Ukrainian and Russian services.

1.5 Predictions

Lemko Translation System. I predicted that the aforementioned translation system would achieve a BLEU score of 15 translating into Lemko from English against the bilingual corpus.

Google Translate

English to Ukrainian Service. I predicted that Google Translate's English to Ukrainian service would achieve a BLEU score of 10 against the bilingual corpus.

English to Russian Service. I predicted that Google Translate's English to Russian service would achieve a BLEU score of 1 against the bilingual corpus.

1.6 Methods and Justification

In the interest of speed, resource conservation, and ruggedizability, a laptop computer discarded as obsolete by my employer was configured to translate into Lemko and make calls to the Google Cloud Platform Google Translate service, as well as configured to evaluate said translations using the industry standard BLEU metric.

1.7 Principal Results

The English to Lemko translation system achieved a cumulative BLEU score of `6.28431824990417`. Meanwhile, Google Translate's Ukrainian service scored BLEU `2.16830846776652`, its Russian service BLEU `1.10424105952048`, and the control of Polish transliterated into the Cyrillic alphabet BLEU `1.70036447680114`.

2 Materials and Methods

The above hypothesis was tested by calculating BLEU quality scores for each translation system set up in the manner detailed below.

2.1 Setup

Hardware. The experiment was conducted on an HP Elitebook 850 G2 laptop with a Core i7-5600U 2.6 GHz processor and 16 GB of random-access memory. It had been discarded by my employer as obsolete and listed for sale at USD 450 at time of press.

Configuration. In the basic input/output system (BIOS) menu, the device was configured to enable Virtualization Technology (VTx).

Operating System. Windows 10 Professional 64 bit had been installed on bare metal. It was ensured that `Virtual Machine Platform` and `Windows Subsystem for Linux` Windows features were enabled. Next, the `WSL2 Linux kernel update for x64` machines (wsl_update_x64.msi) available from Microsoft at https://aka.ms/wsl2kernel was installed.

Software. The Docker Desktop for Windows version 4.4.3 (73365) installer was downloaded from https://www.docker.com/get-started and run with the option to `Install required Windows components for WSL 2` selected.

Packages. The experiment depended on the below packages from the Python Package Index.

SacreBLEU. Version 2.0.0 was installed using the Python package documented at the following universal resource locator (URL):
https://pypi.org/project/sacrebleu/2.0.0/

Google Cloud Translation API Client Library. Version 2.0.1 was installed using the Python package documented at the universal resource locator (URL) https://pypi.org/project/google-cloud-translate/2.0.1/

The above dependencies were specified in the requirements file as follows:

```
google-cloud-translate==2.0.1
sacrebleu==2.0.0
```

Container

Build. The experiment was run in a Docker container featuring the latest version of the Python programming language, which was version 3.10.2 at the time, running on the Debian Bullseye 11 Linux operating system of AMD64 architecture, of Secure Hash Algorithm 2 shortened digest `bcb158d5ddb6`, obtainable via the following command:

```
docker pull
python@sha256:bcb158d5ddb636fa3aa567c987e7fcf6111330782
0d466813527ca90d60fedc7
```

Runtime. The container was configured to save raw experiment data files to a local bind mounted volume.

Translation Quality Scoring

Translation quality scores were calculated according to the BLEU metric using version 2.0.0 of the *SacreBLEU* tool invented by Post [20].

Case Sensitivity. The evaluation was performed in a case-sensitive manner.

Tokenization. Segments were tokenized using version 13a of the Workshop on Statistical Machine Translation standard scoring script metric internal tokenization procedure.

Smoothing Method. The smoothing technique developed at the National Institute of Standards and Technology by United States Federal Government employees for their Multimodal Information Group BLEU toolkit, being the third technique described by Chen and Cherry [21, p. 363], was employed by default.

Signature. The above settings produced the following signature:

```
nrefs:1|case:mixed|eff:no|tok:13a|smooth:exp|
  version:2.0.0
```

Calibration. Configured as above, the machine produces the following output:

Segment 1031

English source	Everything was there.	
Lemko reference and transliteration	Вшытко там было.	Všŷtko tam bŷlo.
Lemkotran.com hypothesis and transliteration	Вшытко там было.	Všŷtko tam bŷlo.
Score	BLEU = 100.00 100.0/100.0/100.0/100.0 (BP = 1.000 ratio = 1.000 hyp_len = 4 ref_len = 4)	

Explanation. The hypothesis segment was identical to the reference one and the machine achieved a perfect score of BLEU 100.

Segment 179

English source	I don't remember what year.	
Lemko reference and transliteration	Не памятам в котрым роцi.	Ne pamjatam v kotrŷm roci.
Lemkotran.com hypothesis and transliteration	Нi памятам, в котрым роцi.	Ni pamjatam, v kotrŷm roci.
Score	BLEU = 43.47 71.4/50.0/40.0/25.0 (BP = 1.000 ratio = 1.167 hyp_len = 7 ref_len = 6)	

Explanation. The hypothesis was different from the reference by two characters. The machine mistranslated the particle negating the verb, using the word for "no" (*ni*) instead of the expected word for "not" (*ne*). This has since been largely fixed. The machine also added a comma after *pamjatam*, which means "I remember." That dropped the score from what would have been a perfect score of 100 to 43.47.

Control. As the corpus is based on interviews conducted in Poland, translations into Polish were used as a control. They were transliterated into the Cyrillic alphabet by reversing the rules for transliterating Lemko names established by Poland's Ministry of the Interior and Administration [22, p. 6564]. Polish nasal vowels were decomposed into a vowel plus a nasal stop, except before approximants, where they were directly denasalized. Word-finally, the front nasal vowel /ę/ was simply denasalized, and the back one /ą/ was transliterated as if followed by a dental stop.

3 Results

The engine available to the public at www.LemkoTran.com took first place with a cumulative translation quality score of BLEU 6.28, nearly three times that of the runner-up, Google Translate's English-Ukrainian service (BLEU 2.17). Next was its English-Polish service (BLEU 1.70), with its English-Russian service in last place (BLEU 1.10) (Table 1).

Table 1. English to Lemko translation quality: LemkoTran.com versus Google Translate

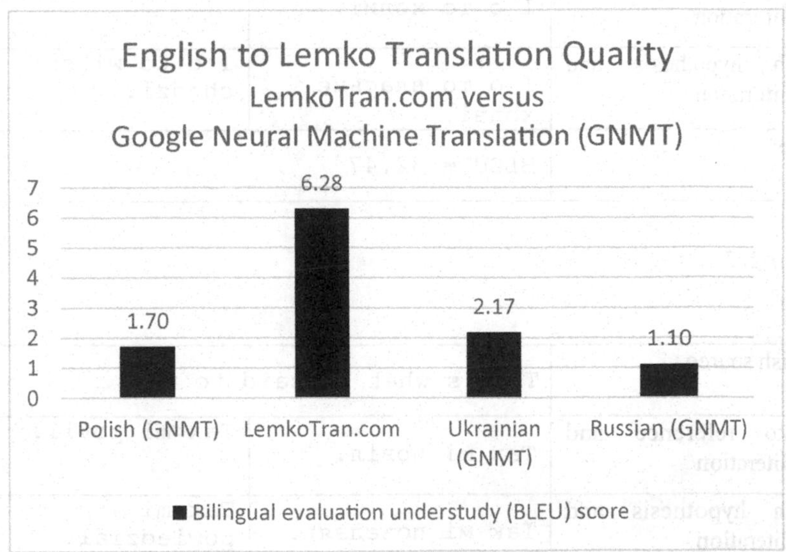

3.1 Results by Machine Translation Service

Control. When transliterated into the Cyrillic alphabet, Google Translate's translations into Standard Polish achieved a corpus-level BLEU score of 1.70. Samples of its performances are as follows:

Segment 2174

<table>
<tr><td>English source</td><td colspan="2">We had still been in Izby, right.</td></tr>
<tr><td>Lemko reference and transliteration</td><td>То мы іщы были в Ізбах, так.</td><td>To mŷ iščŷ bŷly v Izbach, tak.</td></tr>
<tr><td>Polish hypothesis and transliteration</td><td>Билісьми єще в Ізбах, так.</td><td>Byliśmy jeszcze w Izbach, tak.</td></tr>
<tr><td>Score</td><td colspan="2">BLEU = 46.20</td></tr>
</table>

Segment 854

<table>
<tr><td>English source</td><td colspan="2">And that's what it's all about.</td></tr>
<tr><td>Lemko reference and transliteration</td><td>І о то ходит.</td><td>I o to chodyt.</td></tr>
<tr><td>Polish hypothesis and transliteration</td><td>І о то власьнє ходзі.</td><td>I o to właśnie chodzi.</td></tr>
<tr><td>Score</td><td colspan="2">BLEU = 32.47</td></tr>
</table>

Segment 217

<table>
<tr><td>English source</td><td colspan="2">That's what he said to me.</td></tr>
<tr><td>Lemko reference and transliteration</td><td>Так мі повіл.</td><td>Tak mi povil.</td></tr>
<tr><td>Polish hypothesis and transliteration</td><td>Так мі повєдзял.</td><td>Tak mi powiedział.</td></tr>
<tr><td>Score</td><td colspan="2">BLEU = 35.36</td></tr>
</table>

Hybrid English-Lemko Engine. The engine freely available to the public at the URL www.LemkoTran.com achieved a corpus-level BLEU score of 6.28.

Segment 1031

English source	Everything was there.	
Lemko reference and transliteration	Вшытко там было.	Všŷtko tam bŷlo.
Lemkotran.com hypothesis and transliteration	Вшытко там было.	Všŷtko tam bŷlo.
Score	BLEU = 100.00	

Segment 1445

English source	But that officer took that medal and said,	
Lemko reference and transliteration	Але тот офіцер взял тот медаль і повідат:	Ale tot oficer vzial tot medal' i povidat:
Lemkotran.com hypothesis and transliteration	Але тот офіцер взял тот медаль і повіл:	Ale tot oficer vzial tot medal' i povil:
Score	BLEU = 75.06	

Segment 217

English source	That's what he said to me.	
Lemko reference and transliteration	Так мі повіл.	Tak mi povil.
Lemkotran.com hypothesis and transliteration	Так мі повіл.	Tak mi povil.
Score	BLEU = 100.00	

Ukrainian. Google Translate's translations into Standard Ukrainian achieved a corpus-level BLEU score of 2.17.

Segment 2419

English source	Where and when?	
Lemko reference and transliteration	Де і коли?	De i koly?
Ukrainian hypothesis and transliteration	Де і коли?	De i koly?
Score	BLEU = 100.00	

Segment 1096

English source	We were there for three months.	
Lemko reference and transliteration	Там зме были три місяці.	Tam zme bŷly try misjaci.
Ukrainian hypothesis and transliteration	Ми були там три місяці.	My buly tam try misjaci.
Score	BLEU = 30.21	

Segment 2513

English source	Well, here to the west.	
Lemko reference and transliteration	Но то ту на захід.	No to tu na zachid.
Ukrainian hypothesis and transliteration	Ну, тут на захід.	Nu, tut na zachid.
Score	BLEU = 30.21	

Russian. Google Translate's English to Russian service achieved a corpus-level BLEU score of 1.10.

Segment 432

English source	Nobody knew.	
Lemko reference and transliteration	Нихто не знал.	Nychto ne znal.
Russian hypothesis and transliteration	Никто не знал.	Nikto ne znal.
Score	BLEU = 59.46	

Segment 2751

English source	What did they expel us for?	
Lemko reference and transliteration	За што нас выгнали?	Za što nas vŷhnaly?
Russian hypothesis and transliteration	За что нас выгнали?	Za čto nas vyg-nali?
Score	BLEU = 42.73	

Segment 2164

English source	Brother went off to war.	
Lemko reference and transliteration	Брат пішол на войну.	Brat pišol na vojnu.
Russian hypothesis and transliteration	Брат ушел на войну.	Brat ušel na vojnu.
Score	BLEU = 42.73	

4 Discussion

The Lemko translation system corpus-level BLEU score of 6.28 indicates that while there is much still to be done, things are on track. The Standard Russian score of BLEU 1.10 indicates that Lemko is less similar to Russian than it is to Polish (BLEU 1.70). Perhaps using pre-revolutionary orthography could boost Russian's score, but that would be an expensive experiment with little obvious benefit.

The transliterated Standard Polish control similarity score of BLEU 1.70 indicates less interference from the dominant language in Poland than might be expected. It would be interesting to redesign the experiment where a handful of computationally inexpensive and obvious sound correspondences (for example, denasalization of *ę to /ja/ and *ǫ to /u/, retraction of *i to /y/, and change of *g to /h/ [23]) were applied to Polish to see if it then scored higher than Standard Ukrainian.

In summary, Lemko has been synthesized in the lab and the power to produce it placed in the hands of speakers both new and native. After a thorough engine overhaul and glossary ramp-up, the next step is to objectively measure, and if feasible, have speakers subjectively rate, the quality of synthetic Lemko versus that produced by native speakers. The day when new speakers of low-resource languages can use machine translation to start communicating in their language overnight is closer, as is the day the Lemko language joins the ranks of those previously endangered, but now revitalized.

Acknowledgements. I would like to thank my colleague Ming Qian of Peraton Labs for inspiring me to conduct this experiment, and Brian Stensrud of Soar Technology, Inc. for introducing us, as well as his encouragement.

I would also like to thank my friend Corinna Caudill for her encouragement and personal interest in the project, as well as for introducing me to Carpatho-Rusyn Society President Maryann Sivak of the University of Pittsburgh, whom I would like to thank for the opportunity to present my work.

I would also like to thank Maria Silvestri of the John and Helen Timo Foundation for conducting interviews with Lemko native speakers and donating the transcripts and my translations of them to research and development.

I would like to thank Achim Rabus of the University of Freiburg and Yves Scherrer of the University of Helsinki for their interest in the project and ideas.

I would also like to thank Myhal' Lŷžečko of the minority-language technology blog InterFyisa for his early interest in the project and community outreach.

I would also like to thank fellow son of Zahoczewie Marko Łyszyk for his interest in the project and community outreach.

Finally, I would like to thank my co-author and Antech Systems Inc. colleague Tom Dobry for his encouragement and guidance.

References

1. Graddol, D.: The future of language. Science **303**(5662), 1329–1331 (2004). https://doi.org/10.1126/science.1096546

2. Eberhard, D.M., Simons, G.F., Fennig, C.D.: Ethnologue: Languages of the World, SIL International, 24th edn. SIL International, Dallas (2021). Online version: How many languages are endangered? https://www.ethnologue.com/guides/how-many-languages-endangered. Accessed 11 Feb 2022
3. ISO 639 Code Tables. https://iso639-3.sil.org/code_tables/639/data. Accessed 11 Feb 2022
4. Language support. https://cloud.google.com/translate/docs/languages. Accessed 11 Feb 2022
5. Select language. https://m.facebook.com/language.php. Accessed 11 Feb 2022
6. Orynycz, P., Dobry, T., Jackson, A., Litzenberg, K.: Yes I Speak… AI neural machine translation in multi-lingual training. In: Proceedings of the Interservice/Industry Training, Simulation, and Education Conference (I/ITSEC) 2021, Paper no. 21176. National Training and Simulation Association, Orlando (2021). https://www.xcdsystem.com/iitsec/proceedings/index.cfm?Year=2021&AbID=96953&CID=862
7. Duć-Fajfer, O.: Literatura a proces rozwoju i rewitalizacja tożsamości językowej na przykładzie literatury łemkowskiej. In: Olko, J., Wicherkiewicz, T., Borges, R. (eds.) Integral Strategies for Language Revitalization, 1st edn., pp. 175–200. Faculty of "Artes Liberales", University of Warsaw, Warsaw (2016)
8. Scherrer, Y., Rabus, A.: Neural morphosyntactic tagging for Rusyn. In: Mitkov, R., Tait, J., Boguraev, B. (eds.) Natural Language Engineering, vol. 25, no. 5, pp. 633–650. Cambridge University Press, Cambridge (2019). https://doi.org/10.1017/S1351324919000287
9. Reservations and Declarations for Treaty No.148 - European Charter for Regional or Minority Languages (ETS No. 148). https://www.coe.int/en/web/conventions/full-list?module=declarations-by-treaty&numSte=148&codeNature=1&codePays=POL. Accessed 11 Feb 2022
10. Formularz indywidualny. https://stat.gov.pl/download/gfx/portalinformacyjny/pl/defaultstronaopisowa/5781/1/1/nsp_2011_badanie__pelne_wykaz_pytan.pdf. Accessed 11 Feb 2022
11. Narodowy Spis Powszechny Ludności i Mieszkań 2002 r. z 20 maja (formularz A). https://stat.gov.pl/gfx/portalinformacyjny/userfiles/_public/spisy_powszechne/nsp2002-form-a.pdf. Accessed 11 Feb 2022
12. IV Raport dotyczący sytuacji mniejszości narodowych i etnicznych oraz języka regionalnego w Rzeczypospolitej Polskiej – 2013. http://mniejszosci.narodowe.mswia.gov.pl/download/86/14637/TekstIVRaportu.pdf. Accessed 11 Feb 2022
13. Vaňko, J.: The Language of Slovakia's Rusyns. East European Monographs, New York (2000)
14. Forston, B., IV.: Indo-European Language and Culture. Blackwell Publishing, Oxford (2004)
15. Pokorny, J.: Indogermanisches etymologisches Wörterbuch, Bern (1959)
16. Horoszczak, J.: Słownik łemkowsko-polski, polsko-łemkowski. Rutenika, Warsaw (2004)
17. Vasmer, M.: Russisches etymologisches Wörterbuch. Zweiter Band. Carl Winter, Universitätsverlag, Heidelberg (1955)
18. Monier-Williams, M.: A Sanskrit-English Dictionary Etymologically and Philologically Arranged with Special Reference to Cognate Indo-European Languages. The Clarendon Press, Oxford (1899)
19. Derksen, R.: Etymological dictionary of the slavic inherited lexicon. In: Lubotsky, A. (ed.) Leiden Indo-European Etymological Dictionary Series, vol. 4, Koninklijke Brill, Leiden (2008)
20. Post, M.: A call for clarity in reporting BLEU scores. In: Proceedings of the Third Conference on Machine Translation (WMT), vol. 1, pp. 186–191. Association for Computational Linguistics, Brussels (2018). https://aclanthology.org/W18-63
21. Chen, B., Cherry, C.: A systematic comparison of smoothing techniques for sentence-level BLEU. In: Proceedings of the Ninth Workshop on Statistical Machine Translation, pp. 362–367. Association for Computational Linguistics, Baltimore (2014). http://dx.doi.org/10.3115/v1/W14-33

22. Ministerstwo Spraw Wewnętrznych i Administracji: Rozporządzenie Ministra Spraw Wewnętrznych i Administracji z dnia 30 maja 2005 r. w sprawie sposobu transliteracji imion i nazwisk osób należących do mniejszości narodowych i etnicznych zapisanych w alfabecie innym niż alfabet łaciński. In: Dziennik Ustaw Nr 102, pp. 6560–6573. Rządowe Centrum Legislacji, Warsaw (2005)
23. Shevelov, G.: On the chronology of H and the new G in Ukrainian. In: Harvard Ukrainian Studies, vol. 1, no. 2, pp. 137–152. Harvard Ukrainian Research Institute, Cambridge (1977). https://www.jstor.org/stable/40999942

Extracting and Re-mapping Narrative Text Structure Elements Between Languages Using Self-supervised and Active Few-Shot Learning

Ming Qian[1(✉)] and Eve Zhu[2]

[1] Peraton Labs, Basking Ridge, NJ, USA
ming.qian@mail.peratonlabs.com
[2] Translation and Interpretation Program, Middlebury Institute of International Studies at Monterey, Monterey, CA, USA
qzhu@middlebury.edu

Abstract. Transcreators extract crucial information from text written in one language for a specific media type and translate this text into a different language and a different media type. Multiple factors drive changes in narrative structures in different languages for different media platforms. AI-based approaches can be used to extract critical information elements from text and augment human analysis and insight to facilitate transcreation. In this study, we apply self-supervised learning and active few-shot learning based on generative pretrained transformer models (e.g. GPT-N) to perform information extraction. We also used Wikifier (https://wikifier.org/) to annotate the related text with links to relevant Wikipedia concepts to augment human users with additional explanations. The performance statistics were collected using four news stories, and the results show that self-supervised approach is error-prone because the GPT-3 pretrained language model can generate synthetic information based on patterns learned from its huge training corpus instead of reflecting only relevant facts in the prompted text. On the other hand, active few-shot learning worked very well with 87.5% accuracy on the experimental examples. Wikifier also provides a large number of correct and useful links to named entities such as human names, locations, organizations, and concepts. Transcreators can leverage these AI tools to augment their ability to effectively perform their tasks.

Keywords: Active learning · Few-shot learning · Self-supervised learning · Generative language modeling · AI · Machine learning · AI/ML · Natural language processing · Natural language understanding · NLP · NLU · Named entity linking · Transcreation

1 Introduction

AI systems can be used to extract critical information elements from text and augment human analysis and insight. In this study, we apply self-supervised learning and active few-shot learning based on generative pretrained transformer models (e.g. GPT-N) to

H. Degen and S. Ntoa (Eds.): HCII 2022, LNAI 13336, pp. 581–593, 2022.
https://doi.org/10.1007/978-3-031-05643-7_38

perform information extraction. We also used Wikifier (https://wikifier.org/) to annotate the related text with links to relevant Wikipedia concepts to augment human users with additional explanations.

In the use case of translating English articles from a professional institute's website (https://www.middlebury.edu/institute/) into producing Chinese articles for the official WeChat social media platform of the Middlebury Institute of International Studies (MIIS) at Monterey, change in narrative structure from English into Chinese is mostly driven by three factors (Fig. 1):

First, the English news articles on the school's official website are work products from multiple departments, each with its own distinctive writing style. The Career Development Center publishes interviews with alums or current students sometimes in the traditional question-answer fashion or produces a long article detailing the student's journey before and after MIIS. The Admissions Office tends to issue short notices reminding prospective students of upcoming deadlines or admitted students of the resources available on campus to help them settle in. Different departments have different priorities, and hence different ways of communicating the information. The WeChat team, on the other hand, is a small, close-knit group where they hope to keep the content versatile but the style coherent. This brings a challenge: How does one take distinctively different sources of English content and create a relatively coherent line of Chinese articles to formulate their own style?

Second, WeChat articles are, in nature, new media products. The news-release part of the school's official website functions more like a traditional news outlet. For new media content to succeed, and this is true across the entire spectrum of new media including Twitter, Tik Tok, Facebook, etc., there are certain rules that need to be followed. The content needs to be short and attention-grabbing, because modern readers are so spoiled by the fast-paced quick-turnaround outpour of information coming from every corner of the Internet. If the editors want to keep their readers engaged and read the whole article that they post, rule No. 1 is to keep it short, which is usually not the case with the English sources. In addition, most of readers read WeChat articles on their smartphones. Accessing the full article usually requires scrolling down two or three times. Studies have shown that most readers of WeChat articles tend to lose interest after three scrolls, which means in an ideal situation, WeChat articles shouldn't exceed the length of three screens. With limitation in lengths comes prioritization of the information. Only the so-called "hard facts" will be included, which are usually the standard 5W1H (what, who, where, when, how and why) questions. Details of the story will be added depending on their relevance to the storyline and page limits.

Third, the official WeChat account of the MIIS has a targeted viewership and audience group. The WeChat account operates essentially as an outreach of the MIIS Chinese community and part of MIIS's external liaisons. To better service this goal, content needs to be produced with a visible MIIS imprint, usually in the form of stressing the protagonist's connection to MIIS or the part MIIS has played in their academic or career development. This is a staple conclusion segment for our articles, a repeated characteristic in narrative structure that could be seen in almost every article that have been published. We are interested in automatic discovery of cultural knowledge, something that would allow digital assistants equipped with the automatic mechanism to help a user to discover culture-sensitive knowledge, avoid cultural miscommunication, and prevent negative and unintended consequences. Cultural schemas are a generalized collection of knowledge of past experiences that are organized into knowledge groups and guide human behaviors in familiar situations.

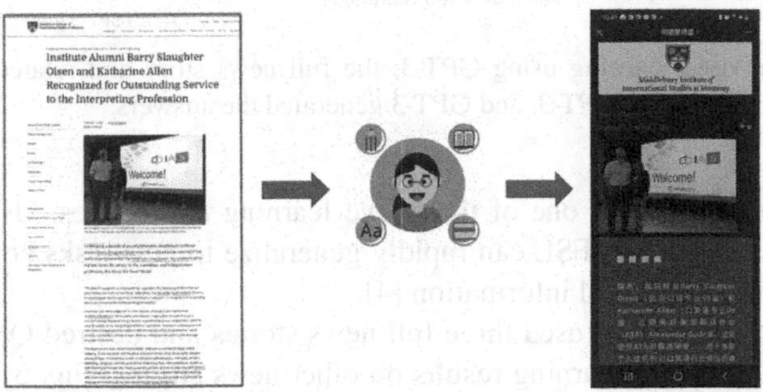

Fig. 1. Narrative structure changes for converting alumina news articles from a MIIS website to their equivalents on social media platforms are motivated by three factors: (1) to take different sources with distinctive style and map them to unified style; (2) Social media content needs to be short and attention-grabbing; (3) A staple conclusion segment in the form of stressing the protagonist's connection to MIIS or the part MIIS has played in their academic or career development.

While human translators can extract the information by reading an original article in the source language (English) and translate/remap the extracted information into the social media article in the target language manually. An AI-based extraction mechanism can provide a much faster knowledge representation, and also provide links to relevant Wikipedia concepts to augment human users with external knowledge.

2 Methodologies

2.1 Self-supervised Learning Using Generative Pretrained Transformer-Based Language (GPT-3)

GPT-3 is a transformer-based language model [1] that takes input and generates text from it. GPT-3 takes any text prompt, such as several phrases or sentences and returns a text completion in natural language. Users can also program GPT-3 by showing just a few examples (few shots) [2]. A full-version of GPT-3 model has 175 billion machine learning parameters.

For our experiment, we send the full news story as the prompted text, and then asked a few related questions, to check if the GPT-3 language model can produce answers that are accurate and/or relevant (Fig. 2).

2.2 Active Few-Shot Learning Using GPT-3

Active learning is a special case of machine learning in which a user can interactively teach a learning algorithm by labeling new data points with the desired outputs [3].

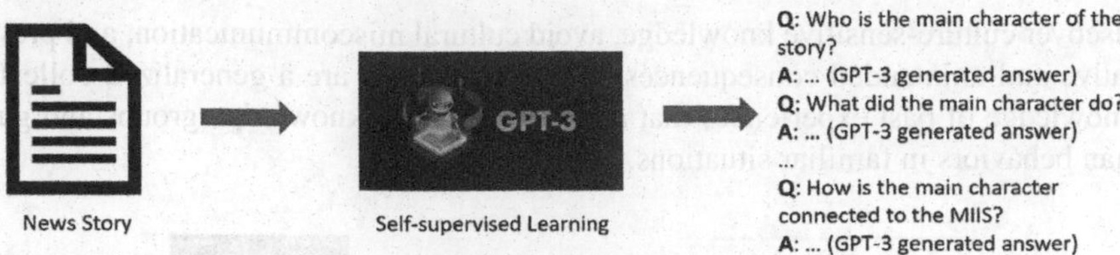

Fig. 2. Self-supervised learning using GPT-3: the full news story and related questions were entered as prompted text for GPT-3, and GPT-3 generated the answers.

Few-shot learning (FSL) is one of the active learning approaches. Using pre-trained knowledge such as GPT-3, FSL can rapidly generalize to new tasks containing only a few samples with supervised information [4].

For our experiment, we used three full news stories and desired Q&A contents as examples, and tested the learning results on other news stories (Fig. 3). The objective was to test if the GPT-3 language model can learn sophisticated patterns illustrated by the few-shot examples and provide accurate and relevant answers to a new story.

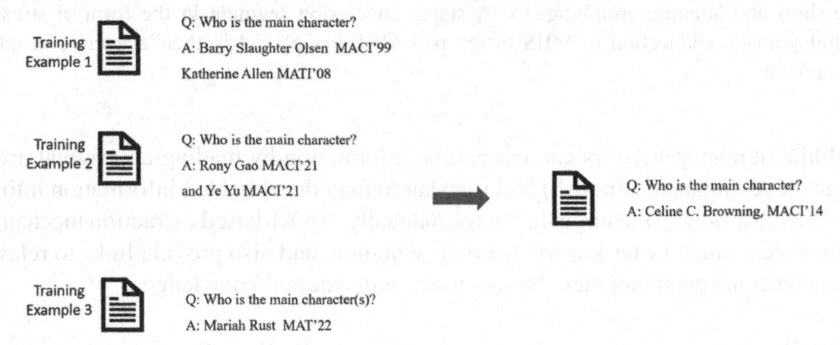

Fig. 3. Active few-shot learning using GPT-3: several news stories were entered as teaching examples for few-shot learning using GPT-3, and then GPT-3 extracted the related information based on the patterns defined by the teaching examples.

2.3 Named Entity Linking Using Wikifier

Named Entity Linking (EL) is the task of recognizing and disambiguating named entities to a knowledge base (e.g. Wikidata, DBpedia, or YAGO). We add this feature using Wikifer [5] to quickly link the users to the related knowledge (see examples on Fig. 4).

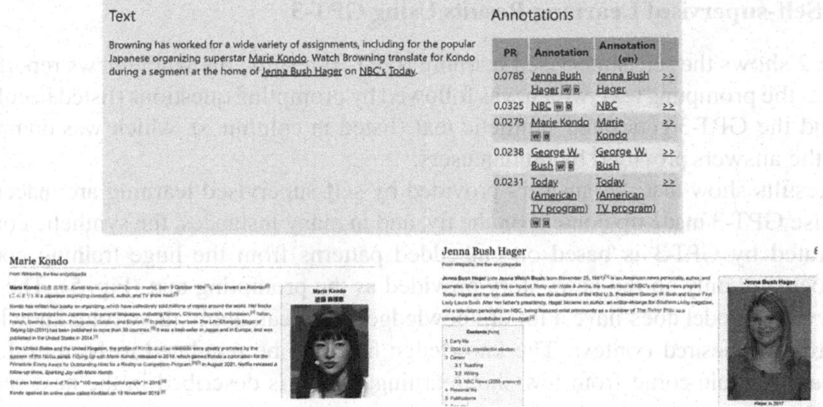

Fig. 4. Named entity linking, using Wikifier semantic annotation services, can quickly link the users to related knowledge on related named entities such as person, location, organization.

3 Results and Evaluations

In this section, we describe the details of our experiments on applying self-supervised learning, active few-shot learning, and named entity linking on specific news stories. We evaluate the performance by comparing the results with human experts' opinions.

3.1 News Reports Data

The following news reports were used as experimental data for this study (Table 1).

Table 1. Titles and web links for the four reports used as experimental data.

Reports	Title and Weblink
1	"Alum Receives Rising Star Award from American Translators Association" https://www.middlebury.edu/institute/advancing-your-career/career-guide/alum-receives-rising-star-award-american-translators-association
2	"Institute Alumni Barry Slaughter Olsen and Katharine Allen Recognized for Outstanding Service to the Interpreting Profession" https://www.middlebury.edu/institute/advancing-your-career/career-guide/institute-alumni-barry-slaughter-olsen-and-katharine-allen
3	"Recent Graduates Win International Interpretation Competition" https://www.middlebury.edu/institute/news/recent-graduates-win-international-interpretation-competition
4	"Student Wins Leading International Literary Journal's Translation Prize" https://www.middlebury.edu/institute/news/student-wins-leading-international-literary-journals-translation-prize

3.2 Self-supervised Learning Results Using GPT-3

Table 2 shows the self-supervised learning (GPT-3) results: the whole news report was used as the prompting text, which was followed by prompting questions (listed in column 1), and the GPT-3 generated synthetic text (listed in column 3), which was compared with the answers provided by human users.

Results show that the answers provided by self-supervised learning are inaccurate because GPT-3 made up content on the fly, and in many instances, the synthetic content generated by GPT-3 is based on embedded patterns from the huge training corpus, not focusing only on the news story provided as the prompting text (Fig. 5). The self-supervised model does have a lot of knowledge, but it can apply the wrong knowledge towards the desired context. The knowledge needs to be regulated to be useful. The regulation could come from few-shot learning, which is described in the next section (Fig. 6).

Table 2. Self-supervised learning (GPT-3) results using story 1 as prompting text. We can observe that many generated answers are unrelated to the prompting text (marked in bold and italicized font), therefore are wrong.

Prompting questions	Ground truth provided by human judgment	GPT-3 results (self-supervised learning)
Who is the main character?	Celine C. Browning	(1) Browning, Céline C (☑) (2) American Translators Association ATA (3) The JLD Language Professionals Division Japanese Language Division Lelia
What did the main character(s) win?	1. Received Rising Star Award from ATA 2. Graduated from MIIS in 2014 3. Established her own translation company 4. Worked on a variety of assignments, including a TV show with Marie Kondo	The Rising Star Award ***includes $1,000 along with an engraved crystal and a plaque*** The Rising Star Award is ***presented to a translator, interpreter, or entity that:*** Browning is one of the recipients of ATA's 2021 ***Lifetime Achievement Award and a member of the ATA Strategic Planning Team***

(continued)

Table 2. (*continued*)

Prompting questions	Ground truth provided by human judgment	GPT-3 results (self-supervised learning)
What is the prize is about?	"Recognizes an early-career translator, interpreter, or entity that is seen as having already 'made a mark' on ATA and seen as having great potential to positively impact ATA and the language professions in the future"	The Rising Star Award was established in 2012 to recognize translators of exceptional talent who are ***under the age of 35***. Recipients are recognized for their contributions to the translation, interpreting, and language professions. The award also celebrates the exceptional work of young translators who represent the next generation of ATA leaders
The main character's connection to MIIS	MACI'14 "MIIS helped create a strong foundation for me to build my career upon, and once I joined the ATA and the JLD, getting involved was such a natural progression of events," said Browning	***"I chose to attend MIIS because it was the first school that I applied to. I was accepted and enrolled within 2 months. It was a great decision! When I first arrived in San Francisco, I was immediately invited to join the JLD where I met many of the people who are still my closest friends today"***

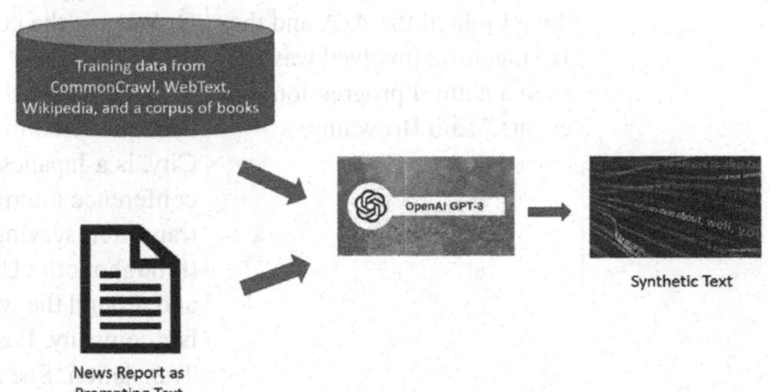

Fig. 5. Synthetic texts generated by self-supervised learning models are influenced by the huge training corpus and the prompting text, leading to inaccurate answers towards questions aiming towards the facts/concepts embedded in the prompting text.

Table 3. Active few-shot learning results for 4 stories. The results align well with the human-generated solutions (14 out of 16 answers are accurate).

Report being tested	Comparison between human judgment and active few-shot learning results	
	Human Judgments (also used as the training examples for few-shot learning)	Active few-shot learning answers
"Alum Receives Rising Star Award from American Translators Association" https://www.middlebury.edu/institute/advancing-your-career/career-guide/alum-receives-rising-star-award-american-translators-association	Q: Who is the main character? A: Celine C. Browning MACI'14 Q: What is the main event? A: Received Rising Star Award from ATA Q: What is the prize about? A: "recognizes an early-career translator, interpreter, or entity that is seen as having already 'made a mark' on ATA and seen as having great potential to positively impact ATA and the language professions in the future." Q: What is the connection to MIIS? A: "MIIS helped create a strong foundation for me to build my career upon, and once I joined the ATA and the JLD, getting involved was such a natural progression of events," said Browning	Q: Who is the main character? A: Céline C. Browning MACI'14 (☑) Q: What is the main event? A: The American Translators Association (ATA) presented its 2021 Rising Star Award to Institute alum Céline C. Browning MACI'14… (☑) Q: What is the prize about? A: According to the ATA, the Rising Star Award "recognizes an early-career translator, interpreter, or entity that is seen as having already 'made a mark' on ATA and seen as having great potential to positively impact ATA and the language professions in the future." (☑) Q: What is the connection to MIIS? A: Browning, who is headquartered in Salt Lake City, is a Japanese/English conference interpreter and translator, serving clients throughout the United States and around the world through her company, Found in Translation. She also serves as a contract interpreter with the U.S. Department of State (☒)

(continued)

Table 3. (*continued*)

Report being tested	Comparison between human judgment and active few-shot learning results	
	Human Judgments (also used as the training examples for few-shot learning)	Active few-shot learning answers
"Institute Alumni Barry Slaughter Olsen and Katharine Allen Recognized for Outstanding Service to the Interpreting Profession" https://www.middlebury.edu/institute/advancing-your-career/career-guide/institute-alumni-barry-slaughter-olsen-and-katharine-allen	Q: Who is Main Character(s)? A: Barry Slaughter Olsen MACI'99 Katherine Allen MATI'08 Q: What is the main event? They received Alexander Gode Prize at ATA Q: What is the prize about? A: The ATA's most prestigious award, is given to an individual or institution "in recognition of outstanding service to the translation and interpreting professions." Q: What is the connection to MIIS? A: InterpretAmerica was born when Olsen, at the time a professor in the MA in Translation and Interpretation degree program at the Institute, asked second-year student Allen—the former president of the California Healthcare Interpreting Association—if she would be interested in collaborating, combining her expertise as a community and medical interpreter with his as a conference interpreter to form a team spanning a substantial portion of the range of subdisciplines within their diverse profession	Q: Who is the main character? A: Barry Slaughter Olsen MACI'99 and Katharine Allen MATI'08 (☑) Q: What is the main event? A: They were recently awarded the American Translators Association's (ATA) highest honor for service to the translation and interpretation profession, the Alexander Gode Medal. (☑) Q: What is the prize about? A: The Alexander Gode Medal, the ATA's most prestigious award, is given to an individual or institution "in recognition of outstanding service to the translation and interpreting professions." (☑) Q: What is the connection to MIIS? A: Olsen, at the time a professor in the MA in Translation and Interpretation degree program at the Institute, asked second-year student Allen—the former president of the California Healthcare Interpreting Association—if she would be interested in collaborating, combining her expertise as a community and medical interpreter with his as a conference interpreter to form a team spanning a substantial portion of the range of subdisciplines within their diverse profession. (☑)

(*continued*)

Table 3. (*continued*)

Report being tested	Comparison between human judgment and active few-shot learning results	
	Human Judgments (also used as the training examples for few-shot learning)	Active few-shot learning answers
"Recent Graduates Win International Interpretation Competition" https://www.middlebury.edu/institute/news/recent-graduates-win-international-interpretation-competition	Q: Who is the main character? A: Rony Gao MACI'21 And Ye Yu MACI'21 Q: What is the main event? A: The two won first prize in the Simultaneous Interpreting Invitational Tournament at the 10th International Translation and Interpreting Competition organized by Beijing Language and Culture University Q: What is the prize about? A: Online and onsite contestants were from major Chinese-English translation and interpretation programs in the world, including Beijing Foreign Studies University, Shanghai International Studies University, Guangdong University of Foreign Studies, University of International Business and Economics, Fudan University, University of Bath, and the University of Leeds Q: What is the connection to MIIS? A: A Supportive Academic Community Both students emphasized the role that the supportive academic community at MIIS played in their success. Said Yu, "I could never have won the prize without the help and support of my professors. I would also like to thank all of my classmates for their encouragement. You all mean so much to me!"	Q: Who is the main character? A: Ye Yu MACI'21 and Rony Gao MACI'21 (☑) Q: What is the main event? A: Won the Simultaneous Interpreting Invitational Tournament at the 10th International Translation and Interpreting Competition organized by Beijing Language and Culture University. (☑) Q: What is the prize about? A: Other online and onsite contestants were from major Chinese-English translation and interpretation programs in the world, including Beijing Foreign Studies University, Shanghai International Studies University, Guangdong University of Foreign Studies, University of International Business and Economics, Fudan University, University of Bath, and the University of Leeds. (☑) Q: What is the connection to MIIS? A: Both students emphasized the role that the supportive academic community at MIIS played in their success. Said Yu, "I could never have won the prize without the help and support of my professors. I would also like to thank all of my classmates for their encouragement. (☑)

(*continued*)

Table 3. (*continued*)

Report being tested	Comparison between human judgment and active few-shot learning results	
	Human Judgments (also used as the training examples for few-shot learning)	Active few-shot learning answers
"Student Wins Leading International Literary Journal's Translation Prize" https://www.middlebury.edu/institute/news/student-wins-leading-international-literary-journals-translation-prize	Q: Who is the main character(s)? A: Mariah Rust MAT'22 Q: What is the main event? A: She won the prose category of the World Literature Today Student Translation Prize for 2021 Q: What is the prize about? A: Now in its fourth year, the annual contest is judged by the editorial team of the leading literary journal World Literature Today and "recognizes the talent and promise of translation students worldwide." Q: What is the connection to MIIS? A: Rust was encouraged and sponsored in the contest by Professor George Henson. "When Mariah notified me that she had won, I was delighted," he says. Unlike his student, though, "I wasn't surprised, because I knew Mariah was an excellent translator"	Q: Who is the main character? A: Mariah Rust MAT'22 (☑) Q: What is the main event? A: She won the prose category of the World Literature Today Student Translation Prize for 2021. (☑) Q: What is the prize about? A: The annual contest is judged by the editorial team of the leading literary journal World Literature Today and "recognizes the talent and promise of translation students worldwide." (☑) Q: What is the connection to MIIS? A: Her submission for the contest, a translation from French of an excerpt from "Gare du Nord," a story by Kinshasa-born author Albertine M. Itela, was "the first time I sent any translation out to be considered for publication." (☒)

3.3 Active Few-Shot Learning

Table 3 shows the active few-shot learning (also using GPT-3) results. Altogether, we used four news stories for a 4-fold cross-validation—three stories were used as the training examples and the other one was used to test the example.

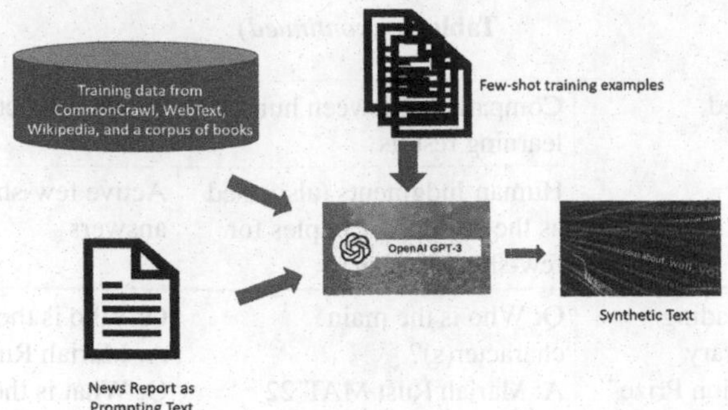

Fig. 6. Once the self-supervised learning language (e.g. GPT-3) is regulated by the few-shot learning examples, the synthetic text generated become much more accurate towards the facts/concepts embedded in the prompting text.

3.4 Named Entity Linking

Table 2 shows the results of named entity linking using Wikifier. We only tested the named entities in the results of few-shot learning for the four stories. Many proper links towards the named entities were properly identified and linked. This could help the translators/editors a lot if they are not familiar with these entities. Instead of relying on individual searches online, a user can have the links highlighted on the same page, and the links are clickable (Table 4 and Fig. 7).

Table 4. Named entity linking results.

Story no.	Named entity linking correctness
1	ATA (American Translation Association) (☑) Salt Lake City (☑) US Department of State (☑)
2	ATA (American Translation Association) (☒fail to detect)
3	10 universities on the list (☑) The short-form expression of Middlebury Institute of International Study (MIIS) (☒)
4	World Literature Today (☑) Gare du Nord (☑) Kinshasa (☒fail to detect)

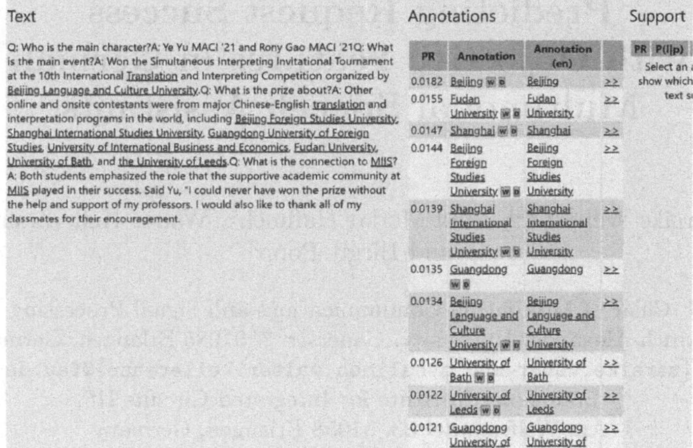

Text
Annotations
Support
Q: Who is the main character?A: Ye Yu MACI '21 and Rony Gao MACI '21Q: What is the main event?A: Won the Simultaneous Interpreting Invitational Tournament at the 10th International Translation and Interpreting Competition organized by Beijing Language and Culture University.Q: What is the prize about?A: Other online and onsite contestants were from major Chinese-English translation and interpretation programs in the world, including Beijing Foreign Studies University, Shanghai International Studies University, Guangdong University of Foreign Studies, University of International Business and Economics, Fudan University, University of Bath, and the University of Leeds.Q: What is the connection to MIIS? A: Both students emphasized the role that the supportive academic community at MIIS played in their success. Said Yu, "I could never have won the prize without the help and support of my professors. I would also like to thank all of my classmates for their encouragement.
PR
Annotation
Annotation (en)
0.0182 Beijing Beijing
0.0155 Fudan University Fudan University
0.0147 Shanghai Shanghai
0.0144 Beijing Foreign Studies University Beijing Foreign Studies University
0.0139 Shanghai International Studies University Shanghai International Studies University
0.0135 Guangdong Guangdong
0.0134 Beijing Language and Culture University Beijing Language and Culture University
0.0126 University of Bath University of Bath
0.0122 University of Leeds University of Leeds
0.0121 Guangdong University of Guangdong University of
PR P(l|p)
Select an
show which
text s

Fig. 7. An example of using Wikifier on the answers towards the story 3. The links to 10 universities on the list were properly identified.

4 Conclusion

Multiple factors drive changes in narrative structures for reports written in different language based on different media platforms. AI-based approaches can be used to extract critical information elements from text and augment human analysis and insight to facilitate the transcreation process across languages and media platforms. In this study, we apply self-supervised learning and active few-shot learning based on generative pretrained transformer models (e.g. GPT-N) to perform information extraction. We also used Wikifier (https://wikifier.org/) to annotate the related text with links to relevant Wikipedia concepts to augment human users with additional explanations. The performance statistics were collected using four news stories, and the results show that self-supervised approach is error-prone because the GPT-3 pretrained language model can generate synthetic information based on patterns learned from its huge training corpus instead of reflecting only relevant facts from the prompted text. On the other hand, active few-shot learning worked very well with 87.5% accuracy on the experimental examples. Wikifier also provides a large number of correct and useful links to named entities such as human names, locations, organizations, and concepts. Transcreators across language and media platforms can leverage these AI tools to augment their ability to effectively perform their tasks.

References

1. Vaswani, A., et al.: Attention is all you need. arXiv preprint arXiv:1706.03762 (2017)
2. Brown, T.B., et al.: Language models are few-shot learners. arXiv preprint arXiv:2005.14165 (2020)
3. Settles, B.: Active learning literature survey (2009)
4. Wang, Y., Yao, Q., Kwok, J.T., Ni, L.M.: Generalizing from a few examples: A survey on few-shot learning. ACM Comput. Surv. (CSUR) **53**(3), 1–34 (2020)
5. Wikifier semantic annotation service for 100 languages. https://wikifier.org/

Predicting Request Success with Objective Features in German Multimodal Speech Assistants

Mareike Weber[1(✉)], Mhd Modar Halimeh[1], Walter Kellermann[1], and Birgit Popp[2]

[1] Chair of Multimedia Communications and Signal Processing, Friedrich-Alexander University, Cauerstr. 7, 91085 Erlangen, Germany
{mareike.weber,mhd.m.halimeh,walter.kellermann}@fau.de
[2] Fraunhofer Institute for Integrated Circuits IIS, Am Wolfsmantel 33, 91058 Erlangen, Germany
birgit.popp@iis.fraunhofer.de

Abstract. We investigate whether objective features, like occurrence of an error and number of turns, can automatically predict success in interactions with multimodal speech assistants. We used interactions from the SmartKom corpus, a data set on multimodal interactions with virtual assistants in German. In a first step, we segmented the interactions into requests and labeled them as successful or unsuccessful. Afterwards, we defined task success as the average of request success rate. Next, we investigated whether subjective features such as emotions expressed by users show a relation to task success. We find no significant correlation. Finally, we exploited objective features, e.g., number of turns to predict request success. We find that objective features suffice to reach F_1 scores over 0.9 (prediction of successful requests) and F_0 scores above 0.83 (prediction of unsuccessful requests). Finally, we discuss implications of our findings for automatic evaluation of pragmatic aspects of user experience.

Keywords: Task success · Request success · Multimodal · Speech assistant · German · Logistic regression · Random forest

1 Introduction

There is a rising trend to use *Speech Assistants* (SAs) all over the world [1]. At the same time, product reviews of Speech Assistants (SAs) criticize their ability to understand users [2–4]. Such reviews present a paradox: products which are attested a low usability, are attractive enough for users to spend money on. This paradox might be solved by distinguishing different aspects of *User Experience* (UX), namely pragmatic and hedonic User Experience (UX) [5,6]. Pragmatic UX describes – among others – how efficient and useful a system is, whereas hedonic aspects involve how attractive, fun and engaging a system is [5,7]. Merčun and Žumer [7] find that task success affects pragmatic aspects of UX more than

H. Degen and S. Ntoa (Eds.): HCII 2022, LNAI 13336, pp. 594–609, 2022.
https://doi.org/10.1007/978-3-031-05643-7_39

hedonic aspects. Minge and Thüring [6] suggest that emotions expressed by users are linked to hedonic UX. In our work, we consider interaction success as a proxy for pragmatic UX and user emotions as a proxy for hedonic UX.

Developers of task-oriented SAs aim to optimize their task success [8], which means that task success is considered to be an important metric in development of SAs. In earlier studies we found that task success and UX are only moderately correlated for SAs and differences found in UX do not translate into differences in task success [9,10]. This suggests that systems which are similar in their ability to successfully complete interactions with users can differ significantly in their UX. In our present work, we investigate this further by correlating task success with emotions expressed by users.

We set out to analyze interaction success of virtual assistants together with subjective reactions, like emotions expressed by the user. To this end, various approaches can be realized. One approach is to conduct surveys and questionnaires [11,12]. However, this can be done only in retrospect to an interaction. Consequently, results can not be incorporated directly into ongoing interactions. Moreover, this performance analysis method is costly and time-consuming [13,14]. In contrast, automatic performance analysis can be considered directly during the interaction, which introduces the possibility of an empathetic response to a system failure. This can positively impact the UX [15]. Various performance measures can be used to realize such an approach. Developers invest, for example, in the recognition of user's emotions to predict the success of a user-system interaction [15]. On the one hand, the consideration of subjective features is found to create more human-like and intelligent assistants [16], making them more engaging [17] and trustworthy [18,19]. On the other hand, emotion recognition is an involved task due to aspects such as subjectivity, cultural or environmental variations [20,21].

Our work focuses on analyzing the success of interactions with multimodal SAs. Schiel [22] showed that objective features correlate with system performance and we build on these results. In contrast to subjective features, objective features can be objectively assessed from a dialogue, e.g., the occurrence of an error or number of turns. Request success contributes to system predictability and efficacy, which are pragmatic qualities of UX [5,23]. Thus, our work can be seen as a step towards automatically predicting pragmatic UX quality of interactions with multimodal SAs.

In this work, we aim to answer the following research questions:

1. Does task success correlate with emotions expressed by users?
2. Can objective features predict request success?
3. Which features are most important when predicting request success?

2 Methods

To address our research questions, we utilized the SmartKom corpus, a data set of user interactions with a multimodal virtual assistant [24] (see Sect. 2.1).

We segmented the interactions in this data set into so-called requests and labeled them as successful or unsuccessful based on the system's response. In a next step, we calculated task success as the average request success of an interaction per domain. Afterwards, we investigated the relationship between emotions and task success. Finally, we developed several classification methods to predict request success.

2.1 Data Set

The SmartKom corpus [24] is, to our knowledge, the largest data set of interactions carried out in German with multimodal virtual assistants. It consists of interactions in which users were asked to complete a specific task using a Wizard-of-Oz simulation of a multimodal assistant [25]. The data set covers several domains, namely, *cinema*, *restaurant*, *hotel*, *tourism*, *navigation*, *calendar*, *music*, and *television*. Interactions were recorded in a session-based manner, resulting in a maximum recording duration of five minutes. Additionally, interactions are transcribed, and transcripts are segmented into user and system turns. Furthermore, gestures and emotions are annotated. Emotions are annotated as holistic and mimic user state. *Holistic User State (HUS)* is annotated based on video and audio recording of the user-system interaction. Consequently, annotators are aware of the content of the dialogue when labeling Holistic User State (HUS). In contrast, the *Mimic User State (MUS)* is annotated based solely on the video recording of the user-system interaction (without audio) and thus lacking context information.

We augmented the data set by annotating success of interactions using two measures, request success and task success.

A request is initiated by a question or command formulated by the user followed by a system response or a dialogue of multiple turns. Each request was labeled as successful or unsuccessful depending on whether or not the question was answered correctly or the command was carried out successfully. Here we provide an example of a successful request (interactions were translated from German to English):

[In the previous interaction the user asked for details about the movie "Four Weddings and a Funeral"]
***User**: Where can I find a cinema on the city map?*
***Assistant**: On the map you can see the cinemas where the movie "Four Weddings and a Funeral" is being shown.*

In contrast, a request is unsuccessful if the system does not answer the question. This can be true, either if a wrong response is given or if an error message is provided by the system as in the following example:

***User**: Where is the pedestrian zone here?*
***Assistant**: Sorry, this information is not available at the moment.*

Finally, a task is defined as a thematically coherent section of an interaction. The definition is derived from the study design of the SmartKom project. Prior to the interaction the users were instructed to complete a specific task using the system, e.g. "Plan a [...] cinema trip in the evening.". Consequently, we defined task success as the average request success rate, defined by Eq. 1. Task success is computed as the number of successful requests ($\#\ successful\ requests$) within a task divided by the number of requests ($\#\ requests$) within the same task. Task success is a relevant metric in the dialogue system community and used to evaluate and optimize task-oriented dialogue systems [8].

$$Task\ success = \frac{\#\ successful\ requests}{\#\ requests} \tag{1}$$

2.2 Emotion Scores

To evaluate whether there is a statistically significant relation between emotions and task success, we used both types of annotated user emotions: HUS and Mimic User State (MUS). In addition, emotions are divided into three categories: negative (neg), positive (pos), and neutral. We focus on negative and positive emotions in our further analysis. Neutral emotions are not further investigated as they are neither negative nor positive and thus we assume that those are not related to task success.

To quantify user emotions during a task, we use the unweighted measure *Total*, calculated for both annotated user emotions HUS and MUS. *HUS Total* is calculated as defined by Eq. 2, where $category \in \{-1, 1\}$ depending on the type of recognized emotion during the task, e.g., negative emotions result in $category = -1$. N refers to the total number of emotions recognized during a task. *MUS Total* is calculated analogously. In addition, a weighted measure is utilized by weighting the recognized user emotions by their *duration* and *intensity*, resulting in the *HUS Score*, and *MUS Score*, respectively. Equation 3 defines the calculation of *HUS Score*, where $intensity \in \{1, 2\}$, with weak intensity resulting in $intensity = 1$ and strong intensity in $intensity = 2$. *MUS Score* is calculated in a similar manner, with the only difference being that the MUS type of emotion annotation was taken as basis for computation. Intensity and duration of emotions were annotated by multiple annotators.

Based on the existing annotations of user emotions we compute five features for both holistic and mimic. For the consideration of solely positive emotions, e.g. *HUSpos Score*, we compute the equations for all n with $category = 1$, and for solely negative emotions, e.g. *HUSneg Score*, the equations are computed for all n with $category = -1$. See Sect. 3.2 for an overview of computed emotion scores and their correlation with task success.

$$HUS\ Total = \sum_{n=1}^{N} category_n \tag{2}$$

$$HUS\ Score = \sum_{n=1}^{N} duration_n \times intensity_n \times category_n \tag{3}$$

2.3 Classification of Request Success

As mentioned earlier, in this work, request success is predicted using objective features. More specifically, the following features are considered: *number of turns*, *number of words*, *request duration*, *number of gestures*, *number of sentences*, the *number of overlapping words* as well as the *ratio of overlapping words* and *occurrence of error message*. *Occurrence of error message* is defined as a binary variable and each request can only result in one error. Table 1 lists all selected features and subcategories the feature is computed for. The subcategories are *total*, *user*, and *system*. Subcategory *total* refers to the feature computed for the whole request. Furthermore, *system* means the feature is only computed for the system's part of the request, while *user* means the feature is only computed for the user's part. In summary, we computed 18 features. We decided on these features as Schiel [22] showed them to correlate with interaction success.

Table 1. Selected 18 objective features to predict request success.

Feature	Subcategory
Number of turns	Total, system, user
Number of words	Total, system, user
Number of sentences	Total, system, user
Number of overlapping words	Total, system, user
Ratio of overlapping words	Total, system, user
Request duration	Total
Number of gestures	Total
Occurrence of error message	Total

These features are used to predict the request success rate by state-of-the-art classifiers. We decided for a broad range of classifiers to test different methods. More specifically, we implemented six models, namely Logistic Regression (LR) [26,27], Random Forest (RF) [28,29], Decision Tree (DT) [30,31], AdaBoost (AB) [32,33], Naive Bayes (NB) [34,35], and Linear Support Vector Machine (SVM) [36]. We compare these models in base implementation, meaning using hyperparameter presettings of the Python package scikit-learn [37,38] without further fine-tuning. Subsequently, we examine the impact of fine-tuning on performance for two of the six models: Random Forest (RF) and Logistic Regression (LR). Further performance gains are investigated by employing class weighting [39] whereas feature space reduction is examined by utilizing Sequential Forward Search (SFS) as feature selection algorithm such that the most important features for request success classification are identified.

In order to ensure unbiased comparison between classifiers, we randomly separate the data set 100 times into training and test data sets using the scikit-learn library *train_test_split* [38]. For the split into training and test data we decided for 70% of data for training and 30% of data for testing.

Prior to the separation, we sorted the data set according to the recording session a request belongs to. Thereby, we ensured that a recording session does not occur in both the test and the training data sets. Thus, the model performance when evaluated using the test data sets reflects its generalization performance. In other words, this ensures that overfitting to user-system interactions in the training data set is accounted for when testing. The sorting was not carried out based on tasks as two tasks could be completed in a single session.

Many performance metrics require a nearly balanced data set. For an unbalanced data set, these goodness-of-fit metrics are biased in favor of models that are more likely to represent the more frequent class. Misclassification of each class is considered equal, resulting in such measures being an unsatisfactory metric for unbalanced data sets [40]. As the data set used in this work is not balanced, we decided to exploit *F-metric* as performance measure. *F-metric* defines the harmonic mean of precision and recall, taking both metrics into account as seen in Eq. 4. It prefers high values of both precision and recall. Consequently, it is suitable for imbalanced data sets [41]. More specifically, we employed the *mean F-metric* as defined in Eq. 5, with F_0 as F-score of unsuccessful requests and F_1 as F-score of successful requests.

$$\textit{F-metric} = 2 \cdot \frac{\textit{Precision} \cdot \textit{Recall}}{\textit{Precision} + \textit{Recall}} \tag{4}$$

$$\textit{mean F-metric} = \frac{1}{2} \cdot (F_0 + F_1) \tag{5}$$

3 Results

3.1 Data Preparation

The duration of recording sessions was limited to five minutes, and not all tasks were completed in this time. If a task is not recorded completely, we can not evaluate if it was successful or not, and thus, these tasks were excluded in the analysis. We identified 179 tasks that were recorded completely. These tasks consist of 1116 requests. Of those, 686 requests (61.5%) were successful and 430 were unsuccessful (38.5%). The annotated request success was the basis for calculating task success as described in Sect. 2.1. The distribution of task success per domain can be found in Fig. 1. The median task success across all domains is 0.667. The domain *music* attains the best score with a median task success of 1.0. In contrast, the domain *tourism* scores worst with a median task success of 0.333.

3.2 Relation Between Emotions and Task Success

In order to investigate the linear dependency between task success and user's emotions (as quantified by the measures introduced in Sect. 2.2), Pearson and Spearman's rank correlation coefficients are evaluated. We did not find significant correlations between emotions and task success, neither when using Pearson correlation nor Spearman rank-order correlation (see Table 2 for correlation results).

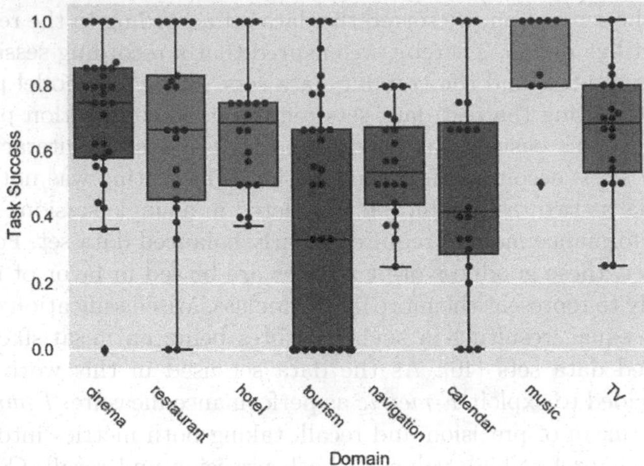

Fig. 1. Distribution of task success per domain. For definition of task success see Sect. 2.1.

3.3 Classifier Performance

In the first step of the analysis, we implemented the six classifiers using hyperparameter presettings of the Python package scikit-learn [37,38]. During training, the entire set of features is used for each classifier. The performance of each employed classifier can be seen in Fig. 2 and Table 3. The RF performs best with a *mean F-metric* of 0.875. The second-best model is AdaBoost (AB) (*mean F-metric* = 0.855). Moreover, these models also exhibit the least variance. The performance of LR is the third-best (*mean F-metric* = 0.849). In general, all models perform better when classifying successful requests (measured by the F_1*-metric*) than when classifying unsuccessful requests (measured by the F_0*-metric*).

When examining the significance of each of the proposed features, the implemented Sequential Forward Search (SFS) for LR showed slightly different results when applying it with and without class weighting. Figure 3 depicts the effect on performance (Δ *mean F-metric*) when adding an additional feature to the model for classification. The effect converges towards zero and does not take on any negative values, since an additional feature is only added in the respective run if this results in an improvement of the performance measure. Starting with the base implementation (blue line in Fig. 3), without class weighting, in all runs at least two features were selected. The first selected feature, in all runs *occurrence of error message*, already adds the most performance improvement. Further selected features, such as *total number of turns* or *number of user turns*, add a performance improvement of around 0.02 in the *mean F-metric*.

Table 2. Correlation coefficients between features computed from annotations of user emotions and task success. None of the correlations is statistically significant (all $p > 0.05$). For definition of emotion scores see Sect. 2.2.

User Emotion score	Pearson correlation	Spearman rank-order
HUS[a] score	0.03187	0.06614
HUSpos score	0.00514	0.00611
HUSneg score	0.04952	0.09326
HUSpos total	0.00558	–0.04179
HUSneg total	–0.07098	–0.11091
MUS[b] score	–0.0161	0.01894
MUSpos score	0.01606	0.02329
MUSneg score	–0.04723	0.0384
MUSpos total	0.03501	–0.00447
MUSneg total	–0.01012	–0.07073

Note. [a] HUS = Holistic user state, [b] MUS = Mimic user state.

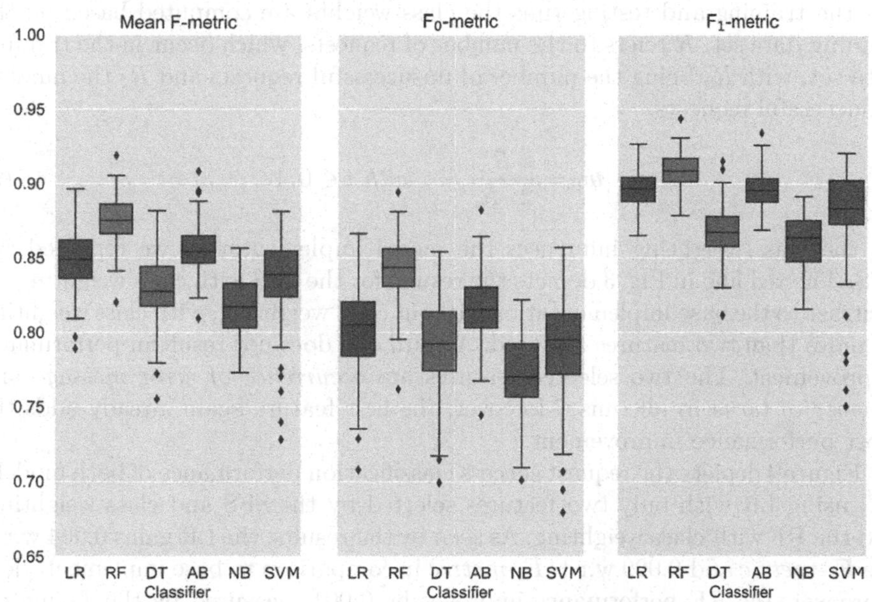

Fig. 2. Performance of the classifiers in their default implementation in scikit-learn. Classifier names are abbreviated as follows: Logistic Regression (LR), Random Forest (RF), Decision Tree (DT), AdaBoost (AB), Naive Bayes (NB), and Linear Support Vector Machine (SVM). For definition of *F-metric* see Sect. 2.3.

Table 3. Mean performance of classifiers in basic implementation using default settings of scikit-learn [37,38]. Classifier names are abbreviated as follows: Logistic Regression (LR), Random Forest (RF), Decision Tree (DT), AdaBoost (AB), Naive Bayes (NB), and Linear Support Vector Machine (SVM). For definition of *F-metric* see Sect. 2.3.

Classifier	F_0-*metric*	F_1-*metric*	*Mean F-metric*
LR	0.801	0.896	0.849
RF	0.842	0.909	0.875
DT	0.791	0.868	0.829
AB	0.815	0.896	0.855
NB	0.771	0.862	0.817
SVM	0.790	0.881	0.835

To further improve the classification performance when predicting request success, class weighting is employed to counteract the data set imbalance. To this end, the training error resulting from each class is weighted by the so-called class weights. Equation 6 shows how the class weights w_0 and w_1 are computed. For the training and testing runs the class weights are computed based on the training data set. R refers to the number of requests, which occur in the training data set, with R_0 being the number of unsuccessful requests and R_1 the number of successful requests.

$$w_i = \frac{R}{2 \cdot R_i} \qquad with\ i \in 0, 1 \tag{6}$$

As the class weighting influences the model implementation we repeated the SFS. The red line in Fig. 3 depicts the results for the SFS with class weighting. In contrast to the base implementation without class weighting, with class weighting no more than two features are used. A third one does not result in performance improvement. The two selected features are *occurrence of error message* and *number of turns* in all runs. Moreover, the first feature again already adds the most performance improvement.

Figure 4 depicts the request success classification performance of both models, i.e., using LR with only two features selected by the SFS and class weighting, and the RF with class weighting. As seen by the results, the LR gains 0.004 w.r.t. the F_1-*metric* and 0.029 w.r.t. F_0-*metric* in comparison to base implementation. Moreover, the RF performance improves by 0.001 measured by the F_1-*metric* and 0.008 measured by the F_0-*metric* in comparison to base implementation. In summary, when comparing the performance between the models RF and LR without class weighting and without a feature space limitation, the performance differs by 0.026 (see Table 3). In contrast, as seen in Table 4 class weighting and the feature space limitation for the model LR, decreases the gap to 0.008.

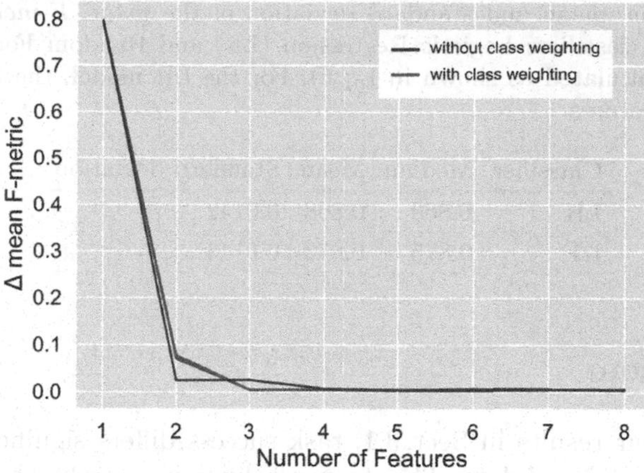

Fig. 3. *Mean F-metric* improvement (*Δ mean F-metric*) of the model Logistic Regression (LR) by successive addition of features. The definition of *F-metric* can be found in Sect. 2.3. (Color figure online)

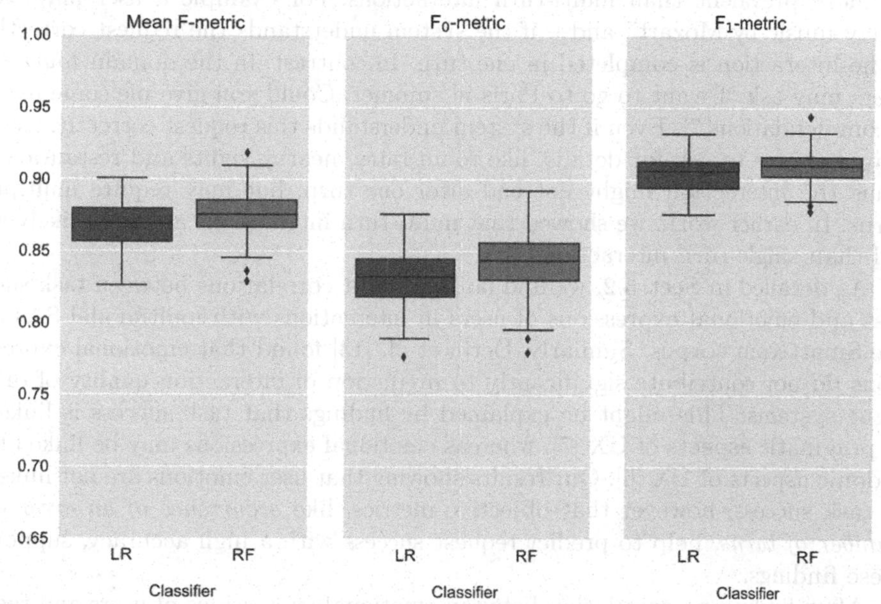

Fig. 4. Model performance estimating request success. Classifier names are abbreviated as follows: Logistic Regression (LR) and Random Forest (RF). For definition of *F-metric* see Sect. 2.3.

Table 4. Median, mean and standard deviation of the *mean F-metric* (defined in Sect. 2.3) of the classifiers Logistic Regression (LR) and Random Forest (RF) using class weights (calculated as shown in Eq. 6). For the LR model, the feature space is limited to two features.

Classifier	Median	Mean	Standard deviation
LR	0.869	0.868	0.0142
RF	0.875	0.876	0.0144

4 Discussion

According to our results in Sect. 3.1, task success differs significantly between domains in the analyzed data. The strongest difference can be observed between the domains *music* and *tourism*. While tasks in the domain *music* are likely to be successful, tasks in the domain *tourism* result in comparably low task success. One explanation may be that in the domain *music* single turn interactions may be more prevalent than multi-turn interactions. For example a user may ask "Play music by Mozart" and – if the system understands the request correctly – the interaction is completed in one turn. In contrast, in the domain *tourism*, users may ask "I want to go to Paris in summer. Could you give me some hotel recommendations?". Even if the system understands this request correctly, users may continue to ask for details, like room rates, nearby sights and restaurants. Thus the interaction might not end after one turn, but may require multiple turns. In earlier work, we showed that multi-turn interactions are more likely to fail than single-turn interactions [10].

As detailed in Sect. 3.2, we find no significant correlations between task success and emotional expressions of users in interactions with multimodal SAs in the SmartKom corpus. Similarly, Deriu et al. [13] found that emotional expressions do not contribute significantly to prediction of interaction quality of dialogue systems. This might be explained by findings that task success is linked to pragmatic aspects of UX [7], whereas emotional expressions may be linked to hedonic aspects of UX [6]. Our results showing that user emotions are not linked to task success, however that objective metrics, like *occurrence of an error* or *number of turns*, help to predict request success with a high accuracy, support these findings.

After finding no correlation between emotional expressions of users and task success, we decided to investigate approaches to automatically predict interaction success with objective features. We chose to predict request success instead of task success because of methodological considerations. More specifically, tasks vary considerably in the number of turns across domains. For example, the planning of a day of tourism activity takes more turns than asking to play a song. This difference in number of turns affect all objective features that count occurrences, e.g., number of turns, number of words, and number of gestures. This means that some objective features, like number of turns within a task, would be confounded by the domain the task is executed in. In contrast, requests are mostly limited to one to three turns, independent of their domain. Thus, requests allow us to analyze occurrences of objective features and control for number of turns across domains.

Furthermore, we chose to focus on predicting request success using objective features rather than subjective features, like emotional expressions of users. One reason for this decision was that we found no significant correlation between task success and emotional expressions in the first step of our analysis. Another important reason to focus on objective features is the relative ease of keeping track of objective features compared to subjective features. For example, a system can log by default if an error message occurs and thus can use this information to predict request success. Similarly, number of turns can be computed from system logs. In contrast, tracking emotions from voice, as well as facial expressions and gestures in video recordings has to cope with major challenges, such as the subjectivity of emotion perception, as well as cultural, linguistic and environmental variations [20,21,42,43]. Thus, objective features may be an attractive alternative for estimating the success of interactions with dialogue systems. Moreover, predicting request success with objective metrics in real-time might enable SAs to appropriately detect and react when requests fail.

As detailed in Sect. 3.3, when investigating performance of machine learning models to predict request success, different models performed differently w.r.t. their performance to predict successful requests (F_1-*metric*) and their performance of predicting unsuccessful requests (F_0-*metric*). We find that the prediction of successful requests is more accurate across models than the prediction of unsuccessful requests. This might be due to the unbalanced distribution of the data set: about two thirds of requests are successful. However, it might also suggest that unsuccessful requests are inherently more difficult to identify than successful requests. One reason for this might be the variety of failure reasons, e.g., misunderstanding, wrong answer and error message. Therefore, we suggest that future work should investigate the prediction of unsuccessful requests in more detail taking the failure reason into consideration as well as repeating the study with a balanced data set.

Furthermore, we find that ensemble classifiers, namely AB and RF, perform better than other classifiers. This could be either due to recursive data consideration [30], built-in feature selection [31] or the power of ensemble classifiers in general [29,32,44].

To investigate the third research question regarding the most important features when predicting request success, we made use of SFS. We find that the LR model requires only two objective features with class weighting applied, namely *occurrence of error message* and *number of turns* to reach F_1 scores over 0.9 (prediction of successful requests) and F_0 scores above 0.83 (prediction of unsuccessful requests). Of the two features used by LR, the most significant feature is *occurrence of error messages*. In addition, the *number of turns* enhances prediction performance. This suggests that if the system does not provide an error message and the user does not repeatedly issue the same command, the request is likely to be successful.

4.1 Limitations

Our work is subject to a number of limitations. While we do not find significant correlations between user emotions and task success, we can not rule out that there is a relationship. Other studies suggest that subjective features may enhance system effectiveness [45], and this should be further investigated.

Only one researcher annotated request success. Therefore, our labels of request success may be influenced by subjective factors. Moreover, we assume that interaction success is a proxy for pragmatic UX [5,7], however there is more work to be done to verify this hypothesis. The same is true for our assumption that emotional expressions of users are a proxy for hedonic UX quality [6]. If true, conflicting findings to the usefulness of tracking user emotions in dialogue systems [13,45] might be explained by the two-factor model of Hassenzahl [5]. User emotions may not be useful to predict pragmatic UX, however they might be useful to predict hedonic UX, which in turn could affect product attractiveness of virtual agents [46]. This might explain why sales numbers continue to rise for SAs when at the same time product reviews attest to their limited ability to correctly understand users.

5 Conclusion

In summary, we find that objective features suffice to reach F_1 scores over 0.9 (prediction of successful requests) and F_0 scores above 0.83 (prediction of unsuccessful requests). This suggests that objective features explain most of request success. In fact, the LR model requires two features only, namely *occurrence of error message* and the *number of turns*, to explain most of request successes and failures in the analyzed data.

In conclusion, the results corroborate and extend the findings of Schiel [22] by showing that a small number of objective features suffices to predict request success with high accuracy. This suggests that it may be possible to use automatic performance analysis based on objective features to predict request success in SAs. Moreover, our results indicate that objective features might suffice to predict pragmatic UX aspects. Past research shows contradictory results regarding the usefulness of subjective features, like user emotions to predict UX [13,45]. We propose that distinguishing pragmatic and hedonic UX qualities [5,23] may help to reconcile contradictory findings: While objective features may suffice to predict pragmatic UX, subjective features might predict hedonic UX qualities like engagement and trustworthiness [46]. Future work should further investigate the assumed link between different aspects of UX, task success and emotional expressions in dialogue systems.

Acknowledgments. Our work is partially funded by the German Federal Ministry for Economic Affairs and Energy as part of their AI innovation initiative (funding code01MK20011A).

References

1. Tractica. Anzahl der Nutzer virtueller digitaler Assistenten weltweit in den Jahren von 2015 bis 2021 (in Millionen). Statista (2016)
2. Porter, J., Pino, N., Leger, H.: Amazon Echo vs Apple HomePod vs Google Home: the battle of the smart speakers (2019). https://www.techradar.com/news/amazon-echo-vs-homepod-vs-google-home-the-battle-of-the-smart-speakers. Accessed 29 Nov 2021
3. Gebhart, A., Price, M.: The best smart speakers for 2019 (2019). https://www.cnet.com/news/best-smart-speakers-for-2019-amazon-echo-dot-google-nest-mini-assistant-alexa/. Accessed 29 Nov 2021
4. Van Camp, J.: The 8 best smart speakers with Alexa and Google Assistant (2019). https://www.wired.com/story/best-smart-speakers/. Accessed 29 Nov 2021
5. Hassenzahl, M.: The hedonic/pragmatic model of user experience. Towards a UX manifesto (2007)
6. Minge, M., Thüring, M.: Hedonic and pragmatic halo effects at early stages of user experience. Int. J. Hum.-Comput. Stud. **109**, 13–25 (2018). ISSN 1071-5819. https://doi.org/10.1016/j.ijhcs.2017.07.007
7. Merčun, T., Žumer, M.: Exploring the influences on pragmatic and hedonic aspects of user experience. Inf. Res. **22**(1) (2017)
8. Gao, J., Galley, M., Li, L.: Neural approaches to conversational AI. In: The 41st International ACM SIGIR Conference on Research and Development in Information Retrieval, SIGIR 2018, pp. 1371–1374. Association for Computing Machinery, New York (2018). ISBN 9781450356572, https://doi.org/10.1145/3209978.3210183
9. Brüggemeier, B., Breiter, M., Kurz, M., Schiwy, J.: User experience of alexa, siri and google assistant when controlling music – comparison of four questionnaires. In: Stephanidis, C., Marcus, A., Rosenzweig, E., Rau, P.-L.P., Moallem, A., Rauterberg, M. (eds.) HCII 2020. LNCS, vol. 12423, pp. 600–618. Springer, Cham (2020). https://doi.org/10.1007/978-3-030-60114-0_40
10. Kurz, M., Brüggemeier, B., Breiter, M.: Success is not final; failure is not fatal – task success and user experience in interactions with alexa, google assistant and siri. In: Kurosu, M. (ed.) HCII 2021. LNCS, vol. 12764, pp. 351–369. Springer, Cham (2021). https://doi.org/10.1007/978-3-030-78468-3_24
11. Lewis, J., Sauro, J.: Can i leave this one out? the effect of dropping an item from the sus. J. Usabil. Stud. **13**(1), 38–46 (2017)
12. Kocabalil, A., Laranjo, L., Coiera, E.: Measuring user experience in conversational interfaces: a comparison of six questionnaires. In: Proceedings of the 32nd International BCS Human Computer Interaction Conference, vol. 32, pp. 1–12 (2018)
13. Deriu, J., Rodrigo, A., Otegi, A., Echegoyen, G., Rosset, S., Agirre, E., Cieliebak, M.: Survey on evaluation methods for dialogue systems. Artif. Intell. Rev. **54**(1), 755–810 (2020). https://doi.org/10.1007/s10462-020-09866-x
14. McLafferty, S.: Conducting questionnaire surveys. Key Methods Geogr. **1**, 87–100 (2003)
15. Fedotov, D., Matsuda, Y., Minker, W.: From smart to personal environment: Integrating emotion recognition into smart houses. In: IEEE International Conference on Pervasive Computing and Communications Workshops (PerCom Workshops), pp. 943–948 (2019). https://doi.org/10.1109/PERCOMW.2019.8730876
16. Shamekhi, A., Czerwinski, M., Mark, G., Novotny, M., Bennett, G.A.: An exploratory study toward the preferred conversational style for compatible virtual agents. In: Traum, D., Swartout, W., Khooshabeh, P., Kopp, S., Scherer, S.,

Leuski, A. (eds.) IVA 2016. LNCS (LNAI), vol. 10011, pp. 40–50. Springer, Cham (2016). https://doi.org/10.1007/978-3-319-47665-0_4
17. Cassell, J., Thórisson, K.: The power of a nod and a glance: envelope vs. emotional feedback in animated conversational agents. Appl. Artif. Intell. **13**, 519–538 (1999). https://doi.org/10.1080/088395199117360
18. Hamacher, A., Bianchi-Berthouze, N., Pipe, A.G., Eder, K.: Believing in bert: using expressive communication to enhance trust and counteract operational error in physical human-robot interaction. In: 25th IEEE International Symposium on Robot and Human Interactive Communication, pp. 493–500 (2016)
19. Bickmore, T., Cassell, J.: Social Dialongue with Embodied Conversational Agents, pp. 23–54. Springer, Dordrecht (2005). https://doi.org/10.1007/1-4020-3933-6_2
20. Schuller, B., et al.: Cross-corpus acoustic emotion recognition: variances and strategies. IEEE Trans. Affect. Comput. **1**(2), 119–131 (2010)
21. Lim, N.: Cultural differences in emotion: differences in emotional arousal level between the east and the west. Integr. Med. Res. **5**(2), 105–109 (2016)
22. Schiel, F.: Evaluation of Multimodal Dialogue Systems, pp. 617–643. Springer, Heidelberg (2006)
23. Hassenzahl, M., Platz, A., Burmester, M., Lehner, K.: Hedonic and ergonomic quality aspect determine a software's appeal. In: Proceedings of the SIGCHI Conference on Human Factors in Computing Systems, pp. 201–208 (2000)
24. Wahlster, W. (ed.): SmartKom: Foundations of Multimodal Dialogue Systems. Springer, Heidelberg (2006). https://doi.org/10.1007/3-540-36678-4
25. Beringer, N.: SmartKom - Datensammlung und Evaluation. Technical Report Memo Nr. 2, Ludwig-Maximilians-Universität München (2000). https://www.phonetik.uni-muenchen.de/Forschung/SmartKom/Memo-NR-02.ps
26. Kleinbaum, D.G., Klein, M.: Logistic Regression. SBH, Springer, New York (2010). https://doi.org/10.1007/978-1-4419-1742-3
27. Bishop, C.: Pattern Recognition and Machine Learning. Springer, Heidelberg (2006)
28. Breiman, L.: Random forests. Mach. Learn. **45**(1), 5–32 (2001). ISSN 1573–0565, https://doi.org/10.1023/A:1010933404324
29. Breiman, L.: Bagging predictors. Mach. Learn. **24**(2), 123–140 (1996). https://doi.org/10.1007/bf00058655
30. Louppe, G.: Understanding Random Forests: From Theory to Practice. PhD thesis, University of Liège (2014)
31. Breiman, L., Friedman, J.H., Olshen, R., Stone, C.J.: Classification and Regression Trees. Wadsworth International Group (1984)
32. Schapire, R., Freund, Y., Bartlett, P., Lee, W.: Boosting the margin: a new explanation for the effectiveness of voting methods. Ann. Statist. **26**(5), 1651–1686 (1998). https://doi.org/10.1214/aos/1024691352
33. Freund, Y., Schapire, R.E.: A decision-theoretic generalization of on-line learning and an application to boosting. In: Vitányi, P. (ed.) EuroCOLT 1995. LNCS, vol. 904, pp. 23–37. Springer, Heidelberg (1995). https://doi.org/10.1007/3-540-59119-2_166
34. Ng, A.Y., Jordan, M.I.: On discriminative vs. generative classifiers: a comparison of logistic regression and naive bayes. Adv. Neural Inf. Process. Syst. **14**, 841–848 (2002)
35. Zhang, H.: The optimality of naive bayes. Assoc. Adv. Artif. Intell. **1**(2), 3 (2004)
36. Cortes, C., Vapnik, V.: Support-vector networks. Mach. Learn. **20**(3), 273–297 (1995). ISSN 1573–0565, https://doi.org/10.1007/BF00994018

37. scikit learn. scikit-learn user guide. https://scikit-learn.org/stable/user_guide.html. Accessed 12 Dec 2021
38. Pedregosa, F., et al.: Scikit-learn: machine learning in python. J. Mach. Learn. Res. **12**, 2825–2830 (2011)
39. King, G., Zeng, L.: Logistic regression in rare events data. Polit. Anal. **9**(2), 137–163 (2001). https://doi.org/10.1093/oxfordjournals.pan.a004868
40. Liu, M., Xu, C., Luo, Y., Xu, C., Wen, Y., Tao, D.: Cost-sensitive feature selection by optimizing f-measures. IEEE Trans. Image Process. **27**(3), 1323–1335 (2018). ISSN 1941–0042, https://doi.org/10.1109/TIP.2017.2781298
41. Parambath, S., Usunier, N., Grandvalet, Y.: Optimizing f-measures by cost-sensitive classification. Adv. Neural Inf. Process. Syst. **27**, 2123–2131 (2014). http://papers.nips.cc/paper/5508-optimizing-f-measures-by-cost-sensitive-classification.pdf
42. Steininger, S., Schiel, F., Rabold, S.: Annotation of multimodal data. In: SmartKom: Foundations of Multimodal Dialogue Systems, pp. 571–596 (2006)
43. Budkov, V., Prischepa, M., Ronzhin, A., Karpov, A.: Multimodal human-robot interaction. In: International Congress on Ultra Modern Telecommunications and Control Systems, pp. 485–488. IEEE (2010). https://doi.org/10.1109/ICUMT.2010.5676593
44. Kuncheva, L.: Combining Pattern Classifiers: Methods and Algorithms. John Wiley & Sons, Hoboken (2014)
45. Shi, W., Yu, Z.: Sentiment adaptive end-to-end dialog systems (2019)
46. McDuff, D., Czerwinski, M.: Designing emotionally sentient agents. Commun. ACM **61**(12), 74–83 (2018). https://doi.org/10.1145/3186591

Author Index